Literature Without Borders

LITERATURE WITHOUT BORDERS

International Literature in English For Student Writers

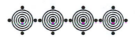

GEORGE R BOZZINI
CYNTHIA A LEENERTS
The George Washington University

Prentice Hall

Upper Saddle River, New Jersey 07458

Literature without borders : international literature in English for student writers / [compiled by] George R. Bozzini [and] Cynthia A. Leenerts.
p. cm.
Includes index.
ISBN 0-13-016665-0
1. College readers. 2. English language—Rhetoric—Problems, exercises, etc. 3. Commonwealth literature (English) 4. English literature. I. Bozzini, George R. II. Leenerts, Cynthia A.

PE1417.L6435 2000
808′.0427—dc21

99-086961

Editor in Chief: Leah Jewell
Senior Acquisitions Editor: Carrie Brandon
Editorial Assistant: Sandy Hrasdzira
Managing Editor: Mary Rottino
Production Liaison: Fran Russello
Editorial/Production Supervision: Marianne Hutchinson (Pine Tree Composition)
Prepress and Manufacturing Buyer: Mary Ann Gloriande
Manufacturing Manager: Nick Sklitsis
Marketing Manager: Brandy Dawson
Cover Designer: Robert Farrar-Wagner
Cover Image: Rene Magritte (1898–1967), "La Grande Famille," 1947. Oil on canvas, 100 × 81 cm © Copyright Charly Herscovici/ARS, NY. Private Collection. Art Resource, NY.

For permission to use copyrighted material, grateful acknowledgment is made to the copyright holders on pages 641–645, which are hereby made part of this copyright page.

This book was set in 10/12 Galliard by Pine Tree Composition, Inc., and was printed and bound by R.R. Donnelley & Sons Company. The cover was printed by Phoenix Color Corp.

Prentice Hall

Printed in the United States of America

10 9 8 7 6 5 4 3 2 1

ISBN 0-13-016665-0

Prentice-Hall International (UK) Limited, *London*
Prentice-Hall of Australia Pty. Limited, *Sydney*
Prentice-Hall Canada Inc., *Toronto*
Prentice-Hall Hispanoamericana, S.A., *Mexico*
Prentice-Hall of India Private Limited, *New Delhi*
Prentice-Hall of Japan, Inc., *Tokyo*
Pearson Education Asia Pte. Ltd., *Singapore*
Editora Prentice-Hall do Brasil, Ltda., *Rio de Janeiro*

To Dal and to Richard

Contents

OUR UNCOMMON HUMANITY

To the Reader

English has evolved not merely as *a* world language but as *the* world language of our time. It is the native tongue of the majority of the populations of its "mother lands"—England, Scotland, Wales, and Ireland; and of the "settler" nations—the United States, Canada, Australia, New Zealand, and South Africa, as well as Jamaica, Trinidad, Barbados, the Leeward and Windward Islands, the Bahamas, and other islands in the Caribbean, and of Belize and Guyana in Central and South America, respectively. As a result of British colonial expansion in the eighteenth and nineteenth centuries, it ultimately became the language of government, trade, and education in India, Pakistan, Nepal, Sri Lanka, and Bangladesh. British colonial rule established English as an official state language in the African nations of Liberia, Nigeria, Ghana, Sierra Leone in the west; of Kenya, Tanzania, Malawi, Cameroon, Uganda, and Zambia in central Africa; and of Namibia, Botswana, Swaziland, and Lesotho in the south. The British left the legacy of English in Singapore and Hong Kong, and the Americans did the same in the Philippines, Micronesia, and Puerto Rico.

Further to British (and a bit of American) colonialism in the nineteenth century, American military and economic might, and the global pervasiveness of American popular culture in the twentieth—and a considerable amount of religious missionary activity in both centuries—the spread of English accelerated.

In most non-anglophone countries of the world, English is by far the foreign language most often taught in the schools; often it is a language of instruction, or the language in which many of the textbooks are written, in the colleges and universities. Students from all over the world travel to the anglophone countries to learn English and pursue their studies in English.

Additionally, English is the principal language of international business and trade, air-traffic control, science and technology, diplomacy, and international conferences, as well as international sports competitions. Of particular relevance to this textbook is the fact that English has become an international literary language of astonishing reach and diversity.

We would note here that when a language spreads as a result of political, military, and economic power, it is not received enthusiastically by its inheritors. Rather than being viewed as empowerment, in many respects it is viewed as a diminishment of local languages and cultures. Ironically, however, as a result of its global hegemony, English has spawned numerous spoken and written varieties that in turn have become such powerful symbols of national and cultural identity that it can be rightly said that "ownership" of the English language is indeed in question.

One issue in this regard concerns the dual nationalities of many of our authors, in particular those of the "postcolonial" texts. In compiling a geographical index for this anthology, we discovered so much overlapping that we abandoned the effort, thus reinforcing our fervently held view that English literature today is truly a literature without borders.

Texts offered in this anthology that specifically address identity issues include Chinua Achebe's essay "The Song of Ourselves" and Salman Rushdie's essay "There Is No Such Thing as 'Commonwealth' Literature." Additionally, stories and poems by writers from all our categories of anglophone countries—and within each of those countries as well—attest to the fact that literature in the English language around the world exhibits extraordinary vigor.

This literature, written over the past fifty or so years—the era of independence for many new nations, and the era of diminished empire for some older nations—is rapidly taking its rightful and long-overdue place at the "table" of English departments' course offerings under the rubric of "postcolonial studies" (rather than appearing as a subset of "British literature"), in much the same way as African American and Asian American surveys have come into their own, after having been read as a sort of afterthought to "American literature." Particularly encouraging is the advent of postcolonial surveys, which give students a chance, quite often, to "discover" this body of texts for the first time, and to follow up on their interests with upper-level and graduate courses.

The word "postcolonial" itself (often applied to most of the texts in this anthology) can be, to use some favorite buzzwords, "problematic," often "vexing." *Lingua Franca*, a professional journal, devoted its September/October 1995 issue to such problems, and essays and essay-collections without number have addressed its "identity crisis," as critic Russell Jacoby and others have called it. The concept of postcoloniality can become so all-inclusive as to lose its meaning. Just exactly what, these days, is *not* postcolonial? At the beginning of coauthor Cynthia Leenerts's postcolonial survey, she asks students to name a nation, or some other designated piece of land, that is not, and has not been, on one side or the other of the "equation" of power: either colonizer or colonized. She is usually greeted by a buzz of thinking-out-loud as students consider, then reconsider, their initial responses. The field of possibilities includes not only today's world, but all configurations of the globe back through the times of ancient empires. Go back far enough in history—or not so far—and even colonizers such as Great Britain and France were once colonized by Rome, which itself experienced its own power struggles in the early days amongst the Latin and Etruscan tribes. Typically, someone will volunteer, "Antarctica!"—to which someone else may respond with "Little America," or with allusion to any of the other bases established by nations with a stake at the South Pole. The moon itself doubtless still has displayed, since 1969, the Stars and Stripes not-flapping in the breezeless Sea of Tranquillity.

The issue of "raw power," then—what group dominates what other group?—is one of the first things we may notice when approaching postcolonial literature. But it is not the only thing. Neither is it as simple as, say, Great Britain dominating India, for India itself, as with many other former British colonies, has its elite and subaltern (its favored and disfavored, its dominating and dominated) groups. To best appreciate the nuances of power, it is important to investigate the histories of the nations or groups in which literature is embedded: to look into the narratives that define, or attempt to define, a people. At the very least, one should learn who the relevant "players" are (and remember at the same time that history itself is "story" and that the points of view will generally differ). *Caveat lector*—reader, beware. But, *tolle, lege*—take up and read—for as flawed as history may be, it always helps provide *some* sort of understanding of a "new" area—some sort of jumping-off place for further exploration.

And, what helps the exploration? At the time of this writing, it is very likely that first-year students, unless they are particularly fortunate, did not get much of a chance in high school to venture beyond U.S. and British literatures; and, even there, quite often didn't get to read much of anything beyond the "center"—the "classics"—which often are taught uncritically, without much appreciation for the creative tensions that went into their making. Even so, for many students—at least those from the "majority" populations—those texts are somehow more "familiar," more accessible, more in tune with "majority" culture. Less troubling. Less likely to keep one awake at night. Ultimately, if taught in ways that empty them of any potential internal struggle, quite unlikely to be anything more than a passing read, something to be learned for an exam, a paper, then mentally trash-compacted to make room for the next assignment.

Postcolonial works (and by those we mean not only literature of formerly colonized peoples, but also literatures sensitive to postcolonial issues of power and relationship, literatures that pose postcolonial questions about the human condition) demand that we pay attention to many things at once. Salman Rushdie, in his 1990 novel *Haroun and the Sea of Stories* (which is a children's book in the same sense that *The Wizard of Oz* is a children's film) illustrates this point particularly well with his character Blabbermouth, who dazzles Haroun with a display of juggling, concluding with, "I just wanted you to *know* who you were *dealing* with here." All reading requires skill in juggling, but postcolonial literature, especially in its initial unfamiliarity, demands finesse. Yet it is potentially the most exciting branch of "literature in English," and rewards the "taking up and reading"—depending upon the background of the individual reader—by introducing her or him to new perspectives, or honouring those who, up to the most recent years, have had to face hostile canons.

In surveys devoted to international English, whether of people formerly colonizing or colonized, some of the issues thus kept "circulating" include

- Cultural theories;
- Histories of each region;

- Style: form and function of each text;
- Language: the use of "proper English," new "englishes," and other languages;
- Audience: often a function of the language(s) used;
- Traditions and their co-optations, erasures, and revivals; and
- Women's voices, and other voices not always heard.

Some issues apply more directly to literature of formerly colonized peoples. These would include, but not be limited to

- Colonizers' perceptions of colonized people;
- Colonized people's perceptions of themselves, and of the colonizers;
- Enfeminization of colonized men; the body politic as female;
- "Whiteness" and "color," self-perceived and otherwise;
- Racial differences in colonizers' treatment of colonists;
- Settler colonists' "colonization," in turn, of the indigenous population;
- The fights for Independence, or the peaceful transitions thereto;
- Post Independence disenchantment, despair, hope; and
- Other concerns not yet mapped.

Of course, not all of these issues are present in all of the texts, all of the time. With some texts, perhaps only one or two will "work" in a meaningful way, although upon subsequent readings, and with deeper experience in reading and responding to this literature, you may notice some additional issues coming to the surface. And, to that end, collaborative discussions and projects will enrich the responses to these texts.

Finally, the last issue listed—other concerns not yet mapped—is one that we hope will continue to expand with each reading of each text. The writers have launched their texts in the 1950s and in each succeeding decade, but what will we make of them in our times? And, how will they change us?

In selecting texts, we have striven for a balance of stories and poems, with the occasional memoir or essay. We have sought as well to achieve broad coverage geographically in the categories noted above—the mother lands, the settler nations, and the postcolonial nations. Likewise, we have fostered diversity within categories with regard to gender, generation, and ethnicity.

In setting up thematic units, we inevitably found that complex literary works do not lend themselves to easy classification, that there is much overlapping. Nonetheless, the units as they stand offer a practical pedagogical focus.

Finally, bearing in mind that our audience will consist largely of students in the early stages of their higher education, we have included texts that simply provide delightful, challenging, engaging reading. *Literature Without Borders* is a textbook to enjoy as well as to learn from.

A WORD ABOUT THE APPARATUS

The apparatus in this anthology provides a useful, uniform framework in which to study each text. Though individual instructors may use it differently, selectively, or not at all, we wish to share here our sense of how the exercises were designed to work.

It should be noted here that each type of exercise makes particular assumptions about teaching and learning literature. PERSPECTIVES assumes that students have developed—in nearly two decades or more of life experience—a fundamental knowledge of their own world, well-defined cultural values, and a burgeoning worldview. Thus, this section prepares them to read meaningfully by first probing their experience with and their feelings about central issues that will be addressed in the text. Where familiarity with an issue might be lacking—and in many cases we assume it will be—we encourage the students themselves to research the issues through their school library or over the Internet. We invite students to share their ideas in a class discussion before charting the text.

The CHARTING THE TEXT section assumes that, to be appreciated fully, a literary text must be read carefully, deliberately, and interactively from beginning to end. Thus, we have shaped our questions to address, in addition to the comprehension of ideas, a text's meaningful divisions, its narrative or poetic structure, the power of its ideas to engage the reader. We further encourage students to put themselves into the text and to interact with it, manifestly by marking and annotating it and responding to it all the while they read.

CONSIDERATIONS OF STYLE focuses students' attention on the literary devices that give the text—be it narrative or poetic—its lifeblood: images, symbols, sound patterns, an "attitude." Our major assumption here is that exploring the nuances of language is essential to fully appreciating and delighting in a work of literature.

The AFTERTHOUGHTS section addresses issues that arise from having "read between the lines" of the text, having connected with it personally, having reflected upon it, and having put it in perspective with self-experience, or with other texts (in the anthology or elsewhere).

Our final assumption underlying the apparatus is that, in the study of literature, reading and writing constantly and necessarily interconnect and reinforce each other. To this end, THE WRITER'S CRAFT section offers students a variety of writing tasks, such as retelling part of the story from another point of view, or extending the story beyond its present ending; writing a critical or argumentative essay on a poignant issue in the text; comparing the treatment of an issue in two or more texts.

Taken together, each element of the apparatus invites a different type of response to the selection that it accompanies—in sum, making some or other aspect of the text a meaningful part of the student's ongoing personal narrative.

George R Bozzini
Cynthia A Leenerts

Acknowledgments

We gratefully acknowledge the help and encouragement that we received from numerous individuals. From the staff at Prentice Hall, we note Allyson Williams, who first reported the project to English Editor Leah Jewell, who encouraged its development and in turn transferred the project to Carrie Brandon, who, with assistants Gianna Caradonna and Sandy Hrasdzira, guided us through various stages of the manuscript. We thank our colleagues at The George Washington University, Miriam Dow and Judith Plotz, for their generous support and thoughtful advice. We thank Nirupana Penumella and Bill Koffenberger for their invaluable assistance with the computer.

Lastly, we thank the writers whose work it has been our pleasure to include in this anthology, for their contribution to the global education of our students.

Our Common Humanity

Part One
Heritage, Family, Community

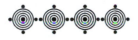

Afterward, he stood in the door to his own room, turning the idea over in his mind like a bright coin. Perhaps he had loved his father, he told himself. Next to respect and obedience, love had always been excess to their relationship. But the more he thought it the more he believed it, until it seemed to him like a sharp point of truth.

PETER HO DAVIES, *The Next Life*

LESLIE MARMON SILKO

LESLIE MARMON SILKO, *of Mexican, Anglo, and Laguna Pueblo ancestry, was born in Albuquerque, New Mexico in 1948. She grew up on the Laguna Pueblo reservation, where she learned the lore of her people from female relatives. Silko was graduated from the University of New Mexico in 1969. She has taught at Navajo Community College in Many Farms, Arizona and at the University of New Mexico, and currently teaches at the University of Arizona at Tucson.*

Silko's works include a collection of stories, The Man to Send Rain Clouds *(1974); a book of poems,* Laguna Woman *(1974); the novels* Ceremony *(1977)—the first by a Native American woman—and* Almanac of Death *(1991); and a miscellany,* Storyteller *(1981), which combines family history, fiction, photographs, and poetry, including "[It Was a Long Time Before]."*

PERSPECTIVES

1 How are the elderly generally treated in Western culture today? In your family, or among your ethnic group, are the old treated differently than they are in the nation at large? What about them is valued (or disvalued), and how are they encouraged to live as full members of society (or to stay ghettoized)?

2 If you spent time with your grandparents, did you have a baby name for them? If so, how did the name, or names, come to be? Did you or your family members continue to use the baby name(s) into adulthood?

[It Was a Long Time Before]

It was a long time before
I learned that my Grandma A'mooh's
real name was Marie Anaya Marmon.
I thought her name really was "A'mooh."
I realize now it had happened when I was a baby
and she cared for me while my mother worked.
I had been hearing her say
"*a'moo'ooh*"

which is the Laguna expression of endearment
for a young child
spoken with great feeling and love.

Her house was next to ours
and as I grew up
I spent a lot of time with her
because she was in her eighties
and they were worried about her falling.
So I would go check up on her—which was really
an excuse to visit her.
After I had to go to school
I went to carry in the coal bucket
which she still insisted on filling.
I slept with her
in case she fell getting up in the night.

She still washed her hair with yucca roots
or "soap weed" as she called it. She said
it kept white hair like hers from yellowing.
She kept these yucca roots on her windowsill
and I remember I was afraid of them for a long time
because they looked like hairy twisted claws.

I watched her make red chili on the grinding stone
the old way, even though it had gotten difficult for her
to get down on her knees.
She used to tell me and my sisters
about the old days when they didn't have toothpaste
and cleaned their teeth with juniper ash,
and how, instead of corn flakes, in the old days they ate
"maaht'zini" crushed up with milk poured over it.

Her last years they took her away to Albuquerque
to live with her daughter, Aunt Bessie.
But there was no fire to start in the morning
and nobody dropping by.
She didn't have anyone to talk to all day
because Bessie worked.
She might have lived without watering morning glories
and without kids running through her kitchen
but she did not last long
without someone to talk to.

CHARTING THE POEM

1 Why did the narrator spend so much time with her grandmother, and what made it possible for her to have all this time with her? Apart from Laguna or other Native American societies, where else might this be possible?

2 What natural, indigenous products does the grandmother use, and what does the narrator learn about them? How do they seem to compare, in the view of A'mooh and the narrator, with store-bought products or foods?

3 What might have motivated the decision to remove A'mooh from her old home, probably in a less urban area than Albuquerque?

CONSIDERATIONS OF STYLE

1 Does the poem appear to be autobiographical as well as a narrative, poetic memoir? What makes it seem this way, and how does this affect its "credibility" to you as a reader (or does it matter)?

2 A'mooh spends four stanzas in company with the rest of the family, and the final stanza cooped up in her daughter Bessie's house. Why the disproportionate amounts of word space for each environment?

3 The narrator refers to "they" in the second and in the last stanzas. Who are "they"? What is implied about the role of the narrator in decisions affecting her grandmother by the use of this pronoun?

4 Rewrite the first three stanzas as narrative prose. Read the text aloud. How does it differ from the same story told in poetic form?

AFTERTHOUGHTS

1 In our society, who tends to make decisions concerning where the old will live, and with whom? Does this poem change your mind in any significant way regarding proper behavior toward old people?

2 If we are all going to grow old (we hope so, anyway), why do we, at least in the United States, often confine the elderly to a world that is so nasty—so sense-deprived, isolated, and impoverished?

THE WRITER'S CRAFT

1 Write a short essay about some traditional, natural botanicals or foods that surpass commercial products in effectiveness or quality. Connect the botanicals or foods, in some way, with the culture in which they were first discovered.

2 Write an essay, story, or poem, dwelling in detail upon an elder, or some other beloved relative, contrasting your view of this person with how this person might be viewed by a stranger.

SHIRLEY GEOK-LIN LIM

SHIRLEY GEOK-LIN LIM *was born in Malacca, Malaysia, a colonized and immigrant country whose diverse cultures with sometimes conflicting social values both enriched and challenged Lim's early life. She was educated by European, Chinese, and Eurasian nuns in a Malaccan convent school.*

Lim is currently a professor of English and Women's Studies at the University of California in Santa Barbara. She is a prize-winning poet and short story writer, and a well-regarded critic in the commonwealth literature of Southeast Asia, Asian American literature of the United States, and in feminist studies.

"Ah Mah" is a poetic memoir of the eight-year-old speaker's grandmother, who had been raised in a traditional Confucian patriarchal society from which the granddaughter's generation has markedly distanced itself. The poem reveals a touching, intimate portrait of its subject.

PERSPECTIVES

1 Foot-binding was practiced among the upper classes in China by many (with the exception of some communities like the Manchu) until it was outlawed by the Communists when they came to power in 1948–49. What might account for this practice, as well as for its outlawing?

2 What other practices have been done to women, especially those of elite societies, that affected them as foot-binding affected Chinese women?

Ah Mah

Grandmother was smaller
than me at eight. Had she
been child forever?

Helpless, hopeless, chin sharp
as a knuckle, fan face
hardly half-opened, not a scrap

of fat anywhere: she tottered
in black silk, leaning on
handmaids, on two tortured

fins. At sixty, his sons all
married, grandfather bought her,
Soochow flower song girl.

Every bone in her feet
had been broken, bound tighter
than any neighbor's sweet

daughter's. Ten toes and instep
curled inwards, yellow petals
of chrysanthemum, wrapped

in gold cloth. He bought the young
face, small knobby breasts
he swore he'd not dress in sarong

of maternity. Each night
he held her feet in his palms,
like lotus in the tight

hollows of celestial lakes.
In his calloused flesh, her
weightless soles, cool, and slack,

clenched in his stranger's fever.

CHARTING THE POEM

1 What divisions—"logical paragraphs," they could be called—can you find in this poem? How do they flow through the poem's ten stanzas? What is the effect of the last, single-line stanza?
2 How does intimate knowledge of Ah Mah such as the physical description of her bound feet, her betrothal to the speaker's grandfather, and the couple's lovemaking inform this poem?
3 Although the grandfather "swore he'd not dress [her] in sarong/of maternity," his wife apparently has become Grandmother. What connections, if any, does this event have with the practice of foot-binding?
4 Why is the grandfather referred to as a stranger to his wife (Line 28)?

CONSIDERATIONS OF STYLE

1 Grandmother and grandfather images are frequently brought together as a juxtaposition of opposites. How does this add to the portrayal of each character?

2 What purposes are served by the narrator's use of her own body to measure against that of her grandmother?

AFTERTHOUGHTS

1 Does the grandmother seem to be an immigrant to the West? If so, or if not, how can this be ascertained from the poem?

2 The image of "two tortured fins" (Lines 3 & 4) resonates with that of stories of mermaids who have come to live on land, and who pay for that transition by a pain as sharp as knives with each step that they take with their transformed feet (read Hans Christian Andersen's "The Little Mermaid"—the original—to best appreciate this image). Besides the obvious connection with the image itself, what does this resonance bring to the poem?

THE WRITER'S CRAFT

1 Write a poem from the grandmother's point of view, or from that of the grandfather. Or from that of one of the handmaids, or any others in the household.

2 Write an essay discussing the effects of a practice like foot-binding on its subjects. If the practice is continued today, you might want to consider addressing the thoughts of the subject her-/himself. Or, you may want to write from the point of view of those whose interest lies in perpetuating this practice.

JULIAN SAMUEL

Born in 1950 in Lahore, Pakistan, JULIAN SAMUEL, *whose family converted from Sikhism to Christianity several general generations ago, and who himself, as a Marxist, is quite innocent of any professed religion, lives and works as a writer and documentary filmmaker in Montreal.*

First appearing as a chapter in his 1995 novel A Passage to Lahore, *the narrative is shaped by the author's memory of unforgettable summers at his grandparents' home in Lahore while radical social and political changes were taking place in Pakistan. The memoir was subsequently published in the Quebecois journal* Jouvert.

PERSPECTIVES

1 What knowledge of Pakistan, of the 1947 Partition, and specifically of Lahore, do you bring to your reading? What sources have contributed to this knowledge?

2 Look up information about the poet Tahar Ben Jelloun. What are some highlights of his life and career? What does the epigrammatic poem talk about?

Grandfather at Noon: Lahore, 1957

Il quitta sa famille
laissa pousser la barbe
et remplit sa solitude de pierres et de brume

Ill arriva au désert
la tête enroulée dans un linceul
le sang versé
en terre occupé

Il n'était
ni héros ni martyr
il était
citoyen de la blessure

—Tahar Ben Jelloun, *Les amandiers sont morts de leurs blessures* (Paris: Maspero, 1976)

It was a hot day and the publishers had been talking with my grandfather about his next technical drawing book. They were in the hall of his narrow three-storey house. While Mohammed Raffi was singing love songs on the radio, my brother was having an attack of worms, amoebic dysentery, and radioitis in the backyard, sitting on the potty. He sang along loudly. My olfactory skills were acute. Smoky worms as long as the Shalimar Express.

The walls of my grandfather's house were yellowish, cool even during the summers. The bedrooms had a slightly greenish tinge in the late afternoon, and over the centre of each bed drooped gauzy white mosquito netting. During the day, shoeless servants would twist and knot these nets high above the beds, where they hung like cloth chandeliers. In the night the netting imprisoned my grandparents' snoring bodies.

He had the house built during the summer of 1947, a summer unlike any other British India had endured. Coincidentally, on 15 August of that year, Independence Day in Pakistan, miles away in Palestine the farmhouse of the Abu Laban family was blown up by the Haganah, the Zionist military organization. Another partition and independence was about to transpire.

The Moslem publishers were discussing aspects of the trade: how many copies of which books, what schools to distribute them in, which teachers would use them. My grandfather was speaking quickly. I had the impression that these business matters had to be cleared up before the family left for a hill station—a summer resort—in Mussourie, where he would rest from the busy schedule of writing, publication, and publicity. In these hill stations he would venture out into ancient markets, selectively buying amaryllis bulbs for his roof garden. His ability to make the bulbs burst into passionate pink and red petals was renowned throughout Christian Lahore. As a drafting teacher he was very well-known throughout Pakistan, and later India. He was a sort of James Joyce of the drafting textbook world in post-Partition Pakistan. Strangely enough, although he was Christian, he still wore his *turra* headdress, symbolically acknowledging his Sikh past.

His asthma caused him to spit a lot, especially in the morning but never 5
in public; never near Rang Mahal Mission High School where he taught. This school was founded, my tall uncle tells me, by the famous American Presbyterian educationist and missionary The Reverend Dr. Charles W. Foreman, DD. Apparently my grandfather never spat near the Lahore Cathedral, either.

He gave private lessons to students in his office, which had greener walls than the rest of the house. Students would use thumb tacks to pin down the corners of sheets of very expensive drafting paper. They would hold T-squares along the drafting board's edge with their left hand while their right would carefully, under the supervision of their greying teacher, draw the finest lines in the world with H2 pencils. I would, when I was allowed to pass through this office, see the time-consuming drafting of square tables with elephantine legs, muscular chairs, toilets that faced in such a way as to avoid direct sunlight as well as any potential insult to anyone's religion. Once in a while I would see small English houses with sloping roofs emerging on the thin paper. English matriculation classes were, I am told, filled with poetry about dogs and wolves barking in cool valleys in Welsh villages. Who in Pakistan has a sloping roof, I wondered.

My grandfather's technical books have been published in four languages: English, Hindi, Gurmukhi, and of course Urdu. The house was divided linguistically; he spoke Punjabi with his wife, because that was the language they most shared, and Urdu with the children, because it, like English, was to become the lingua franca of Pakistan.

I would find at least five excuses to interrupt their drafting lessons. Bringing in water or tea for my grandfather to drink, I would see objects emerging on the tracing paper in oblique projection, side elevation, top plans. The students worked diligently because they had to pay for these lessons. I had the nagging suspicion that he did not charge the poorer students, or at least he charged them less. Secularism.

Many technical students still know about my grandfather's contribution to the art of drafting plans for a house, a table, or a chair. In fact, a few years ago, when I met a Lahorie engineering student at an international party in Montréal and told him my full historical name and where I was born, a smile broke across his face. He told me he had studied my grandfather's books, although now these books are not much used. Mohammed Malikshah, the man from Lahore, was now doing research in atomic power at McGill and would soon be returning to Pakistan to contribute to the weapons program.

My grandfather wrote *A Manual of Scale Drawing* and *Technical Geo-* 10
metrical Drawing, among other titles. Generations have been educated by his books and have helped, consequently, to reconstruct Pakistan from the chair up, as it were. He was also a landscape painter, but he did not become famous for his impressionistic renditions of British India. He depicted passive nature scenes: brooks flowing in and around trees with dark barks without a hint of modernist contortion; his paintings looked very English. There was a spatial ambiguity to the way he drew streams and small waterfalls: one can never really tell which way the stream moves—into or out of the picture, or if the stream is just hanging in mid-air. He was not a great draughtsman in the pictorial sense. I have inherited some of this ambiguous spatial relationship, a kind of rendition of reality that did not do much for my reputation during my phase as an undergraduate student painter.

My grandfather really had no excuse not to have been at least somewhat angsty in his landscapes, like the German expressionists who had seen some of what he had seen. The Germans saw Germany in the nineteen-thirties and -forties. My grandfather saw divisions between people and communal violence in the context of the Two Nation Theory, which was supposed to recognize a nation of Hindus and a nation of Moslems so that everything would work out. So much for the "Lahore" or "Pakistan Resolution." One has to look hard to find any conflict within his pictorial work. Not a very political man. In fact, he once did a loosely composed pen-and-water-colour drawing of flower petals. Of course, the flowers had been drafted in barely visible trace lines first, and then were built up with tiny brush strokes until they became real-looking. I suspect that he may have copied them from a *National Geographic* of the time. I have never been able to understand why he inscribed "God is Love" in old-fashioned English writing below this painted arrangement. The writing probably took as long as the execution of the flowers themselves.

His chalk drawings have a pristine luminosity, but I have the feeling they will always live outside the official art history of Pakistan. Understandable, of course; he had given up his religion to adopt another one, one from the West, or at least a religion which the West had reformulated and that grew up nearer Asia. And, as it was turning out, the promises of a secular state, as Mohammed Ali Jinnah, the leader of the Islamic state, had implied in his many pre-Partition speeches, were far from sight.

In the late fifties this religion was splintering and shattering my grandfather's family from the inside. Western ideas, such as Webberian sociology, were laid down as career options. He thought he was just listening to the American missionaries, but there was another process he did not anticipate: religion, in conjunction with other factors such as two-piece bathing suits and Two Nation Theories, indirectly created a dissatisfaction with Pakistan and what it could not offer. This feeling of Pakistani inadequacy pulled the younger generations to London, Toronto, and Washington. It was as though this Western religion were a kind of seed planted in the older generation, to find fruition in subsequent generations abroad.

The fecund garden on the roof of my grandfather's house was L-shaped; the end of the long side overlooked the banana trees, the other side gave out to a military academy. The flowers grew behind gauze so that the savage and hungry Lahore birds would not peck off the effulgent petals. My grandfather thought the petals would bleed, he was that tender about his flowers. There might have been a problem with mice also. Missionaries picked the flowers when they came to visit: "It would be nice if your children's children could come to Sunday school." The missionaries spoke Urdu with sufficient skill to throw their victims into affectionate innocent smiles. This made their task easier.

There were large church picnics under righteous white tablecloths spread 15
on the ground in sunny parks with fruit bats. Stern obedient servants dusted off plates before sitting many yards away to have a slightly lesser version of the same food. Pakistani men stood around with hands in their pockets, jackets done up, shoes shining. No one in full traditional garb. An occasional touch to the Sunday trimmed mustache. Wives helped by giving the servants orders: "No, over there. Bring some cutlets here and take more salad over there." Black Morrises with wooden steering wheels. This was my Lahore.

My grandfather's house was large, filled with visitors. A community of sweepers, servants, and beggars lived below us in shacks made of materials so flimsy a rainstorm would damage them irreparably. Some of the smaller buildings were made of mud. The hutty houses were brown and tidy, and I would whisk past them with my father on the back of his Triumph 175 cc motorbike.

One summer day a servant was killed because he washed an electric fan with a very wet rag. His blue and bloated body was brought out into the open and everybody wept. I only learned to fully redirect my guilt years later in Montréal, when I began to use Marxism to understand the underlying social process of self-imposed guilt.

In the blustery August of 1947 there was an attempt to burn down the house owned by Kahan Singh, which was my grandfather's original name. My short uncle was to tell me years later, "A good soul, however, came to the rescue when he revealed to the militant group that the owner of the house was in fact a Christian and not a Sikh." So really the family name is Kahan-Singh, thanks to all the kind missionaries—the ones that came to Lahore during the time of the Slave Kings of Delhi and the others who had a comparatively shorter stay. There was modernity attached to the act of becoming victims to the sweet proselytization of the pink souls from America and London.

I am not sure if my grandfather continued to paint after Partition. His house was generous, a continual train of visitors; and he had long walks after supper, often buying my grandmother a *paan*.

One memorable summer before we left Pakistan, my brother and I spent a couple of months at our grandparents'. In the hot evenings we would sleep on the open roof, exposed to the Lahore sky and the circling satellites. "Here is the Russian one," my grandmother would say. We would try ten different ways to pronounce Sputnik. It always resulted in giggling fits. My brother and I would fight with each other to get on the fan side of the grandparents. He usually won because he was younger. The electric fan reluctantly blew a more or less cool breeze across our noses. There was moonlight everywhere.

My grandmother's neck was soft. I'd place the tips of my fingers in the skin folds of her neck and count the gold balls in her necklace. If she moved in the right way during one of her boring accounts of what shapes stars would make if connected, I saw star clusters reflected in gold balls.

I countered her astrological wisdom with little stories of what I had seen during the day; for instance, how the hermaphrodite street dancers—the *Khusras*—danced. I semi-invented a story about snake charmers; stories about a fight between a cobra and a mongoose. A yellow liquid came from the mongoose's gaping mouth as the snake slowly erased the mongoose's memory by coiling around it with a steel grip. I told her about the salt taste in my mouth when I saw the thing die. I once compared her hands, pointing to the heavens, with the paws of the dead mongoose who, I claimed, was pointing to the heavens, not from a nice bed, but from the gutter three floors below us.

One of those nights the whole family, including an otherwordly religious aunt, was sleeping on the roof. We were having a riot of a time throwing things at one another while our grandparents tried to tell us mythical bullshit stories about crows and bits of cheese, foxes who would get married when it rained and shone at the same time; stories of princes and queens and aging elephants in the Lahore zoo. My grandmother claimed that an elephant was lopped up into a hundred grey pieces which were buried throughout the twelve-gated city. In the middle of her story, the sky suddenly changed colour and became a deep blue, as in one of my grandfather's more sombre paintings. The moon also deepened in tone, going from bluish to grey, then suddenly to purple. We rushed indoors. I remember saying to my grandmother that we ought to bring in my *surukhs,* my tiny pet birds. But no sooner had I spoken than I heard them behind us in the room adjoining the large roof patio. The swirling dust must have upset them. The small, burgundy-coloured birds flew in tightly arched paths in the cage. They had white spots near their eyes, sharp pointed scarlet beaks, and were tremendous fun to feed.

Some months after we had arrived in England, my mother got a letter from my grandmother saying that there had been another dust storm "just like the one when the boys were here" and the birds had been accidentally left out in all its raging twelve-gated fury. They were hurled thirty-seven feet into the banana trees.

My brother and I drove our grandparents around the bend in four days; we broke some beds by jumping on them from an eight-foot-high wall. It was a summer of homemade ice-cream, personally selected watermelons, rides in *tongas* to Chandini Chouk to see the toy sellers, green parrots in murderously claustrophobic cages, visits to people who had pet squirrels, and servants who had baths in the afternoons. We visited my grandfather's childhood schools at Kot Radha Kirshan, about three miles from Clarkabad, and Mission School in Narowal, sixty miles southwest of Lahore. Some summer afternoons I climbed a *jamun* tree to eat the berries.

There were scented rituals connected when this house on McLeod Road. There were the Moslem feasts when the moon became a sliver. We joyfully responded by taking candles to the houses of neighbours. We practised a very healthy secularism, though not really out of fear. My grandfather never ate meat when Hindus were in the house. Even then, I had developed a neutrality towards Christmas, and later on, a neutrality towards the Christian faith as well. Flowers behind gauze.

In the cool evenings when the sun was going down and the emerald parrots were returning in dusky blue spirals to their trees, we would have a reddish drink. There was chatter as the ice clinked and tinkered against the inside of the jug. Smooth dissatisfied servants wearing *shalwar kamezes* silkenly brushed the evening into blackness. The drink became pinkish when poured from the deep jug. I could see the faces of my grandparents through the glass; they looked distorted and unhappy. Multicoloured lizards with big blue-green eyes would climb high up into the night and stars. My grandparents refused to let me have a BB gun.

When my grandmother moved to Toronto after her husband died, she told me that they used to let the hut dwellers peek inside their living room to watch their television set. Now some of those hut dwellers have jobs in Oman, Bahrain, Kuwait, and various other Gulf States. And with this injection of money into Pakistan, the Pakistani workers and prostitutes can now buy VCRs and colour TVs. All this took some fifteen years.

There were many jokes about TV; people in 1982 used to say that they had mullahs stuck in their sets who did not disappear even when the power was cut off. General Zia or his ubiquitous representatives were, it seemed, on the air every second of any Islamic day. After the 1979 revolution in Iran, Iranians used to say that their televisions had grown beards, beards oozing out onto the living room floor. Grey beards and, very unfortunately, some young raven-black ones also.

Outside, right near the front door of my grandfather's house, there was a 30
network of open drainage that had not changed since the time Alexander the Great had paid us a visit. They were called *nalies.* The colour of the water interested me very much. At the age of eight I was able to show an occidental experimental filmmaker's sense of fascination at the changes in the colour of the bathwater, at the spirals of moving hair and soap suds in the warm water, caught by the occasional twig.

I claimed that I could tell which person had had a bath. One day after a temporary servant took a bath, the water in the *nalie* changed to burgundy, with hair oil superimposed onto the smell of Pear's soap. The spirals moved slowly and travelled down the open duct; I followed them until they changed shape and slipped under Lahore.

My grandmother had most likely given this servant the soap. Otherwise how would she have gotten it? Possession of the soap was a question of class and relative power. The servant was having her bath on the open roof near the water tank. I was not supposed to be looking at her. She was soaping her brown body unhurriedly in the sun; suds were running through her toes, which were more elongated than moon shaped.

When I look back at the event, for it was certainly an event, I feel guilty because of a highly progressive left-wing film I saw in India sometime during my first return, some twenty years later. This film depicted a landlord doing the same thing I had done as a child. I saw myself as the loathsome landlord, watching his servant taking her bath without her knowing. The landlord used to fuck her. There were no words between them. This initial sight had given me a bit of power, but I could not touch her. I suppose that feeling between guilt and access converted later in life into a phoney solidarity with the women's movement in the West.

It was a large house, but still my grandfather's children were restless to leave the country for England or America. Some even left for Frankfurt to await the ineluctable unification of the two Germanies in 1990. The first documents had already started to arrive at the offices of immigration departments. For my parents, Lahore was becoming like a train station during Partition. The grandparents were unhappy, and I see misery prevailing in their eyes in the photographs they sent over to Toronto during the following decades. Christmas 1968: long faces. Christmas 1972: longer faces. And in the mid-seventies, photographs of one prestigious funeral taken in a big church. A Christian family in a confessional Islamic state.

Soon they would all be gone. At seventy-two my grandfather died of coronary thrombosis. He lies at the cemetery on Central Road. After he died, my grandmother boarded a plane for the first time in her life. It was her first sight of Lahore from the view of the parrots. She joined us in Toronto. The other grandmother is buried in Glasgow.

Sunset. October, some year in the late nineteen-fifties. We have pushed up through the Suez Canal. The sea pulls us down, the sea pushes us up. Salt spray all around. Flying fish dead on the deck, snagged on rigging in the night. Wings of flesh. Elvis in Karachi. Elvis becoming the sea, the air. I remind my mother that if she had paid a particular radio station in Karachi more money, perhaps they would have played Paul Anka's "Oh, Diana" on my birthday. On my birthday we waited, but no Paul Anka. Instead, they aired a bit of semi-classical music by Ravi Shankar accompanied by that famous fiddler from the West—Yehudi Menuhin.

There is a man talking to my mother. He is British and she is beautiful. My father is already in England, living in a small flat with a newly bought gramophone. We are moving up through the Red Sea. The Englishman has on a blue blazer and holds a tall flared sweating glass of cool beer in his stubby English hand. His shirt is open and the collar is folded out over the blazer. Still, he does not look good. My sister is sitting on a deck chair, reading *Jane Eyre*. We are on the promenade deck. The man's fingers are nicotine-stained. A plume of smoke floats towards Pakistan. He inches nearer my mother. Her scarf flutters like Isadora Duncan's when she dies at the end of a black-and-white film.

The white captain with a megaphone tells us, in Urdu, which surprises us, to move away from the deck's edge. Stormy weather. Human cotton moving into Britain.

It was late afternoon when we boarded a large passenger ship with an oily black hull. I sat, waiting for the vessel to pull out of Karachi harbour so I could see Pakistan fade into the Arabian Sea. When I awoke it was night, nothing but the rising and falling of sea and the hissing darkness. Lunar sounds of the inky water. We had departed. Liverpool was to come much later, two or three weeks later, in a northern sunset. We stopped in Aden, and then slowly moved up through Gamel Abdel Nasser's well-organized Suez Canal. Out on the sandy distance I could see people picking dates. Groups of camels stooped in twos and threes out on the watery desert.

Port Said. Dolphins in the smelly Mediterranean. The Rock of Gibraltar and the Bay of Biscay. A strike by dock workers at Liverpool—a vision of the great West.

The Lahore house was empty. In Agincourt, a plaza-ridden suburb of Toronto, there was talk that we ought to sell the old house to a Christian family. When I went back to Lahore in 1982, a carpet dealer had a *soosth* shop there. The carpet dealers were discussing General Zia in very negative terms, which made me feel good despite the initial shock of seeing my family history turned into the fine, redundant weaves of moderately priced carpets from Kabul.

The grandparents had failed to hold things together. A persistent cool breeze, like the one that deepened the colour of the moon and killed my pet birds, had blown their kids into the distance; my mother, father, and brothers and sister had made the dusty train journey to Karachi, then by ship to the port of Liverpool. They rode an old smoky coal-driven train to Middlesex and Wimbledon with its sunny gardens and the smashed shell of a pet tortoise. The English neighbours were disgusted by the Pakistani kids who had used tennis rackets to open its shell.

CHARTING THE MEMOIR

1. What evidence does Samuel present of the complexity of his grandfather's life and—subsequently, perhaps—of his personality?
2. What images of natural and human-made violence move the narrative, and how do they work with the more peaceful images than can be found in it?
3. How does Samuel portray the missionaries who proselytized the Subcontinent?
4. Samuel observes at the end of his memoir that "the grandparents had failed to hold things together." What might have been required to hold things together, and what might account for his grandparents' inability to do so?

CONSIDERATIONS OF STYLE

1. Locate at least three poignant color images in the text. What sort of backdrop do the images provide for the narrative?
2. Do you get the impression that the narrator is observing the events through the eyes of a child or through those of an adult? Give reasons for your response.

AFTERTHOUGHTS

1 As the narrator observes, "There was modernity attached to the act of becoming victims to the sweet proselytization of the pink souls from America and London." What is being implied by this statement, particularly since Sikhism (and Islam, for that matter) was revealed many centuries after Christianity? What images are bound up with the concept of "modernity," according to Julian Samuel, and according to the culture in which you live?

2 What common experiences and beliefs do Julian Samuel and Tahar Ben Jelloun share?

THE WRITER'S CRAFT

1 Write a short memoir centering upon a brief moment in your early childhood, drawing upon as many sharp sensory images as possible, appealing to various senses.

2 Write a brief travelogue in the style of Paragraphs 39 and 40, which describe the family's two-to-three-week passage from Karachi to Liverpool with poignant flashes of imagery that show places on the way. Note in particular—and imitate—the brevity and the diversity of the images.

ANDREW LAM

ANDREW LAM *was born in Saigon, Vietnam. At the end of the Vietnam War, when he was eleven years old, he came to the United States and settled in California. He is an associate editor with the Pacific News Service, where he has worked since 1989. He is also a regular commentator on National Public Radio. Lam has received numerous awards for his writing, including the Society of Professional Journalist Outstanding Young Journalist Award, The Media Alliance Meritorious awards, and The World Affairs Council's Excellence in International Journalism Award. In 1992, he received a Rockefeller Fellowship to study at the University of California at Los Angeles. He lives in northern California.*

Lam's short stories have been published in The Vietnam Review, Zyzzyva, *and* Transfer Magazine.

In "Grandma's Tale," the narrator's Vietnamese immigrant grandmother dies finding solace in the fact that "Buddha has given her the gift to live twice in one life." The story is anthologized in Sudden Fiction: 60 New Short Stories, *ed. Robert Shapard and James Thomas (1996).*

PERSPECTIVES

1 Which world religions, as well as many localized ones, teach a belief in reincarnation? How might this influence the way one lives—and ends—life on earth? What is reincarnation's counterpart in religions such as Judaism, Christianity, and Islam?

2 How is one "supposed" to act when a relative dies, no matter how old the decedent or how expected the death? What procedures are required by law, and what courses of action are prescribed by custom?

Grandma's Tales

The day after Mama and Papa took off to Las Vegas, Grandma died. Nancy and I, we didn't know what to do, Vietnamese traditional funerals with incense sticks and chanting Buddhist monks not being our thing. We have a big freezer, Nancy said. Why don't we freeze her. Really. Why bother Mama and Papa. What's another day or two for Grandma now anyway?

Nancy's older than me, and since I didn't have any better idea, we iced her.

Grandma was 94 years, 8 months, and 6 days old when she died. She lived through three wars, two famines, and a full hard life. America, besides, was not all that good for her. She had been confined to the second floor of our big Victorian home, as her health was failing, and she did not speak English, only a little French, like *Oui monsieur, c'est evidemment un petit monstre,* and, *Non, Madame, vous n'êtes pas du tout enceinte, je vous assure.* She was a head nurse in the maternity ward of the Hanoi hospital during the French colonial time. I used to love her stories about delivering all these strange two-headed babies and Siamese triplets connected at the hip whom she named Happy, Liberation, and Day.

Grandma's death came when she was eating spring rolls with me and Nancy. Nancy was wearing a nice black miniskirt and her lips were painted red, and Grandma said you look like a high-class whore. Nancy made a face and said she was preparing to go to one of her famous San Francisco artsy cocktail parties where waiters were better dressed than most upper-class Vietnamese men back home, and there were silver trays of duck paté and salmon mousse, and ice sculptures with wings and live musicians playing Vivaldi.

So get off my case, Grandma, because I'm no whore.

It was a compliment, Grandma said, winking at me, but I guess it's wasted on you, child. Then she laughed, as Nancy prepared to leave. Child, do the cha-cha-cha for me. I didn't get to do it when I was young, with my clubbed foot and the wars and everything else.

Sure, Grandma, Nancy said, and rolled her pretty eyes.

Then Grandma dropped her chopsticks on the hardwood floor—clack, clack, clatter, clack, clack—closed her eyes, and stopped breathing. Just like that.

So we iced her. She was small, the freezer was large. We wrapped her body in plastic wrap first, then sent a message to Circus-Circus, where Mama and Papa were staying.

Meanwhile Nancy had a party to go to, and I had to meet Eric for a movie.

I didn't care about the movie, but cared about Eric. He's got eyes so blue you can swim in them, and a warm laugh, and is really beautiful, a year older than me, a senior. Eric liked Grandma. Neither one knew the other's language, but there was this thing between them, mutual respect, like one cool old chic to one cool young dude. (Sometimes I would translate but not always 'cause my English is not all that good and my Vietnamese sucks.) What was so cool about Grandma was she was the only one who knew I'm bisexual. Even though she was Confucian bound and trained and a Buddhist and all, she was really cool about it.

One night, we were sitting in the living room watching a John Wayne movie together, *The Green Berets,* and Eric was there with me and Grandma. (Mama and Papa had just gone to bed and Nancy was at some weird black and white ball or something like that.) And Eric leaned over and kissed me on the lips and Grandma said, That's real nice, and I translated and we all laughed and John Wayne shot dead five guys. Just like that. But Grandma didn't mind, really. She's seen Americans like John Wayne shooting her people in the movies before. She always thought of him as a bad guy, uglier than a water buffalo's ass. And she'd seen us more passionate than a kiss on the lips and didn't mind. She used to tell us to be careful and not make any babies—obviously a joke—'cause she'd done delivering them. So you see, we liked Grandma a lot.

Anyway, after Nancy and I packed Grandma down into the 12 degree Fahrenheit, I went out to meet Eric, and later we came back to the house. We made out on the couch. After a while I said, Eric, I have to tell you something. Grandma's dead. You're kidding me, he whispered, with his beautiful smile. I kid you not, I said. She's dead, and Nancy and me, we iced her. Shit! He said. Why? 'Cause otherwise she would start to smell, duh, and we have to wait for my parents to perform a traditional Vietnamese funeral. We fell silent. Then Eric said, can I take a peek at Grandma? Sure, I said, sure you can, she was as much yours as she was mine, and we went to the freezer and looked in.

The weird thing was the freezer was on defrost and Grandma was nowhere in sight. There was a trail of water and plastic wrap leading from the freezer to her bedroom. We followed it. On the bed, all wet, sat Grandma, counting her Buddhist rosary and chanting her diamond sutra. What's weirder is that she looked real young. I mean around 54 now, not 94, the high cheeks, the rosy lips. When she saw us she smiled and said: "What do you say we all go to one of those famous cocktail parties that Nancy's gone to, the three of us?" I wasn't scared because she said it in English, I mean accentless, Californian English.

Wow, Grandma, Eric said, your English is excellent. 15

"I know," Grandma said, "that's just a side benefit of being reborn. But enough with compliments, we got to party."

Cool, said Eric. Cool, I said, though I was a little jealous 'cause I had to go through junior high and high school and all those damn ESL classes and everything to learn the same language while Grandma just got it down cold because she was reborn. Grandma put on this nice brocaded red blouse and black silk pants and sequined velvet shoes and fixed her hair real nice and we drove off downtown.

Boy, you should've seen Nancy's face when we arrived at her cocktail party. She nearly tripped over herself. She laid her face against the wing of an ice sculpture to calm herself. Then she walked straight up to us, haughty, and said, It's invitation only, how'd ya'll get in?

"Calm yourself, child," said Grandma, "I told them that I was a board member of the Cancer Society and flashed my jade bracelet and diamond ring and gave the man a forty dollar tip."

Nancy had the same reaction Eric and I had: Grandma, your English is 20
flawless! Grandma was oblivious to compliments. She went straight to the

punch bowl for some spirits. Since her clubbed foot was cured she had an elegant grace about her. Her hair floated like gray-black clouds behind her. Everyone stared, mesmerized.

Needless to say Grandma was the big hit of the party. She had so many interesting stories to tell. The feminists, it seemed, loved her the most. They crowded around her as she told them how she'd been married early and had eight children while being the matriarch of a middle-class family during the Viet Minh uprising. She told them about my grandfather, a brilliant man who was well versed in Moliére and Shakespeare and who was an accomplished violinist but who drank himself to death because he was helpless against the colonial powers of the French. She told everyone how single-handedly she had raised her children after his death and they all became doctors and lawyers and pilots and famous composers. Then she started telling them how the twenty-four-year-old civil war divided her family up and brothers fought brothers over ideological notions that proved bloody pointless. Then she told them about our journey across the Pacific Ocean in a crowded fishing boat where thirst and starvation nearly did us all in until it was her idea to eat some of the dead and drink their blood so that the rest of us could survive to catch glimpses of this beautiful America and become Americans.

She started telling them, too, about the fate of Vietnamese women who had to marry and see their husbands and sons go to war and never come back. Then she recited poems and told fairy tales with sad endings, fairy tales she herself had learned as a child, the kind she used to tell me and my cousins when we were young. There was this princess, you see, who fell in love with a fisherman and he didn't know about her 'cause she only heard his beautiful voice singing from a distance, so when he drifted away downriver one day she died, her heart turning into this ruby with the image of his boat imprinted on it. (In Grandma's stories, the husbands and fishermen always come home, but they come home always too late and there was nothing they could do but mourn and grieve.)

Grandma's voice was sad and seductive and words came pouring out of her like rain and the whole place turned quiet and Nancy sobbed because she understood and Eric stood close to me and I cried a little, too. "I lost four of my children," Grandma said, "twelve of my grandchildren, and countless relatives and friends to wars and famines and I lost everything I owned when I left my beautiful country behind. Mine is a story of suffering and sorrow, suffering and sorrow being the way of Vietnamese life. But now I have a second chance and I am not who I was, and yet I have all the memories, so wherever I go I will keep telling my stories and songs."

Applause broke out, then a rich-looking man with gray hair came up to Grandma and they talked quietly for a while. When they were done Grandma came to me and Nancy and Eric and said goodbye. She said she was not going to wait for my parents to come home for a traditional funeral. She had a lot of living still to do since Buddha had given her the gift to live twice in one life and this man, some famous novelist from Colombia, was going to take her places. He might even help her write her book. So she was going to the *mediteranée* to get a tan and to Venice to see the festivals and ride the gondolas and maybe afterward she'd go by Hanoi and see what they'd done to her childhood home and visit some long-forgotten ancestral graves and relatives and then who knows where she'd go. She'd send postcards though and don't you wait up. Then before we knew it Grandma was already out of the door with the famous novelist and the music started up again. Eric and I ran out after her but outside there was only this city under a velvety night sky, its highrises shining like glass cages, with little diamonds and gold coins kept locked inside them.

Mama and Papa came home two days later. They brought incense sticks 25
and ox-hide drums and wooden fish and copper gongs and jasmine wreaths and Oolong tea and paper offerings, all the things that we were supposed to have for a traditional funeral. A monk had even sent a fax of his chanting rate and schedule because he was real busy, and the relatives started pouring in.

It was hard to explain then what had happened, what we had always expected as the tragic ending of things, human frailty the point of mourning and grief. And wasn't epic loss what made us tell our stories? It was difficult for me to mourn now, though. Difficult 'cause while the incense smoke drifted all over the mansion and the crying and wailing resounded like cicadas humming on the tamarind tree in the summer back in Vietnam, Grandma wasn't around.

CHARTING THE STORY

1 What three major wars has Grandma lived through? How has each of these wars affected her country, Vietnam?

2 Why does life seem to go on as usual—without overt mourning—immediately after Grandma's death?

3 What suggests that the narrator may have had a warmer, closer relationship with his grandmother than with his parents? What cultural and social factors may account for this?

CONSIDERATIONS OF STYLE

1 How, where, and—do you suppose—why is humor imbued in the narrator's telling of his grandmother's death?

2 How do imaginative and autobiographical fiction work together in this narrative? Which of the two genres seems to prevail?

3 The narrator writes in Paragraph 11, "My English is not all that good and my Vietnamese sucks." How is this statement belied in his narrative? What might the narrator mean by "English"?

AFTERTHOUGHTS

1 Compare this story with John Ho Davies' "The Next Life" (in this anthology), noting how the two—while bearing some noteworthy similarities—treat the subject of life and death of an elder in sharply different ways.

2 Why does the funeral still take place, despite the fact that Grandma quite literally "wasn't around"? What does this imply about either the parents or the narrator?

3 Translate Grandmother's French utterances. What do they signify to her characterization? How do they tie in with other things she says, both as the 94-year-old Grandma and her 54-year-old "incarnation"?

THE WRITER'S CRAFT

1 Write a memoir about an elderly person who has influenced you profoundly, and whose "story," you feel, it is incumbent upon you to tell.

2 Expand upon any one of Grandma's "tales" and tell it as you would imagine her telling it—either as a sharp old lady or as a worldly woman of late middle age.

SHASHI DESHPANDE

SHASHI DESHPANDE, *daughter of playwright and Sanskrit scholar Shiranga, was born in Dharwad, India. She has degrees in economics and in law, and has also worked as a journalist, as well as raising her children. She has written numerous short stories, four children's books, and six novels, of which the best known are* The Dark Holds No Terrors *(1980) and* That Long Silence *(1988), the latter of which won the Sahitya Akademi Award. Deshpande presently lives in Bangalore with her husband, who is a pathologist.*

Many of Deshpande's works reveal a pathology of relationships. Similarly, "Why a Robin?" is the story of a woman estranged from her daughter and her husband. It comes from The Intrusion and Other Stories *(1993).*

PERSPECTIVES

1 What cultures are you familiar with in which marriages are arranged? What might be advantages of such a marriage? What disadvantages come to mind?

2 In your experience, as well as in your reading, does a mother-daughter relationship differ significantly from a father-daughter relationship, particularly in late childhood and early adolescence? If so, how; if not, why not? (You might want to compare your perspectives with those of others, particularly with those coming from other cultures.)

3 What, in your view, constitutes "the exotic"? What images are conjured up by the terms "exotic" and "domestic," and how, if at all, would these clusters of images differ in another locale?

Why a Robin?

'Tell me something about it,' she says. 'About a robin.' 'But why a robin?'

'I don't know,' she says carelessly. Then, firmly, 'Teacher said so. Teacher said a robin.'

Foolishly I ignore the finality of her words and blunder on. 'Why not a bird we know something about? A sparrow, or a . . . a . . . a . . . myna, or even . . . a peacock?'

'No. Not those. I want a robin,' she says with childish petulance. Her lower lip is thrust forward, her forehead is furrowed, her eyes are angry. But I am amazed at her beauty. How did I, so plain, so common, get a daughter like her? Her beauty always gives me a physical wrench. And saddens me. It puts distance between us. Can one envy one's own daughter? I think I do. She gets so much out of life, effortlessly, gracefully. While I . . .?

'Tell me something about the robin.'

This is almost the first time my daughter is appealing to me for help. And I cannot help her. I frown in my turn, perplexed and worried. What shall I say?

'I don't know,' I say at last. 'I know nothing about it. Except that it's a pretty bird. With a red breast . . .? And it comes in winter . . .? Children feed it bread crumbs . . .?'

The words come out haltingly, hesitantly; I feel like I did when I was a child, answering questions I was not very sure of. Her expectant look unnerves me even more. She is looking at me, head held on one side, almost like a bird herself. But not one that will let me ruffle its feathers. Not one that will come and peck from my hands.

As I stop, she bursts out, 'Oh! Is that all! What's the use of that? I'm supposed to do a two-page composition on the robin and you tell me two words. You can't help me, you're no use at all.' I'm conscious that I've failed her, I try to make amends. 'Why don't you write about a peacock? That's a beautiful bird.'

'Teacher said no ex-o-tic birds.' She pronounces the new word carefully and with pride.

'But a peacock isn't exotic. It belongs here. In some places it's quite common.'

'You don't understand,' she says scornfully, looking down at me. Already at twelve, she seems taller than me. Already at her age, she knows more than I do. There is no awkwardness in her; she holds herself with a grace and poise I have never achieved. 'We can't choose the subject ourselves. You don't understand. You don't know anything.'

I look at her terrified. She has already judged me and found me wanting. There is nothing more I can say.

'I'll ask Papa. He's sure to know, he'll help me.'

She begins to gather her books. For some reason, I don't want her to go. I want to hold on to the moment, to her.

'A peacock,' I say helplessly, feebly. 'I'll tell you about a peacock.'

'I said a robin.' She bites off her words sharply, irritated and impatient with my obtuseness. She is sharp, almost like a blade. When I was a girl, a friend told me to use a blade to keep my legs smooth and clean. I was clumsy and the sharp blade gave me little nicks, cuts that bled profusely, briefly, then healed fast. Now my daughter's words, her glances, lacerate me that way. Sometimes I feel I have bleeding nicks all over me, cuts that bleed profusely and heal fast.

'Why a robin?' I ask again, and this time I'm talking to myself. She isn't there any more. Why a robin?

How often have I wanted to ask my husband—why me? But I know he would walk out on me the way the child has, irritated, impatient, but not angry. He is rarely moved to anger. But his silences, more eloquent than any anger, freeze me. And I don't really need to ask the question—why me? Because I know. It was because of the speeding truck which rammed into a car on the highway. And a girl who died. Anyone, he is supposed to have said, my husband, just anyone. But why was it me?

20 As I sit thinking about this, she comes back into the room and I am filled with hope and eagerness. I half rise from my chair. 'I have a peacock's feather, let me show it to you,' I say to her. But she picks up a book and walks away from me, her long, slim brown legs taking her away from me remorselessly. I stare at her slender back, at the thin neck, where little curls grow, endearingly feminine, giving her a childish, vulnerable look. I long to fondle her, to pass my hands over her neck. But I am afraid of being rebuffed. I know she won't respond. I don't have the key to open up this beautiful child, though she is mine. I don't have the key to her father, either. It is as if I am, in my own house, confronted with two closed rooms. I am condemned to sit outside and gaze helplessly at the closed doors.

I force myself to get up. I begin rummaging among my things for the peacock's feather. I have lost, misplaced so many things in my life, but I find the peacock's feather. As I look at it, I am overcome by an onrush of memories. My grandmother used to take me to a temple. I would go with her, quivering in delighted anticipation, for there were peacocks there. I had taken it for granted then, but now I wonder—peacocks in a temple? I can remember how breathless I would be when I reached the temple. Would the peacocks come out and dance for me?

'Can I get a feather? Can I?' I would ask over and over again.

'If you're a lucky girl,' she would say.

And one day I did. I want to share it with my daughter—the peacock, my excitement, the memory of my beautiful grandmother and the peacock's feather. But she won't listen to me, it's too late.

25 Sometimes I think we are all chameleons. We change colour, become different beings with different people. With my servants I am authoritative, with my parents, irresponsible, happy-go-lucky, but with my husband and child I am foolish, stupid, inarticulate. When I am with them, I become dull and brown—no, not even that. I lose colour completely. And with his family too. They can never forget that he married 'beneath him'. Neither can I. Before they visit us, I take endless trouble to tidy the house. But it remains dull, dead. Till he, or the child, does something. A small touch and the house looks different. I slog in the kitchen for his family; I must impress them, show them he's well looked after. They sit at the table, carelessly eating the food I have prepared, and talk of many things, ignoring me. The talk flows above and around

me, leaving me untouched. An outsider in my own home. Have they locked me out or have I locked myself in?

I am full of guilt these days. I am a failure—as a wife, as a companion, as a mother. Between my husband and myself there is a blankness—we never even quarrel. And with my daughter, I am helpless. Her fits of excitement, her questions, her rage, her tantrums, her ideas—I can cope with none of these. She fills me with the same delight the peacock did. And I have no more in common with her than I had with the beautiful peacock I saw that day in the temple.

Now she is asking her father about the robin. She listens eagerly as he talks and explains. They are looking at a book, their faces eager and alive. The reading lamp casts a halo of light around their glowing faces but the light does not reach the corner where I am sitting. I am conscious of an ache within me, an ache I cannot dignify with the name of grief. Even my emotions and feelings refuse to take on larger dimensions. But nothing can ease my ache. I get up and go closer to them. The vivid colour of the birds in the book dazzle my eyes after the dark. I am suddenly reminded of my childhood, filled with nostalgia for a home that exists no more.

When I was a child, we lived in a house surrounded by trees. I often woke up to see a sparrow hopping into the window near my bed. Plain, brown and dull, it was sure of itself. Self-assured and confident. And there were also vivid streaks of colour flying out of trees. I never knew the names of these birds, I could never identify the various cries that blended in some mysterious way into a harmonious melody. But they were part of my life. Now, listening to my husband telling the child about the robin, I am conscious again of my ignorance.

'Let me tell you about the peacock,' I had said. But what could I have told her? Only that I saw it dancing once, brazenly exhibiting the glory of its fan, the sunlight flecking the blue and green and bronze with a golden dust that dazzled my eyes, made it for me, forever, the most enchanting moment of my life. But I cannot say any of this to these two—my husband and my child. We belong to different species. I am an interloper. I do not belong. I move away from them resolutely.

I dawdle over my work deliberately, so that I am going to bed. Two sin- 30
gle beds. Two islands that nothing can bridge. Not the child. Not even the bridge of passion. He has not come to bed when I go into our room. He sits and listens to music every night. I lie on my bed, eyes open, listening to the music streaming across the dark. I cannot understand this music, it is as incomprehensible to me as he is. At first, I wanted to sit with him, to try and share his enjoyment, to ask him to open my ears to the sounds so that they would become a melody. But I was afraid. Now I know I will never do it. It is his special place, his retreat, the place where he can be most alone. I will not intrude. And the worst, most frightening thought is that he may ask me—what do you want?

What do I want? What a large, what a cosmic question that is! What do I want? I will have to live the whole of my life to know what I want. And even then I will have no words to frame my wants. And now I realize I have no wants. I have whittled them down out of fear. I have hoped to give myself a stature I think I do not have by self-abnegation. Instead, I have dwindled. Without wants, there is no 'I'. That is why they so often look at me without seeing me.

The music comes to an end. He comes to bed. I lie still, not wanting to reveal that I am awake. After some time I hear his steady breathing. I can look at him now. He is lying in his usual hunched position, his back towards me. The back is mute, but his neck is like the child's, thin and somehow vulnerable. It makes him seem accessible. I can almost imagine myself going to him, talking to him without inhibitions, without fears. But I know I will not.

As I try to force myself to sleep. I hear a muffled sound from the other room. I hold my breath, waiting for the cry to be repeated. Perhaps he will hear, perhaps he will get up. When she was a baby, he woke up for her feeds, he never let me do it. I hear the sound again, but he does not stir. I know now that she is crying into her pillow. I hesitate to intrude, but the sounds tear at me. I stare, almost in anger, at his humped figure, willing him to wake up, to go to her. As I stare at the motionless figure, the conviction grows within me that bridges have to be built. They do not come out of nothing, they have to be created.

I get hurriedly out of bed, I pull my sari around me. The ground feels cool and smooth to my bare feet.

Her face is buried in the pillow. The young body is utterly still, but there is a tenseness about it that tells me she knows I am there, though my feet have made no sound. I bend down and call her name. She does not respond.

'Shall I get Papa?' I whisper, remembering how, when she had the measles, she had wanted him all the time. She gets up abruptly, showing me her tear-stained face. She has given herself totally to grief. Whatever the cause, her grief is large, real.

'No', she says. 'No, not him.'

'You want me?' Joy is surfacing through the scum of my distress.

Her eyes are distant. 'No,' she says again. 'No one.' Suddenly her eyes fill with tears, they spill over. Her face is contorted, her mouth is working. She looks almost ugly. I sit down and put my arms around her. 'What is it?' I ask her.

When she can control her sobs, she tells me. I look at her with conflicting feelings. My daughter—on the brink of womanhood? This child a woman? Suddenly I feel joyous, exalted, as if I have found one key, opened one door. But her frightened eyes bring me back to myself. I remember how I had once tried to tell her about the process of growing up. She had impatiently rebuffed me. 'Pooh! That! Who doesn't know about all that!'

Now all her self-possession has deserted her; she is only a woeful, frightened child. It is as if she is facing forces she cannot understand or control. I talk to her gently, trying to make her feel it is natural, a part of growing up, something to be welcomed, accepted. She listens to me silently, lying with her knees drawn up to her chest. Like an unborn foetus—waiting to be born again.

'I have a pain,' she says. The tears spill over. I wipe them with the end of my sari. I make her get up and show her what is to be done. I get her a hot water bottle for the pain. I bring her a cup of hot milk and sit by her side as she drinks it. She is unexpectedly docile and childlike, this child who has just become a woman. But the clouds of hurt and bewilderment are dissolving from her eyes. As she sips the milk, she sits up with a new dignity and grace that shows me she is accepting what has happened.

'Can you sleep now?' I ask her when she finishes the milk. She does not reply. I switch off the light and go to cover her up. Her fingers suddenly tighten round my hand. 'No, don't go,' she says with her old vigour. 'Talk to me, talk to me of something.' And suddenly I am my old self too. What can I talk to her about, what can I tell her?

'Were you frightened too?' she asks me shyly.

Yes, I tell her. I tell her how I too had cried and how my grandmother had held my hand as I am now holding hers.

'Your grandmother...?' she says wonderingly, as if surprised I had one. 'Tell me about her.'

'She was beautiful,' I say. 'You look like her.'

'Do I?' I can't see her distinctly, but I can visualize her lips curving into an enchanting smile. 'Tell me about her,' she repeats.

I begin to talk. I tell her how I went to the temple with her every day. And how one day I saw the peacock dance. I tell her how the sunlight had glinted on its many-hued fan and dazzled our eyes so that the world had become a different place. 'I still have the peacock's feather,' I tell her.

Bridges have to be built. I feel I am doing just that.

'Show it to me tomorrow.' Her voice is slurred with sleep. Drowsily she says, 'I'll ask teacher—why not a peacock?'

'Why not a robin?' I say slowly, trying to formulate my thoughts. I remember the sparrow that had hopped onto my window-sill every morning. What if it had seen the peacock? And what if the peacock were more beautiful? It would have strutted just the same.

'Why not a robin? We all belong.'

But she is sleeping, her fingers loosely clasped round my hand. I sit still and quiet. Unmoving.

CHARTING THE STORY

1 What appears, when first you first read the text, to account for the estrangement between the narrator and her daughter, and between the narrator and her husband? Does this impression change at any point in the story? In what ways?

2 How does the daughter's predicament with her homework assignment parallel (or contrast with) the narrator's dilemma of connecting with daughter and husband? How are mother and daughter, wife and husband, themselves similar and dissimilar?

3 What does the narrator take for granted in relating the story of mother's and daughter's reconciliation? Is *menarche* (the onset of the first menstrual period) capable of creating a lasting bond between these two—and, in some way, of eroding the father-daughter bond? If so, in what ways? If not, why not? If your answer is more complex, what issues are at stake in this narrative?

CONSIDERATIONS OF STYLE

1 Deshpande frequently employs transitionary images to move the reader between parts of the narrative. At which points does she make these shifts, and how does she accomplish them? Does the effect seem subtle, overt, or somewhere in between?
2 What stylistic purposes are served by the image of the music that the husband listens to at night? From what is suggested in the text, does the music appear to be Indian or non-Indian? Upon what do you base your point of view?
3 What do the three types of birds—robin, peacock, and sparrow—symbolize to you in the context of this story?

AFTERTHOUGHTS

1 Teacher demands "a robin," and Teacher specifies "no ex-o-tic birds." Apart from a rather rigid methodology of teaching composition, what is suggested about Teacher from this narrative?
2 How might the mother's recollection of the "nicks and cuts" she received from shaving her legs be considered to foreshadow the resolution of the conflict between the mother and daughter?

THE WRITER'S CRAFT

1 In many cultures, *menarche* is marked in rites of passage with ceremony and joy (see Punyakante Wijenaike's "Anoma" in this anthology for comparison). In other cultures, it seems to be met as a burden, with some sort of foreboding, with a sense of "the curse" of womanhood. Write about one such custom, whether within your own culture or another, examining the relative joy, solemnity, or even aversion marking this event.
2 What are girls led to believe concerning menstruation, and how does this affect their experience of *menarche* itself? What analogous transitions exist for boys, and how does this affect their views of themselves as they reach adolescence?
3 Compare the mother-daughter relationship in this story with that in Alice Munro's "Friend of My Youth" and/or in Edna O'Brien's "A Rose in the Heart of New York," or Jamaica Kincaid's "My Mother." In each story, how have bridges been built?

ALICE MUNRO

ALICE MUNRO *was born in Wingham, Ontario in 1931. She spent her early years in western Ontario until she married her first husband, James Munro, and moved with him to Vancouver, where she lived until returning to Ontario in 1972. She currently lives in the small town of Clinton, Ontario, the sort of place that figures in most of her stories.*

Munro's published works consist exclusively of short story collections (even one published novel, The Progress of Love *(1986), is really a collection of related stories), which to date number ten. Early prize-winning collections include:* Dance of the Happy Shades *(1968),* Lives of Girls and Women *(1971), and* The Beggar Maid *(1978). She was awarded the Canada-Australia Literary Prize in 1977. Her most recent collections include* Selected Stories *(1996) and* The Love of a Good Woman *(1998).*

"Friend of My Youth" is the title story in a collection published in 1990. Typically of Munro's works, it is set in rural Ontario. Also typically, her mother's life and death figure prominently in it. In particular, the narrator daughter chronicles her mother's experience as a progressive young teacher who boards at the home of a conservative, deeply religious farm family.

PERSPECTIVES

1 How do individuals in a family, particularly those who for one reason or another seem to be at a disadvantage (at least physically), strive amongst each other for power? How successful as a "trump card" to play is illness? Or martyrdom?

2 Discuss the psychological desirability—or lack thereof—of excoriating one's feelings, verbally or in writing about them.

Friend of My Youth

WITH THANKS TO R. J. T.

I used to dream about my mother, and though the details in the dream varied, the surprise in it was always the same. The dream stopped, I suppose because it was too transparent in its hopefulness, too easy in its forgiveness.

In the dream I would be the age I really was, living the life I was really living, and I would discover that my mother was still alive. (The fact is, she died when I was in my early twenties and she in her early fifties.) Sometimes I would find myself in our old kitchen, where my mother would be rolling out piecrust on the table, or washing the dishes in the battered cream-colored dish-pan with the red rim. But other times I would run into her on the street, in places where I would never have expected to see her. She might be walking through a handsome hotel lobby, or lining up in an airport. She would be looking quite well—not exactly youthful, not entirely untouched by the paralyzing disease that held her in its grip for a decade or more before her death, but so much better than I remembered that I would be astonished. Oh, I just have this little tremor in my arm, she would say, and a little stiffness up this side of my face. It is a nuisance but I get around.

I recovered then what in waking life I had lost—my mother's liveliness of face and voice before her throat muscles stiffened and a woeful, impersonal mask fastened itself over her features. How could I have forgotten this, I would think in the dream—the causal humor she had, not ironic but merry, the lightness and impatience and confidence? I would say that I was sorry I hadn't been to see her in such a long time—meaning not that I felt guilty but that I was sorry I had kept a bugbear in my mind, instead of this reality—and the strangest, kindest thing of all to me was her matter-of-fact reply.

Oh, well, she said, better late than never. I was sure I'd see you someday.

When my mother was a young woman with a soft, mischievous face and shiny, 5
opaque silk stockings on her plump legs (I have seen a photograph of her, with her pupils), she went to teach at a one-room school, called Grieves School, in the Ottawa Valley. The school was on a corner of the farm that belonged to the Grieves family—a very good farm for that country. Well-drained fields with none of the Precambrian rock shouldering through the soil, a little willow-edged river running alongside, a sugar bush, log barns, and a large, unornamented house whose wooden walls had never been painted but had been left to weather. And when wood weathers in the Ottawa Valley, my mother said, I do not know why this is, but it never turns gray, it turns black. There must be something in the air, she said. She often spoke of the Ottawa Valley, which was her home—she had grown up about twenty miles away from Grieves School—in a dogmatic, mystified way, emphasizing things about it that distinguished it from any other place on earth. Houses turn black, maple syrup has a taste no maple syrup produced elsewhere can equal, bears amble within sight of farmhouses. Of course I was disappointed when I finally got to see this place. It was not a valley at all, if by that you mean a cleft between hills; it was a mixture of flat fields and low rocks and heavy bush and little lakes—a scrambled, disarranged sort of country with no easy harmony about it, not yielding readily to any description.

The log barns and unpainted house, common enough on poor farms, were not in the Grieveses' case a sign of poverty but of policy. They had the money but they did not spend it. That was what people told my mother. The Grieveses worked hard and they were far from ignorant, but they were very backward. They didn't have a car or electricity or a telephone or a tractor. Some people thought this was because they were Cameronians—they were the only people in the school district who were of that religion—but in fact their church (which they themselves always called the Reformed Presbyterian) did not forbid engines or electricity or any inventions of that sort, just card playing, dancing, movies, and, on Sundays, any activity at all that was not religious or unavoidable.

My mother could not say who the Cameronians were or why they were called that. Some freak religion from Scotland, she said from the perch of her obedient and lighthearted Anglicanism. The teacher always boarded with the Grieveses, and my mother was a little daunted at the thought of going to live in that black board house with its paralytic Sundays and coal-oil lamps and primitve notions. But she was engaged by that time, she wanted to work on her trousseau instead of running around the country having a good time, and she figured she could get home one Sunday out of three. (On Sundays at the Grieveses' house, you could light a fire for heat but not for cooking, you could not even boil the kettle to make tea, and you were not supposed to write a letter or swat a fly. But it turned out that my mother was exempt from these rules. "No, no," said Flora Grieves, laughing at her. "That doesn't mean you. You must just go on as you're used to doing." And after a while my mother had made friends with Flora to such an extent that she wasn't even going home on the Sundays when she'd planned to.)

Flora and Ellie Grieves were the two sisters left of the family. Ellie was married, to a man called Robert Deal, who lived there and worked the farm but had not changed its name to Deal's in anyone's mind. By the way people spoke, my mother expected the Grieves sisters and Robert Deal to be middle-aged at least, but Ellie, the younger sister, was only about thirty, and Flora seven or eight years older. Robert Deal might be in between.

The house was divided in an unexpected way. The married couple didn't live with Flora. At the time of their marriage, she had given them the parlor and the dining room, the front bedrooms and staircase, the winter kitchen. There was no need to decide about the bathroom, because there wasn't one. Flora had the summer kitchen, with its open rafters and uncovered brick walls, the old pantry made into a narrow dining room and sitting room, and the two back bedrooms, one of which was my mother's. The teacher was housed with Flora, in the poorer part of the house. But my mother didn't mind. She immediately preferred Flora, and Flora's cheerfulness, to the silence and sickroom atmosphere of the front rooms. In Flora's domain it was not even true that all amusements were forbidden. She had a crokinole board—she taught my mother how to play.

The division had been made, of course, in the expectation that Robert 10
and Ellie would have a family, and that they would need the room. This hadn't happened. They had been married for more than a dozen years and there had not been a live child. Time and again Ellie had been pregnant, but two babies had been stillborn, and the rest she had miscarried. During my mother's first year, Ellie seemed to be staying in bed more and more of the time, and my mother thought that she must be pregnant again, but there was no mention of it. Such people would not mention it. You could not tell from the look of Ellie, when she got up and walked around, because she showed a stretched and ruined though slack-chested shape. She carried a sickbed odor, and she fretted in a childish way about everything. Flora took care of her and did all the work. She washed the clothes and tidied up the rooms and cooked the meals served in both sides of the house, as well as helping Robert with the milking and separating. She was up before daylight and never seemed to tire. During the first spring my mother was there, a great housecleaning was embarked upon, during which Flora climbed the ladders herself and carried down the storm windows, washed and stacked them away, carried all the furniture out of one room after another so that she could scrub the woodwork and varnish the floors. She washed every dish and glass that was sitting in the cupboards supposedly clean already. She scalded every pot and spoon. Such need and energy possessed her that she could hardly sleep—my mother would wake up to the sound of stovepipes being taken down, or the broom, draped in a dish towel, whacking at the smoky cobwebs. Through the washed uncurtained windows came a torrent of unmerciful light. The cleanliness was devastating. My mother slept now on sheets that had been bleached and starched and that gave her a rash. Sick Ellie complained daily of the smell of varnish and cleansing powders. Flora's hands were raw. But her disposition remained topnotch. Her kerchief and apron and Robert's baggy overalls that she donned for the climbing jobs gave her the air of a comedian—sportive, unpredictable.

My mother called her a whirling dervish.

"You're a regular whirling dervish, Flora," she said, and Flora halted. She wanted to know what was meant. My mother went ahead and explained, though she was a little afraid lest piety should be offended. (Not piety exactly—you could not call it that. Religious strictness.) Of course it wasn't. There was not a trace of nastiness or smug vigilance in Flora's observance of her religion. She had no fear of heathens—she had always lived in the midst of them. She liked the idea of being a dervish, and went to tell her sister.

"Do you know what the teacher says I am?"

Flora and Ellie were both dark-haired, dark-eyed women, tall and narrow-shouldered and long-legged. Ellie was a wreck, of course, but Flora was still superbly straight and graceful. She could look like a queen, my mother said—even riding into town in that cart they had. For church they used a buggy or a cutter, but when they went to town they often had to transport sacks of wool—they kept a few sheep—or of produce, to sell, and they had to bring provisions home. The trip of a few miles was not made often. Robert rode in front, to drive the horse—Flora could drive a horse perfectly well, but it must always be the man who drove. Flora would be standing behind holding on to the sacks. She rode to town and back standing up, keeping an easy balance, wearing her black hat. Almost ridiculous but not quite. A gypsy queen, my mother thought she looked like, with her black hair and her skin that always looked slightly tanned, and her lithe and bold serenity. Of course she lacked the gold bangles and the bright clothes. My mother envied her her slenderness, and her cheekbones.

Returning in the fall for her second year, my mother learned what was the matter with Ellie.

"My sister has a growth," Flora said. Nobody then spoke of cancer.

My mother had heard that before. People suspected it. My mother knew many people in the district by that time. She had made particular friends with a young woman who worked in the post office; this woman was going to be one of my mother's bridesmaids. The story of Flora and Ellie and Robert had been told—or all that people knew of it—in various versions. My mother did not feel that she was listening to gossip, because she was always on the alert for any disparaging remarks about Flora—she would not put up with that. But indeed nobody offered any. Everybody said that Flora had behaved like a saint. Even when she went to extremes, as in dividing up the house—that was like a saint.

Robert came to work at Grieveses' some months before the girls' father died. They knew him already, from church. (Oh, that church, my mother said, having attended it once, out of curiosity—that drear building miles on the other side of town, no organ or piano and plain glass in the windows and a doddery old minister with his hours-long sermon, a man hitting a tuning fork for the singing.) Robert had come out from Scotland and was on his way west. He had stopped with relatives or people he knew, members of the scanty congregation. To earn some money, probably, he came to Grieveses'. Soon he and Flora were engaged. They could not go to dances or to card parties like other couples, but they went for long walks. The chaperone—unofficially—was Ellie. Ellie was then a wild tease, a long-haired, impudent, childish girl full of lolloping energy. She would run up hills and smite the mullein stalks with a stick, shouting and prancing and pretending to be a warrior on horseback. That, or the horse itself. This when she was fifteen, sixteen years old. Nobody but Flora could control her, and generally Flora just laughed at her, being too used to her to wonder if she was quite right in the head. They were wonderfully fond of each other. Ellie, with her long skinny body, her long pale face, was like a copy of Flora—the kind of copy you often see in families, in which because of some carelessness or exaggeration of features or coloring, the handsomeness of one person passes into the plainness—or almost plainness—of the other. But Ellie had no jealousy about this. She loved to comb out Flora's hair and pin it up. They had great times, washing each other's hair. Ellie would press her face into Flora's throat, like a colt nuzzling its mother. So when Robert laid claim to Flora, or Flora to him—nobody knew how it was—Ellie had to be included. She didn't show any spite toward Robert, but she pursued and waylaid them on their walks; she sprung on them out of the bushes or sneaked up behind them so softly that she could blow on their necks. People saw her do it. And they heard of her jokes. She had always been terrible for jokes and sometimes it had got her into trouble with her father, but Flora had protected her. Now she put thistles in Robert's bed. She set his place at the table with the knife and fork the wrong way around. She switched the milk pails to give him the old one with the hole in it. For Flora's sake, maybe, Robert humored her.

The father had made Flora and Robert set the wedding day a year ahead, and after he died they did not move it any closer. Robert went on living in the house. Nobody knew how to speak to Flora about this being scandalous, or looking scandalous. Flora would just ask why. Instead of putting the wedding ahead, she put it back—from next spring to early fall, so that there should be a full year between it and her father's death. A year from wedding to funeral—that seemed proper to her. She trusted fully in Robert's patience and in her own purity.

So she might. But in the winter a commotion started. There was Ellie, vomiting, weeping, running off and hiding in the haymow, howling when they found her and pulled her out, jumping to the barn floor, running around in circles, rolling in the snow. Ellie was deranged. Flora had to call the doctor. She told him that her sister's periods had stopped—could the backup of blood be driving her wild? Robert had had to catch her and tie her up, and together he and Flora had put her to bed. She would not take food, just whipped her head from side to side, howling. It looked as if she would die speechless. But somehow the truth came out. Not from the doctor, who could not get close enough to examine her, with all her thrashing about. Probably, Robert confessed. Flora finally got wind of the truth, through all her high-mindedness. Now there had to be a wedding, though not the one that had been planned.

No cake, no new clothes, no wedding trip, no congratulations. Just a shameful hurry-up visit to the manse. Some people, seeing the names in the paper, thought the editor must have got the sisters mixed up. They thought it must be Flora. A hurry-up wedding for Flora! But no—it was Flora who pressed Robert's suit—it must have been—and got Ellie out of bed and washed her and made her presentable. It would have been Flora who picked one geranium from the window plant and pinned it to her sister's dress. And Ellie hadn't torn it out. Ellie was meek now, no longer flailing or crying. She let Flora fix her up, she let herself be married, she was never wild from that day on.

Flora had the house divided. She herself helped Robert build the necessary partitions. The baby was carried full term—nobody even pretended that it was early—but it was born dead after a long, tearing labor. Perhaps Ellie had damaged it when she jumped from the barn beam and rolled in the snow and beat on herself. Even if she hadn't done that, people would have expected something to go wrong, with that child or maybe one that came later. God dealt out punishment for hurry-up marriages—not just Presbyterians but almost everybody else believed that. God rewarded lust with dead babies, idiots, harelips and withered limbs and clubfeet.

In this case the punishment continued. Ellie had one miscarriage after another, then another stillbirth and more miscarriages. She was constantly pregnant, and the pregnancies were full of vomiting fits that lasted for days, headaches, cramps, dizzy spells. The miscarriages were as agonizing as full-term births. Ellie could not do her own work. She walked around holding on to chairs. Her numb silence passed off, and she became a complainer. If anybody came to visit, she would talk about the peculiarities of her headaches or describe her latest fainting fit, or even—in front of men, in front of unmarried girls or children—go into bloody detail about what Flora called her "disappointments." When people changed the subject or dragged the children away, she turned sullen. She demanded new medicine, reviled the doctor, nagged Flora. She accused Flora of washing the dishes with a great clang and clatter, out of spite, of pulling her—Ellie's—hair when she combed it out, of stingily substituting water-and-molasses for her real medicine. No matter what she said, Flora soothed her. Everybody who came into the house had some story of that kind to tell. Flora said, "Where's my little girl, then? Where's my Ellie? This isn't my Ellie, this is some crosspatch got in here in place of her!"

In the winter evenings after she came in from helping Robert with the barn chores, Flora would wash and change her clothes and go next door to read Ellie to sleep. My mother might invite herself along, taking whatever sewing she was doing, on some item of her trousseau. Ellie's bed was set up in the big dining room, where there was a gas lamp over the table. My mother sat on one side of the table, sewing, and Flora sat on the other side, reading aloud. Sometimes Ellie said, "I can't hear you." Or if Flora paused for a little rest Ellie said, "I'm not asleep yet."

What did Flora read? Stories about Scottish life—not classics. Stories about urchins and comic grandmothers. The only title my mother could remember was *Wee Macgregor*. She could not follow the stories very well, or laugh when Flora laughed and Ellie gave a whimper, because so much was in Scots dialect or read with that thick accent. She was surprised that Flora could do it—it wasn't the way Flora ordinarily talked, at all.

(But wouldn't it be the way Robert talked? Perhaps that is why my mother never reports anything that Robert said, never has him contributing to the scene. He must have been there, he must have been sitting there in the room. They would only heat the main room of the house. I see him black-haired, heavy-shouldered, with the strength of a plow horse, and the same kind of sombre, shackled beauty.)

Then Flora would say, "That's all of that for tonight." She would pick up another book, an old book written by some preacher of their faith. There was in it such stuff as my mother had never heard. What stuff? She couldn't say. All the stuff that was in their monstrous old religion. That put Ellie to sleep, or made her pretend she was asleep, after a couple of pages.

All that configuration of the elect and the damned, my mother must have meant—all the arguments about the illusion and necessity of free will. Doom and slippery redemption. The torturing, defeating, but for some minds irresistible pileup of interlocking and contradictory notions. My mother could resist it. Her faith was easy, her spirits at that time robust. Ideas were not what she was curious about, ever.

But what sort of thing was that, she asked (silently), to read to a dying woman? This was the nearest she got to criticizing Flora.

The answer—that it was the only thing, if you believed it—never seemed to have occurred to her.

By spring a nurse had arrived. That was the way things were done then. People died at home, and a nurse came in to manage it.

The nurse's name was Audrey Atkinson. She was a stout woman with corsets as stiff as barrel hoops, marcelled hair the color of brass candlesticks, a mouth shaped by lipstick beyond its own stingy outlines. She drove a car into the yard—her own car, a dark-green coupé, shiny and smart. News of Audrey Atkinson and her car spread quickly. Questions were asked. Where did she get the money? Had some rich fool altered his will on her behalf? Had she exercised influence? Or simply helped herself to a stash of bills under the mattress? How was she to be trusted?

Hers was the first car ever to sit in the Grieveses' yard overnight.

Audrey Atkinson said that she had never been called out to tend a case in so primitive a house. It was beyond her, she said, how people could live in such a way.

"It's not that they're poor, even," she said to my mother. "It isn't, is it? That I could understand. Or it's not even their religion. So what is it? They do not care!"

She tried at first to cozy up to my mother, as if they would be natural allies in this benighted place. She spoke as if they were around the same age—both stylish, intelligent women who liked a good time and had modern ideas. She offered to teach my mother to drive the car. She offered her cigarettes. My mother was more tempted by the idea of learning to drive than she was by the cigarettes. But she said no, she would wait for her husband to teach her. Audrey Atkinson raised her pinkish-orange eyebrows at my mother behind Flora's back, and my mother was furious. She disliked the nurse far more than Flora did.

"I knew what she was like and Flora didn't," my mother said. She meant that she caught a whiff of a cheap life, maybe even of drinking establishments and unsavory men, of hard bargains, which Flora was too unworldly to notice.

Flora started into the great housecleaning again. She had the curtains spread out on stretchers, she beat the rugs on the line, she leapt up on the stepladder to attack the dust on the molding. But she was impeded all the time by Nurse Atkinson's complaining.

"I wondered if we could have a little less of the running and clattering?" said Nurse Atkinson with offensive politeness. "I only ask for my patient's sake." She always spoke of Ellie as "my patient" and pretended that she was the only one to protect her and compel respect. But she was not so respectful of Ellie herself. "Allee-oop," she would say, dragging the poor creature up on her pillows. And she told Ellie she was not going to stand for fretting and whimpering. "You don't do yourself any good that way," she said. "And you certainly don't make me come any quicker. What you just as well might do is learn to control yourself." She exclaimed at Ellie's bedsores in a scolding way, as if they were a further disgrace of the house. She demanded lotions, ointments, expensive soap—most of them, no doubt, to protect her own skin, which she claimed suffered from the hard water. (How could it be hard, my mother asked her—sticking up for the household when nobody else would—how could it be hard when it came straight from the rain barrel?)

Nurse Atkinson wanted cream, too—she said that they should hold some 40
back, not sell it all to the creamery. She wanted to make nourishing soups and puddings for her patient. She did make puddings, and jellies, from packaged mixes such as had never before entered this house. My mother was convinced that she ate them all herself.

Flora still read to Ellie, but now it was only short bits from the Bible. When she finished and stood up, Ellie tried to cling to her. Ellie wept, sometimes she made ridiculous complaints. She said there was a horned cow outside, trying to get into the room and kill her.

"They often get some kind of idea like that," Nurse Atkinson said. "You mustn't give in to her or she won't let you go day or night. That's what they're like, they only think of themselves. Now, when I'm here alone with her, she behaves herself quite nice. I don't have any trouble at all. But after you been in here I have trouble all over again because she sees you and she gets upset. You don't want to make my job harder for me, do you? I mean, you brought me here to take charge, didn't you?"

"Ellie, now, Ellie dear, I must go," said Flora, and to the nurse she said, "I understand. I do understand that you have to be in charge and I admire you, I admire you for your work. In your work you have to have so much patience and kindness."

My mother wondered at this—was Flora really so blinded, or did she hope by this undeserved praise to exhort Nurse Atkinson to the patience and kindness that she didn't have? Nurse Atkinson was too thick-skinned and self-approving for any trick like that to work.

"It is a hard job, all right, and not many can do it," she said. "It's not like 45
those nurses in the hospital, where they got everything laid out for them." She

had no time for more conversation—she was trying to bring in "Make-Believe Ballroom" on her battery radio.

My mother was busy with the final exams and the June exercises at the school. She was getting ready for her wedding in July. Friends came in cars and whisked her off to the dressmaker's, to parties, to choose the invitations and order the cake. The lilacs came out, the evenings lengthened, the birds were back and nesting, my mother bloomed in everybody's attention, about to set out on the deliciously solemn adventure of marriage. Her dress was to be appliquéd with silk roses, her veil held by a cap of seed pearls. She belonged to the first generation of young women who saved their money and paid for their own weddings—far fancier than their parents could have afforded.

On her last evening, the friend from the post office came to drive her away, with her clothes and her books and the things she had made for her trousseau and the gifts her pupils and others had given her. There was great fuss and laughter about getting everything loaded into the car. Flora came out and helped. This getting married is even more of a nuisance than I thought, said Flora, laughing. She gave my mother a dresser scarf, which she had crocheted in secret. Nurse Atkinson could not be shut out of an important occasion—she presented a spray bottle of cologne. Flora stood on the slope at the side of the house to wave goodbye. She had been invited to the wedding, but of course she had said she could not come, she could not "go out" at such a time. The last my mother ever saw of her was this solitary, energetically waving figure in her housecleaning apron and bandanna, on the green slope by the black-walled house, in the evening light.

"Well, maybe now she'll get what she should've got the first time round," the friend from the post office said. "Maybe now they'll be able to get married. Is she too old to start a family? How old is she, anyway?"

My mother thought that this was a crude way of talking about Flora and replied that she didn't know. But she had to admit to herself that she had been thinking the very same thing.

When she was married and settled in her own home, three hundred miles away, 50
my mother got a letter from Flora. Ellie was dead. She had died firm in her faith, Flora said, and grateful for her release. Nurse Atkinson was staying on for a little while, until it was time for her to go off to her next case. This was late in the summer.

News of what happened next did not come from Flora. When she wrote at Christmas, she seemed to take for granted that information would have gone ahead of her.

"You have in all probability heard," wrote Flora, "that Robert and Nurse Atkinson have been married. They are living on here, in Robert's part of the house. They are fixing it up to suit themselves. It is very impolite of me to call her Nurse Atkinson, as I see I have done. I ought to have called her Audrey."

Of course the post-office friend had written, and so had others. It was a great shock and scandal and a matter that excited the district—the wedding as secret and surprising as Robert's first one had been (though surely not for the same reason), Nurse Atkinson permanently installed in the community, Flora losing out for the second time. Nobody had been aware of any courtship, and they asked how the woman could have enticed him. Did she promise children, lying about her age?

The surprises were not to stop with the wedding. The bride got down to business immediately with the "fixing up" that Flora mentioned. In came the electricity and then the telephone. Now Nurse Atkinson—she would always be called Nurse Atkinson—was heard on the party line lambasting painters and paperhangers and delivery services. She was having everything done over. She was buying an electric stove and putting in a bathroom, and who knew where the money was coming from? Was it all hers, got in her deathbed dealings, in shady bequests? Was it Robert's, was he claiming his share? Ellie's share, left to him and Nurse Atkinson to enjoy themselves with, the shameless pair?

All these improvements took place on one side of the house only. Flora's side remained just as it was. No electric lights there, no fresh wallpaper or new venetian blinds. When the house was painted on the outside—cream with dark-green trim—Flora's side was left bare. This strange open statement was greeted at first with pity and disapproval, then with less sympathy, as a sign of Flora's stubbornness and eccentricity (she could have bought her own paint and made it look decent), and finally as a joke. People drove out of their way to see it.

There was always a dance given in the schoolhouse for a newly married couple. A cash collection—called "a purse of money"—was presented to them. Nurse Atkinson sent out word that she would not mind seeing this custom followed, even though it happened that the family she had married into was opposed to dancing. Some people thought it would be a disgrace to gratify her, a lap in the face to Flora. Others were too curious to hold back. They wanted to see how the newlyweds would behave. Would Robert dance? What sort of outfit would the bride show up in? They delayed a while, but finally the dance was held, and my mother got her report.

The bride wore the dress she had worn at her wedding, or so she said. But who would wear such a dress for a wedding at the manse? More than likely it was bought specially for her appearance at the dance. Pure-white satin with a sweetheart neckline, idiotically youthful. The groom was got up in a new dark-blue suit, and she had stuck a flower in his buttonhole. They were a sight. Her hair was freshly done to blind the eye with brassy reflections, and her face looked as if it would come off on a man's jacket, should she lay it against his shoulder in the dancing. Of course she did dance. She danced with every man present except the groom, who sat scrunched into one of the school desks along the wall. She danced with every man present—they all claimed they had to do it, it was the custom—and then she dragged Robert out to receive the money and to thank everybody for their best wishes. To the ladies in the cloakroom she even hinted that she was feeling unwell, for the usual newlywed reason. Nobody believed her, and indeed nothing ever came of this hope, if she really had it. Some of the women thought that she was lying to them out of malice, insulting them, making them out to be so credulous. But nobody challenged her, nobody was rude to her—maybe because it was plain that she could summon a rudeness of her own to knock anybody flat.

Flora was not present at the dance.

"My sister-in-law is not a dancer," said Nurse Atkinson. "She is stuck in the olden times." She invited them to laugh at Flora, whom she always called her sister-in-law, though she had no right to do so.

My mother wrote a letter to Flora after hearing about all these things. 60
Being removed from the scene, and perhaps in a flurry of importance due to her own newly married state, she may have lost sight of the kind of person she was writing to. She offered sympathy and showed outrage, and said blunt disparaging things about the woman who had—as my mother saw it—dealt Flora such a blow. Back came a letter from Flora saying that she did not know where my mother had been getting her information, but that it seemed she had misunderstood, or listened to malicious people, or jumped to unjustified conclusions. What happened in Flora's family was nobody else's business, and certainly nobody needed to feel sorry for her or angry on her behalf. Flora said that she was happy and satisfied in her life, as she always had been, and she did not interfere with what others did or wanted, because such things did not concern her. She wished my mother all happiness in her marriage and hoped that she would soon be too busy with her own responsibilities to worry about the lives of people that she used to know.

This well-written letter cut my mother, as she said, to the quick. She and Flora stopped corresponding. My mother did become busy with her own life and finally a prisoner in it.

But she thought about Flora. In later years, when she sometimes talked about the things she might have been, or done, she would say, "If I could have been a writer—I do think I could have been; I could have been a writer—then I would have written the story of Flora's life. And do you know what I would have called it? 'The Maiden Lady.'"

The Maiden Lady. She said these words in a solemn and sentimental tone of voice that I had no use for. I knew, or thought I knew, exactly the value she found in them. The stateliness and mystery. The hint of derision turning to reverence. I was fifteen or sixteen years old by that time, and I believed that I could see into my mother's mind. I could see what she would do with Flora, what she had already done. She would make her into a noble figure, one who accepts defection, treachery, who forgives and stands aside, not once but twice. Never a moment of complaint. Flora goes about her cheerful labors, she cleans the house and shovels out the cow byre, she removes some bloody mess from her sister's bed, and when at last the future seems to open up for her—Ellie will die and Robert will beg forgiveness and Flora will silence him with the proud gift of herself—it is time for Audrey Atkinson to drive into the yard and shut Flora out again, more inexplicably and thoroughly the second time than the first. She must endure the painting of the house, the electric lights, all the prosperous activity next door. "Make-Believe Ballroom," "Amos n' Andy." No more Scottish comedies or ancient sermons. She must see them drive off to the dance—her old lover and that coldhearted, stupid, by no means beautiful woman in the white satin wedding dress. She is mocked. (And of course she has made over the farm to Ellie and Robert, of course he has inherited it, and now everything belongs to Audrey Atkinson.) The wicked flourish. But it is all right. It is all right—the elect are veiled in patience and humility and lighted by a certainty that events cannot disturb.

That was what I believed my mother would make of things. In her own plight her notions had turned mystical, and there was sometimes a hush, a solemn thrill in her voice that grated on me, alerted me to what seemed a personal danger. I felt a great fog of platitudes and pieties lurking, an incontestable crippled-mother power, which could capture and choke me. There would be no end to it. I had to keep myself sharp-tongued and cynical, arguing and deflating. Eventually I gave up even that recognition and opposed her in silence.

This is a fancy way of saying that I was no comfort and poor company to her when she had almost nowhere else to turn.

I had my own ideas about Flora's story. I didn't think that I could have written a novel but that I would write one. I would take a different tack. I saw through my mother's story and put in what she left out. My Flora would be as black as hers was white. Rejoicing in the bad turns done to her and in her own forgiveness, spying on the shambles of her sister's life. A Presbyterian witch, reading out of her poisonous book. It takes a rival ruthlessness, the comparatively innocent brutality of the thick-skinned nurse, to drive her back, to flourish in her shade. But she is driven back; the power of sex and ordinary greed drive her back and shut her up in her own part of the house with the coal-oil lamps. She shrinks, she caves in, her bones harden and her joints thicken, and—oh, this is it, this is it, I see the bare beauty of the ending I will contrive!—she becomes crippled herself, with arthritis, hardly able to move. Now Audrey Atkinson comes into her full power—she demands the whole house. She wants those partitions knocked out that Robert put up with Flora's help when he married Ellie. She will provide Flora with a room, she will take care of her. (Audrey Atkinson does not wish to be seen as a monster, and perhaps she really isn't one.) So one day Robert carries Flora—for the first and last time he carries her in his arms—to the room that his wife Audrey has prepared for her. And once Flora is settled in her well-lit, well-heated corner Audrey Atkinson undertakes to clean out the newly vacated rooms, Flora's rooms. She carries a heap of old books out into the yard. It's spring again, housecleaning time, the season when Flora herself performed such feats, and now the pale face of Flora appears behind the new net curtains. She has dragged herself from her corner, she sees the light-blue sky with its high skidding clouds over the watery fields, the contending crows, the flooded creeks, the reddening tree branches. She sees the smoke rise out of the incinerator in the yard, where her books are burning. Those smelly old books, as Audrey has called them. Words and pages, the ominous dark spines. The elect, the damned, the slim hopes, the mighty torments—up in smoke. There was the ending.

To me the really mysterious person in the story, as my mother told it, was Robert. He never has a word to say. He gets engaged to Flora. He is walking beside her along the river when Ellie leaps out at them. He finds Ellie's thistles in his bed. He does the carpentry made necessary by his and Ellie's marriage. He listens or does not listen while Flora reads. Finally he sits scrunched up in the school desk while his flashy bride dances by with all the men.

So much for his public acts and appearances. But he was the one who started everything, in secret. He *did it to* Ellie. He did it to that skinny wild girl at a time when he was engaged to her sister, and he did it to her again and again when she was nothing but a poor botched body, a failed childbearer, lying in bed.

He must have done it to Audrey Atkinson, too, but with less disastrous results.

Those words, *did it to*—the words my mother, no more than Flora, 70
would never bring herself to speak—were simply exciting to me. I didn't feel any decent revulsion or reasonable indignation. I refused the warning. Not even the fate of Ellie could put me off. Not when I thought of that first encounter—the desperation of it, the ripping and striving. I used to sneak longing looks at men in those days. I admired their wrists and their necks and any bit of their chests a loose button let show, and even their ears and their feet in shoes. I expected nothing reasonable of them, only to be engulfed by their passion. I had similar thoughts about Robert.

What made Flora evil in my story was just what made her admirable in my mother's—her turning away from sex. I fought against everything my mother wanted to tell me on this subject; I despised even the drop in her voice, the gloomy caution, with which she approached it. My mother had grown up in a time and in a place where sex was a dark undertaking for women. She knew that you could die of it. So she honored the decency, the prudery, the frigidity, that might protect you. And I grew up in horror of that very protection, the dainty tyranny that seemed to me to extend to all areas of life, to enforce tea parties and white gloves and all other sorts of tinkling inanities. I favored bad words and a breakthrough, I teased myself with the thought of a man's recklessness and domination. The odd thing is that my mother's ideas were in line with some progressive notions of her times, and mine echoed the notions that were favored in my time. This in spite of the fact that we both believed ourselves independent, and lived in backwaters that did not register such changes. It's as if tendencies that seem most deeply rooted in our minds, most private and singular, have come in as spores on the prevailing wind, looking for any likely place to land, any welcome.

Not long before she died, but when I was still at home, my mother got a letter from the real Flora. It came from that town near the farm, the town that Flora used to ride to, with Robert, in the cart, holding on to the sacks of wool or potatoes.

Flora wrote that she was no longer living on the farm.

"Robert and Audrey are still there," she wrote. "Robert has some trouble with his back but otherwise he is very well. Audrey has poor circulation and is often short of breath. The doctor says she must lose weight but none of the diets seem to work. The farm has been doing very well. They are out of sheep entirely and into dairy cattle. As you may have heard, the chief thing nowadays is to get your milk quota from the government and then you are set. The old stable is all fixed up with milking machines and the latest modern equipment, it is quite a marvel. When I go out there to visit I hardly know where I am."

She went on to say that she had been living in town for some years now, and that she had a job clerking in a store. She must have said what kind of a store this was, but I cannot now remember. She said nothing, of course, about what had led her to this decision—whether she had in fact been put off her own farm, or had sold out her share, apparently not to much advantage. She stressed the fact of her friendliness with Robert and Audrey. She said her health was good.

"I hear that you have not been so lucky in that way," she wrote. "I ran into Cleta Barnes who used to be Cleta Stapleton at the post office out at home, and she told me that there is some problem with your muscles and she said your speech is affected too. This is sad to hear but they can do such wonderful things nowadays so I am hoping that the doctors may be able to help you."

An unsettling letter, leaving so many things out. Nothing in it about God's will or His role in our afflictions. No mention of whether Flora still went to that church. I don't think my mother ever answered. Her fine legible handwriting, her schoolteacher's writing, had deteriorated, and she had difficulty holding a pen. She was always beginning letters and not finishing them. I would find them lying around the house. *My dearest Mary,* they began. *My darling Ruth, My dear little Joanne (though I realize you are not little anymore), My dear old friend Cleta, My lovely Margaret.* These women were friends from her teaching days, her Normal School days, and from high school. A few were former pupils. I have friends all over the country, she would say defiantly. I have dear, dear friends.

I remember seeing one letter that started out: *Friend of my Youth.* I don't know whom it was to. They were all friends of her youth. I don't recall one that began with *My dear and most admired Flora.* I would always look at them, try to read the salutation and the few sentences she had written, and because I could not bear to feel sadness I would feel an impatience with the flowery language, the direct appeal for love and pity. She would get more of that, I thought (more from myself, I meant), if she could manage to withdraw with dignity, instead of reaching out all the time to cast her stricken shadow.

I had lost interest in Flora by then. I was always thinking of stories, and by this time I probably had a new one on my mind.

80 But I have thought of her since. I have wondered what kind of a store. A hardware store or a five-and-ten, where she has to wear a coverall, or a drugstore, where she is uniformed like a nurse, or a Ladies' Wear, where she is expected to be genteelly fashionable? She might have had to learn about food blenders or chain saws, negligees, cosmetics, even condoms. She would have to work all day under electric lights, and operate a cash register. Would she get a permanent, paint her nails, put on lipstick? She must have found a place to live—a little apartment with a kitchenette, overlooking the main street, or a room in a boarding house. How could she go on being a Cameronian? How could she get to that out-of-the-way church unless she managed to buy a car and learned to drive it? And if she did that she might drive not only to church but to other places. She might go on holidays. She might rent a cottage on a lake for a week, learn to swim, visit a city. She might eat meals in a restaurant, possibly in a restaurant where drinks were served. She might make friends with women who were divorced.

She might meet a man. A friend's widowed brother, perhaps. A man who did not know that she was a Cameronian or what Cameronians were. Who knew nothing of her story. A man who had never heard about the partial painting of the house or the two betrayals, or that it took all her dignity and innocence to keep her from being a joke. He might want to take her dancing, and she would have to explain that she could not go. He would be surprised but not put off—all that Cameronian business might seem quaint to him, almost charming. So it would to everybody. She was brought up in some weird religion, people would say. She lived a long time out on some godforsaken farm. She is a little bit strange but really quite nice. Nice-looking, too. Especially since she went and got her hair done.

I might go into a store and find her.

No, no. She would be dead a long time now.

But suppose I had gone into a store—perhaps a department store. I see a place with the brisk atmosphere, the straightforward displays, the old-fashioned modern look of the fifties. Suppose a tall, handsome woman, nicely turned out, had come to wait on me, and I had known, somehow, in spite of the sprayed and puffed hair and the pink or coral lips and fingernails—I had known that this was Flora. I would have wanted to tell her that I knew, I knew her story, though we had never met. I imagine myself trying to tell her. (This is a dream now, I understand it as a dream.) I imagine her listening, with a pleasant composure. But she shakes her head. She smiles at me, and in her smile there is a degree of mockery, a faint, self-assured malice. Weariness, as well. She is not surprised that I am telling her this, but she is weary of it, of me and my idea of her, my information, my notion that I can know anything about her.

85 Of course it's my mother I'm thinking of, my mother as she was in those dreams, saying, It's nothing, just this little tremor; saying with such astonishing

lighthearted forgiveness, Oh, I knew you'd come someday. My mother surprising me, and doing it almost indifferently. Her mask, her fate, and most of her affliction taken away. How relieved I was, and happy. But I now recall that I was disconcerted as well. I would have to say that I felt slightly cheated. Yes. Offended, tricked, cheated, by this welcome turnaround, this reprieve. My mother moving rather carelessly out of her old prison, showing options and powers I never dreamed she had, changes more than herself. She changes the bitter lump of love I have carried all this time into a phantom—something useless and uncalled for, like a phantom pregnancy.

The Cameronians, I have discovered, are or were an uncompromising remnant of the Covenanters—those Scots who in the seventeenth century bound themselves, with God, to resist prayer books, bishops, any taint of popery or interference by the King. Their name comes from Richard Cameron, an outlawed, or "field," preacher, soon cut down. The Cameronians—for a long time they have preferred to be called the Reformed Presbyterians—went into battle singing the seventy-fourth and the seventy-eighth Psalms. They hacked the haughty Bishop of St. Andrews to death on the highway and rode their horses over his body. One of their ministers, in a mood of firm rejoicing at his own hanging, excommunicated all the other preachers in the world.

CHARTING THE STORY

1. What did the narrator's mother find unusual about the Ottawa Valley? What effect does the valley's uniqueness have upon the mood of the story?
2. The narrator's mother was a practitioner of Anglicanism, whose "faith was easy" (Paragraph 28), whose "spirits . . . [were] robust" (Paragraph 28), while Flora was an uncompromisingly devout "Cameronian." How did the two manage to maintain their deep friendship?
3. What may have contributed to the marked transformation in Ellie from a spirited young woman—"a wild tease, a long-haired, impudent childish girl full of lolloping energy" (Paragraph 18)—to a physical and psychological "wreck"?

CONSIDERATIONS OF STYLE

1. How does the attitude of the daughter-narrator toward her mother contrast in the beginning and at the end of the story?
2. Of what relevance is the Cameronian religion to the events and characters in the narrative, as well as to the narrator's way of relating the story of her relationship with her mother and of the mother's experiences with Flora, Ellie, and Robert?
3. What is the significance to the story of the last paragraph, a sort of postscript about the Cameronians?

AFTERTHOUGHTS

1 Compare and contrast the mother-daughter relationship in this story with that in "A Rose in the Heart of New York."

2 Why do you suppose the daughter appropriates her mother's story of Flora as *The Maiden Lady* and reinvents the subject as a ruthless witch?

3 Discuss their roles in this story of two rather mysterious characters: Robert, the major male character in the story, who keeps a very low profile in a cast that includes self-assured women such as Flora, Audrey, and the narrator's mother; and mother's friend from the post office, Cleta, who isn't even named until near the end of the story.

THE WRITER'S CRAFT

1 Write a fictive or nonfictive profile of a close friend of one of your parents or grandparents, a person perhaps alluded to in the family stories.

2 The mother constantly left unfinished letters lying around. Write a short essay exploring the significance of these half-started letters, connecting them with similar images in the rest of the narrative.

3 Write a retelling of one episode in this story from the point of view of a marginal character.

EDNA O'BRIEN

EDNA O'BRIEN *was born in Tuamgraney, County Clare in 1930. She was educated at the National School in Scariff, the Convent of Mercy at Loughrea, and the Pharmaceutical College in Dublin.*

O'Brien has populated many of her novels and stories with people from County Clare. She has also drawn much from Irish lore, history, and geography. She has resided in London since 1959, though she returns often to Ireland.

O'Brien is the author of fourteen novels, including The Country Girls, August Is a Wicked Month, Casualties of Peace, *and* A Pagan Place; *five collections of short stories, including* The Love Object, A Scandalous Woman, *and* Lantern Slides; and *the plays* A Pagan Place, Virginia, *and* Beloved. *She has received numerous awards, including the European Literature Prize (1995), the Italia Prima Cavour, and the Writers' Guild of Great Britain Prize.*

This story traces an intense relationship between a mother and daughter. It first appeared in The New Yorker *and is included in two of O'Brien's story collections,* A Rose in the Heart *(1978) and* A Fanatic Heart *(1984).*

PERSPECTIVES

1 What attitudes underlie such expressions as "Mama's boy" or "Daddy's girl"? Are the converse expressions "Mama's girl" and "Daddy's boy" as common in English?

2 What are some little pleasures that you shared as a child with your parents together or individually? With siblings?

3 What are things about home and your family that you missed most when you first left home for school or to make your own life elsewhere?

A Rose in the Heart of New York

December night. Jack Frost in scales along the outside of the windows giving to the various rooms a white filtered light. The ice like bits of mirror beveling the puddles of the potholes. The rooms were cold inside, and for the most part identically furnished. The room with no furniture at all—save for the apples gathered in the autumn—was called the Vacant Room. The apples were all over the place. Their smell was heady, many of them having begun to rot. Rooms into which no one had stepped for days, and yet these rooms and their belongings would become part of the remembered story. A solemn house, set in its own grounds, away from the lazy bustle of the village. A lonesome house, it would prove to be, and with a strange lifelikeness, as if it were not a house at all but a person observing and breathing, a presence amid a cluster of trees and sturdy wind-shorn hedges.

The overweight midwife hurried up the drive, her serge cape blowing behind her. She was puffing. She carried her barrel-shaped leather bag in which were disinfectant, gauze, forceps, instruments, and a small bottle of holy water lest the new child should prove to be in danger of death. More infants died around Christmastime than in any other month of the year. When she passed the little sycamore tree that was halfway up, she began to hear the roaring and beseeching to God. Poor mother, she thought, poor poor mother. She was not too early, had come more or less at the correct time, even though she was summoned hours before by Donal, the serving boy who worked on the farm. She had brought most of the children of that parish into the world, yet had neither kith nor kin of her own. Coming in the back door, she took off her bonnet and then attached it to the knob by means of its elastic string.

It was a blue room—walls of dark wet morose blue, furniture made of walnut, including the bed on which the event was taking place. Fronting the fireplace was a huge lid of a chocolate box with the representation of a saucy-looking lady. The tassel of the blind kept bobbing against the frosted windowpane. There was a washstand, a basin and ewer of off-white, with big roses splashed throughout the china itself, and a huge lumbering beast of a wardrobe. The midwife recalled once going to a house up the mountain, and finding that the child had been smothered by the time she arrived, the fatherless child had been stuffed in a drawer. The moans filled that room and went beyond the distempered walls out into the cold hall outside, where the black felt doggie with the amber eyes stood sentinel on a tall varnished whatnot. At intervals the woman apologized to the midwife for the untoward commotion, said sorry in a gasping whisper, and then was seized again by a pain that at different times she described as being a knife, a dagger, a hell on earth. It was her fourth labor. The previous child had died two days after being born. An earlier child, also a daughter, had died of whooping cough. Her womb was sick unto death. Why be a woman. Oh cruel life; oh, merciless fate; oh, heartless man, she sobbed. Gripping the coverlet and remembering that between those selfsame, much-patched sheets, she had been prized apart, again and again, with not a word to her, not a little endearment, only rammed through and told to open up. When she married she had escaped the life of a serving girl, the possible experience of living in some grim institution, but as time went on and the bottom drawer was emptied of its gifts, she saw that she was made to serve in an altogether other way. When she wasn't screaming she was grinding her head into the pillow and praying for it to be all over. She dreaded the eventual bloodshed long before they saw any. The midwife made her ease up as she put an old sheet under her and over that a bit of oilcloth. The midwife said it was no joke and repeated the hypothesis that if men had to give birth there would not be a child born in the whole wide world. The husband was downstairs getting paralytic. Earlier when his wife had announced that she would have to go upstairs because of her labor, he said, looking for the slightest pretext for a celebration, that if there was any homemade wine or altar wine stacked away, to get it out, to produce it, and also the cut glasses. She said there was none and well he knew it, since they could hardly afford tea and sugar. He started to root and to rummage, to empty cupboards of their contents of rags, garments, and provisions, even to put his hand inside the bolster case, to delve into pillows; on he went, rampaging until he found a bottle in the wardrobe, in the very room into which she delivered her moans and exhortations. She begged of him not to, but all he did was to wield the amber-colored bottle in her direction, and then put it to his head so that the spirit started to go glug-glug. It was intoxicating stuff. By a wicked coincidence a crony of his had come to sell them another stove, most likely another crock, a thing that would have to be coaxed alight with constant attention and puffing to create a draft. The other child was with a neighbor, the dead ones in a graveyard six or seven miles away, among strangers and distant relatives, without their names being carved on the crooked rain-soaked tomb.

"O Jesus," she cried out as he came back to ask for a knitting needle to skewer out the bit of broken cork.

"Blazes," he said to her as she coiled into a knot and felt the big urgent 5
ball—that would be the head—as it pressed on the base of her bowels and battered at her insides.

Curses and prayers combined to issue out of her mouth, and as time went on, they became most pitiful and were interrupted with screams. The midwife put a facecloth on her forehead and told her to push, in the name of the Lord to push. She said she had no strength left, but the midwife went on enjoining her and simulating a hefty breath. It took over an hour. The little head showing its tonsure would recoil, would reshow itself, each time a fraction more, although, in between, it was seeming to shrink from the world that it was hurtling toward. She said to the nurse that she was being burst apart, and that she no longer cared if she died, or if they drank themselves to death. In the kitchen they were sparring over who had the best greyhound, who had the successor to Mick the Miller. The crucifix that had been in her hand had fallen out, and her hands themselves felt bony and skinned because of the way they wrenched one another.

"In the name of God, push, missus."

She would have pushed everything out of herself, her guts, her womb, her craw, her lights, and her liver, but the center of her body was holding on and this center seemed to be the governor of her. She wished to be nothing, a shell, devoid of everything and everyone, and she was announcing that, and roaring and raving, when the child came hurtling out, slowly at first, as if its neck could not wring its way through, then the shoulder—that was the worst bit—carving a straight course, then the hideous turnabout, and a scream other than her own, and an urgent presage of things, as the great gouts of blood and lymph followed upon the mewling creature itself. Her last bit of easiness was then torn from her, and she was without hope. It had come into the world lop-sided, and the first announcement from the midwife was a fatality, was that it had clubbed feet. Its little feet, she ventured to say, were like two stumps adhering to one another, and the blasted cord was bound around its neck. The result was a mewling piece of screwed-up, inert, dark-purple misery. The men subsided a little when the announcement was shouted down and they came to say congrats. The father waved a strip of pink flesh on a fork that he was carrying and remarked on its being unappetizing. They were cooking a goose downstairs and he said in future he would insist on turkey, as goose was only for gobs and goms. The mother felt green and disgusted, asked them to leave her alone. The salesman said was it a boy or a child, although he had just been told that it was a daughter. The mother could feel the blood gushing out of her, like water at a weir. The midwife told them to go down and behave like gentlemen.

Then she got three back numbers of the weekly paper, and a shoe box with a lid, and into it she stuffed the mess and the unnecessaries. She hummed as she prepared to do the stitching down the line of torn flesh that was gaping and coated with blood. The mother roared again and said this indeed was her vinegar and gall. She bit into the crucifix and dented it further. She could feel her mouth and her eyelids being stitched, too; she was no longer a lovely body, she was a vehicle for pain and for insult. The child was so quiet it scarcely breathed. The afterbirth was placed on the stove, where the dog, Shep, sniffed at it through its layers of paper and for his curiosity got a kick in the tail. The stove had been quenched, and the midwife said to the men that it was a crying shame to leave a good goose like that, neither cooked nor uncooked. The men had torn off bits of the breast so that the goose looked wounded, like the woman upstairs, who was then tightening her heart and soul, tightening inside the array of catgut stitches, and regarding her whole life as a vast disappointment. The midwife carried the big bundle up to the cellar, put an oil rag to it, set a match to it, and knew that she would have to be off soon to do the same task elsewhere. She would have liked to stay and swaddle the infant, and comfort the woman, and drink hot sweet tea, but there was not enough time. There was never enough time, and she hadn't even cleaned out the ashes or the cinders in her grate that morning.

The child was in a corner of the room in a brown cot with slats that rat- 10
tled because of the racket they had received from the previous children. The mother was not proud, far from it. She fed the child its first bottle, looked down at its wizened face, and thought, Where have you come from and why? She had no choice of a name. In fact, she said to her first visitor, a lieutenant

from the army, not to tell her a pack of lies, because this child had the ugliest face that had ever seen the light of day. That Christmas the drinking and sparring went on, the odd neighbor called, the mother got up on the third day and staggered down to do something about the unruly kitchen. Each evening at nightfall she got a bit of a candle to have handy and reoiled the Sacred Heart lamp for when the child cried. They both contracted bronchitis and the child was impounded in masses of flannel and flannelette.

Things changed. The mother came to idolize the child, because it was so quiet, never bawling, never asking for anything, just weirdly still in its pram, the dog watching over it, its eyes staring out at whatever happened to loom in. Its very ugliness disappeared. It seemed to drink them in with its huge, contemplating, slightly hazed-over, navy eyes. They shone at whatever they saw. The mother would look in the direction of the pram and say a little prayer for it, or smile, and often at night she held the candle shielded by her hand to see the face, to say pet or tush, to say nonsense to it. It ate whatever it was given, but as time went on, it knew what it like and had a sweet tooth. The food was what united them, eating off the same plate, using the same spoon, watching another's chews, feeling the food as it went down the other's neck. The child was slow to crawl and slower still to walk, but it knew everything, it perceived everything. When it ate blancmange or junket, it was eating part of the lovely substance of its mother.

They were together, always together. If its mother went to the post office, the child stood in the middle of the drive praying until its mother returned safely. The child cut the ridges of four fingers along the edge of a razor blade that had been wedged upright in the wood of the dresser, and seeing these four deep, horizontal identical slits the mother took the poor fingers into her own mouth and sucked them, to lessen the pain, and licked them to abolish the blood, and kept saying soft things until the child was stilled again.

Her mother's knuckles were her knuckles, her mother's veins were her veins, her mother's lap was a second heaven, her mother's forehead a copybook onto which she traced A B C D, her mother's body was a recess that she would wander inside forever and ever, a sepulcher growing deeper and deeper. When she saw other people, especially her pretty sister, she would simply wave from that safe place, she would not budge, would not be lured out. Her father took a hatchet to her mother and threatened that he would split open the head of her. The child watched through the kitchen window, because this debacle took place outdoors on a hillock under the three beech trees where the clothesline stretched, then sagged. The mother had been hanging out the four sheets washed that morning, two off each bed. The child was engaged in twisting her hair, looping it around bits of white rag, to form ringlets, decking herself in the kitchen mirror, and then every other minute running across to the window to reconnoiter, wondering what she ought to do, jumping up and down as if she had a pain, not knowing what to do, running back to the mirror, hoping that the terrible scene would pass, that the ground would open up and swallow her father, that the hatchet would turn into a magic wand, that her mother would come through the kitchen door and say "Fear not," that travail would be all over. Later she heard a verbatim account of what had happened. Her father demanded money, her mother refused same on the grounds that she had none, but added that if she had it she would hang sooner than give it to him. That did it. It was then he really got bucking, gritted his teeth and his muscles, said that he would split the head of her, and the mother said that if he did so there was a place for him. That place was the lunatic asylum. It was twenty or thirty miles away, a big gray edifice, men and women lumped in together, some in straitjackets, some in padded cells, some blindfolded because of having sacks thrown over their heads, some strapped across the chest to quell and impede them. Those who did not want to go there were dragged by relatives, or by means of rope, some being tied on to the end of a plow or a harrow and brought in on all fours, like beasts of the earth. Then when they were not so mad, not so rampaging, they were let home again, where they were very peculiar and given to smiling and to chattering to themselves, and in no time they were ripe to go off again or to be dragged off. March was the worst month, when everything went askew, even the wind, even the March hares. Her father did not go there. He went off on a batter and then went to a monastery, and then was brought home and shook in the bed chair for five days, eating bread and milk and asking who would convey him over the fields, until he saw his yearlings, and when no one volunteered to, it fell to her because she was the youngest. Over in the fields he patted the yearlings and said soppy things that he'd never day indoors, or to a human, and he cried and said he'd never touch a drop again, and there was a dribble on his pewter-brown mustache that was the remains of the mush he had been eating, and the yearling herself became fidgety and fretful as if she might bolt or stamp the ground to smithereens.

The girl and her mother took walks on Sundays—strolls, picked blackberries, consulted them for worms, made preserve, and slept side by side, entwined like twigs of trees or the ends of the sugar tongs. When she wakened and found that her mother had got up and was already mixing meals for the hens or stirabout for the young pigs, she hurried down, carrying her clothes under her arm, and dressed in whatever spot she could feast on the sight of her mother most. Always an egg for breakfast. An egg a day and she would grow strong. Her mother never ate an egg but topped the girl's egg and fed her it off the tarnished eggy spoon and gave her little sups of tea with which to wash it down. She had her own mug, red enamel and with not a chip. The girl kept looking back as she went down the drive for school, and as time went on, she mastered the knack of walking backward to be able to look all the longer, look at the aproned figure waving or holding up a potato pounder or a colander, or whatever happened to be in her hand.

The girl came home once and the mother was missing. Her mother had actually fulfilled her promise of going away one day and going to a spot where she would not be found. That threatened spot was the bottom of the lake. But in fact her mother had gone back to her own family, because the father had taken a shotgun to her and had shot her but was not a good aim like William Tell, had missed, had instead made a hole in the Blue Room wall. What were they doing upstairs in the middle of the day, an ascent they never made except the mother alone to dress the two beds. She could guess. She slept in a neighbor's house, slept in a bed with two old people who reeked of eucalyptus. She kept most of her clothes on and shriveled into herself, not wanting to touch or be touched by these two old people buried in their various layers of skin and hair and winceyette. Outside the window was a climbing rose with three or four red flowers along the bow of it, and looking at the flowers and thinking of the wormy clay, she would try to shut out what these two old people were saying, in order that she could remember the mother whom she despaired of ever seeing again. Not far away was their own house, with the back door wide open so that any stranger or tinker could come in or out. The dog was probably lonely and bloodied from hunting rabbits, the hens were forgotten about and were probably in their coops, hysterical, picking at one another's feathers because of their nerves. Eggs would rot. If she stood on the low whitewashed wall that fronted the cottage, she could see over the high limestone wall that boundaried their fields and then look to the driveway that led to the abandoned house itself. To her it was like a kind of castle where strange things had happened and would go on happening. She loved it and she feared it. The sky behind and above gave it mystery, sometimes made it broody, and gave it a kind of splendor when the red streaks in the heavens were like torches that betokened the performance of a gory play. All of a sudden, standing there, with a bit of grass between her front teeth, looking at her home and imagining this future drama, she heard the nearby lych-gate open and then shut with a clang, and saw her father appear, and jumped so clumsily she thought she had broken everything, particularly her ribs. She felt she was in pieces. She would be like Humpty-Dumpty, and all the king's horses and all the king's men would not be able to put her together again. Dismemberment did happen, a long time before, the time when her neck swelled out into a big fleshed balloon. She could only move her neck on one side, because the other side was like a ball and full of fluid and made gluggles when she touched it with her fingers. They were going to lance it. They placed her on a kitchen chair. Her mother boiled a saucepan of water. Her mother stood on another chair and reached far into the rear of a cupboard and hauled out a new towel. Everything was in that cupboard, sugar and tea and round biscuits and white flour and linen and must and mice. First one man, then another, then another man, then a last man who was mending the chimney, and then last of all her father each took hold of her—an arm, another arm, a shoulder, a waist, and her two flying legs that were doing everything possible not to be there. The lady doctor said nice things and cut into the big football of her neck, and it was like a pig's bladder bursting all over, the waters flowing out, and then it was not like that at all; it was like a sword on the bone of her neck sawing, cutting into the flesh, deeper and deeper, the men pressing upon her with all their might, saying that she was a demon, and the knife went into her swallow or where she thought of forever more as her swallow, and the lady doctor said, "Drat it," because she had done the wrong thing—had cut too deep and had to start scraping now, and her older sister danced a jig out on the flagstones so that neighbors going down the road would not get the impression that someone was being murdered. Long afterward she came back to the world of voices, muffled voices, and their reassurances, and a little something sweet to help her get over it all, and the lady doctor putting on her brown fur coat and hurrying to her next important work of mercy.

When she slept with the neighbors the old man asked the old woman were they ever going to be rid of her, were they going to have this dunce off their hands, were they saddled with her for the rest of their blooming lives. She declined the milk they gave her because it was goat's milk and too yellow and there was dust in it. She would answer them in single syllables, just yes or no, mostly no. She was learning to frown, so that she, too, would have A B C's. Her mother's forehead and hers would meet in heaven, salute, and all their lines would coincide. She refused food. She pined. In all, it was about a week.

The day her mother returned home—it was still January—the water pipes had burst, and when she got to the neighbors' and was told she could go on up home, she ran with all her might and resolution, so that her windpipe ached and then stopped aching when she found her mother down on her knees dealing with pools of water that had gushed from the red pipes. The brown rag was wet every other second and had to be wrung out and squeezed in the big chipped basin, the one she was first bathed in. The lodges of water were everywhere, lapping back and forth, threatening to expand, to discolor the tiles, and it was of this hazard they talked and fretted over rather than the mother's disappearance, or the dire cause of it, or the reason for her return. They went indoors and got the ingredients and the utensils and the sieve so as to make an orange cake with orange filling and orange icing. She never tasted anything so wonderful in all her life. She ate three big hunks, and her mother put her hand around her and said if she ate any more she would have a little corporation.

The father came home from the hospital, cried again, said that sure he wouldn't hurt a fly, and predicted that he would never break his pledge or go outside the gate again, only to Mass, never leave his own sweet acres. As before, the girl slept with her mother, recited the Rosary with her, and shared the small cubes of dark raisin-filled chocolate, then trembled while her mother went along to her father's bedroom for a tick, to stop him bucking. The consequences of those visits were deterred by the bits of tissue paper, a protection between herself and any emission. No other child got conceived, and there was no further use for the baggy napkins, the bottle, and the dark-brown mottled teat. The cot itself was sawn up and used to back two chairs, and they constituted something of the furniture in the big upstairs landing, where the felt dog still lorded over it now but had an eye missing because a visiting child had poked wire at it. The chairs were painted oxblood red and had the sharp end of a nail dragged along the varnish to give a wavering effect. Also on the landing was a bowl with a bit of wire inside to hold a profusion of artificial tea roses. These tea roses were a two-toned color, were red and yellow plastic, and the point of each petal was seared like the point of a thorn. Cloth flowers were softer. She had seen some once, very pale pink and purple, made of voile, in another house, in a big jug, tumbling over lady's bureau. In the landing at home, too, was the speared head of Christ, which looked down on all the proceedings with endless patience, endless commiseration. Underneath Christ was a pussy cat of black papier-mâché which originally had sweets stuffed into its middle, sweets the exact image of strawberries and even with a little leaf at the base, a leaf made of green-glazed angelica. They liked the same things—applesauce and beetroot and tomato sausages and angelica. They cleaned the windows, one the inside, the other the outside, they sang duets, they put newspapers over the newly washed dark-red tiles so as to keep them safe from the muck and trampalations of the men. About everything they agreed, or almost everything.

In the dark nights the wind used to sweep through the window and out on the landing and into the other rooms, and into the Blue Room, by now uninhabited. The wardrobe door would open of its own accord, or the ewer would rattle, or the lovely buxom Our Lady of Limerick picture would fall onto the marble washstand and there was a rumpus followed by prognostications of bad luck for seven years. When the other child came back from boarding school, the girl was at first excited, prepared lovingly for her, made cakes, and, soon after, was plunged into a state of wretchedness. Her mother was being taken away from her, or, worse, was gladly giving her speech, her attention, her hands, and all of her gaze to this intruder. Her mother and her older sister would go upstairs, where her mother would have some little treat for her, a hanky or a hanky sachet, and once a remnant that had been got at the mill at reduced price, due to a fire there. Beautiful, a flecked salmon pink.

Downstairs *she* had to stack dishes onto the tray. She banged the cups, she put a butter knife into the two-pound pot of black-currant jam and hauled out a big helping, then stuck the greasy plates one on top of the other, whereas normally she would have put a fork in between to protect the undersides. She dreamed that her mother and her rival sister were going for a walk and she asked to go too, but they sneaked off. She followed on a bicycle, but once outside the main gate could not decide whether to go to the left or the right, and then, having decided, made the wrong choice and stumbled on a herd of bullocks, all butting one another and endeavoring to get up into one another's backside. She turned back, and there they were strolling up the drive, like two sedate ladies linking and laughing, and the salmon-flecked remnant was already a garment, a beautiful swagger coat which her sister wore with a dash.

"I wanted to be with you," she said, and one said to the other, "She wanted to be with us," and then no matter what she said, no matter what the appeal, they repeated it as if she weren't there. In the end she knew that she would have to turn away from them, because she was not wanted, she was in their way. As a result of that dream, or rather the commotion that she made in her sleep, it was decided that she had worms, and the following morning they gave her a dose of turpentine and castor oil, the same as they gave the horses.

When her sister went back to the city, happiness was restored again. Her mother consulted her about the design on a leather bag which she was making. Her mother wanted a very old design, something concerning the history of their country. She said there would have to be battles and then peace and wonderful scenes form nature. Her mother said that there must be a lot of back history to a land and that education was a very fine thing. Preferable to the bog, her mother said. The girl said when she grew up that she would get a very good job and bring her mother to America. Her mother mentioned the street in Brooklyn where she had lodged and said that it had adjoined a park. They would go there one day. Her mother said maybe.

The growing girl began to say the word "backside" to herself and knew that her mother would be appalled. The girl laughed at bullocks and the sport they had. Then she went one further and jumped up and down and said "Jumping Jack," as if some devil were inside her, touching and tickling the lining of her. It was creepy. It was done outdoors, far from the house, out in the fields, in a grove, or under a canopy of rhododendrons. The buds of the rhododendrons were sticky and oozed with life, and everything along with herself was soaking wet, and she was given to wandering flushes and then fits of untoward laughter, so that she had to scold herself into some state of normality and this she did by slapping both cheeks vehemently. As a dire punishment she took cups of Glauber's salts three times a day, choosing to drink it when it was lukewarm and at its most nauseating. She would be told by her father to get out, to stop hatching, to get out from under her mother's apron strings, and he would send her for a spin on the woeful brakeless bicycle. She would go to the chapel, finding it empty of all but herself and the lady sacristan, who spent her life in there polishing and rearranging the artificial flowers; or she would go down into a bog and make certain unattainable wishes, but always at the end of every day, and at the end of every thought, and at the beginning of sleep and the precise moment of wakening, it was of her mother and for her mother she existed, and her prayers and her good deeds and her ringlets and the ire on her legs—created by the serge of her gym frock—were for her mother's intention, and on and on. Only death could part them, and not even that, because she resolved that she would take her own life if some disease or some calamity snatched her mother away. Her mother's three-quarter-length jacket she would don, sink her hands into the deep pockets, and say the name "Delia," her mother's, say it in different tones of voice, over and over again, always in a whisper and with a note of conspiracy.

A lovely thing happened. Her mother and father went on a journey by hire car to do a transaction whereby they could get some credit on his lands, and her father did not get drunk but ordered a nice pot of tea, and then sat back gripping his braces and gave her mother a few bob, with which her mother procured a most beautiful lipstick in a ridged gold case. It was like fresh fruit, so moist was it, and coral red. Her mother and she tried it on over and over again, were comical with it, trying it on, then wiping it off, trying it on again, making cupids so that her mother expostulated and said what scatterbrains they were, and even the father joined in the hilarity and daubed down the mother's cheek and said Fanny Anny, and the mother said that was enough, as the lipstick was liable to get broken. With her thumbnail she pressed on the little catch, pushing the lipstick down into its case, into its bed. As the years went on, it dried out and developed a peculiar shape, and they read somewhere that a lady's character could be told by that particular shape, and they wished that they could discover whether the mother was the extrovert or the shy violet.

The girl had no friends, she didn't need any. Her cup was full. Her mother was the cup, the cupboard, the sideboard with all the things in it, the tabernacle with God in it, the lake with the legends in it, the bog with the wishing well in it, the sea with the oysters and the corpses in it, her mother a gigantic sponge, a habitation in which she longed to sink and disappear forever and ever. Yet she was afraid to sink, caught in that hideous trap between fear of sinking and fear of swimming, she moved like a flounderer through this and that; through school, through inoculation, through a man who put his white handkerchief between naked her and naked him, and against a galvanized outhouse door came, gruntling and disgruntling like a tethered beast upon her; through a best friend, a girl friend who tried to clip the hairs of her vagina with a shears. The hairs of her vagina were mahogany-colored, and her best friend said that that denoted mortal sin. She agonized over it. Then came a dreadful blow. Two nuns called her and her mother and her father said that she was to stay outside in the kitchen and see that the kettle boiled and then lift it off so that water would not boil over. She went on tiptoe through the hall and listened at the door of the room. She got it in snatches. She was being discussed. She was being sent away to school. A fee was being discussed and her mother was asking if they could make a reduction. She ran out of the house in a dreadful state. She ran to the chicken run and went inside to cry and to go beserk. The floor was full of damp and gray-green mottled droppings. The nests were full of sour sops of hay. She thought she was going out of her mind. When they found her later, her father said to cut out the "bull," but her mother tried to comfort her by saying they had a prospectus and that she would have to get a whole lot of new clothes in navy blue. But where would the money come from?

In the convent to which they sent her she eventually found solace. A nun became her new idol. A nun with a dreadfully pale face and a master's degree in science. This nun and she worked out codes with the eyelids, and the flutter of the lashes, so they always knew each other's moods and feelings, so that the slightest hurt imposed by one was spotted by the other and responded to with a glance. The nun gave another girl more marks at the mid-term examination, and did it solely to hurt her, to wound her pride; the nun addressed her briskly in front of the whole class, said her full name and asked her a theological conundrum that was impossible to answer. In turn, she let one of the nun's holy pictures fall on the chapel floor, where of course it was found by the cleaning nun, who gave it back to the nun, who gave it to her with a "This seems to have got mislaid." They exchanged Christmas presents and notes that contained blissful innuendos. She had given chocolates with a kingfisher on the cover, and she had received a prayer book with gilt edging and it was as tiny as her little finger. She could not read the print but she held it to herself like a talisman, like a secret scroll in which love was mentioned.

Home on holiday it was a different story. Now *she* did the avoiding, the shunning. All the little treats and the carrageen soufflé that her mother had prepared were not gloated over. Then the pink crepe-de-Chine apron that her mother had made from an old dance dress did not receive the acclamation that the mother expected. It was fitted on and at once taken off and flung over the back of a chair with no praise except to remark on the braiding, which was cleverly done.

"These things are not to be sniffed at," her mother said, passing the plate of scones for the third or fourth time. The love of the nun dominated all her thoughts, and the nun's pale face got between her and the visible world that she was supposed to be seeing. At times she could taste it. It interfered with her studies, her other friendships, it got known about. She was called to see the Reverend Mother. The nun and she never had a tête-à-tête again and never swapped holy pictures. The day she was leaving forever they made an illicit date to meet in the summerhouse, out in the grounds, but neither of them turned up. They each sent a message with an apology, and it was, in fact, the messengers who met, a junior girl and a postulant carrying the same sentence on separate lips—"So-and-so is sorry—she wishes to say she can't . . ." They might have broken down or done anything, they might have kissed.

Out of school, away from the spell of nuns and gods and flower gardens and acts of contrition, away from the chapel with its incense and its brimstome sermons, away from surveillance, she met a bakery man who was also a notable hurley player and they started up that kind of courtship common to their sort—a date at Nelson's pillar two evenings a week, then to a café to have coffee and cream cakes, to hold hands under the table, to take a bus to her digs, to kiss against a railing and devour each other's face, as earlier they had devoured the mock cream and the sugar-dusted sponge cakes. But these orgies only increased her hunger, made it into something that could not be appeased. She would recall her mother from the very long ago, in the three-quarter-length jacket of salmon tweed, the brooch on the lapel, the smell of face powder, the lipstick hurriedly put on so that a little of it always smudged on the upper or the lower lip and appeared like some kind of birthmark. Recall that they even had the same mole on the back of the left hand, a mole that did not alter winter or summer and was made to seem paler when the fist was clenched. But she was recalling someone whom she wanted to banish. The bakery man got fed up, wanted more than a cuddle, hopped it. Then there was no one, just a long stretch, doing novenas, working in the library, and her mother's letters arriving, saying the usual things, how life was hard, how inclement the weather, how she's send a cake that day or the next day, as soon as there were enough eggs to make it with. The parcels arrived once a fortnight, bound in layers of newspaper, and then a strong outer layer of brown paper, all held with hideous assortments of twines—binding twine, very white twine, and colored plastic string form the stools that she had taken to making; then great spatters of sealing wax adorning it. Always a registered parcel, always a cake, a pound of butter, and a chicken that had to be cooked at once, because of its being nearly putrid form the four-day journey. It was not difficult to imagine the kitchen table, the bucket full of feathers, the moled hand picking away at the pin feathers, the other hand plunging in and drawing out all the undesirables, tremulous, making sure not to break a certain little pouch, since its tobacco-colored fluid could ruin the taste of the bird. Phew. Always the same implications in each letter, the same cry—

"Who knows what life brings. Your father is not hard-boiled despite his failings. It makes me sad to think of the little things that I used to be able to do for you." She hated those parcels, despite the fact that they were most welcome.

She married. Married in haste. Her mother said from the outset that he was as odd as two left shoes. He worked on an encyclopedia and was a mine of information on certain subjects. His specialty was vegetation in pond life. They lived to themselves. She learned to do chores, to bottle and preserve, to comply, to be a wife, to undress neatly at night, to fold her clothes, to put them on a cane chair, making sure to put her corset and her underthings respectfully under her dress or her skirt. It was like being at school again. The mother did not visit, being at odds with the censuring husband. Mother and daughter would meet in a market town midway between each of their rural homes, and when they met they sat in some hotel lounge, ordered tea, and discussed things that can easily be discussed—recipes, patterns for knitting, her sister, items of furniture that they envisaged buying. Her mother was getting older, had developed a slight stoop, and held up her hands to show the rheumatism in her joints. Then all of a sudden, as if she had just remembered it, she spoke about the cataracts, and her journey to the specialist, and how the specialist had asked her if she remembered anything about her eyes and how she had to tell him that she had lost her sight for five or six minutes one morning and that then it came back. He had told her how lucky it was, because in some instances it does not come back at all. She said yes, the shades of life were closing in on her. The daughter knew that her marriage would not last, but she dared not say so. Things were happening such as that they had separate meals, that he did not speak for weeks on end, and yet she defended him, talked of the open pine dresser he had made, and her mother rued the fact that she never had a handyman to do odd things for her. She said the window had broken in a storm and that there was still a bit of cardboard in it. She said she had her heart on two armchairs, armchairs with damask covers. The daughter longed to give them to her and thought that she might steal from her husband when he was asleep, steal the deposit, that is, and pay for them on hire purchase. But they said none of the things that they should have said.

"You didn't get any new style," the mother said, restating her particular dislike for a sheepskin coat.

"I don't want it," the girl said tersely.

"You were always a softie," the mother said, and inherent in this was disapproval for a man who allowed his wife to be dowdy. Perhaps she thought that her daughter's marriage might have amended for her own.

When her marriage did end, the girl wrote and said that it was all over, and the mother wrote posthaste, exacting two dire promises—the girl must write back on her oath and promise her that she would never touch an alcoholic drink as long as she lived and she would never again have to do with any man in body or soul. High commands. At the time the girl was walking the streets in a daze and stopping strangers to tell of her plight. One day in a park she met a man who was very sympathetic, a sort of a tramp. She told him her story, and then all of a sudden he told her this terrible dream. He had wakened up and he was swimming in water and the water kept changing color, it was blue and red and green, and these changing colors terrified him. She saw that he was not all there and invented an excuse to go somewhere. In time she sold her bicycle and pawned a gold bracelet and a gold watch and chain. She fled to England. She wanted to go somewhere where she knew no one. She was trying to start afresh, to wipe out the previous life. She was staggered by the assaults of memory—a bowl with her mother's menstrual cloth soaking in it and her sacrilegious idea that if lit it could resemble the heart of Christ, the conical wick of the Aladdin lamp being lit too high and disappearing into a jet of black; the roses, the five freakish winter roses that were in bloom when the pipes burst; the mice that came out of the shoes, then out of the shoe closet itself, onto the floor where the newspapers had been laid to prevent the muck and manure of the trampling men; the little box of rouge that almost asked to be licked, so dry and rosy was it; the black range whose temperature could be tested by just spitting on it and watching the immediate jig and trepidation of the spit; the pancakes on Shrove Tuesday (if there wasn't a row); the flitches of bacon hanging to smoke; the forgotten jam jars with inevitably the bit of moldy jam in the bottom; and always, like an overseeing spirit, the figure of the mother, who was responsible for each and every one of these facets, and always the pending doom in which the mother would perhaps be struck with the rim of a bucket, or a sledgehammer, or some improvised weapon; struck by the near-crazed father. It would be something as slight as that the mother had a splinter under her nail and the girl felt her own nail being lifted up, felt hurt to the quick, or felt her mother's sputum, could taste it like a dish. She was possessed by these thoughts in the library where she worked day in and day out, filing and cataloguing and handing over books. They were more than thoughts, they were the presence of this woman whom she resolved to kill. Yes, she would have to kill. She would have to take up arms and commit a murder. She thought of choking or drowning. Certainly the method had to do with suffocation, and she foresaw herself holding big suffocating pillows or a bolster, in the secrecy of the Blue Room, where it had all begun. Her mother turned into the bursting red pipes, into the brown dishcloths, into swamps of black-brown blooded water. Her mother turned into a streetwalker and paraded. Her mother was taking down her knickers in public, squatting to do awful things, left little piddles, small as puppies' piddles, her mother was drifting down a well in a big bucket, crying for help, but no help was forthcoming. The oddest dream came along. Her mother was on her deathbed, having just given birth to her—the little tonsured head jutted above the sheet—and had a neck rash, and was busy trying to catch a little insect, trying to cup it in the palms of her hands, and was saying that in the end "all there is, is yourself and this little insect that you're trying to kill." The word "kill" was everywhere, on the hoardings, in the evening air, on the tip of her thoughts. But life goes on. She bought a yellow two-piece worsted, and wrote home and said, "I must be getting cheerful, I wear less black." Her mother wrote, "I have only one wish now and it is that we will be buried together." The more she tried to kill, the more clinging the advances became. Her mother was taking out all the old souvenirs, the brown scapulars salvaged from the hurtful night in December, a mug, with their similar initial on it, a tablecloth that the girl had sent from her first earnings when she qualified as a librarian. The mother's letters began to show signs of wandering. They broke off in midsentence; one was written on blotting paper and almost indecipherable; they contained snatches of information such as "So-and-so died, there was a big turnout at the funeral," "I could do with a copper bracelet for rheumatism," "You know life gets lonelier."

She dreaded the summer holidays, but still she went. The geese and the gander would be trailing by the riverbank, the cows would gape at her as if an alien had entered their terrain. It was only the horses she avoided—always on the nervy side, as if ready to bolt. The fields themselves as beguiling as ever, fields full of herbage and meadowsweet, fields adorned with spangles of gold as the buttercups caught the shafts of intermittent sunshine. If only she could pick them up and carry them away. They sat indoors. A dog had a deep cut in his paw and it was thought that a fox did it, that the dog and the fox had tussled one night. As a result of this, he was admitted to the house. The mother and the dog spoke, although not a word passed between them. The father asked pointed questions, such as would it rain or was it teatime. For a pastime they then discussed all the dogs that they had had. The mother especially remembered Monkey and said that he was a queer one, that he'd know what you were thinking of. The father and daughter remembered further back to Shep, the big collie, who guarded the child's pram and drove thoroughbred horses off the drive, causing risk to his own person. Then there were the several pairs of dogs, all of whom sparred and quarreled throughout their lives, yet all of whom died within a week of one another, the surviving dog dying of grief for his pal. No matter how they avoided it, death crept into the conversation. The mother said unconvincingly how lucky they were never to have been crippled, to have enjoyed good health and enough to eat. The curtains behind her chair were a warm red velveteen and gave a glow to her face. A glow that was reminiscent of her lost beauty.

She decided on a celebration. She owed it to her mother. They would meet somewhere else, away from that house, and its skeletons and its old cunning tug at the heartstrings. She planned it a year in advance, a holiday in a hotel, set in beautiful woodland surroundings on the verge of the Atlantic Ocean. Their first hours were happily and most joyfully passed as they looked at the rooms, the view, the various tapestries, found where things were located, looked at the games room and then at the display cabinets, where there were cutglass and marble souvenirs on sale. The mother said that everything was "poison, dear." They took a walk by the seashore and remarked one to the other on the different stripes of color on the water, how definite they were, each color claiming its surface of sea, just like oats or grass or a plowed land. The brown plaits of seaweed slapped and slathered over rocks, long-legged birds let out their lonesome shrieks, and the mountains that loomed beyond seemed to hold the specter of continents inside them so vast were they, so old. They dined early. Afterward there was a singsong and the mother whispered that money wasn't everything; to look at the hard-boiled faces. Something snapped inside her, and forgetting this was her errand of mercy, she thought instead how this mother had a whole series of grudges, bitter grudges concerning love, happiness, and her hard impecunious fate. The angora jumpers, the court shoes, the brown and the fawn garments, the milk complexion, the auburn tresses, the little breathlessnesses, the hands worn by toil, the sore feet, these were but the trimmings, behind them lay the real person, who demanded her pound of flesh from life. They sat on a sofa. The mother sipped tea and she her whiskey. They said, "Cheers." The girl tried to get the conversation back to before she was born, or before other children were born, to the dances and the annual race day and the courtship that preempted the marriage. The mother refused to speak, balked, had no story to tell, said that even if she had a story she would not tell it. Said she hated raking up the past. The girl tweezed it out of her in scraps. The mother said yes, that as a young girl she was bold and obstinate and she did have fancy dreams but soon learned to toe the line. Then she burst out laughing and said she climbed up a ladder once into the chapel, and into the confessional, so as to be the first person there to have her confession heard by the missioner. The missioner nearly lost his life because he didn't know how anyone could possibly have got in, since the door was bolted and he had simply come to sit in the confessional to compose himself, when there she was, spouting sins. What sins?

The mother said, "Oh, I forget, love. I forget everything now."

The girl said, "No, you don't."

They said night-night and arranged to meet in the dining room the following morning.

The mother didn't sleep a wink, complained that her eyes and her nose were itchy, and she feared she was catching a cold. She drank tea noisily, slugged it down. They walked by the sea, which was now the color of gunmetal, and the mountains were no longer a talking point. They visited a ruined monastery where the nettles, the sorrel, the clover, and the seedy dock grew high in a rectangle. Powder shed from walls that were built of solid stone. The mother said that probably it was a chapel, or a chancery, a seat of sanctity down through the centuries, and she genuflected. To the girl it was just a ruin, unhallowed, full of weeds and buzzing with wasps and insects. Outside, there was a flock of noisy starlings. She could feel the trouble brewing. She said that there was a lovely smell, that it was most likely some wild herb, and she got down on her knees to locate it. Peering with eyes and fingers among the low grass, she came upon a nest of ants that were crawling over a tiny bit of ground with an amazing amount of energy and will. She felt barely in control.

They trailed back in time for coffee. The mother said hotel life was demoralizing as she bit into an iced biscuit. The porter fetched the paper. Two strange little puppies lapped at the mother's feet, and the porter said they would have to be drowned if they were not claimed before dusk. The mother said what a shame and recalled her own little pups, who didn't eat clothes on the line during the day but when night came got down to work on them.

"You'd be fit to kill them, but of course you couldn't," she said lamely. She was speaking of puppies from ten or fifteen years back.

He asked if she was enjoying it, and the mother said, "I quote the saying 'See Naples and die,' the same applies to this."

The daughter knew that her mother wanted to go home there and then, but they had booked for four days and it would be an admission of failure to cut it short. She asked the porter to arrange a boat trip to the island inhabited by seabirds, then a car drive to the Lakes of Killarney and another to see the home of the liberator Daniel O'Connell, the man who had asked to have his dead heart sent to Rome, to the Holy See. The porter said certainly and made a great to-do about accepting the tip she gave him. It was he who told them where Daniel O'Connell's heart lay, and the mother said it was the most rending thing she had ever heard, and the most devout. Then she said yes, that a holiday was an uplift, but that it came too late, as she wasn't use to the spoiling. The girl did not like that. To change the conversation the girl produced a postcard that she used as a bookmark. It was a photograph of a gouged torso and she told the porter that was how she felt, that was the state of her mind.

The mother said later she didn't think the girl should have said such a thing and wasn't it a bit extreme. Then the mother wrote a six-page letter to her friend Molly and the girl conspired to be the one to post it so that she could read it and find some clue to the chasm that stretched between them. As it happened, she could not bring herself to read it, because the mother gave it to her unsealed, as if she had guessed those thoughts, and the girl bit her lower lip and said, "How's Molly doing?"

The mother became very sentimental and said, "Poor creature, blind as a bat," but added that people were kind and how when they saw her with the white cane, they knew. The letter would be read to her by a daughter who was married and overweight and who suffered with her nerves. The girl recalled an autograph book, the mother's, with its confectionery-colored pages and its likewise rhymes and ditties. The mother recalled ice creams that she had eaten in Brooklyn long before. The mother remembered the embroidery she had done, making the statement in stitches that there was a rose in the heart of New York. The girl said stitches played such an important role in life and said, "A stitch in time saves nine." They tittered. They were getting nearer. The girl delicately inquired into the name and occupation of the mother's previous lover, in short, the father's rival. The mother would not divulge, except to say that he loved his mother, loved his sister, was most thoughtful, and that was that. Another long silence. Then the mother stirred in her chair, coughed, confided, said that in fact she and this thoughtful man, fearing, somehow sensing, that they would not be man and wife, had made each other a solemn pact one Sunday afternoon in Coney Island over an ice. They swore that they would get in touch with each other toward the end of their days. Lo and behold, after fifty-five years the mother wrote that letter! The girl's heart quickened, and her blood danced to the news of this tryst, this long-sustained clandestine passion. She felt that something momentous was about to get uttered. They could be true at last, they need not hide from one another's gaze. Her mother would own up. Her own life would not be one of curtained shame. She thought of the married man who was waiting for her in London, the one who took her for delicious weekends, and she shivered. The mother said that her letter had been returned; probably his sister had returned it, always being jealous. The girl begged to know the contents of the letter. The mother said it was harmless. The girl said go on. She tried to revive the spark, but the mother's mind was made up. The mother said that there was no such thing as love between the sexes and that it was all bull. She reaffirmed that there was only one kind of love and that was a mother's love for her child. There passed between them then such a moment, not a moment of sweetness, not a moment of reaffirmation, but a moment dense with hate—one hating and the other receiving it like rays, and then it was glossed over by the mother's remark about the grandeur of the ceiling. The girl gritted her teeth and resolved that they would not be buried in the same grave, and vehemently lit a cigarette, although they had hardly tasted the first course.

"I think you're very unsettled," her mother said.

"I didn't get that from the ground," the daughter said.

The mother bridled, stood up to leave, but was impeded by a waiter who was carrying a big chafing dish, over which a bright blue flame riotously spread. She sat down as if pushed down and said that that remark was the essence of cruelty. The girl said sorry. The mother said she had done all she could and that without maid or car or checkbook or any of life's luxuries. Life's dainties had not dropped on her path, she had to knit her own sweaters, cut and sew her own skirts, be her own hairdresser. The girl said for God's sake to let them enjoy it. The mother said that at seventy-eight one had time to think.

"And at thirty-eight," the girl said.

She wished then that her mother's life had been happier and had not exacted so much from her, and she felt she was being milked emotionally. With all her heart she pitied this woman, pitied her for having her dreams pulped and for betrothing herself to a life of suffering. But also she blamed her. They were both wild with emotion. They were speaking out of turn and eating carelessly; the very food seemed to taunt them. The mother wished that one of those white-coated waiters would tactfully take her plate of dinner away and replace it with a nice warm pot of tea, or better still, that she could be home in her own house by her own fireside, and furthermore she wished that her daughter had never grown into the cruel feelingless hussy that she was.

"What else could I have done?" the mother said.

"A lot," the girl said, and gulped at once.

The mother excused herself.

"When I pass on, I won't be sorry," she said.

Up in the room she locked and bolted the door, and lay curled up on the bed, knotted as a foetus, with a clump of paper handkerchiefs in front of her mouth. Downstairs she left behind her a grown girl, remembering a woman she most bottomlessly loved, then unloved, and cut off from herself in the middle of a large dining room while confronting a plate of undercooked lamb strewn with mint.

Death in its way comes just as much of a surprise as birth. We know we will die, just as the mother knows that she is primed to deliver around such and such a time, yet there is a fierce inner exclamation from her at the first onset of labor, and when the water breaks she is already a shocked woman. So it was. The reconciliation that she had hoped for, and indeed intended to instigate, never came. She was abroad at a conference when her mother died, and when she arrived through her own front door, the phone was ringing with the news of her mother's death. The message though clear to her ears was incredible to her. How had her mother died and why? In a hospital in Dublin as a result of a heart attack. Her mother had gone there to do shopping and was taken ill in the street. How fearful that must have been. Straightaway she set back for the airport, hoping to get a seat on a late-night flight.

Her sister would not be going, as she lived now in Australia, lived on a big farm miles from anywhere. Her letters were always pleas for news, for gossip, for books, for magazines. She had mellowed with the years, had grown fat, and was no longer the daffodil beauty. To her it was like seeing pages of life slip away, and she did not bend down to pick them up. They were carried away in the stream of life itself. And yet something tugged. The last plane had gone, but she decided to sit there until dawn and thought to herself that she might be sitting up at her mother's wake. The tube lighting drained the color from all the other waiting faces, and though she could not cry, she longed to tell someone that something incalculable had happened to her. They seemed as tired and as inert as she did. Coffee, bread, whiskey, all tasted the same, tasted of nothing, or at best of blotting paper. There was no man in her life at the moment, no one to ring up and tell the news to. Even if there was, she thought that lovers never know the full story of one another, only know the bit they meet, never know the iceberg of hurts that have gone before, and therefore are always strangers, or semi-strangers, even in the folds of love. She could not cry. She asked herself if perhaps her heart had turned to lead. Yet she dreaded that on impulse she might break down and that an attendant might have to lead her away.

When she arrived at the hospital next day, the remains had been removed and were now on their way through the center of Ireland. Through Joyce's Ireland, as she always called it, and thought of the great central plain open to the elements, the teeming rain, the drifting snow, the winds that gave chapped faces to farmers and cattle dealers and croup to the young calves. She passed the big towns and the lesser towns, recited snatches of recitation that she remembered, and hoped that no one could consider her disrespectful because the hire care was a bright ketchup red. When she got to her own part of the world, the sight of the mountains moved her, as they had always done—solemn, beautiful, unchanging except for different ranges of color. Solid and timeless. She tried to speak to her mother, but found the words artificial. She had bought a sandwich at the airport and now removed the glacé paper with her teeth and bit into it. The two days ahead would be awful. There would be her father's wild grief, there would be her aunt's grief, there would be cousins and friends, and strays and workmen; there would be a grave wide open and as they walked to it they would walk over other graves, under hawthorn, stamping the nettles as they went. She knew the graveyard very well, since childhood. She knew the tombs, the headstones, and the hidden vaults. She used to play there alone and both challenge and cower from ghosts. The inside of the grave was always a rich broody brown, and the gravedigger would probably lace it with a trellis of ivy or convolvulus leaf.

At that very moment she found that she had just caught up with the fu- 60
neral cortege, but she could hardly believe that it would be her mother's. Too much of a coincidence. They drove at a great pace and without too much respect for the dead. She kept up with them. The light was fading, the bushes were like blurs, the air bat-black; the birds had ceased, and the mountains were

dark bulks. If the file of cars took a right from the main road toward the lake town, then it must certainly be her mother's. It did. The thought of catching up with it was what made her cry. She cried with such delight, cried like a child who has done something good and is being praised for it and yet cannot bear the weight of emotioin. She cried the whole way through the lakeside town and sobbed as they crossed the old bridge toward the lovely dark leafy country road that led toward home. She cried like a homing bird. She was therefore seen as a daughter deeply distressed when she walked past the file of mourners outside the chapel gate, and when she shook the hands or touched the sleeves of those who had come forward to meet her. Earlier a friend had left flowers at the car-hire desk and she carried them as if she had specially chosen them. She thought, They think it is grief, but it is not the grief they think it is. It is emptiness more than grief. It is a grief at not being able to be wholehearted again. It is not a false grief, but it is unyielding, it is blood from a stone.

Inside the chapel she found her father howling, and in the first rows closest to the altar and to the coffin the chief mourners, both men and women, were sobbing, or, having just sobbed, were drying their eyes. As she shook hands with each one of them, she heard the same condolence—"Sorry for your trouble, sorry for your trouble, sorry for your trouble."

That night in her father's house people supped and ate and reminisced. As if in mourning a huge bough of a nearby tree had fallen down. Its roots were like a hand stuck up in the air. The house already reeked of neglect. She kept seeing her mother's figure coming through the door with a large tray, laden down with things. The undertaker called her out. He said since she had not seen the remains he would bring her to the chapel and unscrew the lid. She shrank from it, but she went, because to say no would have brought her disgrace. The chapel was cold, the wood creaked, and even the flowers at night seemed to have departed form themselves, like ghost flowers. Just as he lifted the lid he asked her to please step away, and she thought, Something fateful has happened, the skin has turned black or a finger moves or, the worst, she is not dead, she has merely visited the other world. Then he called her and she walked solemnly over and she almost screamed. The mouth was trying to speak. She was sure of it. One eyelid was not fully shut. It was unfinished. She kissed the face and felt a terrible pity. "O soul," she said, "where are you, on your voyaging, and O soul, are you immortal."

Suddenly she was afraid of her mother's fate and afraid for the fact that one day she, too, would have to make it. She longed to hold the face and utter consolations to it, but she was unable. She thought of the holiday that had been such a fiasco and the love that she had first so cravenly and so rampantly given and the love that she had so callously and so pointedly taken back. She thought why did she have to withdraw, why do people have to withdraw, why?

After the funeral she went around the house tidying and searching, as if for some secret. In the Blue Room damp had seeped through the walls, and there were little burrs of fungus that clung like bobbins on a hat veiling. In drawers she found bits of her mother's life. Emblems. Wishes. Dreams contained in such things as an exotic gauze rose of the darkest drenchingest red. Perfume bottles, dance shoes, boxes of handkerchiefs, and the returned letter. It was to the man called Vincent, the man her mother had intended to marry but whom she had forsaken when she left New York and came back to Ireland, back to her destiny. For the most part it was a practical letter outlining the size of her farm, the crops they grew, asking about mutual friends, his circumstances, and so forth. It seems he worked in a meat factory. There was only one little leak—"I think of you, you would not believe how often." In an instinctive gesture she crumpled the letter up as if it had been her own. The envelope had marked on the outside—*Return to sender*. The words seemed brazen, as if he himself had written them. There were so many hats, with flowers and veiling, all of light color, hats for summer outings, for rainless climes. Ah, the garden parties she must have conceived. Never having had the money for real style, her mother had invested in imitation things—an imitation crocodile handbag and an imitation fur bolero. It felt light, as if made of hair. There were, too, pink embroidered corsets, long bloomers, and three unworn cardigans.

For some reason she put her hand above the mantelpiece to the place 65
where they hid shillings when she was young. There wrapped in cobweb was an envelope addressed to her in her mother's handwriting. It sent shivers through her, and she prayed that it did not bristle with accusations. Inside, there were some trinkets, a gold sovereign, and some money. The notes were dirty, crumpled, and folded many times. How long had the envelope lain there? How had her mother managed to save? There was no letter, yet in her mind she concocted little tendernesses that her mother might have written—words such as "Buy yourself a jacket," or "Have a night out," or "Don't spend this on Masses." She wanted something, some communiqué. But there was no such thing.

A new wall had arisen, stronger and sturdier than before. Their life together and all those exchanges were like so many spilt feelings, and she looked to see some sign or hear some murmur. Instead, a silence filled the room, and there was a vaster silence beyond, as if the house itself had died or had been carefully put down to sleep.

CHARTING THE STORY

1. Trace the bonding process between the mother and daughter, from the daughter's birth (Paragraph 8) to the day the daughter came home to find her mother missing (Paragraph 15). Why did the mother leave? Why does she come back? How has her absence affected the mother-daughter relationship?
2. What sort of relationship does the father in this story have with his wife and daughters? What relationship exists between the two sisters? What purpose do the father and the sister seem to serve in the narrative?

3 What amorous relationships does the daughter experience? How do these affect her relationship with her mother?

CONSIDERATIONS OF STYLE

1 At which points in the story do images of death seem to take center stage? What differing circumstances evoke death references? What differing attitudes do the references convey?
2 What is the effect of recounting dreams in this story?
3 How do descriptions of the Blue Room differ in various places in the story?
4 The image of the "rose" recurs at various times throughout the story. What significance do roses possess? What connections might one be able to make between the rose and Ireland itself, considering that the rose has both national and religious significance?

AFTERTHOUGHTS

1 How do our perceptions of our parents change when we can finally ascribe to them sexuality and romance?
2 Find a poem or song that relies on a rose for its central image and discuss ramifications of that image, comparing and contrasting them with rose images in this story.

THE WRITER'S CRAFT

1 Throughout the story, objects link the mother and daughter emotionally, especially in the end, after the mother's death. Write about an object or objects that you hold dear as a memento of someone who has died.
2 Using the description of the letter that came back "Return to Sender," write a letter such as the mother might have written to Vincent.

JAMAICA KINCAID

JAMAICA KINCAID *was born Elaine Potter Richardson in 1949 in Antigua. She spent her childhood in the Caribbean, and, at seventeen, left for the United States. She entered the United States using her present name, worked as an au pair in New York City, later studied photography at the New School for Social Research, attended Franconia College in New Hampshire, and returned to New York without having taken a degree. She was a regular contributor to* The New Yorker *for twenty years, and her stories have also appeared in* Ms, Rolling Stone, *and* The Paris Review. *Her first collection of short stories,* At the Bottom of the River *(1983), won the Morton Dauwen Zabel Award of the American Academy and Institute of Arts and Letters.*

Other works of fiction include Annie John *(1985),* Annie, Gwen, Lilly, Pam, and Tulip *(1986),* Lucy *(1990), and* Autobiography of My Mother *(1996).*

PERSPECTIVES

1 Look up "authority" and "power" in a dictionary. What nuances differentiate the two words? How might these words characterize/categorize good and bad human relationships in general, and between parents and their children in particular?

2 In your view, is there such a thing as a pure, unconditional love? If so, in what types of relationship does it best flourish; and if not, why is such a love unattainable?

My Mother

Immediately on wishing my mother dead and seeing the pain it caused her, I was sorry and cried so many tears that all the earth around me was drenched. Standing before my mother, I begged her forgiveness, and I begged so earnestly that she took pity on me, kissing my face and placing my head on her bosom to rest. Placing her arms around me, she drew my head closer and closer to her bosom, until finally I suffocated. I lay on her bosom, breathless, for a time uncountable, until one day, for a reason she has kept to herself, she shook me out and stood me under a tree and I started to breathe again. I cast a sharp glance at her and said to myself, 'So.' Instantly I grew my own bosoms, small mounds at first, leaving a small, soft place between them, where, if ever necessary, I could rest my own head. Between my mother and me now were the tears I had cried, and I gathered up some stones and banked them in so that they formed a small pond. The water in the pond was thick and black and poisonous, so that only unnamable invertebrates could live in it. My mother and I now watched each other carefully, always making sure to shower the other with words and deeds of love and affection.

I was sitting on my mother's bed trying to get a good look at myself. It was a large bed and it stood in the middle of a large, completely dark room. The room was completely dark because all the windows had been boarded up and all the crevices stuff with black cloth. My mother lit some candles and the room burst into a pink-like, yellow-like glow. Looming over us, much larger than ourselves, were our shadows. We sat mesmerized because our shadows had made a place between themselves, as if they were making room for someone else. Nothing filled up the space between them, and the shadow of my mother sighed. The shadow of my mother danced around the room to a tune that my own shadow sang, and then they stopped. All along, our shadows had grown thick and thin, long and short, had fallen at every angle, as if they were controlled by the light of day. Suddenly my mother got up and blew out the candles and our shadows vanished. I continued to sit on the bed, trying to get a good look at myself.

My mother removed her clothes and covered thoroughly her skin with a thick gold-coloured oil, which had recently been rendered in a hot pan from the livers of reptiles with pouched throats. She grew plates of metal-coloured scales on her back, and light, when it collided with this surface, would shatter and collapse into tiny points. Her teeth now arranged themselves into rows that reached all the way back to her long white throat. She uncoiled her hair from her head and then removed her hair altogether. Taking her head into her large palms, she flattened it so that her eyes, which were by now ablaze, sat on top of her head and spun like two revolving balls. Then, making two lines on the soles of each foot, she divided her feet into crossroads. Silently, she had instructed me to follow her example, and now I too travelled along on my white underbelly, my tongue darting and flickering in the hot air. 'Look,' said my mother.

My mother and I were standing on the sea-bed side by side, my arms laced loosely around her waist, my head resting securely on her shoulder, as if I needed the support. To make sure she believed in my frailness I sighed occasionally—long soft sighs, the kind of sigh she had long ago taught me could evoke sympathy. In fact, how I really felt was invincible. I was no longer a child but I was not yet a woman. My skin had just blackened and cracked and fallen away and my new impregnable carapace had taken full hold. My nose had flattened; my hair curled in and stood out straight from my head simultaneously; my many rows of teeth in their retractable trays were in place. My mother and I wordlessly made an arrangement—I sent out my beautiful sighs, she received them; I leaned ever more heavily on her for support, she offered her shoulder, which shortly grew to the size of a thick plank. A long time passed, at the end of which I had hoped to see my mother permanently cemented to the sea-bed. My mother reached out to pass a hand over my head, a pacifying gesture, but I laughed and, with great agility, stepped aside. I let out a horrible roar, then a self-pitying whine. I had grown big, but my mother was bigger, and that would always be so. We walked to the Garden of Fruits and there ate to our hearts' satisfaction. We departed through the south-westerly gate, leaving as always, in our trail, small colonies of worms.

With my mother, I crossed, unwillingly, the valley. We saw a lamb grazing and 5
when it heard our footsteps it paused and looked up at us. The lamb looked cross and miserable. I said to my mother, 'The lamb is cross and miserable. So would I be, too, if I had to live in a climate not suited to my nature.' My mother and I now entered the cave. It was the dark and cold cave. I felt something growing under my feet and I bent down to eat it. I stayed that way for years, bent over eating whatever I found growing under my feet. Eventually, I grew a special lens that would allow me to see in the darkest of darkness; eventually, I grew a special coat the kept me warm in the coldest of coldness. One day I saw my mother sitting on a rock. She said, 'What a strange expression you have on your face. So cross, so miserable, as if you were living in a climate not suited to your nature.' Laughing, she vanished. I dug a deep, deep hole. I built a beautiful house, a floorless house, over the deep, deep hole. I put in lattice windows, most favoured of windows by my mother, so perfect for looking out at people passing by without her being observed. I painted the house itself yellow, the windows green, colours I knew would please her. Standing just outside the door, I asked her to inspect the house. I said, 'Take a look. Tell me if it's to your satisfaction.' Laughing out of the corner of a mouth I could not see, she stepped inside. I stood just outside the door, listening carefully, hoping to hear her land with a thud at the bottom of the deep, deep hole. Instead, she walked up and down in every direction, even pounding her heel on the air. Coming outside to greet me, she said, 'It is an excellent house. I would be honoured to live in it,' and then vanished. I filled up the hole and burnt the house to the ground.

My mother has grown to an enormous height. I have grown to an enormous height also, but my mother's height is three times mine. Sometimes I cannot see from her breasts on up, so lost is she in the atmosphere. One day, seeing her sitting on the seashore, her hand reaching out in the deep to caress the belly of a striped fish as he swam through a place where two seas met, I glowed red with anger. For a while then I lived alone on the island where there were eight full moons and I adorned the face of each moon with expressions I had seen on my mother's face. All the expressions favoured me. I soon grew tired of living in this way and returned to my mother's side. I remained, though glowing red with anger, and my mother and I built houses on opposite banks of the dead pond. The dead pond lay between us; in it, only small invertebrates with poisonous lances lived. My mother behaved towards them as if she had suddenly found herself in the same room with relatives we had long since risen above. I cherished their presence and gave them names. Still I missed my mother's close company and cried constantly for her, but at the end of each day when I saw her return to her house, incredible and great deeds in her wake, each of them singing loudly her praises, I glowed and glowed again, red with anger. Eventually, I wore myself out and sank into a deep, deep sleep, the only dreamless sleep I have ever had.

One day my mother packed my things in a grip and, taking me by the hand, walked me to the jetty, placed me on board a boat, in care of the captain. My mother, while caressing my chin and cheeks, said some words of comfort to me because we had never been apart before. She kissed me on the forehead and turned and walked away. I cried so much my chest heaved up and down, my whole body shook at the sight of her back turned toward me, as if I had never seen her back turned toward me before. I started to make plans to get off the boat, but when I saw that the boat was encased in a large green bottle, as if it were about to decorate a mantelpiece, I fell asleep, until I reached my destination, the new island. When the boat stopped, I got off and I saw a woman with feet exactly like mine, especially around the arch of the instep. Even though the face was completely different from what I was used to, I recognized this woman as my mother. We greeted each other at first with great caution and politeness, but as we walked along, our steps became one, and as we talked, our voices became one voice, and we were in complete union in every other way. What peace came over me then, for I could not see where she left off and I began, or where I left off and she began.

My mother and I walk through the rooms of her house. Every crack in the floor holds a significant event: here, an apparently healthy young man suddenly dropped dead; here a young woman defied her father and, while riding her bicycle to the forbidden lovers' meeting place, fell down a precipice, remaining a cripple for the rest of a very long life. My mother and I find this a beautiful house. The rooms are large and empty, opening on to each other, waiting for people and things to fill them up. Our white muslin skirts billow up around our ankles, our hair hangs straight down our backs as our arms hang straight at our sides. I fit perfectly in the crook of my mother's arm, on the curve of her back, in the hollow of her stomach. We eat from the same bowl, drink from the same cup; when we sleep, our heads rest on the same pillow. As we walk through the rooms, we merge and separate, merge and separate; soon we shall enter the final stage of our evolution.

The fishermen are coming in from sea; their catch is bountiful, my mother has seen to that. As the waves plop, plop against each other, the fishermen are happy that the sea is calm. My mother points out the fishermen to me, their contentment is a source of my contentment. I am sitting in my mother's enormous lap. Sometimes I sit on a mat she has made for me from her hair. The lime trees are weighed down with limes—I have already perfumed myself with their blossoms. A humming-bird has nested on my stomach, a sign of my fertileness. My mother and I live in a bower made from flowers whose petals are imperishable. There is the silvery blue of the sea, criss-crossed with sharp darts of light, there is the warm rain falling on the clumps of castor bush, there is the small lamb bounding across the pasture, there is the soft ground welcoming the soles of my pink feet. It is in this way my mother and I have lived for a long time now.

CHARTING THE STORY

1 What are some of the powers that the mother possesses, noted in the first two paragraphs?
2 What do the monstrous, reptilian transformations of mother and daughter in Paragraphs 3 and 4 signify? At what stage of the daughter's development might such a transmogrification have occurred?
3 What stages do mother and daughter go through in their "evolution"? What could be considered the turning point in their relationship—bearing in mind that a "turning point" typically involves a decision that leads to the resolution of a story?
4 What images in the final paragraph of the story suggest that it is indeed "the final stage of [their—or mostly, the daughter's?] evolution"? What does the narrator seem to imply will be the future of mother and daughter, and what in the text suggests so?

CONSIDERATIONS OF STYLE

1 Highlight or copy the dialogue in this story. What does its sparseness suggest? What examples of non-verbal communication—like cues in a stage play—accompany the lines of dialogue?
2 What dream-logic connects the "evolutionary stages" of this relationship? How does the narrator, or the reader, segue from image to image?
3 What does the lamb in the story—first "cross and miserable," then "the *small* lamb bounding across the pasture"—signify?
4 Magical realism is, for some, an acquired taste, and for many, a delicious one. What elements of the story mark it as different from a more customarily "realistic"

story such as Edna O'Brien's mother-daughter story, "A Rose in the Heart of New York," which is also anthologized in this book?

AFTERTHOUGHTS

1 Go back over this "(auto-)biographical" story and chart the stages in the narrator/daughter's development from birth to the time in her adulthood when she makes an accommodation with her mother, and is content to share the beautiful, spacious house with her. Why does it seem to make sense to consider this story "autobiographical," even though it is entitled "My Mother"? (Note that one of Kincaid's recent novels is entitled *Autobiography of My Mother*.)

2 Would this sort of story work as a father-son narrative? Mother-son? Father-daughter? If so, what images might be evoked in each of the three alternatives; if not, what about this story makes it uniquely and totally female, by gender untranslatable?

3 Compare the life-journey shared by mother and daughter in this story with that in Edna O'Brien's "A Rose in the Heart of New York."

4 The daughter/narrator here and the daughter in Alice Munro's "Friend of My Youth" and in Edwidge Danticat's "New York Day Women" appropriate their mothers' stories. How do the stories differ? How does the fact that they have been "reauthored" (again, consider the etymology of "authority") speak to the mother-daughter relationship in each text?

THE WRITER'S CRAFT

1 In a critical essay, compare the imagery in this story with the mother-daughter images in Jamaica Kincaid's *Annie John* or *Autobiography of My Mother*, both of which are relatively easily attainable. How does "My Mother" differ from those two texts, and what binds it to them?

2 How would the mother in this story have narrated the "same" events? Choose one paragraph and recast it from her point of view.

PUNYAKANTE WIJENAIKE

PUNYAKANTE WIJENAIKE *has lived most of her life in Colombo, Sri Lanka, where she has had a long writing career. Critic Alastair Niven has called her "one of the most underestimated fiction writers currently at work in the English language," though her fiction has been taught in university courses in Britain, Australia, and elsewhere. Her first novel was* The Wailing Earth. *She has also published a collection of short stories,* The Third Woman.

"Anoma," originally published in Commonwealth Currents *in 1996, is a tale of a fourteen-year-old "neither child nor woman" who is left to care for her father, grandmother, and younger brother while her mother is working in the Middle East. The story shared first prize in the Commonwealth Short Story Competition shortly after its appearance.*

PERSPECTIVES

1 What constitutes "incest" in various cultures? Are there any commonalities that seem to be universal taboos? If there are, what might account for this? If not, what might account for the variance in responses? (This works best as a collaborative exercise.)

2 In your opinion or experience, what connections or bonds are formed between a mother and her unborn child? What may arise to threaten that bond?

Anoma

—I HAVE GOT AN IDEA.

—Why don't I call you Anoma?

—Then you are identified.

—Anoma—a girl, my friend and confidante.

—After all, we are both in this together, are we not?

—My grandmother keeps asking why I talk to myself.

—My grandmother, my archi-amma, does not know of your existence.

—I am talking to you because only you are in a position to understand what I am talking about. The Story behind your creation.

—You are still an embryo. Nature protects you from outside harm.
—When I talk you will listen but it will not disturb your sleep the way mine is disturbed. You will not be disturbed by the nightmares I suffer.
—But can you feel me toss and turn in our bed at night?
—Unfortunately, I am neither child nor woman. If I were as small as you, still an embryo curled in my mother's womb, I would be yet untouched by anyone.
—I would have not the need to talk to anyone.
—I am fourteen years old and missing from my mother far away in the Middle East.
—Why did she have to go?
—She went to earn a pot of gold for us.
—Was money more important than being together?
—I remember mother before she went away. She used to comb my hair, wash my face clean and starch my one and only white school uniform.
—Now I don't need the white uniform any more because I no longer go to school.
—My brother still goes to school.
—He is eleven years old but he does not miss mother the way I do because I wash his school clothes for him and cook his lunch. But he will not look me in the face nor talk to me.
—This hurts but I know why he avoids me. He thinks I have robbed mother of her place with father. He does not go anywhere near father at all.
—Archi-amma, my grandmother, cannot hear nor see very well. She never asks why I don't go to school any more. She is only glad I am at home to help her scrape a coconut or grind the chilly into a paste.
—You are the only one I can talk to, Anoma. I need to talk to someone.
—I am sick and afraid all the time.
—What will mother say, what will mother do when she finds out?
—I have to do something before she returns and finds out.
—During the day father neither looks at me nor comes near me.
—It is only at night, when he misses mother, that he calls for me.
—He does not think of my loneliness, only his.
—I can see brother does not sleep well at night either. Both of us wait night after night, dreading father's call. Often he smells of alcohol.
—Grandmother is too old to look after this household. Mother should have left someone younger in charge, like mother's sister, my Punchi-amma, my aunt. Someone who could cope with father's needs. Did she forget father's needs?
—I must warn you, Anoma, that it will not be by appointment that I disturb you when I need to communicate. It will be solely through my need to cry, to talk to someone when I cannot sleep at night. After all, it is not only father who needs comforting. His needs are physical. My need is to communicate.
—I am sure mother never wanted this to happen to me. She wanted me to remain chaste, a virgin until her return. When I attained age I remember her shielding me from the eyes of men. Even father and brother were not permit-

ted near me until I ceased to menstruate and she had bathed me, pouring potful after potful of water over my head. She had gifted me with gold ear-studs and washed my soiled garment clean. That is why it is all so confusing. Why did she leave me unprotected after all that care?

—It is that pot of gold. It has ruined us.

—For evil crept into the house after she left. I cannot get rid of the smell of soiled garments in the night. Father's and mine.

—However much I bathe, pouring potful after potful of water over me, I cannot get rid of this dirty smell.

—Anoma, Anoma, where are you? Are you hiding from me? Of late it is as if you are not there, safe and warm, within me, consoling me. It seems the more I talk to you, the more you withdraw from me. Have I touched you, even in the womb? Is that why you lie so still and quiet, not moving any more, within me?

—Anoma, you are making me afraid. It is as if suddenly you have identified yourself and you have become suspicious of my talking to you.

—You are no longer an embryo, a silent, sympathetic listener. You are challenging me. You have escaped your protective shell.

—You are hurt and accusing me.

—You are asking, without being a silent listener, "Have I got a future? Will I be born or are you contemplating my destruction before birth?"

—Anoma, you are not giving me time to come to terms with the situation.

—By talking you have roused my conscience.

—This is terrible, I feel betrayed, destroyed. Why can't you remain a silent listener?

—Please understand I did not create you willingly.

—Father created you within me.

—You are his grandchild, not my child.

—I need to grow into full womanhood and carry my own child from a man who is not my father.

—There, I have hurt and confused you again.

—You can no longer remain silent within me now. You ask, "Will I be born?" How can I answer that, Anoma?

—It's your life against mine.

—If you are born I will die. In shame.

CHARTING THE STORY

1. What does the narrator mean when she refers to herself as "neither child nor woman"? How might this self-designation be stated more accurately, given her circumstances?
2. How do the other family members—the younger brother, the grandmother, the father—respond to the narrator's crisis? In particular, what might account for the

speaker's grandmother, who ostensibly does not know of her granddaughter's pregnancy, to not be surprised that her granddaughter no longer goes to school?

3 What turn does the monologue take when Anoma ceases to be "a silent, sympathetic listener"?

CONSIDERATIONS OF STYLE

1 What is the effect of writing the first sentence of this monologue in capital letters?

2 The story is told as a series of utterances, most of which are no longer than one or two sentences, and all of which are directed at Anoma. What does this technique bring to the telling of the "Story behind [Anoma's] creation"?

3 Does the narrative appear to take place at one point in time, or to spread out over a series of instances? What in the text supports a unitary time or a longer span of time?

AFTERTHOUGHTS

1 Although many persons who argue against abortion make exceptions in cases of rape or incest, some hold that the circumstances of conception should not affect the decision whether to abort or to carry the pregnancy to term. What is your position on this matter, and how would you apply it to the narrator?

2 What do you predict would happen, were the narrative to move forward in time? What in the story (whether explicit or implicit) leads you to make this prediction?

THE WRITER'S CRAFT

1 Rewrite the lines of the monologue in which the speaker's brother, grandmother, and father are mentioned in their own voices, respectively. How does the inclusion of additional voices change the text as a dramatic presentation?

2 Tell Anoma's story, in her own voice, from the moment she ceases to be a "silent, sympathetic listener."

3 Suppose that an observant neighbor or some other person has reported the conditions in the narrator's family to local authorities, and a social worker is dispatched to interview the persons in the narrator's family. Write a report containing your observations as the social worker, outlining the positions of each family member, and recommending further action.

LI-YOUNG LEE

LI-YOUNG LEE *was born in Jakarta, Indonesia in 1957, of Chinese parents. His father was jailed during the Sukarno regime. Upon his release the family fled to Hong Kong, later lived in Macau and Japan, and settled in western Pennsylvania when Lee was seven. Lee has published two volumes of poetry:* Rose *(1986), in which "The Gift" appears, and* The City in Which I Love You *(1990). He has also published a memoir,* The Winged Seed *(1995). Lee currently lives in Chicago.*

PERSPECTIVES

1 What perspectives do you bring to your reading concerning the bonds between father and son?

2 How do parents typically balance the need both to love and to discipline their children?

3 What images come to mind when you consider the joined hands of a parent and child, and the joined hands of spouses or lovers?

The Gift

To pull the metal splinter from my palm
my father recited a story in a low voice.
I watched his lovely face and not the blade.
Before the story ended, he'd removed
the iron sliver I thought I'd die from.

I can't remember the tale,
but hear his voice still,
a well of dark water, a prayer.
And I recall his hands,
two measures of tenderness
he laid against my face,

the flames of discipline
he raised above my head.

Had you entered that afternoon
you would have thought you saw a man
planting something in a boy's palm,
a silver tear, a tiny flame.
Had you followed that boy
you would have arrived here,
where I bend over my wife's right hand.

Look how I shave her thumbnail down
so carefully she feels no pain.
Watch as I lift the splinter out.
I was seven when my father
took my hand like this,
and I did not hold that shard
between my fingers and think,
Metal that will bury me,
christen it Little Assassin,
One Going Deep for My Heart.
And I did not lift up my wound and cry,
Death visited here!
I did what a child does
when he's given something to keep.
I kissed my father.

CHARTING THE POEM

1 What incidents are recounted in the poem? What is the role of the speaker in each? How are they connected?
2 What similarities and differences do you note between the way the child apparently experienced the removal of the splinter from his hand and the way the adult remembers the event later in life?
3 What is the "Little Assassin"? Why does the narrator refer to it as such?

CONSIDERATIONS OF STYLE

1 With what images does the narrator convey his father's character? Do you see an elegantly simple presentation of the father, or a more layered complexity? What images seem consistent, and what (if any) break the consistency?

2 How does the author use parallelism and symmetry in the overall structure of the poem, as well as in lines within each stanza?

3 In motion picture making the technique of "cross-cutting" is used to create the illusion of simultaneity—for example, moving back and forth between shots of the pursued and the pursuer in a chase scene. How does Lee use a similar technique in this poem? What are its effects?

4 What purpose does the scene with the narrator and his wife serve? If it were removed, how would the poem change?

AFTERTHOUGHTS

1 What "gifts" are bestowed in this poem?

2 What similarities and differences do you observe between the father-son relationship in this poem and that in the stories "Cricket," "In the Shadow of War," and "A Family Supper"? How about between this poem and Seamus Heaney's poem "Digging"?

3 In what texts that you have read in this anthology, do mother-daughter relationships show the same closeness and affection as is seen between the speaker and his father in "The Gift"? In what texts do the parent-child relationships differ significantly?

THE WRITER'S CRAFT

1 Write a personal narrative describing how a particular act of parental kindness influenced you later in life.

2 Write a poem, or a short essay, about a "gift" that you have received, and have been able to pass on in turn.

3 Look most carefully at your hands, or at those of someone deeply meaningful to you, and write a short story, essay, or poem that features these hands.

RUDY THAUBERGER

RUDY THAUBERGER *was born in Saskatoon, Saskatchewan in 1961 and was graduated from the University of British Columbia Creative Writing Program. His works include short stories, articles, and plays, including* The Rhino Brothers, *his first feature-length screenplay.*

His story "Goalie" first appeared in 1988 in The Rocket, The Hammer, the Flower and Me *anthology of hockey stories edited by Doug Beardsley, and was later anthologized in* The Last Map Is the Heart: An Anthology of Western Canadian Fiction *in 1989.*

PERSPECTIVES

1 Hockey is considered to be one of the roughest of team sports. To what extent is this reputation due to the nature of the sport? To what extent to the environment in which it is played?

2 At what point in a young person's life must his or her parents learn to let go? In your experience, how do parents and children start to send each other signals during that critical time?

Goalie

Nothing pleases him. Win or lose, he comes home angry, dragging his equipment bag up the driveway, sullen eyes staring down, seeing nothing, refusing to see. He throws the bag against the door. You hear him, fumbling with his keys, his hands sore, swollen and cold. He drops the keys. He kicks the door. You open it and he enters, glaring, not at you, not at the keys, but at everything, the bag, the walls, the house, the air, the sky.

His clothes are heavy with sweat. There are spots of blood on his jersey and on his pads. He moves past you, wordless, pulling his equipment inside, into the laundry room and then into the garage. You listen to him, tearing the equipment from the bag, throwing it. You hear the thump of heavy leather, the clatter of plastic, the heavy whisper of damp cloth. He leaves and you enter. The equipment is everywhere, scattered, draped over chairs, hung on hooks, thrown on the floor.

You imagine him on the ice: compact, alert, impossibly agile and quick. Then you stare at the equipment: helmet and throat protector, hockey pants, jersey, chest and arm protectors, athletic supporter, knee pads and leg pads, blocker, catching glove and skates. In the centre of the floor are three sticks, scattered, their broad blades chipped and worn. The clutter is deliberate, perhaps even necessary. His room is the same, pure chaos, clothes and magazines everywhere, spilling out of dresser drawers, into the closet. He says he knows where everything is. You imagine him on the ice, focused, intense, single-minded. You understand the need for clutter.

When he isn't playing, he hates the equipment. It's heavy and awkward and bulky. It smells. He avoids it, scorns it. It disgusts him. Before a game, he gathers it together on the floor and stares at it. He lays each piece out carefully, obsessively, growling and snarling at anyone who comes too close. His mother calls him a gladiator, a bullfighter. But you know the truth, that gathering the equipment is a ritual of hatred, that every piece represents, to him, a particular variety of pain.

There are black marks scattered on the white plastic of his skates. He treats them like scars, reminders of pain. His glove hand is always swollen. His chest, his knees and his biceps are always bruised. After a hard game, he can barely move. "Do you enjoy it?" you ask, "Do you enjoy the game at least? Do you like playing?" He shrugs. "I love it," he says.

Without the game, he's miserable. He spends his summers restless and morose, skating every morning, lifting weights at night. He juggles absent-mindedly; tennis balls, coins, apples, tossing them behind his back and under his leg, see-sawing two in one hand as he talks on the phone, bouncing them off the walls and knees and feet. He plays golf and tennis with great fervour, but you suspect, underneath, he is indifferent to these games.

As fall approaches, you begin to find him in the basement, cleaning his skates, oiling his glove, taping his sticks. His hands move with precision and care. You sit with him and talk. He tells you stories. This save. That goal. Funny stories. He laughs. The funniest stories are about failure: the goal scored from centre ice, the goal scored on him by his own defenceman, the goal scored through a shattered stick. There is always a moral, the same moral every time. "You try your best and you lose."

He starts wearing the leg pads in September. Every evening, he wanders the house in them, wearing them with shorts and a T-shirt. He hops in them, does leg lifts and jumping jacks. He takes them off and sits on them, folding them into a squat pile to limber them up. He starts to shoot a tennis ball against the fence with his stick.

As practices begin, he comes home overwhelmed by despair. His skill is an illusion, a lie, a magic trick. Nothing you say reassures him. You're his father. Your praise is empty, invalid.

The injuries begin. Bruises. Sprains. His body betrays him. Too slow. Too clumsy. His ankles are weak, buckling under him. His muscles cramp. His nose bleeds. A nerve in his chest begins to knot and fray. No one understands. They believe he's invulnerable, the fans, his teammates. They stare at him blankly while he lies on the ice, white-blind, paralyzed, as his knee or his toe or his hand or his chest or his throat burns.

To be a goalie, you realize, is to be an adult too soon, to have too soon an intimate understanding of the inevitability of pain and failure. In the backyard, next to the garage, is an old garbage can filled with broken hockey sticks. The blades have shattered. The shafts are cracked. He keeps them all, adding a new one every two weeks. You imagine him, at the end of the season, burning them, purging his failure with a bonfire. But that doesn't happen. At the end of the season, he forgets them and you throw them away.

You watch him play. You sit in the stands with his mother, freezing, in an arena filled with echoes. He comes out without his helmet and stick, skating slowly around the rink. Others move around him deftly. He stares past them, disconnected, barely awake. They talk to him, call his name, hit his pads lightly with their sticks. He nods, smiles. You know he's had at least four cups of coffee. You've seen him, drinking, prowling the house frantically.

As the warm-up drills begin, he gets into the goal casually. Pucks fly over the ice, crashing into the boards, cluttering the net. He skates into the goal, pulling on his glove and blocker. He raps the posts with his stick. No one seems to notice, even when he starts deflecting shots. They come around to him slowly, firing easy shots at his pads. He scoops the pucks out of the net with his stick. He seems bored.

You shiver as you sit, watching him. You hardly speak. He ignores you. You think of the cost of his equipment. Sticks, forty dollars. Glove, one hundred and twenty. Leg pads, thirteen hundred dollars. The pads have patches. The glove is soft, the leather eaten away by his sweat.

The game begins, casually, without ceremony. The scoreboard lights up. The ice is cleared of pucks. Whistles blow. After the stillness of the face-off, you hardly notice the change, until you see him in goal, crouched over, staring.

You remember him in the backyard, six years old, standing in a ragged net, wearing a parka and a baseball glove, holding an ordinary hockey stick, sawed off at the top. The puck is a tennis ball. The ice is cement. He falls down every time you shoot, ignoring the ball, trying to look like the goalies on TV. You score, even when you don't want to. He's too busy play-acting. He smiles, laughs, shouts.

You buy him a mask. He paints it. Yellow and black. Blue and white. Red and blue. It changes every month, as his heroes change. You make him a blocker out of cardboard and leg pads out of foam rubber. His mother makes him a chest protector. You play in the backyard, every evening, taking shot after shot, all winter.

It's hard to recall when you realize he's good. You come to a point where he starts to surprise you, snatching the ball out of the air with his glove, kicking it away with his shoe. You watch him one Saturday, playing with his friends.

He humiliates them, stopping everything. They shout and curse. He comes in, frozen, tired and spellbound. "Did you see?" he says.

He learns to skate, moving off the street and onto the ice. The pain begins. A shot to the shoulder paralyzes his arm for ten minutes. You buy him pads, protectors, thinking it will stop the pain. He begins to lose. Game after game. Fast reflexes are no longer enough. He is suddenly alone, separate from you, miserable. Nothing you say helps. Keep trying. Stop. Concentrate. Hold your stick blade flat on the ice.

He begins to practice. He begins to realize that he is alone. You can't help him. His mother can't help him. That part of his life detaches from you, becoming independent, free. You fool yourself, going to his games, cheering, believing you're being supportive, refusing to understand that here, in the rink, you're irrelevant. When you're happy for him, he's angry. When you're sad for him, he's indifferent. He begins to collect trophies.

You watch the game, fascinated. You try to see it through his eyes. You watch him. His head moves rhythmically. His stick sweeps the ice and chops at it. When the shots come, he stands frozen in a crouch. Position is everything, he tells you. He moves, the movement so swift it seems to strike you physically. How does he do it? How? You don't see the puck, only his movement. Save or goal, it's all the same.

You try to see the game through his eyes, aware of everything, constantly alert. It's not enough to follow the puck. The position of the puck is old news. The game. You try to understand the game. You fail.

He seems unearthly, moving to cut down the angle, chopping the puck with his stick. Nothing is wasted. You can almost feel his mind at work, watching, calculating. Where does it come from, you wonder, this strange mind? You try to move with him, watching his eyes through his cage, and his hands. You remember the way he watches games on television, cross-legged, hands fluttering, eyes seeing everything.

Suddenly you succeed, or you think you do. Suddenly, you see the game, not as a series of events, but as a state, with every moment in time potentially a goal. Potentiality. Probability. These are words you think of afterwards. As you watch, there is only the game, pressing against you, soft now, then sharp, then rough, biting, shocking, burning, dull, cold. No players. Only forces, feelings, the white ice, the cold, the echo, all joined. A shot crashes into his helmet. He falls to his knees. You cry out.

He stands slowly, shaking his head, hacking at the ice furiously with his stick. They scored. You never noticed. Seeing the game is not enough. Feeling it is not enough. He wants more, to understand completely, to control. You look out at the ice. The game is chaos again.

He comes home, angry, limping up the driveway, victorious. You watch him, dragging his bag, sticks in his hand, leg pads over his shoulder. You wonder when it happened, when he became this sullen, driven young man. You hear whispers about scouts, rumours. Everyone adores him, adores his skill.

But when you see his stiff, swollen hands, when he walks slowly into the kitchen in the mornings, every movement agony, you want to ask him why. Why does he do it? Why does he go on?

But you don't ask. Because you think you know the answer. You imagine him, looking at you and saying quietly, "What choice do I have? What else have I ever wanted to do?"

CHARTING THE STORY

1 What are some contradictions—surprising, at times even disturbing—in the young goalie's life?

2 What differing roles do the mother and the father play in the "making of a hockey player" of their son?

3 In Paragraph 4, the narrator speaks of a "ritual of hatred." What set pattern of actions does the son follow in this paragraph, and later on in the story? What characteristic rituals are followed by either or both parents? What purposes do such rituals seem to serve?

4 How does the game change for the father as he comes to better understand his son?

CONSIDERATIONS OF STYLE

1 What is the effect of the narrator's withholding the identity of "you" until one-third of the way into the story?

2 What is the effect of telling this story from the father's point of view?

3 In Paragraphs 16 through 20, the narrator flashes back to the goalie's childhood. What purposes does this remembrance serve?

AFTERTHOUGHTS

1 In what ways is the position of goalie different from those of the forward, the half-back, and the fullback? How does this affect the character of the son? Were he playing any other position, how might the story be affected?

2 If the goalie had been "your" daughter, do you think her character would have been portrayed differently? If so, how would it come across? If not, why would it not change?

3 Read a general article on the concept in psychology called the "self-fulfilling prophecy"—also called the "Pygmalion Effect." What is the origin of the latter term? How does the concept apply to the story "The Goalie"?

THE WRITER'S CRAFT

1 Write an essay chronicling your training for excellence in a sport such as swimming, tennis, archery—or hockey. Emphasize the extreme physical and psychological demands that challenged you in the process.

2 Write an essay describing how, with great diligence, determination, and "the inevitability of pain and failure" (Paragraph 11), you mastered a demanding skill such as playing a musical instrument, painting or sculpting, writing, or public speaking.

3 Do sports or other competitive activities tend to produce "sullen, driven" players? In an essay, or in some other venue, discuss some advantages and disadvantages of such intense pursuit. If you have experience in playing noncompetitive games, you may wish to examine their effects by way of comparison.

SEAMUS HEANEY

SEAMUS HEANEY *won the Nobel Prize for Literature in 1995—the first Irish poet to win the prize since William Butler Yeats in 1923. A Catholic born on a farm in Northern Ireland in 1939, Heaney moved to Dublin in 1976 and has lived mostly there since. His first volume of poetry,* Death of a Naturalist, *published when he was twenty-seven, won him several literary prizes. He has won numerous major literary awards, and is considered by many critics to be one of the three greatest living poets, along with Russian-born American Joseph Brodsky and the Caribbean poet Derek Walcott.*

In this warm, familial poem, Heaney shares a vignette of his family story set in the stark simplicity of the Irish countryside. "Digging" *is included in Heaney's* Selected Poems, 1966–1987.

PERSPECTIVES

1 The term "generation gap" is said to have first been used by anthropologist Margaret Mead in the early 1960s. Can you apply the term—now in common use—in your own life? What are both positive and negative effects of a wide generation gap?

2 In your experience, is writing "hard labor"? Can gardening be poetry?

Digging

Between my finger and my thumb
The squat pen rests; snug as a gun.

Under my window, a clean rasping sound
When the spade sinks into gravelly ground:
My father, digging. I look down

Till his straining rump among the flowerbeds
Bends low, comes up twenty years away
Stooping in rhythm through potato drills
Where he was digging.

The coarse boot nestled on the lug, the shaft
Against the inside knee was levered firmly.
He rooted out tall tops, buried the bright edge deep
To scatter new potatoes that we picked
Loving their cool hardness in our hands.

By God, the old man could handle a spade.
Just like his old man.

My grandfather cut more turf in a day
Than any other man on Toner's bog.
Once I carried him milk in a bottle
Corked sloppily with paper. He straightened up
To drink it, then fell to right away

Nicking and slicing neatly, heaving sods
Over his shoulder, going down and down
For the good turf. Digging.

The cold smell of potato mould, the squelch and slap
Of soggy peat, the curt cuts of an edge
Through living roots awaken in my head.
But I've no spade to follow men like them.

Between my finger and my thumb
The squat pen rests.
I'll dig with it.

CHARTING THE POEM

1 Where is this poem set in place and time? Are the characters mentioned in the poem physically together in the setting?
2 The poem begins and ends with an image of the poet-narrator at work writing. How do the beginning and ending images differ? How do they connect with the intervening images of the poem?

CONSIDERATIONS OF STYLE

1 The vocabulary of this poem is simple, direct, and palpably Anglo-Saxon. How does the vocabulary fit with the imagery and the tone of the poem?
2 What sensory impressions do various stanzas in this poem evoke?
3 What is the effect of the spare use of rhyming and alliteration in this poem?

AFTERTHOUGHTS

1 This poem could be called an *apologia pro vita sua*—a defense or justification of the poet-narrator's choice not to follow in his father's and grandfather's footsteps. What purpose does such an *apologia* serve?

2 How has the father's digging changed since he himself was younger? What does this imply about him—not only physically, but socioeconomically?

THE WRITER'S CRAFT

1 Discuss some generational differences between your parents that have caused conflict. How have you collectively sought to resolve the conflict?

2 Write a narrative poem—fictional or factual—chronicling three generations in your family.

3 From the point of view of the father outside digging, write a poem about your adult child inside, writing.

PETER HO DAVIES

PETER HO DAVIES *was born in England in 1966 to a Welsh father and a Chinese Malaysian mother. He received a B.S. in physics and the history of philosophy and science from the University of Manchester, a B.A. in English from Cambridge University in England, and an M.A. in creative writing from Boston University.*

His book of short stories, The Ugliest House in the World, *published in 1997, won an O Henry Award and an NEA Fellowship. His newest collection is entitled* Equal Love.

Davies is an assistant professor in the Creative Writing Program at the University of Oregon.

"The Next Life," to be included in the collection Equal Love, *appeared in the March 1999 issue of* Harper's Magazine. *It chronicles the lavish funeral that a Chinese American son gives for his father, who in life had earned his respect and obedience, and who now in death receives his unqualified love.*

PERSPECTIVES

1 Given that a funeral is a significant cultural act, what "mainstream" American cultural values do you consider a typical American funeral to reflect?

2 In your culture or religious tradition, what customs surround death and the mourning process, including notions about "respect for the dead"? Have they changed since your childhood, and if so, how and why?

3 What attitudes about gambling do you bring to your reading of this text? What attitudes seem to be present in the culture that surrounds you (including the system of laws under which you live)?

The Next Life

The mourners were playing poker around the rosewood table the night before his father's funeral, and Lim was winning.

They had begun the game to help themselves stay awake during the vigil. Pang had produced the new deck from a pocket of his white mourning suit and asked Lim's permission earlier in the evening. "It'll amuse the ghost," he said, indicating the casket. "Being able to see all our cards."

Now it was almost dawn, and Lim had been winning for an hour or more. It was uncomfortable. Where before they had talked softly among themselves, now they played in silence. Lim wished he could get up and leave, but it seemed improper to end the game ahead. Every time he told himself to fold he would look at his cards and find a pair of aces, a wild card, four cards to a flush, something too good to turn down. He bet heavily on mediocre hands, hoping to have his bluff called, but the others were afraid of his good fortune now. When one of them did stay in, Lim made a hand with his last card and still took the pot.

He fanned his cards to study them and thought of the coffin over his shoulder.

Lim had been determined to give his father the finest possible funeral. Old Lim 5
had been the proprietor of the longest established Chinese newspaper on the West Coast. The day after his death of a second stroke, Lim had driven his father's prized Cadillac gingerly into Chinatown, to the corner of Jackson and Powell and the shop of Mr. Pang, the maker of grave goods.

The shop was on the second floor of a brick warehouse opposite the old Kong Chow Temple. At the top of the stairs a lighted glass cabinet was bright with spirit money, bricks of red-and-gold notes in neat, squat stacks. Beside them, through the narrow open door, Lim could see white paper furniture and, farther back, life-size paper suits hanging on the wall. He would need to buy all these items to burn at the funeral. Their smoke and ash would rise to heaven, where his father would be well provided for—as wealthy in the next life as in this.

Inside, he found Pang himself, seated at a long work table fitting thin canes together to make the frame of a model house. Behind him a bundle of bamboo rested in a pan of boiling water, softening until it could be bent and shaped. Sheets of rice paper hung on wire racks above, fluttering gently in the breeze from the door. It was warm in the shop. Pang himself wore only shorts and a singlet, and his shaved head, above his half-moon glasses, shone under the bright silver work lights. He stood as Lim came forward and dried his hands on a rag, apologizing for the heat. "Air-conditioning dries the paper." He rubbed his thumb against his fingertips. "Makes it hard to work."

He led Lim into the back room of the shop, which doubled as a showroom and storage space. It was filled with paper houses and cars and, farther back, whole rooms of ghost furniture. Everything was white, but the different items were to mismatched scales: the furniture would not fit in the houses; the cars reached as high as the rooftops. There was something toylike about the displays that reminded Lim of childhood, and yet he walked among them like a giant. So this, he thought, is what the afterlife looks like.

With Pang's help he chose the best house in stock, with a balcony and verandah, and an almost life-size paper sedan, with the three-pointed Mercedes star fashioned in straw on its hood. Pang nodded his approval and went to the stairs and called his assistant to come and move the pieces to the back of the shop. A door opened, the sound of a television—the stuttered blows and grunts of a martial-arts movie—floated down to them, and a stocky, muscular young man appeared. Pang gestured to him impatiently, pointing out with his chin the pieces Lim had chosen and whistling angrily when the youth stooped over the wrong item. Lim watched as he lifted the house and then the car high overhead and carried them away. At the door a breeze filled the paper shells with a snap, and the boy had to steady himself to steer them through the opening while Pang hissed with displeasure.

They moved on to the furniture, and Lim chose the best tables and chairs, even a paper TV and VCR. By the time Pang left him to write up the order, he had bought up almost half the stock. Alone in the showroom, Lim paced back and forth between the houses of the dead. Over the rooftops he saw the youth—a young man really, he decided—lighting a cigarette. He held the match in his hand, watched it burn down slowly till the yellow flame touched his fingertips, let it fall. When he noticed Lim watching, he stared back blankly and pantomimed the offer of a cigarette, but Lim shook his head. He heard Pang's footsteps returning and went to meet him.

"You make all the pieces yourself?" he asked, looking down the list the old man presented to him. "Or does your assistant build some?"

"They're all my own work," Pang told him. "My son runs the press. To print the hell notes." Lim had bought several million dollars in the best gold-leaf spirit money.

He complimented the workmanship, while Pang calculated the bill on an abacus. In the whiteness of the shop, the dark beads clacked back and forth. There was something soothing to Lim about the transaction and the other man's quiet business manner. "Isn't it hard to see your work burn?" he asked, and Pang nodded without looking up. He checked his figures twice and then named a price. It was a large sum, but Lim reached for his wallet and counted the bills out, one by one, with no word of bargaining. Pang blinked as each note was laid down, then shuffled them into a neat pile and put them in his pocket. "My condolences," he said. "Your father was a great man."

Lim gave instructions for delivery to the cemetery and thanked Pang for his time. He made to leave but paused and turned back. "Tell me," he said, "do you know where I might hire professional mourners?"

Pang looked doubtful. "It is the old custom."

Lim watched him tip the abacus slightly, the beads sliding silently to one side, erasing the last calculation.

"I would be very grateful," he began.

"My own family, in fact, were once mourners," Pang said slowly. "I could perhaps find some to attend you."

Lim thanked him for his kindness.

The day before the funeral, with the casket lying behind screens in the house 20
on Diamond Hill, friends and family members came to pay their respects. The casket was closed, but Lim's mother placed a gold-framed photograph of the deceased on the lid. It was an old studio pose of an intense young man in a dark suit and narrow tie, his hair shining like a movie star's. The photograph had been taken before Lim was born, and he hardly recognized his father. He complained to his mother. "He looks like a stranger."

"Such talk!" she cried. "How can he be a stranger? He looks like you in this picture."

Mr. Pang arrived early with three others. Two were old men: one a retired grocer, the other a former butcher, cousins of Pang's. The third was his brawny son. He helped move the deceased's favorite chair beside the casket while the old men laid out a table with old Lim's glasses; Luckies, his preferred brand of cigarettes; and a bottle of Courvoisier. Pang poured a glass of brandy, lit a cigarette, and set it in a jade ashtray for the spirit to enjoy. Lim showed them where the bottles of liquor and the cartons of cigarettes his father used to bring back from his business trips to Taiwan were kept. "Duty-free," he told Pang's son, who whistled softly when he saw the hoard. The mourners would ensure that fresh cigarettes were lit every half hour or so.

Dishes of Old Lim's favorite foods had already been prepared by the cook, and these were brought out now and set beside the coffin. The ginger bass, Lim saw, was a fish his father had caught himself and frozen. Fishing had become the old man's passion at the end of his life. Lim remembered one afternoon off Duxbury Reef. They were out for striped bass, but his father could reel in nothing but rockfish. He kept throwing them back and hooking another. The weather had begun to worsen and the fog roll in, but he refused to turn back without a bass. And all the time he kept hooking rockfish. Finally, in frustration, he had started to use his pocket knife to blind the fish, gouging their eyes before tossing them, still thrashing, back into the water. "Teach them to take my bait." Lim had turned away but said nothing. He hung over the side staring into the dark water and feigned seasickness all the way in. Even as a grown man, he found, he had been afraid of his father.

Pang sniffed appreciatively over the dish. "The spirit will smell the delicious aroma and come closer." Lim thought of the blind fish swimming in the darkness.

As the first guests came up the drive Pang's son began to wail and the 25
older men bent their heads. When they looked up they had tears in their eyes. Lim was impressed. He had begun to worry about the extravagance of hiring

mourners, but now, as he went to greet his visitors, he felt a deep satisfaction. These men would help the family shoulder the burden of grief.

He was gratified when his father's business partners and his older relatives complimented him on finding such skillful mourners. He noticed a change in the way these people treated him now. Some of the journalists and editors were of his own age, but previously at his father's office or the golf club they had merely nodded to him or smiled politely while they addressed his father. Now they caught his eye and drew him aside to express their sympathy. His father had been a giant. He was a dutiful son. They were sure the newspaper would prosper. They had always known how proud his father was of him. Lim nodded. The old man had made a point of bringing his partners past his son's desk, testing him on figures, or summoning him with a snap of his fingers to bring new copy to his office while they sat and sipped tea. His father liked to boast about Lim's education—Berkeley, his M.B.A.—but also to joke about what they didn't teach you in college: greed, luck, how to cut throats. Lim supposed he had resented it, but abstractly. Whatever he felt toward his father had always come second to what his father thought of him.

Every so often Lim excused himself to see that the flow of refreshments from the kitchen was running smoothly. The faces of Mr. Pang and the older mourners, he noticed, were still wet with tears. He could not imagine how the dried-up old men could cry so long. Pang's son did not cry, but he was still wailing lustily, and Lim thought it had been a wise choice on Pang's part to bring a young man with such strong lungs. Some of his guests had told him that the wailing could be heard from the street. Even his mother, who had been concerned about the expense, was moved. She had scolded him that his father, who had always been careful with money, would not have appreciated such excess. But she took one look at the mourners and her own tears began to flow so swiftly that she was surprised and tried to cup them in her hands.

In the evening, as the last guests departed, there was a small commotion. The wails of Pang's son suddenly ceased, and at the door, saying good-bye, Lim and his guests fell silent momentarily. When he had seen them off he came back into the house, and Pang's son approached him with a carton of cigarettes, almost crushed, gripped in his hand.

He held them out to Lim without a word.

"He means to apologize," Pang said in a pinched voice. "He was taking these." Lim took the small box and stared at it dumbly. It felt so light in his hands. The young man stood before him, his head bowed, shoulders raised, hands behind his back, as if expecting a blow. Pang was waiting for him, he knew, but in his confusion Lim could only thank the youth.

"It's nothing," Lim said. "It's not important." He almost pressed the box back into the boy's hands, but he could see the flush on Pang's face and bald head, and he could not meet his eyes. He felt as if the old man were angry with him, but he did not know what to say, and he excused himself to lead his mother to bed.

She leaned heavily on the arm he offered her. "If you had done anything like that your father would have whipped you," she whispered on the stairs. Lim nodded. He wondered if he had done the right thing, but he was glad he had stayed calm. He didn't want to be angry at the funeral. It would be unseemly. At her door, his mother turned. "You have honored Bar-Bar today," she said. "He was always such a superstitious man. You remember? When you were a small boy he used to call you names. Little pig. Ugly dog. He made you cry." She smiled ruefully. "You didn't understand. He was so proud of you. He thought if he praised you, demons would know how valuable you were and take you."

"I know," Lim told her. "I do understand. It's the custom."

"All this," she said, squeezing his hand. "I never knew you loved him so much."

Afterward, he stood in the door to his own room, turning the idea over in his mind like a bright coin. Perhaps he had loved his father, he told himself. Next to respect and obedience, love had always been excess to their relationship. But the more he thought it the more he believed it, until it seemed to him like a sharp point of truth.

He stared at his bed, but for the first time that day he felt relaxed, not tired. He decided to go down again to where the mourners were sitting up beside the casket to keep the spirit company.

Lim found them playing cards. He had wondered briefly if it was proper, but he trusted Pang not to suggest any impropriety. He was a professional, after all. He had even asked for their fee in advance so that they could divide it up and have something to gamble with. Now he formally complimented Lim on the success of the day and, after a moment of awkwardness, invited him to join them and make a fifth.

"I haven't played since I was a student," Lim told them, but he pulled up a stool and Pang dealt him in. He had thought himself a skillful player in college, betting quarters, but he felt out of his depth with stakes of ten or twenty dollars. He watched the other players carefully, but they betrayed little. Pang's son never looked up from his cards, and the faces of the older mourners were perfectly still, resting. Lim lost hand after hand.

"Your luck is lousy," Pang told him, less with sympathy than approval. "Only natural."

Lim played on, but his concentration was poor. He was restless, thinking about reopening his father's office, the huge rolls of white paper waiting for ink. He didn't mind that he was losing. He had taken a kind of pride in spending money on the funeral arrangements. The mourners had done a good job, and he told himself he would think of his losses as a tip, but after a while he grew bored. He had such bad cards that the game held no interest. He folded again and got up to stretch his legs. The others played on—Pang was betting hard and winning, mostly at his son's expense—while he walked slowly over to his father's casket. He ran his finger along the rich teak and sat for a moment in the chair, listening to the bets being called from the table. The ginger fish was cold and congealed. He picked up his father's spectacles from the table beside him and slipped them over his own ears, as he had as a child. He blinked, dizzied by the blurred images through the thick glass. Over the lenses, he saw that the cigarette in its jade ashtray was out, and he tapped another from the pack and put it between his lips and lit it. His father had smoked to the end, but Lim had not had a cigarette for years. He took the smoke into his lungs and held it for a long moment before exhaling. He rested the cigarette on the ashtray. The smell reminded him of his father. He watched the smoke swim upward and thought of Old Lim inhaling in heaven. He picked up the glass and watched the brandy cling to its sides as he swirled it around. The rich sweet smell filled his nostrils as he held it close to his nose. He took a deep breath, as if for a dive, and before he knew it he'd put the glass to his lips. He held the brandy in his mouth for a second and swallowed. It was good. He set the glass down and refilled it carefully from the bottle and went back to the game.

They were playing five-card draw now and Lim threw in his ante. His cards were poor, but out of decency he stayed in, made a flush on his last card, and won his first hand of the night. The others seemed surprised. They looked at the cards he had laid down, and he waited a moment before pulling the pot toward him.

"Luck," he said, shrugging.

After that he began to play with more care and found himself drawing better cards. He played out a few more hands and won two or three in a row. The pile of notes in front of him began to grow. He felt pleased but a little embarrassed. These men were gambling with money he had paid them and he was taking it back. The grocer and the butcher looked away now when he won and would not meet his eyes. After a while he noticed the silence, and to break it he asked the mourners about their work.

"It must be hard," he said. "Mourning someone you never knew."

"My father taught me little," Pang said. "When I was young he never let me cry. He used to threaten me with a cane. When a pet died or when a toy broke, he told me to laugh. That way mourners saved up their tears for when they needed them."

"And does it work?" Lim asked. He found it hard to imagine Pang as a child with a father. He took two cards. He was working, skeptically, on a low straight, thinking if he made it he would win; if he didn't he could give back some of the money he'd taken.

"For me," Pang said. He drew one card. "I've known others taught to wail and scream as children to build their strength." He shrugged, and Lim decided, almost with relief, that he had made a flush or a full house.

"Your bet."

Lim threw in money, and the bet was seen until it came round to Pang, who raised it with a small flourish. The light glinted off his glasses as he dipped his head to study his hand. His son looked at the crumpled notes still in front of him—he had lost almost all his earnings from the mourning—and scattered them over the center of the table. But at the next raise, he folded out of turn.

Pang gave a little snort and lay down a fifty.

Lim saw the bet and, after a moment, raised. What did it matter? he thought. His father was dead. Losing was nothing. He welcomed it. Dawn was breaking over the curving palms, and the gulls, clustered on the telegraph lines, were waking.

The bet revolved until Pang raised it once more. He looked around the table confidently, and the old men folded, wearily, one after the other until only Lim remained. He could have called—should have—but instead he raised again. Pang studied him closely, and Lim looked back at his own cards fanned in his hand suddenly ashamed of his recklessness, embarrassed by his play.

"You're wasting your money, I think," Pang said. He raised again.

Lim looked back at his cards, looked at the pile of notes by his elbow, but all he could think of was the trace of emphasis Pang had placed on the word "your." He felt something pressing him on, and he slid the cash into the center of the table. He regretted it immediately, hunched his shoulders and covered his cards, but when he glanced up, just for a moment, he saw a look of fear on Pang's face and felt a kind of thrill.

Pang gathered up his own stack of remaining notes, counted them slowly from one hand to the other, straightened them into a neat bundle.

"Call," he said at length. "With this," he pushed the money forward, "and I refund you for the grave goods, yes?"

Lim stared at him and Pang nodded fiercely.

"The funeral," he whispered. "For free."

Lim rested his cards on edge against the table for a second, tapped them one, finally let them fall open. He'd made his low straight, but the cards in their whiteness seemed so insubstantial to him. He stared at a small crease across the corner of one of them. Just paper after all, he thought. There must have been $900 on the table. Lim shuddered a little in the morning chill. Opposite him, Pang's son sat very still. But Pang himself just shook his head and started to laugh. "Take it," he said, smiling crookedly at the money. "Take it. It's yours." Lim looked at him and began to smile, too. He saw the flicker of distaste on the faces of the older mourners, but that, too, seemed funny. He was still smiling as he drew the money into his arms, like an embrace.

The funeral took place in the old Chinese cemetery at Colma. Lim dimly recalled a festival day, years earlier, white ash, like snow, rising from every part of the dark graveyard. Now he watched the paper Mercedes burn. He stared into the leaping, dancing fire, letting the heat wash over him until he felt his eyes begin to smart and finally prick with tears. Pang had told him that it took almost thirty hours to build such a car; the house, another thirty hours; and every piece of paper furniture, three or four hours each. Lim saw the flames eat them, lighting them like festive lanterns before stripping the paper from the bamboo skeletons. He stepped forward to lay one of the empty paper suits on the smoldering coals, but it fluttered in the smoke, and he had to hold it until it flared. He felt the hairs on his knuckles shrink and pull tight. The heat caused an updraft, and the smoke and ashes ascended almost vertically. With them went the wails of the mourners, their voices cracking in the parched air, and Lim marveled, with a new appreciation, at their art.

He caught Pang's eye, and as the old man paused to fill his lungs, Lim bent and threw another bundle of spirit money into the brazier at the foot of the grave. He watched as the notes turned white and scattered in the wind of the flames. The scorched breeze flickered over him, plucking at his sleeve, his lapel, as if it might swirl him away with the ashes falling softly into the sky above. And for a moment he felt himself rise up with them—light as paper, buoyant with heat—until the cries of the mourners sounded only faintly below him.

CHARTING THE STORY

1 What evidence is given at Pang's grave goods shop that whatever the Next Life is, it is distinctly different from life as we know it here and now, on earth? On the other hand, what commonalities do the Here and There seem to share?

2 "Your father was a great man," remarks Pang to Lim. What attitudes toward his father does Lim exhibit, and what attitudes does his mother exhibit? Other attendees at the funeral? To what extent are the attitudes caught up in conventionality, and why might this be so? Where do the attitudes appear genuine, and what might account for this?

3 What recollections of Lim's childhood shed light on his father's character? On the father-son relationship?

4 What does Lim do with the proceeds of the gambling, and why does he do what he does? What did you, as a reader, expect him to do?

CONSIDERATIONS OF STYLE

1 The color "white" is used throughout the narrative. In connection with what is it used, and why is "white" meaningful here rather than another color?

2 As the story starts out, the mourners have been playing poker while observing the vigil of the dead man. This scene, however, is interrupted and taken up again at the end. What is the stylistic effect of the narrator's truncating this scene?

AFTERTHOUGHTS

1 If you have recently been to a funeral, and have sufficient distance from it to be able to analyze it, what sort of discourse can you recall surrounding the deceased person? How is it similar or dissimilar to that surrounding Old Lim, and why?

2 Davies, in a 1998 *Atlantic Unbound* cyberinterview, notes that, while his parents are not storytellers, he has been able to draw upon their stories by "fill[ing] in the gaps between all the little snippets that [he] slowly gleaned from them over the years." What "snippets"—as opposed to whole stories—have you gleaned from your forebears that might conceivably tell fictionalized whole stories some day?

THE WRITER'S CRAFT

1 In the form of a short essay or poem, write what Old Lim might have thought, were he observing all that had been said or done about him.

2 Find an incident within the story "The Next Life" that is narrated only briefly, and write a few paragraphs to expand it, while at the same time remaining within the "world" of the text.

KAZUO ISHIGURO

KAZUO ISHIGURO *was born in Nagasaki, Japan in 1954. Six years later, his family moved to Britain. At the time, they intended to return to Japan, but ended up staying, and Ishiguro grew up bilingual in English and Japanese and straddling his heritage and adopted cultures. He studied at the universities of Kent at Canterbury and East Anglia. His first recognition as a writer came at the age of twenty-five, for an anthologized short story. His novels include* A Pale View of Hills *(1982), which won the Holtby Prize of the Royal Society of Literature;* An Artist of the Floating World *(1986), winner of the Whitbread Book of the Year Award; and* The Remains of the Day, *which was awarded the 1989 Booker Prize and was the basis for a critically acclaimed film; and* The Unconsoled *(1995).*

The story "A Family Supper" first appeared in the collection Firebird 2 *in 1982. This story, like much of Ishiguro's writing, though traditionally English in style, is imbued with Japanese perspectives and reminiscences.*

PERSPECTIVES

1 What artifacts of Japanese culture—food, clothing, art, manufactured goods—have you come in contact with as export items? What do these items suggest to you about a Japanese esthetic?

2 What happens when an irresistible force meets an immovable object? How has this Greek conundrum played itself out in your experience?

A Family Supper

Fugu is a fish caught off the Pacific shores of Japan. The fish has held a special significance for me ever since my mother died after eating one. The poison resides in the sex glands of the fish, inside two fragile bags. These bags must be removed with caution when preparing the fish, for any clumsiness will result in the poison leaking into the veins. Regrettably, it is not easy to tell whether or not this operation has been carried out successfully. The proof is, as it were, in the eating.

Fugu poisoning is hideously painful and almost always fatal. If the fish has been eaten during the evening, the victim is usually overtaken by pain during his sleep. He rolls about in agony for a few hours and is dead by morning. The fish became extremely popular in Japan after the war. Until stricter regulations were imposed, it was all the rage to perform the hazardous gutting operation in one's own kitchen, then to invite neighbors and friends round for the feast.

At the time of my mother's death, I was living in California. My relationship with my parents had become somewhat strained around that period and consequently I did not learn of the circumstances of her death until I returned to Tokyo two years later. Apparently, my mother had always refused to eat fugu, but on this particular occasion she had made an exception, having been invited by an old school friend whom she was anxious not to offend. It was my father who supplied me with the details as we drove from the airport to his house in the Kamakura district. When we finally arrived, it was nearing the end of a sunny autumn day.

"Did you eat on the plane?" my father asked. We were sitting on the tatami floor of his tearoom.

"They gave me a light snack."

"You must be hungry. We'll eat as soon as Kikuko arrives."

My father was a formidable-looking man with a large stony jaw and furious black eyebrows. I think now, in retrospect, that he much resembled [Chinese Communist leader] Chou En-lai, although he would not have cherished such a comparison, being particularly proud of the pure samurai blood that ran in the family. His general presence was not one that encouraged relaxed conversation; neither were things helped much by his odd way of stating each remark as if it were the concluding one. In fact, as I sat opposite him that afternoon, a boyhood memory came back to me of the time he had struck me several times around the head for "chattering like an old woman." Inevitably, our conversation since my arrival at the airport had been punctuated by long pauses.

"I'm sorry to hear about the firm," I said when neither of us had spoken for some time. He nodded gravely.

"In fact, the story didn't end there," he said. "After the firm's collapse, Watanabe killed himself. He didn't wish to live with the disgrace."

"I see."

"We were partners for seventeen years. A man of principle and honor. I respected him very much."

"Will you go into business again?" I asked.

"I am... in retirement. I'm too old to involve myself in new ventures now. Business these days has become so different. Dealing with foreigners. Doing things their way. I don't understand how we've come to this. Neither did Watanabe." He sighed. "A fine man. A man of principle."

The tearoom looked out over the garden. From where I sat I cold make out the ancient well that as a child I had believed to be haunted. It was just visible now through the thick foliage. The sun had sunk low and much of the garden had fallen into shadow.

"I'm glad in any case that you've decided to come back," my father said. "More than a short visit, I hope."

"I'm not sure what my plans will be."

"I, for one, am prepared to forget the past. Your mother, too, was always ready to welcome you back—upset as she was by your behavior."

"I appreciate your sympathy. As I say, I'm not sure what my plans are."

"I've come to believe now that there were no evil intentions in your mind," my father continued. "You were swayed by certain . . . influences. Like so many others."

"Perhaps we should forget it, as you suggest."

"As you will. More tea?"

Just then a girl's voice came echoing through the house.

"At last." My father rose to his feet. "Kikuko has arrived."

Despite our differences in years, my sister and I had always been close. Seeing me again seemed to make her excessively excited, and for a while she did nothing but giggle nervously. But she calmed down somewhat when my father started to question her about Osaka and her university. She answered him with short, formal replies. She in turn asked me a few questions, but she seemed inhibited by the fear that her questions might lead to awkward topics. After a while, the conversation had become even sparser than prior to Kikuko's arrival. Then my father stood up, saying: "I must attend supper. Please excuse me for being burdened by such matters. Kikuko will look after you."

My sister relaxed quite visibly once he had left the room. Within a few minutes, she was chatting freely about her friends in Osaka and about her classes at university. Then quite suddenly she decided we should walk in the garden and went striding out onto the veranda. We put on some straw sandals that had been left along the veranda rail and stepped out into the garden. The light in the garden had grown very dim.

"I've been dying for a smoke for the last half hour," she said, lighting a cigarette.

"Then why didn't you smoke?"

She made a furtive gesture back toward the house, then grinned mischievously.

"Oh, I see," I said.

"Guess what? I've got a boyfriend now."

"Oh, yes?"

"Except I'm wondering what to do. I haven't made up my mind yet."

"Quite understandable."

"You see, he's making plans to go to America. He wants me to go with him as soon as I finish studying."

"I see. And you want to go to America?"

"If we go, we're going to hitchhike." Kikuko waved a thumb in front of my face. "People say it's dangerous, but I've done it in Osaka and it's fine."

"I see. So what is it you're unsure about?"

We were following a narrow path that wound through the shrubs and finished by the old well. As we walked, Kikuko persisted in taking unnecessarily theatrical puffs on her cigarette.

"Well, I've got lots of friends now in Osaka. I like it there. I'm not sure I want to leave them all behind just yet. And Suichi . . . I like him, but I'm not sure I want to spend so much time with him. Do you understand?"

"Oh, perfectly."

She grinned again, then skipped on ahead of me until she had reached the well. "Do you remember," she said as I came walking up to her, "how you used to say this well was haunted?"

"Yes, I remember."

We both peered over the side.

"Mother always told me it was the old woman from the vegetable store you'd seen that night," she said. "But I never believed her and never came out here alone."

"Mother used to tell me that too. She even told me once the old woman had confessed to being the ghost. Apparently, she'd been taking a shortcut through our garden. I imagine she had some trouble clambering over these walls."

Kikuko gave a giggle. She then turned her back to the well, casting her gaze about the garden.

"Mother never really blamed you, you know," she said, in a new voice. I remained silent. "She always used to say to me how it was their fault, hers and Father's, for not bringing you up correctly. She used to tell me how much more careful they'd been with me, and that's why I was so good." She looked up and the mischievous grin had returned to her face. "Poor Mother," she said.

"Yes. Poor Mother."

"Are you going back to California?"

"I don't know. I'll have to see."

"What happened to . . . to her? To Vicki?"

"That's all finished with," I said. "There's nothing much left for me now in California."

"Do you think I ought to go there?"

"Why not? I don't know. You'll probably like it." I glanced toward the house. "Perhaps we'd better go in soon. Father might need a hand with the supper."

But my sister was once more peering down into the well. "I can't see any ghosts," she said. Her voice echoed a little.

"Is Father very upset about his firm collapsing?"

"Don't know. You never can tell with Father." Then suddenly she straightened up and turned to me. "Did he tell you about old Watanabe? What he did?"

"I heard he committed suicide."

"Well, that wasn't all. He took his whole family with him. His wife and his two little girls."

"Oh, yes?"

"Those two beautiful little girls. He turned on the gas while they were all asleep. Then he cut his stomach with a meat knife."

"Yes, Father was just telling me how Watanabe was a man of principle."

"Sick." My sister turned back to the well.

"Careful. You'll fall right in."

"I can't see any ghost," she said. "You were lying to me all that time."

"But I never said it lived down the well."

"Where is it then?"

We both looked around at the trees and shrubs. The daylight had almost gone. Eventually I pointed to a small clearing some ten yards away.

"Just there I saw it. Just there."

We stared at the spot.

"What did it look like?"

"I couldn't see very well. It was dark."

"But you must have seen something."

"It was an old woman. She was just standing there, watching me."

We kept staring at the spot as if mesmerized.

"She was wearing a white kimono," I said. "Some of her hair came undone. It was blowing around a little."

Kikuko pushed her elbow against my arm. "Oh, be quiet. You're trying to frighten me all over again." She trod on the remains of her cigarette, then for a brief moment stood regarding it with a perplexed expression. She kicked some pine needles over it, then once more displayed her grin. "Let's see if supper's ready," she said.

We found my father in the kitchen. He gave us a quick glance, then carried on with what he was doing.

"Father's become quite a chef since he's had to manage on his own," Kikuko said with a laugh.

He turned and looked at my sister coldly. "Hardly a skill I'm proud of," he said. "Kikuko, come here and help."

For some moments my sister did not move. Then she stepped forward and took an apron hanging from a drawer.

"Just these vegetables need cooking now," he said to her. "The rest just needs watching." Then he looked up and regarded me strangely for some seconds. "I expect you want to look around the house," he said eventually. He put down the chopsticks he had been holding. "It's a long time since you've seen it."

As we left the kitchen I glanced toward Kikuko, but her back was turned.

"She's a good girl," my father said.

I followed my father from room to room. I had forgotten how large the house was. A panel would slide open and another room would appear. But the rooms were all startlingly empty. In one of the rooms the lights did not come on, and we stared at the stark walls and tatami in the pale light that came from the windows.

"This house it too large for a man to live in alone," my father said. "I don't have much use for most of these rooms now."

But eventually my father opened the door to a room packed full of books and papers. There were flowers in vases and pictures on the walls. Then I noticed something on a low table in the corner of the room. I came nearer and saw it was a plastic model of a battleship, the kind constructed by children. It had been placed on some newspaper; scattered around it were assorted pieces of gray plastic.

My father gave a laugh. He came up to the table and picked up the model.

"Since the firm folded," he said, "I have a little more time on my hands." He laughed again, rather strangely. For a moment his face looked almost gentle. "A little more time."

"That seems odd," I said. "You were always so busy."

"Too busy, perhaps." He looked at me with a small smile. "Perhaps I should have been a more attentive father."

I laughed. He went on contemplating his battleship. Then he looked up. "I hadn't meant to tell you this, but perhaps it's best that I do. It's my belief that your mother's death was no accident. She had many worries. And some disappointments."

We both gazed at the plastic battleship.

"Surely," I said eventually, "my mother didn't expect me to live here forever."

"Obviously you don't see. You don't see how it is for some parents. Not only must they lose their children, they must lose them to things they don't understand." He spun the battleship in his fingers. "These little gunboats here could have been better glued, don't you think?"

"Perhaps. I think it looks fine."

"During the war I spent some time on a ship rather like this. But my ambition was always the air force. I figured it like this: If your ship was struck by the enemy, all you could do was struggle in the water hoping for a lifeline. But in an airplane—well, there was always the final weapon." He put the model back onto the table. "I don't suppose you believe in war."

"Not particularly."

He cast an eye around the room. "Supper should be ready by now," he said. "You must be hungry."

Supper was waiting in a dimly lit room next to the kitchen. The only source of light was a big lantern that hung over the table, casting the rest of the room in shadow. We bowed to each other before starting the meal.

There was little conversation. When I made some polite comment about the food, Kikuko giggled a little. Her earlier nervousness seemed to have returned to her. My father did not speak for several minutes. Finally he said:

"It must feel strange for you, being back in Japan."

"Yes, it is a little strange."

"Already, perhaps, you regret leaving America."

"A little. Not so much. I didn't leave behind much. Just some empty rooms."

"I see."

I glanced across the table. My father's face looked stony and forbidding in the half-light. We ate on in silence.

Then my eye caught something at the back of the room. At first I continued eating, then my hands became still. The others noticed and looked at me. I went on gazing into the darkness past my father's shoulder.

"Who is that? In that photograph there?"

"Which photograph?" My father turned slightly, trying to follow my gaze.

"The lowest one. The old woman in the white kimono."

My father put down his chopsticks. He looked first at the photograph, then at me.

"Your mother." His voice had become very hard. "Can't you recognize your own mother?"

"My mother. You see, it's dark. I can't see it very well."

No one spoke for a few seconds, then Kikuko rose to her feet. She took the photograph down from the wall, came back to the table, and gave it to me.

"She looks a lot older," I said.

"It was taken shortly before her death," said my father.

"It was dark. I couldn't see very well."

I looked up and noticed my father holding out a hand. I gave him the photograph. He looked at it intently, then held it toward Kikuko. Obediently, my sister rose to her feet once more and returned the picture to the wall.

There was a large pot left unopened at the center of the table. When Kikuko had seated herself again, my father reached forward and lifted the lid. A cloud of steam rose up and curled toward the lantern. He pushed the pot a little toward me.

"You must be hungry," he said. One side of his face had fallen into shadow.

"Thank you." I reached forward with my chopsticks. The steam was almost scalding. "What is it?"

"Fish."

"It smells very good."

In the soup were strips of fish that had curled almost into balls. I picked one out and brought it to my bowl.

"Help yourself. There's plenty."

"Thank you." I took a little more, then pushed the pot toward my father. I watched him put several pieces to his bowl. Then we both watched as Kikuko served herself.

My father bowed slightly. "You must be hungry," he said again. He took some fish to his mouth and started to eat. Then I, too, chose a piece and put it in my mouth. It felt soft, quite fleshy against my tongue.

The three of us ate in silence. Several minutes went by. My father lifted the lid and once more steam rose up. We all reached forward and helped ourselves.

"Here," I said to my father, "you have this last piece."

"Thank you."

When we had finished the meal, my father stretched out his arms and yawned with an air of satisfaction. "Kikuko," he said, "prepare a pot of tea, please."

My sister looked at him, then left the room without comment. My father stood up.

"Let's retire to the other room. It's rather warm in here."

I got to my feet and followed him into the tearoom. The large sliding windows had been left open, bringing in a breeze from the garden. For a while we sat in silence.

"Father," I said, finally.

"Yes?"

"Kikuko tells me Watanabe-san took his whole family with him."

My father lowered his eyes and nodded. For some moments he seemed deep in thought. "Watanabe was very devoted to his work," he said at last. "The collapse of the firm was a great blow to him. I fear it must have weakened his judgment."

"You think what he did . . . it was a mistake?"

"Why, of course. Do you see it otherwise?"

"No, no. Of course not."

"There are other things besides work," my father said.

"Yes."

We fell silent again. The sound of locusts came in from the garden. I looked out into the darkness. The well was no longer visible.

"What do you think you will do now?" my father asked. "Will you stay in Japan for a while?"

"To be honest, I hadn't thought that far ahead."

"If you wish to stay here, I mean here in this house, you would be very welcome. That is, if you don't mind living with an old man."

"Thank you. I'll have to think about it."

I gazed out once more into the darkness.

"But of course," said my father, "this house is so dreary now. You'll no doubt return to America before long."

"Perhaps. I don't know yet."

"No doubt you will."

For some time my father seemed to be studying the back of his hands. Then he looked up and sighed.

"Kikuko is due to complete her studies next spring," he said. "Perhaps she will want to come home then. She's a good girl."

"Perhaps she will."

"Things will improve then."

"Yes, I'm sure they will."

We fell silent once more, waiting for Kikuko to bring the tea.

CHARTING THE STORY

1 What has the narrator done that had so gravely upset his parents? How do his father and sister deal with this transgression? How do father and son articulate their diverging views over the son's "past"?

2 This story is dominated by uncertainty, ambiguity, and obscurity. Find examples of these qualities in the setting, in the characters' conversations, in their personal histories, and in their destinies within the confines of the plot.

3 What external behaviors and mannerisms of the characters do you find to be reflective of their Japanese cultural identity?

CONSIDERATIONS OF STYLE

1 What connections, both symbolic and concrete, can you find between the picture of the mother in a white kimono that is briefly brought to the supper table and the ghost woman wearing a white kimono at the well in the garden?

2 What conceivable connection might there be between the reference to the potentially lethal fugu fish at the story's opening and the detailed description of the fish in the soup served at supper?

3 Where are the son and father, brother and sister, speaking indirectly with each other, and directly with each other? To what purposes do they shape their responses and conversational gambits?

AFTERTHOUGHTS

1 What aspects of the interpersonal relationships among the family members in this story would you consider to be typically Japanese? Or typically Asian? Which might simply be peculiar to this family? What is the basis of your observation?

2 Do you foresee either the narrator or Kikuko returning home to live with the father? How do you envision the rest of the father's life?

THE WRITER'S CRAFT

1 Were the mother's ghost to speak, what would it say? Relate the closing events of her life from her point of view.

2 Rewrite the family supper scene (Paragraphs 100-134) from a distinctly American or other cultural point of view. What contrasts stand out?

PATRICIA GRACE

Of Maori descent (three different bloodlines, and affiliated to a fourth one by marriage), PATRICIA GRACE *was born in Wellington, New Zealand in 1937, and along with working as a writer and as a mother of several children, has taught in primary and secondary schools. Her first story collection,* Waiariki *(1975), was the first publication of a short story collection by a Maori woman writer. She has also published the collections* The Dream Sleepers *(1980) and* Electric City and Other Stories *(1987), as well as the novels* Mutuwhenua, The Moon Sleeps *(1978) and* Potiki *(1986), among others.*

In this story, when a poor Maori family strikes it rich, they find that wealth brings with it challenges both new and old. "It Used to Be Green Once" was published in Patricia Grace's Selected Stories *in 1987.*

PERSPECTIVES

1. What knowledge (historical and otherwise) of Maori and white cultures in New Zealand do you bring to your reading of this text?
2. Look up information on New Zealand's Maori people. What is their socioeconomic standing relative to that of other ethnic New Zealanders? What causes are posited for the disparity?
3. Winning the lottery is the hope of millions who bet both big and small amounts of their paycheck on it. Research the odds of winning big in a lottery. What is the lot of those who lose time after time?

It Used To Be Green Once

We were all ashamed of our mother. Our mother always did things to shame us. Like putting red darns in our clothes, and cutting up old swimming togs and making two—girl's togs from the top half for my sister, and boy's togs from the bottom half for my brother. Peti and Raana both cried when Mum made them take the togs to school. Peti sat down on the road by our gate and yelled out she wasn't going to school. She wasn't going swimming. I didn't blame my sister because the togs were thirty-eight chest and Peti was only ten.

But Mum knew how to get her up off the road. She yelled loudly, 'Get up off that road, my girl. There's nothing wrong with those togs. I didn't have any togs when I was a kid and I had to swim in my nothings. Get up off your backside and get to school.' Mum's got a loud voice and she knew how to shame us. We all dragged Peti up off the road before our mates came along and heard Mum. We pushed Peti into the school bus so Mum wouldn't come yelling up the drive.

We never minded our holey fruit at first. Dad used to pick up the cases of over-ripe apples or pears from town that he got cheap. Mum would dig out the rotten bits, and then give them to us to take for play-lunch. We didn't notice much at first, not until Reweti from down the road yelled out to us one morning, 'Hey you fullas. Who shot your pears?' We didn't have anywhere to hide our lunch because we weren't allowed schoolbags until we got to high school. Mum said she wasn't buying fourteen schoolbags. When we went to high school we could have shoes too. The whole lot of us gave Reweti a good hiding after school.

However, this story is mainly about the car, and about Mum and how she shamed us all the time. The shame of rainbow darns and cut-up togs and holey fruit was nothing to what we suffered because of the car. Uncle Raz gave us the car because he couldn't fix it up any more, and he'd been fined because he lived in Auckland. He gave the car to Dad so we could drive our cream cans up to the road instead of pushing them up by wheelbarrow.

It didn't matter about the car not having brakes, because the drive from 5
our cowshed goes down in a dip then up to the gate. Put the car in its first gear, run it down from the shed, pick up a bit of speed, up the other side, turn it round by the cream stand so that it's pointing down the drive again, foot off the accelerator and slam on the handbrake. Dad pegged a board there to make sure it stopped. Then when we'd lifted the cans out onto the stand, he'd back up a little and slide off down the drive—with all of us throwing ourselves in over the sides as if it were a dinghy that had just been pushed out into the sea.

The car had been red once, because you could still see some patches of red paint here and there. And it used to have a top too, that you could put down or up. Our uncle told us that when he gave it to Dad. We were all proud about the car having a top once. Some of the younger kids skited to their mates about our convertible and its top that went up and down. But that was before our mother started shaming us by driving the car to the shop.

We growled at Mum and we cried but it made no difference. 'You kids always howl when I tell you to get our shopping,' she said.

'We'll get it, Mum. We won't cry.'

'We won't cry, Mum. We'll carry the sack of potatoes.'

'And the flour.' 10

'And the bag of sugar.'

'And the tin of treacle.'

'We'll do the shopping, Mum.'

But Mum would say, 'Never mind. I'll do it myself.' And after that she wouldn't listen any more.

How we hated Wednesdays. We always tried to be sick on Wednesdays, or to miss the bus. But Mum would be up early yelling at us to get out of bed. If we didn't get up when we were told she'd drag us out and pull down our pyjama pants and set our bums on the cold lino. Mum was cruel to us.

Whoever was helping with the milking had to be back quickly from the shed for breakfast, and we'd all have to rush through our kai and get to school. Wednesday was Mum's day for shopping.

As soon as she had everything tidy she'd change into her good purple dress that she'd made from a Japanese bedspread, pull on her floppy, brimmed blue sunhat and her slippers and galoshes, and go out and start up the car.

We tried everything to stop her shaming us all.

'You've got no licence, Mum.'

'What do I want a licence for? I can drive, can't I? I don't need the proof.'

'You got no warrant.'

'Warrant? What's warrant?'

'The traffic man'll get you, Mum.'

'That rat. He won't come near me after what he did to my niece. I'll hit him right over his smart head with a bag of riwais and I'll hit him somewhere else as well.'

We never could win an argument with Mum.

Off she'd go on a Wednesday morning, and once out on the road she'd start tooting the horn. This didn't sound like a horn at all but more like a flock of ducks coming in for a feed. The reason for the horn was to let all her mates and relations along the way know she was coming. And as she passed each one's house, if they wanted anything they'd have to run out and call it out loud. Mum couldn't stop because of not having breaks. 'E Kiri,' each would call. 'Mauria mai he riwai,' if they wanted spuds; 'Mauria mai he paraoa,' if they wanted bread. 'Mauria mai he tarau, penei te kaita,' hand spread to show the size of the pants they wanted Mum to get. She would call out to each one and wave to them to show she'd understood. And when she neared the store she'd switch the motor off, run into the kerbing and pull on the handbrake. I don't know how she remembered all the things she had to buy—I only know that by the time she'd finished, every space in that car was filled and it was a squeeze for her to get into the driver's seat. But she had everything there, all ready to throw out on the way back.

As soon as she'd left the store she'd begin hooting again, to let the whole district know she was on her way. Everybody would be out on the road to get their shopping thrown at them, or just to watch our mother go chuffing past. We always hid if we heard her coming.

The first time Mum's car and the school bus met was when they were both approaching a one-way bridge from opposite directions. We had to ask the driver to stop and give way to Mum because she had no brakes. We were all ashamed. But everyone soon got to know Mum and her car and they always stopped whenever they saw her coming. And you know, Mum never ever had an accident in her car, except for once when she threw a side of mutton out to Uncle Peta and it knocked him over and broke his leg.

After a while we started walking home from school on Wednesdays to give Mum a good chance of getting home before us, and so we wouldn't be in the bus when it had to stop and let her past. The boys didn't like having to walk home, but we girls didn't mind because Mr. Hadly walked home too. He was a new teacher at our school and he stayed not far from where we lived. We girls thought he was really neat.

But one day, it had to happen. When I heard the honking and tooting behind me I wished that a hole would appear in the ground and that I would fall in it and disappear for ever. As Mum came near she started smiling and waving and yelling her head off. 'Anyone wants a ride,' she yelled, 'they'll have to run and jump in.'

We all turned our heads the other way and hoped Mr. Hadly wouldn't notice the car with our mother in it, and her yelling and tooting, and the brim of her hat jumping up and down. But instead, Mr. Hadley took off after the car and leapt in over the back seat on top of the shopping. Oh, the shame.

But then one day something happened that changed everything. We arrived home to find Dad in his best clothes, walking round and grinning, and not doing anything like getting the cows in, or mending a gate, or digging a drain. We said, 'What are you laughing at, Dad? What are you dressed up for? Hey Mum, what's the matter with Dad?'

'Your dad's a rich man,' she said. 'Your dad, he's just won ten thousand pounds in a lottery.'

At first we couldn't believe it. We couldn't believe it. Then we all began running round and laughing and yelling and hugging Dad and Mum. 'We can have shoes and bags,' we said. 'New clothes and swimming togs, and proper apples and pears.' Then do you know what Dad said? Dad said, 'Mum can have a new car.' This really astounded and amazed us. We went numb with excitement for five minutes then began hooting and shouting again, and knocking Mum over.

'A new car!'

'A new car?'

'Get us a Packard, Mum.'

'Or a De Soto. Yes, yes.'

Get this, get that...

Well, Mum bought a shiny green Chevrolet, and Dad got a new cowshed with everything modernised and water gushing everywhere. We all got our new clothes—shoes, bags, togs—and we even started taking posh lunches to school. Sandwiches cut in triangle, bottles of cordial, crisp apples and pears, and yellow bananas.

And somehow all of us kids changed. We started acting like we were 40
somebody instead of ordinary like before. We used to whine to Dad for money to spend, and he'd always give it to us. Every week we'd nag Mum into taking us to the pictures, or if she was tired we'd go ourselves by taxi. We got flash bedspreads and a piano and we really thought we were neat.

As for the old car—we made Dad take it to the dump. We never wanted to see it again. We all cheered when he took it away, except for Mum. Mum stayed inside where she couldn't watch, but we all stood outside and cheered.

We all changed, as though we were really somebody, but there was one thing I noticed. Mum didn't change at all, and neither did Dad. Mum had a new car all right, and a couple of new dresses, and a new pair of galoshes to put over her slippers. And Dad had a new modern milking shed and a tractor, and some other gadgets for the farm. But Mum and Dad didn't change. They were the same as always.

Mum still went shopping every Wednesday. But instead of having to do all the shopping herself, she was able to take all her friends and relations with her. She had to start out earlier so she'd have time to pick everyone up on the way. How angry we used to be when Mum went past with her same old sunhat and her heap of friends and relations, and them all waving and calling out to us.

Mum sometimes forgot that the new car had brakes, especially when she was approaching the old bridge and we were coming the opposite way in the school bus. She would start tooting and the bus would have to pull over and let her through. That's when all our aunties and uncles and friends would start waving and calling out. But some of them couldn't wave because they were too squashed by people and shopping, they'd just yell. How shaming.

There were always ropes everywhere over Mum's new car holding bags of 45
things and shovel handles to the roof and sides. The boot was always hanging open because it was too full to close—things used to drop out on to the road all the time. And the new car—it used to be green once, because if you look closely you can still see some patches of green paint here and there.

CHARTING THE STORY

1. Why are the children so frequently "shamed" by their mother? Why does it appear to be the case that the mother shames them far more than does the father?
2. This is clearly Mum's story and Dad keeps a low profile. On the other hand, what does the story say about the division of labor in their marriage?
3. What does the character Mr Hadley contribute to the story?
4. What effects of the sudden riches show up in the family? Who and what changes and does not change, and what might account for some things changing and others staying more or less the same?

CONSIDERATIONS OF STYLE

1 How can you determine whether the family is of Maori or of *pakeha* (white) background? How relevant is the family's cultural background to the text?

2 How does Grace contextualize Maori expressions to make them comprehensible to anglophone readers?

3 If the story had been told from a third-person point of view, how might it have differed? What does the author achieve by putting the narrative in the voice of one of the children of the family? Can you tell whether the narrator is a girl or a boy? If so, what suggests gender?

AFTERTHOUGHTS

1 In her memoir *Among the White Moon Faces,* Shirley Geok-lin Lim, rediscovering the grandeur of her grandfather's home, feels "a pride not of possession but of identity push[ing] the exploration." How is such a feeling shared by Mum in this story?

2 Persons from New Zealand generally resent others' lumping them in with Australians. What differences do you find between the various texts from New Zealand and Australia in this book, and between the nations themselves? What similarities do you find (not only between these antipodal works, but amongst them and works from other primarily English-speaking nations)?

3 "Use it up, wear it out, make it do, or do without": a watchword amongst some "old-money" families who do not flaunt their wealth. Can this adage be practiced in the same way in poor and working-class households? Why, or why not?

THE WRITER'S CRAFT

1 Compose a two- to three-page "rags-to-riches" story in which the characters struggle not to be spoiled by fortune.

2 Write a short essay describing a "shaming" incident occurring amongst family or friends.

3 Especially in the first few paragraphs of the story, Grace graphically presents images of poverty at home in the cut-down swimming togs and the "holey" fruit, and the lack of shoes and bookbags. Write an essay, story, or poem conveying the atmosphere of your or someone else's home, foregrounding poverty, riches, or somewhere in between.

FAYE MOSKOWITZ

FAYE MOSKOWITZ *grew up in Jackson and Detroit, Michigan. She attended Wayne State University in Detroit and The George Washington University in Washington, DC, where she now teaches in the creative writing program.*

Moskowitz's writing typically reflects her life as the child of Jewish immigrants growing up in a non-Jewish community. Her work includes the collection of stories Whoever Finds This: I Love You *(1991), and the collections of memoirs and essays,* A Leak in the Heart: Personal Essays and Life Stories *(1985) and* And the Bridge Is Love *(1991). She has also edited an anthology of Jewish women's writing about mothers and daughters,* Her Face in the Mirror *(1994).*

"Jewish Christmas"—from And the Bridge is Love*—is a richly crafted memoir about Chanukah—nowise a simple Jewish equivalent of Christmas.*

PERSPECTIVES

1 What meaning does Chanukah hold for you? If you celebrate Chanukah, what customs do you follow, what family traditions do you observe? If you are not Jewish, what do you know of the origins of and ways of celebrating this holiday?

2 How do religious holidays both bring people together and set them apart? How have you celebrated the religious holidays of your tradition? Or, has the absence of a religious tradition set you apart from others?

3 How did special foods highlight holidays in general in your childhood? Are traditional victuals still a part of your life today?

Jewish Christmas

"Jewish Christmas"—that's what my gentile friends called Chanukah when I was growing up in Michigan in the thirties and forties. Anachronistic, yes, but they had a point. Observing the dietary laws of separating milk and meat dishes was far easier for the handful of Jewish families in our little town than getting through December without mixing the two holidays.

Christmas was a miserable time for Jewish children in those days, nothing short of quarantine could have kept us from catching the Christmas fever. My parents were no help. Immigrants who had fled pogroms in Russia and Poland, they were world-class outsiders. If tee shirts with mottos had been in fashion then, our shirts would surely have read Keep a Low Profile. My mother would never have considered going to my school to complain about the Christmas tree in the lobby or the creche in our principal's office or the three life-size wise men, complete with camels, that we cut out of construction paper in Art and hung on our classroom walls.

If I still wasn't convinced Christmas was coming after all those reminders, I had only to look at the advent calendar hanging behind my teacher's desk or walk downtown, where carols blared out over loudspeakers and built to a crescendo in front of the six-foot neon cross decorating our largest department store. And as for keeping a low profile, try it when yours is the only neighborhood house in work clothes while every other is dressed for a party.

By the time we moved to the Jewish section of Detroit, I was old enough to accept Christmas as a holiday other people celebrated. Chanukah was our winter holiday, not a substitute at all, but a minor-league festival that paled before Passover, Rosh Hashanah, and Yom Kippur. All the cousins gathered at our grandparents' house where we lined up to get Chanukah gelt from the uncles: quarters and half dollars, and dollar bills, perhaps, for the older children. Mostly we ran around a lot, got very flushed, and ate latkes, plenty of them.

My own children were raised in a diverse neighborhood in Washington, 5
D.C. The Ghost of Christmas Past clanked its chains for a while, and my husband and I learned to make a few concessions. Still, we never sunk to the Chanukah bush or an actual Christmas tree, though we knew Jews who did, we lit the menorah, bought presents for each of the eight nights, decorated our house with blue and white paper chains, and played with dreidels. In spite of that, our kids were pretty disgruntled for most of December, although even their non-Jewish friends had to concede we had something with those latkes.

For the past few years, with our children grown, my husband and I have cut off the Chanukah/Christmas debate entirely. We distribute the Chanukah gelt early and then leave the country. That's going to a lot of trouble to avoid office parties and the egg nog and pfeffernuss for which we never did develop a taste, but at least we don't have to get caught up in the general depression that afflicts not only the people who celebrate Christmas but all the rest who don't and wish they did.

Several years ago, we found ourselves in Venice during the holidays. In spite of all our rationalizations, we missed being home with our children, missed the ritual of lighting the menorah, the tacky paper chains, the dreidel game we play, gambling for raisins or nuts, and at that moment we would have traded any pasta dish, no matter how delectable, for potato latkes like the ones we ate at Chanukah as far back as we both could remember.

So maybe that's why, with the help of guidebooks and our faltering Italian, we threaded our way through the city's bewildering twists and turns until we suddenly emerged into a spacious square that marks the old Jewish ghetto of Venice. The clip-clop of our heels on cobblestones and the flutter of pigeons punctuated a silence that might have existed for centuries or only on that particular rest day, we didn't know. "There's an old synagogue at the other end of the square," my husband said. "Let's go see if maybe it's open for visitors." We pulled at the heavy brass-studded wooden door, and far down a long corridor I heard the sound of many voices chattering in Italian. "I'm probably hallucinating," I whispered to my husband, "but I swear I smell latkes."

In that musty, crumbling building, the memories flooded back as clear as the icicles we licked in those nose-numbing December days of my Michigan childhood. Bundled against the stunning cold, we walked hand in hand, my mother and father, my brothers and I, along darkened streets where orange candles in brass menorahs bravely illuminated each front window we passed.

In my grandparents' vestibule, we shed our snowy boots. The welcoming 10
warmth of the coal furnace promised more coziness deep inside, there my aunts sucked in their bellies as they elbowed past one another in and out of Bobbe's tiny kitchen, from which they pulled a seemingly endless array of delicious dishes as if from a magician's opera hat: platters of bagels slathered with cream cheese, smoked fish with skins of irridescent gold, pickled herring, thick slices of Bermuda onion strong enough to prompt a double-dare, boiled potatoes with their red jackets on, wallowing in butter. Best of all were the crisp potato latkes, hot from Bobbe's frying pan, to eat swaddled in cool sour cream, the contrasting textures and temperatures indelibly printing themselves on our memory.

Though our mothers' cooking styles were virtually interchangeable, my husband and I used to quarrel every year about whose family made the better latkes. My mother's potato pancakes were thin and lacy, delicate enough to float in their hot cooking oil. His mother's latkes, I pointed out at every opportunity, utterly lacked refinement: colossal, digestion-defying pancakes the size of hockey pucks, they were each a meal in themselves. "Just the way I like them," my husband would tell me as he wolfed yet another one.

I never learned to make my mother's latkes. She died just before my husband and I were married, and when we came to Washington we brought my mother–in-law with us, so her potato latkes won by default and became part of our children's Chanukah tradition. Which is not to say I ever accepted them graciously, and as we moved into our middle years, and cholesterol moved into our lexicon, my husband, too, scorned the latkes of his childhood. "The Israeli secret weapon," he called them when his mother wasn't listening. "Eat two, and you're on sick call for at least a week."

But friends came each Chanukah and brought their children to celebrate with ours. We exchanged small gifts: boxes of crayons, pretty bars of soap, cellophane bags of sour candies for Grandma, who, of course, supplied the latkes. Early in the afternoon, she would begin grating potatoes on a vicious four-sided grater, the invention of some fiendish anti-Semite who must have seen the opportunity to maim half the Jewish population each December.

The trick was to finish grating just before the guests arrived so the potatoes would not blacken, as they have a discouraging tendency to do. Meanwhile, as she mixed in eggs, matzo meal, salt, and baking powder, Grandma heated a frying pan with enough oil to light the Chanukah lamps into the next century. The finished latkes were drained on supermarket paper bags that promptly turned translucent with fat. Still, we ate them: great, golden, greasy, dolloped-with-sour-cream latkes, and our complaints became part of our Chanukah tradition, too.

15 The Venetian latkes didn't taste very much like Grandma's, but there was enough resemblance to quell our homesickness. Well, that was a while ago. Today, though November leaves, red and brown and gold, still hang on stubbornly, the Christmas drumming has already begun. My morning's *Washington Post* bursts with ads like a ripe pomegranate spewing seeds. Overnight, green wreaths have sprouted on our neighbors' doors, and the Salvation Army kettle, come out of storage, stands on its tripod in front of the Giant food store once again. I remember how little I cared for this time. For a moment, the buried stones of jealousy and of shame and not belonging work themselves to the surface with a speed that surprises me.

But this year something is different, suddenly, finally, *I* am the grandma who makes the latkes. Two little grandchildren, both named for my mother-in-law (may she rest in peace), will come to our house to watch us light the menorah. Baby Helen at two and a half can already say the Hebrew blessing over the candles, and if my joy in that could translate to Chanukah gelt, all the banks in America would be forced to close.

I close my eyes and think of Grandma tasting a bit of her childhood each Chanukah when she prepared the latkes as her mother had made them before her. My mother, my aunts, my own grandmothers float back to me, young and vibrant once more, making days holy in the sanctuaries of their kitchens, feeding me, cradling me, connecting me to the intricately plaited braid of their past, and even at this moment, looking down the corridor of what's to come, I see myself join them as they open their arms wide to enfold my children and grandchildren in their embrace.

CHARTING THE MEMOIR

1. What signs of approaching Christmas does the author notice in her childhood, and how do they compare with the signs of Christmas-yet-to-come in her maturity? What are her reactions as a child, and how does she react as an adult, to the inevitable, relentless "Christmas time in the city"?
2. Moskowitz recalls her gentile friends referring to Chanukah as "Jewish Christmas." How is this received? How accurate can such a description be?

3 How do public schools in the United States today acknowledge and/or celebrate different religious holidays? How would the celebration of Christmas, as Moskowitz describes it in her memoirs of her Michigan childhood, be viewed today?

CONSIDERATIONS OF STYLE

1 In this memoir, references to Chanukah such as the menorah, dreidels, blue and white paper chains, and latkes are discussed as casually as Christmas trees, the crèche, carols, egg nog and pfeffernuss—without explanation for a non-Jewish audience. What assumptions might the narrator be making here?

2 Of what importance are *latkes* for this memoir? What other domestic items, pieces of "material culture," does Moskowitz feature? How do these images reflect the times of which she writes; that is, if her mother-in-law had used a food processor, how might have Moskowitz's memoir changed?

3 How does Moskowitz's vignette about her holiday visit to Venice enhance her memoir about the celebration of Chanukah in the United States? Do we know who was making the latkes and who invited the narrator and her husband to taste of them?

AFTERTHOUGHTS

1 Compare the descriptions of the simultaneous celebrations of Christmas and Chanukah in Moskowitz's memoir and in Jane Shore's poem "The Holiday Season."

2 It has been noted that in an immigrant culture's process of assimilation into a new country/culture, "the food (if it goes) is the last to go." Does this observation seem accurate? If so, choose a culture for which you have noticed this occurrence; and what cultural phenomena "went" (either disappeared or were assimilated), in approximately what order? What may account for this process? If not, or if not always, in what ways have you observed phenomena of a given culture maintain their distinction?

3 This memoir records an almost completely matriarchal "bridge of love" across the generations. How would it differ if it were written by a man, relating connections from grandfathers to grandsons, to their grandsons in turn?

THE WRITER'S CRAFT

1 Write an essay showing how the commercialization of holidays in the United States in general, or of a specific holiday that is meaningful to you, marginalizes their/its significance. You might recall Moskowitz's warm recollections of tradition, family, and food as a point of departure.

2 Write of a particularly evocative family tradition, in which a grandparent or other elder has passed on something of great meaning to you. How do you foresee passing this tradition on to later generations?

JANE SHORE

JANE SHORE *has been a member of the English faculty at the George Washington University since 1991. She has also taught at the Universities of Iowa, Washington, and Hawaii (Manoa), at Tufts and Harvard Universities, and at MIT and Sarah Lawrence College. She holds a bachelor's degree from Goddard College and an MFA from the University of Iowa.*

Her books include Music Minus One, *from which* The Holiday Season *is taken, and which was a finalist for the 1996 National Book Critics Circle award in poetry;* The Minute Hand, *winner of the 1986 Lamont Poetry Prize from the American Academy of Poets; and a new collection,* Happy Family. *Her poems have also been widely anthologized.*

PERSPECTIVES

1 What are your fondest childhood memories of a major religious holiday? How has your feeling for that holiday, and for its attendant rituals and customs, changed over the years? If your childhood was bereft of religious tradition, did you feel the lack of one as others around you celebrated theirs?

2 As you were growing up, what differing religious traditions did you encounter either in your own family or in your community? In what respects can a child's awareness of religious diversity be positive and instructive? In what respects can it be confusing?

The Holiday Season

The electric eye of the mezuzah
guarded our apartment over the store
as innocent of Christmas
as heaven, where God lived,
how many stories above the world?
Was He angry when He saw
all the windows on my street—

the assimilated grocer's, druggist's,
even my father's store—lit up
like windows in an Advent calendar?

Alone in my bedroom
the nights my parents worked late,
I'd hear voices and laughter
floating up through the floor—
customers trying on dressy dresses
in the fitting rooms below.
The store was dressed up, too,
with tinsel, icicles,
everything but a Christmas tree—
"Over my dead body," my mother said.

Christmas was strictly business
in my parents' store.
Fourteen shopping days to go,
my class sang carols
in front of the school assembly.
In starched white blouses
we marched up to the stage,
our mouths a chain of O's.
When we came to the refrain
"Christ the Savior is born,"
as if on cue all the Jewish kids
were silent, except me,
absentmindedly humming along
until the word Christ slipped out.
It was an accident!
Gentiles believed in Christ.
We Jews believed in a God
Whose face we were forbidden to see,
Whose name we were forbidden
to say out loud, or write completely.

We had to spell it G-d,
the missing o dashing into its hole.
That afternoon after school,
I sat near an empty fitting room
folding cardboard gift boxes,
carefully locking the flaps in place.
Was God going to punish me?

My father knelt in the window display
among the mannequins
like one of the Magi in a crèche,

dusting a plastic angel three feet tall.
Stored in the cellar under the stairs,
draped in her dusty cellophane caul,
waiting to be reborn,
she lorded it over the old mannequins,
naked, bald, their amputated limbs
piled in the corner like firewood.
The Sunday before the holiday season
she ascended, one floor, to the store,
trailing a tail of electric cord.

After my father plugged her in,
she glowed from halo-tip to toe,
faith—a fever—warming her cheeks,
her insides lit by a tiny bulb.
I longed to smuggle her up to my room,
to have some company at night
when the store was open late.
I gazed down the darkening street,
Seventy-ninth to Boulevard East,
and out over the Hudson.
At sundown, I went upstairs.
Dinner was defrosting in the oven.
The last night of Chanukah,
eight candles, like eight crayons,
wobbled in the brass menorah.
My father struck the match.
Flame wavering in my hand,
I lit the candles from left
to right, like a line of English writing,
and numbly sang the blessing.

as if the words on my breath
could sweep away the word
I'd sung earlier that day.
Was God going to punish me?
I'd have to ask the Magic 8 Ball,
my gift the first night of Chanukah.
For the last seven nights,

before going to sleep,
instead of saying my prayers,
I'd consulted the 8 Ball.

It could predict the future.
You asked it a yes-or-no question,
you turned it over,
and the answer slowly floated up
through the inky liquid
to the round window on top.
I held the black ball
firmly in my hands.
"Is God going to punish me?"
"CONCENTRATE AND ASK AGAIN"

I stared out my bedroom window
across the back alley
at the rabbi's house,
and watched him walk from room
to room, his windows
like frames on a strip of film.
He vanished through his kitchen door
and reappeared a moment later
a shadow, a hazy nimbus rippling
his bathroom's glazed window glass.
Swaying before his mirrored ark's
two fluorescent scrolls of light,
he performed his evening ritual—
brushing his teeth,
washing his hands, then
sinking discreetly out of sight.
For spying on the rabbi,
I'd added on another sin!
I concentrated, closed my eyes,
again, I asked the question:

"Is God going to punish me?"
"REPLY HAZY TRY AGAIN"
"Is God going to punish me?"
"BETTER NOT TELL YOU NOW"
"Is God going to punish me?"
"IT IS DECIDELY SO"
"Is God going to punish me?"
"MY REPLY IS NO"

"8 Ball, what is your answer?"
"ASK AGAIN LATER"

I had to see what was inside.
I took a hammer to the ball,
and whacked. Not a crack;
I'd barely scratched its shell.
I looked into its eye,
the dark unblinking eye,
as far as I could see inside the skull
where, floating together in ink
(so many I couldn't see them all)
were all the answers possible.

CHARTING THE POEM

1 What various traditions does the eponymous Holiday Season involve in the speaker's family? How and why does the speaker's perception of the Holiday Season differ from that of her parents?

2 How does the speaker's "spying on the rabbi" complicate her moral conundrum? Does she resolve the issue within her conscience?

3 Why does the speaker consult the Magic 8 Ball so many times, even after getting one definitive answer? Why would she consult *it* rather than her parents, or even the rabbi?

CONSIDERATIONS OF STYLE

1 What do the speaker's perceptions of the Christian and Jewish religious traditions say about her assimilation into a multicultural society in which religion plays a socially defining role?

2 Of what relevance is the electric angel to the development of the poem's narrative?

3 What, would you say, does the Magic 8 Ball symbolize in this poem?

AFTERTHOUGHTS

1 What are some social, historical, and/or political forces that militate against the easy assimilation of immigrants into "the American Way of Life"? What motives can you ascribe to those in a dominant culture who encourage assimilation? To those who resist it? To those who strive for a compromise?

2 The Magic 8 Ball can still be found in toy stores. Obtain one, then get a good look ino it, as the speaker in the poem did. What do you see inside? How would it fasci-

nate a child, and of what might it be suggestive? Why would it be different from a folding paper "fortune teller" or other childhood method of divination?

3 What other "eyes" can be found in the poem? How do they connect, thematically?

THE WRITER'S CRAFT

1 Write a brief account, in prose or poetic form, of your attempt—as a child or young adult—to resolve a religious conundrum.

2 Ask a deep, dark question of the Magic 8 Ball and record your dialogue, and either analyze this "conversation" or use it to build an essay or poem.

3 In a short essay, compare Jane Shore's poem with Faye Moskowitz's memoir "Jewish Christmas." What commonalities do they share (not only of theme but of technique); how were the girls' Christmas and Chanukah experiences different?

Our Common Humanity

Part Two
Identity and Autonomy

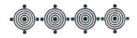

After her second cigarette and her resolute refusal to apologise, the family seriously thought of sending Bineeta off to the Sharada Ashram for some discipline and ascetic thoughts.

SUBHADRA BEN GUPTA, *Good Girls Are Bad News*

MARGARET WALKER

MARGARET WALKER *was one of the last surviving members of the generation of black female writers who became prominent in the 1940s, after the Harlem Renaissance, whose lights, she noted, had no "real conception of the problems of black people being basically economic and political."*

Walker herself was a third-generation college graduate, the daughter of a Methodist minister, born in Birmingham, Alabama. She graduated from Northwestern University in 1935 and received a Master of Arts degree from the University of Iowa in the difficult Depression years. She later earned a PhD and worked as a newspaper reporter and a social worker. She taught at Jackson State University, where she founded the Institute for the Study of the History, Life, and Culture of Black People in 1968.

Walker's first book, For My People, *was written in 1942, when she was only 22 years old.*

She worked nearly three decades on her one novel, Jubilee, *which was finally published in 1966. She also authored a book about Richard Wright,* Richard Wright: Daemonic Genius.

Margaret Walker received the Mississippi Arts Commission's lifetime achievement award in 1992. She died in 1998.

The title poem of Walker's first book, "For My People" won the Yale Younger Poets competition in 1942, despite the fact that it had been rejected the first three times she submitted it. Written with intense imagery and passionate vision, this poem evokes the hardships of the poet's people in nine building stanzas, and provides a resolution and a demand for change in the final stanza. The poem reflects a very militant civil rights position for its time, and continues to inspire and uplift more than a half-century later.

PERSPECTIVES

1 Which social group(s) do you consider to be "your people"? What various criteria would you apply in setting up categories that help "define" you as a member of a particular?

2 Politicians tend to bandy about the term "the American people." How does the meaning of this term differ depending upon who is using it? Consider other generalized usage of nationality terms—e g, "Australians," "Africans," "Indians"—in this anthology.

For My People

For my people everywhere singing their slave songs repeatedly:
their dirges, and their ditties and their blues and jubilees,
praying their prayers nightly to an unknown god, bending their
knees humbly to an unseen power;

For my people lending their strength to the years, to the gone
years and the now years and the maybe years, washing ironing
cooking scrubbing sewing mending hoeing plowing digging
planting pruning patching dragging along never gaining never
reaping never knowing and never understanding;

For my playmates in the clay and dust and sand of Alabama backyards
playing baptizing and preaching and doctor and jail and soldier
and school and mama and cooking and playhouse and concert and
store and hair and Miss Choomby and company;

For the cramped bewildered years we went to school to learn to know
the reasons why and the answers to and the people who and the
places where and the days when, in memory of the bitter hours
when we discovered we were black and poor and small and
different and nobody cared and nobody wondered and nobody understood;

For the boys and girls who grew up in spite of these things to be man
and woman, to laugh and dance and sing and play and drink their
wine and religion and success, to marry their playmates and
bear children and then die of consumption and anemia and lynching;

For my people thronging 47th Street in Chicago and Lenox Avenue in
New York and Rampart Street in New Orleans, lost disinherited
dispossessed and happy people filling the cabarets and taverns
and other people's pockets needing bread and shoes and milk and
land and money and something—something all our own;

For my people walking blindly spreading joy, losing time being
lazy, sleeping when hungry, shouting when burdened, drinking
when hopeless, tied and shackled and tangled among ourselves by
the unseen creatures who tower over us omnisciently and laugh;

For my people blundering and groping and floundering in the dark of
churches and schools and clubs and societies, associations and

councils and committees and conventions, distressed and
disturbed and deceived and devoured by money-hungry glory-
craving leeches, preyed on by the facile force of state and fad and
novelty, by false prophet and holy believer;

For my people standing staring trying to fashion a better way from
confusion, from hypocrisy and misunderstanding, trying to
fashion a world that will hold all the people, all the faces
all the adams and eves and their countless generations;

Let a new earth rise. Let another world be born. Let a bloody peace
be written in the sky. Let a second generation full of courage
issue forth; let a people loving freedom come to growth. Let a
beauty full of healing and a strength of final clenching be the
pulsing of our spirits and our blood. Let the martial songs be
written, let the dirges disappear. Let a race of men now rise
and take control.

CHARTING THE POEM

1 In what respect was the god to whom Walker's people prayed (Line 3) "an unknown god," and an "unseen power" (Line 4)? What connection can you make between this god and the "unseen creatures" in Line 31?

2 What do Walker's playmates appear to have in common with children everywhere? Where in the poem does pretending become hoping?

3 The poem is written in ten stanzas. What significances arise from that number, especially to a Western audience?

CONSIDERATIONS OF STYLE

1 How do the poem's frequent repetitions affect its musical and rhetorical qualities?

2 What is the dramatic effect of the poem's sentence structure?

3 Nine stanzas delineate one aspect or another of the audience. At great length, the tenth stanza, beginning "Let a new earth rise," brings about a sense of resolution. What is the poet achieving—stylistically and polemically—by delaying the resolution?

AFTERTHOUGHTS

1 It has often been said that "the poet is a seer." In what respect do the exhortations in the final stanza make Margaret Walker a seer?

2 On the other hand, the poem was written in 1937, and published in 1942. Since then, at least three "second generations" have "issued forth." How fully has the author's vision been realized? Where has it been, in the words of Lorraine Hansberry, author of the play *Raisin in the Sun*, a "dream deferred"?

3 The African American hymn "Lift Ev'ry Voice and Sing," written by James Weldon Johnson in 1942, and since anthologized in many hymnals, is also written for Walker's and Johnson's "people." Compare and contrast the effects of the poem and the hymn—and if you know the music, consider that, too, in of your response.

THE WRITER'S CRAFT

1 Fashion a stanza about "your people" in their world of work (as in the second stanza), in their associations (as in the eighth stanza), or in their political environment (as in the ninth stanza).

2 Stand up, straighten your shoulders, take a deep breath, and belt out this poem. Loud, passionately; quiet, tenderly. Give it a voice. Shout it out a window, declaim it in a stairwell, tell it to the trees. Then write about how you experienced the poem before your dramatic reading, and after. If the poem seemed to change, what accounts for the change?

NICK CARBÓ

NICK CARBÓ *was born in Legazpi, Albay in the Philippines in 1964. He received an M.F.A. from Sarah Lawrence College and served as Resident Poet at Bucknell University and Writer-in-Residence at American University. "El Grupo McDonald's" is the title poem in a collection published in 1995. Carbó has also edited an anthology of poems by Filipino and Filipino American poets,* Returning a Borrowed Tongue, *published in 1996.*

Bud Leenerts, the father of Cynthia Leenerts, co-author of this anthology, is a Monday-morning regular of a group of men, mostly retired military officers, who call themselves "the University of Greers Ferry Lake" and who meet at a local convenience store/gas station/bait shop in Heber Springs, Arkansas. This poem describes a similar group, who live in the Philippines.

PERSPECTIVES

1 How have Tagalog, Spanish, and English evolved into major languages in the Philippines today?

2 If you are a "regular" at a neighborhood restaurant, have you noticed any groups of friends, particularly of the older generation, who tend to gather there frequently? How would you describe them? Why do you think they meet at the same place on a regular basis, and what seems to draw them together?

3 What interests keep you together with your friends? If you are part of a group of people who enjoy each other's company, what are your dynamics of friendship? What topics do you discuss? Where do you tend to meet?

El Grupo McDonald's

My father is seventy-seven and meets
with a group of "old-timers"
every other day in a McDonald's
in the heart of Makati.
These men have worked
for the prestigious firms of Soriano,

Ayala, and Elizalde. Accountants,
Managing Vice-Presidents, District
Consultants, and Sales Representatives.
A white long-sleeved shirt, white trousers,
and a black leather belt is the dress code
for these retired *Ilustrados.*

The coffee is always hot and *los temas*
de conversación son, las bases Americanas,
el cambio del Dollar, la Cory Aquino,
y el tiempo distante cuando Manila
era la perla del oriente.
The city is changing color, fresh air
from the bay does not blow into Makati
and the pollution lingers all night.

My father tells me that Enrique,
the ex-Jai-alai star, died
over the summer, Ralph Zulueta is also dead.
He tells me that even if the group is shrinking
every year, they still talk about the idiots
in the government, the American bases,
the exchange rate of the Dollar, Cory Aquino,
and the days when Manila was still
the pearl of the orient.

CHARTING THE POEM

1. Why do the retired men in the poem continue to observe a dress code? Do you think they dress now as they did when they worked as professionals for prestigious firms?
2. What aspects of Philippine culture are reflected in the fact that there are no women in the group of old-timers? That the retired men are referred to as *Ilustrados*?
3. In the second stanza, the topics of conversation are given in Spanish, and are then translated in the third stanza. What is the significance of the topic that is added in the English translation?

CONSIDERATIONS OF STYLE

1. Why does Carbó have the men in the group speaking Spanish, instead of Tagalog, the native language of Manila?
2. What is the significance of the poem's setting—in a McDonald's in the heart of Makati, one of the more elegant neighborhoods of Manila?

3 In what sense does the city seem to be "changing color," and what does the metaphor of the lack of fresh air, and the presence of pollution suggest about the world that the men of El Grupo inhabit?

AFTERTHOUGHTS

1 The Filipino national hero José Rizal, martyred during the revolution against Spain in the late nineteenth century, referred to Manila as *la perla del mar del oriente*—the pearl of the Orient. The poem suggests that Manila has lost this distinction. What other great cities of the world—in your experience or in your reading, in the stories of your parents or grandparents—have been diminished in the course of one or two generations?

2 What major U.S. corporations can be found almost worldwide, and how do the "locals" overseas react to what Gita Mehta and others have referred to as the "Coca-Colonization" of the world? How do these expatriate corporations adapt themselves to their local market, and how do they influence consumer spending habits there? What sort of *cachet* do U.S. exports of this nature enjoy in various overseas markets? Compare their relative status levels overseas and at home in the United States.

THE WRITER'S CRAFT

1 In essay, short-short story, or poetic format, write about a group similar to El Grupo McDonald's; if you do not know them, try to interview them.

2 Retirement is probably very distant for most of you. Nevertheless, write a description—in prose or poetic form—about a typical day in your life as a retiree, around 2045 or earlier.

3 Using the example of one global corporation, write in detail about its reception both at home and overseas, using the questions in AFTERTHOUGHTS 2 as a jumping-off point.

LAWSON FUSAO INADA

LAWSON FUSAO INADA, *born in 1939, is a third-generation Japanese American. He was one of the youngest residents of the American internment camps during World War II, and has written about that experience in his collection of poems* Legends from Camp *(1993). Other works include* Before the War: Poems as They Happened *(1971) and, with Eichiro Azuma,* In This Great Land of Freedom: The Japanese Pioneers in Oregon *(1993).*

"Kicking the Habit" is a fast-moving poem that shows how a hard-working writer escapes from his demanding routine into a world dominated by nature. The poem appeared first in Ergo! *and was nominated for inclusion in* Pushcart Poetry 1994–95.

PERSPECTIVES

1 Describe a burdensome (but necessary) activity in your life—nonacademic as well as academic. What motivates you to keep on with that activity? If you could escape from it just for a day, where would you hide out? What would you do "there"?

2 How does the phenomenon of "workaholism" affect social relationships? How does it affect the workaholic self?

Kicking the Habit

Late last night, I decided to
stop using English.
I had been using it all day—

    talking all day,
    listening all day,
    thinking all day,
    reading all day,
    remembering all day,
    feeling all day,

and even driving all day,
in English—

when finally I decided to
stop.

So I pulled off the main highway
onto a dark country road
and kept on going and going
until I emerged in another nation and
stopped.

There, the insects
inspected my passport, the frogs
investigated my baggage, and the trees
pointed out lights in the sky,
saying

“Shhhhlllyyymmm”—

and I, of course, replied.
After all, I was a foreigner,
and had to comply...

Now don’t get me wrong:
There’s nothing “wrong”
with English,
and I’m not complaining
about the language
which is my “native tongue.”
I make my living with the lingo;
I was even in England, once.

So you might say I’m actually
addicted to it;
yes, I’m an Angloholic,
and I can’t get along without the stuff:
It controls my life.

Until last night, that is.
Yes, I had had it
with the habit.

I was exhausted,
burned out,

by the habit.
And I decided to
kick the habit
cold turkey
right then and there,
on the spot!

And, in so doing, I kicked
open the door of a cage
and stepped out from confinement
into the greater world.

Tentatively, I uttered

"Chemawa? Chinook?"—

and the pines said

"Clackamas. Siskiyou."

And before long, everything else
chimed in with their two cents' worth
and we had a fluid and fluent
conversation going,

communicating, expressing,
echoing, whatever we needed to
know, know, know...

What was it like?
Well, just listen:

Ah, the exquisite seasonings
of syllables, the consummate consonants, the vigorous
vowels of varied vocabularies

clicking, ticking, humming,
growling, throbbing, strumming—

coming from all parts of orifices, surfaces,
in creative combinations, orchestrations,
resonating in rhythm with the atmosphere!

I could have remained there
forever—as I did, and will.

And, when I resumed my way,
my stay could no longer be

"ordinary"—
as they say,
as *we* say, in English.

For on the road of life,
in the code of life,

there's much more to red than

"stop,"

there's much more to green than

"go,"

and there's much, much more to yellow than

"caution,"

for as the yellow
sun clearly enunciated to me this morning:

"Fusao. Inada."

CHARTING THE POEM

1 Discuss Stanzas 1–7 and the narrator's escape from the drudgery of "using English all day" as a transition from the concrete to the metaphorical.
2 Discuss the narrator's explanation (Stanzas 9–11) for his "addiction" to English.
3 Linguists have pointed out that language utterances are used not only to *say*, but to *do:* e g "I'm sorry" both says something and apologizes; "Watch out!" both says something and warns. How is this fundamental concept shown in Inada's poem?
4 What does the narrator mean at the end of the poem in his references to the red, green, and yellow road codes?

CONSIDERATIONS OF STYLE

1 What differences can we find between the style of vocabulary in Lines 29–68 and 69–76? How would the poem "feel" if the two styles of vocabulary were reversed?
2 Additionally, what stylistic devices are employed in Lines 69–76?

AFTERTHOUGHTS

1 With what cognitive and linguistic skills does the speaker in the poem associate the act of driving? How is this rather mundane act elevated by the end of the poem?
2 What do you think the narrator suggests in Lines 30 and 34 by putting "wrong" and "native tongue" in quotation marks?
3 What does the word "Shhhlllyyymmm" mean to you? To the narrator? To this poem?
4 Why does the sun "enunciate" to the narrator, "Fusao. Inada," and not "Lawson"?

THE WRITER'S CRAFT

1 Inada's escape from the "confinement" that is his writer's life into "the greater world" is described vividly in Lines 52–76. Describe, in poetic or prose form, a favorite place of escape from the routine of your life.
2 A poem by Ezra Pound, "The Lake Isle" (1916), ends:

> O God, O Venus, O Mercury, patron of thieves,
> Lend me a little tobacco-shop,
> 		Or install me in any profession
> Save this damn'd profession of writing,
> 		Where one needs one's brains all the time.

Clearly, if writing were an act of pure intelligence/brains, more intelligent people would be better writers. Conversely, of course, within the community of writers, intelligence varies. What, then, does the "damn'd profession of writing" require in addition to brains? What have you in particular striven to bring to your most successful writing?
3 As transcendent and as liberating as this poem may be, it is still in English. Rewrite it—or write your own—in "found noises."

JEAN RHYS

In the introduction to JEAN RHYS's *novel* The Wide Sargasso Sea, *editor Francis Wyndham notes that Rhys was born in Roseau, Dominica to a Welsh doctor and a Creole (white West Indian) mother. Rhys grew up in Dominica, and went to Great Britain at the age of sixteen, which was at about the time of World War I. She was married to a Dutch poet and lived in Paris and Vienna for about ten years (during the 1920s). At first she wrote prodigiously: a series of essays and sketches,* The Left Bank *(1927); and novels* Quartet *(1928),* After Leaving Mr Mackenzie *(1930),* Voyage in the Dark *(1934), and* Good Morning, Midnight *(1939). Then she vanished from the literary scene, to re-emerge in 1958, when she was traced to Cornwall by people interested in her work. There she was found to have many unpublished short stories (which were subsequently urged into publication and later appeared in* Jean Rhys: The Collected Short Stories*), and to be at work on* The Wide Sargasso Sea, *which was published in 1966.*

Jean Rhys, in many respects a sort of Greta Garbo of the literary world, died in 1979. "The Day They Burned the Books" is from Rhys's collection Tales of the Wide Caribbean, *published in 1985.*

PERSPECTIVES

1 What half-dozen books in your lifetime of reading would you include on a shelf of "my greatest books"? Discuss your criteria for individual books as well as for the collection as a whole.

2 What instances of book-burning throughout history are you familiar with? What were the effects of such burnings on those who lost the books? On those who burned them? What connotations arise from book-burning itself?

3 Discuss the advantages and disadvantages of marriages that intersect race, ethnicity, nationality, or class. Cite examples—personal or public—to support your ideas.

4 With what creole societies—those stratified into European-born; European-descended, locally born (Creole); *mestizo* (mixed); and indigenous peoples—are you presently familiar, in your historical studies? Why do those born in Europe draw distinctions between themselves and those who are of the same cultural background, but actually born in the colonized society rather than at "Home"? Why, and how, do both distinguish themselves from the mixed and indigenous populations?

The Day They Burned the Books

My friend Eddie was a small, thin boy. You could see the blue veins in his wrists and temples. People said that he had consumption and wasn't long for this world. I loved, but sometimes despised him.

His father, Mr Sawyer, was a strange man. Nobody could make out what he was doing in our part of the world at all. He was not a planter or a doctor or a lawyer or a banker. He didn't keep a store. He wasn't a schoolmaster or a government official. He wasn't—that was the point—a gentleman. We had several resident romantics who had fallen in love with the moon on the Caribees—they were all gentlemen and quite unlike Mr Sawyer who hadn't an 'h' in his composition. Besides, he detested the moon and everything else about the Caribbean and he didn't mind telling you so.

He was agent for a small steamship line which in those days linked up Venezuela and Trinidad with the smaller islands, but he couldn't make much out of that. He must have a private income, people decided, but they never decided why he had chosen to settle in a place he didn't like and to marry a coloured woman. Though a decent, respectable, nicely educated coloured woman, mind you.

Mrs Sawyer must have been very pretty once but, what with one thing and another, that was in days gone by.

When Mr Sawyer was drunk—this often happened—he used to be very rude to her. She never answered him.

'Look at the nigger showing off,' he would say; and she would smile as if she knew she ought to see the joke but couldn't. 'You damned, long-eyed gloomy half-caste, you don't smell right,' he would say; and she never answered, not even to whisper, 'You don't smell right to me, either.'

The story went that once they had ventured to give a dinner party and that when the servant, Mildred, was bringing in coffee, he had pulled Mrs Sawyer's hair. 'Not a wig, you see,' he bawled. Even then, if you can believe it, Mrs Sawyer laughed and tried to pretend that it was all part of the joke, this mysterious, obscure, sacred English joke.

But Mildred told the other servants in the town that her eyes had gone wicked, like a soucriant's eyes, and that afterwards she had picked up some of the hair he pulled out and put it in an envelope, and that Mr Sawyer ought to look out (hair is obeah as well as hands).

Of course, Mrs Sawyer had her compensations. They lived in a very pleasant house in Hill Street. The garden was large and they had a fine mango tree, which bore prolifically. The fruit was small, round, very sweet and juicy—a lovely, red-and-yellow colour when it was ripe. Perhaps it was one of the compensations, I used to think.

Mr Sawyer built a room onto the back of this house. It was unpainted inside and the wood smelt very sweet. Bookshelves lined the walls. Every time the Royal Mail steamer came in it brought a package for him, and gradually the empty shelves were filled.

Once I went there with Eddie to borrow *The Arabian Nights.* That was on a Saturday afternoon, one of those hot, still afternoons when you felt that everything had gone to sleep, even the water in the gutters. But Mrs Sawyer was not asleep. She put her head in at the door and looked at us, and I knew that she hated the room and hated the books.

It was Eddie with the pale blue eyes and straw-coloured hair—the living image of his father, though often as silent as his mother—who first infected me with doubts about 'home', meaning England. He would be so quiet when others who had never seen it—none of us had ever seen it—were talking about its delights, gesticulating freely as we talked—London, the beautiful, rosy-cheeked ladies, the theatres, the shops, the fog, the blazing coal fires in winter, the exotic food (whitebait eaten to the sound of violins), strawberries and cream—the word 'strawberries' always spoken with a guttural and throaty sound which we imagined to be the proper English pronunciation.

'I don't like strawberries,' Eddie said on one occasion.

'You *don't like* strawberries?'

'No, and I don't like daffodils either. Dad's always going on about them. He says they lick the flowers here into a cocked hat and I bet that's a lie.'

We were all too shocked to say, 'You don't know a thing about it.' We were so shocked that nobody spoke to him for the rest of the day. But I for one admired him. I also was tired of learning and reciting poems in praise of daffodils, and my relations with the few 'real' English boys and girls I had met were awkward. I had discovered that if I called myself English they would snub me haughtily: 'You're not English; you're a horrid colonial.' 'Well, I don't much want to be English,' I would say. 'It's much more fun to be French or Spanish or something like that—and, as a matter of fact, I am a bit.' Then I was too killingly funny, quite ridiculous. Not only a horrid colonial, but also ridiculous. Heads I win, tails you lose—that was the English. I had thought about all this, and thought hard, but I had never dared to tell anybody what I thought and I realized that Eddie had been very bold.

But he was bold, and stronger than you would think. For one thing, he never felt the heat; some coldness in his fair skin resisted it. He didn't burn red or brown, he didn't freckle much.

Hot days seemed to make him feel especially energetic. 'Now we'll run twice round the lawn and then you can pretend you're dying of thirst in the desert and that I'm an Arab chieftain bringing you water.'

'You must drink slowly,' he would say, 'for if you're very thirsty and you drink quickly you die.'

So I learnt the voluptuousness of drinking slowly when you are very thirsty—small mouthful by small mouthful, until the glass of pink, iced Coca-Cola was empty.

Just after my twelfth birthday Mr Sawyer died suddenly, and as Eddie's special friend I went to the funeral, wearing a new white dress. My straight hair was damped with sugar and water the night before and plaited into tight little plaits, so that it should be fluffy for the occasion.

When it was all over everybody said how nice Mrs Sawyer had looked, walking like a queen behind the coffin and crying her eyeballs out at the right moment, and wasn't Eddie a funny boy? He hadn't cried at all.

After this Eddie and I took possession of the room with the books. No one else ever entered it, except Mildred to sweep and dust in the mornings and gradually the ghost of Mr Sawyer pulling Mrs Sawyer's hair faded though this took a little time. The blinds were always half-way down and going in out of the sun was like stepping into a pool of brown-green water. It was empty except for the bookshelves, a desk with a green baize top and a wicker rocking-chair.

'My room,' Eddie called it. 'My books,' he would say, 'my books.'

I don't know how long this lasted. I don't know whether it was weeks after Mr Sawyer's death or months after, that I see myself and Eddie in the room. But there we are and there, unexpectedly, are Mrs Sawyer and Mildred. Mrs Sawyer's mouth tight, her eyes pleased. She is pulling all the books out of the shelves and piling them into two heaps. The big, fat glossy ones—the good-looking ones, Mildred explains in a whisper—lie in one heap. The *Encyclopaedia Britannica, British Flowers, Birds and Beasts,* various histories, books with maps, Froude's *English in the West Indies* and so on—they are going to be sold. The unimportant books, with paper covers or damaged covers or torn pages, lie in another heap. They are going to be burnt—yes, burnt.

Mildred's expression was extraordinary as she said that—half hugely delighted, half-shocked, even frightened. And as for Mrs Sawyer—well, I knew bad temper (I had often seen it), I knew rage, but this was hate. I recognized the difference at once and stared at her curiously. I edged closer to her so that I could see the titles of the books she was handling.

It was the poetry shelf. *Poems,* Lord Byron, *Poetical Works,* Milton, and so on. Vlung, vlung, vlung—all thrown into the heap that were to be sold. But a book by Christina Rossetti, though also bound in leather, went into the heap that was to be burnt, and by a flicker in Mrs Sawyer's eyes I knew that worse than men who wrote books were women who wrote books—infinitely worse. Men could be mercifully shot; women must be tortured.

Mrs Sawyer did not seem to notice that we were there, but she was breathing free and easy and her hands had got the rhythm of tearing and pitching. She looked beautiful, too—beautiful as the sky outside which was a very dark blue, or the mango tree, long sprays of brown and gold.

When Eddie said 'No,' she did not even glance at him.

'No,' he said again in a high voice. 'Not that one. I was reading that one.'

She laughed and he rushed at her, his eyes starting out of his head, shrieking, 'Now I've got to hate you too. Now I hate you too.'

He snatched the book out of her hand and gave her a violent push. She fell into the rocking-chair.

Well, I wasn't going to be left out of all this, so I grabbed a book from the condemned pile and dived under Mildred's outstretched arm.

Then we were both in the garden. We ran along the path, bordered with crotons. We pelted down the path, though they did not follow us and we could hear Mildred laughing—kyah, kyah, kyah, kyah. As I ran I put the book I had taken into the loose front of my brown holland dress. It felt warm and alive.

When we got into the street we walked sedately, for we feared the black children's ridicule. I felt very happy, because I had saved this book and it was my book and I would read it from the beginning to the triumphant words 'The End'. But I was uneasy when I thought of Mrs Sawyer.

'What will she do?' I said.

'Nothing,' Eddie said. 'Not to me.'

He was white as a ghost in his sailor suit, a blue-white even in the setting sun, and his father's sneer was clamped on his face.

'But she'll tell your mother all sorts of lies about you,' he said. 'She's an awful liar. She can't make up a story to save her life, but she makes up lies about people all right.'

'My mother won't take any notice of her,' I said. Though I was not at all sure.

'Why not? Because she's . . . because she isn't white?'

Well, I knew the answer to that one. Whenever the subject was brought up—people's relations and whether they had a drop of coloured blood or whether they hadn't—my father would grow impatient and interrupt, 'Who's white?' he would say. 'Damned few.'

So *I* said, 'Who's white? Damned few.'

'You can go to the devil,' Eddie said. 'She's prettier than your mother. When she's asleep her mouth smiles and she has curling eyelashes and quantities and quantities and *quantities* of hair.'

'Yes,' I said truthfully. 'She's prettier than my mother.'

It was a red sunset that evening, a huge, sad, frightening sunset.

'Look, let's go back,' I said. 'If you're sure she won't be vexed with you, let's go back. It'll be dark soon.'

At his gate he asked me not to go. 'Don't go yet, don't go yet.'

We sat under the mango tree and I was holding his hand when he began to cry. Drops fell on my hand like the water from the dripstone in the filter in our yard. Then I began to cry too and when I felt my own tears on my hand I thought, 'Now perhaps we're married.'

'Yes, certainly, now we're married,' I thought. But I didn't say anything. I didn't say a thing until I was sure he had stopped. Then I asked, 'What's your book?'

'It's *Kim*,' he said. 'But it got torn. It starts at page twenty now. What's the one you took?'

'I don't know; it's too dark to see,' I said.

When I got home I rushed into my bedroom and locked the door because I knew that this book was the most important thing that had ever happened to me and I did not want anybody to be there when I looked at it.

But I was very disappointed, because it was in French and seemed dull. *Fort Comme La Mort,* it was called. . . .

CHARTING THE STORY

1 In what respects does the Sawyer family appear to be "dysfunctional"? On the other hand, what are some of the strengths of each member—the wife, the son, and, yes, the husband—alluded to in the story?

2 In each of its five characters, and in relationships between and among them, how does the story inform us about social relationships in the Caribbean country in which it is set?

3 Mr Sawyer "hadn't an 'h' in his composition," according to the narrator. What does this infer about him? What motivations might he have had for having married Mrs Sawyer? What, if anything, is suggested in the text?

4 What motivates Mrs Sawyer, with Mildred's help, to burn the books? How, if at all, do her motivations differ from those throughout history that you identified in the PERSPECTIVES Question 2?

5 What is the translation of the book title *Fort Comme la Mort*? Who wrote it? Why do you suppose Rhys hasn't translated it for her readers?

CONSIDERATIONS OF STYLE

1 How does Rhys use color images to brighten what might otherwise have been a psychologically dark narrative?

2 What particularly Caribbean and British expressions can you identify from the text, and what are their literal and figurative significations?

3 Paragraphs 10 and 23 dwell upon the ambience of Mr Sawyer's reading room. How is it distinguished from the rest of the house, and from the other places where the children play? How does its significance change for Eddie before and after his father's death?

AFTERTHOUGHTS

1 What sort of political or social statement was Eddie making when he announced that he did not like strawberries or daffodils? What sort of fruits and flowers are mentioned in the text, or that you associate with the Caribbean region, and how do they compare with strawberries and daffodils?

2 What does the narrator's father imply by his comment, "Who's white? Damned few"? How does Eddie understand this comment?

3 Of what significance is the fact that Eddie was able to save Rudyard Kipling's *Kim*?

4 In a book of quotations, find three under the heading "books" that you personally consider significant. Working in small groups, compare your quotations and discuss their relevance to the story.

THE WRITER'S CRAFT

1 Describe, in an essay, what you predict will be the dynamic of the relationships between Eddie and his mother, and Eddie and the narrator, in the ensuing years.

2 From the point of view of Mildred, describe the incident of the book-burning, including the reasons for her laughter.

STUART DYBEK

STUART DYBEK, *a second-generation Polish American, was born in Chicago in 1942. He attended Catholic schools throughout his childhood and majored in English literature at Loyola University, where he was graduated in 1964. He received his MFA in 1973 from the University of Iowa.*

Dybek is the author of the short-story collections Childhood and Other Neighborhoods *(1980) and* The Coast of Chicago *(1990) and the collection of poems* Brass Knuckles *(1979). His fiction, poetry, and nonfiction have been published in* The New Yorker, Atlantic, Harper's, Paris Review, Ploughshares, *and other major publications, and his work has been translated into several languages and is frequently anthologized. He lives in Kalamazoo, Michigan, and is professor of English at Western Michigan University, where he has taught since 1974.*

The narrator in "Thread" is an exemplary Catholic fourth-grader, a member of the esteemed organization for boys, the Knights of Christ, "an essential step up the staircase of sanctity" to altar boy, torch bearer, subdeacon, deacon, and priest. But before ascending that staircase, he is foiled by a piece of thread from his Knight's sash and his fear of mortal sin.

This memoir appeared in the September 1998 issue of Harper's Magazine.

PERSPECTIVES

1 What rituals—religious or other—were a part of your childhood that involved special dress, or uniforms? How did wearing a uniform in the performance of the ritual set you apart from your peers?

2 What were the religious landmarks—institutions, places, events, authority figures—of your childhood? In the absence of an institutional religion, what educational, social or spiritual landmarks charted your childhood years? How did your perception of these landmarks change as you became an adult?

Thread

The year after I made my first Holy Communion, I joined the Knights of Christ, as did most of the boys in my fourth-grade class. We'd assemble before Mass on Sunday mornings in the sunless, concrete courtyard between the convent and the side entrance to the sacristy. The nuns' courtyard was private, off-limits, and being allowed to assemble there was a measure of the esteem in which the Knights were held.

Our uniforms consisted of the navy blue suits we'd been required to wear for our first Holy Communion, though several of the boys had already outgrown them over the summer. In our lapels we wore tiny bronze pins of a miniature chalice engraved with a cross, and across our suit coats we fit the broad satin sashes that Sister Mary Barbara, who coached the Knights, would distribute. She had sewn them herself. At our first meeting Sister Mary Barbara instructed us that just as in the days of King Arthur, the responsibility of the Knights was to set an example of Christian gentlemanliness. If ever called upon to do so, each Knight should be ready to make the ultimate sacrifice for his faith.

Our sashes came in varying shades of gold, some worn to a darker luster and a bit threadbare at the edges, and others crisp and shining like newly minted coins. We wore them diagonally in the swashbuckling style of the Three Musketeers. It felt as if they should have supported the weight of silver swords ready at our sides.

Once outfitted, we marched out of the courtyard into the sunlight, around St. Roman church, and through its open massive doors, pausing to dip our fingers in the marble font of holy water and cross ourselves as if saluting our Lord—the bloodied, life-size Christ crowned with thorns and crucified in the vestibule. Then we continued down the center aisle to the front pews that were reserved for the Knights.

In the ranking order of the Mass we weren't quite as elite as the altar boys, who got to dress in actual vestments like the priest, but being a Knight seemed an essential step up the staircase of sanctity. Next would be torch bearer, then altar boy, and beyond that, if one had a vocation, subdeacon, deacon, priest.

Although I couldn't have articulated it, I already understood that nothing was more fundamental to religion than hierarchies. I was sort of a child prodigy when it came to religion, in the way that some kids had a gift for math or were spelling whizzes. Not only did I always know the answer in catechism class, I could anticipate the question. I could quote Scripture and recite almost any Bible story upon command. Although I couldn't find my way out of our parish, the map of the spiritual world was inscribed on my consciousness. I could enumerate the twelve choirs of angels. From among the multitude of saints, I could list the various patrons—not just the easy ones like St. Nicholas, Patron of Children, or St. Jude, Patron of Hopeless Cases, but those that most people didn't even know existed: St. Brendan the Navigator, Patron of Sailors and Whales; St. Anthony of Padua, whose name I would take later when I was confirmed, Patron of the Poor; St. Bonaventure of Potenza, Patron of Bowel Disorders; St. Fiacre, an Irish hermit, Patron of Cabdrivers; St. Alban, Patron of Torture Victims; St. Dismas, the Good Thief who hung beside Christ, Patron of Death Row Inmates; St. Mary Magdalen, Patron of Perfume.

I could describe their powers with the same accuracy that kids described the powers of superheroes—Batman and Robin, Green Lantern, the Flash—but I knew that, unlike comic-book heroes, saints were real.

That was an era for ceremony, a time before what my Aunt Zosha came to derisively refer to as Kumbaya Catholicism, when the Mass was still in Latin and, on Good Fridays, weeping old women in babushkas would walk on their knees up the cold marble aisle to kiss the glass-encased sliver of the True Cross that the priest presented at the altar rail. After each kiss, he would wipe the glass with a special silk kerchief for sanitary purposes.

It was a time of Cold War when each Sunday Mass ended with a prayer "for the conversion of Russia," a more severe time when eating meat on Friday, the day of Christ's crucifixion, could send a soul to hell. Before receiving Communion, one was required to fast from the night before. To receive Communion without fasting was a mortal sin, and there could be no greater blasphemy than to take the body and blood of Christ into one's mouth with mortal sin on the soul. Sometimes at Sunday Mass, women, weak from fasting, would faint at church.

Once Mass began, the Knights would rise in unison and stand and kneel 10
to the ebb and flow of the ceremony with a fierce attention that should have been accompanied by the rattling of our sabers and spurs against the marble. Our boyish, still unbroken voices were raised in prayer and hymn. At Communion time, it was the privilege of the Knights to be the first to file from the pews, leading the rest of the congregation to the Communion rail. There we would kneel in a long row of navy blue slashed with diagonals of gold awaiting the priest. Often the priest was Father Fernando, the first Mexican priest at our parish. He'd served as a chaplain in the Marine Corps and lost an eye to shrapnel while administering the last rites to dying soldiers in Korea, and he distributed the Eucharist to us as if reviewing the troops. Usually, Father Fernando wore a brown glass eye, but he'd been shattering glass eyes lately—the rumor was he'd been going out drinking with Father Boguslaw—and when he'd break one he'd wear a pair of sunglasses with the lens over the good eye popped out.

Sometimes, approaching the Communion rail, I'd be struck by the sight of my fellow Knights, already kneeling, by their frayed cuffs and the various shades of socks and worn soles. It never failed to move me to see my classmates from the perspective of their shoes.

One Sunday, sitting in the pew, watching flashes of spring lightning illuminate the robes of the angels on the stained-glass windows, my mind began to drift. I studied my gold sash, upon which the tarnishing imprint of raindrops had dried into vague patterns—it had begun to rain just as we marched in off the street. There was a frayed edge to my sash, and I wrapped a loose thread around my finger and gently tugged. The fabric bunched, and the thread continued to unwind until it seemed that the entire sash might unravel. I pinched the thread and broke it off, then wound it back around my finger tightly enough to cut off my circulation.

When my fingertip turned white, I unwound the thread from my finger and weighed it on my open hand, fitting it along the various lines on my palm. I opened my other palm and held my hands out to test if the balance between them was affected by the weight of the thread. It wasn't. I placed the thread on my tongue and let it rest there where its weight was more discernible. I half expected a metallic taste of gold, but it tasted starchy, like any other thread. Against the pores of my tongue, I could feel it growing thicker with the saliva that was gathering in my mouth. I swallowed both the saliva and the thread.

Immediately after, when it was already too late, it occurred to me that I had broken my fast.

It would be a mortal sin for me to receive the host. Yet the primary duty of a Knight was to march to the Communion rail, leading the congregation. Not only was the enormous humiliation I would feel if I remained seated while the others filed up to the altar more than I was willing to face; in a sudden panic I worried that I'd be kicked out of the Knights, my ascent up the staircase of sanctity over almost before it had begun. I sat trying to figure a way out of the predicament I'd created, feeling increasingly anxious, a little sick, actually, as if the thread were winding around my stomach. I thought about how not one of my classmates would have even realized that his fast had been broken by swallowing a thread, and since he wouldn't have realized it was a sin, then it wouldn't have been one. It didn't seem quite fair that my keener understanding made me more culpable. Perhaps a thread didn't count as food, I thought, but I knew I was grasping for excuses—it seemed a dubious distinction to risk one's soul upon. The choir was singing the Agnus Dei; Communion would be next. My suit coat pasted to my back by a clammy sweat, I thought up various plans at what seemed a feverish pace and rejected them just as feverishly. Maybe I could pretend to be even sicker than I was feeling and run from church with my hand over my mouth as if I were about to vomit; or I could pretend to faint. But the notion of making up a lie in order to not receive Communion seemed too devious, and I didn't have the nerve to carry a spectacle like that off. To do so would probably be a mortal sin against the Eighth Commandment; I'd just be getting myself in deeper.

Then a detail mentioned in passing by Sister Aurelia back in third grade 15
when we practiced for our first Holy Communion occurred to me. She'd told us that if at the Communion rail one should ever realize he had a mortal sin on his soul that he'd somehow forgotten about until that moment, then he was merely to clasp a hand in mea culpa over his heart and bow his head, and the priest would understand and move on.

Communion time arrived, and on trembling legs I marched to the rail with the other Knights. How fervently I wished that I was simply going to receive Communion. I felt alone, separated from the others by my secret, and yet I became aware of an odd kind of excitement bordering on exhilaration at what

I was about to do. Father Fernando, wearing his one-eyed pair of dark glasses, approached, an altar boy at his elbow, holding a paten to catch the host in case it should slip from the priest's hand. I could hear their soles on the carpet as they paused to deliver a host and moved to the next Knight, I could hear Father Fernando muttering the Latin prayer over and over as he deposited a host upon each awaiting tongue. *Corpus domini nostri Jesu Christi*... May the body of our Lord, Jesus Christ, preserve your soul in everlasting life.

This is the aching flush of anticipation, I thought, that a penitent sinner would feel, a murderer perhaps, or a thief, someone who had committed terrible crimes and found himself at the Communion rail.

Father Fernando paused before me, and I clapped a fist against my heart and bowed my head. He stopped and squinted down at me through the missing lens of his dark glasses, trying to catch my eyes and having a hard time doing it with his single good eye. Finally, he shrugged and moved on, wondering, I was sure, what grievous sin I had committed.

I never told him or anyone else. I had swallowed a thread. No one but God would ever be the wiser. It was my finest hour as a theologian. Only years later did I realize it would be that moment I'd think back to when I came to wonder how I'd lost my faith.

CHARTING THE MEMOIR

1 The narrator notes in Paragraph 6 that "nothing was more fundamental to [his Catholic] religion than hierarchies." How is this shown in the story? To what degree might this statement apply to other religions?

2 "Kumbaya" (see Paragraph 8) is a West African folksong sung by a number of popular singers of the 1950s and 1960s like Neil Diamond and the Seekers. Why do you think Aunt Zosha uses the song title to describe Catholicism after the Vatican II Council, in the 1960s, had adopted some fairly radical theological and liturgical changes?

3 Discuss the significance of the unraveling thread in the sash, and of the narrator's picking at it and playing with it, not only as a central element of the plot, but also as a symbolic foreshadowing device.

CONSIDERATIONS OF STYLE

1 How do the narrator's subtly humorous descriptions of the Knights of Christ and the multitudes of saints, the clearly comic characterization of Father Fernando, and tensely amusing Communion scene relate to his professed loss of faith as his childlike earnestness is undermined by his adult worldliness?

2 What is the effect of the marked shift of focus from contextual or background information in Paragraphs 1-9 to the narrator's detailed observations of his fellow

Knights "from the perspective of their shoes" (Paragraph 11), to the "flashes of spring lightning illuminat[ing] the robes of the angels on the stained-glass windows," to the crucial thread incident?

3 Poet Don Lee has said of Dybek that he is inclined to "mimic the emotion of music with prose." In this regard, Dybek himself has noted: "What's come to fascinate me more and more is trying to use language the way that the mediums of other arts—music in particular—are used so that they lead you to nonverbal places . . ., to something unsayable." Can you find any suggestion of these notions in "Thread"?

AFTERTHOUGHTS

1 The narrator, later in life, connects the Communion incident of the thread with the loss of his Catholic faith. What aspects of religion described through the child's eyes in "Thread" might be embodied in the use of the term *faith* here? What aspects of religious faith seem to be missing in the story?

2 In legal discussions, one should distinguish between the "letter of the law" and the "spirit of the law." How does this dichotomy apply to religious dogma? Give evidence from the allusions to Catholic ritual and lore in "Thread."

3 Apart from the nuns, everyone in the hierarchy of the narrator's church is male. What advantages and disadvantages arise from having such a clearly defined hierarchical vocational path?

THE WRITER'S CRAFT

1 Children often feel deluded or disappointed when they realize the world around them is not what adults have claimed it to be. Discuss an event in your childhood that was brought on by your discovery that things were not what they were "supposed to be."

2 Write a vignette from your childhood describing a religious or secular ritual. Try to convey the sense of place and sense of immediacy that Dybek conveys so vividly in "Thread."

3 The narrator's misunderstanding of theology largely depends upon his passively receiving information and not raising questions about it. Discuss a similar incident from your experience or readings, where silence has played a critical role.

SUBHADRA SEN GUPTA

SUBHADRA SEN GUPTA *was born and raised in Old Delhi (the old section of town, which has an artistic, Mughlai* cachet*). She has published children's books including* This Is Earth Calling: A Child's Eye-View of the Earth's Population and Environment Problems; *a ctitical study,* The Art of Bernard Shaw; *and* The Sword of Dara Shikoh and Other Stories from History. *"Good Girls Are Bad News," a story of a "good" Bengali girl in the 1950s who shocks the town by smoking a cigarette in public at a religious service, comes from the eponymous collection, which was published by Rupa in Calcutta in 1992.*

PERSPECTIVES

1. What constitutes a "good girl," in your view, and how do these qualities contrast with those of "good boys"? How do both sets of qualities contrast with those associated with a "good person"?
2. What knowledge of sexual or gender "revolution," nationally or internationally, do you bring to this text?

Good Girls Are Bad News

It all began when Bineeta Sen lit a cigarette in the middle of a crowded Durga Puja pandal at Delhi's Kashmere Gate grounds.

It was the balmy month of October, in the year 1953, and the morning of Ashtami. Everyone had fasted, then prayed and thrown flowers at the resplendent Durga idol and obediently chanted the mantras after the pandit. Now the hungry mob of the Durga-devotees was moving like an inexorable force towards the food stalls.

At the biryani and kabab corner—"Mughlai Parathas, ghooghni, kababs. Try please!"—Pratap and his gang were bracing for the onslaught behind tall minars of plates and trays of spoons. At the sweets counter.—"Sandesh, mishti doi, kochuri. Once eaten never forgotten!"—Kali babu was sweating over a huge karhai of frying singaras.

At this exact juncture, right there in view of hundreds, beside the ice cream and Coca Cola stall, Bineeta Sen held a cigarette to her mouth, struck a match with slightly shaky fingers, lit the cigarette, took a drag and inexpertly blew out a cloud of shocking smoke.

The wave of mashimas and kakababus faltered. Isn't that our Bineeta? 5
Professor Dibanath Sen's daughter? She's smoking! Is she inhaling? She blew smoke out of her nose! Are you sure it's our Bineeta?

In a pool of growing silence, watched by a sea of open mouths and swivelling heads, Bineeta finished the cigarette with only one small revealing cough. She dropped the butt and stubbed it out with her chappal. Then she turned to the two girls standing beside her and said with a slight quaver, "Okay. Where's the tenner?"

In the few minutes that it took her to smoke the cigarette, Bineeta was transformed into the local scandal. You see, the most astounding thing was that it was Bineeta. She was "Our Bineeta", the quintessential Good Girl. The kind that are the bane of the existence of lively young girls with sanctimonious "respectable" parents.

She was the good student who had won a string of prizes in mathematics and debating. She was the good daughter who always helped her mother make papads and never forgot to brew a cup of Horlicks for her father every night. She was the good neighbourhood girl who sang Rabindra Sangeet, knew alpana designs, and knitted pullovers in winter. She spoke quietly, never screamed after film stars and always bent and touched the feet of every adult within reach. She wore demure dhonekhali saris in pastels, long sleeved blouses, small earrings, never any lipstick or nail polish, and her long hair was always in two tight plaits snaking down her back.

Bineeta smoking a cigarette, and in public, was as remote a possibility as Nidhubabu, the President of the Puja Committee addressing the congregation in shorts and a T-shirt.

Bineeta took the two five-rupee notes from her friends Romola and 10
Sudha and forced a small grin. When they had dared her to smoke, all she had thought was that a tenner was just what she needed to buy those books she had been drooling over at the bookshop. Now she had a feeling that such an impulsive decision hadn't been a good idea at all.

Stuffing the notes into her wallet, without looking around, she ducked past the biryani stall and hotfooted home. She hadn't seen her parents in the gawking crowd but such news travels faster than light and the prospect of a face-to-face encounter with her mother was making her throat dry up.

What she faced was more like a combination of court martial and the Spanish Inquisition. She stood before her parents and grandmother, with her brother, the maid, and the cook as the audience. The living room was gloomy in the afternoon; faintly she could hear a sad tune in the air as if someone had died in a film.

"Did you smoke a cigarette?"

"It was just a bet Baba, and I . . ."

"That's no excuse!"

"What will people say?"

"Did you really smoke it?"

"You usually do. You can't chew a . . ."

"Stop being impudent in front of your father!"

"But . . ."

As she had turned the name of her family into mud in the locality, Bineeta was ordered to stay in her room for the rest of the day to think over the terrible consequences of her action. She was not to go to the puja pandal for the evening arati and was debarred from watching the plays and music programmes.

In the evening, as the family left, sitting by the window staring at the traffic of Faiz Bazar, Bineeta thought, very logically, step by step, like the binary equations she was so good at. If anything had saved her good-girl image from tarnishing, it had been that logical, unsentimental mind of hers, that now reasoned out the pluses and minuses of the day's happenings.

As she worked it out—for nineteen years she had not taken a wrong step. If one cigarette could wipe out all those years of good behaviour, if one cloud of tobacco smoke was more important than a first in mathematics at graduation, then she did not like the equation at all.

She had obediently emulated all the Good Girls that had been held up before her. Maybe she should have become a good-time girl instead, like Meenakshi, who wore sleeveless blouses, nail polish and lipstick and maybe Meenakshi had more fun when she went to eat pastries at Volga with guys like Pratap and Mohit. She even shaved her legs and once wore a transparent red sari over a bottle-green petticoat. When they met her, the mashimas gave tight little smiles and the older men always guffawed indulgently around her. Maybe that was what one should be.

The cool logical mind clicked on. Bineeta had to admit it was hard work being a good-time girl. Taking all the trouble over make-up and clothes, having to constantly put on an act, flatter and flirt with the boys. Just a movie and pastries in return was not really enough. For Bineeta the returns had to be higher. Clean cash was a better idea.

Next morning Bineeta walked with her family to the puja in a pool of clenched-teeth silence. Only her brother looked sympathetic. Entering the pandal she braved the barrage of eyes and wondered idly why the reporters holding notepads and the flash bulbs were missing. Then Romola and Sudha came loyally to her side and she felt better. The crowd was beginning to lose interest. Bineeta was on her way to becoming a one-day wonder, soon to be forgotten.

A couple of hours later, the three girls once again stood by the biryani stall sipping Cokes. Romola was busy filling in the details of her own ordeal at home. After all to be found standing next to a girl smoking Red & White was pretty shocking too.

"By the way", Bineeta asked casually, "where did you find the cigarette and matches yesterday?"

"Got it from Pratap," Sudha explained.

"Would he have some more?"

"What! Are you mad!"

"Nope. If you two are willing to raise the bet I'll smoke again today." But Sudha and Romola were shying away from her as if they didn't like the gleam in her eyes when, "How much?" asked a voice from behind and Bineeta turned to find Pratap at the biryani stall, leaning eagerly against the plates and spoons. "How much, Bini?" he repeated. Bineeta thought quickly. Why plan to buy more books when just one more smoke could pay for a whole new polished ebony bookcase.

"Fifty", she said.

"Done", said Pratap. "Red & White or Charminar?"

Bineeta realised she was enjoying all the attention.

Of course, Bineeta calmly repeated the feat, collected her money, bought the bookcase and went on to beat everyone in the M.A. exam. But what she began inadvertently was a revolution.

At the next Puja Committee meeting of the Bengalee Club a resolution was brought forward by Nidhubabu the President, that from then on all girls below the voting age were to be escorted at all times by parents inside the pandal. At which the girls of the locality gheraoed Nidhubabu on stage and made such a clamour that the resolution could not be passed because no one could hear anything. Then Meenakshi marched up demanding that girls and boys should be allowed to act together in plays as girls in false moustaches and boys in falsetto were equally ridiculous. This resolution was passed with the enthusiastic support of all the young members of the Club. And at the following Kali Puja, two girls wore high heels and a third came with short hair. The revolution in Kashmere Gate had begun.

Bineeta went her serene way. As she told Romola, she had come to the logical conclusion that the whole Good Girl criterion of do's and don'ts had been created by parents for their own convenience and had nothing to do with being good. Docile girls could be abysmally boring but they were no trouble. And, continued Bineeta with devastating logic, the rules of the good-time girl had been made by men for their convenience. They were fun to have on your arm in the corridors of Connaught Place and show off at parties but no one expected you to marry them. As Bineeta concluded, it was no fun being a good girl and too much hard work with clothes, make up, keeping slim, and smiling at boring parties to be a good-time girl.

"I'll be neither," she ended firmly. "One can have the pleasures of both though. I'm going to be me."

After her second cigarette and her resolute refusal to apologise, the family seriously thought of sending Bineeta off to the Sharada Ashram for some discipline and ascetic thoughts. So Dibanath decided to have a quiet chat with his daughter. After an hour with her when he came out he had the dazed look and glazed eyes you see nowadays after a person's first encounter with a computer. He mumbled to his waiting wife, "She wants me to hold the punishment until her M.A. exams. She says that if her two cigarettes affect her result she'll enter the ashram the next day."

"Where's she now?"

"Gone to get my Horlicks."

Just then the maid entered, "Nidhubabu is here." They turned to find Nidhubabu standing at the door, dramatically framed by the setting sun, his face flushed to match, as his hands shook on top of his cane like all the angry fathers in melodramatic films.

"Your daughter's responsible for this!"

"What's happened now?"

"The girls disrupted the committee meeting and all the boys supported them. They cancelled my resolution and it had taken me all of..."

"But that was a month ago!"

"That's not all!"

"No?"

"My son Pratap wants to marry her!" There was a resounding crash behind them. Bineeta had dropped the cup of Horlicks.

Thirty-five years later my aunt Bineeta at a svelte 54, is the principal of one of the best colleges in the city. She has a head of snowwhite hair that she crops short and has recently added two streaks of turquoise rinse over the temples. Funnily enough she doesn't smoke. Through the years she has shamelessly encouraged her nephews and nieces to be trouble to their parents. Applauding jeans, safety pins instead of shirt buttons, singing in beat groups and shocking careers in hotels and advertising. Her daughter, a gentle, restrained singer, is quietly convinced her mother is mad. My uncle Pratap has always found his wife a handful but he has an unbeatable formula to get her to do what he wants. He first reasons it out very logically and if that fails, he lays a bet with her.

CHARTING THE STORY

1 Why does Bineeta smoke her first cigarette? Why is that first cigarette not her last? What do you make of her motivations, in terms of being "good" or "good-time"?

2 In this text laced with references to Indian culture, what Western ways, products, and/or artifacts are evident? How do the traditional and the borrowed seem to be accommodated by the characters in the story?

3 In Paragraph 38, Bineeta pronounces her opinions on who benefits from the rules for "good girls" and who benefits from the rules for "good-time girls." How does she resolve to negotiate these sets of rules; and, in your opinion, does her exchange with Pratap confirm or undercut this resolve? What leads you to make this evaluation?

CONSIDERATIONS OF STYLE

1 Sen Gupta has related to Rupa, her publishers, that she "loves the city of Delhi and has an inexplicable passion for cats." Also, "she is addicted to detective novels and enjoys dreaming up comic strips." What elements of "detective fiction" or "comic strips" enjoyed by the author seem to make their way into the story? What other genres come into play?

2 How does Sen Gupta use irony in this story both satirically and seriously?

3 At Bineeta's confrontation with her parents, and with the arrival of the enraged Nidhubabu, "a sad tune in the air as if someone had died in a film" and "angry fathers in melodramatic films," respectively, are mentioned. For what sort of effect does the author seem to be reaching?

AFTERTHOUGHTS

1 In some strata of United States culture, at least until recently (and some would argue this is still the case), a "lady" does not smoke, or eat, on the street. What appear to be the rules in Bineeta's surroundings? What is so shocking about her lighting up? If a young man were to light a cigarette under the same circumstances (after all, Pratap is the supplier of the Red & Whites), what might the repercussions be? Were Bineeta to have smoked at home, how might her parents have reacted?

2 Brainstorm (or research) associations with the goddess Durga, who is being worshipped as Bineeta lights up. What is particularly meaningful, or ironic, about the choice of such deity as the object of veneration at the moment of Bineeta's transgression?

THE WRITER'S CRAFT

1 From the perspective of Bineeta's "gentle, restrained" daughter, or of "good-time girl" Meenakshi, or of any other character, human or divine, write your views of Bineeta's actions.

2 Write an account of what you would consider a "liberating" experience in your life, one in which your poise and self-assuredness suddenly and inalterably took shape as a result of a gesture as simple as Bineeta's smoking in public on a bet.

3 Retell Bineeta's story in the form of a comic strip. If you have a chance to see the Amar Chitra Katha comic-book series, you might find it inspiring. If you can do only a few panels, you might take inspiration from Roy Lichtenstein.

MAXINE CLAIR

Poet and fiction writer MAXINE CLAIR *is a native of Kansas City, Kansas. Her works include:* Coping with Gravity, *a collection of poems;* October Brown, *a fiction chapbook; and* Rattlebone, *a collection of stories which won the Friends of American Literature Fiction Award, the American Library Association's Black Caucus Award for fiction, and the* Chicago Tribune's *Heartland Prize for Fiction. She has just completed the novel* A Letter to Vergie, *a story set in the Midwest.*

Clair is an associate professor of English at The George Washington University in Washington, DC, where she teaches creative writing.

"The Creation" is a moving coming-of-age story included in Rattlebone.

PERSPECTIVES

1 Research over the Internet, or in another source, the events leading up to the 1954 Supreme Court decision *Brown vs the Board of Education of Topeka, Kansas.* How did the decision change public-school education in the United States inalterably? If racial segregation is no longer *de jure* in US schools, can one still observe instances of its being *de facto*?

2 Discuss your educational experience in the light of ethnic and social diversity.

The Creation

If I had not seen my life sinking in the unhip backwater of high school, I would not have prayed night after night for something big to happen to me, the way it seemed to be happening to everyone else. By everyone else I meant Carol Walker who had to be "stabilized" at the hospital after eating crackers and water for two weeks because her boyfriend quit her. And Wanda. She had become one of the exalted. A senior, and crowned by the entire school when the police caught her drinking liquor at Shady Maurice's, where she placed second in the Friday-night talent show. Not a month went by that I didn't observe Jewel Hicks's wan return to school after being stupefied with morphine her doctor gave her for the cramps. If such events shook up their existences to make those girls aware of living, not a single event disrupted mine. I spent my time walking around looking for something I could not describe, until I found it in the Red Quanders.

I was only six or seven when Dottie, my play aunt from church, first took Wanda and me to the colored lights strung around the pony rides, tubs of cotton candy, and stalls of hit-the-target games we called the carnival. Instead of taking us the long way down Tenth and across Walrond, she walked us along the railroad tracks to the trestle high over the open sewer of Skagg Creek.

"Don't look down at the water or you'll fall in," she yelled, then ran off and left us.

The trestle, higher than Union Hall in Rattlebone, might as well have been a tightrope. Dizzy above the leaden, gray stream, I had nothing to hold on to. I knelt down. Wanda kept walking ahead of me. Then when neither of them would come back, I crawled on hands and knees, afraid to keep my eyes shut, afraid to open them. That's how I got across. That's how I remember the first time I saw Red Quanders.

5 I passed their strange district as I lagged behind alone. The dozen or so shotgun shacks and outhouses pushed up close to the railroad tracks reminded me of how scared I had been of spiders and daddy longlegs in the outhouse we used before we were hooked up to the city. Long before the day Obadele Quander first knocked on our door selling fresh-dressed chickens, I was passing near his house looking at chicken coops, goat stalls, and gardens, wondering who were all these people living between the tracks and the woods. At the time, nothing was as puzzling as the way all of them had their heads covered in fire-red satin, the men in a do-rag style, and the women in a kind of wrapped gèle.

Finally, my play aunt came back for me.

"Who are they?" I asked her.

"Red Quanders," she said. "This is Redtown and those obeah women will get you if they catch you looking at them, so stop staring and come on."

None of the dark men with braided beards, and none of the dark women cooking over wash-tub fires seemed to notice us.

10 Years went by. Redtown was there, a part of our part of the city. I was familiar with Folami and Akin, the Red Quanders everybody knew because they went to our high school. They were twins, not identical, but you could tell they were related. Aside from them, I seldom saw any of the others, they seldom came over our way. So what led Obadele Quander to my house that September? And on a Saturday morning, too, when I looked like Hooty Coot in my mother's faded sack dress and my hair not even combed. Of all the doors he could have knocked on, why did ours stand out to him? And when I opened it and he saw my face, did he think of cinnamon, or tobacco juice? With that hair I must have resembled a picked chicken.

"Is your mamma home?"

"Yes," I said, holding down my hair with both hands.

"Can you go get her? I got only two corn-fed chickens left. Fresh-dressed this morning. I got a few brown eggs on the truck too."

"Just a minute," I said and went to get my mother. I thought, This boy doesn't go to our school, I won't have to see him, what do I care. I wondered why they wore white shirts when white was the hardest to keep clean. Was he Folami and Akin's brother? Because by then I knew that all of the Reds were Quanders, and few of them ever went to our schools.

At first my curiosity about Obadele, Folami, and Akin was casual. Other 15
matters concerned me more. For instance, why I had never heard about squaring a corner until my turn in the tryouts for the Drill Team. Why, after a month of school, no boy except the doofus Alvin Kidd had ever called me up. And the school's upcoming speech competition. The way I saw it, the competition was the only imminent thing whose outcome I could influence in the least. I hoped that Mrs. Welche, our new white teacher, would select me to represent our class.

Mrs. Welche had made *The Kansan* the spring before with her insistence that as an exercise "for all involved," she and one of our English teachers at Douglass should exchange schools. It would be a "first." At that point we had two white students at Douglass and no white teachers. The two students were sisters who had come by choice and with much fanfare. A reluctant superintendent had made it clear that a few more years would pass before the new desegregation law would take effect districtwide.

But Mrs. Welche was having none of it. At one time her husband had been a member of the Board of Education, and people said she must have known something damaging to hold over the superintendent's head. People said the school would go to pot, that there would be no discipline with a white woman coming in and changing the rules. Others thought it was a show of good faith.

I didn't mind that she had come. Her blue eyes and brown hair didn't seem to matter to anybody, and I was flattered by the fact that she noticed my small talent for public speaking. I liked her even more when she suggested I learn "Annabel Lee" by Edgar Allan Poe, and represent our class in the competition.

Wanda was a convenient, if reluctant, practice audience. Her mother, eager for Wanda's interest in anything other than her "Annie Had a Baby," record, encouraged me to come and recite for them some evenings. And one of those evenings she brought out a slim volume of poems called *God's Trombones.*

"This belongs to Reverend's wife," she said. "It's a nice book, but 20
Wanda isn't ever going to make use of it." She said that if I wanted I could keep it for a while.

I took the book home. The more I read, the more excited I became about the poems. They reminded me of spirituals. I wouldn't have been surprised to find that Reverend had borrowed some of these lines to use in his sermons. Any one of these poems was sure to make an audience sit up and take notice.

"If you really feel that strongly about it," Mrs. Welche said, "then I'm willing to let you switch. Choose one poem and we'll see how it goes."

And God stepped out on space,
And He looked around and said:
I'm lonely—I'll make Me a world.

That was it. "The Creation." I was set.

"We'll try it tomorrow after school," Mrs. Welche said.

Perhaps I thought Folami would make an exotic critic. True, I wanted her to hear my recitation, but that wasn't all. I was curious. She had attracted me and everyone else precisely because of our superstition, based on hearsay, that she had powers. Her face was no different from any of our faces—moon-round, dark as Karo syrup, with big black eyes, nothing unusual. She was a little stout, but she didn't have to worry, Red Quander women never wore store-bought clothes. We all wondered why they made no effort at being stylish.

"Don't you feel funny being the only girl with wraparound skirts down to your ankles?" I asked her.

"It's all I've ever worn. All of my friends at home wear them too, you all just don't get to see them."

"But your skirts are too straight, you can't walk that good, let alone run in them."

"Yes I can," she said.

I didn't know how to ask her about those sloppy-looking blouses that didn't match the skirts. Why didn't they wear them tucked in? And what kind of hairstyle was up under that gèle?

We had physical education, English, and algebra together. Wanda claimed that Folami smelled, but that was after Folami showed us the stone she rubbed under her arms instead of using baking soda or Mum.

"You're smelling your upper lip," I told Wanda. "I'm around her a lot and I never smell anything."

"Well, she doesn't ever take showers after gym."

"At her house they probably still have to heat water for a bath. Maybe she isn't ready for showers. She always looks clean."

Folami was careful always to slip into her one-piece gym suit beneath her long skirt, then go through contortions getting the top part on under her long-sleeved blouses, all the while holding on to her gèle. And after gym she reversed the careful plan so that no one would ever see any part of her without clothes, except of course her arms and legs. We all hated the common shower too. Granted, the rest of us didn't have to worry about headwraps, but we couldn't afford to get *our* hair wet either. We managed by putting on shower caps and running through. I thought Folami was silly to risk getting an F for the semester just because she was modest. Anyhow, I couldn't reconcile her modesty with her powers. Finally, though, Folami stopped getting dressed at all for gym, and when we suited up, she went to Study Hall with the girls who were on their periods.

"Why don't you ever suit up anymore?" I asked her.

"Too much trouble," she said.

I thought about those hideous scars on the bodies of young African girls pictured in the encyclopedia.

"It's only twice a week," I said. "Why don't you take your gym suit home every day and wear it to school under your dress?"

She didn't seem moved by my idea, but she thanked me. No one else had bothered to notice her problem.

I wouldn't say we were friends after that, but we were okay. Since Wanda usually talked to, walked with, or hid from some boy every morning, Folami and I began meeting on the corner in front of Doll's Market to walk to school. Generally she had little to say, but she waited there each morning with her brother—Akin of the white shirt and flimsy brown trousers. I never saw either of them eating in the cafeteria, yet every morning they had delicious-smelling, paper-wrapped lunches that disappeared before they walked to Redtown in the evening.

I knew in my heart that Folami didn't want to bring me home with her. I considered myself clever enough, though, to talk her into it.

"That's okay, my mother is a little peculiar too," I told her. And when she mentioned dinner, I told her, "Don't worry about that. I'll wait until I go home to eat dinner."

"How long is this poem?" she asked me. I assured her that it wouldn't take more than five or ten minutes. I didn't want her to think I was going to bore her with some dry speech.

"Are you sure you want to hear me do my poem?" I said. I didn't think that she would refuse me. She told me that it was usually the old people who recited things to them in Redtown. I let her know that I wouldn't be too embarrassed if somebody else listened.

And so, for the first time, I went to Redtown and into a Red Quander house. What was so different there? The strangely heady, earth-oil smell. The glow from a kerosene lamp. The cloth on the wall, the circle of chairs. The shiny coal of an old woman, her skinny white braids sprouting like a fringe from her red gèle. The carved stool in the corner of the first room where she sat. The snuff she packed into her lower lip. The second room and the low table with no chairs. Akin in gray overalls. And Folami's mother, with a figure and a gèle fuller and more regal than Folami's.

"Who is this girl?" her mother asked Folami.

Folami answered that I was a friend who had helped her at school.

"What is she doing here?"

"I'm helping her learn a poem."

"Hi, Mrs. Quander," I said.

At that greeting she flashed a mouthful of square white teeth, then burst out with laughter so deep that at first I started to laugh too. Softening it a bit, she shook her head and went back to the kitchen.

Akin brought a plate of strange candy. "Crystal ginger," Folami said. "Take one, it's good. It's rolled in sugar."

Folami sat down in the first room on one of the wooden, straight-back chairs. I stood before her.

And as far as the eye of God could see,
Darkness covered everything . . .

"Wait," Folami said. "You look dead. You ought to move around. When we tell stories, we move our arms and look at people. We make faces and jump around. Don't just stand there. *Do* something!"

And the light that was left from making the sun
God gathered it up in a shining ball
And flung it against the darkness,
Spangling the night with the moon and stars.

When Folami's mother came to sit and listen, I hesitated.

"Keep going. Suppose somebody at school walks in while you're up there. Are you going to stop?" Folami asked.

Then down between
The darkness and the light
He hurled the world;
Then He stopped and looked and saw
That the earth was hot and barren.
So God stepped over to the edge of the world
And He spat out the seven seas—

Another woman, stout and wearing a robe affair, came walking from the kitchen through the eating room to stand outside the circle of chairs and listen. Then still another woman. Then a girl about Folami's age entered, and they sat in the circle of chairs.

And the waters above the earth came down,
The cooling waters came down.

They held themselves, listening intently, rocked and looked at the floor. Now and again someone hummed. When finally I finished, they were quiet.

"They tell you this story at school?" Folami's mother asked, casually.

"Irene is going to say this poem in front of the whole school," Folami said.

"You like this story too?" her mother asked Folami.

"It's just a poem out of a book. It doesn't mean anything," Folami said.

Her mother stood abruptly, and pointed a long finger nearly touching my chest. "Don't come back here to our place with stories," she said. "When you talk, you talk to them that understands you. Not us."

Immediately I was out the door. And there he was, the boy with the chickens. The lean, smooth boy, taller this time, white teeth, ripe lips, sloe eyes.

"Scared you, didn't she?" he said. I ignored him. He walked at my heels, teasing.

"What you scared of, somebody gonna sprinkle dust? Take some of your hair? Turn you into a dog? Guess you won't be coming around here singing your sweet little songs."

That broke the spell. I surely wasn't going to let some boy, Red Quander or not, make fun of me.

"If you have the nerve to come over to Tenth Street trying to sell those puny guinea hens and sorry brown eggs, I can come over in Redtown to see my friend."

"What you mean guineas? Your mother sure doesn't mind giving me a dollar every Saturday."

I turned around and looked at him. "Those women in there would just as soon bawl me out as look at me. At least my mother is nice to you."

That caught him off guard.

"What was that you were telling them, anyway?" he asked.

"It was a poem I have to memorize for school."

"Oh. Well, you better be careful about what you do in Redtown, especially in that house," he said, and he smiled. "My name is Obadele."

Every Saturday my mother bought her usual chickens and eggs and teased with Wanda about our Red Quander eggman. She watched me, though. By the way I washed and braided my hair late Friday nights to get up straightening it early Saturdays before Dele came with the eggs, she knew. She knew by the school clothes I put on just to have on. I was at least fascinated.

"Who's that egg boy and how you know them Red Quanders?" she asked me.

"I've been to one of their houses," I said. "And his name is Obadele Quander. He's some kin to Folami, the one who goes to our school."

"I see he got a funny name too, but you know all of them is Quanders. Every last one of them."

"That's just like us. All of us are Wilsons."

"In *this* house," my mother said. "Not in the whole city. Don't make no sense one man having so many women. You stay away from there."

I saw Folami every day at school. She was apologetic about her mother's ways, but until I pressed her, she didn't say any more.

"Who is your father?" I asked.

"His name is Oba Quander," she said. "Why?"

"I don't know. Curious, I guess. And what's your mother's name?"

She told me that her mother had died when she and Akin were born, but the woman I saw—her Mamma Mandisa—had raised them. Those other women were all sorts of aunts of hers.

No mystery there. I thought about the play aunt I once had. I told Folami what my mother had said about their unusual ways, especially about how men could have several wives. She said it was true, but she said, "So what? To us every father is Oba—that means king. We're just a family that keeps to itself. Only bigger."

I didn't quite get it. If so many had the same father and every father had the same name, how would I know one Oba Quander from another?

"*You* wouldn't," she said. "*I* would."

The evening Obadele first walked with Folami, Akin, and me down by the creek, he itched to tell me how pure the Quanders were, how, across generations, their blood had seldom been mixed.

"Who cares?" I said. "Besides, lots of people say that, but how do you know?"

"I know because I'm my father's son, and my father came from his pure-blooded father, and we go on back just like that to the time we were first brought here. Same is true with my mother."

"Why don't you speak African, then? You all sound just like us to me. Like you're from around here."

"I do, a little," he said. "Anyway, we can use the same words you use, but it doesn't mean we speak the same language. We don't want to be like you," he said.

"Well, you sure do go through a lot of trouble trying to be different," I said.

"Us? What about you? You can't be what you really are at your school," Obadele said.

"I knew you'd say that, but it's not true." I tried to sell him on the advantages of common knowledge, but he wasn't interested.

"Look," he said. And he untied his red satin. I think I expected a conk because the red cloth fit his head as closely as the do-rags my father sometimes wore. I wasn't prepared for the way Dele's naps grew in perfect swirls around his head, like a cap.

He said to me, "Cut off all your hair and let it be, then see what happens. I dare you."

No wonder Folami had held on to her gèle at school. Was he crazy? The last thing I wanted was hair shorter than mine already was. Who wanted to look like an African, even a civilized one?

I didn't want to look like him, but I wouldn't have minded having his gift for storytellling. He knew he was good. 100

"This is the way it was," he would say. And then he would become quiet as if he were recalling all the details of a life he once knew. This set a certain mood. Then he would begin:

"At first there was no solid land. There were only two kingdoms. There was the sky, the domain of the *orisha* Olorun, the Sky God. And far below that, the watery mists, the domain of Olukun, a female *orisha*. The two kingdoms existed separately, and they let each other alone. Back then, all of life was in the sky, where Olorun lived with many other powerful *orishas*.

"There was Ifa, who could see the future and who was in charge of Fate; Eshu, who was made of chance and whim, and who causes the unforeseen troubles and pleasures in our lives. There was Agemo, the chameleon, and many others, but the most important was Obatala, the Sky God's son."

Obadele went on to tell how it was Obatala who formed the earth. How he hooked a gold chain onto the edge of the sky and descended to the water below, carrying with him a snail's shell filled with sand, a pouch of palm nuts, and the egg that contained the essence of all the *orishas*. The story explained how, when he reached the end of the golden chain, Obatala poured out the sand and dropped the egg, releasing an exquisite bird who scattered the sand, along with the traits of the *orishas*, throughout the mists. In this way he created solid land with hills and valleys. And when he planted his palms nuts, vegetation sprang up on all the earth. Then he saw a reflection of himself in a shallow pool, and began to make figures from the clay, human figures imbued with the personalities of all the *orishas*. He made them carefully and set them in the sun to dry while he quenched his thirst on palm wine. When he resumed his work, because he was intoxicated he made mistakes—the disfigured, the blind, the lame, the deaf. Then the Sky God's breath set the earth spinning, and washed across the figures drying in the sun, bringing them to life. One by one, they rose from the earth and began to do all the things people do. And Obatala, the Sky God's son, became the chief of all the earth.

But every so often, the *orisha* of the watery mists casts powerful juju on the earth, which once was her domain. 105

I liked Obadele's story, but I was even more fascinated with his version of the mystery of Folami and Akin and their Mamma Mandisa. According to Dele, the twins were not ordinary people. All twins, he said, have the power to bring good fortune into the lives of those who treat them well. Whatever they want, they get. The wise do everything they can to make twins happy.

Obadele said that Akin, the second born, sent Folami into the world first to see if life was worth living. Their mother was suffering great pains at that moment and Folami made this known to Akin. A whole day later, the reluctant Akin arrived, and sure enough, their mother died.

Mandisa was another of their father's wives. Apparently she was always a mean woman. Dele said only that she "used to be troublesome." At any rate, she was hard to get along with and she made an enemy of a neighbor woman, inviting that other woman's juju. And powerful it was. The woman, whose name Dele would not say, caused what he called an *abiku* child to enter Mandisa's womb. This was a child that was born over and over again, a child that died shortly after each birth just to torment Mandisa. But Mandisa was more clever. She took the newborn twins into her house and succeeded in nullifying all of the obeah woman's power.

Week after week, Dele mesmerized me with stories of *orishas,* of lost kingdoms and ancient rulers, and of people—Hausas and Zulus—he claimed I had to thank for more than my black skin. Squat on his haunches on the bank of the creek, he talked about how his father's father's father was the end-all, be-all keeper of the secrets of life, how the old man could recite, for days, every event since the beginning of time without one mistaken word. I was convinced that at least *he* believed what he was saying.

And when Folami gave me an amulet, I pinned it to my brassiere. For an unbeliever, an amulet has no charm. But I liked the idea of it, and maybe it worked because a certain kind of luck followed me to school, right to the stage of our auditorium. Whoever won the competition would represent Douglass in the state competition at KU that next month. Thanks to Mrs. Welche, it was the first year our school would participate. The reading, a kind of oratorical talent show, would be judged by several teachers.

I had decided to wear my navy blue chemise dress with the white collar because I would be standing, and it would show off what I hoped was my slinky-but-not-skinny figure. On the stage, we sat facing the student body and the scattered teacher-judges with their tablets and pens poised. According to their lottery, I was to go third. The Girls' Ensemble sang two selections, we were introduced, and the contest was on.

First the one white student who was competing, Ann Marie Cooper, walked to the podium. I was immediately struck by how confident she seemed. She threw her golden hair back over her shoulder and said good morning to the audience, then turned to greet her fellow schoolmates on the stage. Though brief, her background comments, in which she explained why she had chosen the Gettsyburg Address, were more successful than her overheated rendition of Lincoln's speech. I was heartened, but also frustrated. I had not prepared an introduction. Were we expected to follow her example?

John Goodson went next. He towered over the podium. He clutched it, preacher-like, rolled up on the balls of his feet, and in his sonorous best, all but shook the place. *Out of the night that covers me, Black as the Pit from pole to pole!* The assembly sat entirely still. Not once did John let up until he had built to the final *I am the master of my fate; I am the captain of my soul!* with such power that half the students jumped to their feet in applause. Well, okay, I hadn't prepared a nice introduction to put everybody at ease. And "The Creation" certainly couldn't begin on a loud note.

When I stood up, I smoothed the lap creases of my dress and walked deliberately to the podium. I felt the sweat on my palms. Despite my three-inch, pointed-toe shoes, I was short. Nevertheless, in a sudden inspired moment I stepped to the side of the podium and gently opened my arms. Unhurried, I looked from one side of the auditorium to the other, then began. *And God stepped out on space, and He looked around and said: I'm lonely—I'll make Me a world.* I swept out an arm. *And as far as the eye of God could see, darkness covered everything, blacker,* I said "blacker" with a rasp: ... *blacker than a hundred midnights down in a cypress swamp.* I paused, dropped my arms, turned my head away from the audience, and walked a few steps across the stage. I faced them again, loosely folded my hands in a prayer stance and smiled, nodding my head. *Then God smiled, and the light broke, and the darkness rolled up on one side* ... and when I said "rolled up," I sang the O sound and made grand loops in the air with one hand, then finished: ... *and the light stood shining on the other.* I sang "shining" and flung up my other hand. With my entire being bent on heaven, the rest was automatic. *And God said: That's good!*

Some other, bolder Irene had taken over, and batted her eyes hard when 115
she came to *batted His eyes and the lightning flashed*... and she clapped the thunder and toiled with her hands until anyone watching would be hard put to deny that she held an actual lump of clay. As that Irene *blew into it the breath of life*... six hundred souls in the auditorium held their breath, quiet, until Mr. Harris's "Amen!" released them to clap hard and long.

Donald South closed with Tennyson's "Ulysses," potentially a good choice, since the last line, *To strive, to seek, to find, and not to yield,* had been selected for the senior class motto. Unfortunately for Donald, that fact contributed to his undoing when several seniors shouted out the line a beat ahead of him, destroying his delivery of the final words.

I won. Obadele was not impressed. What was the point? What did it mean to win? So I could recite a poem—was it an important poem? Why would I want to do that for a school that taught me nothing relevant? Why was I so bent on impressing a white woman teacher?

He's jealous, I thought. I realized that in some ways he was smarter than he knew. He could discuss a simple story with a depth no one in my class would attempt. The Red Quander men and women mainly taught their children at home. I suppose they had books to augment all of that reciting the old folks did. But wasn't I the one who watched John Cameron Swayze explain the world several times a week on our new television, something Dele could see only if he dared to take his Red Quander self into the Montgomery Ward store on the avenue? Didn't I know the facts he dismissed outright about the girl ironically named Brown who lived in Topeka, just fifty miles away, and who had been named in the Supreme Court case that was changing everything? Ours was the school that had maps and literature. Mine was the mother who saw to it that I went there every day. I knew more facts. He was jealous. I knew more.

The next time he knew more. He knew that if he carried a load of chicken wire and rags in his Oba-fixed truck, the state patrol would not stop a Red Quander riding out in the county on a Friday night. He knew the place in the hills at Wyandotte Lake where, if you stood on the edge of a boulder, you could see the whole of the winding water. He knew that the moon affects everything it shines on. He knew that I was afraid to be with him and the dark trees, and how a scent is a charm, how the nose can catch what the eye misses. He was the one who explained the rot of Skagg Creek as something to get beyond. That in it I could discover the wonder of everything turning to dust, and my hunger for the smell of earth's dark life. Obadele knew the effect that smell would have on me as he oiled it into his pores.

I had never talked the talk for hours on the telephone with him, never 120
drank a single Nehi with him at Nettie's Dinette. He had never been past the front door of my house, or seen me dressed up at church, never even heard of Al Hibbler and "Unchained Melody." We had never slow-danced.

"It's all right," he said. Inside his truck, on a bed of soft rags, we took off our clothes. Without light to see by, he touched me as if, slowly and gently, he were shaping my body into a woman. He opened door after door. This was the slow-dance I had wanted to learn. I found the steps awkward, but he was a born dancer. Instinctively, he set a rhythm and unchained us both.

For someone who loved school, I became a slouch. I ignored poetry and logarithms. My mind busied itself with logistics. Meeting Dele. At first it didn't matter that he had no telephone, I saw him every morning and every evening unless he had to go hauling or selling in his father's truck too early and too late. Or unless Mrs. Welche pressed me about staying after school to practice my speech. Or unless Folami stuck to me like warm mush and asked too many questions, unless Akin spied, unless Wanda used her sixth sense.

"Hope you know you can get pregnant," Wanda said. "Red Quanders don't play. They'll be workin hoodoo on you, and you won't even know it."

Then it mattered that he had no phone. Even when I came early and stayed late, I couldn't be sure he would be under the trestle. He said that people like us who were forced to hide had to be careful. We were to act as if nothing had changed. But it was impossible. I lived to see Dele, and looked for him every chance I got, despite his father and my schedule and my friends. I didn't care what time I got home, or what time I got to school.

Once, I even met him after the morning classes had already begun. The 125
crisp November air was filled with him. In the truck we drove right past the school, out to the highway and up through Olathe. To Leavenworth to see anything we had never seen, which turned out to be the prison and the army base. I wished for a gèle and long skirt so that people could see that we belonged together.

"It's more than the clothes," Dele said. "You have to *be* one of us, or at least see yourself as we do."

"Who knows," I told him, "maybe someday I will."

As we rode out Highway 40, the designation "great" came easily to my mind when I looked at the plains. Fields of winter wheat, undulant and green, surged to recede into pale seas of corn, or plowed black acreage, or loam as brown as the bread it supported. It seemed that if we could rise high enough above those vast stretches, we would see that they formed the very center of a continent. And if we focused closely, a certain symmetry would emerge with our highway as the dividing line, and a boy who was Obadele and a girl who was my very self as the axis from which it all sprang.

We drove on to Topeka that afternoon, licking his salt fish from our fingers. I wanted to show him the streets where history had begun to unfold.

"It isn't going to make any difference," Dele said. "White people don't 130
want you all in their schools, and no court can change that. You should keep to your own, forget about them."

He didn't understand, but I was in no mood to spoil our adventure. When we got home, I saw no reason for him to drop me off anywhere but in front of my house. Of course I didn't expect to see my mother watching for me out the front door. My mother was never tempted to mince words. I knew what was coming when she yelled, "Just a minute," and came out to the truck.

"I know what you're doing and I'm not going to allow it," she said to Dele. "Irene is not one of y'all and I don't want her around y'all. Don't make me come over to Redtown looking for your people, because that's just what I'm going to do if I catch you around here again. You can consider that a promise," she told Dele.

"You can't do that!" I said.

"Don't try me, Irene. Get your hind parts out of that truck."

Given my opinion on how little my mother knew about love, I was furi- 135
ous. As soon as Dele left I told her I loved him. "I'm not going to stop just because you don't understand him."

She attempted to pull rank with "You ain't too grown yet for me to whip."

"I don't care," I told her. "You can't stop me."

"I can tell your daddy," she said. She was losing ground.

"I don't care. Tell him."

My love for a Red Quander had made me my own woman. 140

Later that same week, I missed seeing Folami and noted that she had been absent for several days. I asked Dele about her.

"I don't know. I'm not her keeper," he said. "Maybe she's had enough of y'all's school."

And I asked Akin about her.

"She's at home," he said.

"What's the matter with her?" 145

"Nothing," Akin said. "She's just not coming back to school anymore."

At the first glimmer of a realization, it's hard to distinguish titillation from dread. I wondered if Folami's absence had anything to do with Obadele and me. Friday of that week my mother and I stood in the door waving Wanda on, when who else but Dele rode by in his truck. I remember clearly that it was a Friday evening because I had decided against going to the football game with Wanda.

Since the confrontation with my mother, Dele had made me promise that we would be more careful. Although I had missed him under the trestle that morning, I was shocked that he would provoke my mother by coming to our street, and thrilled that he would defy her to see me. His truck didn't stop, though. Just rattled on by.

"He can drive on any street he wants to," my mother said. "It's a free country. But he better not be looking for you." She had already heard me tell Wanda that I wasn't going to the game, and so I couldn't get out to talk to him that night.

Wanda did, however. First thing Saturday morning she came over to get me.

"Come on, we got to walk to the store. Mamma needs some milk," she said. Wanda never got up early on Saturday mornings. I hurried to finish curling my hair, just in case. Once we were outside my house, walking fast, our breath disappearing in the fog, I urged her, "Tell me what's up."

"Nothing, why?"

"I know something is up. Your mother probably doesn't even know you're out of bed."

"Okay, I just want us to talk," Wanda said.

"About what? Did you see Dele last night? Did he ask you to get me out of the house this morning?"

"Yeah, I saw him last night. Let's go over to my house. It's too cold out here."

Appeal moved toward alarm. I dismissed the fantasy of seeing the truck in the alley behind her house and went quickly with her up to her attic bedroom.

"Sit down," she said. I sat down. She looked out her window and shook her head. Then she sat down beside me and surrendered.

"You know Folami, right?

"Yeah."

"Well, she's pregnant."

"What?"

"Yeah," Wanda said, letting it register.

"So that's why she can't come back to school. How did you find out?"

"How do you think? Obadele told me."

"I just asked him—why would he tell *you?*" My stomach began to float up.

"So I could tell you what he didn't have the guts to tell you himself. He's about to become a little king in Redtown. Full-fledged man. No more nigger girls."

I didn't want to hear any more from Wanda.

"Look, don't blame me," she said. "I wasn't there to hold the light while he did it to her. I just told him I'd tell you."

I understood the words, but it didn't make sense to me. There had to be 170
something Wanda missed. That, or Obadele must have told Wanda a half-truth because of the pressure from the world.

It took a Monday morning under the trestle waiting in the cold, and a Monday afternoon in gym class hearing about Folami, and a Monday evening walking around outside Redtown with Wanda, hoping to see Dele's truck—it took all that for me to allow that it could even be possible. On Wednesday, after Wanda left me under the trestle in the cold morning, cursed me out in the evening, and threatened to go get my mother, I was only slightly more convinced that Dele could have done this.

By Friday it became clear that it would take a lot more than Wanda's word or my mother's threats to bring the fullness of it home. Why go to school when what I needed to know was in Redtown? I fastened my car coat, tied my scarf, collected my books, and left the house.

So what if I didn't have the slightest clue to where Dele lived? I would look for the truck.

Instead, when I got to Redtown, I headed for the only familiar place, Folami's house. My father used to say, when somebody burns down a house, he can't hide the smoke. I had to see her with my own eyes first. As I tramped up to the door, her Mamma Mandisa opened it, filling the doorway, hands on her hips, superiority beaming on her face.

"What you want, girl?" 175

"Can I speak to Folami?"

"Nothing around here for you. She's not coming back to the school, so you may as well get on away from here." She didn't wait for me to respond before she closed the door.

I found the truck parked in front of a house covered in brown tar-paper siding. I knocked loudly on the front door. When that didn't rouse anyone, I knocked again, with both fists, and when that didn't do it, I went to the back of the house and knocked on the door with my feet. When that didn't bring Dele outside to tell me that I had it all wrong, I got into the truck and laid on the horn. Surely he would hear, surely he would see me sitting out there. The horn blasted a minute or two, then gave up in a hoarse bleat. I got out of the truck, with its cracked window and wrong-color fender and its smell of kerosene and earth.

Where could I go? I wanted to be some other place, anywhere except this red town where I was certain that red eyes watched my foolish misery and cackled their red pleasure. I followed the railroad tracks, where I could be lost without losing my way.

For hours I walked. Through the woods, outside other neighborhoods, 180
along the river, and into the outskirts of Rattlebone. I was one with the fallow fields I passed through, and with the harvested ones too, where sheaves stood like empty spools. How could he? How could this be happening to me?

I got home after dark that night. Through the window in the front door I could see the kitchen and Wanda at the table with my mother and father, chattering to distract them. I could have been a ghost the way my mother flinched when she saw me.

Wanda said, “Girl, we were really worried—weren’t we, Miss Wilson?” I knew it was her attempt to diffuse the tightness in the air.

“You ain’t got no business wandering around by yourself this late,” my father said. “I was waiting till nine. You better be glad you got some sense and came on home before I had to come after you.” His speech sounded rehearsed.

My mother went to the stove and dipped up a bowl of oxtail stew. She unbuttoned my car coat for me and touched her fingers to my cheek.

“Too cold for you to be out with nothing on,” she said. “Sit down and eat.” I obeyed.

Days later, Wanda broached the subject again. “Welcome to the club,” she said. “I could have told you. They’re all alike. Dogs, all of them. Forget him. You have to tell yourself nothing happened. Nothing at all happened. After all,” she said, “I’m the only one at school who knows the whole story, and I know how to keep it to myself. There’s nothing else to do unless you plan to jump in the river.”

I tried following Wanda’s expert advice, act as if nothing had happened. Forget Obadele Quander. He wasn’t anyone, anyway. If my life was going to be a mess, it wasn’t going to show.

I had missed several rehearsals with Mrs. Welche. I frightened myself with the possibility that I had ruined my chances for the competition.

“I understand you’ve been having some problems at home,” she said. I wondered who she had been talking to.

“I hope whatever is going on, you won’t miss any more days of school or we may have to reconsider the tournament,” she said.

That short-circuited my cure. What I needed now was a victory. Mrs. Welche was offering that possibility, and I would focus all my energy on claiming it.

“I’m fine now,” I said. I wanted to give the right slant to what she had heard. “I won’t have to miss any more days of school.”

“You know,” she said, “those students of ours that live in Redtown, from what I understand, you’ve been spending a lot of time with them. I’m not so sure they’re the kind of influence you should be exposed to. Most of them aren’t even interested in school.”

“Yes, ma’am, I know,” I said. I could not look at her.

“They have strange ideas,” she said.

“Yes, ma’am,” I said.

“They don’t believe in God, and they don’t believe in washing themselves,” she said.

I didn’t say anything.

“They’re all related, yet they marry each other.”

“I’m having a little trouble with the last part of my introduction,” I said.

The tournament was to be held on the Sunday after Thanksgiving. Mrs. Welche had already arranged for me to ride with her and a student from her old school. Of the twenty-five contestants, I suspected, few to none would look like me. I considered it an initiation into the world I would move through if and when I went to college.

Usually I rehearsed twice a week in the auditorium after school with Mrs. Welche sitting at various places to see how well I projected. Occasionally another teacher would sit in, or a student would sneak in to watch. About ten days before Thanksgiving, Mrs. Welche asked me to meet her in her classroom instead of going to the auditorium. When I got there she sat on her desk with her arms folded.

"I received some bad news a couple of days ago," she said. "I've been wondering how to tell you. Why don't you sit down?"

She picked up the letter from her desk. "I want you to know that if I had known this, I would have never even mentioned the state competition to you. I've been involved with it for years. I just didn't think."

She was looking at the letter, but of course, I already knew.

"They won't let me be in it, will they?" I said.

"I'm sorry," she said. "The contest has never been open to you all. They say in the future . . . "

"But isn't that against the law now?"

"Well, sort of," she said. "But things take time."

This was not news. I told myself that perhaps it had happened this way for a good reason. Maybe I would have frozen up on that stage. Those people probably had never even heard of James Weldon Johnson. From the way Mrs. Welche had responded at first, I believed she had never heard of him herself.

Then Mrs. Welche said, "I was just thinking, you've done all this work for nothing. Wouldn't it be wonderful if we could salvage some of it, put it to good use?"

"Yes, but how?" I asked her.

"Well, you know, Ann Marie Cooper is a pretty good speaker. She has poise and she can project. I had her read "The Creation" for me yesterday, and she wasn't nearly as good as you are, but she could probably learn to do it your way. I thought if you would teach it to her, you know, teach her your inflections and gestures, all the drama you put into it, she could take it to state."

I gathered my books without answering. Outside, November trees had lost their leaves, and their branches showed crooked against the clouds. I took the shortcut along the tracks past Redtown. Without looking down, I crossed the narrow trestle and went home.

CHARTING THE STORY

1 Why does integration of the faculty at Douglass High School, with the transfer of Mrs Welche, appear to cause more of a stir than does the integration of the student body, with the admission of the two white sisters?

2 What cultural differences are apparent between the African American communities of the narrator and the Red Quanders? Do these differences impinge upon the friendship between Irene and Folami and between Irene and Obadele—or are other forces at play in their ultimate estrangements?

3 Why does Folami's family react so negatively to Irene and her poem recital?

4 How is the "Otherness" of the Quanders conveyed? How do other African Americans view them? How do whites view them? How do they view themselves? In what ways is Irene reciprocally "othered" by the Quanders?

CONSIDERATIONS OF STYLE

1 How does the interspersion of the poem by James Weldon Johnson, "The Creation"—first in Irene's reading of it for herself and later in her reciting it in public—enrich the narrative? How does the story line of "The Creation" differ from the creation story that Obadele tells? How do you account for the differences?

2 What "creation" metaphors enrich the story? What purpose does each serve, in the plot and thematically?

AFTERTHOUGHTS

1 Was the "bad news" scene with Mrs Welche inevitable? Why would Mrs Welche have been so unaware that African American students were not allowed to compete in the statewide contest? Why, after the *Brown vs Board of Education* decision, would she fall back lamely on "things take time"?

2 Although school segregation was declared unconstitutional by the Supreme Court in 1954, how do we account for the current racial/ethnic imbalances in many schools in the United States today? Do such imbalances diminish significantly as one progresses to higher education? Why, why not?

3 Find a copy of "The Creation" (over the Internet or in your school or public library) and read it as a performance piece, per Irene's cues in Paragraphs 114 and 115.

THE WRITER'S CRAFT

1 Write a personal narrative about a literary text that strongly influenced your formative years, just as "The Creation" influenced Irene Wilson's.

2 Write a short essay about the role of *obeah* in this story, or in any of the other stories in this anthology that feature it. ("Easter Sunday Morning" by Hazel D Campbell is a fine example.) Why are *obeah*, "Hoodoo," and *Santería*-related religions so marginalized, particularly in the United States?

RUKUN ADVANI

RUKUN ADVANI *was born in Lucknow, India. He was educated in Lucknow, Delhi, and Cambridge. His first story was published in* First Fiction *in 1992. He has also written a story collection,* Beethoven among the Cows. *Advani lives in New Delhi.*

For two brothers preoccupied with death and desire, desire wins the day—with the help of Beethoven's Emperor Concerto *and Elizabeth Taylor in her Cleopatric splendor. "Death by Music" appears in* Katha Prize Stories, Volume 2 *(1992), as well as in* Beethoven among the Cows.

PERSPECTIVES

1. As a child, in what forms of fantasy games did you indulge yourself? Assuming that "pretending" is a lifelong activity, how does the pretending of adults differ from that of children?
2. Discuss a crush that you have had on some celebrity and what that individual has contributed to your life.
3. Did any piece of music make a profound impression upon you as an adolescent? Does any piece produce similar effects on you today?

Death by Music

FOR MARTIN AND JANE—R.A.

'If suicide wasn't such a permanent thing,' said my brother, 'I'd commit it once a day. Some days maybe twice.' I wasn't surprised. He was looking at film magazines which had pictures of Elizabeth Taylor.

The cup of my brother's life brimmed over with a shallow wit. We looked quite different from each other, but he felt the same way as me; every time we saw beautiful women the injustice of life came home to us and, like Hamlet, we weighed the pros and cons of doing ourselves in. A battle between desire and death raged within us all the time.

Looking at those pictures and gauging our impossible distance from Hollywood, I agreed with my brother, though I knew that on other days, when the blues hadn't struck with their habitual ferocity, life seemed tolerably livable, occasionally even ecstatic. It was that oscillation between feeling traumatically low and excitedly high which sank me in gloom, making me sceptical about living out life with an emotional gas regulator, always checking on how much feeling to let flow, how high to keep the flame without burning other people or burning out, how much of myself to express without feeling vulnerable, exposed, misunderstood.

Of course we weren't serious about suicide, desisting out of fear of pain: my brother said Hamlet's problem with suicide wasn't that it was unaesthetic but that he didn't have an anaesthetic. It would certainly have hurt to have passed into a realm where one couldn't even savour apple tart the next day. In some vague way we felt there lay ahead of us a future pregnant with possibilities. Our palate for what it held in taste for us dampened the desire for self-slaughter, and so the native hue of resolution was sicklied o'er with the pale cast of a proven pudding. Desire won the day; death might have seemed acceptable if it didn't cut us off so dismayingly from the senses, or if it took us off painlessly to some undiscovered country from whose bourne no traveller returns.

'Hey man, put on the Emperor Concerto,' said my brother, scattering 5
the magazines all over the bed.

'Okay,' I said. I opened our record box and put Beethoven's Emperor Concerto on the record-changer.

In those adolescent days, when life seemed a balancing beam between perdition at one end and orgasm at the other, music served in some ways as a ready-to-hand substitute for sex. My brother and I had immunized ourselves against the possibilities of lust and intimations of mortality with Beethoven's Emperor Concerto, in which the melodies seemed to give sufficient form to all the feelings we had ever harboured. Earlier, I had fretted awhile over the words to choose in some stupendous literary endeavour to transform soulful torment into aesthetic torrent, but the flow of my phrases got nowhere near the tunes in the Emperor Concerto. That music set in perspective everything else in life and seemed the highest cathartic interruption within the general desirability of silence.

Not that it was possible to get away from desire. Even the act of putting on that music had a faintly sexual tinge. Our record-changer had an erect metallic obelisk wedged into the centre of a rotating disk. The record sat on this Cleopatric needle for a few seconds and then, with a subtle bit of foreplay, the needle nudged the record right down its firm length, onto the rotator. Now it was time for the record-changer to use its arm: it had a phallic arm with a gentle curve and a hard tip. For a few seconds that arm hovered in the air, as though searching an entrance, and then gently but firmly it closed in over the Emperor Concerto. As that diamond tip nestled into the opening groove and the orchestra came alive with a triumphant orgasmic crash, we felt our veins flood with the sound of salvation. We closed our eyes and felt our bodies embrace something as sweet as Elizabeth Taylor.

'Lower the volume for God's sake,' yelled Amma from her bedroom. We paid no heed and she came in storming. 'For God's sake,' she said, softening the Emperor and closing the magazines full of Liz Taylor, 'can't you boys do anything better with your lives than mooning around filmstars?'

'Elizabeth Taylor is my birthright,' said my brother with gusto, 'and I shall have her.'

Amma raised an eyebrow, angling her disdain in our general direction. In her hierarchy neither plastic film nor orchestrally manufactured sound could surpass the hum of domestic contentment. She knew the difference between illusion and reality and patted each into its proper place, smoothing their creases. She clicked mostly to the music of knitting needles, which communicated present tranquillity and future warmth. My brother and I took the sounds of domestic bliss for granted; we were in search of the exotic and the extraordinary.

'I had a dream recently,' he explained, 'a very strange one. I dreamt I was playing the lyre in Sparta, near Mount Olympus, and out of the blue who should come walking down to me but Elizabeth Taylor, arm in arm with Zeus.'

'I'm surprised,' said Amma, smiling. 'Are you sure she wasn't arm in arm with you?' She walked off towards the reality of her cushions, which needed to be tidied, and the music of her whistling pressure-cooker.

My brother explained the rest of his convoluted dream to me, a happy frolicsome dream which contrived to pull together so many of the images which rotated like planets upon the disk of our minds. In his dream my brother attempted the sweet violence of the Emperor Concerto on the lower tones of his antique instrument, and the nobility of this ridiculous effort, spotted by Zeus, made the god so full of mirth that in a fit of magnanimity he offered to make Paris out of my brother as reward for his next life, when he could have Helen all to himself and sway to the rhythms of her dance in all the Hindi films that ever came out of Bombay.

But my brother, desiring his companion Elizabeth Taylor instead, was intemperately changed into a Golden Retriever by the irate god, being retrieved from a canine end only by the divine intervention of Miss Taylor, who liked Golden Retrievers. One day, with Zeus asnooze, she disguised one of her hundred husbands as Achilles, then asked him to take the kennel and fling it with all his might, dog and all, into the River Gomti, which filtered unnoticed past the obscurest town in all Asia, where Zeus would never look. She also ordained that before the kennel fell upon the river it would change its form to a basket made of bulrushes anxiously awaited by a horde of barren washerwomen, all in search of forlorn babies which might float past their river in baskets made of bulrushes. When the women had done killing themselves over this scarce resource, the only survivor among them, after drowning the rest along the prescribed rules of Indian capitalism, would find inside a musical baby with hearing so perfect he would be the envy of Ludwig van Beethoven when he was full-grown. To this full-grown inheritor of the Emperor Concerto, declared my brother, Elizabeth Taylor had made it known that she would some day return. 'And if I remember the whole dream right,' he said, 'she's going to arrive in the shape of a queen. Yes, that's right, she'll come like an empress.'

The level of anarchy in that dream somehow faded out of our bodies as we grew older, but in those days it made perfect sense to me. That dream seemed a premonition, or the articulation of an exciting possibility, or at worst a sensuous alchemy of exaltation and despair which found symbolic form in that strange pairing of Emperor and empress. The incredible harmony of tempestuous impulse and quiet sadness which moved within the grooves of the Emperor Concerto seemed linked, with an eccentricity which fortified us against the inequities of life, with the always restless, always mobile, forever beautiful form of Elizabeth Taylor.

Something of this same restless, questing, searching feeling lay in the ample bosom of Elizabeth Taylor as she stepped out of the cinema screen of the Mayfair Theatre in Lucknow, leaving Mark Antony, Octavius Caesar and a swimming pool of asses' milk to play out the rest of *Cleopatra*.

It was perhaps a fortnight after that dream. My brother and I were part of a normal, sexually-repressed crowd of fellow natives watching the late show of that film in our small city theatre, when she calmly detached herself from tinsel and celluloid, stepped into our little movie hall, walked down the four wooden steps that separated the screen from the audience, and came straight towards our seats.

There were perhaps five hundred people in the audience, all erotically hungry for Elizabeth Taylor. English movies had begun giving way to the Hindi cinema, and the crowds only paid money to watch Hollywood heroines if they knew they were getting sex in return for their investment. 'Strictly for Adults,' the tag attached to *Cleopatra*, partly betokened the censor board's antediluvian notion of sex—which was a white woman who revealed anything between her neck and her knees—but mostly it served to draw in the throngs. In our town that label usually brought in every man to leer awhile and return home cheered.

News had got around that there were juicy tidbits in *Cleopatra* which in- 20
volved some queen floating about in an untransparent pool of milk, so a full house watched the film eagerly, hoping the milk in Egypt was as diluted as in India, at least enough to reveal the erogenous zones of a Nubian empress. Sitting by their side were other voyeurs like my brother and me, who had one foot in Los Angeles and the other in Lucknow. It was a motley crew that lay in wait for burnished gold to barge Cleopatra into view.

We hadn't bargained for her barging into contemporary India in a debut quite as casually spectacular as this.

'Hello,' she said softly, 'd'you think I can squeeze in somewhere for a bit?'

'Sure Cleopatra,' I replied coolly in her own sort of Hollywood drawl to aid instantaneous comprehension, 'you c'n sit right here between us.' The armrest between my brother and me seemed to have vanished with her appearance, and she squeezed between us to watch the rest of the movie.

Naturally, we waited for the hall to erupt in pandemonium with her entry. But to our amazement the consternation which ensued from her caesura out of ancient Egypt was visible only on screen; there seemed not the slightest evidence of it in our theatre. We looked this way and that, we rubbed our eyes and adjusted our vision, but no change of focus followed. Cleopatra sat beside us, watching what would happen next in *Cleopatra,* apparently invisible to our fellow watchers.

25 The movie was still running, except Mark Antony and Octavius Caesar were no longer antagonists; they had come close to each other and were looking aghast in our general direction For some reason, which I saw as a lack of vision, they couldn't see beyond the screen which separated them from us; their world lay in illusion. Behind them we saw a slowly gathering herd of asses alongside an army of extras. The asses brayed vigorously in our direction before wandering offscreen to waste their snorts upon the desert air. The extras scratched themselves here and there, accustoming their bodies to the fact that in such sandy climes even a substantial woman might prove a mirage and just thinly vanish.

We watched the move hypnotised, held in thrall by what was happening. Yet only my brother and I seemed to see that the woman who sat near us, all scented and Oriented, smiling at the bewilderment of her co-stars on screen, was the missing Cleopatra. Age had not withered her, nor husbands staled her infinite desirability. If it wasn't Elizabeth Taylor sitting by our side, it could only be her ideal Platonic form come straight out of the shadowy world of Hollywood.

Meanwhile the movie was running on, perplexing us with new evidence on the decline of the Roman empire. An odd fate seemed to have struck the emperors into an open-mouthed and paralyzed inertia uncharacteristic of that period of swashbuckling Roman history. Caesar, Antony, the asses, the extras, were all searching diffidently about them, and it was soon clear to our theatre audience that the missing object of their phallic gaze was Cleopatra.

'Hey Caesar,' shouted Mark Antony, 'does she know how to swim?'

Caesar looked in alarm at the pool of milk. Four little donkeys joined him and stared down too, moved by a different intention. They bent their heads and began lapping up the pool.

30 'Maybe she's down there somewhere,' said Caesar, now frenzied.

More donkeys crowded around the pool, and soon there was a whole circle of asses drinking up the bath. In a minute it was quite drained, but there was no African queen at the bottom. The crowd had paid good money to see Cleopatra emerge in the nude and patiently awaited her return on their investment.

But to little profit. The passionate international relationship between Rome and Egypt remained, unfortunately for the investors, material for future speculation. For, just at this crucial juncture of history, there was a blackout.

It was an electricity failure, organised specially by all state governments in India to keep citizens in mind of exactly which set of pussy-stroking political villains were currently in power. In the theatre everyone groaned in one go, for the energy required to keep the illusion alive was at least temporarily at an end. The exit lights glowed brighter and several shrill wolf-whistles—directed from the audience at the film operators to get their generator going—got no response at all. People were stirring irritably in their seats, wondering what was going on, exasperated by the emptiness of the pool and the capricious twists of history, and then by the film's frustrating cut before the empress with no clothes could reveal all. But everyone seemed oblivious of the most obvious truth, that Cleopatra had appeared and was now one of us.

'Excuse me,' said Cleopatra to us, loud and clear in the encompassing penumbra, 'could you direct me to a hotel anywhere downtown, if there's one near here, maybe?'

My brother was still adjusting his eyesight but I, though a bit obtuse, was readier with high sentence.

'Sure Liz,' I said, 'we c'n show you some reel cool places downtown.' I spoke as though those words had lodged within me all my life, awaiting only the appearance of a nubile empress to shape my utterance.

'Gee thanks honey,' she said. 'Let's go then,' she said more urgently, as we shuffled out to the sound of louder wolf-whistles in the diminishing dark. I looked nervously about, certain they were directed at the two of us and Cleopatra, certain they'd stop her for leaving with us and put her back on screen to get their money's worth when the generator got going. But no one closed in upon us, no one seemed to see us, and I realized like a one-eyed man that in the country of the blind people see only as much as they are allowed by the shared social vision which constitutes each man's cornea.

As we moved out of the Mayfair Theatre, I saw her ruffle her hair and put a hanky to her eyelids, which she vigorously wiped, and there lay the rub—she seemed to know she couldn't be seen. The liquefaction of her clothes, in which she flowed with us to the foyer, attracted no comment either, even though what she wore was as flamboyantly outlandish as some of the things I'd seen on many of the Anglo-Indian Sandras and Teresas who went arm in arm and cheap high heels down Lovers Lane or the Shahnajaf Road.

Outside the hall, on the M.G. Road which blackened every Indian town as memorial to Mahatma Gandhi's abbreviated life, rickshawallahs huddled meagrely on their enlarged tricycles and a paanwallah's rope burnt its slow way towards a swimming pool of betel leaf and white lime.

We made our way through faceless throngs towards the diurnal round of parked rickshaws, the skeletons on them crying out in the dark to attract our custom. My brother and I directed her with complete confidence now, caring nothing, while Cleopatra followed where we led. We would normally have walked to our house, only a mile away, but had telepathicaly decided that travel with Cleopatra would be more pleasantly tactile, at least for us, if we squeezed into a rickshaw.

There were several people about. Two pregnant men approaching labour scratched their scrotae and had developed white moustaches eating Tootie

Frooties. A Bengali gent clutched the tail of his dhoti and repeatedly insulted the nearest wall with vermilion spittle. Jesus, hoist with his own petard on the church steeple opposite, felt helplessly cross carrying the weight of avian multitudes which gurgled and crowned his nest of thorns. Below him university criminals roamed in small bands, combing their hair and then the streets for passing women. A pavement loudspeaker with a sore throat, long devoid of song, screeched its undirected abuse of music alongside the local Come September Brass Band, which brayed encouragement to a three-piece groom already astride his nag. Skeletons plied aimless rickshaws and a South Indian lady, buying a flower garland, whispered to her husband, 'Do you think that was cent per cent donkey milk in which she would be taking her bath?' They all saw straight through Cleopatra, looking at us briefly but seeing nothing amiss.

We knew where to take her, naturally. Every American who ever visited our small town was on his way to a tiger, just as in Africa they were all hunting for their roots. We knew exactly where, within our little urban jungle, she might find what she was looking for.

'Excuse me Miss Cleopatra,' said my brother, 'we can drop you off at a hotel near here which is quite nice, if you like.'

'You c'n call me Liz,' she said, so we gave her our names, and fishing in her dress pocket she added: 'Sure, any place you c'n recommend should do for now, s'long as it's kinda quiet and large and if they'll take dollars.'

We were getting on quite well, I thought, and wondered at her lack of nervousness, hopping off the screen and onto a rickshaw with her first two men in a strange city. I guessed she was a traveller, like the two of us, and felt at home being always on the move. I sensed in particular the affinity between my brother and her from the air of ease they both radiated, from that capacity some people have to appear equally relaxed among schoolchildren or lawyers, golfers or historians, strangers or friends, in the most odd or unlikely circumstances. Even in that short space I had intimations that something of my brother lay in Elizabeth Taylor too, a shared impulse which drove her all that distance from pyramid and sand dune to the obscurest theatre in all Asia.

But the precise contours of a symmetry which linked her world and ours only became obscurely clear to me towards the end of her stay in Lucknow.

All the obvious questions crowded our minds as we huddled into the rickshaw and a skeleton stood on his pedals to move us towards the Carlton Hotel, where a stuffed tiger with permed coat and waxed moustaches glared out a reception from his glass case at the entrance door. How had she made her appearance? Why had she come here, of all places? Was it really true that she sat ensconced between us, being pulled on a rickshaw so soon after rolling out of a rug to a concert of emperors? What was going to happen now? Would she stay a while or return like a mirage to the screen?

There were so many questions to ask that to ask one or the other seemed futile. There were likely to be so many answers, and all so confusing to our emotions, that silence seemed that most obvious and desired conditions of being. We stayed quiet, and so did Liz, warming to each other in the solitude of that shared cold air through the slowly passing sights, the yowl of stray dogs against the temperature, the whiff of open rubbish dumps mingling with the scent of burning eucalyptus where three men crouched to hide a glow.

We were now at the tail end of a straining spine, wondering how it managed to heft three substantial people so lavishly clad. It deserved a thousand dollars, I thought, so it could get itself some warm skin from the morgue. Watching all the absent muscle as that cadaver moved us in the direction of the Carlton Hotel was like taking in an anatomy lesson. His bones were clanking and gleamed white with the oil that dropped down to keep them from rusting. But our sympathy for him was finite; we disembarked at the Carlton Hotel.

A taxidermic tiger gaped at the arrival of Elizabeth Taylor to his hotel, his 50
incisors gleaming at her as though awaiting his dentist. Fortunately he made no other move to receive us, and while my brother haggled with our rickshawallah we waited by his flanks at the reception desk. I watched my brother bargain with some embarrassment on account of Cleopatra's obvious concern for the pedaller. Socially, we were always under great pressure never to give anything to beggars, lepers, cadavers and the poor, lest the sin of richness deny them the kingdom of heaven, and so that we could spend all we saved on Tootie Frootie and Kassata ice cream. I tried telepathy and got through. He gave the rickshawallah a thousand dollars, which was the new currency of our country, and the bones cycled away saying salaam.

There was no one behind the reception desk. We rang an electric bell which broadcast a low whine and two cockroaches. The cockroaches had their antennae out in alarm but retreated into the bell after giving some thought to our circumstances. No one else appeared. We rang and rang again, but in Lucknow it little profits a hotel rich in vermin to employ receptionists.

'Mebbe they're full up, d'you think?' said Liz finally. 'Can we try someplace else?'

My brother ran after the pedalling silhouette to re-engage his services, and we hopped on once more.

'We live just round the corner from here,' said my brother. 'With our mother,' he added, to suggest she was safe with us.

'We could go home and you could stay overnight in our mother's room, 55
if that's okay by you.'

'Okay,' said Cleopatra with an imperial smile, 'if that's okay with your mama.'

We had no doubt that Amma, after the initial shock, wouldn't refuse a night's shelter to our stray Cleopatra at that hour of the night. But she surprised us with her perspicacity, saying she was expecting this all along, and merely scolded Cleopatra for being out so late and out of date.

'A girl your age ought to know better than to be gallivanting about at this time of night with these two,' she said. 'I knew these brats would bring you home one day, but I thought you'd be here much earlier.'

We knew she wasn't really upset, of course, recognizing the obliqueness of her affection from the timbre of her scolding. She'd already left Cleopatra her second-best bed, and towel, soap and nightie for the nonce.

Falling asleep on my pillow I remembered asking Amma once how the 60
emperor Babur, walking thrice around the bed of his sick son Humayun, took the disease upon himself.

'I can't tell you how,' Amma replied, adding one of her parables. 'Some things just happen and it's best to take them as they come. Edison said Let there be Light, and there was.'

I awoke the next morning as usual to the opening crescendo of the Emperor Concerto, proclaiming the triumph with which it makes sense to start the superhuman endeavours of each new day. I liked silence in the early mornings and Amma liked bed-tea, but my brother had hegemonized us both into waking up to that music. Liz was still there. She was awake too, alert and listening, which was conclusive proof for us that she hadn't been pulling the rug over our eyes.

'I need a break,' she was telling Amma through Klemperer's majestic conducting. 'I'm through with playing Cleopatra. 'Fact I'm through with playing this queen, that queen, all the time. Gimme a break I said to all those men. Men, men, men, day and night. Makes me sick. Have you noticed how there only seem to have become more and more men and then some in the world lately? Anyhow, I just need a break. I'm through with moving beds and roles and husbands, the whole lot. I need a break. I'm looking for something different, and maybe that something's brought me here.' She paused, searching for some clearer definition of her restlessness, then shrugged.

Amma was the eternal mother and understood the emotional fatigue of continuous travel. We did too, having moved restlessly from one thing to another, unsure of what we searched, certain only of the need to persist in always seeking something other than what we possessed, distrusting the immobility of comfort and accepting instead an unquenchable wanderlust which moved us towards periods of short-lived exhaustion and defined the way we were. We saw Liz as one of us and accepted her presence in our home, refusing to ask the obvious questions and taking it for granted that her visit was something both she and we wanted, or needed, or that was mysteriously but happily fated for us. Her instinctive need was to feel free to say only as much as she wished.

Two days' rest cleared some of the cobwebs in her mind. She said she had 65
felt imprisoned for ages by men, relationships, routine, and the omniscient clamour of human beings, and one day, when it all got too much and she felt herself at the edge of suicidal despair, she thought she saw in front of her eyes a solitary grave where a tree rose out of the earth in the shape of an upturned woman, an image of overpowering beauty towards which she had taken some sort of plunge, finding herself thereafter seated in spacious comfort, and assured of movement towards an area of blissful solitude, space and silence. She

couldn't recollect anything more, no more than a child recollects its plunge into the world, nor no more than does a transformed Golden Retriever when washed amnesiac down an obscure river to a new shore. It had seemed a sudden relief to shed the past, to feel free of lovers, husbands, and the stars which directed her destiny, to watch the huge and sudden gap between herself and the people who had wrenched her insides, to be distant for a short space.

All this made sense to us. It was superficially illogical, but it had an inner emotional logic beyond which questions became transgressions. The episode fitted no formula, its causes were happily unknown and beyond the tax of ascertainment. Liz Taylor had come to us because she wanted a break, because she felt some unknown pull in our direction, and because we possessed that silent state of mind by which hospitality, being unspoken, is doubly communicated. We knew her visit would last only as long as the electric current which all three of us had generated held us together, that power breakdowns were inevitable, and that she would, like every wayfarer who makes a sojourn, soon enter that undiscovered country from whose bourne no traveller returns.

A few days went happily by and we showed her all the famous historic sights, the fading palaces, the arenas of war, the residences of conquerors, the tombs where flowers disguised the conquests of death.

'Gee honey,' said Liz by way of admiration after each monument, 'that looks kinda neat.'

But she seemed in search of something else for the old restive feeling came crowding back in her, and the sound of the Emperor Concerto which caused the sun to rise each morning troubled in her an old vision, stirring within her the sight of a solitary grave in which a tree rose out of the earth in the shape of an upturned woman. With the ebb of fatigue her vision improved and she described it to us with greater clarity. 'Have either of you ever seen anything like that?" she asked. 'I'm trying to figure out what pulled me here.'

We were puzzling over this when my brother said again, in that way he always did, 'Hey man, put on the Emperor Concerto.'

'Okay,' I said. I opened our record box and put Beethoven's concerto on the slim, taut shaft of our record-changer, watching as it edged the record towards the inevitable orgasm. It was at that very moment, with the opening crash of an allegro, that we linked Liz's vision to what was commonplace in our lives, and which connected her with an unforeseen symmetry to people so distant from her world. We had seen precisely what she described. Suddenly that instant, switching on the Emperor, we knew it had switched on in Elizabeth's mind the exact location of suicidal despair, which we saw every day on our way to school.

We knew it all our lives as the grave of an unknown woman who died mysteriously during the Mutiny of 1857, leaving only a note that her remains be spared a churchyard, and that a single tree be planted by her side as protection. The tree that emerged had a double trunk which, at the appropriate height, overlapped and gave out the appearance of a woman's thighs. That grave, that tree, were almost the epicentre of our lives, lying halfway in our history, equidistant between the unspoken warmth of our mother's knitting needles and the dictations in reason we received at our school. They were for us a sight both beautiful and moving, connected through the current of our emotions and associations with the Emperor Concerto, suddenly confirmed now by the vision which linked us to Liz.

I think it may have been at this point that some suspicion of the name of the woman in that grave began to grow within us, making us wonder at the strange contours of an emotional convergence between our world and the one from which Liz had arrived.

No official history of the Indian Mutiny of 1857 records the story of an English woman who, during the siege of the Residency, gave solace to the ears of the besieged with the only piano left in Lucknow. Her music was not of sufficient consequence for history, the sound of her instrument drowned out by cannon and musket, the crowds closing in upon the precincts and leaving no room for softness or melody, leaving room only for the suicidal despair in which the woman wrote her note, asking only solitude, silence and space in the hereafter.

There was little left for us to do now, except get confirmation of what we 75
suspected. We summoned the skeleton again and were pulled by him towards the grave where our unknown woman rested in peace, guarded by a solitary tree which grew with silent grace along the lines of her body.

Elizabeth paid him for the long haul and he left our world grinning. Elizabeth scraped the moss that obscured an epitaph.

We were right, of course, and as Elizabeth Taylor vanished from our sight we read what we had recently guessed but never bothered before to notice.

HERE LIES ELIZA TAYLOR
1827–1857
WHO WITH MELODY AND MUSIC LIT . . .

The gravestone broke off at that point, leaving us in the dark with further obvious questions—Who, How, What, Where, When, and Why.

Now, looking back, I attribute our feeling for the Emperor Concerto and that singular perception of Elizabeth Taylor to an uncommon Anglicization which sensitized us to the beauties of the West, until the clamour of local historians sternly warned us against being so ideologically evil as to desire white before brown. In later years we went native and adored the acceptably off-white Shabana Azmi to atone for our misguided youth, by which time the nationalist noise had given way to the feminist, dampening our desire altogether with Wills Filter evidence on the wicked lashings of power within all male sexuality.

But in those days of adolescent dreams, when we had the power to make 80
the images of our minds come alive almost at will, the shadows of doubt cast

upon us by that grave would likely have taken up the rest of our short lives to pose and answer all those profound and overwhelming questions about the visionary and the real. We could have asked those questions endlessly, then posed them again and answered them a different way: they would have yielded no satisfactory answers. That was not a time for answers. To be alive then was to revel in the illogic of our minds and feelings, to witness the inner struggle of death and desire, to dream of Elizabeth Taylor and bring her home to bed, to listen to Beethoven and connect his music with the image of a tree or the silent beauty of a grave. The happiness of our youth was no different from the ease with which our wildest dreams and desires came so intensely alive, assuming shapes with a furious, unpredictable anarchy. I remember now those wild, speculative days, when our images of passion culminated in that brief fusion of tempestuous impulse and suicidal despair which gave us, so strangely and unaccountably, the company of Elizabeth Taylor and the Emperor Concerto.*

*I claim no originality in attempting a convergence of 'fact' and 'fiction' within this story. The device is commonplace; in recent times it has been used with comic brilliance in at least two works by Woody Allen: his short story 'The Kugelmass Episode,' and his film *The Purple Rose of Cairo.*

CHARTING THE STORY

1 How, for the brothers, is playing a phonograph (vinyl) record a quasi-sexual act? Could their playing a cassette tape or a CD have achieved a similar thematic effect? If not, why not; if so, how?

2 What seems to be Amma's attitude towards the sexual coming of age of her sons? How does this play in the story?

3 Explain the role of Eliza Taylor's grave and the tree that grew by it (Paragraph 72) as "almost the epicentre" of the narrator's and his brother's] lives, equidistant between their home and their school.

4 In the second-to-last paragraph, the narrator confesses that later his attention would turn to Shabana Azmi, an Indian film star. What is operating—ideologically and psychologically—with the brothers' change of fascination? How does the narrator account for this redirection of fantasy?

CONSIDERATIONS OF STYLE

1 What would seem to be the correlates in reality of the skeletons pulling the rickshaws? Of the stuffed tiger and the cockroaches at the Carlton Hotel? Of the Golden Retriever in Paragraphs 15 and 65?

2 How does the author weave together images of sex, music, and Elizabeth Taylor? Where are the blendings most effective?

3 What are some of the more graphic sexual images presented in the narrative? How are they gradually softened by the end of the story?

4 What elements of the story—of image and plot—move it into the realm of magical realism? What seems magical, and what seems realistic about this text?

AFTERTHOUGHTS

1 How many references to major Western texts (Shakespeare or otherwise) can you find? Of what relevance is Elizabeth Taylor's starring role in the film *Cleopatra* to the imagery—as opposed to, say, her roles in *Cat on a Hot Tin Roof* or *Night of the Iguana*, or, for that matter, as opposed to Julie Andrews's film *The Sound of Music*, which was also popular in the mid-1960s in India? Similarly, why would the boys be aroused by the *Emperor Concerto* rather than by the equally (some would say "more") passionate *Ninth Symphony*?

2 How is the story legitimately informed by Indian history of the past two centuries?

THE WRITER'S CRAFT

1 Research the "Mutiny of 1857"—in particular the siege of the Residency (British cantonment) at Lucknow—and write a short essay discussing its employment in Advani's story.

2 Having seen the film *Cleopatra*, write an appraisal of the allure of Cleopatra to Julius Caesar and Marc Antony, or of Elizabeth Taylor to masses of viewers, alluding to episodes from "Death by Music" if you desire.

3 Compare the fantasy-play that dominates "Death by Music" with that in one or more other texts in this anthology, such as "Yellow Woman," "Waiting for a Turn," or "Kicking the Habit." Write a critical response based on your observations.

CRAIG RAINE

Born in Bishop Auckland, Durham, England in 1944, CRAIG RAINE *was educated at Oxford and for some years lectured there. Since 1981, he has served as poetry editor for the publishing house Faber & Faber Ltd, a post once held by T S Eliot.*

Raine's verse often confronts the reader with its opaqueness, yet it has drawn a large audience, and the poet is highly regarded among contemporary English poets.

The poems in this lesson share a common theme, domesticity, though this theme is manifested quite differently in each poem.

Additionally, these poems have been selected because of their critical success. "Flying to Belfast, 1977" and "Mother Dressmaking" won a first prize in the Cheltenham Festival of Literature in 1977 and 1978 respectively. "A Martian Sends a Postcard Home" won the Prudence Farmer Award in 1978, awarded annually for the best poem to appear in The New Statesman. *All three poems are included in the collection* A Martian Sends a Postcard Home, *published by Oxford University Press in 1979.*

PERSPECTIVES

1 What are some constructive activities—cooking, sewing, building something—that you, as a child, enjoyed sharing with a parent or other adult, as either a helper or a bystander?

2 This poem reminds one of an interior genre scene by seventeenth-century Dutch painter Jan Vermeer. Consult an art history book, a book on Vermeer, or a museum publication that contains examples of Vermeer's work to get a sense of such a domestic scene.

Mother Dressmaking

The budgerigar pecks at the millet,
his beak prised apart like a pistachio nut

by the fat kernel of tongue. I draw,
wet profiles on the window pane.

We are immersed in making things.
The clock clicks its tongue...

trial and error. She tries her shapes
in different ways like a collage,

until they are close without touching...
Pinned in place, they are packed

like a suitcase. She takes
a prehistoric triangle of chalk

and leaves a margin for the seams.
Her scissors move through the material

like a swimmer doing crawl,
among the archipelago of tissue paper.

We are immersed, with our tongues out.
Waiting for the time when profiles run.

CHARTING THE POEM

1 This poem works in small detailed images drawn around the simple act of the mother making a dress in the presence of the child narrator. What details suggest that the mother is an accomplished seamstress? What do the accompanying images—of the budgerigar, of the child drawing on the windowpane, of the clock, of the "swimmer doing crawl" contribute to the scene?

2 What is the significance of the line—which appears twice in the poem—"We are immersed..."? Who does the author's "we" include, and why does this appear to be so?

CONSIDERATIONS OF STYLE

1 How do *sound* associations such as alliteration and onomatopoeia inform the images in this poem?

2 Why does the speaker call the piece of chalk "prehistoric"?

AFTERTHOUGHTS

1 We've noted above that meaning in Raine's poems is sometimes elusive. A case in point may be the last stanza of "Mother Dressmaking." How do you interpret it?

THE WRITER'S CRAFT

1 Write a description of an interior genre scene from a picture, such as Vermeer painting or a similarly constructed photograph.

2 Describe a domestic scene, such as the one in "Mother Dressmaking," of your own invention.

PERSPECTIVES

1 Describe your sensations in flying into a particular city for the first time.
2 Discuss the associations that apply to Belfast, particularly to the Belfast of the 1970s.

Flying to Belfast, 1977

It was possible to laugh
as the engines whistled to the boil,

and wonder what the clouds looked like—
shovelled snow, Apple Charlotte,

Tufty Tails . . . I enjoyed
the Irish Sea, the ships were faults

in a dark expanse of linen.
And then Belfast below, a radio

with its back ripped off,
among the agricultural abstract

of the fields. Intricate,
neat and orderly. The windows

gleamed like drops of solder—
everything was wired up.

I thought of wedding presents,
white tea things

grouped on a dresser,
as we entered the cloud

and were nowhere—
a bride in a veil, laughing

at the sense of event, only
half afraid of an empty house

with its curtains boiling
from the bedroom window.

CHARTING THE POEM

1. What is "actually" taking place throughout the poem, and how does this "event" connect, if at all, with the similes used throughout?
2. What is the significance of laughter—alluded to twice—in this "serious" poem?
3. Five of the poem's 12 stanzas tell of a "bride in a veil," "wedding presents, white tea things grouped on a dresser" in "an empty house with its curtains boiling from the bedroom window." How does this scene inform the poem, which is narrated from an airplane flying overhead?

CONSIDERATIONS OF STYLE

1. The sentences in this poem vary in length, and are threaded throughout the poem, often ending in mid-stanza. What is the narrative effect of such a pattern?
2. Of what might the imaged bride be afraid, concerning the "empty house," and how does this relate to the mood of the poem?

AFTERTHOUGHTS

1. The media nowadays report often—frequently in graphic detail—on war. What are typical scenes of war you might witness on TV, or in newspapers and news magazines? By comparison, Raine's description of war-weary Belfast is just a "snapshot" of "a radio with its back ripped off" among images of clouds, of orderly fields, of a bride and wedding presents. What is the effect of such a contextualization of war's effects?

THE WRITER'S CRAFT

1. Compare how the "Belfast below" presented in the poem might contrast with a description of Belfast as it would be if the speaker in the poem were on the ground.

PERSPECTIVES

1. Recall a time when you entered a different culture—in another country, perhaps on another continent. Or, when you stepped into a milieu which was so unfamiliar to you that you felt like a *complete outsider*. How did you come to interpret the new environment? In effect, to make sense out of it?

A Martian Sends a Postcard Home

Caxtons are mechanical birds with many wings
and some are treasured for their markings—

they cause the eyes to melt
or the body to shriek without pain.

I have never seen one fly, but
sometimes they perch on the hand.

Mist is when the sky is tired of flight
and rests its soft machine on ground:

then the world is dim and bookish
like engravings under tissue paper.

Rain is when the earth is television.
It has the property of making colours darker.

Model T is a room with the lock inside—
a key is turned to free the world

for movement, so quick there is a film
to watch for anything missed.

But time is tied to the wrist
or kept in a box, ticking with impatience.

In homes, a haunted apparatus sleeps,
that snores when you pick it up.

If the ghost cries, they carry it
to their lips and soothe it to sleep

with sounds. And yet, they wake it up
deliberately, by tickling with a finger.

Only the young are allowed to suffer
openly. Adults go to a punishment room

with water but nothing to eat.
They lock the door and suffer the noises

alone. No one is exempt
and everyone's pain has a different smell.

At night, when all the colours die,
they hide in pairs

and read about themselves—
in colour, with their eyelids shut.

CHARTING THE POEM

1 Image by image, ascertain what the Martian is describing; in other words, decode the poem. (This works very interestingly if at first done individually before comparing your findings with those of others.)
2 What are some of the marvels of technology that the Martian witnesses in the exotic culture that he is visiting?
3 In what contexts does the Martian witness human beings?

CONSIDERATIONS OF STYLE

1 "Mist is when the sky is tired of flight." "But time is tied to the wrist or kept in a box. . . ." How do such examples of the Martian narrator's language brand him as an outsider? On the other hand, in what ways is his language shaped to communicate to his audience?

AFTERTHOUGHTS

1 When we enter an unfamiliar culture, we tend—not unlike the Martian in the poem—to perceive that culture through our own worldview. What sort of world do you think the Martian inhabits "back home"?
2 Interplanetary mail service being what it is, how might the Martian be sending a postcard home? (Note: this poem was written before *ET.*)

THE WRITER'S CRAFT

1 Bearing in mind how you have answered the previous questions, make a visit to Mars and write a postcard home to Earth describing your impressions of Martian civilization.

DANNIE ABSE

DANNIE ABSE *was born in 1923 in Cardiff, South Wales, where he also received his early education. He later studied medicine in London. Since receiving his medical degree, he has worked both as a physician and a freelance writer. He is a Fellow of the Royal Society of Literature and is President of the Welsh Academy of Letters.*

*Abse has published collections of poetry—*Walking under Water, A Small Desperation, Selected Poems, Collected Poems 1948–1976, Remembrance of Crimes Past *(1993), and* White Coat, Purple Coat *(1998); plays—*Three Questor Plays, The Dogs of Pavlov, *and* Pythagoras *(1979); novels—*Ash on a Young Man's Sleeve, O. Jones, O. Jones; *an autobiography; several volumes of essays; and a book on the medical profession in England.*

His latest book of poems is Arcadia, One Mile *(1999). He is the editor, with Carey Archard, of* Welsh Perspectives *and of* Twentieth Century Anglo-Welsh Poetry *(1998). With his wife, art historian Joan Abse, he has co-edited* Voices from the Gallery, *an anthology of poems and paintings commissioned by the Tate Gallery, London.*

The three poems presented here all mention a disadvantaged, "down and out" person who has overcome his or her plight through faith: the blind man in "Of Rabbi Yose" who carries the torch in the night so that others may see him and save him from danger; the lonely nonagenarian in the park in "A Winter Visit" who holds on to life like a flamingo standing, "one-legged on ice"; or old Itzig who petitions to a God that "always makes... the dog's tail wag."

The poems are collected in One-Legged on Ice *(1981).*

PERSPECTIVES

1 The first five books of the Hebrew Bible constitute the core of Jewish sacred literature, referred to as the Torah. Consult the Old Testament of a Bible to determine what themes are discussed in these books. Read Deuteronomy 28:29 for the reference to the blind groping at midday alluded to in "Of Rabbi Yose."

2 Why is Jerusalem's Western Wall—also known as the Wailing Wall—an important site of pilgrimage, lamentation, and prayer?

Of Rabbi Yose

I know little except he would ponder
on the meaning of words in the Torah
till those words became more mysterious
became an astonishment and an error.

'Thou shalt grope at noonday
as the blind gropeth in darkness.'
Soon Yose's eyebrows raised
from that poetry page of curses.
Instead he stared at the adventure
of a white wall and said, 'What difference
to a blind man, noon or midnight?'

All that week, all that month
he puzzled it, '. . . as the blind gropeth . . .',
not reading it as a child would
without obstruction, nor understanding it
as a child could. He thought, too,
of his neighbour, the blind man.

Then coming home late one night
after discussing the Torah with a pupil,
or sickness with a sick man,
one suffering perhaps from the botch
of Egypt, or from emerods, or the scab,

he saw near the darkest foliage
the plumed yellow flame of a torch
moving towards him, held high in the hand
of his neighbour, the blind man.

'Neighbour,' he cried, 'why this torch
since you are blind?' The night waited
for an answer: the wind in a carob tree,
two men, one blind, both bearded, so many
shadows thrown and fleeing from the torch.

'So that others may see me, of course,'
replied the neighbour, 'and save me
from quicksand and rock, from the snake asleep,
from cactus, from thistle and from thornbush,
from the deep potholes in the roadway.'

Year after year, to pupil after pupil,

Yose told of this night-meeting,
told it as parable, told it smiling,
satisfied, with clear-seeing eyes,
and never again pondered the true
lucid meaning of the words:
'Thou shalt grope at noonday
as the blind gropeth in darkness.'

CHARTING THE POEM

1 What puzzles Rabbi Yose about the sentence "Thou shalt grope at noonday as the blind gropeth in darkness"? How is his question ultimately answered?
2 What parallels can be made between a blind man's not knowing the difference between noon and midnight (Lines 10–11) and a child who could read scripture "without obstruction" (Lines 14–15)?
3 What connections can be made between the suffering of the student of the Torah and the sick man (Lines 18–22)?

CONSIDERATIONS OF STYLE

1 What Biblical images does the poet use, and to what effect?
2 What methods of storytelling does this poem partake of? How do these methods uniquely shape it?
3 Does the "I know little except" opening of the poem, and the indeterminacy of part of the narrative (the fourth stanza, the "coming home late one night" episode) support or undercut the veracity of the story that it relates? In what ways?

PERSPECTIVES

1 Discuss the effects of extreme old age on one's body and mind. How do younger persons generally react to such elders?
2 Who were the sibyls of Ancient Greece and Rome?

A Winter Visit

Now she's ninety I walk through the local park
where, too cold, the usual peacocks do not screech

and neighbouring lights come on before it's dark.

Dare I affirm to her, so aged and so frail,
that from one pale dot of peacock's sperm
spring forth all the colours of a peacock's tail?

I do. But she like the sibyl says, 'I would die';
then complains, 'This winter I'm half dead, son.'
And because it's true I want to cry.

Yet must not (although only Nothing keeps)
for I inhabit a white coat not a black
even here—and am not qualified to weep.

So I speak of small approximate things,
of how I saw, in the park, four flamingoes
standing, one-legged on ice, heads beneath wings.

CHARTING THE POEM

1 In what ways does the subject of this poem resemble a sibyl?
2 What might be a subtext of the narrator's affirmation to the aged woman regarding the peacock sperm?
3 Why is the narrator "not qualified to weep" over the woman's plight? Of what significance is his reference to white coats and black coats?

CONSIDERATIONS OF STYLE

1 Why does the narrator consider the image of the flamingoes at the end of the poem a small, approximate, and—perhaps—appropriate thing to talk about with the old woman?
2 What patterns—actual and approximate—of rhyme and scansion exist in the poem, and what effects do they create? (You may want to compare this poem with the other Abse poems anthologized.)

PERSPECTIVES

1 What kind of relationship with God—particularly in the matter of prayer—is a person usually encouraged to have?

Of Itzig and His Dog

To pray for the impossible,
says Itzig, is disgraceful.
I prefer, when I'm on my own,
when I'm only with my dog,
when I can't go out
because of the weather,
because of my shoes,
to talk very intimately to God.

        Itzig, they nag, why do that,
    what's the point of that?
    God never replies surely?

Such ignorance! Am I at the Western Wall?
Am I on spacious Mount Sinai?
Is there a thornbush in this murky room?
God may never say a word,
may never even whisper, Itzig, hullo.

But when I'm talking away
to the right and to the left,
when it's raining outside,
when there's rain on the glass,
when I say please God this
and thank God that,
then God always makes, believe me,
the dog's tail wag.

CHARTING THE POEM

1 What limitations does Itzig place on his petitions to God? And by extension, on himself as a believer?

2 What Biblical reference(s) to thorns—such as in Hosea 9:6—might explain Itzig's reference to "a thornbush in this murky room"?

CONSIDERATIONS OF STYLE

1 Of what significance are the images of the Western Wall, Mount Sinai, and the thornbush?

2 What does the aberrant format of the second stanza reflect?
3 Where does the poem use repetition, and to what effect?

AFTERTHOUGHTS

1 It has been observed that the mystics, the contemplatives, of all faith traditions, have much more in common with each other than any one of them would have with his or her co-religionists who are not mystics or contemplatives. Taking all three poems into account, does this observation seem true? Why or why not?
2 In what ways is each of the poems a variation on their common theme?

THE WRITER'S CRAFT

1 Write of a moment when you understood, in an epiphany, some idea, problem, or situation that had previously baffled you. What led up to the epiphany, and what have been its consequences?
2 Describe, in prose or poetic form, a "down-and-out" individual whom you have observed, about whom you have wondered, who has taught you to appreciate more fully your own blessings.

Our Common Humanity

Part Three
Love and Commitment

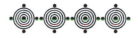

Frankie raised his arms in the air, clutched at his hair, threw down his red and green flag and stomped on them. "God help this country with lovers like you," he said finally. Then he took Shiv by the arm, and took him home, to Frankie's lair, and began to plan.

VIKRAM CHANDRA, *Shanti*

RICHARD HAGOPIAN

RICHARD HAGOPIAN *was born in Revere, Massachusetts in 1914. He first studied singing at the New England Conservatory of Music. While on a concert tour in Maine, he met poet Robert P Tristram Coffin, to whom he showed some short stories he had written. With the poet's encouragement, he eventually produced a book of stories,* The Dove Brings Peace, *published in 1944. Many of his later stories have been published in* The Atlantic Monthly, *and he also wrote two novels,* Faraway the Spring *and* Wine for the Living. *Much of his fiction centers around the everyday struggles and joys of Armenians and Italians in and around Boston.*

"Wonderful People" is a short, short love story—the kind that might appear in a newspaper on Valentine's Day to illustrate love's many possibilities.

PERSPECTIVES

1 What do "serious" poetry and music contribute to our lives? What sort of "so-called" poetry and music might not be considered "serious"?

2 What understandings do you bring to your reading of the relatedness of physical characteristics such as tallness and shortness with psychological makeup?

Wonderful People

I saw her and liked her because she was not beautiful. Her chin was not just right and something about her nose fell short of perfection. And when she stood up, well, there wasn't much to see but her tallness, the length from her hips to her feet, and the length from her hips to her shoulders. She was a tall girl and that was all. She was the first tall girl I had ever liked, perhaps because I had never watched a tall girl get up from a table before; that is, get up the way she did, everything in her rising to the art of getting up, combining to make the act look beautiful and not like just another casual movement, an ordinary life motion.

Maybe I liked her because when I talked to her for the first time I found that she had tall ideas too, ideas which like her chin and nose did not seem just right to me, but like her getting up were beautiful. They hung together. They were tall ideas, about life and people, morals and ethics. At first they seemed shockingly loose to me, but when I saw them all moving together, like her body, they hung together. They looked naturally beautiful. They had the same kind of pulled-out poetry that sometimes defies the extra-long line and hangs together; hangs together when you see the whole thing finished, when you've scanned it up and down and seen all the line endings melt into a curious kind of unity, which makes strange music—strange because everything is long yet compact. She was music. I see it now, her getting up impressed me at the time because for the first time I felt poetry in a person rising—music in body parts moving in natural rhythms. I liked the tall girl.

By stature I was not tall. I was built almost too close to the ground. Perhaps that is why I had old-fashioned ideas, ideas as simple and as pure as the good soil. Maybe my eyes saw more in the ground than other people's because I was closer to it. I was what you might call compact. Everything was knitted together strongly, like my ideas about life, morals and ethics, all squeezed together, rhyming easily, making music of a strong, dominant sort. Call it smugness if you wish. But I really couldn't move far without taking along everything I had. My ideas were like that too. I could take a radical fling once in a while, but sooner or later, mostly sooner, the rest of me ganged up and compressed the wild motion with one easy squeeze.

We were a funny pair, the tall girl and I, funny because we were so different in everything. She was a slow walker and I had to hold back. She talked in long lines and I used the short one. She ate easily and I ate hard and fast. We were different.

5 The tall girl and I fell in love with each other. Why, I do not know. We just did, that's all. We did crazy things: tall things and compact things, like running madly up and down a beach laughing and feeling loose and free, or like sitting down and knitting our minds together to feel after a piece of music or a problem. Something made us agree. We couldn't figure out what, but we agreed. And after looking at each other and seeing our bodies and the stuff behind them, we couldn't quite understand, but we accepted our good luck and we called ourselves wonderful people.

After a while we talked about marriage, children, and a home. For a few months we didn't agree on a couple of things, but, as I said, we were wonderful people, and one day we decided to get married.

But the tall girl and I didn't get married. For one moment somewhere I think we stopped being wonderful people, and she must have felt her tallness for the first time, and maybe the ground came up too close to my face. But that was all; it was the end. Something had come between the tall girl and me. I don't know what it was, but something died and with it went all the funny music and poetry in people.

Many years have passed and sometimes I get a strange feeling—I mean about walking and getting up. I don't seem to hang together as I used to. Only last week my best friend told me to pull myself together. And when I looked around, I'll be dammed if I wasn't just all pieces and parts, going this way and that, down and . . . up. Up! That was it. I felt taller. And I felt good. I liked the freedom. I could reach for an idea now without straining everything in me to hold it; and I didn't care about the rest of me. What music there was left in me, what must I heard in others, was the strange kind one finds in long-line poetry. It made me happy.

Sometimes I think of the tall girl; but she doesn't seem tall any more. She just seems natural—arms, legs, ideas, and everything. I wonder what I thought was *tall*? Sometimes I wonder if she is the same girl I first saw rising from a table. I don't know. But people grow taller, I know that. Perhaps they grow shorter and more compact too. Maybe that's what makes us wonderful people.

CHARTING THE STORY

1 How does the narrator put the physical shortcomings of the tall girl and of himself in perspective?

2 Of what significance is "long-line poetry" to the narrator, and how does it relate to the other images in the story?

3 By the end of the story, what is your understanding of the term "wonderful people" as the narrator uses the term?

CONSIDERATIONS OF STYLE

1 What effects does the relative lack of particulars—names, places, specific events, and emotions—have on your reaction to this narrative? Of what importance are such particulars to a reader of a "love story"—or is this, ultimately, a "love story" at all?

2 Does this narrative appear to be "tall," or "compact"—or something else entirely?

AFTERTHOUGHTS

1 What attitudes about love and "marriage, children, and a home" underlie the narrative? How does love appear to come about or disappear? Can the narrator or anyone else do anything about such love?

2 Compare this story to another story—or poem or essay—about a relationship. With what does the narrator "walk away" at the end of each text, and what might account for the differences?

THE WRITER'S CRAFT

1 Given that the woman seems to have tall, loose, elongated, graceful ideas and mannerisms, write about the relationship from her point of view.

2 Discuss a piece of music, a set of musical lyrics, or a poem that you associate with a memorable romantic relationship or moment in your life.

BHARATI MUKHERJEE

BHARATI MUKHERJEE *was born in Calcutta in 1940. She studied at the universities of Calcutta and Baroda, and came to the United States in 1961 to attend the Writers Workshop at the University of Iowa, where she later took her PhD. She married Canadian author Clark Blaise in 1963, became a Canadian citizen, and taught English at McGill University in Montreal. It was there that she began writing fiction.*

Mukherjee and her husband moved to the United States and took US citizenship. She taught creative writing at Columbia University, New York University, and Queens College, and is currently professor of English at the University of California at Berkeley.

"The Tenant" comes from the collection The Middleman and Other Stories *(1988).*

PERSPECTIVES

1 Look up the term "Brahmin" in a dictionary. Besides denoting a member of the highest Hindu caste, what spiritual connections does it denote? Are such connections pertinent in the American usage in the expression "Boston Brahmin"? Why?/Why not?

2 The landlord-tenant relationship is charged with issues of power and dependency. What associations do you bring concerning "tenancy" to your reading?

The Tenant

Maya Sanyal has been in Cedar Falls, Iowa, less than two weeks. She's come, books and clothes and one armchair rattling in the smallest truck that U-Haul would rent her, from New Jersey. Before that she was in North Carolina. Before that, Calcutta, India. Every place has something to give. She is sitting at the kitchen table with Fran drinking bourbon for the first time in her life. Fran Johnson found her the furnished apartment and helped her settle in. Now she's brought a bottle of bourbon which gives her the right to stay and talk for a bit. She's breaking up with someone named Vern, a pharmacist. Vern's father is also a pharmacist and owns a drugstore. Maya has seen Vern's father on TV twice already. The first time was on the local news when he spoke out against the selling of painkillers like Advil and Nuprin in supermarkets and gas stations. In the matter of painkillers, Maya is a universalist. The other time he was in a barbershop quartet. Vern gets along all right with his father. He likes the pharmacy business, as business goes, but he wants to go back to graduate school and learn to make films. Maya is drinking her first bourbon tonight because Vern left today for San Francisco State.

"I understand totally," Fran says. She teaches Utopian Fiction and a course in Women's Studies and worked hard to get Maya hired. Maya has a Ph.D. in Comparative Literature and will introduce writers like R. K. Narayan and Chinua Achebe to three sections of sophomores at the University of Northern Iowa. "A person has to leave home. Try out his wings."

Fran has to use the bathroom. "I don't feel abandoned." She pushes her chair away from the table. "Anyway it was a sex thing totally. We were good together. It'd be different if I'd loved him."

Maya tries to remember what's in the refrigerator. They need food. She hasn't been to the supermarket in over a week. She doesn't have a car yet and so she relies on a corner store—a longish walk—for milk, cereal, and frozen dinners. Someday these exigencies will show up as bad skin and collapsed muscle tone. No folly is ever lost. Maya pictures history as a net, the kind of safety net travelling trapeze artists of her childhood fell into when they were inattentive, or clumsy. Going to circuses in Calcutta with her father is what she remembers vividly. It is a banal memory, for her father, the owner of a steel company, is a complicated man.

Fran is out in the kitchen long enough for Maya to worry. They need food. 5
Her mother believed in food. What is love, anger, inner peace, etc., her mother used to say, but the brain's biochemistry. Maya doesn't want to get into that, but she is glad she has enough stuff in the refrigerator to make an omelette. She realizes Indian women are supposed to be inventive with food, whip up exotic delights to tickle an American's palate, and she knows she should be meeting Fran's generosity and candor with some sort of bizarre and effortless countermove. If there's an exotic spice store in Cedar Falls or in neighboring Waterloo, she hasn't found it. She's looked in the phone book for common Indian names, especially Bengali, but hasn't yet struck up culinary intimacies. That will come—it always does. There's a six-pack in the fridge that her landlord, Ted Suminski, had put in because she'd be thirsty after unpacking. She was thirsty, but she doesn't drink beer. She probably should have asked him to come up and drink the beer. Except for Fran she hasn't had anyone over. Fran is more friendly and helpful than anyone Maya has known in the States since she came to North Carolina ten years ago, at nineteen. Fran is a Swede, and she is tall, with blue eyes. Her hair, however, is a dull, darkish brown.

"I don't think I can handle anything that heavy-duty," Fran says when she comes back to the room. She means the omelette. "I have to go home in any case." She lives with her mother and her aunt, two women in their mid-seventies, in a drafty farmhouse. The farmhouse now has a computer store catty-corner from it. Maya's been to the farm. She's been shown photographs of the way the corner used to be. If land values ever rebound, Fran will be worth millions.

Before Fran leaves she says, "Has Rab Chatterji called you yet?"

"No." She remembers the name, a good, reliable Bengali name, from the first night's study of the phone book. Dr. Rabindra Chatterji teaches Physics.

"He called the English office just before I left." She takes car keys out of her pocketbook. She reknots her scarf. "I bet Indian men are more sensitive than Americans. Rab's a Brahmin, that's what people say."

A Chatterji has to be a Bengali Brahmin—last names give ancestral secrets 10
away—but Brahminness seems to mean more to Fran than it does to Maya. She was born in 1954, six full years after India became independent. Her India was Nehru's India: a charged, progressive place.

"All Indian men are wife beaters," Maya says. She means it and doesn't mean it. "That's why I married an American." Fran knows about the divorce, but nothing else. Fran is on the Hiring, Tenure, and Reappointment Committee.

Maya sees Fran down the stairs and to the car which is parked in the back in the spot reserved for Maya's car, if she had owned one. It will take her several months to save enough to buy one. She always pays cash, never borrows. She tells herself she's still recovering from the U-Haul drive halfway across the country. Ted Suminski is in his kitchen watching the women. Maya waves to him because waving to him, acknowledging him in that way, makes him seem less creepy. He seems to live alone though a sign, THE SUMINSKIS, hangs from a metal horse's head in the front yard. Maya hasn't seen Mrs. Suminski. She hasn't seen any children either. Ted always looks lonely. When she comes back from campus, he's nearly always in the back, throwing darts or shooting baskets.

"What's he like?" Fran gestures with her head as she starts up her car. "You hear these stories."

Maya doesn't want to know the stories. She has signed a year's lease. She doesn't want complications. "He's all right. I keep out of his way."

"You know what I'm thinking? Of all the people in Cedar Falls, you're 15
the one who could understand Vern best. His wanting to try out his wings, run away, stuff like that."

"Not really." Maya is not being modest. Fran is being impulsively democratic, lumping her wayward lover and Indian friend together as headstrong adventurers. For Fran, a utopian and feminist, borders don't count. Maya's taken some big risks, made a break with her parents' way. She's done things a woman from Ballygunge Park Road doesn't do, even in fantasies. She's not yet shared stories with Fran, apart from the divorce. She's told her nothing of men she picks up, the reputation she'd gained, before Cedar Falls, for "indiscretions." She has a job, equity, three friends she can count on for emergencies. She is an American citizen. But.

Fran's Brahmin calls her two nights later. On the phone he presents himself as Dr. Chatterji, not Rabindra or Rab. An old-fashioned Indian, she assumes. Her father still calls his closest friend, "Colonel." Dr. Chatterji asks her to tea on Sunday. She means to say no but hears herself saying, "Sunday? Fiveish? I'm not doing anything special this Sunday."

Outside, Ted Suminski is throwing darts into his garage door. The door has painted-on rings: orange, purple, pink. The bull's-eye is gray. He has to be fifty at least. He is a big, thick, lonely man about whom people tell stories. Maya pulls the phone cord as far as it'll go so she can look down more directly on her landlord's large, bald head. He has his back to her as he lines up a dart. He's in black running shoes, red shorts, he's naked to the waist. He hunches his right shoulder, he pulls the arm back; a big, lonely man shouldn't have so much grace. The dart is ready to cut though the September evening. But Ted Suminski doesn't let go. He swings on worn rubber soles, catches her eye in the window (she has to have imagined this), takes aim at her shadow. Could she have imagined the noise of the dart's metal tip on her windowpane?

Dr. Chatterji is still on the phone. "You are not having any mode of transportation, is that right?"

Ted Suminski has lost interest in her. Perhaps it isn't interest, at all; perhaps it's aggression. "I don't drive," she lies, knowing it sounds less shameful than not owning a car. She has said this so often she can get in the right degree of apology and Asian upper-class helplessness. "It's an awful nuisance."

"Not to worry, please." Then, "It is a great honor to be meeting Dr. Sanyal's daughter. In Calcutta business circles he is a legend."

On Sunday she is ready by four-thirty. She doesn't know what the afternoon holds; there are surely no places for "high tea"—a colonial tradition—in Cedar Falls, Iowa. If he takes her back to his place, it will mean he has invited other guests. From his voice she can tell Dr. Chatterji likes to do things correctly. She has dressed herself in a peach-colored nylon georgette sari, jade drop-earrings and a necklace. The color is good on dark skin. She is not pretty, but she does her best. Working at it is a part of self-respect. In the mid-seventies, when American women felt rather strongly about such things, Maya had been in trouble with her women's group at Duke. She was too feminine. She had tried to explain the world she came out of. Her grandmother had been married off at the age of five in a village now in Bangladesh. Her great-aunt had been burned to death over a dowry problem. She herself had been trained to speak softly, arrange flowers, sing, be pliant. If she were to seduce Ted Suminski, she thinks as she waits in the front yard for Dr. Chatterji, it would be minor heroism. She has broken with the past. But.

Dr. Chatterji drives up for her at about five ten. He is a hesitant driver. The car stalls, jumps ahead, finally slams to a stop. Maya has to tell him to back off a foot or so; it's hard to leap over two sacks of pruned branches in a sari. Ted Suminski is an obsessive pruner and gardener.

"My sincerest apologies, Mrs. Sanyal," Dr. Chatterji says. He leans across the wide front seat of his noisy, very old, very used car and unlocks the door for her. "I am late. But then, I am sure you're remembering that Indian Standard Time is not at all the same as time in the States." He laughs. He could be nervous—she often had that effect on Indian men. Or he could just be chatty. "These Americans are all the time rushing and rushing but where it gets them?" He moves his head laterally once, twice. It's the gesture made famous by Peter Sellers. When Peter Sellers did it, it had seemed hilarious. Now it suggests that Maya and Dr. Chatterji have three thousand years plus civilization, sophistication, moral virtue, over people born on this continent. Like her, Dr. Chatterji is a naturalized American.

"Call me Maya," she says. She fusses with the seat belt. She does it because she needs time to look him over. He seems quite harmless. She takes in the prominent teeth, the eyebrows that run together. He's in a blue shirt and a beige cardigan with the K-Mart logo that buttons tightly over the waist. It's hard to guess his age because he has dyed his hair and his moustache. Late thirties, early forties. Older than she had expected. "Not Mrs. Sanyal."

This isn't time to tell about ex-husbands. She doesn't know where John is these days. He should have kept up at least. John had come into her life as a graduate student at Duke, and she, mistaking the brief breathlessness of sex for love, had married him. They had stayed together two years, maybe a little less. The pain that John had inflicted all those years ago by leaving her had subsided into a cozy feeling of loss. This isn't the time, but then she doesn't want to be a legend's daughter all evening. She's not necessarily on Dr. Chatterji's side is what she wants to get across early; she's not against America and Americans. She makes the story—of marriage outside the Brahminic pale, the divorce—quick, dull. Her unsentimentality seems to shock him. His stomach sags inside the cardigan.

"We've each had our several griefs," the physicist says. "We're each required to pay our karmic debts."

"Where are we headed?"

"Mrs. Chatterji has made some Indian snacks. She is waiting to meet you because she is knowing your cousin-sister who studied in Scottish Church College. My home is okay, no?"

Frank would get a kick out of this. Maya has slept with married men, with nameless men, with men little more than boys, but never with an Indian man. Never.

The Chatterjis live in a small blue house on a gravelly street. There are at least five or six other houses on the street; the same size but in different colors and with different front yard treatments. More houses are going up. This is the cutting edge of suburbia.

Mrs. Chatterji stands in the driveway. She is throwing a large plastic ball to a child. The child looks about four, and is Korean or Cambodian. The child is not hers because she tells it, "Chung-Hee, ta-ta, bye-bye. Now I play with guest," as Maya gets out of the car.

Maya hasn't seen this part of town. The early September light softens the construction pits. In that light the houses too close together, the stout woman in a striped cotton sari, the child hugging a pink ball, the two plastic lawn chairs by a tender young tree, the sheets and saris on the clothesline in the back, all seem miraculously incandescent.

"Go home now, Chung-Hee. I am busy." Mrs. Chatterji points the child homeward, then turns to Maya, who has folded her hands in traditional Bengali greeting. "It is an honor. We feel very privileged." She leads Maya indoors to a front room that smells of moisture and paint.

In her new, deliquescent mood, Maya allows herself to be backed into 35
the best armchair—a low-backed, boxy Goodwill item draped over with a Rajasthani bedspread—and asks after the cousin Mrs. Chatterji knows. She doesn't want to let go of Mrs. Chatterji. She doesn't want husband and wife to get into whispered conferences about their guest's misadventures in America, as they make tea in the kitchen.

The coffee table is already laid with platters of mutton croquettes, fish chops, onion pakoras, ghugni with puris, samosas, chutneys. Mrs. Chatterji has gone to too much trouble. Maya counts four kinds of sweetmeats in Corning casseroles on an end table. She looks into a see-through lid; spongy, white dumplings float in rosewater syrup. Planets contained, mysteries made visible.

"What are you waiting for, Santana?" Dr. Chatterji becomes imperious, though not unaffectionate. He pulls a dining chair up close to the coffee table. "Make some tea." He speaks in Bengali to his wife, in English to Maya. To Maya he says, grandly, "We are having real Indian Green Label Lipton. A nephew is bringing it just one month back."

His wife ignores him. "The kettle's already on," she says. She wants to know about the Sanyal family. Is it true her great-grandfather was a member of the Star Chamber in England?

Nothing in Calcutta is ever lost. Just as her story is known to Bengalis all over America, so are the scandals of her family, the grandfather hauled up for tax evasion, the aunt who left her husband to act in films. This woman brings up the Star Chamber, the glories of the Sanyal family, her father's philanthropies, but it's a way of saying, *I know the dirt.*

The bedrooms are upstairs. In one of those bedrooms an unseen, tor- 40
mented presence—Maya pictures it as a clumsy ghost that strains to shake off the body's shell—drops things on the floor. The things are heavy and they make the front room's chandelier shake. Light bulbs, shaped like tiny candle flames, flicker. The Chatterjis have said nothing about children. There are no tricycles in the hallway, no small sandals behind the doors. Maya is too polite to ask about the noise, and the Chatterjis don't explain. They talk just a little louder. They flip the embroidered cover off the stereo. What would Maya like to hear? Hemanta Kumar? Manna Dey? Oh, that young chap, Manna Dey! What sincerity, what tenderness he can convey!

Upstairs the ghost doesn't hear the music of nostalgia. The ghost throws and thumps. The ghost makes its own vehement music. Maya hears in its voice madness, self-hate.

Finally the water in the kettle comes to a boil. The whistle cuts through all fantasy and pretense. Dr. Chatterji says, "I'll see to it," and rushes out of the room. But he doesn't go to the kitchen. He shouts up the stairwell. "Poltoo, kindly stop this nonsense straightaway! We're having a brilliant and cultured lady-guest and you're creating earthquakes?" The kettle is hysterical.

Mrs. Chatterji wipes her face. The face that had seemed plump and cheery at the start of the evening now is flabby. "My sister's boy," the woman says.

So this is the nephew who has brought with him the cartons of Green Label tea, one of which will be given to Maya.

Mrs. Chatterji speaks to Maya in English as though only the alien language can keep emotions in check. "Such an intelligent boy! His father is government servant. Very highly placed."

Maya is meant to visualize a smart, clean-cut young man from south Calcutta, but all she can see is a crazy, thwarted, lost graduate student. Intelligence, proper family guarantee nothing. Even Brahmins can do self-destructive things, felt unsavory urges. Maya herself had been an excellent student.

"He was First Class First in B. Sc. from Presidency College," the woman says. "Now he's getting Master's in Ag. Science at Iowa State."

The kitchen is silent. Dr. Chatterji comes back into the room with a tray. The teapot is under a tea cozy, a Kashmiri one embroidered with the usual chinar leaves, loops, and chains. "*Her* nephew," he says. The dyed hair and dyed moustache are no longer signs of a man wishing to fight the odds. He is a vain man, anxious to cut losses. "Very unfortunate business."

The nephew's story comes out slowly, over fish chops and mutton croquettes. He is in love with a student from Ghana.

"Everything was A-Okay until the Christmas break. Grades, assistantship for next semester, everything."

"I blame the college. The office for foreign students arranged a Christmas party. And now, *baapre baap!* Our poor Poltoo wants to marry a Negro Muslim."

Maya is known for her nasty, ironic one-liners. It has taken her friends weeks to overlook her malicious, un-American pleasure in others' misfortunes. Maya would like to finish Dr. Chatterji off quickly. He is pompous; he is reactionary; he wants to live and work in America but give back nothing except taxes. The confused world of the immigrant—the lostness that Maya and Poltoo feel—that's what Dr. Chatterji wants to avoid. She hates him. But.

Dr. Chatterji's horror is real. A good Brahmin boy in Iowa is in love with an African Muslim. It shouldn't be a big deal. But the more she watches the physicist, the more she realizes that "Brahmin" isn't a caste; it's a metaphor. You break one small rule, and the constellation collapses. She thinks suddenly that John Cheever—she is teaching him as a "world writer" in her classes, cheek-by-jowl with Africans and West Indians—would have understood Dr. Chatterji's dread. Cheever had been on her mind, ever since the late afternoon light slanted over

Mrs. Chatterji's drying saris. She remembers now how full of a soft, Cheeverian light Durham had been the summer she had slept with John Hadwen; and how after that, her tidy graduate-student world became monstrous, lawless. All men became John Hadwen; John became all men. Outwardly, she retained her poise, her Brahminical breeding. She treated her crisis as a literary event; she lost her moral sense, her judgment, her power to distinguish. Her parents had behaved magnanimously. They had cabled from Calcutta: WHAT'S DONE IS DONE. WE ARE CONFIDENT YOU WILL HANDLE NEW SITUATIONS WELL. ALL LOVE. But she knows more than do her parents. Love is anarchy.

Poltoo is Mrs. Chatterji's favorite nephew. She looks as though it is her fault that the Sunday has turned unpleasant. She stacks the empty platters methodically. To Maya she says, "It is the goddess who pulls the strings. We are puppets. I know the goddess will fix it. Poltoo will not marry that African woman." Then she goes to the coat closet in the hall and staggers back with a harmonium, the kind sold in music stores in Calcutta, and sets it down on the carpeted floor. "We're nothing but puppets," she says again. She sits at Maya's feet, her pudgy hands on the harmonium's shiny, black bellows. She sings, beautifully, in a virgin's high voice, "Come, goddess, come, muse, come to us hapless peoples' rescue."

Maya is astonished. She has taken singing lessons at Dakshini Academy in 55
Calcutta. She plays the sitar and the tanpur, well enough to please Bengalis, to astonish Americans. But stout Mrs. Chatterji is a devotee, talking to God.

A little after eight, Dr. Chatterji drops her off. It's been an odd evening and they are both subdued.

"I want to say one thing," he says. He stops her from undoing her seat belt. The plastic sacks of pruned branches are still at the corner.

"You don't have to get out," she says.

"Please. Give me one more minute of your time."

"Sure."

"Maya is my favorite name."

She says nothing. She turns away from him without making her embarrassment obvious.

"Truly speaking, it is my favorite. You are sometimes lonely, no? But you 60
are lucky. Divorced women can date, they can go to bars and discos. They can see mens, many mens. But inside marriage there is so much loneliness." A groan, low, horrible, comes out of him.

She turns back toward him, to unlatch the seat belt and run out of the car. She sees that Dr. Chatterji's pants are unzipped. One hand works hard under his Jockey shorts; the other rests, limp, penitential, on the steering wheel.

"Dr. Chatterji—*really!*" she cries.

The next day, Monday, instead of getting a ride home with Fran—Fran says she *likes* to give rives, she needs the chance to talk, and she won't share gas expenses, absolutely not—Maya goes to the periodicals room of the library.

There are newspapers from everywhere, even from Madagascar and New Caledonia. She thinks of the periodicals room as an asylum for homesick aliens. There are two aliens already in the room, both Orientals, both absorbed in the politics and gossip of their far off homes.

She goes straight to the newspapers from India. She bunches her raincoat like a bolster to make herself more comfortable. There's so much to catch up on. A village headman, a known Congress-Indira party worker, has been shot at by scooter-riding snipers. An Indian pugilist has won an international medal—in Nepal. A child drawing well water—the reporter calls the child "a neo-Buddhist, a convert from the now-outlawed untouchable caste"—has been stoned. An editorial explains that the story about stoning is not a story about caste but about failed idealism; a story about promises of green fields and clean, potable water broker, a story about brides paid and wells not dug. But no, thinks Maya, its' about caste.

Out here, in the heartland of the new world, the India of serious newspapers unsettles. Maya longs again to feel what she had felt in the Chatterjis' living room: virtues made physical. It is a familiar feeling, a longing. Had a suitable man presented himself in the reading room at that instant, she would have seduced him. She goes on to the stack of *India Abroads,* reads through matrimonial columns, and steals an issue to take home.

Indian men want Indian brides. Married Indian men want Indian mistresses. All over America, "handsome, tall, fair" engineers, doctors, data processors—the new pioneers—cry their eerie love calls.

Maya runs a finger down the first column; her fingertip, dark with newsprint, stops at random.

> Hello! Hi! Yes, you *are* the one I'm looking for. You are the new emancipated Indo-American woman. You have a zest for life. You are at ease in USA and yet your ethics are rooted in Indian tradition. The man of your dreams has come. Yours truly is handsome, ear-nose-throat specialist, well-settled in Connecticut. Age is 41 but never married, physically fit, sportsmanly, and strong. I adore idealism, poetry, beauty. I abhor smugness, passivity, caste system. Write with recent photo. Better still, call!!!

Maya calls. Hullo, hullo, hullo! She hears immigrant lovers cry in crowded shopping malls. Yes, you who are at ease in both worlds, you are the one. She feels she has a fair chance.

A man answers. "Ashoke Mehta speaking."

She speaks quickly into the bright-red mouthpiece of her telephone. He will be in Chicago, in transit, passing though O'Hare. United counter, Saturday, two p.m. As easy as that.

"Good," Ashoke Mehta says. "For these encounters I, too, prefer a neutral zone."

On Saturday at exactly two o'clock the man of Maya's dreams floats toward her as lovers used to in shampoo commercials. The United counter is a loud, harassed place but passengers and piled-up luggage fall away from him. Full-cheeked and fleshy-lipped, he is handsome. He hasn't lied. He is serene, assured, a Hindu god touching down in Illinois.

She can't move. She feels ugly and unworthy. Her adult life no longer seems miraculously rebellious; it is grim, it is perverse. She has accomplished nothing. She has changed her citizenship but she hasn't broken though into the light, the vigor, the *hustle* of the New World. She is stuck in dead space.

"Hullo, hullo!" Their fingers touch.

Oh, the excitement! Ashoke Mehta's palm feels so right in the small of her back. Hullo, hullo, hullo. He pushes her out of the reach of anti-Khomeini Iranians, Hare Krishnas, American Fascists, men with fierce wants, and guides her to an empty gate. They have less than an hour.

"What would you like, Maya?"

She knows he can read her mind, she knows her thoughts are open to him. *You,* she's almost giddy with the thought, with simple desire. "From the snack bar," he says as though to clarify. "I'm afraid I'm starved."

Below them, where the light is strong and hurtful, a Boeing is being serviced. "Nothing," she says.

He leans forward. She can feel the nap of his scarf—she recognizes the Cambridge colors—she can smell the wool of his Icelandic sweater. She runs her hand along the scarf, then against the flesh of his neck. "Only the impulsive ones call," he says.

The immigrant courtship proceeds. It's easy, he's good with facts. He knows how to come across to a stranger who may end up a lover, a spouse. He makes over a hundred thousand. He owns a house in Hartford, and two income properties in Newark. He plays the market but he's cautious. He's good at badminton but plays handball to keep in shape. He watches all the sports on television. Last August he visited Copenhagen, Helsinki and Leningrad. Once upon a time he collected stamps but now he doesn't have hobbies, except for reading. He counts himself an intellectual, he spends too much on books. Ludlum, Forsyth, MacInnes; other names she doesn't catch. She suppresses a smile, she's told him only she's a graduate student. He's not without his vices. He's a spender, not a saver, He's a sensualist: good food—all foods, but easy on the Indian—good wine. Some temptations he doesn't try to resist.

And I, she wants to ask, do I tempt?

"Now tell me about yourself, Maya." He makes it easy for her. "Have you ever been in love?"

"No."

"But many have loved you, I can see that." He says it not unkindly. It is the fate of women like her, and men like him. Their karmic duty, to be loved.

It is expected, not judged. She feels he can see them all, the sad parade of need and demand. This isn't the time to reveal all.

And so the courtship enters a second phase.

When she gets back to Cedar Falls, Ted Suminski is standing on the front porch. It's late at night, chilly. He is wearing a down vest. She's never seen him on the porch. In fact there's no chair to sit on. He looks chilled through. He's waited around a while.

"Hi." She has her keys ready. This isn't the night to offer the six-pack in 85
the fridge. He looks expectant, ready to pounce.

"Hi." He looks like a man who might have aimed the dart at her. What has he done to his wife, his kids? Why isn't there at least a dog? "Say, I left a note upstairs."

The note is written in Magic Marker and thumb-tacked to her apartment door. DUE TO PERSONAL REASONS, NAMELY REMARRIAGE, I REQUEST THAT YOU VACATE MY PLACE AT THE END OF THE SEMESTER.

Maya takes the note down and retacks it to the kitchen wall. The whole wall is like a bulletin board, made of some new, crumbly building-material. Her kitchen, Ted Suminski had told her, was once a child's bedroom. Suminski in love: the idea stuns her. She has misread her landlord. The dart at her window speaks of no twisted fantasy. The landlord wants the tenant out.

She gets a glass out of the kitchen cabinet, gets out a tray of ice, pours herself a shot of Fran's bourbon. She is happy for Ted Suminski. She is. She wants to tell someone how moved she'd been by Mrs. Chatterji's singing. How she'd felt in O'Hare, even about Dr. Rab Chatterji in the car. But Fran is not the person. No one she's ever met is the person. She can't talk about the dead space she lives in. She wishes Ashoke Mehta would call. Right now.

Weeks pass. Then two months. She finds a new room, signs another 90
lease. Her new landlord calls himself Fred. He has no arms, but he helps her move her things. He drives between Ted Suminski's place and his twice in his station wagon. He uses his toes the way Maya uses her fingers. He likes to do things. He pushes garbage sacks full of Maya's clothes up the stairs.

"It's all right to stare," Fred says. "Hell, I would."

That first afternoon in Fred's rooming house, they share a Chianti. Fred wants to cook her pork chops but he's a little shy about Indians and meat. Is it beef, or pork? Or any meat? She says it's okay, any meat, but not tonight. He has an ex-wife in Des Moines, two kids in Portland, Oregon. The kids are both normal; he's the only freak in the family. But he's self-reliant. He shops in the supermarket like anyone else, he carries out the garbage, shovels the snow off the sidewalk. He needs Maya's help with one thing. Just one thing. The box of Tide is a bit too heavy to manage. Could she get him the giant size every so often and leave it in the basement?

The dead space need not suffocate. Over the months, Fred and she will settle into companionship. She has never slept with a man without arms. Two wounded people, he will joke during their nightly contortions. It will shock her, this assumed equivalence with a man so strikingly deficient. She knows she is strange, and lonely, but being Indian is not the same, she would have thought, as being a freak.

One night in spring, Fred's phone rings. "Ashoke Mehta speaking." None of this "do you remember me?" nonsense.

The god has tracked her down. He hasn't forgotten. "Hullo," he says, in their special way. And because she doesn't answer back, "Hullo, hullo, hullo." She is aware of Fred in the back of the room. He is lighting a cigarette with his toes.

"Yes," she says, "I remember."

"I had to take care of a problem," Ashoke Mehta says. "You know that I have my vices. That time at O'Hare I was honest with you."

She is breathless.

"Who is it, May?" asks Fred.

"You also have a problem," says the voice. His laugh echoes.

"You will come to Hartford, I know."

When she moves out, she tells herself, it will not be the end of Fred's world.

CHARTING THE STORY

1 In the first paragraph, Maya muses: "Every place has something to give." How might such a maxim be extended to encounters? Specifically, what does Maya seem to gain from her encounters with Fran, Ted Suminski, Dr Chatterjee, Mrs Chatterji, Fred, and—especially—Ashoke Mehta?

2 "Even Brahmins can do self-destructive things, feel unsavory urges," notes the narrator. What associations does the term have for Maya, for Fran, for the Chatterjis, for Ashoke Mehta?

3 What is the reader led to expect, by Fran's description of him, concerning Mr Chatterji's behavior towards Maya, and how are the expectations met or not met? Of what importance is the Sunday evening to the plot of the story?

4 Throughout the text, Maya must constantly "present" herself in one way or another to Fran, to the Chatterjis, to Ashoke Mehta, and even to her landlords. How do her self-presentations differ, and why?

CONSIDERATIONS OF STYLE

1 At three junctures in the story, a paragraph ends in the single-word sentence "But." What larger meaning does this normally understressed conjunction take on when it stands alone in such a prominent context?

2 What grammatical features mark Dr Chatterji's Indian-style English? How does his speech tend to caricature him?

3 What purpose does the second landlord Fred—who makes only a brief appearance toward the end of the story—serve in the text?

AFTERTHOUGHTS

1 Paragraph 33 describes the setting of the Chatterjis' home: "The early September light softens the construction pits. In that light the houses too close together, the stout woman in a striped cotton sari, the child hugging a pink ball, the two plastic lawn chairs by a tender young tree and saris on the clothesline in the back, all seem miraculously incandescent." Scan the story for other examples of such culturally integrated images. What do these images suggest about the comfortable incongruity of elements in a cross-cultural mix?

2 Projecting into the next generation: if Ashoke and Maya were to have children, what might be their attitudes toward their Indian heritage? On what do you base this prediction?

3 The name "Maya" connotes "illusion." How well chosen is this name for this character? How illusive, illusory, disillusioned, or disillusioning does she seem to be?

THE WRITER'S CRAFT

1 This story shows that in life "dead space need not suffocate." Picking up on this thought, write about an occasion when you overcame adversity by filling in the dead space at some critical juncture in your life.

2 Write a "matrimonial" (or "ISO"—"in search of") ad describing yourself, your image as you'd like to appear to a prospective spouse or partner. Then write such an ad as you would think a parent would write for you, in hopes of catching a "suitable boy" or "suitable girl." How do the ads differ, and what accounts for their differences?

3 Write an account of the Sunday evening at the Chatterjis from the point of view of Poltoo, who could very likely have overheard the conversation being broadcast from downstairs.

Two Poems For a Wedding

ANDREW MOTION

ANDREW MOTION, *born in 1952, is a London poet, critic, biographer, and professor. In May 1999, he was chosen as Britain's poet laureate, succeeding the late poet Ted Hughes.*

Motion was educated at Radley College and at University College, Oxford. He currently teaches creative writing at the University of East Anglia.

Motion's works include eight volumes of his collected poems, biographies of John Keats and Philip Larkin (which won the 1993 Whitbread Prize), critical studies of Edward Thomas and Philip Larkin, and collections of selected poems of William Barnes and Thomas Hardy.

"Epithalamium—St George's Chapel, Windsor," composed only a month after his appointment as poet laureate to celebrate the royal wedding of Prince Edward and Sophie Rhys-Jones, drew a favorable response from critics. Motion has expressed his desire to expand and diversify his job from writing about royal occasions to writing poems on wider national and world issues, as well as promoting poetry in the nation's schools.

PERSPECTIVES

1 Research the position of poet laureate—national and local—in the United States. How does the position differ in the United States and in Britain? Who is the current US poet laureate?

2 What sentiments or thoughts would you wish to have expressed in public, should you marry?

Epithalamium—St George's Chapel, Windsor

St George's Chapel, Windsor
One day, the tissue-light through stained glass falls
on vacant stone, on gaping pews, on air
made up of nothing more than atom storms
which whiten silently, then disappear.

The next, all this is charged with brimming life.
A people-river floods those empty pews,
and music-torrents break—but then stop dead
to let two human voices make their vows:
to work—so what is true today remains the truth;
to hope—for privacy and what its secrets show;
to trust—that all the world can offer it will give;
to love—and what it has to understand to grow.

CHARTING THE POEM

1 What are the poem's divisions? How do they contrast in their respective focus, tone, imagery?

2 How do the couple's vows reflect the fact that they are public persons concerned with public issues as well as personal sentiments? What public issues might have concerned them on this occasion?

CONSIDERATIONS OF STYLE

1 What configurations of accented and unaccented syllables—namely, the rhythm pattern—does the poem contain? What is the rhythmic effect?

2 What sound devices such as rhyme, quasi-rhyme, alliteration, and repetition does the poem contain?

3 Research the poetic genre of "epithalamium." Apart from the occasion for which Motion's poem is written, what marks it as epithalamic in style, mood, and in image? Where does it appear to be different from the standard; i e, what makes it unique?

BENJAMIN ALIRE SAENZ

BENJAMIN ALIRE SAENZ *was born in Old Picacho, New Mexico, a farming community near Las Cruces. He studied theology in Belgium, was ordained a priest, left the priesthood, and married. He studied creative writing at the University of Texas at El Paso, the University of Iowa, and Stanford University, where he was a Wallace Stegner Fellow. Saenz currently teaches Engish at the University of Texas at El Paso.*

His works include: the poetry collections Calendar of Dust *and* Dark and Perfect Angels; *the novels* Carry Me Like Water *and* The House of Forgetting; *the book of short stories,* Flowers of the Broken; *and a children's book,* A Gift from Papa Diego.

PERSPECTIVES

1 What rituals surround the marriage of two persons in your religious and/or ethnic tradition? Typically, how much of the wedding ceremony is conventionally structured, as opposed to that part which might be tailored to the occasion?

2 Read the Biblical account of the wedding feast at Cana (John 2:1–11), noting the major characters, the basic plot, and the theme. Having read it, what are your expectations for this poem?

The Wedding Feast at Cana

This, the first of his miracles, Jesus perfomed at Cana in Galilee, and manifested his glory.

—John 2:11

FOR LARRY AND KATY

A man and woman meet. They fall
in love. This has been written; this
has been read; this is an old story.

In the body there is a place;
those who work will know this space,
will know it's hard and holy, will
know it wears away the heart. We may
curse it day and night; we may
speak of it, point to it, pray to it—
it will not be appeased.

Listen to your names:
their sounds are like
no other: whispers of the world
needing to know if there is joy.
Is there joy? Listen to the hunger

forever—that song will never cease.
The song is sad. *You*
will never be full. Stay. Listen
to the hunger. Do not turn
from that sound. You cannot
run from earth. *Naked*
you came from the dirt. Naked you must
return. Flesh is flesh and it is flesh
till death.

This day, words
like thirst, and flesh, and hunger
mean *marriage.* Water is turned
into wine. This is the day of miracles.
Take. Drink. The best has been
saved for the poor. Taste. This is the cup
of salvation. Be drunk. Touch. Make love
through the lonely night—but when you wake
remember: this wine is good and sweet
but you will thirst again.

The book of life is hard to write:
it is written with bone and blood:
it is written with hearts that labor
and labor, beat and beat until the walls
fall down. Begin. Write: in the kingdom
of the naked, working heart
shame is banished. A man and woman
meet—this is an old—*write it!*
Begin. Begin. Begin.

CHARTING THE POEM

1 What is the operative word in the opening epigraph that sets the tone for the rest of the poem? Where in the poem is this thought reinforced?

2 While the first stanza depicts marriage as a product of romantic love, the poem gives way in the four succeeding stanzas to more somber reflections. Identify these, and consider why the speaker—probably in this case the poet himself—would want to convey his well-wishes to the couple in such a manner.

3 What is the "best" that has "been saved for the poor"? What images of poverty, or need, find their way into the poem, and to what can one connect them, given the Biblical context?

CONSIDERATIONS OF STYLE

1 What seems to be the semantic significance of the differing visual spacing of each consecutive stanza?
2 What use does the poet make of rhyme and repetition as sound devices?
3 What is the significance of the various italicized portions of the text?

AFTERTHOUGHTS

1 How does the relationship between the speaker and the couple differ in each wedding poem? What might account for the difference?
2 Wedding homilies generally emphasize the challenges as well as the joys inherent in a marriage. How does each poem undertake this expectation?
3 Is the "old story" of marriage noted in the first stanza of "The Wedding Feast at Cana"—one of a man and a woman meeting and falling in love—historically accurate? Have there not always been other perfectly acceptable motives for marriage? What other "old stories" are there, and can epithalamia be written to honor them?

THE WRITER'S CRAFT

1 Write a descriptive narrative about a memorable wedding that you have attended. Is the event memorable because the ritual was unfamiliar to you? Or because of its solemnity and simplicity? Or because of its unusual setting?
2 Write an epithalamium on the occasion of the union of two close friends or relatives.
3 Write about an event connected with the Biblical wedding feast of Cana. Why is it significant that the apostle John noted that it was the first of the miracles of Jesus?

HA JIN

HA JIN *was born in Liaoning, China, in 1956. He served in the Chinese People's Liberation Army eight years before coming to the United States to pursue his doctoral degree in American literature at Brandeis University. He had planned to return to China, but after witnessing on television the June 1989 student demonstrations in Beijing's Tiananmen Square, he realized he could not go back. He secured a job at Emory University teaching creative writing and has become an American writer, though to date nearly all of his works have focused on his original homeland.*

He has written two short story collections: Ocean of Words: Army Stories *(1996), which won the Ernest Hemingway Foundation/PEN Award for First Fiction, and* Under the Red Flag, *which won the Flannery O'Connor Award for short fiction from the University of Georgia Press. He has also composed two volumes of poetry and two novels:* In the Pond *(1998) and* Waiting *(1999).*

"The Bridegroom" appeared in Harper's Magazine *in July 1999.*

PERSPECTIVES

1 What makes a marriage a "good marriage"? What, in your view, is absolutely necessary for a marriage to be considered "valid"? What, under the law, must transpire?

2 Of what relevance is the opinion of society at large about the marriage of any couple, and what attitudes do you thereby take for granted in your response to this question?

The Bridegroom

Before Beina's father died, I promised him that I'd take care of his daughter. He and I had been close friends for twenty years. He left his only child with me because my wife and I had no children of our own. It was easy to keep my word when Beina was still a teenager. As she grew older, it became more difficult, not because she was willful or troublesome but because no man was interested in her, a short, homely girl. When she turned twenty-three and still had no boyfriend, I began to worry. Where could I find her a husband? Timid and quiet, she didn't know how to get close to a man. I was afraid she'd become an old maid.

Then out of the blue Baowen Huang proposed to her. I found myself at a loss, because they'd hardly known each other. How could he be serious about his offer? I feared he might make a fool of Beina, so I insisted they get engaged if he meant business. He came to my home with two trussed-up capons, four cartons of Ginseng cigarettes, two bottles of Five Grains' Sap, and one tall tin of oolong tea. I was pleased, though not very impressed by his gifts.

Two months later they got married. My colleagues congratulated me, saying, "That was fast, Old Cheng."

What a relief to me. But to many young women in our sewing-machine factory, Beina's marriage was a slap in the face. They'd say, "A hen cooped up a peacock." Or, "A fool always lands in the arms of fortune." True, Baowen had been one of the most handsome unmarried men in the factory, and nobody had expected that Beina, stocky and stout, would win him. What's more, Baowen was good-natured and well educated—a middle-school graduate—and he didn't smoke or drink or gamble. He had fine manners and often smiled politely, showing his bright, straight teeth. In a way he resembled a woman, delicate, clear-skinned, and soft-spoken; he even could knit things out of wool. But no men dared bully him because he was skilled at martial arts. Three times in a row he had won the first prize for kung fu at our factory's annual sports meet. He was very good at the long sword and freestyle boxing. When he was in middle school, bigger boys had often picked on him, so his stepfather had sent him to the martial arts school in their hometown. A year later nobody would ever bug him again.

Sometimes I couldn't help wondering why Baowen had chosen Beina. 5
What in her had caught his heart? Did he really like her fleshy face, which often reminded me of a globe-fish? Although we had our doubts, my wife and I couldn't say anything negative about the marriage. Our only concern was that Baowen might be too good for our nominal daughter. Whenever I heard that somebody had divorced, I'd feel a sudden flutter of panic.

As the head of the Security Section in the factory, I had some pull and did what I could to help the young couple. Soon after their wedding I secured them a brand-new two-bedroom apartment, which angered some people waiting in line for housing. I wasn't daunted by their criticism. I'd do almost anything to make Beina's marriage stable, because I believed that if it survived the first two years, it might last decades—once Baowen became a father, it would be difficult for him to break loose.

But after they'd been married for eight months, Beina still wasn't pregnant. I was afraid that Baowen would soon grow tired of her and run after another woman, since many young women in the factory were still attracted to him. A brazen one even declared that she'd leave her door open for him all night long. Some of them frequently offered him movie tickets and meat coupons. It seemed that they were determined to wreck Beina's marriage. I hated them, and just the thought of them would give me an earache or a sour stomach. Fortunately, Baowen hadn't yet done anything outside the bounds of a decent husband.

One morning in early November, Beina stepped into my office. "Uncle," she said in a tearful voice, "Baowen didn't come home last night."

I tried to remain calm, though my head began to swim. "Do you know where he's been?" I asked.

"I don't know. I looked for him everywhere." She licked her cracked lips and took off her green work cap, her hair in a huge bun.

"When did you see him last?"

"At dinner yesterday evening. He said he was going to see somebody. He has lots of buddies in town."

"Is that so?" I didn't know he had many friends. "Don't worry. Go back to your workshop and don't tell anybody about this. I'll call around and find him."

She dragged herself out of my office. She must have gained at least a dozen pounds since the wedding. Her blue dungarees had become so tight that they seemed about to burst. Viewed from behind, she looked like a giant turnip.

I called the Rainbow Movie Theater, Victory Park, and a few restaurants in town. They all said they had not seen anyone matching Baowen's description. Before I could phone the City Library, where Baowen sometimes spent his weekends, a call came in. It was from the city's Public Security Bureau. The man on the phone said they'd detained a worker of ours named Baowen Huang. He wouldn't tell me what had happened. He just said, "Indecent activity. Come as soon as you can."

It was a cold day. As I cycled toward downtown, the shrill north wind kept flipping up the front ends of my overcoat. My knees were sore, and I couldn't help shivering. Soon my asthma tightened my throat and I began moaning. I couldn't stop cursing Baowen. "I knew it. I just knew it," I said to myself. I had sensed that sooner or later he'd seek pleasure with another woman. Now he was in the police's hands, and the whole factory would talk about him. How could Beina take this blow?

At the Public Security Bureau I was surprised to see that about a dozen officials from other factories, schools, and companies were already there. I knew most of them, who were in charge of security affairs at their workplaces. A policewoman conducted us into a conference room upstairs, where green silk curtains hung in the windows. We sat down around a long mahogany table and waited to be briefed about the case. The glass tabletop was brand new, its edge still sharp. I saw worry and confusion on the other men's faces. I figured Baowen must have been involved in an organized crime—either an orgy or a gang rape. On second thought I felt he couldn't have been a rapist; by nature he was kindhearted, very gentle. I hoped this was not a political case, which would be absolutely unpardonable. Six or seven years ago a half-wit and a high school graduate had started an association in our city, named the China Liberation Party, which had later recruited nine members. Although the sparrow is small it has a complete set of organs—their party elected a chairman, a secretary, and even a prime minister. But before they could print their manifesto, which expressed their intention to overthrow the government, the police rounded them up. Two of the top leaders were executed, and the rest of the members were jailed.

As I was wondering about the nature of Baowen's crime, a middle-aged man came in. He had a solemn face, and his eyes were half-closed. He took off his dark-blue tunic, hung it on the back of a chair, and sat down at the end of the table. I recognized him; he was Chief Miao of the Investigation Department. Wearing a sheepskin jerkin, he somehow reminded me of Genghis Khan, thick-boned and round-faced. His hooded eyes were shrewd, though they looked sleepy. Without any opening remarks he declared that we had a case of homosexuality on our hands. At that, the room turned noisy. We'd heard of the term but didn't know what it meant exactly. Seeing many of us puzzled, Chief Maio explained, "It's a social disease, like gambling, or prostitution, or syphilis." He kept on squirming as if itchy with hemorrhoids.

A young man from the city's Fifth Middle School raised his hand. He asked, "What do homosexuals do?"

Miao smiled and his eyes almost disappeared. He said, "People of the same sex have a sexual relationship."

"Sodomy!" cried someone.

The room turned quiet for at least ten seconds. Then somebody asked what kind of crime this was.

Chief Miao explained, "Homosexuality originated from Western capitalism and bourgeois lifestyle. According to our law it's dealt with as a kind of hooliganism. Therefore every one of the men we arrested will serve a sentence, from six months to five years, depending on the severity of his crime and his attitude toward it."

A truck blew its horn on the street and made my heart twinge. If Baowen went to prison, Beina would live like a widow, unless she divorced him. Why had he married her to begin with? Why did he ruin her this way?

What had happened was that a group of men, mostly clerks, artists, and schoolteachers, had formed a club called Men's World, a salon of sorts. Every Thursday evening they'd met in a large room on the third floor of the office building of the Forestry Institute. Since the club admitted only men, the police suspected that it might be a secret association with a leaning toward violence, so they assigned two detectives to mix with the group. True, some of the men appeared to be intimate with each other in the club, but most of the time they talked about movies, books, and current events. Occasionally music was played, and they danced together. According to the detectives' account, it was a bizarre, emotional scene. A few men appeared in pairs, unashamed of necking and cuddling in the presence of others, and some would say with tears, "At last we men have a place for ourselves." A middle-aged painter wearing earrings exclaimed, "Now I feel alive! Only in here can I stop living in hypocrisy." Every week two or three new faces would show up. When the club grew close to the size of thirty men, the police took action and arrested the all.

After Chief Miao's briefing, we were allowed to meet with the criminals for fifteen minutes. A policeman led me into a small room in the basement and let me read Baowen's confession while he went to fetch him. I glanced through the four pages of interrogation notes, which stated that Baowen had been new to the club and that he'd joined them only twice, mainly because he was interested in their talks. Yet he didn't deny that he was a homosexual.

The room smelled of urine, since it was next to a bathroom. The policeman took Baowen in and ordered him to sit opposite me at the table. Baowen, in handcuffs, avoided looking at me. His face was bloated, covered with bruises. A broad welt left by a baton, about four inches long, slanted across his forehead. The collar of his jacket was torn open. Yet he didn't appear frightened. His calm manner angered me, though I felt sorry for him.

I kept a hard face and said, "Baowen, do you know you committed a crime?"

"I didn't do anything. I just went there to listen to them talk."

"You mean you didn't do that thing with any man?" I wanted to make sure so that I could help him.

He looked at me, then lowered his eyes, saying, "I might've done something, to be honest, but I didn't."

"What's that supposed to mean?"

"I—I liked a man in the club, a lot. If he'd asked me, I might've agreed." His lips curled upward as if he prided himself on what he had said.

"You're sick!" I struck the table with my knuckles.

To my surprise, he said, "So? I'm a sick man. You think I don't know that?"

I was bewildered. He went on, "Years ago I tried everything to cure myself. I took a lot of herbs and boluses, and even ate baked scorpions, lizards, and toads. Nothing helped me. Still I'm fond of men. I don't know why I'm not interested in women. Whenever I'm with a woman my heart is as calm as a stone."

Outraged by his confession, I asked, "Then why did you marry my Beina? To make fun of her, eh? To throw mud in my face?"

"How could I be that mean? Before we got married, I told her I didn't like women and might not give her a baby."

"She believed you?"

"Yes. She said she wouldn't mind. She just wanted a husband."

"She's an idiot!" I unfolded my hanky and blew my clogged nose into it, then asked, "Why did you choose her if you had no feelings for her at all?"

"What was the difference? For me she was similar to other women."

"You're a scoundrel!"

"If I didn't marry her, who would? The marriage helped us both, covering me and saving face for her. Besides, we could have a good apartment—a home. You see, I tried living like a normal man. I've never been mean to Beina."

"But the marriage is a fake! You lied to your mother too, didn't you?"

"She wanted me to marry."

The policeman signaled that our meeting was over. In spite of my anger, I told Baowen that I'd see what I could do, and that he'd better cooperate with the police and show a sincere attitude.

What should I do? I was sick of him, but he belonged to my family, at least in name, and I was obligated to help him.

On the way home I pedaled slowly, my mind heavy with thoughts. Gradually I realized that I might be able to do something to prevent him from going to jail. There were two steps I could take: first, I would maintain that he had done nothing in the club, so as to isolate him from those real criminals; second, I would present him as a sick man, so that he might receive medical treatment instead of a prison term. Once he became a criminal, he'd be marked forever as an enemy of society, no longer redeemable. Even his children might suffer. I ought to save him.

Fortunately both the Party secretary and the director of our factory were willing to accept Baowen as a sick man, particularly Secretary Zhu, who liked Baowen's kung-fu style and had once let him teach his youngest son how to use a three-section cudgel. Zhu suggested we make an effort to rescue Baowen from the police. He said to me in the men's room inside our office building, "Old Cheng, we must not let Baowen end up in prison." I was grateful for his words.

All of a sudden homosexuality became a popular topic in the factory. A few old workers said that some actors of the Beijing opera had slept together as lovers in the old days, because no women were allowed to perform in any troupe and the actors could spend time with men only. Secretary Zhu, who was well read, said that some emperors in the Han Dynasty had owned male lovers in addition to their large harems. Director Liu had heard that the last emperor, Puyi, had often ordered his eunuchs to suck his penis and caress his testicles. Someone even claimed that homosexuality was an upper-class thing, not something for ordinary people. All the talk sickened me. I felt ashamed of my nominal son-in-law. I wouldn't join them in talking and just listened, pretending I wasn't bothered.

As I expected, rumors went wild in the factory, especially in the foundry shop. Some people said Baowen was impotent. Some believed he was a hermaphrodite, otherwise his wife would've been pregnant long ago.

To console Beina, I went to see her one evening. She had a pleasant home, in which everything was in order. Two bookcases, filled with industrial manuals, biographies, novels, and medical books, stood against the white-washed wall, on either side of the window. In one corner of the living room was a coat tree on which hung the red feather parka Baowen had bought her before their wedding, and in another corner sat a floor lamp. At the opposite end of the room two pots of blooming flowers, one of cyclamens and the other of Bengal roses, were placed on a pair of low stools kept at an equal distance from each other and from the walls on both sides. Near the inner wall, beside a yellow enamel spittoon, was a large sofa upholstered in orange imitation leather. A black-and-white TV perched on an oak chest against the outer wall.

I was impressed, especially by the floor inlaid with bricks and coated with bright red paint. Even my wife couldn't keep a home so neat. No doubt it was Baowen's work, because Beina couldn't be so tidy. Already the room showed the trace of her sloppy habits—in a corner were scattered an empty flour sack and a pile of soiled laundry. Sipping the tea she had poured me, I said, "Beina, I'm sorry about Baowen. I didn't know he was so bad."

"No, he's a good man." Her round eyes looked at me with a steady light.

"Why do you say that?"

"He's been good to me."

"But he can't be a good husband, can he?"

"What do you mean?"

I said bluntly, "He didn't go to bed with you very often, did he?"

"Oh, he can't do that because he practices kung fu. He said if he slept with a woman, all his many years' work would be gone. From the very beginning his master told him to avoid women."

"So you don't mind?" I was puzzled, saying to myself, What a stupid girl.

"Not really."

"But you two must've shared the bed a couple of times, haven't you?"

"No, we haven't."

"Really? Not even once?"

"No." She blushed a little and looked away, twisting her earlobe with her fingertips.

My head was reeling. After eight months' marriage she was still a virgin! And she didn't mind! I lifted the cup and took a large gulp of the jasmine tea.

A lull settled in. We both turned to watch the evening news; my numb mind couldn't take in what the anchorwoman said about a border skirmish between Vietnamese and Chinese troops.

A moment later I told Beina, "I'm sorry he has such a problem. If only we had known."

"Don't feel so bad, Uncle. In fact he's better than a normal man."

"How so?"

"Most men can't stay away from pretty women, but Baowen just likes to have a few buddies. What's wrong with that? It's better this way, 'cause I don't have to worry about those shameless bitches in our factory. He won't bother to give them a look. He'll never have a lifestyle problem."

I almost laughed, wondering how I should explain to her that he could have a sexual relationship with a man and that he'd been detained precisely because of a lifestyle problem. On second thought I realized it might be better for her to continue to think that way. She didn't need more stress at the moment.

Then we talked about how to help Baowen. I told her to write a report, emphasizing what a good, considerate husband he'd been. Of course she must not mention his celibacy in their marriage. Also, from now on, however vicious her fellow workers' remarks were, she should ignore them and never talk back, as if she'd heard nothing.

That night when I told my wife about Beina's silly notions, she smiled, 75
saying, "Compared with most men, Baowen isn't too bad. Beina's not a fool."

I begged Chief Miao and a high-ranking officer to treat Baowen leniently and even gave each of them two bottles of brandy and a coupon for a Butterfly sewing machine. They seemed willing to help but wouldn't promise me anything. For days I was so anxious that my wife was afraid my ulcer might recur.

One morning the Public Security Bureau called, saying they had accepted our factory's proposal and would have Baowen transferred to the mental hospital in a western suburb, provided our factory agreed to pay for his hospitalization. I accepted the offer readily, feeling relieved. Later, I learned that there wasn't enough space in the city's prison for twenty-seven gay men, who couldn't be mixed with other inmates and had to be put in solitary cells. So only four of them were jailed; the rest were either hospitalized (if their work units agreed to pay for the medical expenses) or sent to some labor farms to be reformed. The two Party members among them didn't go to jail, though they were expelled from the Party, a very severe punishment that ended their political lives.

The moment I put down the phone, I hurried to the assembly shop and found Beina. She broke into tears at the good news. She ran back home and filled a duffel bag with Baowen's clothes. We met at my office, then together set out for the Public Security Bureau. I rode my bicycle while she sat behind me, embracing the duffel as if it were a baby. With a strong tailwind, the cycling was easy and fast, so we arrived before Baowen left for the hospital. He was waiting for a van in front of the Police Station, accompanied by two policemen.

The bruises on his face had healed, so he looked handsome again. He smiled at us and said rather secretively, "I want to ask you a favor." He rolled his eyes as the dark-green van rounded the street corner, coming toward us.

"What?" I said. 80

"Don't let my mother know the truth. She's too old to take it. Don't tell her, please!"

"What should we say to her then?" I asked.

"Just say I have a temporary mental disorder."

Beina couldn't hold back her tears anymore, saying loudly, "Don't worry. We won't let her know. Take care of yourself and come back soon." She handed him the duffel, which he took without a word.

I nodded to assure him that I wouldn't reveal the truth. He smiled at her, 85
then at me. For some reason his face turned rather sweet—charming and enticing, as though it were a mysterious female face. I blinked my eyes and wondered if he was really a man. It flashed through my mind that if he were a woman he could've been a beauty—tall, slim, muscular, and slightly languid.

My thoughts were cut short by a metallic screech as the van stopped in front of us. Baowen climbed into it; so did the policemen. I walked around the van, and shook his hand, saying that I'd visit him the next week and that meanwhile, if he needed anything, just to give me a ring.

We waved good-bye as the van drew away, its tire chains clattering and flinging up bits of snow. After a blasting toot, it turned left and disappeared from the icy street. I got on my bicycle as a gust of wind blew up and almost threw me down. Beina followed me for about twenty yards, then leaped on the carrier, and together we headed home. She was so heavy. Thank heaven, I was riding a Great Golden Deer, one of the sturdiest makes.

During the following week I heard from Baowen once. He said on the phone that he felt better now and less agitated. Indeed his voice sounded calm and smooth. He asked me to bring him a few books when I came, specifically his *Dictionary of Universal Knowledge,* which was a hefty, rare book translated from the Russian in the late Fifties. I had no idea how he had come by it.

I went to see him on Thursday morning. The hospital was on a mountain, six miles southwest of Muji City. As I was cycling on the asphalt road, a few tall smokestacks fumed lazily beyond the larch woods in the west. To my right the power lines along the roadside curved, heavy with fluffy snow, which would drop in little chunks whenever the wind blew across them. Now and then I overtook a horse cart loaded with earless sheaves of wheat, followed by one or two foals. After I pedaled across a stone bridge and turned into the mouth of a valley, a group of brick buildings emerged on a gentle slope, connected with one another by straight cement paths. Farther up the hill, past the buildings, there was a cow pen, in which about two dozen milk cows were grazing on dry grass while a few others huddled together to keep warm.

It was so peaceful here that it you hadn't known this was a mental hospi- 90
tal, you might have imagined it was a sanatorium for ranking officials. Entering Building 9, I was stopped by a guard, who then took me to Baowen's room on the ground floor. It happened that the doctor on duty, a tall fortyish man with tapering fingers, was making the morning rounds and examining Baowen. He shook hands with me and said that my son-in-law was doing fine. His surname was Mai; his whiskered face looked very intelligent. When he turned to give a male nurse instructions about Baowen's treatment, I noticed an enormous

wart in his ear almost blocking the ear hole like a hearing aid. In a way he looked like a foreigner. I wondered if he had some Mongolian or Tibetan blood.

"We give him the electric bath," Doctor Mai said to me a moment later.

"What?" I asked, wincing.

"We treat him with the electric bath."

I turned to Baowen. "How is it?"

"It's good, really soothing." He smiled, but there was churlish look in his 95
eyes, and his mouth tightened.

The nurse was ready to take him for the treatment. Never having heard of such a bath, I asked Doctor Mai, "Can I see how it works?"

"All right, you may go with them."

Together we climbed the stairs to the second floor. There was another reason for me to join them. I wanted to find out whether Baowen was a normal man. The rumors in our factory had gotten on my nerves, particularly the one that said he had no penis—that was why he had always avoided bathing in the workers' bathhouse.

After taking off our shoes and putting on plastic slippers, we entered a small room that had pea-green walls and a parquet floor. At its center lay a porcelain bathtub, as ghastly as an apparatus of torture. Affixed along the interior wall of the tub were rectangles of black perforated metal. Three thick rubber cords connected them to a tall machine standing by the wall. A control board full of buttons, gauges, and switches slanted atop the machine. The young nurse, burly and square-faced, turned on the faucet; steaming water began to tumble into the tub. Then he went over to operate the machine. He seemed good-natured; his name was Fuhai Dong. He said he came from the countryside, apparently of peasant stock, and had graduated from Jilin Nursing School.

Baowen smiled at me while unbuttoning his zebra-striped hospital robe. 100
He looked fine now—all the bruises had disappeared from his face, which had become pinkish and smooth. I was scared by the tub. It seemed suitable for electrocuting a criminal. However sick I was, I wouldn't lie in it with my back resting against that metal groove. What if there was an electricity leak?

"Does it hurt?" I asked Baowen.

"No."

He went behind a khaki screen in a corner and began taking off his clothes. When the water half filled the tub, the nurse took a small bag of white powder out of a drawer, cut it open with scissors, and poured the stuff into the water. It must have been salt. He tucked up his shirt sleeves and bent double to agitate the solution with both hands, which were large and sinewy.

To my dismay, Baowen came out in a clean pair of shorts. Without hesitation he got into the tub and lay down, just as one would enter a lukewarm bathing pool. I was amazed. "Have you given him electricity yet?" I asked Nurse Dong.

"Yes, a little. I'll increase it by and by." He turned to the machine and adjusted a few buttons.

"You know," he said to me, "your son-in-law is a very good patient, always cooperative."

"He should be."

"That's why we give him the bath. Others patients get electric cuffs around their limbs or electric rods on their bodies. Some of them scream like animals every time. We have to tie them up."

"When will he be cured?"

"I'm not sure."

Baowen was noiseless in the electrified water, with his eyes shut and his head resting on a black rubber pad at the end of the tub. He looked fine, rather relaxed.

I drew up a chair and sat down. Baowen seemed reluctant to talk, concentrating on the treatment, so I remained silent, observing him. His body was wiry, his legs hairless, and the front of his shorts bulged quite a bit. He looked all right physically. Once in a while he breathed a feeble sigh.

As the nurse increased the electric current, Baowen began to squirm in the tub as if smarting from something. "Are you all right?" I asked and dared not touch him.

"Yeah."

He kept his eyes shut. Glistening beads of sweat gathered on his forehead. He looked pale, his lips curling now and again as though he were thirsty.

Then the nurse gave him more electricity. Baowen began writhing and moaning a little. Obviously he was suffering. This bath couldn't be as soothing as he'd claimed. With a white towel Nurse Dong wiped the sweat off Baowen's face and whispered, "I'll turn it down in a few minutes."

"No, give me more!" Baowen said resolutely without opening his eyes, his face twisted.

I felt as though he was ashamed of himself. Perhaps my presence made this section of the treatment more uncomfortable to him. His hands gripped the rim of the tub, the arched wrists trembling. For a good three minutes nobody said a word; the room was so quiet that its walls seemed to be ringing.

As the nurse gradually reduced the electricity, Baowen calmed down. His toes stopped wiggling.

Not wanting to bother him further with my presence, I went out to look for Doctor Mai, to thank him and find out when Baowen could be cured. The doctor was not in his office, so I walked out of the building for a breath of air. The sun was high and the snow blazingly white. Once outside, I had to close my eyes for a minute to adjust them. I then sat down on a bench and lit a cigarette. A young woman in an ermine hat and army mittens passed by, holding an empty milk pail and humming the song "Comrade, Please Have a Cup of Tea." She looked handsome, and her crisp voice pleased me. I gazed at the pair of thick braids behind her, which swayed a little in the wind.

My heart was full of pity for Baowen. He was such a fine young man that he ought to be able to love a woman, have a family, and enjoy a normal life.

Twenty minutes later I rejoined him in his room. He looked tired, still shivering a little. He told me that as the electric currents increased, his skin had begun prickling as though stung by hundreds of mosquitoes. That was why he couldn't stay in the tub for longer than half an hour.

I felt for him and said, "I'll tell our leaders how sincere your attitude is and how cooperative you are."

"Oh sure." He tilted his damp head. "Thanks for bringing the books."

"Do you need something else?" 125

"No." He sounded sad.

"Baowen, I hope you can come home before the New Year. Beina needs you."

"I know. I don't want to be locked up here forever."

I told him that Beina had written to his mother, saying he'd been away on a business trip. Then the bell for lunch rang in building, and ouside the loudspeaker began broadcasting the fiery music of "March of the Volunteers." Nurse Dong walked in with a pair of chopsticks and a plate containing two corn buns. He said cheerily to Baowen, I'll bring you the dish in a minute. We have tofu stewed with sauerkraut today, also bean sprout soup."

I stood up and took my leave. 130

When I reported Baowen's condition to the factory leaders, they seemed impressed. The term "electric bath" must have given their imagination free rein. Secretary Zhu kept shaking his head and said, "I'm sorry Baowen has to go through such a thing."

I didn't explain that the electric bath was a treatment less severe than the other kinds, nor did I describe what the bath was like. I just said, "They steep him in electrified water every day." Let the terror seize their brains, I thought, so that they might be more sympathetic to Baowen when he is discharged from the hospital.

It was mid-December, and Baowen had been in the hospital for a month already. For days Beina went on saying that she wanted to see how her husband was doing; she was eager to take him home before the New Year. Among her fellow workers rumors persisted. One said the electric bath had blistered Baowen; another claimed that his genitals had been shriveled up by the treatment; another added that he had become a vegetarian, nauseated at the mere sight of meat. The young woman who had once declared she'd leave her door open for him has just married and proudly told everybody she was pregnant. People began to be kind and considerate to Beina, treating her like an abused wife. The leaders of the assembly shop assigned her only the daytime shift. I was pleased that Finance still paid Baowen his wages as though he were on sick leave. Perhaps they did this because they didn't want to upset me.

On Saturday Beina and I went to the mental hospital. She couldn't pedal, and it was too far for me to carry her on my bicycle, so we took the bus. She had been there by herself two weeks ago to deliver some socks and a pair of woolen pajamas she'd knitted for Baowen.

We arrived at the hospital early in the afternoon. Baowen looked healthy, 135
in good spirits. It seemed that the bath had helped him. He was happy to see Beina and even cuddled her in my presence. He gave her two toffees; knowing I disliked candies, he didn't give me one. He poured a large mug of malted milk for both of us, since there was only one mug in the room. I didn't touch the milk, unsure whether homosexuality was communicable. I was glad to see that he treated his wife well. He took a genuine interest in what she said about their comrades in our factory, and now and then laughed heartily. What a wonderful husband he could have been if he were not sick.

Having sat with the couple for a few minutes, I left so that they could be alone. I went to the Nurse's Office upstairs and found Fuhai Dong writing at a desk. The door was open, and knocked on its frame. Startled, he closed his brown notebook and stood up.

"I didn't mean to scare you," I said.

"No, Uncle, I just didn't expect anyone to come up here."

I took a carton of Peony cigarettes out of my bag and put it on the desk, saying, "I won't take too much of your time, young man. Please keep this as a token of my regards." I didn't mean to bribe him. I was sincerely grateful to him for treating Baowen well.

"Oh, don't give me this please." 140

"You don't smoke?"

"I do. Tell you what, give it to Doctor Mai. He'll help Baowen more."

I was puzzled. Why didn't he want the top-quality cigarettes if he smoked? Seeing that I was confused, he went on, "I'll be nice to Baowen without any gift from you. He's a good man. It's the doctor's wheels that you should grease."

"I have another carton for him."

"One carton's nothing here. You should give him at least two." 145

I was moved by his words, thanked him, and said good-bye.

Doctor Mai happened to be in his office. When I walked in, he was reading the current issue of *Women's Life,* whose back cover carried a large photo of Madame Mao on trial—she wore black and stood, handcuffed, between two young policewomen. Doctor Mai put the magazine aside and asked me to sit down. In the room, tall shelves, loaded with books and files, lined the walls. A smell of rotten fruit hung in there. He seemed pleased to see me.

After we exchanged a few words, I took out both cartons of cigarettes and handed them to him. "This is just a small token of my gratitude, for the New Year," I said.

He took the cigarettes and put them away under his desk. "Thanks a lot," he whispered.

"Doctor Mai, do you think Baowen will be cured before the holiday?" I asked.

"What did you say? Cured?" He looked surprised. 150

"Yes."

He shook his head slowly, then turned to check that the door was shut. He motioned me to move closer. I pulled the chair forward a little and rested my forearms on the edge of his Bakelite desktop.

"To be honest, there's no cure," he said.

"What?"

"Homosexuality isn't an illness, so it has no cure. Don't tell anyone I said 155
this."

"Then why torture Baowen like that?"

"The police sent him here and we couldn't refuse. Besides, we ought to make him feel better and hopeful."

"So it isn't a disease?"

Unfortnately no. Let me say this again: there's no cure for your son-in-law, Old Cheng. It's not a disease. It's just a sexual preference; it may be congenital, like being left-handed. Got it?"

"Then why give him the electric bath?" Still I wasn't convinced. 160

"Electrotherapy is prescribed by the book—a standard treatment required by the Department of Public Health. I have no choice but to follow the regulations. That's why I didn't give him any of those harsher treatments. The bath is very mild by comparison. You see, I've done everything in my power to help him. Let me tell you another fact: according to the statistics, so far electrotherapy has cured only one out of a thousand homosexuals. I bet cod liver oil, or chocolate, or fried pork, anything, could produce a better result. All right, enough of this. I've talked too much."

At last his words sank in. For a good while I sat there motionless with a numb mind. A flock of sparrows were flitting about in the naked branches outside the window, chasing the one that held a tiny ear of millet in its bill. Another of them dragged a yellow string tied around its leg, unable to fly as nimbly as the others. I rose to my feet and thanked the doctor for his candid words. He stubbed out his cigarette in the ashtray on the windowsill and said, "I'll take special care of your son-in-law. Don't worry."

I rejoined Beina downstairs. Baowen looked quite cheerful, and it seemed they'd had a good time. He said to me, "If I can't come home soon, don't try too hard to get me out. They won't keep me here forever."

"I'll see what I can do."

In my heart I was exasperated, because if Doctor Mai's words were true, 165
there'd be little I could do for Baowen. If homosexuality wasn't a disease, why had he felt sick and tried to have himself cured? Had he been shamming? It was unlikely.

Beina had been busy cleaning their home since her last visit to the hospital. She bought two young drakes and planned to make drunk duck, a dish she said Baowen liked best. My heart was heavy. On the one hand, I'd have loved to have him back for the holiday; on the other hand, I was unsure what would happen if his condition hadn't improved. I dared not reveal my thoughts to anybody, not even to my wife, who had a big mouth. Because of her, the whole factory knew that Beina was still a virgin, and some people called her the Virgin Bride.

For days I pondered what to do. I was confused. Everybody thought homosexuality was a disease except for Doctor Mai, whose opinion I dared not mention to others. The factory leaders would be mad at me if they knew there was no cure for homosexuality. We had already spent over three thousand yuan on Baowen. I kept questioning in my mind, If homosexuality is a natural thing, then why are there men and women? Why can't two men get married and make a baby? Why didn't nature give men another hole? I was beset by doubts. If only I could have seen a trustworthy doctor for a second opinion. If only there were a knowledgeable, honest friend I could have talked with.

I hadn't yet made up my mind about what to do when Chief Miao called from the Public Security Bureau five days before the holiday. He informed me that Baowen had repeated his crime, so the police had taken him out of the hospital and sent him to the prison in Tangyuan County. "This time he did it," said the chief.

"Impossible!" I cried.

"We have evidence and witnesses. He doesn't deny it himself."

"Oh." I didn't know how to continue.

"He has to be incarcerated now."

"Are you sure he's not a hermaphrodite?" I mentioned that as a last resort.

Miao chuckled drily. "No, he's not. We had him checked. Physically he's a man, healthy and normal. Obviously it's a mental, moral disease, like an addiction to opium."

Putting down the phone, I felt dizzy, cursing Baowen for having totally ruined himself. What had happened was that he and Fuhai Dong had developed a relationship secretly. The nurse often gave him a double amount of meat or fish at dinner. Baowen, in return, unraveled his woolen pajamas and knitted Dong a pullover with the wool. One evening when they were lying in each other's arms in the Nurses' Office, an old cleaner passed by in the corridor and coughed. Fuhai Dong was terrified and convinced that the man had seen what they had been doing. For days, however hard Baowen tried to talk him out of his conviction, Dong wouldn't change his mind, blaming Baowen for having misled him. He said that the old cleaner often smiled at him meaningfully and would definitely turn them in. Finally Fuhai Dong went to the hospital leaders and confessed everything. So unlike Baowen, who got three and a half years in jail, Nurse Dong was merely put on probation; if he worked harder and criticized himself well, he might keep his current job.

That evening I went to tell Beina about the new development. As I was talking, she sobbed continually. Although she'd been cleaning the apartment for several days, her home was in shambles, most of the flowers half-dead, and dishes and pots piled in the sink. Mopping her face with a pink towel, she asked me, "What should I tell my mother-in-law?"

"Tell her the truth."

She made no response. I said again, "You should consider a divorce."

"No!" Her sobbing turned into wailing. "He—he's my husband and I'm his wife. If I die my soul belongs to him. We've sworn never to leave each other. Let others say whatever they want, I know he's a good man."

"Then why did he go to bed with a guy?"

"He just wanted to have a good time. That was all. It's nothing like adultery or bigamy, is it?"

"But it's a crime that got him into jail," I said. Although in my heart I admitted that Baowen in every way was a good fellow except for his fondness for men, I had to be adamant about my position. I was in charge of security for our factory; if I had a criminal son-in-law, who would listen to me? Wouldn't I be removed from my office soon? If I lost my job, who could protect Beina? Sooner or later she would be laid off, since a criminal's wife was not supposed to have the same opportunities for employment as others. Beina remained silent: I asked again, "What are you going to do?"

"Wait for him."

I took a few spiced pumpkin seeds from a bowl, stood up, and went over to the window. Under the sill the radiator was hissing softly with a tiny steam leak. Outside, in the distance, firecrackers one after another scattered clusters of sparks into the indigo dusk. I turned around and said, "He's not worth waiting for. You must divorce him."

"No, I won't," she moaned.

"Well, it's impossible for me to have a criminal as my son-in-law. I've been humiliated enough. If you want to wait for him, don't come to see me again." I put the pumpkin seeds back into the bowl, picked up my fur hat, and dragged myself out the door.

CHARTING THE STORY

1 How is homosexuality presented by Chief Miao to those who are gathered at the Public Security Bureau? How does the narrator react to the news concerning Baowen? Does he present as the only possible view? Where, and in what ways, do you find dissent among other characters?

2 What motivates the narrator to pursue Baowen's defense? What, in the end, causes him to change course?

3 What does the "outing" of Baowen contribute to discussions of homosexuality among the factory workers? How do workers and managers alike seem to "adjudicate" their co-worker?

4 What sort of "treatment" is given to Baowen, and what results from this "therapy"? Why, ultimately, is he given this particular form of treatment?

5 In the end, is Baowen's spirit broken? Why, or why not?

CONSIDERATIONS OF STYLE

1 What attitude toward homosexuality is expressed by the narrator? What attitudes does it seem likely that the author would express, and why? How would the story change, were the narration made by someone sympathetic to Baowen? In your view, which story would be more successful as a polemic, and why?

2 In Paragraph 17, observing the completeness of the tiny, nine-member China Liberation Party, the narrator observes, "Although the sparrow is small, it has a complete set of organs—their party elected a chairman, a secretary, and even a prime minister." In Paragraph 163, toward the end of the story, the narrator comments upon a sparrow who "dragged a yellow string tied around its leg, unable to fly as nimbly as the others." What connections, symbolic and otherwise, may there be between the two imaged sparrows?

3 In what ways does humor humanize the characterization of the narrator, despite his curmudgeonly attitudes?

AFTERTHOUGHTS

1 Is Baowen's and Beina's marriage a success? On what do you base your evaluation of the dynamics of their union? What would be considered a "successful" marriage by the narrator and by the majority of those in his venue?

2 What details in the text make it clear that it is set in the People's Republic of China? Why is it relevant that it be set in China? Where else, conceivably, could this story have been set, and what would lead you to choose these locales?

THE WRITER'S CRAFT

1 Research the "treatments" or "therapies" that once were given (and in some cases, still are) to gay men, lesbians, and young persons sent to mental hospitals to be "cured" of "gender confusion." Compare the attitudes underlying these attempts to eradicate homosexual behavior (or even desire), and explore the issues apparently at stake in the view of the "therapists" in this endeavor.

2 Write "case notes" concerning Baowen, from the points of view of Chief Miao and Doctor Mai (remembering that Doctor Mai's notes will be read by his superiors). Finally, in the *persona* of Baowen, write what you would write if you would not face more punishment thereby.

JOHN UPDIKE

Born in Shillington, Pennsylvania in 1932, JOHN UPDIKE *has lived most of his life in Massachusetts. His most famous novels are* Couples *(1968), and the "Rabbit" trilogy:* Rabbit, Run *(1960),* Rabbit Redux *(1970), and* Rabbit Is Rich, *which won the Pulitzer Prize in 1981, to which he added* Rabbit at Rest *in 1990. His most recent novel,* Toward the End of Time, *appeared in 1997.*

His short story collections include Pigeon Feathers *(1962),* The Music School *(1966), and* Too Far to Go *(1979). An extremely versatile writer, Updike has also written five volumes of poetry, from* The Carpentered Hen and Other Tame Creatures *in 1958 to* Facing Nature *in 1985.*

In "Licks of Love in the Heart of the Cold War," a famous country singer is chosen by the U S Department of State to be a cultural ambassador to the Soviet Union in the 1960s. However, his tour begins rather undiplomatically with a one-night affair that becomes a potential threat to his marriage of fifteen years.

This story appeared in The Atlantic Monthly *in May 1998.*

PERSPECTIVES

1. When and how did the Cold War between the United States and the Soviet Union begin and end? What role did cultural exchange play in mitigating the political and military tensions between the superpowers of that era?
2. John Updike's fiction generally manages to include the "wonderful and strange" aspects of "the way men and women get together." What attitudes about such gettings-together do you bring to your reading; and having read the text, how are they confirmed, challenged, or otherwise gotten together with?

Licks of Love in the Heart of the Cold War

Khrushchev was in power, or we thought he was, that month I spent as cultural ambassador and banjo-picking bridge between the superpowers, helping to stave off nuclear holocaust. It was September into October of 1964. We had a cultural-exchange program with the Soviets at the time. Our State Department's theory was that almost any American paraded before the oppressed Soviet masses would be, just in his easy manner of walking and talking, such an advertisement for the free way of life that cells of subversion would pop up in his wake like dandelions on an April lawn. So my mission wasn't as innocent as it seemed. Still, I was game to undertake it.

My home lies on the far side of the Blue Ridge in western Virginia, which isn't the same as West Virginia, though it's getting close. Washington, D.C., to me spells "big city," and when the official franked letters began to come through, it never occurred to me to resist something as big and beautiful as the pre-Vietnam U.S. government. Russia is just one more struggling country now, run by economists with sweaty palms, but then it was the dark side of the moon. The Aeroflot plane from Paris smelled of boiled potatoes, as I recall, and the stewardesses were as hefty as packed suitcases. When we landed, at midnight, we might have been descending over the ocean, there were so few lights under us.

The airport was illuminated dimly, as if by those bedside lamps that hotels give you, not to read by. One of the young soldiers was pawing through a well-worn *Playboy* that some discomfited fur trader had tried to smuggle in, and my first impression of how life worked under communism was the glare of that poor centerfold's sweet bare skin under those brownish airport lights. The magazine was confiscated, but I don't want to believe that the traveling salesman was sent to the gulag. He had a touch of Asia in his cheekbones—it wasn't as if we had corrupted a pure-blooded Russian. The State Department boys swooped me out the customs door into a chauffeured limo that smelled not of boiled potatoes, exactly, but very deeply of tobacco, another natural product. My granddaddy's barn used to smell like that, even after the cured leaf had been baled and sold. I knew I was going to like it here.

On the airport road into Moscow in those days there was this giant billboard of Lenin, leaning forward with a wicked goateed grin and pointing to something up above with a single finger, like John the Baptist pointing to a Jesus we couldn't see yet. "I love that," my chief State Department escort said from the jump seat. "To three hundred million people—'Up yours.'" He was Bud Nevins, cultural attaché. I saw a lot of Bud, Bud and his lovely wife, April, in the weeks to come.

Washington had been an adventure already. I had been briefed on a cou- 5
ple of afternoons by a combination of our experts and some refugees from the Soviet Union. One portly old charmer, who had been upper-middle management in the KGB, filled a whole afternoon around a long leather-topped table by telling me what restaurants to go to and what food to order—smoked sturgeon, piroshki, mushoom pie. His mouth was watering, though from the look of him he hadn't exactly starved under capitalism. Still, no food like home cooking; I could sympathize with that.

Those Washington people loved to party. Each briefing would be followed by a reception, and at one of the receptions a little black-haired coffee fetcher from that afternoon's briefing came up to me as if this time her breasts were being offered on a tray. They were sizable, pert breasts, in a peach-colored cotton chemise that had just outgrown being a T-shirt.

"Sir, you are my god," she told me. That's always nice to hear, and she shouldn't have spoiled it by adding "Except of course for Earl Scruggs. And that nice tall Allen Shelton, who used to fill in on banjo with the Virginia Boys—oh, he was *cute!* Now, have you heard those new sides the McReynoldses have cut down in Jacksonville, with this boy named Bobby Thompson? *He* is the future! He has this whole new style—you can hear the melody! 'Hard Hearted.' 'Dixie Hoedown.' Oh, my!"

"Young lady, you know I'm not exactly bluegrass," I told her politely. "Earl, well, he's beginning to miss notes, but you can't get away from him; he's a giant, and Don Reno likewise. Nevertheless, my idol intellectually is Pete Seeger, if you must know; he's the one, him and the Weavers, brought back the five-string after the war, after the dance bands all but turned the banjo into a ukelele."

"So folksy and *pokey* and phony, if you're asking me," she said, with a hurried overemphasis that I was beginning to get used to, while her warm black eyes darted back and forth on my face like stirred-up horseflies. "And a traitor to his country besides."

"Well," I admitted, "you won't find him on *Grand Ole Opry* real soon, but the college kids eat him up, and for his sheer sincere picking—none of that show-biz flash that sometimes bothers me about Earl. Young lady, you should calm yourself and sit down and listen sometime to those albums Pete cut with Woody and the Almanacs before the war."

"I did," she said eagerly. "I did, I did. 'Talking Union.' 'Sod Buster Ballads.' Wonderful true-blue lefty stuff. The West Coast Communists must have loved it. Mr. Chester, did you ever in your life listen to a program called *Jamboree,* out of Wheeling?"

"Did I? I got my first air time on it, on good old WWVA. Me and Jim Buchanan on fiddle, before he got big. 'Are You Lost in Sin?' and 'Don't Say Good-bye If You Love Me.' With a little 'Somebody Loves You, Darlin'" for a rideout. Did I catch your name, may I ask?"

"You'll laugh. It's a silly name."

"I bet now it isn't. You got to love the name the good Lord gave you."

"It wasn't the good Lord, it was my hateful mother." Momentarily holding a deep breath that rounded out her cheeks like a trumpet player's, she said, "Imogene." Then she exhaled in a blubbery rush and said, "Imogene Frye. Isn't it silly?"

"No," I said. That was my first lie to her. She seemed a little off-center right from the first, but Imogene could talk banjo, and here, in this city of block-long buildings and charcoal suits, that was as welcome to me as borscht and salted cucumber would have been to that homeless KGB colonel, locked out forever as a traitor from the land he loved.

"I *loved,*" this Imogene was saying, "the licks you took on 'Heavy Traffic Ahead.' And the repeat an octave higher on 'Walking in Jerusalem Just Like John.'"

"It wasn't an octave, it was a fifth," I told her, settling in and lifting two bourbons from a silver tray that a kindly Negro was carrying around. I saw that this was going to be a conversation. Banjos were getting to be hot then, what with that *Beverly Hillbillies* theme, and I didn't want to engage with any shallow groupie. "Do you ever tune in WDBJ, out of Roanoke?" I asked her. "And tell me exactly why you think this Bobby Thompson is the future."

She saw my hurt, with those hot bright eyes that looked to be all pupil, and hastened to reassure me in her hurried, twitchy way of talking that I was the present, the past, and the future as far as she was concerned. Neither of us, I think, had the habit of drinking, but the trays kept coming around, brought by black men in white gloves, and by the time the reception broke up, the whole scene might have been a picture printed on silk, waving gently in and out. The Iron Curtain experts had drifted away to their homes in Bethesda and Silver Spring, and it seemed the most natural thing in the free world that little Imogene, to whom I must have looked a little wavy myself, would be inviting me back to her apartment somewhere off in one of those neighborhoods where they say it's not safe for a white man to show his face late at night.

Black and white, that's most of what I remember. Her hair was black and soft, and her skin was white and soft, and her voice had slowed and gotten girlish with the effects of liquor and being romanced. I was on the floor, peeling down her pantyhose while she rested a hand on the top of my head for balance. Then we were sitting on the bed while she cupped her hands under those sizable breasts, pointing them at me like guns. "I want them to be even bigger," she told me so softly that I strained to hear, "for *you.*" Her breasts being appreciated made her smile in the slanted light from the street like a round-faced cartoon character, a cat-and-canary smile. When I carried the courtesies down below, this seemed to startle her, so she stiffened a bit before relaxing her legs. I was striving to keep my focus amid the swaying caused by government-issue alcohol, the jostling of my conscience, my wondering what time it was, and the glinting strangeness of this environment, with its sadness of the single girl. Black and white—her little room sucked dry of color, like something on early TV; her bureau with its brushes and silver-framed photos of the family that had hatched her; an armchair with a cellophane-wrapped drugstore rental book still balanced on one arm, where she had left it before heading off this morning into her working day; her AM-FM-shortwave portable radio, big enough to pick up stations from Antarctica; her narrow bed with its brass headboard that was no good to lean on when we had done our best and needed to reminisce and establish limits.

"Lordy," I said. This was something of a lie, since when the main event 20
came up, I had lost a certain energy to the good times behind us, beginning hours ago at the party. I had felt lost in her.

She touched my shoulder and said my full name tentatively, as if I wouldn't like it: "Eddie Chester." She was right; it sounded proprietary, and something in me bristled. "You really are a god."

"You should catch me sober sometime."

"When?" Her voice pounced, quick and eager, as it had been at first. The pieces of white beside her swollen pupils glinted like sparkles on TV; her propped-up pillow eclipsed half of her round face and half a head of black hair, mussed out to a wild size.

Mine had been just a manner of speaking. "Not ever, it may be, Imogene," I told her. "I have a week of gigs out west, and then I'm off on this trip, helping to keep your planet safe for democracy."

"But I'll see you when you come back," she insisted.

"You must come back to Washington, to be debriefed. Eddie, Eddie, Eddie," she said, as if knowing it galled me. "I can't ever let you go."

I longed for a taxi out of there. "I got a wife, you know. And three little ones."

"Do you love your wife?"

"Well, honey, I wouldn't say I don't, though after fifteen years a little of the bloom rubs off."

"Do you do to her everything you did to me?"

This seemed downright forward. "I forget," I said, and pushed out of the bed into the bathroom, where the switch brought color back into everything, all those pinks and blues and yellows on her medicine-cabinet shelves; it seemed that she needed a lot of pills to keep herself functional.

"Eddie, don't go," she pleaded. "Stay the night. It's not safe out there. It's so bad the taxis won't come even if you call."

"Young lady, I got a hired car coming to the Willard Hotel at seven-thirty tomorrow morning to carry me back to western Virginia, and I'm going to be there. I may not be the future of banjo picking, but I take a real professional pride in never having missed a date." Putting on my underwear, I remembered how the taxi had gone around past the railroad station and then the Capitol, all lit up, and I figured we hadn't gone so far past it that I couldn't steer myself by its tip, or by the spotlights on the Washington Monument.

"Eddie, you *can't* go; I won't let you," Imogene asserted, out of bed except for one sweet, fat white leg caught in the sheet. Her breasts didn't look quite so cocky without her holding them up for me. That's the trouble with a full figure; it ties you to a bra.

I crooned a few lines of "Don't Say Good-bye If You Love Me" until my memory ran out, though I could see Jim Buchanan's face right across from me, squeezed into its fiddle, at the WWVA microphone. And then I told Imogene, as if still quoting a song, "Little darlin', you ain't keeping me here, though I must say it was absolute bliss." This was my third lie, but a white one, and with some truth in it. "Now, you go save your undying affection for an unattached man."

"You'll be killed!" she shrieked, and clawed at me for a while, but I shushed and sweet-talked her back into her bed, fighting a rising headache all the while, and let myself out into the stairwell. The street, one of those numbered ones, was as still as a stage set, but stepping out firmly in my cowboy boots, I headed what I figured was west—you get a sense of direction growing up in the morning shadow of the Blue Ridge—and, sure enough, I soon caught a peek of the Capitol dome in the distance, white as an egg in an eggcup. A couple of tattered colored gentlemen stumbled toward me from a boarded-up doorway, but I gave them each a dollar and a hearty God bless and strode on. If a man can't walk around in his own country without fear, what business does he have selling freedom to the Russians?

Bud Nevins got me and my banjos—a fine old Gibson mother-of-pearl-trimmed Masterton and an S. S. Stewart backup whose thumb string always sounded a little punky—into Moscow and put us all to bed in a spare room of the big apartment that he and his wife and three children occupied in the cement warehouse where the Russians stashed free-world diplomatic staff. April Nevins was a long-haired strawberry blonde beginning to acquire the tight, worried expression that the wives of ministers and government officials get, from being saddled with the husbands' careers. You get the pecking-order blues. The bygone summer hadn't done much to refresh her freckles, and a long white winter lay ahead. This was late September, shirtless apple-picking time back home. The puff on the bed they put me in smelled old-fashionedly of flake soap, the way my mother's laundry used to when I helped her carry the wet wash basket out back to the clothesline.

As he put me to bed, Nevins said that something had already come for me in the diplomatic pouch. An envelope lay on my pillow, addressed to me care of the embassy APO number in a scrunched-up hand in black ballpoint. Inside was a long letter from Imogene, recounting her sorrowful feelings after I left and guessing that I was still alive because my death in her neighborhood hadn't been in the papers and she had caught on the radio a plug for an appearance of mine in St. Louis. She recalled some sexual details I had half forgotten and wasn't sure needed to be put down on paper, and promised undying love. I just skimmed the second page. Her words weren't easy to read; the individual letters looked like they wanted to double back on themselves, and I was dog-tired from those thousands of miles I had traveled to reach the dark side of the moon.

Now, I've seen a lot of friendly crowds in the course of my professional life, but I must say I've never seen as many lovable, well-disposed people as I did that month in Russia. They were—at least the ones that weren't in any gulag—full of beans, up all night and bouncy the next morning. The young ones didn't have that shadowy look that American children were taking on, as if dragged out from watching television; these young Russians seemed to be looking directly at life. I hated to think it, but they were unspoiled. Grins poured from the students I played for, in one drafty old classroom after another. Converted ballrooms, many of them seemed to be. Or not even converted—they just took the dancers and musicians out and moved the desks in. There were dusty moldings and plaster garlands high along the peeling plaster walls, and velvet czarist drapes rotting around a view of some damp little park where old women in babushkas, so gnarled and hunched our own society would have had them on the junk heap, swept the dirt paths with brooms that were just twigs tied to sticks. Everything was still used here.

I had worked up a little talk. I would begin with the banjo as an African instrument, called *banza* in the French colonies of West Africa and *banjer* in the American South, where in some backwaters you could still hear it called that. Slaves played it, and then there were the traveling minstrel shows, in which white performers like Dan Emmett and Joel Walker Sweeney used the traditional black "stroke" or "frailing" or "claw-hammer" style of striking down across the strings with thumb and the back of the index-finger nail (I would demonstrate). Then (still demonstrating) I would tell of the rise of the "finger-picking" or "guitar" style, adding the middle finger and pulling *up* on the strings with metal picks on those three fingers, and end with bluegrass and traditional folk as revived by my hero, Seeger. When I had said all that, in about half an hour, with samples of what we think minstrel banjo sounded like, and some rags from the 1890s, the way Vess L. Ossman and Fred Van Eps left them on Edison cylinders, and a little Leadbelly at the end, they would ask me why Americans oppressed their black people.

I got better at answering that one, as I strummed and picked and rolled through those echoing classrooms. I stopped saying that slavery had been universal not long ago, that the Russians had had the serfs, that several hundred thousand white men from the North had died so that slaves could be free, that a hundred years later civil-rights laws had been passed and lynching had become a rarity. I would tell, as I stood there listening to myself being translated, that I was losing them. What I was saying was too much like what they heard from their own teachers, too much historical inevitability. I simply said yes, it was a problem, a disgraceful problem, but that I honestly believed America was working at it, and music was one of the foremost ways it was working at it. Listening to myself talk, I would sometimes think that the State Department knew what it was doing, bringing a natural patriotic optimist like me over here. Ever since JFK had been shot, my breed had been harder to find. They must have had a pretty fat file on me somewhere; the thought made me uneasy.

I felt best when I played, played as if for a country-fair crowd back home, and those young Russian faces would light up as if I were telling jokes. They had all heard jazz, and even some twist and early rock on tapes that were smuggled through, but rarely anything so jaunty and tinny and jolly, so *irrepressible,* as banjo music going full steam, when your fingers do the thinking and you listen in amazement yourself. Sometimes thy would pair me with a balalaika player, and one little Azerbaijani—I think he had some Gypsy blood—tried my instrument, and I his. We made an act of it for a few days, touring the Caucasus, where old men with beards would gather outside the auditorium windows as if sipping moonshine. When they had me advertised ahead for a formal concert, the crowds were so big that the Soviet controller cut down on the schedule.

The translator who traveled with me kept changing, but usually it was Nadia, a lean, thin-lipped lady over forty who had learned her English during the war, in the military. She had lost two brothers and a fiancé to Hitler, and was wed to the Red system with bonds of iron and grief. She looked like a skinny, tall, stunned soldier boy herself, just out of uniform—no lipstick, a long, white, waxy nose, and a feathery short haircut with gray coming in, not in strands but in patches. Blank-faced, she would listen to my spiel, give a nod when she'd heard all she could hold, and spout out a stream of this language that was, with all its mushy, twisty sounds, pure music to me. The more she and I traveled together, the better she knew what I was going to say, and the longer she could let me go before translating, and the more I could hear individual words go by, and little transparent phrases through which I seemed to see into her as if into a furnace through a mica window. We traveled on trains in the same compartment, so I could look down from the top bunk and see her hands remove her shoes and her mustard-colored stockings, and then her bare feet and hands flitter out of sight. I would listen, but never heard her breathing relax; she confessed to me toward the end of my stay that she could never sleep on trains. The motion and clicking stirred her up.

An inhibiting factor was Bud Nevins's being in the compartment with us—there were two bunks on two sides—or if, not Bud, another escort from our embassy, and often a fourth, an underling of Bud's or a second escort from the Soviet side, who spoke Armenian or Kazakh or whatever the language was going to be when we disembarked. Sometimes I had more escorts than would fit into one compartment; I think I often got the best night's sleep, with everybody watching everybody else. Nadia was as loyal a Communist as they made, but seemed to need watching anyway. As I got to know her body language, I could tell when we were being crowded, politically speaking.

After a while I tended to bond with the Communists. When we arrived at one of our hinterland destinations, Nadia and her associates would bundle me into a Zil, and then we would share irritation at being tailed by an embassy watchdog in his imported Chevrolet. When we all went south, Bud came along with that willowy, redheaded wife of his. April had, along with her worried look, a plump, pretty mouth a little too full of teeth. For all their three children, they hadn't been married ten years. Out of wifely love and loyalty she wanted to join in what fun the Soviet Union in its sinister vastness offered.

Somewhere in backwoods Georgia we visited a monastery, a showpiece of 45
religious tolerance. The skeleton crew of monks glided around with us in their grim stone rooms. The place had a depressing, stuffy, holy smell—old candle wax and chrism and furniture polish—that I hadn't sniffed for thirty years, and then in the storage closet of a Baptist basement Sunday school. Among the monks with beards down to their bellies was a young one, and I wondered how

he had enlisted himself in this ghostly brotherhood. Demented, or a government employee, I decided. He had silky long hair, like a princess captive in a tower, and the sliding onyx eyeballs of a spy. He was one kind of human animal, and I was another, and when we looked at each other, we each repressed a shudder.

Outside, a little crowd of shepherds and sheep, neither group looking any too clean, had gathered around the automobiles, and when Nadia had made our identities and curious mission clear, the shepherds invited us to dine with them, on one of the sheep. I would have settled for some cabbage soup and blini back at the Tbilisi hotel, but the Nevinses looked stricken, as though this chance at authentic ethnicity and bridge-building would never come again, and I suppose it wouldn't have. Their duty was to see that I did my duty, and my duty was clear: consort with the shepherds, scoring points for the free world. I looked toward Nadia, and with one of her unsmiling nods she approved, though this hadn't been on her schedule. Or—who knows?—maybe it had been. By now I saw her as an ally in my mission to subvert the proletariat, no doubt deluding myself.

We climbed for what seemed like a mile and sat down around a kind of campfire, where an ominous big kettle was mulling over some bony chunks of a recently living creature. The shepherds loved April's long ironed hair and the way her round freckled knees peeped out of her skirt as we squatted on our circle of rock perches. After the goatskin of red wine (as stated before, I'm no connoisseur of alcoholic beverages, but this stuff was so rough that flies kept dying in it, and a full swig removed the paint from the roof of your mouth) had been passed a few times, she began to relish their attention, to glow and giggle and switch her long limbs around and come up with her phrases of language-school Russian. Those shepherds—agricultural workers and livestock supervisors was probably how they thought of themselves—had a number of unsolved dental problems, as we saw when their whiskers cracked open in a laugh, but a lot of love hovered around that simmering pot, a lot of desire for international peace. Even Bud took off his jacket and unbuttoned his top shirt button, and Nadia began to lounge back in the scree and translate me loosely, with what heard as her own original material. The lamb when it came, in tin bowls, could have been mulled somewhat longer, and was mixed with what looked like crabgrass, roots and all, and some little green capers that each had a firecracker inside, but as it turned out, only the Nevinses got sick. Next day they had to stay in their hotel room with the shades lowered while the Communists and I motored out to entertain at a People's War veterans home with a view of Mount Elbrus. The way we all cackled in the car at the expense of the Nevinses and their tender capitalist stomachs was the cruelest thing I saw come to pass in my month in the Soviet Union.

Uzbekistan, Tajikistan, Kazakhstan: you wondered why God ever made so much wasteland in the world, with a gold dome or a blue lake now and then as a sop to the thirsty soul. But here's where the next revolution was coming from, it turned out—out from under those Islamic turbans. When my banjo flashed mother-of-pearl their way, they made the split-finger sign to ward off the evil eye. They knew a devil's gadget when they saw it.

Whenever I showed up back in Moscow, I was solemnly handed packets of letters in Imogene's cramped black hand, pages and pages and pages of them. I couldn't believe the paper she wasted, and the abuse of taxpayer money involved in using the diplomatic pouch. She had heard me take an eight-bar vocal break on my Decca cut of "Somebody Loves You, Darlin'," on a station out of Charlottesville, and had decided that it was a code to announce that I was leaving my wife for her. "I am altogether open and YOURS, my dearest DEAREST Eddie," she wrote, if I can remember one sentence in all that trash. "I will wait for as LONG as it takes, though KINGDOM COME in the meantime," if I can recall another. Then on and on, with every detail of what she did each day, with some about her internal workings that I would rather not be told, though I was happy she had her period, and all about her unhappiness (that I wasn't there with her) and hopefulness (that I soon would be), and her theory that I was in the air talking to her all the time, broadcasting from every frequency on the dial, including the shortwave that brought in stations from the Caribbean and Western Europe. If she caught Osborne and Martin doing "My Lonely Heart" or "You'll Never Be the Same," she knew that I was their personal friend and had asked them to send her a private message—never mind that they had recorded it in the early fifties. I couldn't do more than skim a page here and there; the handwriting would get smaller and scrunchier and then blossom out into some declaration of love printed in capitals and triple underlined. Just the envelopes, the bulky white tumble of them, were embarrassing me in front of Bud Nevins and the whole embassy staff, embattled here in the heartland of godless communism. How could I be a cultural ambassador shouldering this ridiculous load of puling, mewing, conceited infatuation?

Imogene was planning where we would live, how she would dress for her 50
seat of honor at my concerts, what she would do for me in the bedroom and the kitchen to keep my love at its present sky-high pitch. Thinking we were in for a lifetime together, she filled me in on her family—her mother, whom she had maligned but who wasn't all bad, and her father, who was scarcely in her life enough to mention, and her brothers and sisters, who sounded like the worst pack of losers and freeloaders in the Delmarva Peninsula. My fear was that her outpourings would not escape the vigilance of the KGB, x-raying the diplomatic pouch. I would lose face with Nadia, that steely exemplar of doing without. The innocent-eyed gymnasium students would sense my contamination. The homely austerity of Soviet life, with that undercurrent of fear left over from Stalin, made the amorous delusions of this childish American woman repulsive to me. As my month approached its end and the capitalist world was putting out feelers to reclaim me, Imogene's crazy stuff got mixed in with businesslike communications from my agent and colorless but friendly letters

from my wife with notes and dutiful drawings from my children enclosed. This heightened my disgust and helpless indignation. I would have sent a cable—CUT IT OUT, OR YOU AIN'T NO BLUE-EYED SWEETHEART OF MINE—but by some canniness of her warped mind she never gave a return address, and when I tried to think of her apartment, all I got was that black-and-white feeling: the way she fed me her breasts one at a time, the very big radio, and the empty street with the Capitol at the end like a white-chocolate candy. I had simply to endure it, this sore humiliation.

They had saved Leningrad for me to the last, since it was where the Communists, still remembering the siege, were the toughest, and I might run into the most hostility from an audience. But as soon as my Gibson began talking, the picked strings all rolling like the synchronized wheels, big and little, of the *Wabash Cannonball,* the smiles of mutual understanding would start breaking out. I am not a brave man, but I have faith in my instrument and in people's decent instincts. St. Petersburg, as we call it again, is one beautiful city, a Venice where you least expect it, all those big curved buildings in Italian colors. The students in their gloomy old ballrooms were worried about Goldwater getting elected, and I told them that the American people would never elect a warmonger. I was always introduced as a "progressive" American folk artist, but I had to tell them that there wasn't much progressive about me—my folks had been lifelong Democrats, because of a war fought a hundred years ago, and I wasn't going to be the one to change parties.

Then, just as I was about to get back onto Aeroflot, Khrushchev was pushed out of power, and all the Soviets around me tightened up, wary of what was going to happen next. This whole huge empire was run out of some back rooms by a few beetle-browed men. Nadia—my voice, my guide, my protector, closer to me for this month than a wife, because I couldn't have done without her—complimented me by confiding, somewhere out on the Nevsky Prospekt, or in some hallway where no bugs were likely to be placed, "Eddie, it was not civilized. It was not done how a civilized country should do things. We should have said 'Thank you very much for ending the terror.' And then 'You are excused—too much adventurism, okay, failures in agricultural production, and et cetera. Okay, so long, but *bolshoi* thanks.'"

At moments, toward the end of a long public day in, say, Tashkent her English would deteriorate, out of sheer weariness from drawing on two sets of brain cells, and her eyelids and the tip of her long white nose would get pink. We would say goodnight in the hotel lobby, with its musty-attic smell and lamps whose bases were brass bears, and she would give me in her handshake not the palm and the meat of the thumb but four cool fingers, aligned like a sergeant's stripes. That was the way we began to say good-bye in the airport, until we leaped the gulf between our two great countries and I kissed her on one cheek and then the other and hugged her, in proper Slavic style. Her eyes teared up, but it may have been just the start of a cold.

Bud told me in the airport, so casually that I should have smelled trouble, "We took you off the APO number two days ago, so your mail won't show up here after you leave. It will be forwarded to your home."

"Sounds reasonable," I said, not thinking.

Coming back, on the last leg, out of Paris, I had an experience such as I've never had again in all my miles of flying. We came down on the big arc over Gander and Nova Scotia and from five miles up I could see New York, hundreds of miles away, a little blur of light in the cold plastic oval of the plane window which grew and grew, like a fish I was pulling in. My cheek got cold against the plastic as I pressed to keep the light in view, a spot on the invisible surface of the earth like a nebula, like a dust mouse, only glowing, the fuzzy center of our heavenly liberty. Just it and me, there in the night sky, communing. It was a vision.

After I cleared customs at Kennedy, I phoned home, though it was after ten o'clock. I was so happy to be in the land of the free. My wife answered with something in her voice besides welcome, like a fearful salamander under a big warm rock. "Some letters for you came today and yesterday," she said. "All from one person, it looks like."

How bright this airport was, I thought, compared with the one in Moscow. Every corner and rampway was lit as harshly as a mug shot. The place was packed with advertisements and snack bars, sizzling with electricity. "Did you open them?" I asked, my heart suddenly plunked by a heavy hand.

"Just one," she said. "That was enough, Eddie. Oh, my."

"It wasn't anything," I began, which wasn't a hundred percent true. For though I was very unhappy with Imogene for making what looked to be an ongoing mess, you can't blame a person for thinking you're a god. You have to feel a spark of fondness, remembering the way she held up one breast and then the other, each nipple looking in that black-and-white room like the hole of a gun barrel pointed straight at your mouth. You can go to the dark side of the moon and back and see nothing more wonderful and strange than the way men and women get together.

CHARTING THE STORY

1 What motivated each of Eddie's three lies to Imogene in the course of their short encounter?

2 What were Eddie's first impressions of Russia on his Aeroflot flight from Paris? How does his attitude change in the course of the story? For what aspects of Russian society does he express great admiration?

3 What does Eddie consider to be the "official" objective of his being chosen as a cultural ambassador to the Soviet Union? In the end, is this objective realized?

4 How do issues of politics, music and marital infidelity serve both to inform and entertain in this story?

CONSIDERATIONS OF STYLE

1 Describe the narrator's *persona* as characterized in the way he speaks of himself and others. Does he truly seem to be the "country boy" that he describes himself to be? Why, or why not? Were the narrator to have come from another environment (more urban, "less married," different vocation), how might the text be affected?

2 How might the story be different if the narrator had set it down immediately upon returning home, rather than after a hiatus of decades? (How does one know when the story was narrated?)

3 Of what significance is the metaphor of the Cold War? How does it intersect with other images and metaphors in the text?

AFTERTHOUGHTS

1 How has Eddie's month-long stay in the Soviet Union changed his perspectives on both his own and his host country?

2 Do you consider Eddie's attitude towards his marital infidelity typical of most Americans? Does it reflect an attitude typical of your generation or gender?

THE WRITER'S CRAFT

1 From the point of view of one of the Russians, write a short piece reacting to Eddie's visit.

2 Write about an experience abroad that changed your perspective on your own and your host country.

3 Discuss the "hot-button" issue of marital infidelity from a cross-cultural perspective.

LESLIE MARMON SILKO

LESLIE MARMON SILKO, *of Mexican, Anglo, and Laguna Pueblo ancestry, was born in Albuquerque, New Mexico in 1948. She grew up on the Laguna Pueblo reservation, where she learned the lore of her people from female relatives. Silko was graduated from the University of New Mexico in 1969. She has taught at Navajo Community College in Many Farms, Arizona and at the University of New Mexico, and currently teaches at the University of Arizona, Tucson.*

Silko's works include a collection of stories, The Man to Send Rain Clouds *(1974); a book of poems,* Laguna Woman *(1974); the novels* Ceremony *(1977)—the first by a Native American Woman—and* Almanac of Death *(1991); and a miscellany of family history, fiction, photographs, and poems,* Storyteller *(1981).*

"Yellow Woman" makes references to the myths of Native American peoples, who regard them as a way of documenting their histories. It contains evocative descriptions of the Southwest, and is an intriguing love story. It is included in The Man to Send Rain Clouds.

PERSPECTIVES

1 What myths by or about Native Americans did you learn while you were growing up? How did they shape your perceptions of American culture as a whole? How do they define American culture today?

2 What myths and mythological heroes prevail in contemporary American culture?

Yellow Woman

I

My thigh clung to his with dampness, and I watched the sun rising up through the tamaracks and willows. The small brown water birds came to the river and hopped across the mud, leaving brown scratches in the alkali-white crust. They bathed in the river silently. I could hear the water, almost at our feet where the narrow fast channel bubbled and washed green ragged moss and fern leaves. I looked at him beside me, rolled in the red blanket on the white river sand. I cleaned the sand out of the cracks between my toes, squinting because the sun was above the willow trees. I looked at him for the last time, sleeping on the white river sand.

I felt hungry and followed the river south the way we had come the afternoon before, following our footprints that were already blurred by lizard tracks and bug trails. The horses were still lying down, and the black one whinnied when he saw me but he did not get up—maybe it was because the corral was made out of thick cedar branches and the horses had not yet felt the sun like I had. I tried to look beyond the pale red mesas to the pueblo. I knew it was there, even if I could not see it, on the sand rock hill above the river, the same river that moved past me now and had reflected the moon last night.

The horse felt warm underneath me. He shook his head and pawed the sand. The bay whinnied and leaned against the gate trying to follow, and I remembered him asleep on the red blanket beside the river. I slid off the horse and tied him close to the other horse. I walked north with the river again, and the white sand broke loose in footprints over footprints.

"Wake up."

He moved in the blanket and turned his face to me with his eyes still closed. I knelt down to touch him.

"I'm leaving."

He smiled now, eyes still closed. "You are coming with me, remember?" He sat up now with his bare dark chest and belly in the sun.

"Where?"

"To my place."

"And will I come back?"

He pulled his pants on. I walked away from him, feeling him behind me and smelling the willows.

"Yellow Woman," he said.

I turned to face him. "Who are you?" I asked.

He laughed and knelt on the low, sandy bank, washing his face in the river. "Last night you guessed my name, and you knew why I had come."

I stared past him at the shallow moving water and tried to remember the night, but I could only see the moon in the water and remember his warmth around me.

"But I only said that you were him and that I was Yellow Woman—I'm not really her—I have my own name and I come from the pueblo on the other side of the mesa. Your name is Silva and you are a stranger I met by the river yesterday afternoon."

He laughed softly. "What happened yesterday has nothing to do with what you will do today, Yellow Woman."

"I know—that's what I'm saying—the old stories about the ka'tsina spirit and Yellow Woman can't mean us."

My old grandpa liked to tell those stories best. There is one about Badger and Coyote who went hunting and were gone all day, and when the sun was going down they found a house. There was a girl living there alone, and she had light hair and eyes and she told them that they could sleep with her. Coyote wanted to be with her all night so he sent Badger into a prairie-dog hole, telling him he thought he saw something in it. As soon as Badger crawled in, Coyote blocked up the entrance with rocks and hurried back to Yellow Woman.

"Come here," he said gently.

He touched my neck and I moved close to him to feel his breathing and to hear his heart. I was wondering if Yellow Woman had known who she was—if she knew that she would become part of the stories. Maybe she'd had another name that her husband and relatives called her so that only the ka'tsina from the north and the storytellers would know her as Yellow Woman. But I didn't go on; I felt him all around me, pushing me down into the white river sand.

Yellow Woman went away with the spirit from the north and lived with him and his relatives. She was gone for a long time, but then one day she came back and she brought twin boys.

"Do you know the story?"

"What story?" He smiled and pulled me close to him as he said this. I was afraid lying there on the red blanket. All I could know was the way he felt, warm, damp, his body beside me. This is the way it happens in the stories, I was thinking, with no thought beyond the moment she meets the ka'tsina spirit and they go.

"I don't have to go. What they tell in stories was real only then, back in time immemorial, like they say."

He stood up and pointed at my clothes tangled in the blanket. "Let's go," he said.

I walked beside him, breathing hard because he walked fast, his hand around my wrist. I had stopped trying to pull away from him, because his hand felt cool and the sun was high, drying the river bed into alkali. I will see someone, eventually I will see someone, and then I will be certain that he is only a man—some man from nearby—and I will be sure that I am not Yellow Woman. Because she is from out of time past and I live now and I've been to school and there are highways and pickup trucks that Yellow Woman never saw.

It was an easy ride north on horseback. I watched the change from the cottonwood trees along the river to the junipers that brushed past us in the foothills, and finally there were only piñons, and when I looked up at the rim of the mountain plateau I could see pine trees growing on the edge. Once I stopped to look down, but the pale sandstone had disappeared and the river was gone and the dark lava hills were all around. He touched my hand, not speaking, but always singing softly a mountain song and looking into my eyes.

I felt hungry and wondered what they were doing at home now—my mother, my grandmother, my husband, and the baby. Cooking breakfast, saying, "Where did she go?—maybe kidnapped," and Al going to the tribal police with the details: "She went walking along the river."

The house was made with black lava rock and red mud. It was high above the spreading miles of arroyos and long mesas. I smelled a mountain smell of pitch and buck brush. I stood there beside the black horse, looking down on the small, dim country we had passed, and I shivered.

"Yellow Woman, come inside where it's warm."

II

He lit a fire in the stove. It was an old stove with a round belly and an enamel coffeepot on top. There was only the stove, some faded Navajo blankets, and a bedroll and cardboard box. The floor was made of smooth abode plaster, and there was one small window facing east. He pointed at the box.

"There's some potatoes and the frying pan." He sat on the floor with his arms around his knees pulling them close to his chest and he watched me fry the potatoes. I didn't mind him watching me because he was always watching me—he had been watching me since I came upon him sitting on the river bank trimming leaves from a willow twig with his knife. We ate from the pan and he wiped the grease from his fingers on his Levi's.

"Have you brought women here before?" He smiled and kept chewing, so I said, "Do you always use the same tricks?"

"What tricks?" He looked at me like he didn't understand.

"The story about being a ka'tsina from the mountains. The story about Yellow Woman."

Silva was silent; his face was calm.

"I don't believe it. Those stories couldn't happen now," I said.

He shook his head and said softly, "But someday they will talk about us, and they will say, "Those two lived long ago when things like that happened.'"

He stood up and went out. I ate the rest of the potatoes and thought about things—about the noise the stove was making and the sound of the mountain wind outside. I remembered yesterday and the day before, and then I went outside.

I walked past the corral to the edge where the narrow trail cut through the black rim rock. I was standing in the sky with nothing around me but the wind that came down from the blue mountain peak behind me. I could see faint mountain images in the distance miles across the vast spread of mesas and valleys and plains. I wondered who was over there to feel the mountain wind on those sheer blue edges—who walks on the pine needles in those blue mountains.

"Can you see the pueblo?" Silva was standing behind me.

I shook my head. "We're too far away."

"From here I can see the world." He stepped out on the edge. "The Navajo reservation begins over there." He pointed to the east. "The Pueblo boundaries are over here." He looked below us to the south, were the narrow trail seemed to come from. "The Texans have their ranches over there, starting with that valley, the Concho Valley. The Mexicans run some cattle over there too."

"Do you ever work for them?"

"I steal from them," Silva answered. The sun was dropping behind us and shadows were filling the land below. I turned away from the edge that dropped forever into the valleys below.

"I'm cold," I said; "I'm going inside." I started wondering about this man who could speak the Pueblo language so well but who lived on a mountain and rustled cattle. I decided that this man Silva must be Navajo, because Pueblo men didn't do things like that.

"You must be a Navajo."

Silva shook his head gently. "Little Yellow Woman," he said, "you never give up, do you? I have told you who I am. The Navajo people know me, too." He knelt down and unrolled the bedroll and spread the extra blankets out on a piece of canvas. The sun was down, and the only light in the house came from outside—the dim orange light from sundown.

I stood there and waited for him to crawl under the blankets.

"What are you waiting for?" he said, and I lay down beside him. He undressed me slowly like the night before beside the river—kissing my face gently and running his hands up and down my belly and legs. He took off my pants and then he laughed.

"Why are you laughing?"

"You are breathing so hard."

I pulled away from him and turned my back to him.

He pulled me around and pinned me down with his arms and chest. "You don't understand, do you, little Yellow Woman? You will do what I want."

And again he was all around me with his skin slippery against mine, and I was afraid because I understood that his strength could hurt me. I lay underneath him and I knew that he could destroy me. But later, while he slept beside me, I touched his face and I had a feeling—the kind of feeling for him that overcame me that morning along the river. I kissed him on the forehead and he reached out for me.

When I woke up in the morning he was gone. It gave me a strange feeling because for a long time I sat there on the blankets and looked around the little house for some object of his—some proof that he had been there or maybe that he was coming back. Only the blankets and the cardboard box remained. The .30–30 that had been leaning in the corner was gone, and so was the knife I had used the night before. He was gone, and I had my chance to now. But first I had to eat, because I knew it would be a long walk home.

I found some dried apricots in the cardboard box, and I sat down on a rock at the edge of the plateau rim. There was no wind and the sun warmed me. I was surrounded by silence. I drowsed with apricots in my mouth, and I didn't believe that there were highways or railroads or cattle to steal.

When I woke up, I stared down at my feet in the black mountain dirt. Little black ants were swarming over the pine needles around my foot. They must have smelled the apricots. I thought about my family far below me. They would be wondering about me, because this had never happened to me before. The tribal police would file a report. But if old Grandpa weren't dead he would tell them what happened—he would laugh and say, "Stolen by a ka'tsina, a mountain spirit. She'll come home—they usually do." There are enough of them to handle things. My mother and grandmother will raise the baby like they raised me. Al will find someone else, and they will go on like before, except that there will be a story about the day I disappeared while I was walking along the river. Silva had come for me; he said he had. I did not decide to go. I just went. Moonflowers blossom in the sand hills before dawn, just as I followed him. That's what I was thinking as I wandered along the trail through the pine trees. 60

It was noon when I got back. When I saw the stone house I remembered that I had meant to go home. But that didn't seem important anymore, maybe because there were little blue flowers growing in the meadow behind the stone house and the gray squirrels were playing in the pines next to the house. The horses were standing in the corral, and there was a beef carcass hanging on the shady side of a big pine in front of the house. Flies buzzed around the clotted blood that hung from the carcass. Silva was washing his hands in a bucket full of water. He must have heard me coming because he spoke to me without turning to face me.

"I've been waiting for you."

"I went walking in the big pine trees."

I looked into the bucket full of bloody water with brown-and-white animal hairs floating in it. Silva stood there letting his hand drip, examining me intently.

"Are you coming with me?" 65

"Where?" I asked him.

"To sell the meat in Marquez."

"If you're sure it's O.K."

"I wouldn't ask you if it wasn't," he answered.

He sloshed the water around in the bucket before he dumped it out and set the bucket upside down near the door. I followed him to the corral and watched him saddle the horses. Even beside the horses he looked tall, and asked him again if he wasn't Navajo. He didn't say anything; he just shook his head and kept cinching up the saddle. 70

"But Navajos are tall."

"Get on the horse," he said, "and let's go."

The last thing he did before we started down the steep trail was to grab the .30–30 from the corner. He slid the rifle into the scabbard that hung from his saddle.

"Do they ever try to catch you?" I asked.

"They don't know who I am."

"Then why did you bring the rifle?"

"Because we are going to Marquez where the Mexicans live."

III

The trail leveled out on a narrow ridge that was steep on both sides like an animal spine. On one side I could see where the trail went around the rocky gray hills and disappeared into the southeast where the pale sandrock mesas stood in the distance near my home. On the other side was a trail that went west, and as I looked far into the distance I thought I saw the little town. But Silva said no, that I was looking in the wrong place, that I just thought I saw houses. After that I quit looking off into the distance; it was hot and the wildflowers were closing up their deep-yellow petals. Only the waxy cactus flowers bloomed in the bright sun, and I saw every color that a cactus blossom can be; the white ones and the red ones were still buds, but the purple and the yellow were blossoms, open full and the most beautiful of all.

Silva saw him before I did. The white man was riding a big gray horse, coming up the trail toward us. He was traveling fast and the gray horse's feet sent rocks rolling off the trail into the dry tumbleweeds. Silva motioned for me to stop and we watched the white man. He didn't see us right away, but finally his horse whinnied at our horses and he stopped. He looked at us briefly before he loped the gray horse across the three hundred yards that separated us. He stopped his horse in front of Silva, and his young fat face was shadowed by the brim of his hat. He didn't look mad, but his small, pale eyes moved from the blood-soaked gunny sacks hanging from my saddle to Silva's face and then back to my face.

"Where did you get the fresh meat?" the white man asked.

"I've been hunting," Silva said, and when he shifted his weight in the saddle the leather creaked.

"The hell you have, Indian. You've been rustling cattle. We've been looking for the thief for a long time."

The rancher was fat, and sweat began to soak through his white cowboy shirt and the wet cloth stuck to the thick rolls of belly fat. He almost seemed to be panting from the exertion of talking, and he smelled rancid, maybe because Silva scared him.

Silva turned to me and smiled. "Go back up the mountain, Yellow Woman."

The white man got angry when he heard Silva speak in a language he couldn't understand. "Don't try anything, Indian. Just keep riding to Marquez. We'll call the state police from there."

The rancher must have been unarmed because he was very frightened and if he had a gun he would have pulled it out then. I turned my horse around and the rancher yelled, "Stop!" I looked at Silva for an instant and there was something ancient and dark—something I could feel in my stomach—in his eyes, and when I glanced at his hand I saw his finger on the trigger of the .30–30 that was still in the saddle scabbard. I slapped my horse across the flank and the sacks of raw meat swung against my knees as the horse leaped up the trail. It was hard to keep my balance, and once I thought I felt the saddle slipping backward; it was because of this that I could not look back.

I didn't stop until I reached the ridge where the trail forked. The horse was breathing deep gasps and there was a dark film of sweat on its neck. I looked down in the direction I had come from, but I couldn't see the place. I waited. The wind came up and pushed warm air past me. I looked up at the sky, pale blue and full of thin clouds and fading vapor trails left by jets.

I think four shots were fired—I remember hearing four hollow explosions that reminded me of deer hunting. There could have been more shots after that, but I couldn't have heard them because my horse was running again and the loose rocks were making too much noise as they scattered around his feet.

Horses have a hard time running downhill, but I went that way instead of uphill to the mountain because I thought it was safer. I felt better with the horse running southeast past the round gray hills that were covered with cedar trees and black lava rock. When I got to the plain in the distance I could see the dark green patches of tamaracks that grew along the river; and beyond the river I could see the beginning of the pale sandrock mesas. I stopped the horse and looked back to see if anyone was coming; then I got off the horse and turned the horse around, wondering if it would go back to its corral under the pines on the mountain. It looked back at me for a moment and then plucked a mouthful of green tumbleweeds before it trotted back up the trail with its ears pointed forward, carrying its head daintily to one side to avoid stepping on the dragging reins. When the horse disappeared over the last hill, the gunny sacks full of meat were still swinging and bouncing.

IV

I walked toward the river on a wood-hauler's road that I knew would eventually lead to the paved road. I was thinking about waiting beside the road for someone to drive by, but by the time I got to the pavement I had decided it wasn't very far to walk if I followed the river back the way Silva and I had come.

The river water tasted good, and I sat in the shade under a cluster of silvery willows. I thought about Silva, and I felt sad at leaving him; still, there was something strange about him, and I tried to figure it out all the way back home.

I came back to the place on the river bank where he had been sitting the first time I saw him. The green willow leaves that he had trimmed from the branch were still lying there, wilted in the sand. I saw the leaves and I wanted to go back to him—to kiss him and to touch him—but the mountains were too far away now. And I told myself, because I believe it, he will come back sometime and be waiting again by the river.

I followed the path up from the river into the village. The sun was getting low, and I could smell supper cooking when I got to the screen door of my house. I could hear their voices inside—my mother was telling my grandmother how to fix the Jell-O and my husband, Al, was playing with the baby. I decided to tell them that some Navajo had kidnapped me, but I was sorry that old Grandpa wasn't alive to hear my story because it was the Yellow Woman stories he liked to tell best.

CHARTING THE STORY

1 Part I of the story opens with the romantic encounter of a man and a woman on a river bank. Describe the "power dynamic" in the couple's relationship.
2 In Paragraph 20, the story line of the encounter is interrupted by a reference to the Native American myth of Coyote, Badger, and Yellow Woman. How does this myth help to define the female narrator as a character in the story?
3 What light does the reference to the narrator's family in Paragraph 60 shed on the story?
4 How does Part III contribute to the story's narrative development, and how is the conflict resolved in Part IV?

CONSIDERATIONS OF STYLE

1 How does the author temper the sensual description of the romantic encounter on the river bank? Why do you suppose she does this, rather than write it more erotically?
2 Discuss the particular focus of the descriptions of landscape and place in Paragraphs 29, 42, 61, and 78.

AFTERTHOUGHTS

1 What are some possible motivations for the narrator's actions in the story? What might motivate Silva?
2 What does this story seem to say about the toleration of marital infidelity in the mythology of the narrator's culture, as well as in her culture outside the realm of myth? Compare the attitudes of various cultures on this issue.
3 British anthropologist Bronislaw Malinowski noted that "All history is saga and myth." How do saga and myth shape the narrator's perceptions of her people's history?

THE WRITER'S CRAFT

1 Research a myth from a book, a web site, or a storyteller, and analyze its salient features.
2 Compose a myth explaining a phenomenon in contemporary American culture.
3 How would the narrator tell her story, perhaps a few months later, to the spirit of her grandfather? From the point of view of the grandfather listening and asking questions—or of the narrator telling the tale—relate such a narrative.

MARGARET ATWOOD

MARGARET ATWOOD *was born in Ottawa, Ontario in 1939 and spent a large part of her childhood in rural northern Quebec. She went to school in Toronto and earned a BA from Victoria College, University of Toronto and an MA from "the dreaded" Harvard University.*

Atwood is one of Canada's most acclaimed and prolific writers, the author of more than twenty-five books, including novels, poetry and short story collections, books for children, and criticism. She has edited or co-edited several anthologies, and has written dramatic works, television and radio scripts, and libretti—and has produced drawings, watercolors, cover illustrations, and comic strips.

"Postcard" is from the poetry collection True Stories, *published in 1981. While the eponymous postcard concludes with the conventional "Wish you were here," the rest of the message belies the conventional.*

PERSPECTIVES

1. When does Absence Make the Heart Grow Fonder, and when does Out of Sight mean Out of Mind? How do these contradictory notions come together to befuddle separated lovers?
2. When you know you will be receiving a postcard from someone, what things do you expect to find—not only in the message, but in the photograph?

Postcard

I'm thinking of you. What else can I say?
The palm trees on the reverse
are a delusion; so is the pink sand.
What we have are the usual
fractured coke bottles and the smell
of backed-up drains, too sweet,
like a mango on the verge
of rot, which we have also.

The air clear sweat, mosquitoes
& their tracks; birds, blue & elusive.

Time comes in waves here, a sickness, one
day after the other rolling on;
I move up, it's called
awake, then down into the uneasy
nights but never
forward. The roosters crow
for hours before dawn, and a prodded
child howls & howls
on the pocked road to school.
In the hold with the baggage
there are two prisoners,
their heads shaved by bayonets, & ten crates
of queasy chicks. Each spring
there's a race of cripples, from the store
to the church. This is the sort of junk
I carry with me; and a clipping
about democracy from the local paper.
Outside the window
they're building the damn hotel,
nail by nail, someone's
crumbling dream. A universe that includes you
can't be all bad, but
does it? At this distance
you're a mirage, a glossy image
fixed in the posture
of the last time I saw you.
Turn you over, there's the place
for the address. Wish you were
here. Love comes
in waves like the ocean, a sickness which goes on
& on, a hollow cave
in the head, filling and pounding, a kicked ear.

CHARTING THE POEM

1 What expectations might the speaker have harbored of her tropical "paradise"? Which aspects of the place are really "a delusion" and which probably not? How do the delusional and the real combine to create a sense of place in the first stanza of the poem?

2 Who do you suppose are the two prisoners in the hold with the baggage? What is the effect of the change of venue implied in this line?

3 What is "the sort of junk" that the speaker is carrying, literally and figuratively?

CONSIDERATIONS OF STYLE

1 What is the effect on the reader—especially in reading the poem aloud—of the jagged lines? How does form suggest content here?

2 Despite its jagged edges, the poem has an element of symmetry. What is the speaker suggesting by turning the lover into a postcard?

AFTERTHOUGHTS

1 Stanza 2 opens by noting: "Time comes in waves here, a sickness, one/ day after the other rolling on; " and concludes: "...Love comes/ in waves like the ocean, a sickness which goes on/ & on, a hollow cave/ in the head, filling and pounding, a kicked ear." What kind of response do you think the speaker hopes to elicit from the recipient of this postcard?

2 Had the writer travelled to a locale not in the tropics and not in an underdeveloped area, how might the postcard differ? If there were less disparity between the postcard photograph and the actual environment, how might the writer's thoughts about the lover change?

THE WRITER'S CRAFT

1 Having received the postcard, write a response—in poetry or prose.

2 In your own locale, design three sample postcards (illustrating, then writing about your choice of design and location) to elicit three different responses in a lover: renewal of love; "wish I were there"; and ennui or malaise.

TED HUGHES

TED HUGHES *was born Edward James Hughes in Mytholmroyd, Yorkshire, England. He had planned to use the public name E J Hughes, but his wife of seven years, poet Sylvia Plath, submitted one of his poems for publication under the name "Ted" and so the name stuck. Hughes was graduated from Pembroke College, London in 1954 in archeology and anthropology, having become disenchanted with the school's English curriculum.*

In 1956, Hughes met Plath, an American studying in England, and the two shared a deep admiration for each other's poems. They married in 1956. By 1962, their marriage had run into difficulties—which Plath interpreted as a sign of inevitable impermanence, and which is said to have led to her suicide in 1963. Hughes's second wife, Assia Wevill, also took her own life—and that of their young daughter. After an interval marked by many darkly intense poems, Hughes married Carol Orchard, who with whom he enjoyed 28 putatively happy years until his death in 1998.

According to his obituary in the London Times, *Hughes was "perhaps the most widely read serious poet of his time." Hughes was also praised for his contribution to the literary life of Britain, in particular for his sponsorship of young or neglected poets. His appointment as Poet Laureate signaled a turning point in that office, the major function of which is to write verse for state occasions.*

Hughes was a prodigious poet as well as a writer of highly acclaimed children's books, anthologies, and criticism.

"Incompatibilities" comes from his 1957 book The Hawk in the Rain.

PERSPECTIVES

1 What criteria for compatibility do you seek in a casual date? In a more "serious" relationship? In a life-partner?
2 What role does desire play in an erotic relationship? What platitudes are commonly expressed about sexual desire?

Incompatibilities

Desire's a vicious separator in spite
    Of its twisting women round men:

Cold-chisels two selfs single as it welds hot
  Iron of their separates to one.

Old Eden commonplace: something magnets
  And furnaces and with fierce
Hammer-blows the one body on the other knits
  Till the division disappears.

But desire outstrips those hands that a nothing fills,
  It dives into the opposite eyes,
Plummets through blackouts of impassables
  For the star that lights the face,

Each body still straining to follow down
  The maelstrom dark of the other, their limbs flail
Flesh and beat upon
  The inane everywhere of its obstacle,

Each, each second, lonelier and further
  Falling alone through the endless
Without-world of the other, through both here
  Twist so close they choke their cries.

CHARTING THE POEM

1. What negative sentiments, expressed in specific images, does Hughes employ to render the couple "incompatible"?
2. What bodily images track through the poem; do they seem random, or is there a progression? What pattern, or defiance of a pattern, do you observe?

CONSIDERATIONS OF STYLE

1. Read the poem aloud, conveying the sense of its rhythm and alliteration operating as one, as the couple making love become one.
2. What idiosyncratic use does Hughes make of compound (hyphenated) nouns and other word forms? What images do these "semantically full" words convey?

AFTERTHOUGHTS

1. Could this poem speak of homoerotic love in the same terms?
2. What is the "Old Eden commonplace" to which Hughes alludes?

THE WRITER'S CRAFT

1. Biblical accounts wrote of Adam and Eve's (and all other couples') "knowing" one another as a way to convey coitus. Even the expression "sexual intercourse" infers a ground for communication, and so of "knowledge." Contrast these notions with those of this poem. Upon what grounds do Hughes's lovers meet?
2. Compare the notion of incompatibility/incompatibilities in this poem with that in Richard Hagopian's story "Wonderful People."

VIKRAM CHANDRA

VIKRAM CHANDRA *was born in New Delhi in 1961. He attended Pomona College in California and the Columbia University Film School. He holds an M.A. from Johns Hopkins University and an MFA from the University of Houston. Chandra's first novel,* Red Earth and Pouring Rain *(1995), won the David Higham Prize for Fiction and the Commonwealth Writers Prize for Best First Published Book.*

Chandra divides his time between Bombay and Washington DC, where he teaches writing at the George Washington University.

"Shanti," a love story set during World War II, is taken from Chandra's second book, a collection of connected stories, Love and Longing in Bombay *(1997).*

PERSPECTIVES

1 What knowledge of India's precolonial, colonial, and postcolonial history do you bring to this story? What knowledge of its multicultural character?

2 Research India's role in World War II, particularly its continuing struggle for Independence and the phenomenon of the Indian National Army, a breakaway group that forged ties to Japan.

3 Whom would you consider to be "the most evil man in the world," and why?

Shanti

I hate Sunday evenings. It's that slow descent into the dusk that oppresses me, that endless end with its undertaste of death. Not so long ago, one Sunday evening, I flipped the television off and on a dozen times, walked around my room three times, sat on the floor and tried to read a thriller, switched on the television again, and the relentless chatty joyousness finally drove me out of the house. I walked aimlessly through the streets, listening to the long echoes of children's games, tormented by a nostalgia that settled lightly over me. I had not the slightest idea of what I was looking for, but only that I was suddenly aware of my age, and it seemed cruel that time should pass so gently and leave behind long swathes of unremembered years. I walked, then, along the long curve of the seawall at Haji Ali, and came along towards the white shape of the mosque floating on the waters.

Then, at the intersection, I didn't know what to do. I stood, too tired for another long journey and too restless still to go home, and I was swaying a little from side to side. Then I felt a gentle tap on my shoulder. It was Subramaniam.

"Come along," he said. "I'll give you a drink."

He was carrying a tattered *thela,* and we stopped along the way to fill it with bread, marmalade, and bottles of soda. He lived in an old, shabby building near Tardeo, and we went up four flights of stone stairs worn thin in the centre. Inside the door marked "Subramaniam" in brass letters, I bent to take off my shoes, and I could see the space was cool and large. There were those old high ceilings, and walls hung with prints. I sat in the drawing room on a heavy teak couch, on worn cushions, and wriggled my toes on the cold marble. Subramaniam came in carrying a bowl of chips.

"New brand," he said, smiling, and he put the bowl down on the table at 5
my elbow. Then he poured me a drink. He sat in an armchair that creaked slightly, and raised his glass at me.

"Haven't seen you in a while," I said.

"Yes," he said. "Unfortunately my wife has been unwell."

"Sorry," I said. "I hope it's nothing serious."

He raised his shoulders in that awkward little shrug of his. "At a certain age everything is serious, and nothing is serious." He drank, and then put down his glass on the table with a crisp click. He looked keenly at me. "How is that Ayesha?"

"Yesterday, she was very bitter about a patriotic movie she saw," I said. 10
"She is in despair about the state of the country. What are we, she said. For a cynic she despairs a lot. She's my friend, but I don't understand her, not really."

He nodded. "Listen," he said. "I want to tell you a story."

A train drifting across a field of yellow grass. This is what he saw first. A plume of black smoke turning slowly in the white glare. He had gone up the long slope in front of the station, across the three tracks, and then up the rise, to the ridge which had turned out to be much, much further than he had thought. When he had reached it, and gone across, he had found himself on an endless plateau, a plain dotted with scrubby bushes, an endless flatness that vanished into the sky. So he had turned around and come back. He had already forgotten what he had hoped to find on the other side of the ridge, but for two months he had looked at it curling in the distance, and finally he had taken a walk to see the other side of it. Now the sun burnt on his shoulders. Now he came back over the ridge and saw the train drifting across a field of yellow grass.

It was 1945 and he was twenty years old. His name was Shiv, and he had a twin who was dead, killed in Delhi the year before when a Hindu procession had gone the wrong way. The newspapers had regretted the continued communal violence in the city, but had reported with relief that on this day there were only six dead. One of the six was his, one body identical down to the strangely short fifth toe on the left foot. He had never known the bitterness of small statistics, but now he carried it everywhere in his mouth. He had it now, as he stumbled with aching calves, back from his walk of no purpose. The day yawned before him. He lived with his sister and her husband in a large bungalow a minute and a half's walk from the station. In the house there were a dozen novels he had read already, his B.Sc. degree framed on a wall, and two small children he could not bear to play with. He had come to live with his sister and her station-master husband after his silences had frightened his parents. His sister had loved him most, had loved him and his brother best after their birth at her eight years, and even now, grief-stricken, she found happiness and generosity enough in the safety of her home to comfort him. But the day, and life itself, stretched on forever like a bleak plain of yellow grass, and he felt himself walking, and the train drifted with its fantastic uncurling of smoke.

The train slowed imperceptibly as he walked. It must have, because he became aware that it was paused, halted at the station. But even then it moved, shimmering in the heat haze, a long red blur. Then, again, it was stirring, drifting across the yellow. He had no sense of his own movement, only of the shuffling of his feet and the sweat trickling down his back, and somehow the train was drawing away from him. Then he was at the station. He crossed the tracks and climbed onto the main platform. He went past the sign that proclaimed "Leharia" and its elevation of seven hundred and eighteen feet, past the station master's office and the second class waiting room, past the door to the ticketing office and the passengers sprawled on the green benches, and to the arched white entrance to the station. There he stopped, unsure. He looked out across the tracks and there was the slow slope and the faraway rim. He had gone to the edge of his world and come back and he didn't know what was next. The train was now a single oblong to the west. He looked down along the tracks to the west and then back to the east and the thought occurred to him suddenly that he could wait for the next train, and it was a short step off the platform onto the black rails, a drop of three feet. The train would be moving very slowly but it had a great momentum. It could not be stopped. He recognized the melodrama of the thought, and was also surprised that he had not had it before. There was a certain relief in it. It seemed now inevitable, at least as an idea, and he determined that he would wait for the next train to see what happened. That would be the three-thirty from Lucknow.

Now that there was a plan he was released from lethargy. He was sud- 15
denly full of energy and very thirsty. There was a *matka* of water in the first class waiting room. He walked now with a snap, and he waved smartly at Frankie Furtado the assistant station master, who was looking, from a barred window, after the receding smudge on the western sky with an expression that was usually taken for commendable railway concentration and proper serious-

ness. He was actually—Shiv knew—dreaming of Bombay, and now Frankie returned the wave with but a slow raising of the fingers of one elegant hand that rested on an iron bar. There was an entire matinee's worth of tragedy in the single motion, and Shiv smiled a little as he drank the lovely clayey water. It was crisp and cold and the ladle made a deep belling sound as it dipped under the dark surface.

He poured the water into his mouth. It splashed over his neck and chest, and he let it fall on his face, and when he heard the laugh he choked. When he stopped coughing he turned and saw the figure by the window. At first all he could see was hands held together, the furled drapery of a grey sari from knee to ground. Then in a moment or two he could see her. She was thin, very young. She wore no ornaments, not a bangle, no earrings. The eyes were large, there was a thick plait falling over a shoulder, and now she looked down and put a hand over her mouth. Shiv put the ladle back in the *matka,* and it dropped with a rattle into the water. He backed to the door, edged through it, blushing, and then stood on the platform wiping his face.

"Who is that in there?" he asked Frankie Furtado, whose face lit up at the question. Frankie was really a movie star trapped by his railway father and railway grandfathers and various railway uncles in Leharia, which he always called Zinderneuf. He had explained with shining eyes the sentimental possibilities of desert forts, marauding Bedouin, stolen jewels, and violent death. Now he was bright eyed about chance meetings while whistles echoed.

"Second class passenger," Frankie said. "But I put her in first class because she is very beautiful."

"Yes," Shiv said. Actually she was rather plain, but Frankie was dedicated to romance.

Frankie ran his finger down a list on a board. "Mrs. Shanti Chauhan," he said.

"Fine," Shiv said, unaccountably irritated. He walked down the length of the platform, trying to find again his imperturbable velocity of a moment ago. At the end of the platform he waited, sitting on a green bench. He fanned himself with a folded *Times of India* and tried not to think. But as always the images skipped and skittered at the back of his head. He spread the newspaper across his knee but then was drowned by the vast turbulence of the world, its fires and refugees and ruined cities. A letter-writer called "Old Soldier" wrote, "Whether these men of the so-called Indian National Army were prompted by a version of patriotism, or gave in to fear of unspeakable persecutions by the Japanese, is scarcely to the point; that they took up arms against their former comrades is certain. They betrayed their vows to their units and their army and their king, and a soldier who is false to his *namak* can expect only two things: court-martial and the ultimate penalty." Shiv saw them falling, their bodies riddled and holed. He shuddered. So he shut his eyes and with a slow twist of fear in his stomach gave himself up to the uncertain currents of memory. Then Shiv's nostrils were full of Hari's smell, the slightly pungent aroma of life itself, cotton and perspiration and flesh, springing muscle, the same hair oil he used himself but sweeter on Hari. Now Shiv opened his eyes and his face was covered with sweat. There was a whistle, softened by distance.

He stood up and waited. He felt very small now, and under the huge sky he waited for the two events to come together, the busily grinding three-thirty from Lucknow and himself. He could see them moving closer to each other, the loco on its tracks, and his life, brought to each other in a series of spirals. He took a step forward and now it was a matter of another one to the edge. He could see the train, a black circle, huffing smoke and getting bigger. He began to think of calculations, of the time it would take to put one foot in front of another, of velocity and braking distance. He noted the red fragments from a broken *khullar* next to the tracks and determined that he would jump when the shadow of the train fell on them. That was close enough. The train came faster than he had thought it would, and now the sound enveloped him. He felt his legs twitch. He watched the red clay and then at the last moment turned his head to look down the platform. He saw in the swirl of colours a grey figure, motionless. He jerked his head back, felt the huge weight of the engine, its heat, and began his step forward, seeing the black curve of the metal above him, slashed in half by the slanting sun, the rivets through the iron, and then he staggered back, pulled himself back, an arm over his head.

Shiv found himself sitting on the ground, knees splayed outward. The bone at the base of his spine throbbed. He picked himself up and hurried past the first class compartments as the train screeched mournfully. She was stooping to pick up a small brown attaché, and he was sure she saw him coming. But she turned her face away, an expression of anger on her face, and walked resolutely towards the door of a carriage, where Frankie Furtado stood with his clipboard. She went past his smile with her eyes downcast, into the carriage, and afterwards sat in a compartment with half-lowered shades. Shiv stood outside, wondering at himself. He could see her arm. Twelve minutes passed, and then Frankie waved a green flag, leaning suavely to one side, and quite suddenly the train was gone. Leaving only a black wisp fading, and Shiv with his questions.

Frankie had an alphabetical list of names: "Madhosh Kumar, Magan Kumar, Nand Kumar, Narendra Kumar..." He read from these every evening when Shiv visited him in his room behind the National Provision Store, in his desert lair, his lonely eyrie festooned with pictures of Ronald Colman. Frankie was the handsomest man Shiv had ever seen, with his gently wavy hair and his thin moustache and fair skin, and they were trying to find a screen name that would encompass and radiate all the mysterious glamour of his profile. Usually Shiv enjoyed the distraction of holding the name up to imaginary bright lights, of writing it into the magazines which Frankie collected and hoarded with incandescent seriousness. "Nitin Kumar Signs with MovieTone," or "Om Kumar Dazzles in Megabuster" were all tried, tested and classified and estimated and measured, and found wanting in the analysis. This discussion took place always on the little *chabutra* in front of Frankie's room, with the spokes of Frankie's bicycle glinting in the moonlight. There were a few bedraggled bushes at the bottom of a brick wall, and a *chameli* tree overhanging the wall from Lala Manohar Lal's garden. The Lala's two daughters were of course in love with Frankie, but tonight even the sight of them hovering on the rooftop across the way like two bottom-heavy nightingales took nothing from Shiv's enormous yearning.

He was filled with a longing so bitter that he wanted.all over again to die. He felt as if he was gone from himself. This was not the numb descent towards an inevitable stillness, no, not that at all. Now, in the darkness, Shiv felt a quickening in the night, a throb like a pulse that moved far away, and he was acutely aware of the smallness of the *chabutra* and how tiny Frankie's room was, with its one sagging *charpai* and the chipped white plaster on the walls and the crudely shaped green windows that could never completely close. Even the moonlight didn't hide the dirt, the disheveled ugliness and cowpatties of a small *mofussil* town one step away from a village.

"Have you seen her before?" Shiv said. His voice was loud. He was angry, and he didn't know quite why.

"Yes," Frankie said. He stood up straight, alive with pleasure. "Twice before. She comes through every two or three months, I think. Looking so beautiful and so alone."

"Going where?"

"I don't know. She catches a *tonga* outside the station. I think to the cantonment. Her attaché has stencilling on it."

Four miles from the station there was a brigade headquarters and, further away, an aerodrome.

"She's married," Shiv said. "Probably going to visit her army husband."

"Air force," Frankie said. "And why would she be visiting instead of staying in a lovely air force bungalow? And when she showed me her ticket I saw that she had others. Connections to all over the country, man. Why?"

"I don't know." Shiv snapped back. "I don't *know*. And why would it matter to you and me anyway? She's a married woman."

Frankie raised an eyebrow. He put a hand on his hip and his shoulder rose and fell in a long exaggerated shrug. Shiv saw that it was a gesture too large for life, impossible in its elegance, but in the silver light it was entirely conceivable and exactly right, as if the world had suddenly changed, moved and become just a little larger, just enough to contain Frankie Furtado. Frankie, who swept his hair back now and turned majestically away, ridiculous and beautiful. Shiv shut his eyes, pressed on them until he felt pain.

Frankie sang: "*Kahan gaya ranchor? Duniya ke rahane valon bolo, chcheen ke dil mera, kahan gaya ranchor?*" His voice was good, light and yet full of intensity, and ample and rounded with its delight in its own skill. Shiv fled from it.

A cut on the palm of a right hand. Small, not too large, but ferocious in the straightness of its edges, in the geometry of its depth. Another on the left forearm, from the same straight edge. This is what Shiv remembered. As he walked home along a dusty lane he remembered the dark pearls of blood frozen on the pale skin. In the morgue he had found the cuts unbearable to look at, this damage, these rents in the surface and the lewd exposure of what lay underneath. Now he clung to the still shape as the only reality. It was the world stripped of all its fictions, this dead body on a grey stone slab, the smell. In only a minute or two, in a lane off Chandni Chowk, a whole life came to merely this, all of Hari's idealisms, his Congress membership and his Nehru-worhip, his belief in change and the careful asceticism of his three khadi *kurtas* and his blushing appetite for mangoes, all of it gone to an odour of rot. All of it ready for the fire. Shiv held out an arm in the darkness and took careful steps with his fingertips on a wall. In the memory of the dead body of his brother there was a certain safety. There was a certain logic there, a brilliant lesson about the nature of the world. This Shiv knew. In Frankie's falsities, in his fantasies about the past and the future, there was certain disaster. To believe Frankie, to believe in him, that he could exist in Leharia, Shiv knew, was to risk an unfolding in his own chest, an expansion of emotion that would let in, once again, a certain hell of hope and remorse. He had left this behind.

"Did you have a good evening?" Shiv's brother-in-law, Rajan, liked to sit in an armchair in the courtyard of their house after dinner. Shiv could see the curve of his bald head, and the rounded shapes of his shoulders.

"Yes," Shiv said, and shut the door to his room behind him. He knew Anuradha *akka* would hurry out of her bedroom in a moment, and want to give him food. He was unspeakably rude, and they were used to this. They had patience. But Shiv lay on his bed and wrapped death around himself. He could hear a bird calling outside, solitary and plaintive. Shiv knew that finally the bird would stop crying out, his sister and her husband would stop whispering to each other and sleep, the house would settle into a late silence, a quietness that would echo the slow creaking of trees into his head. He would feel his self, his soul turn and turn inwards, again and again, until it was as thin-drawn as a wire, shiny and brittle. It was not a good feeling but he knew it well, and it was better than everything else. He waited.

He found that he was waiting for her. As he cycled around town, from one tuition to another, he anticipated each turn in the rutted lanes, even though on the other side of each corner there was always the same pool of stagnant water, the same goat leaving a trail of perfect black pellets, the same two familiar *dehati* citizens of Leharia with their flapping *pajamias* and "Ram-Ram, Shiv Bhaiyya." At the station, Shiv sat on platform number one and watched the trains. Frankie smiled fondly and hummed *Mere piya gaye Rangoon* under his breath every time he strolled by. Rajan believed that Shiv had at last and only naturally succumbed to the charm of steam, that he had become a lover of the black beauties that raced across the horizon, an aficionado of their hulking grace and their sonorous power. He came and sat beside Shiv often, in the quiet moments of the day. "Beyer Garrat loco, latest model, 1939. Used only on the express. Look at that! The total heating area, including the superheater, is more than four thousand square feet."

Shiv listened to the tales of the trains, and imagined the tracks narrowing 40
across the enormous plains to the north, and to the south across the rocky plateau, and hairpin turns over vertiginous ridges, and through black deserts. He thought of her sitting by a half-closed window, her hands in her lap, and wondered what she was doing. Who was she? Where was she going? Why did she return? As the questions came he understood that everything had changed. Now, at night, instead of long wakefulness and empty, tiring slumber for an hour before dawn, he found a twisting, sweaty, dream-ridden sleep. He saw long visions of childhood, fantastic and drenched with blood, and also adventures in forests, and unspeakable seraglios in which *apsaras* with long black hair twisted against each other. He was hungry all the time, and ate his sister's *uttapam* with a relish that made her beam and write gladdened letters to his parents. And one evening in August he actually asked Frankie Furtado to sing *Kahan gaya ranchor*. Frankie tilted himself against the wall next to a window, a slim streak of white against the black, black clouds, turned his face to the light, and sang as the rain billowed over the green fields.

Shiv believed that he would know, somehow, when she came back, that he would sense her presence in the twisting lanes. Even as he laughed at the Frankie influence on his thoughts he believed this. But when she came he missed her entirely. He was unfastening the cycle-clips from his calves outside the station when Frankie came running out and found him.

"Where were you? She's here," Frankie said, clutching hard at Shiv's shoulder. "She's here."

"Where?" There was a solid sheet of water falling from the crenellated roof of the station, spattering loudly against the flowerpots below.

"On the 24 up. She had to wait quite a while for a *tonga*, all this rain, I suppose. Then finally she left ten, fifteen minutes ago."

Shiv threw his leg over his cycle and skidded out into the rain. His plastic 45
cap tumbled away and splashed into the mud but Shiv rode on, spraying an arc over the road. He rode hard, leaning against the pedals, feeling the water pull at the wheels in the deep parts. The rain hit him violently in the face, coming straight and parallel to the road, and he laughed. His chest was drenched and cool, but under his raincoat he was sweating. He cycled though the main bazaar, where the little shops looked cozy under the darkness of the rain. Then he struggled against the long slope where the road opened out into the orderly rows of the Civil Lines and the cantonment, and the wind pushed against him, but then he saw the shape of the *tonga* ahead, sailing on the water. He pedaled madly, and then he came up on it and slowed. He could hear the muffled clip-clop, the swish of the wheels. There were small curtain-like pieces of cloth

drawn around the back of the *tonga,* but he could see her feet on the backboard. Shiv went along now, not near but not too far. He listened to the rain, and the sound of his own breathing, in and out. He had no idea what to do next.

Shiv stopped at a big double gate. There was a wide curving drive leading up to the square white building Shiv knew was the military hospital. He could see, as he blinked his eyes against the sting of the drops, the *tonga* stopped next to a balustraded entranceway, the dripping horse, her attaché case, and her, as she hurried, head bent, through the doors. Shiv waited, cold now, shivering. Finally, when it was dark and he could only see the rows of lighted windows, glowing and unreadable, he turned and wheeled his cycle home, coughing.

He woke up the next morning with a fever. His sister saw it in his reddened eyes and careful walk, but he burst past her protestations and rode to the station. It was very quiet now, no rain, and the silence was wet and fresh and everywhere green, and he felt himself lost under the enormity of the smooth grey sky. Frankie was waiting for him at the entrance to the station.

"She's in the waiting room," Frankie said.

Shiv nodded impatiently. He walked down the length of the platform, past the fire buckets filled with sand and the two coolies wrapped in checked red sheets and a cloud of *bidi* smoke. Outside the waiting room, he stood for a moment, running hooked fingers through his tangled hair. His eyes burnt drily. He pushed the doors ajar and went in, keeping his gaze on the floor. He found the *matka,* and as he dipped into the water with the ladle he found that he was really thirsty. He poured into a glass, drank, and turned.

"Hello," he said.

She said nothing, and looked solemnly at him. He realized suddenly what it must take from her, how much courage and strength to travel the length and breadth of the country alone, in these times.

"My name is Shiv Subramaniam," he said. She looked down, and he was then ashamed of persecuting her as many others must have done on her travels, and he edged away toward the door. But Frankie was backing in, carrying a tray with a teapot and cups.

"Mrs. Chauhan," Frankie said, swooping down on the small table in front of her. "Tea for you." He laid out the cups with smart little movements. "There. Mr. Subramaniam, who is our esteemed Station Master *saab*'s brother-in-law, will serve." He looked at Shiv. "Please." Then he bowed to Mrs. Chauhan, and was gone.

For a moment Shiv stood absolutely still. He felt dizzy. Then he stepped up to the table, bent over, and picked up the teapot. He was angling awkwardly at the waist and the teapot felt very heavy, but he poured one cup, and then the other. He put the pot down.

"Sugar?" he said.

"No," she said. Her voice was oddly husky. She took the cup and the saucer and held it in her lap. Shiv stood stupidly still, and then realized she was waiting for him. Quickly he picked up his cup and saucer, and tried to keep it steady in his trembling hand. He took a sip, and it was very hot and he usually took sugar, lots of it, but he drank rapidly and watched her. Finally she raised her cup and drank.

"You've come here before," he said.

"I go to the hospital at the base," she said.

"Ah," he said. His legs were shaky, and very carefully he sat on the chair to her left. Looking at her directly, he saw that she was very thin, that the way she held her head alertly above her bony shoulders gave her a kind of intrepid dignity.

"I'm looking for my husband."

"Your husband?"

"He's missing in Burma," she said. "He is a pilot."

There was nothing to say to this.

"He is a fighter pilot," she said. "He was in the first batch of Indian fighter pilots in the RIAF. He was flying a Hurricane over Burma in 1942. They were protecting transports. They were attacked by Japanese fighters. The last his wingman saw of him was the plane losing height over the jungle. The plane was smoking. That was all they saw."

She was speaking in an even voice, and the sentences came steadily after one another, without any emotion. It was a story she had told before.

"So, at the hospital . . .?"

"I talk to the men who come back. Before it was only a few. Now they're all coming back. From the prison camps. And the others, from the INA." She looked at Shiv. "Somebody must have seen him, met him. Only today I met a soldier from the Fourth Gurkhas who said he had heard about a fighter pilot in a camp on the Irrawaddy."

She had complete confidence. The names of the units and of the faraway places came to her easily.

"So I'll go to the army headquarters in Delhi, find out who was in that camp. Talk to them."

She nodded. She finished her tea, and put the cup back on the tray. Then she folded her hands in her lap, and it seemed she was now content to wait, either for the train, or the man from the Fourth Gurkhas, or a flier in a plane above the trees. There was again that strange quietness, as if the world had paused. Again Shiv felt that he was vanishing into the huge wash of grey above, the sudden and endless green to the horizon. He shut his eyes.

"The man in the hospital told me he had seen the most evil man in the world."

Shiv opened his eyes. "Who? The Gurkha told you this?"

"No, no," she said impatiently. "The man in the next bed. He was from the Twenty-third Cavalry."

And then she told him the story of the most evil man in the world. Shiv listened, and the words came to him through the burning of his blood and the din of his pulse. The shadows drifted in the room and then she was finished. Then Frankie came in and said the train was near, and they walked down the platform, and Shiv held her attaché case in his right hand, and walked slowly behind her. They stood on the platform until the train came, and when the train pulled away neither she nor Shiv waved or raised a hand.

Frankie walked up to him. "You don't look very well," Frankie said.

Shiv fainted.

His sister was pressing a glass against his lips. Shiv choked on the hot milk and turned his head away from the bitter metal of the glass.

"You have to drink, Shiv," Anuradha said. "There is this weakness you have to defeat."

He raised himself up against the pillows, and his body felt light, ready to float. He drank the milk, and saw that Frankie was sitting at the far end of the darkened room. Shiv finished, and handed the empty glass to Anuradha, still feeling the hot liquid burble in his throat. After Anuradha left, Frankie opened the window a little, so that Shiv could see the swirling sky. And there were still the steady drops splattering on the stone outside.

"Crazy man," Frankie said. "But you'll be all right. Just a little flu you've got."

Shiv tilted his head, yes, and the room moved around him.

"She was talking to you for a long time," Frankie said, smiling. "I saw. Very seriously. What was she tell you?"

"She," Shiv said. He stopped for the friction in his throat. He tried again. "She told me about the most evil man in the world."

Frankie turned, came and sat next to the bed. "What do you mean?"

Shiv didn't quite know. What she had told him, how she had told him, that day yesterday was now left to him only in fragments. He remembered it now only across the dark sea of sleep, lost behind the distant horizon of sunset and illness. He reached back and held only slivers. But there was something else in his throat, complete and whole. "I think this is what she told me." He cleared his throat. It hurt.

I touched my mother's feet and she sent me to war with an *aarti*. "Ja, beta," she said. And so I left her, and the smell of incense, and went. My grandfather and my father had served in the Twenty-third Cavalry, and there I went. Our colonel McNaughten said our job was to kill Germans, and we killed them. We are fighting evil, he said. In the mess there was a cartoon of Hitler crushing Africa under his jackboots. So we killed them on Ruweisat Ridge, on the Rahman track, on the Aqaqir ridge. I saw huge stony fields and burning tanks and trucks and upended guns till the eye could see no more. Long black columns of smoke and oily burning at the root. We killed them. And they killed us. Mahipal Singh, Jagat Singh, Narain Singh. Kirpal Singh in the night when we ran into the First Life Guards and they shot us and we shot them.

On the Tel the Germans tried a counterattack. They came at night down a narrowing slope, after a barrage with what they had left. Across a narrow wadi, facing the slope, the 1/9th Suffolk had dug in. They had machine gun positions and antitank and mortars sighted in on the slope. All night the Germans came and the Suffolk cut them down. They could hear the Germans calling to each other. Then the light of flares and the Suffolk firing. The Germans came and tried and tried again and then again. All night it went. Then in the morning the Suffolk counterattacked, and then they opened up and let us through, followed by Bren gun carriers. I was driving the lead armoured car, not only in the troop but in the regiment. We came down the Suffolk side of the wadi with the wheels and tracks crunching on the rocks and we could see the bodies of the Germans covering the slope opposite. They had fallen so close, so many, that it was as if all the rock were covered with faded olive cloth, a green carpet. German bodies. Of course not all of them were dead. But we had killed them. We bounced into the bottom of the wadi and the engine growled and we struggled against a lip of rock and the heavy wheels bit into the ground and rocks crumbled and sprayed and then we were almost over and then I stopped.

I stopped the car, I brought it to a halt. Through the driver's slit, through the armour plate, not six feet away and ahead, a German was looking at me. He was very young, propped up on an elbow, that strange golden white hair, and he had the bluest eyes I had ever seen. He was looking at me. He had the bluest eyes I had ever seen, against the dust-covered face, eyes the colour of a sky you or I had never seen. I could not tell if he was dead or alive, and he was looking at me. "Damn it, Huknam," Captain Duff crackled into my ears. "Push on." But I could not tell if the man with the blue eyes was dead or alive, and he was looking at me. "Huknam, you're holding up the whole advance," Captain Duff shouted, and I thought of the troop behind me, and then the regiment, and the army and armies and all the countries beyond, all held up behind me. So I let in the clutch and the man with the blue eyes was looking at me for a few seconds more and then we went over him and up the slope and the regiment followed. The engine was thundering in my ears as we crunched up and up but as we went up I could not have heard it but I heard them, them outside on the ground calling out. "*Mutti,*" they said. "*Mutti.*" We came up over the ridge and they had nothing left, but thirty-four miles on and the next day we came into a line of anti-tank guns. They were very close to the ground and well-camouflaged and they caught us well, two other cars in our troop burning in the first minute. We saw the muzzle-flashes and tumbled one, but then there was a whang behind and above me and I was deaf, and I raised my hatch and jumped out. The sand was on fire and there was a burning behind my ears and on my shoulders. I fell down and got up and ran as I could and then I knew my shoulders were on fire. I rolled and rolled and finally it was out. The car exploded and I never saw any of them again, not Captain Duff or the others. It must have been an eighty-eight.

They put me in a field hospital and finally in Cairo they cut my left arm off. When I had jumped off the car I hadn't known but it had been shattered all to pieces. They cut my arm off and it was strange but I felt no pain, not then and not afterwards. But there was something else. When finally I could walk I went into the courtyard of the hospital, I liked to sit on the bench there. There were

> birds in the roof and in the rafters and they came down to be fed, and there was a fountain. One day I sat on the edge of the fountain, which was dry. But there was a Rajput who brought out a bowl of water for the birds and put it, the bowl, into the fountain. In this bowl of water I saw that my eyes had turned blue. I went inside and found a bathroom with a chipped mirror and still my eyes were blue. My eyes were blue and as I looked at the man, the man who was before me, I saw that his face was cruel and the eyes were blue and still, neither alive nor dead, strange in the brown face. He had the bluest eyes in the world. And this was how I met the most evil man in the world.

When Shiv finished he was exhausted. He lay back on the pillows and let his eyes shut. Yet he was afraid to sleep. He felt Frankie pull the sheet up and lay it over his chest.

"Did she see him?" Frankie whispered. "Did she see his eyes."

"Yes," Shiv said. "She saw him and she said he had the bluest eyes she had ever seen, not only for an Indian but for English or German or anything else."

After a moment, Frankie said, "Sleep."

Shiv stretched under the sheet, turned his neck against the pillow. He felt tired but better, achy but relaxed. He knew he would get better. He slept.

Shiv got so much better that his parents started talking about marriage. He splashed around town on his cycle, singing. He laughed at the yellow furrows that his wheels carved deep in the water. His sister and her husband were relieved and then a little concerned, made uneasy by the sudden change, but in Delhi his parents were convinced that all was now well and it was time for him to settle, everything should be settled. Meanwhile Frankie Furtado watched the trains eagerly, even the ones that were not going towards Bombay. He told Shiv that he would use a network of assistant station masters throughout the country to find her, to trace her movements and predict her return. But Shiv was confident that she would come back, and soon. He said to Frankie, "Not to worry, my friend. She'll come back." Frankie looked disappointed as his dream of a clandestine spy network vanished, but still, a month and three days later, it gave him tremendous satisfaction to discover her name on a list of advance reservations. He found Shiv on platform three, where he was sitting with his arms flung over the back of a bench, looking out at the slow wind swaying the tall grass.

"My friend," Frankie said. "Eleven hundred hours tomorrow."

"What?" Shi said.

"Eleven hundred hours," Frankie said out of the side of his mouth, his hands in his pockets and looking away significantly.

Shiv looked up and down the empty length of the platform. "Yes, that, but what?" he said.

Frankie raised an eyebrow, and Shiv burst out laughing. "What her?"

"Yes, yes, her," Frankie said, a tremendous smile on his face and not a spy anymore.

Shiv got up, put his arm through Frankie's, and led him down the platform. "Frankie Furtado," Shiv said. "You're a madman."

Frankie flung his hair back, and raised a declamatory hand to the sky. "I have drunk of the chalice of wine," he said. "And I am mad." And Shiv thought that Frankie was indeed mad, and he was mad too, and if there was wine the world must have drunk it too.

The next day, though, Shiv was very rational, very cool when she stepped from the train. "Mrs. Chauhan," he said, and carried her attaché case to the *tonga*.

"What did she say?" Frankie said, pulling at Shiv's elbow as the *tonga* 105
pulled away. "What did you say?"

"Nothing," Shiv said. Frankie was stricken. "Don't worry, Frankie. She'll come back and I'll tell her something."

"What?"

"I don't know. Wait and see."

The next day Shiv found her again in the waiting room. Again Frankie brought in a tray with cups and a teapot, and again Shiv poured. She drank the tea without speaking, as before, but afterwards she cleared her throat.

"Did you find anybody from the camp on the Irrawaddy?" Shiv said. 110

"Yes," she said. "But he wasn't in that camp. But there was some other news, of an escape at another place. So many of them are back."

Shiv nodded. They had come back in thousands, from the army, from the prison camps, and from the other army which had fought against its former comrades. And they had hope for her, each of them, and despair.

"But," she said. "But I met somebody, a woman."

"Yes?"

"At the bus station at Bareilly. She was a Congress-*walli*." 115

Shiv nodded. He started to say, my brother was also, but it caught in his throat. "Yes," he said.

"She told me something."

"Yes?"

"She told me about a woman who ran backwards into the future," she said.

Afterwards, when she, Mrs. Chauhan, had gone, gone away on the train 120
without a wave or a backward glance, Frankie put an arm around Shiv's shoulder and walked him to the end of the platform. "So?" Frankie said. "So how did you get along?"

"Swimmingly," Shiv said.

"Tell me all. What did she tell you? Learn anything new?"

"Nothing about her, really."

"But you were in there so long. What, then?"

"Take a walk, Frankie?" 125

"Where? There? No, you must be crazy."

But Shiv could see that Frankie was dying to know, to be told, and so of course Frankie came along with Shiv, in spite of the green grass stains on his white pant legs, and they walked up the slope a far away. And Shiv told him what she had said.

Zingu heard a speech by a politician. Zingu had been coming home to his hut at the end of the day, and it was dark, and so Zingu stood in the dark behind a broken wall and listened to the politician. The politician stood under a petromax lamp and said that all men were equal. The townspeople applauded. Zingu went home in the dark, and he slept quietly, but in the morning he told his wife not to go to work. He told her that there was no need to carry shit anymore. This is what they did, Zingu and his wife. They cleaned the latrines of the twice-born by hand and carried it away on their heads in baskets. But Zingu said his son would be a judge. He told his wife that all men were equal. His wife told him that he was crazy, and took her stinking basket and went to the village. But they killed Zingu anyway, and his son. He wandered around with his son saying all men were equal, and so they caught him in the open fields behind Dhiresa's mansion and cut Zingu and his son to pieces. One of them held up Zingu's foot at the end of a *talwar* and said, look at the size of this thing. All men aren't equal. And that was the end of Zingu, and his son.

But that's not the end of it. Because in Dhiresa's mansion, on the roof, his daughter-in-law Janamohini was drying her hair. In the winter sunlight Janamohini was lying on a *charpai* on the roof, her long, long black hair spread like a cloud, wet and curling and shining and dark. She was young and beautiful and loved, and the mother of two sons and one daughter, and through the delicious sunny sleep of the contented she heard far away the snick and whick of the swords as they cut Zingu. She stretched reluctantly out of her drowsy dreaming, feeling the welcome soreness in the muscles from the night before, sat up, and looked out over the parapet and saw Zingu's foot at the end of a sword. She covered her face and screamed, and many people came running up, uncles and aunts and cousins, and comforted her, and told her it was nothing. And then she was content, and smiling again, and she ate well that night.

But in the darkness, from the roof, she saw a glow. There were fires in the fields. She saw campfires in the fields, and figures dancing about them. She watched them, for a long time, and she could hear singing. She could hear music. Finally her husband called out to her from the courtyard below, and she went down the stairs. She was happy, she laughed and played with her children, yet later she slipped out of the house, by the small door inset into the spiked gate at the back of the house, and she went into the fields. Janamohini walked for a long time, guided by the glow shining off the sky, and finally she found her campfires. There was indeed music, and singing. There were people dancing near the fires. Janamohini saw they were of despised caste, that they were celebrating a wedding, that they were drinking liquor and eating meat, and the music was happy and they welcomed her, and so she danced with them. She drank their liquor and ate their meat. And she whirled around the campfires.

But then her husband and his brothers, who had found the open door, came and took her back to Dhiresa's mansion. Janamohini screamed and fought, but the husband said there had been no campfires, no dancers, no liquor, no meat. He said there had been nothing at all. Now Janamohini shrieked, my feet, my feet, look. She said her feet were pointing the wrong way. Upside down they

> are, she said. Look. And she began to walk backwards. They tried to stop her, but she walked backwards, faster and faster. She began to run backwards. Her husband wept, and she said, can't you see? If I go fast enough, back and back, I will leap into tomorrow. And her husband wept.
>
> They tried many exorcists then, many a priest, two Tantrics, and a doctor from the town. But Janamohini always walked backwards after that, looking for tomorrow.
>
> But that's not the end of it. Because on that night, no, the next morning, when the people in Dhiresa's mansion woke up, the aunts and uncles and cousins, they saw that Janamohini's hair was white. During that night, and that night only, all of her glorious hair, all of it long and luxurious and oiled and to her knees, all of it, turned white. From the scented clinging black of love it went to the white of madness. All in one night. All this happened in one night.

"And," Shiv said, "she, Mrs. Chauhan, that is, she said she asked the woman who told her this, is this true?"

"Yes," Frankie said. "And the woman said?"

"The woman said—yes, it's true, I tell you it's true, because Janamohini was my mother. I saw her hair turn white, she said, I saw it white in the first light of the morning. All of it white. And I am twenty-two and my hair is white. And perhaps my daughter's hair, if I have a daughter, will be white also."

"And it was white, her hair? The woman who told Mrs. Chauhan this?"

"White, yes. She was young but her hair was white as salt on a beach, as metal in the moonlight, as the sun on a flag."

"That's white," Frankie said. "Poor Zingu."

"Poor Zingu."

They walked back towards the long length of the station, with the huge mottled sky above, and the wind pulled at their shoulders.

"What about her, Shiv?" Frankie said. "Did you find out anything about her? The husband?"

Shiv thought, his head tilted back to the grey glory of the clouds. "I don't think so," he said.

"You didn't ask?"

"No."

"Don't you want to know, Shiv?"

Shiv shrugged. He knew he was smiling awkwardly. "I know it's strange," he said. "And I suppose I do want to know. And I suppose I'll find out. But right now, today, I just like her name."

"Shanti?"

"Yes."

Frankie put his hands in his pockets, hunched his shoulders, and laughed. "Some people fall in love with dark eyes. Others with pale hands glimpsed beside the Shalimar. Why not a name then?"

"It's a good name."

"I know," Frankie said, and put an arm around Shiv's shoulder. "But, brother, a fact now and then is a good thing."

"You're talking about facts, Frankie the lover?"

"Lovers are practical, my young friend."

"Really? That's interesting. It means, I think, that I'm not a lover." 155

Frankie nodded gravely. But as he looked away Shiv saw that he was smiling. The grass made a sighing sound as they walked.

Now Shanti—and this was how Shiv thought of her—came to Leharia often. As the trial of Dhillon and Sahgal and Shah Nawaz was argued in Delhi, and lawyers and advocates and judges jousted with each other to establish once and for all who was traitor, who was hero, she followed anecdotes and hints and the visions of delirious men up and down the country. Now she pursued the merest whisper, a shadow seen on a jungled hillside years before, a fevered groan floating across fetid bunks laden with dying men. But each time she came she told Shiv of something that she had heard on the way, the things that came to her on all the ways that she went, some incident, some episode, told to her by an old man, a young bride, a favourite son, an angry daughter-in-law, a mother, an orphan, and all of it true, true, and true. She told him about the Ten Year Old Boy Who Joined the Theatre Company of Death, The Woman Who Traded in Oil and Bought a Flying Racehorse, The Farmer Who Went to America and Fell Through a Hole to the Other Side of the World, The Moneylender Who Saw the True Face of the Creator, Ghurabat and Her Lover the Assassin Who Wept, The Birth of the Holiest Nun in the World and The Downfall of the Mughal Empire. And each time Shiv said, it's true. Of course it's true.

But one day in January she had nothing to tell. Or perhaps she hadn't the strength to speak. She sat in her usual chair, an empty teacup in her lap, and her eyes fluttered shut as Shiv watched. He saw the way her mouth trembled and the slump of her shoulders from the taut line he had come to know. He took the cup from her and put it on the table, and with the tiny rattle she opened her eyes.

"They let them go," she said. "They went home." 160

"Who?"

"Dhillon, Shah Nawaz, and Sahgal."

The papers had exulted in huge black letters: "GUILTY, BUT FREE!" they had gone home, the three, heroes or traitors, finished with it one way or the other. They had been convicted, cashiered, but finally they were told, you're free, you can go. They would go home, and even if nothing was finished, not ever, they would batten away the memories and find new beginnings. All of them were going, going home. Shiv thought of them, the thousands and thousands of them, jostling and jolting across the country in trains, in busses and bullock carts. He pulled a chair toward Shanti, set it squarely in front of her. He sat down in front of her, his hands in his lap. At the back of his neck there was a trembling, as the words pulsed in his chest, exerting a steady pressure against his heart: you're free, you can go.

"I heard something," Shiv said.

"What?"

He cleared his throat, and for a moment he felt fear, blank and overpowering, and he was afraid of speaking, he felt profusion pressing up against the clean prison he had built for himself, but then he looked into Shanti's eyes and he spoke. He told her what he had heard. Afterwards they sat in silence, and Shiv was grateful, because his shoulders ached and he was very tired.

When she was in her compartment, settled in the window, Frankie came strolling down the platform to announce that the train was delayed for twelve minutes. Shanti nodded, but Shiv was too lost in a sudden panic of emotion to say anything. He felt terror and joy mixing in his stomach, and a slow creep of pleasure at the sunlight across his shoulders, and grief. Frankie looked at him, and then took him by the arm and led him away.

"This time you were talking," Frankie said. "And talking and talking. About what?"

"I was telling her something."

"*You* told her a story?"

"Yes."

"Tell me."

Shiv tried. He opened his mouth, and tried to form the words, but they were gone from him. "I can't," he said, trembling. He gestured at his throat, meaning to explain the tumult under the skin.

"All right, sure," Frankie said, baffled but quick to the chase. "I'll ask *her*."

And he did. Frankie stood by the window, his head cocked to one side. Under the long flutter and hiss of steam, Shiv could hear her words.

Amma woke in the morning and cleaned the house. She cleaned the storerooms, the rooms around the courtyard, she swept the dark mud floors and wiped the mantlepieces and the tops of the doorways. She put new wicks in the lanterns and filled them with oil. She washed the red brick of the courtyard and emptied out the ashes from the *choola*. And the children going in and out of the house, through the big door with iron hoops, told their mothers, Amma's cleaning. And the women of the village said, one of her children is coming.

It was a small house, with a granary at the rear and a good well. Amma's grandfather had built it in some time so far away that she thought of it as beyond numbers. He had built it solid and strong, and she came back to it after her school-teacher husband died of typhoid. She came back with four children, two sons and two daughters, the oldest just eleven, to this village called Chandapur, and here she lived and grew old. Her name was Amita but the village called her Amma. She could not read or write, but she educated her children. There was money, just so much, from the farming of her land, and she lived quietly and with a simplicity that was exactly the same as poverty, but she sent her children to school in the city. In her house books were sacred. She wrapped them in red cloth and stacked them on a bed in the biggest of the rooms in her house. Amma lived in a village and ate only twice a day but her children went to boarding school. Her eldest son went to Roorkee and became an engineer. Amma went sometimes to the cities, north, south, east, and west, to visit her children, but came back always to her house in the village, fiercely alone and happy.

It was this engineer son who came home that day. He sat on a *charpai* in the courtyard and spoke to the men from the *panchayat,* who came and sat around him in a circle and smoked. There were women in the kitchen, helping Amma and laughing with her. She had a wicked tongue, and liked to talk. They could hear her laughing in the courtyard, as they listened to the engineer. There were children running in and out of the house. The engineer was telling them, everyone, about the end of the war. He was wearing a white shirt, dark blue pants, and his hair came up on his forehead in a wonderful swell which the villagers, knowing too little, couldn't recognize as stylish. He had a high, querulous voice, and he was telling them about the American bombs.

"The bomb killed a city," he said. "There were two bombs. Each finished a city." He snapped his fingers, high in the air. They looked at him, not saying a word, and he felt the stubborn peasant scepticism gathering around his ankles, that unmovable slow stupidity. He was irritated, rankled now as he used to be when his mother laughed at his modernisms. *Ajihaan,* she would say, unanswerable. It baffled him that his most sophisticated explanations of cause and effect were defeated easily by snorting homespun scepticism, sure-yes, *aji-haan.* He could see her now, standing in the sooty doorway to the kitchen, her arm up on the wall, listening. "Fire," he said. "Whoosh. One moment of fire and a whole city gone."

"How?" It was Amma. Her hair was white, and she was wearing white, and she had a strong nose and direct eyes. The engineer looked up at her, a glass of milk in his left hand. "If you break a speck," he said. He didn't know how to translate "atom." "You release energy. Fire." Amma said, "How?" Now the children were quiet. Amma took two steps forward. "How?" The engineer gestured into the air. "It's like that thing in the *Mahabharata,*" he said finally. "That weapon that Ashwatthaman hurled at Arjun." "The Brahmasira?" Amma said. "That was stopped." "Not this one," the engineer said, turning his hand palm down. "They used it." Then the food was ready and he ate.

Nobody noticed until the next morning that Amma had stopped talking. "What happened?" the engineer asked. "Why aren't you talking?" A little later he asked, "Are you angry with me? Did I do something?" Amma shook her head but said nothing. She refused to talk to her friends, and to their children. Now some people thought she had taken a vow of silence, like Gandhi-ji, and others thought that she had been witchcrafted by some secret hater. The engineer was annoyed, and then concerned. He wanted to take her to the city, to a doctor. She put a hand on the ground and shook her head. But she wouldn't talk, couldn't. Finally he left, her son. In the weeks after her other children came, one by one, and still she spoke to nobody. She smiled, she went about her daily business, but her silence was complete and eternal.

First it was just one child, Nainavati's daughter, eight years old. Her skin cracked on her hands. Her mother rubbed her skin with *neem*-leaf oil, and held her close. The next morning the cracks were open, a little wider, and spreading to the elbows. And that afternoon Narain Singh's son had it too. There was no bleeding, no pain, only the lurch of Nainavati's heart when she looked at her daughter's hand and saw the white of bone at the wrist. A week later all the children in the village were splintered from head to toe. Looking at each other they wept with fear, and their parents were afraid to hold them. Pattadevi said it first. One morning her baby, ten months old, gurgled against her thigh, and Pattadevi raised her head, forgetful and so smiling, and she saw the pulsating beat of a tiny heart. Pattadevi shut her eyes tight, and in her anguish she said, "Amma's son brought it home, with his Japanese bomb." That was then the understanding of the village, true and agreed upon.

Finally the horror was that they grew used to it. The months passed and they were shunned by the neighbouring settlements, and certainly they did not want to go anywhere. Life had to go on, and so they tended the crops, saw to the animals, built and repaired, and lived in a sort of bleak satisfaction, and expectation of precisely nothing. On the three hundred and sixtieth day Amma came to the *panchayat*.

They were sitting at their usual places under the *pipal* tree, the old men, and the powerful, and then the others. They fell silent when Amma walked among them, surprised by her appearance in an assembly of men, and a little afraid of her, her witchy quiet and her confident walk. She sat under the pipal tree. In her hand she had a letter.

"What is that, Amma?" the *sarpanch* said. "A letter from your son? What does he write?" He took the letter from her, as he usually did, tore it open, and began to read. "Respected mother . . ."

"I want to praise," Amma said. 185

"What?" the *sarpanch* said, dropping the letter.

"The kindness of postmen, their long walks in the summer sun, their aching feet. The mysterious and generous knowledge of all those who cook, their intimate and vast power over us. The unsung courage of young brides, their sacrifices beyond all others, their patience. The age of trees, the years of their lives and their companionship. The sleeping ferocity of dogs—I saw two kill another last week—and their stretching muscles, their complete and deep and good happiness with a full stomach and a long sleep."

The *sarpanch* opened and closed his mouth. Before long all the women gathered too, with their children, and the whole village listened to Amma.

"The long song of those who drive trucks on the perpetual roads. The black faces of the diggers of coal, and their wives who try ever not to hear the sound of rushing water under their feet. The staggering smell of the birds that clean bones, their drunken walk with its anxious greed. The roofs of the village houses in the morning, seen from the *ghats* above the river, and the white glimmer of the temple above the trees. The roaring familiarity of the dusty brickmakers with fire. The painful faith of unrequited lovers."

The villagers listened to her. One of the children noticed it first. He tugged 190
at his mother's hand, but she was rapt. He held her index finger and pulled it to and fro, and the gold bangles on her wrist jingled, and she looked down. He held up his arm to her, and she saw the cracks were gone. Then others saw it too. No one could see it happening, not one fissure or the other closing, but if they looked and looked away and looked back, they could see the skin becoming whole. And

> Amma was talking. She praised the sky, the earth, and every woman in the village, and each of the men, even the ones known for sloth, or cruelty. Then they brought her food, and water, and she talked.
>
> When she finished talking the next day the children were well. Much later, the *sarpanch,* who was sitting on a *charpai* in her courtyard, said to her, "Well, Amma, your son brought the sickness, and you fixed it."
>
> "What did you say?" Amma said, and for a moment the *sarpanch* was afraid that for all his dignity she would throw the teacup she was holding at his head. "My son brought it?"
>
> "You have to admit that he came, and then they were sick."
>
> But Amma rolled her eyes. "*Aji-haan,*" she said, and that was that.

By the time Shanti had finished telling the story, the train was an extra two minutes late, and Rajan came out of his office and looked angrily down the platform. Frankie waved his flag and the bogie began to move. Shiv walked beside the window, and he watched the shadows from the bars move across Shanti's face. With every step he had to walk a little faster.

"Will you marry me?" he said.

"What?"

"Will you marry me?"

A shudder passed over Shanti's cheeks, a twist of emotion like a wave, and she turned her face to the side in pain, as if he had hit her. But then she looked up at him, and he could see that her eyes were full. He was running now.

"Yes," she said.

He raised a hand to the window as she leaned forward, but the train was away, and the platform came suddenly to an end. Shiv stood poised at the drop, one hand raised.

"Is it true?" It was Frankie, eager and open-faced, "Is it true?"

"What?"

"Your story, you stupid man, is it true?"

"Of course it is," Shiv said, waving his arm in front of Frankie's face. "It is. Look."

Frankie was looking past the arm with a deductive frown.

"What happened to you? Why are you grinning like that?"

"She's going to marry me."

"She is? She? You mean you asked?"

"And she said yes."

"But where is she going now?"

"I don't know."

Frankie raised his arms in the air, clutched at his hair, threw down his red flag and green flag and stomped on them. "God help this country, with lovers like you," he said finally. Then he took Shiv by the arm, and took him home, to Frankie's lair, and began to plan.

Two months and three days later, in a train to Bombay, Shanti slept with her head on Shiv's knee. They were in an unreserved third class compartment, and Shiv was thinking about the four hundred and twenty-two rupees in his wallet. Next to the notes he had a folded yellow slip of paper with the address of one Benedicto Fernandes, who was Frankie's first cousin and an old Bombay hand. In the sleeping dimness of the compartment Shiv could see the nodding heads and swaying shoulders of his fellow travelers, two salesmen on their way back from their territories, a farmer with his feet propped up on a huge cloth bundle, his wife, a muscular mechanic, and others. They had made space on the one berth for the newlyweds.

They had been married in a civil ceremony in Delhi. This after Shiv 215
had written to his father, "My Dear Papa," and "I must ask your blessing in a momentous decision," and had received a curt reply telling him to come home, and containing no blessing, or word of affection. He had written again, and this time received two pages of fury, "disobedience" and "disgrace to the family" and "that woman, whoever or whatever she may be." Meanwhile Anuradha was tremulous, and Rajan had muttered about what one owed to one's parents, and what a bad influence that Furtado fellow was. But finally Frankie had saved them. He had found Shanti, her letters and Shiv's had gone to his address, and he had made the arrangements, set up their rendezvous, lent money, and had gone with Shiv to wait for the night bus at the crossroads.

"What if they do something, Frankie? What if you lose your job?"

"All to the good, my friend. I shall be free." In the moonlight Frankie threw his head back. They stood arm in arm, with fields and bunds stretching away on all sides. Frankie was humming something, a song that faded gently under the chittering of the crickets. When the headlights appeared to the east, appeared and disappeared, Shiv said, "Thanks, *yaar*."

"*Yaars* don't say thanks," Frankie said. Then the bus roared up to them, heavingly full of passengers, and luggage, and a half dozen goats. Frankie found a place for Shiv's suitcase on the roof, and a space for him to squat in the doorwell. Shiv hugged him, hard, and Frankie held him close.

"Go," Frankie said.

"Frankie, come to Bombay," Shiv said as the bus pulled away. Frankie 220
raised a hand, and that was the last Shiv saw of him, in a silvery swirl of dust and a fading light.

Now Shiv looked down at the head on his knee, at the rich thickness of the dark hair. It occurred to him that they hadn't kissed yet. After they had signed the register they had both paused, and then Shiv had thanked the registrar. Then they had gone to the station, awkward in the tonga, each keeping to one side of the cracked leather seat. Shiv had seen kisses in the movies, but he hadn't ever kissed anyone. He looked around the compartment, and then, with the very tips of his fingers, he touched Shanti's cheek. It was very soft, and he was overcome by a knowledge of complete unfamiliarity, of wonderment, and complete tenderness. "Shanti," he whispered under his breath. "Shanti." How strange it was, how unknown. How unknowable.

Shiv's fingers moved over her cheekbone, and now she stirred. He watched her come awake, the small stirrings. Then she tried to stretch, and found the hardness of his hip, and the end of the berth, and woke up. He could see memory coming back, shiverings of happiness and loss. She sat up, rubbed her face. He smiled.

"Do you have a photo of yourself?" she said.

"What?"

"A photo. Of yourself."

"You woke up thinking about this?"

"I went to sleep thinking I don't have one."

Shiv leaned back, raised his hip with a curl of pain through his back, and found his wallet. Under the four hundred and twenty-two rupees and behind Frankie's cousin's address he found a creased snapshot.

"Here," he said. "Actually it's Hari. But it doesn't matter. We're identical."

She was looking down at the photo, smoothing away the ridges. "No, you're not."

"Yes, we are."

"No, really, you look different. Very different. See?"

He looked, and there was the well-known twist of the torso, the smile. He knew exactly and well the leaves behind the hair, the tree, and the garden.

"Maybe," he said. "Maybe."

"It is," she said, certain. "You are." She took the photo from him and opened her purse, found a small black diary and put the picture away.

"How about one of yourself?" he said.

She hesitated, then opened the diary to the back. In the picture she gave him she was laughing, leaning towards the lense. But in front of her, there was a smiling man, very handsome, dark hair and keen pilot's eyes, and her hand rested on the epaulettes of his jacket.

"You're different, too," Shiv said.

"I was younger, yes." Shanti said.

"More beautiful now, I meant," Shiv said, and she smiled at him, and he wanted very much to kiss her but the compartment was stirring now. They sat back and away from each other as the travellers awakened themselves with thunderous yawns. Shiv put the photo in his shirt pocket, and raised the shutter on the window. He leaned into the fresh wash of air, the glad early grey of the land. You are changed, Shiv thought, and I am, and we are all something new now. And then he looked up, and saw the red sun on a ridge, and he was filled with excitement and foreboding. The mountains here were unfamiliar to him, different in their age, their ridges, and the shape of their rivers.

"We must be near Bombay," he said.

One of the salesmen leaned over to the window, scratched at an armpit, looked about with the certainty of a professional traveler, and shook his head. "No, not quite," he said. "Not yet, *beta*."

Shiv laughed. He looked at Shanti. She was laughing with him. "We'll get there," he said.

Now there was night outside. In the dark I wiped at my face, and listened to the clear clink of ice in Subramaniam's glass. There was something I wanted to say, but it seemed impossible to speak. Then I heard a key turning in the door.

"That must be my wife," he said, and got up. "She and her friends have a Ladies' Tea on Sundays. Where they drink anything but tea." A light came on in the corridor.

"Are you sitting in the dark?" she called, and another light flickered, a lamp just inside the room. She had the same white hair as him, and round gold-rimmed glasses, and she was wearing a dark red sari.

"This is young Ranjit Sharma," Subramaniam said. "From the bar, you remember."

"*Namaste, namaste, Ranjit,*" she said in answer to me. "Sit, sit. And you, you've been giving him those horrible chips? Has he been eating them, Ranjit? And drinking? He's not supposed to, you know. And did you go to Dr. Mehdi's for the medicine?"

He hadn't, and so she shooed him out, and I made her a drink. She drank Scotch and water and talked about horses. Also about a long vacation that they were to take, and their reservations.

"You're feeling better, then?" I said.

"Me? Me? Oh, I see. You mustn't believe a word he says, you know." She took off her glasses. Her eyes were a lovely flecked brown in the lamplight. He had said nothing about her eyes. "The medicine is for him, not for me."

"Is it serious?"

"Yes."

"I'm sorry."

She shrugged, just like him, and I thought they looked exactly like each other, transformed by the years together, and I tried to smile.

"Don't be sad," she said. "We've had our life, our Bombay life. Come on, you'll stay for dinner. But you'll cut onions before."

It is night, and I am walking in my city. After dinner, Subramaniam came down to the road with me, and walked a little way. What happened to Frankie, I asked. Did he come to Bombay and become a movie star? For a long moment Subramaniam said nothing, and we walked together. No, he said, no, to tell you the truth, Frankie died. He was killed. Those were bad times. But there was somebody else who came to Mumbai and became a movie star. When I come back from vacation, he said, "I'll tell you that one. You had better, I said. At the *naka* he shook my hand. Goodbye, chief, I said.

I am walking in my city. The island sleeps, and I can feel the jostling of its dreams. I know they are out there, Mahalaxmi, Mazagaon, Umerkhadi, Pydhuni, and the grand melodrama of Marine Drive. I have music in my head, the jingle of those old names, Wadala, Matunga, Koliwada, Sakinaka, and as I cross the causeway I can hear the steady, eternal beat of the sea, and I am filled with a terrible longing. I know I am walking to Bandra, and I know I am looking for Ayesha. I will stand before her building, and when it is morning I will call up to her. I might ask her to go for a walk, I might ask her to marry me. If we search together, I think, we may find in Andheri, in Colaba, in Bhuleshwar, perhaps not heaven, or its opposite, but only life itself.

CHARTING THE STORY

1 What major conceptual divisions of this story are reflected in its physical divisions?
2 What motivates Subramaniam to tell his story to the narrator? What has seemingly triggered this mass of stories-within-story?
3 To whom and to what are Shiv and Frankie, respectively or together, attracted, and why? How would you explain their virtual absence of jealousy concerning Shanti?

CONSIDERATIONS OF STYLE

1 How many stories are told within this hefty narrative? By whom? How are the stories thematically connected? Of what relevance is each of the enclosed narratives to the story as a whole? What is the holistic effect of the stories-within-story technique?
2 The Mahabharata, the great Indian epic mentioned on page 294, is structured as a series of stories within stories, contained in a text that is eight times the length of the Iliad and the Odyssey combined, or fifteen times the length of the Bible. Although one cannot reduce its plot or theme to a few sentences, it concerns, in the main, a struggle between larger-than-life antagonists from two sides of a divided family. How "Mahabharatic" is "Shanti"? Where is its style "epic," and how and where does it depart from that style? Of what other genres meaningful to Chandra, and to many Indians, does this story partake?
3 Discuss the stylistic and other rhetorical devices in Amma's "I want to praise" panegyric, which begins on page 295. What is she accomplishing with her praise, and what seems to motivate her to rise to this height?

AFTERTHOUGHTS

1 Shanti's prolonged, unescorted travel would have been strongly disapproved of in 1945, and would be almost impossible to pull off, even today. Apart from being reminiscent of the Mahabharata's stories of Damayanti and Nala and of Savitri and

Satyavan (both concerning a woman searching for her absent husband), how do various characters in the story react to Shanti? Why do Shiv and Frankie seem supportive of her quest?

2 How does Shiv's telling of his story (and Shanti's addendum) affect the narrator? Were Frankie to have narrated his part of it, how would the overall effect change?

THE WRITER'S CRAFT

1 Write about the eventual leave taking from the point of view of Frankie, or from that of any of the members of Shiv's family.

2 Paragraph 157 evokes a plethora of stories told by Shanti to Shiv: "The Ten Year Old Boy Who Joined the Theatre Company of Death, The Woman Who Traded in Oil and Bought a Flying Racehorse, The Farmer Who Went to America and Fell Through a Hole to the Other Side of the World, The Moneylender Who Saw the True Face of the Creator, Ghurabat and Her Lover the Assassin Who Wept, the Birth of the Holiest Nun in the World, and The Downfall of the Mughal Empire." Choose one of these titles, or make up one equally as wondrous, and relate the tale.

Part Four
(Post) Colonization

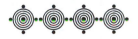

One day these wazungu would go!
One day his people would be free! Then, then—he did not know what he would do. However, he bitterly assured himself no one would ever flout his manhood again.

NGUGI WA THIONG'O, *The Return*

SALMAN RUSHDIE

SALMAN RUSHDIE *was born in Bombay in 1947, the same year India gained its independence from Britain. He attended a British-style private school in Bombay, lived briefly in Pakistan, and later went to Rugby School in England. He received a degree in Islamic history from Cambridge University.*

Rushdie's first novel, Grimus, *was published in 1975; his second,* Midnight's Children *(1981), won the prestigious Booker Prize; his third,* Shame, *was published in 1983; his fourth novel,* The Satanic Verses *(1988), earned him a death warrant, or* fatwa, *for "blasphemy" from the late Ayatollah Khomeini of Iran. Later works include the short story collection* East, West *(1994), and the novels* Haroun and the Sea of Stories *(1990),* The Moor's Last Sigh *(1995), and* The Ground Beneath Her Feet *(1999). He has also written the major nonfiction works* The Jaguar Smile, The Wizard of Oz, *and* Imaginary Homelands: Essays and Criticism *(1981).*

The government of Iran recently lifted the fatwa, *and, while no longer living in underground seclusion in England, Rushdie makes only guarded, usually unpublicized appearances.*

In this essay, from Imaginary Homelands, *Rushdie argues strongly against the "ghettoization" of literature in English.*

PERSPECTIVES

1 Research the history of the British Commonwealth. What do the member countries have in common? How do they differ? How does the use of the term "commonwealth" differ in the United States? In the post-Soviet Commonwealth of Independent States, or CIS?

2 In your view, or in that of your English Department, what constitutes "English literature"? What constitutes "Commonwealth" or "postcolonial" literature? Are these terms interchangeable? Are there discrepancies of opinion? If so, what might account for them?

'Commonwealth Literature' Does Not Exist

When I was invited to speak at the 1983 English Studies Seminar in Cambridge, the lady from the British Council offered me a few words of reassurance. "It's all right," I was told, "for the purposes of our seminar, English studies are taken to include Commonwealth literature." At all other times, one was forced to conclude, these two would be kept strictly apart, like squabbling children, or sexually incompatible pandas, or, perhaps, like unstable, fissile materials whose union might cause explosions.

A few weeks later I was talking to a literature don—a specialist, I ought to say, in *English* literature—a friendly and perceptive man. "As a Commonwealth writer," he suggested, "you probably find, don't you, that there's a kind of liberty, certain advantages, in occupying, as you do, a position on the periphery?"

And then a British magazine published, in the same issue, interviews with Shiva Naipaul, Buchi Emecheta and myself. In my interview, I admitted that I had begun to find this strange term, "Commonwealth literature," unhelpful and even a little distasteful; and I was interested to read that in *their* interviews, both Shiva Naipaul and Buchi Emecheta, in their own ways, said much the same thing. The three interviews appeared, therefore, under the headline: "Commonwealth writers... but don't call them that!"

By this point, the Commonwealth was becoming unpopular with me.

Isn't this the very oddest of beasts, I thought—a school of literature 5
whose supposed members deny vehemently that they belong to it. Worse, these denials are simply disregarded! It seems the creature has taken on a life of its own. So when I was invited to a conference about the animal in—of all places—Sweden, I thought I'd better go along to take a closer look at it.

The conference was beautifully organized, packed with erudite and sophisticated persons capable of discoursing at length about the new spirit of experiment in English-language writing in the Philippines. Also, I was able to meet writers from all over the world—or, rather, the Commonwealth. It was such a seductive environment that it almost persuaded me that the subject under discussion actually existed, and was not simply a fiction, and a fiction of a unique type, at that, in that it has been created solely by critics and academics, who have then proceeded to believe in it wholeheartedly... but the doubts did, in spite of all temptations to succumb, persist.

Many of the delegates, I found, were willing freely to admit that the term "Commonwealth literature" was a bad one. South Africa and Pakistan, for instance, are not members of the Commonwealth, but their authors apparently belong to its literature. On the other hand, England, which, as far as I'm aware, has not been expelled from the Commonwealth quite yet, has been excluded from its literary manifestation. For obvious reasons. It would never do to include English literature, the great sacred thing itself, with this bunch of upstarts, huddling together under this new and badly made umbrella.

At the Commonwealth literature conference, I talked with and listened to the Australian poet Randolph Stow; the West Indian, Wilson Harris; Ngugi wa Thiong'o from Kenya; Anita Desai from India and the Canadian novelist Aritha van Herk. I became quite sure that our differences were so much more signficant than our similarities, that it was impossible to say what "Commonwealth literature"—the idea which had, after all, made possible our assembly—might conceivably mean. Van Herk spoke eloquently about the problem of drawing imaginative maps of the great emptinesses of Canada; Wilson Harris soared into great flights of metaphysical lyricism and high abstraction; Anita Desai spoke in whispers, her novel the novel of sensibility, and I wondered what on earth she could be held to have in common with the committed Marxist Ngugi, an overtly political writer, who expressed his rejection of the English language by reading his own work in Swahili, with a Swedish version read by his translator, leaving the rest of us completely bemused. Now obviously this great diversity would be entirely natural in a general literature conference—but this was a particular school of literature, and I was trying to work out what that school was supposed to be.

The nearest I could get to a definition sounded distinctly patronizing: "Commonwealth literature," it appears, is that body of writing created, I think, in the English language, by persons who are not themselves white Britons, or Irish, or citizens of the United States of America. I don't know whether black Americans are citizens of this bizarre Commonwealth or not. Probably not. It is also uncertain whether citizens of Commonwealth countries writing in languages other than English—Hindi, for example—or who switch out of English, like Ngugi, are permitted into the club or asked to keep out.

By now "Commonwealth literature" was sounding very unlikeable in- 10
deed. Not only was it a ghetto, but it was actually an exclusive ghetto. And the effect of creating such a ghetto was, is, to change the meaning of the far broader term "English literature"—which I'd always taken to mean simply the literature of the English language—into something far narrower, something topographical, nationalistic, possibly even racially segregationist.

It occurred to me, as I surveyed this muddle, that the category is a chimera, and in very precise terms. The word has of course come to mean an unreal, monstrous creature of the imagination; but you will recall that the classical chimera was a monster of a rather special type. It had the head of a lion, the body of a goat and a serpent's tail. This is to say, it could exist only in dreams, being composed of elements which could not possibly be joined together in the real world.

The dangers of unleashing such a phantom into the groves of literature are, it seems to me, manifold. As I mentioned, there is the effect of creating a ghetto, and that, in turn, does lead to a ghetto mentality amongst some of its occupants. Also, the creation of a false category can and does lead to excessively narrow, and sometimes misleading, readings of some of the artists it is held to include; and again, the existence—or putative existence—of the beast distracts attention from what is actually worth looking at, what is actually going on. I thought it might be worth spending a few minutes reflecting further on these dangers.

I'll begin from an obvious starting place. English is by now the world language. It achieved this status partly as a result of the physical colonization of a quarter of the globe by the British, and it remains ambiguous but central to the affairs of just about all the countries to whom it was given, along with mission schools, trunk roads and the rules of cricket, as a gift of the British colonizers.

But its present-day pre-eminence is not solely—perhaps not even primarily—the result of the British legacy. It is also the effect of the primacy of the United States of America in the affairs of the world. This second impetus towards English could be termed a kind of linguistic neo-colonialism, or just plain pragmatism on the part of many of the world's governments and educationists, according to your point of view.

As for myself, I don't think it is always necessary to take up the anti-colonial—or is it post-colonial?—cudgels against English. What seems to me to be happening is that those peoples who were once colonized by the language are now rapidly remaking it, domesticating it, becoming more and more relaxed about the way they use it—assisted by the English language's enormous flexibility and size, they are carving out large territories for themselves within its frontiers.

To take the case of India, only because it's the one with which I'm most familiar. The debate about the appropriateness of English in post-British India has been raging ever since 1947; but today, I find, it is a debate which has meaning only for the older generation. The children of independent India seem not to think of English as being irredeemably tainted by its colonial provenance. They use it as an Indian language, as one of the tools they have to hand.

(I am simplifying, of course, but the point is broadly true.)

There is also an interesting North-South divide in Indian attitudes to English. In the North, in the so-called "Hindi belt," where the capital, Delhi, is located, it is possible to think of Hindi as a future national language; but in South India, which is at present suffering from the attempts of central government to *impose* this national language on it, the resentment of Hindi is far greater than of English. After spending quite some time in South India, I've become convinced that English is an essential language in India, not only because of its technical vocabularies and the international communication which it makes possible, but also simply to permit two Indians to talk to each other in a tongue which neither party hates.

Incidentally, in West Bengal, where there is a State-led move against English, the following graffito, a sharp dig at the State's Marxist chief minister, Jyoti Basu, appeared on a wall, in English: it said, "My son won't learn English; your son won't learn English; but Jyoti Basu will send his son abroad to learn English."

One of the points I want to make is that what I've said indicates, I hope, that Indian society and Indian literature have a complex and developing relationship with the English language. This kind of post-colonial dialectic is propounded as one of the unifying factors in "Commonwealth literature"; but it clearly does not exist, or at least is far more peripheral to the problems of literatures in Canada, Australia, even South Africa. Every time you examine the general theories of "Commonwealth literature" they come apart in your hands.

English literature has its Indian branch. By this I mean the literature of the English language. This literature is also Indian literature. There is no incompatibility here. If history creates complexities, let us not try to simplify them.

So: English is an Indian literary language, and by now, thanks to writers like Tagore, Desani, Chaudhuri, Mulk Raj Anand, Raja Rao, Anita Desai and others, it has quite a pedigree. Now it is certainly true that the English-language literatures of England, Ireland and the USA are older than, for example, the Indian; so it's possible that "Commonwealth literature" is no more than an ungainly name for the world's younger English literatures. If that were true or, rather, if that were all, it would be a relatively unimportant misnomer. But it isn't all. Because the term is not used simply to describe, or even misdescribe, but also to *divide.* It permits academic institutions, publishers, critics and even readers to dump a large segment of English literature into a box and then more or less ignore it. At best, what is called "Commonwealth literature" is positioned *below* English literature "proper"—or, to come back to my friend the don, it places Eng. Lit. at the centre and the rest of the world at the periphery. How depressing that such a view should persist in the study of literature long after it has been discarded in the study of everything else English.

What is life like inside the ghetto of "Commonwealth literature"? Well, every ghetto has its own rules, and this one is no exception.

One of the rules, one of the ideas on which the edifice rests, is that literature is an expression of nationality. What Commonwealth literature finds interesting in Patrick White is his Australianness; in Doris Lessing, her Africanness; in V. S. Naipaul, his West Indianness, although I doubt that anyone would have the nerve to say so to his face. Books are almost always praised for using motifs and symbols out of the author's own national tradition, or when their form echoes some traditional form, obviously pre-English, and when the influences at work upon the writer can be seen to be wholly internal to the culture from which he "springs." Books which mix traditions, or which seek consciously to break with tradition, are often treated as highly suspect. To give one example. A few years ago the Indian poet, Arun Kolatkar, who works with equal facility in English and Marathi, wrote, in English, an award-winning series of poems called *Jejuri,* the account of his visit to a Hindu temple town. (Ironically, I should say, it won the Commonwealth Poetry Prize.) The poems are marvellous, contemporary, witty, and in spite of their subject they are the work of a non-religious man. They aroused the wrath of one of the doyens of Commonwealth literary studies in India, Professor C. D. Narasimhaiah, who, while admitting the brilliance of the poems, accused Kolatkar of making his work irrelevant by seeking to defy tradition.

What we are facing here is the bogy of Authenticity. This is something which the Indian art critic Geeta Kapur has explored in connection with modern Indian painting, but it applies equally well to literature. "Authenticity" is the respectable child of old-fashioned exoticism. It demands that sources, forms, style, language and symbol all derive from a supposedly homogeneous and unbroken tradition. Or else. What is revealing is that the term, so much in use inside the little world of "Commonwealth literature," and always as term of praise, would seem ridiculous outside this world. Imagine a novel being eulogized for being "authentically English," or "authentically German." It would seem absurd. Yet such absurdities persist in the ghetto.

In my own case, I have constantly been asked whether I am British, or Indian. The formulation "Indian-born British writer" has been invented to explain me. But, as I said last night, my new book deals with Pakistan. So what now? "British-resident Indo-Pakistani writer"? You see the folly of trying to contain writers inside passports.

One of the most absurd aspects of this quest for national authenticity is that—as far as India is concerned, anyway—it is completely fallacious to suppose that there is such a thing as a pure, unalloyed tradition from which to draw. The only people who seriously believe this are religious extremists. The rest of us understand that the very essence of Indian culture is that we possess a mixed tradition, a *mélange* of elements as disparate as ancient Mughal and contemporary Coca-Cola American. To say nothing of Muslim, Buddhist, Jain, Christian, Jewish, British, French, Portuguese, Marxist, Maoist, Trotskyist, Vietnamese, capitalist, and of course Hindu elements. Eclecticism, the ability to take from the world what seems fitting and to leave the rest, has always been a hallmark of the Indian tradition, and today it is at the centre of the best work being done both in the visual arts and in literature. Yet eclecticism is not really a nice word in the lexicon of "Commonwealth literature." So the reality of the mixed tradition is replaced by the fantasy of purity.

You will perhaps have noticed that the purpose of this literary ghetto—like that of all ghettos, perhaps—is to confine, to restrain. Its rules are basically conservative. Tradition is all; radical breaches with the past are frowned upon. No wonder so many of the writers claimed by "Commonwealth literature" deny that they have anything to do with it.

I said that the concept of "Commonwealth literature" did disservice to some writers, leading to false readings of their work; in India, I think this is true of the work of Ruth Jhabvala and, to a lesser extent, Anita Desai. You see, looked at from the point of view that literature must be nationally connected and even committed, it becomes simply impossible to understand the cast of mind and vision of a rootless intellect like Jhabvala's. In Europe, of course, there are enough instances of uprooted, wandering writers and even peoples to make Ruth Jhabvala's work readily comprehensible; but by the rules of the Commonwealth ghetto, she is beyond the pale. As a result, her reputation in India is much lower than it is in the West. Anita Desai, too, gets into trouble when she states with complete honesty that her work has no Indian models.

The novel is a Western form, she says, so the influences on her are Western. Yet her delicate but tough fictions are magnificent studies of Indian life. This confuses the cohorts of the Commonwealth. But then, where "Commonwealth literature" is concerned, confusion is the norm.

I also said that the creation of this phantom category served to obscure 30
what was really going on, and worth talking about. To expand on this, let me say that if we were to forget about "Commonwealth literature," we might see that there is a kind of commonality about much literature, in many languages, emerging from those parts of the world which one could loosely term the less powerful, or the powerless. The magical realism of the Latin Americans influences Indian language writers in India today. The rich, folk-tale quality of a novel like *Sandro of Chegem,* by the Muslim Russian Fazil Iskander, finds its parallels in the work—for instance—of the Nigerian, Amos Tutuola, or even Cervantes. It is possible, I think, to begin to theorize common factors between writers from these societies—poor countries, or deprived minorities in powerful countries—and to say that much of what is new in world literature comes from this group. This seems to me to be a "real" theory, bounded by frontiers which are neither political nor linguistic but imaginative. And it is developments of this kind which the chimera of "Commonwealth literature" obscures.

This transnational, cross-lingual process of pollination is not new. The works of Rabindranath Tagore, for example, have long been widely available in Spanish-speaking America, thanks to his close friendship with the Argentinian intellectual Victoria Ocampo. Thus an entire generation, or even two, of South American writers have read *Gitanjali, The Home and the World* and other works, and some, like Mario Vargas Llosa, say that they found them very exciting and stimulating.

If this "Third World literature" is one development obscured by the ghost of "Commonwealth literature," then "Commonwealth literature's" emphasis on writing in English distracts attention from much else that is worth our attention. I tried to show how in India the whole issue of language was a subject of deep contention. It is also worth saying that major work is being done in India in many languages other than English; yet outside India there is just about no interest in any of this work. The Indo-Anglians seize all the limelight. Very little is translated; very few of the best writers—Premchand, Anantha Moorthy—or the best novels are known, even by name.

To go on in this vein: it strikes me that, at the moment, the greatest area of friction in Indian literature has nothing to do with English literature, but with the effects of the hegemony of Hindi on the literatures of other Indian languages, particularly other North Indian languages. I recently met the distinguished Gujarati novelist, Suresh Joshi. He told me that he could write in Hindi but felt obliged to write in Gujarati because it was a language under threat. Not from English, or the West: from Hindi. In two or three generations, he said, Gujarati could easily die. And he compared it, interestingly, to the state of the Czech language under the yoke of Russian, as described by Milan Kundera.

This is clearly a matter of central importance for Indian literature. "Commonwealth literature" is not interested in such matters.

It strikes me that my title may not really be accurate. There is clearly such 35
a thing as "Commonwealth literature," because even ghosts can be made to exist if you set up enough faculties, if you write enough books and appoint enough research students. It does not exist in the sense that writers do not write it, but that is of minor importance. So perhaps I should rephrase myself: "Commonwealth literature" should not exist. If it did not, we could appreciate writers for what they are, whether in English or not; we could discuss literature in terms of its real groupings, which may well be national, which may well be linguistic, but which may also be international, and based on imaginative affinities; and as far as Eng. Lit. itself is concerned, I think that if all English literatures could be studied together, a shape would emerge which would truly reflect the new shape of the language in the world, and we could see that Eng. Lit. has never been in better shape, because the world language now also possesses a world literature, which is proliferating in every conceivable direction.

The English language ceased to be the sole possession of the English some time ago. Perhaps "Commonwealth literature" was invented to delay the day when we rough beasts actually slouch into Bethlehem. In which case, it's time to admit that the centre cannot hold.

CHARTING THE ESSAY

1. What is ironic, to Rushdie, about the inclusion or exclusion of some Commonwealth (or non-Commonwealth) national literatures from the category of "Commonwealth literature"? What might account for these "extra" or "missing" national literatures?
2. Give at least three reasons why so-called "Commonwealth writers" object to that term to describe themselves. According to Rushdie, what do these writers share that is of far greater importance than nationality or historical association with the British Commonwealth?
3. What are some of the "rules" of the Commonwealth "ghetto" to which Rushdie begins to refer in Paragraph 23? How does he argue against them?
4. Why do you suppose Rushdie rephrases the title of his essay at the end?

CONSIDERATIONS OF STYLE

1. To what audience does this essay appear to be directed? What tone is he taking with his readers? What evidence in the text would lead you to these conclusions?
2. What is the effect of the animal references (Paragraphs 1, 5, 11, 36) used by Rushdie to describe "Commonwealth literature"?

3 How do Rushdie's accounts of the English Studies Seminar, the conversation with a colleague, and the magazine article (Paragraphs 1–3) work stylistically in this essay? Had he not included this material, and instead launched right into his argument, how would the essay be different?

AFTERTHOUGHTS

1 How does the debate over "Commonwealth literature" parallel that over "ethnic literature" in the United States, Canada, Australia, or New Zealand?

2 In the last paragraph, Rushdie writes: "Perhaps 'Commonwealth literature' was invented to delay the day when we rough beasts actually slouch into Bethlehem. In which case, it's time to admit that the centre cannot hold." Rushie is alluding to William B Yeats's poem *The Second Coming:*

Turning and turning in the widening gyre
The falcon cannot hear the falconer;
Things fall apart; the centre cannot hold;
Mere anarchy is loosed upon the world,
The blood-dimmed tide is loosed, and everywhere
The ceremony of innocence is drowned;
The best lack all conviction, while the worst
Are full of passionate intensity.
Surely some revelation is at hand;
The Second Coming! Hardly are those words out
Surely the Second Coming is at hand.

When a vast image out of *Spiritus Mundi*
Troubles my sight: somewhere in the sand of the desert
A shape with lion body and the head of a man,
A gaze blank and pitiless as the sun,
Is moving its slow thighs, while all about it
Reel shadows of the indignant desert birds.
The darkness drops again; but now I know
That twenty centuries of stony sleep
Were vexed to nightmare by a rocking cradle,
And what rough beast, its hour come round at last,
Slouches towards Bethlehem to be born?

Taking both Yeats's poem and Rushdie's essay together, what is Rushdie accomplishing with this allusion?

THE WRITER'S CRAFT

1 Compare the texts of any three writers from different countries found in this anthology in terms of the literary commonality noted by Rushdie in Paragraph 30.

2 Outline Rushdie's argument against the notion of a "commonwealth literature" in terms of its major claims and counterclaims (rebuttals), stated reasons, grounds, qualifications, and underlying assumptions.

3 Propose a syllabus for your ideal literature class. What texts would you wish to feature, and why?

CHINUA ACHEBE

CHINUA ACHEBE *was born in 1930 in the Igbo region of eastern Nigeria. He was educated at mission schools, where he learned English and was converted to Christianity. The inherent tension of his dual heritage—pre-colonial and colonial—is prominent in his works. Achebe's first novel,* Things Fall Apart *(1959), written when he was in his twenties, has become a classic. His later works include the poetry collection* Christmas in Biafra and Other Poems *(1969),* Girls at War and Other Stories *(1972), and the novel* Anthills of the Savannah *(1983).*

Achebe is one of Nigeria's best-known writers. He has been a steadfast activist concerned about the disappearance of democracy in his country.

"The Song of Ourselves" is from a talk that Achebe gave for the LWT South Bank Show *in 4 February 1990, and was published in* New Statesman & Society's *9 February 1990 issue.*

PERSPECTIVES

1 Before commencing your undergraduate studies, what African writers could you have named, and how prevalent were they in your reading curriculum? (Compare answers with fellow students; do you find common threads? What would account for the commonality or lack thereof?)

2 In your view, is "literature" a thing that can be disconnected from a writer's or reader's gender, race, class, or worldview, that it somehow transcends these categories? How so, or how not?

The Song of Ourselves

Just under two years ago, I was one of a dozen or so foreign guests at a writers' symposium in Dublin. The general theme chosen, I believe, by the novelist Anthony Cronin, was "Literature as celebation." Some of my colleagues appeared to have difficulty with that subject. For my part, I found it almost perfect; it rendered in a simple form of words a truth about art which accorded with my traditional inheritance and satisfied my personal taste. A kind columnist referred to me as the man who invented African literature. I took the opportunity given me at the symposium to dissociate myself from that well-meant but blasphemous characterization. My refusal was due rather to an artistic taboo among my people the Igbo of Nigeria, a prohibition—on pain of being finished off rather quickly by the gods—from laying a proprietary hand on even the smallest item in that communal enterprise in creativity.

I offer this to you as one illustration of my pre-colonial inheritance—of art as celebration of my reality; of art in its social dimension; of the creative potential in all of us and of the need to exercise this latent energy again and again in artistic expression and communal, cooperative enterprises.

Now I come to my colonial inheritance. To call my colonial experience an inheritance may surprise some people. But everything is grist to the mill of the artist. True, one grain may differ from another in its powers of nourishment; still, we must accord appropriate recognition to every grain that comes our way.

It is not my intention to engage in a detailed evaluation of the colonial experience, but merely to ask what possibility, what encouragement there was in this episode of our history for the celebration of our own world, for the singing of the song of ourselves, in the din of an insistent world and song of others.

Colonization may indeed be a very complex affair, but one thing is certain; you do not walk in, seize the land, the person, the history of another, and then sit back and compose hymns of praise in his honor. To do that would amount to calling yourself a bandit; and you don't want to do that. So what do you do? You construct very elaborate excuses for your action. You say, for instance, that the man in question is worthless and quite unfit to manage himself or his affairs. If there are valuable things like gold or diamonds which you are carting away from this territory, you proceed to prove that he doesn't own them in the real sense of the word—that he and they just happened to be lying around the same place when you arrived. Finally, if the worse comes to the worst, you may even be prepared to question whether such as he can be, like you, fully human. From denying the presence of a man standing there before you, you end up questioning his very humanity. 5

In the colonial situation, *presence* was the critical question, the crucial word. Its denial was the keynote of colonialist ideololgy.

Question: Were there people there?

Answer: Well . . . not really, you know people of sorts, perhaps, but not as you and I understand the word.

From the period of the slave trade, through the age of colonization to the present day, the catalog of what Africa and Africans have been said not to have or not to be is a pretty extensive list. Churchmen at some point wondered about the soul itself. Did the black man have a soul? Lesser attributes such as culture and religion were debated extensively by others and generally ruled out as far as Africa was concerned. African history seemed unimaginable except perhaps for a few marginal places like Ethiopia, where Gibbon tells us of a short burst of activity followed from the seventh century by 1,000 years in which she fell into a deep sleep, "forgetful of the world by whom she was forgot," to use his own famous phrase.

A habit of generosity to Africa has not grown since Gibbon's time; on the 10
contrary, it seems to have diminished. If we shift our focus from history to literature we find the same hardening of attitude.

In *The Tempest,* Caliban is not specifically African; but he is the quintessential colonial subject created by Shakespeare's genius at the very onset of Europe's Age of Expansion. To begin with, Caliban knew not his own meaning but "wouldst gabble like a thing most brutish." However, Shakespeare restores humanity to him in many little ways, but especially by giving him not just speech but great poetry to speak before the play's end. Contrast this with Joseph Conrad's *Heart of Darkness* 300 years later. His Calibans make "a violent babble of uncouth sounds" and go on making it right through the novel.

So these African creatures have no soul, no religion, no culture, no history, no human speech, no IQ. Any wonder then that they should be subjected by those who are endowed with these human gifts?

A character in John Buchan's colonial novel *Prester John* says:

> I knew then the meaning of the white man's duty. He has to take all the risks. . . . That is the difference between white and black, the gift of responsibility, the power of being in a little way a king, and so long as we know and practice it we will not rule in Africa alone but wherever there are dark men who live only for their bellies.

John Buchan, by the way, was a very senior colonial administrator and novelist. One suspects he knew his terrain. So let us add to our long list of absences this last item—the absence of responsibility. If we add up all the absences reported from Africa, our grand total would equal one great absence of the Human Mind and Spirit.

I am not quite certain whether all the fieldworkers who reported these absences genuinely believed their report or whether it was some kind of make-believe, the kind of alibi we might expect a man arraigned for a serious crime to put together. It is significant, for example, that the moment when churchmen began to worry and doubt the existence of the black man's soul was the same moment when the black man's body was fetching high prices in the market place.

On the other hand, these reporters may well have believed their own sto- 15
ries—such was the complex nature of the imperial vocation. The picture of Africa and Africans which they carried in their minds did not grow there adventitiously, but was planted and watered by careful mental and educational husbandry. In an important study, Philip Curtin tells us that Europe's image of Africa which began to emerge in the 1870s was:

> found in children's books, in Sunday school tracts, in the popular press. Its major affirmations were the "common knowledge" of the educated classes. Thereafter,

> when new generations of explorers and administrators went to Africa, they went with a prior impression of what they would find. Most often, they found it...

Conrad's *Heart of Darkness,* first published in 1899, portrays Africa as a place where the wandering European may discover that the dark impulses and unspeakable appetites he has suppressed and forgotten through ages of civilization may spring into life again in answer to Africa's free and triumphant savagery. In one striking passage, Conrad reveals a very interesting aspect of the question of presence. It is the scene where a French gunboat is sitting on the water and firing rockets into the mainland. Conrad's intention, high minded as usual, is to show the futility of Europe's action in Africa:

> Pop would go one of the six-inch guns; a small flame would dart and vanish, a tiny projectile would give a feeble screech—and nothing happened. Nothing could happen. There was a touch of insanity in the proceeding.

About sanity I cannot speak. But futility, good heavens, no! By that crazy act of shelling the bush, France managed to acquire an empire in West and Equatorial Africa nine to ten times its own size. Whether there was method in the madness or not, there was profit, quite definitely.

Conrad was giving vent to one popular conceit that Europe's devastation of Africa left no mark on the victim. Africa is presumed to pursue its dark, mysterious ways and destiny untouched by explorations and expeditions. Sometimes Africa as an anthropomorphic personage steps out of the shadows and physically annihilates the invasion—which of course adds a touch of suspense and even tragedy to Europe's enterprise. One of the best images in *Heart of Darkness* is of a boat going upstream and the forest stepping across to bar its return. Note, however, that it is the African forest that takes the action: The Africans themselves are absent.

Contrast Conrad's episode of the French gunboat with the rendering of an analogous incident in *Ambiguous Adventure,* a powerful novel of colonization by the Muslim writer Cheikh Hamidou Kane, from Senegal—a country colonized by the French. Conrad insists on the futility of the bombardment but also the absence of human response to it. Cheikh Hamidou Kane, standing as it were at the explosive end of the trajectory, tells a different story. The words are those of the Most Royal Lady, a member of the Diallobe aristocracy:

> A hundred years ago our grandfather, along with all the inhabitants of this countryside, was awakened one morning by an uproar arising from the river. He took his gun and, followed by all the elite of the region, he flung himself upon the newcomers. His heart was intrepid and to him the value of liberty was greater than the value of life. Our grandfather, and the elite of the country with him, was defeated. Why? How? Only the newcomers know. We must ask them: We must go to learn from them the art of conquering without being in the right.

Conrad portrays a void, Hamidou Kane celebrates a human presence and a heroic struggle.

The difference is very clear. You might say *that* difference was the very reason the African writer came into being. His story has been told for him and he found the telling quite unsatisfactory. I went to a good school modeled on British public schools. I read lots of English books there; *Treasure Island* and *Gulliver's Travels* and *Prisoner of Zenda,* and *Oliver Twist* and *Tom Brown's School Days* and such books in their dozens. But I also encountered Ryder Haggard and John Buchan and the rest, and their "African" books.

I did not see myself as an African to begin with. I took sides with the white men against the savages. In other words, I went through my first level of schooling thinking I was of the party of the white man in his hair-raising adventures and narrow escapes. The white man was good and reasonable and intelligent and courageous. The savages arrayed against him were sinister and stupid or, at the most, cunning. I hated their guts.

But a time came when I reached the appropriate age and realized that 20
these writers had pulled a fast one on me! I was not on Marlowe's boat steaming up the Congo in *Heart of Darkness.* I was one of those strange beings jumping up and down on the river bank, making horrid faces.

That was when I said no, and realized that stories are not innocent; that they can be used to put you in the wrong crowd, in the party of the man who has come to dispossess you.

And talking of dispossession, what about language itself? Does my writing in the language of my colonizer not amount to acquiescing in the ultimate dispossession? This is a big and complex matter I cannot go into fully here. Let me simply say that when at the age of thirteen I went to that school modeled after British public schools, it was not only English literature that I encountered there. I came in contact also for the first time in my life with many boys of my own age who did not speak my Igbo language. And they were not foreigners, but fellow Nigerians. We lived in the same dormitories, attended the same morning assembly and classes, and gathered in the same playing fields. To be able to do all that we had to put away our different mother tongues and communicate in the language of our colonizers. This paradox was not peculiar to Nigeria. It happened in every colony where the British put diverse people together under one administration.

Some of my colleagues, finding this too awkward, have tried to rewrite their story into a straightforward case of oppression by presenting a happy monolingual African childhood brusquely disrupted by the imposition of a domineering foreign language. This historical fantasy demands that we throw out the English language in order to restore linguistic justice and self-respect to ourselves.

My position is that anyone who feels unable to write in English should follow their desires. But they must not take liberties with our history. It is simply not true that the English forced us to learn their language. On the contrary, British colonial policy in Africa and elsewhere emphasized again and again its preference for native languages. We see remnants of that preference today in the Bantustan policies of South Africa. We chose English not because the British desired it, but because having tacitly accepted the new nationalities into which colonialism had grouped us, we needed its language to transact our business, including the business of overthrowing colonialism itself in the fullness of time.

25 Now, that does not mean that our indigenous languages should now be neglected. It does mean that these languages must coexist and interact with the newcomer now and in the foreseeable future. For me, it is not *either* English or Igbo, it is *both.* Twenty-one years ago when Christopher Okigbo, our finest poet, fell in the Biafran battlefield, I wrote for him one of the best poems I have ever written, in the Igbo language, in the form of a traditional dirge sung by his age-grade. Fifteen years ago I wrote a different kind of poem, in English, to commemorate the passing way of the Angolan poet and President, Agostinho Neto.

It is inevitable, I believe, to see the emergence of modern African literature as a return of celebration. It is tempting to say that this literature came to put people back into Africa. But that would be wrong because people never left Africa except in the guilty imagination of Africa's antagonists.

CHARTING THE ESSAY

1. In the first paragraph, Achebe relates his response to a "kind columnist" who referred to him as "the man who invented African literature." Why did he respond in the way that he did? How might others have responded? Do you find that most would share the Igbo perspective of the "ownership" of creativity?
2. What are the basic positions upon African languages vs English that Achebe delineates, what viewpoint does he express, and for what reasons?

CONSIDERATIONS OF STYLE

1. In Achebe's contrast of Joseph Conrad's *Heart of Darkness* and Hamidou Kane's *Ambiguous Adventure,* what issue is at stake between Conrad's and Kane's visions of African resistance, and what tone does Achebe take in juxtaposing the two outlooks?
2. Achebe intersperses stories of himself as a writer and as a reader through his narrative. How do these stories serve to carry out his ideas? Were he to have stayed with the third-person point of view, how would his essay have changed?
3. Cite several places where Achebe's talk is infused with irony. How do you think his audience (collectively and individually) might have reacted to his presentation?

AFTERTHOUGHTS

1. Achebe notes, in Paragraphs 19 through 22, a sort of "de-Africanization" worked upon him by the texts that he read, which leads him to realize that "stories are not

innocent; that they can be used to put you in the wrong crowd, in the party of the man who has come to dispossess you." In any of your reading, have you found yourself degendered, deraced, denationalized, dehumanized, etc? If so, how did you respond? Were you aware of it at the time, or did you later realize it? If this has not happened, can you explain why this is so?

2 How complicit have colonizers been in the project of dehumanizing Africans? What were some of the actions taken, and how did they build upon one another? What, if anything, would you add to Achebe's historical narrative?

THE WRITER'S CRAFT

1 Compare this essay with Salman Rushdie's "'Commonwealth Literature' Does Not Exist," in this anthology. How do the authors' ideas and views mesh with each other's? What attitudes do they share concerning postcolonial English and englishes? In what ways do their perspectives differ?

2 Write a poem or a short story expanding upon, or responding to, any one of the issues that Achebe has discussed in this essay.

MUTABARUKA

MUTABARUKA *was born Allen Hope in Kingston, Jamaica in 1953. He changed his name to honor the poet Jean Batiste Mutabaruka. A rebellious youth, Mutabaruka was strongly influenced by the writings of Malcolm X and Black Panther Eldridge Cleaver, which fueled his criticism of the Jamaican political authorities. His militant style of poetry and reggae music invites comparisons to the more affectionate style of Bob Marley and Peter Tosh.*

Mutabaruka gave up urban life in Kingston for a back-to-nature existence in the Jamaican countryside, although he continues to host a controversial radio show, The Cutting Edge, *on which he debates social and political issues. He has released seven albums, appeared in two films (*Sankora *and* Land of Look Behind*), and has written four books of poetry. His gripping public performances have earned him an international reputation.*

This dub poem chronicles black people's struggle against racism and oppression along a historical continuum with no end yet in sight. At the same time, it serves as a manifesto of the poet's response to that struggle. It is recorded on Mutabaruka's 1999 CD, The Ultimate Collection *and is also included in* The Routledge Reader in Caribbean Literature *(1996).*

PERSPECTIVES

1 Cite some instances of revolutionary change—within the past two to three hundred years—that have been brought about by either violent or nonviolent means. How, would you say, have different means effected different ends?

2 Recall "protest songs" from the 1960s up to the present. How effective were they in galvanizing populations to achieve political change?

3 What reactions do you have to metapoetry (i e, poetry about poetry)?

dis poem

dis poem
shall speak of the wretched sea
that washed ships to these shores

of mothers cryin for their
young swallowed up by the sea
dis poem shall say nothin new
dis poem shall speak of time
time unlimited time undefined
dis poem shall call names names
like lumumba kenyatta nkrumah
hannibal akenaton malcolm garvey
haile selassie
dis poem is vex about apartheid racism fascism
the ku klux klan riots in brixton atlanta
jim jones
dis poem is revoltin against 1st world 2nd world
3rd world—division man made decision
dis poem is like all the rest
dis poem will not be amongst great literary works
will not be recited by poetry enthusiasts
will not be quoted by politicians nor men of religion
dis poem is knives bombs guns blood fire
blazin for freedom
yes dis poem is a drum
ashanti mau mau ibo yoruba nyahbingi warriors
uhuru uhuru
uhuru namibia
uhuru soweto
uhuru afrika
dis poem will not change things
dis poem need to be changed
dis poem is a rebirth of a people
arizin awakin understandin
dis poem speak is speakin have spoken
dis poem shall continue even when poets have stopped writin
dis poem shall survive u me it shall linger in history
in your mind
in time   forever
dis poem is time only time will tell
dis poem is still not written
dis poem has no poet
dis poem is just part of the story his-story her-story our-story
        the story still untold
is now ringin talkin irritatin
makin u want to stop it
but dis poem will not stop
dis poem is long cannot be short

dis poem cannot be tamed cannot be blamed
the story is still not told about dis poem
dis poem is old new
dis poem was copied from the bible your prayer book
playboy magazine the n.y. times readers digest
the c.i.a. files the k.g.b. files
dis poem is no secret
dis poem shall be called borin stupid senseless
dis poem is watchin u tryin to make sense from dis poem
dis poem is messin up your brains
makin u want to stop listenin to dis poem
but u shall not stop listenin to dis poem
  u need to know what will be said next in dis poem
    dis poem shall disappoint u
      because
        dis poem is to be continued in your mind
          in your mind in your mind your mind

CHARTING THE POEM

1 At what point does this poem cease to allude to specific historical events, personages, policies, or ideologies to postulate [itself?] as a musical manifesto?
2 What are the accomplishments of the black leaders cited in Lines 10–13? What do the disparate figures have in common that would place them on Mutabaruka's high altar?/give them nearly iconic status in Mutabaruka's poem?
3 What are the historical references that the poem "is vex about" in Lines 13–15?
4 Cite some obvious contradictions in the poem. Might some/most of these be considered stylistic rather than rhetorical?

CONSIDERATIONS OF STYLE

1 What are some features of Jamaican dialect reflected in the poem's expression? Is the poet consistent in representing dialect speech in every line?
2 What is the effect of the progressive indentation of the last five lines?
3 What effects does Mutabaruka achieve by "calling names" of the black leaders cited in Lines 10–13? Why simply "call them out"?

AFTERTHOUGHTS

1 When asked to explain the differences between his music and the music of other reggae musicians, Mutabaruka responded: "The difference between my music and

others is that I'm a poet just saying the poetry. The others are making the poems become songs." Relate that response to "dis poem," which is also recorded as a song on a CD collection, *The Ultimate Collection*.

2 In what ways is "dis poem," in the words of the author, copied from your bible your prayer book/ playboy magazine the n. y. times readers digest/ the c .i. a. files the k. g. b. files"?

3 Why does the speaker say "dis poem will not be amongst great literary works/ will not be recited by poetry enthusiasts/ will not be quoted by politicians nor men of religion"?

THE WRITER'S CRAFT

1 Write an essay comparing Mutabaruka with Derek Walcott, whose poem "The Season of Phantasmal Peace" appears in this anthology. What commonalities do the two poems share? What differences do you see between them? The two writers, who are of African origin but are native to the Caribbean region?

2 Continue the poem "in your mind," and when you're ready, write out your vision of its continuation.

3 Take any one of Mutabaruka's "lists" within the poem, and discuss the relevance of each of the items on it, to the other items in the list, and to the poem as a whole.

CHINUA ACHEBE

CHINUA ACHEBE *was born in 1930 in the Igbo region of eastern Nigeria. He was educated at mission schools, where he learned English and was converted to Christianity. The inherent tension of his dual heritage—pre-colonial and colonial—is prominent in his works. Achebe's first novel,* Things Fall Apart *(1959), written when he was in his mid-twenties, has become a classic. His later works include a book of poems* Christmas in Biafra and Other Poems *(1969), a collection of stories* Girls at War and Other Stories *(1972), and a novel* Anthills of the Savannah *(1983).*

Achebe is one of Nigeria's best-known writers. He has been a steadfast activist concerned about the disappearance of democracy in his country.

The tension in "Dead Men's Path" between British colonizers and colonized Nigerians—as well as that between Westernized and non-Westernized Africans—parallels that in Achebe's own past. In the course of his British mission school education, he admits to seeing himself not as an African but "of the party of the white man," with the African natives arrayed against him. In the end, however, through his literary works, Achebe has experienced a return to the celebration of his native past.

"Dead Men's Path" is taken from Girls at War and Other Stories.

PERSPECTIVES

1. The word *colony* has a rather benign etymology: from the Latin, *colonia, colonus,* settler; *colere,* to cultivate. How does the history of this word square with the reality of colonialism in recent history?
2. What are some lingering effects of nineteenth- and early twentieth-century colonialism in the world today? In Western Africa in particular?

Dead Men's Path

Michael Obi's hopes were fulfilled much earlier than he had expected. He was appointed headmaster of Ndume Central School in January 1949. It had always been an unprogressive school, so the Mission authorities decided to send a young and energetic man to run it. Obi accepted this responsibility with enthusiasm. He had many wonderful ideas and this was an opportunity to put them into practice. He had had sound secondary school education which designated him a "pivotal teacher" in the official records and set him apart from the other headmasters in the mission field. He was outspoken in his condemnation of the narrow views of these older and often less-educated ones.

"We shall make a good job of it, shan't we?" he asked his young wife when they first heard the joyful news of his promotion.

"We shall do our best," she replied. "We shall have such beautiful gardens and everything will be just *modern* and delightful . . ." In their two years of married life she had become completely infected by his passion for "modern methods" and his denigration of "these old and superannuated people in the teaching field who would be better employed as traders in the Onitsha market." She began to see herself already as the admired wife of the young headmaster, the queen of the school.

The wives of the other teachers would envy her position. She would set the fashion in everything . . . Then, suddenly, it occurred to her that there might not be other wives. Wavering between hope and fear, she asked her husband, looking anxiously at him.

"All our colleagues are young and unmarried," he said with enthusiasm which for once she did not share. "Which is a good thing," he continued.

"Why?"

"Why? They will give all their time and energy to the school."

Nancy was downcast. For a few minutes she became sceptical about the new school; but it was only for a few minutes. Her little personal misfortune could not blind her to her husband's happy prospects. She looked at him as he sat folded up in a chair. He was stoop-shouldered and looked frail. But he sometimes surprised people with sudden bursts of physical energy. In his present posture, however, all his bodily strength seemed to have retired behind his deep-set eyes, giving them an extraordinary power of penetration. He was only twenty-six, but looked thirty or more. On the whole, he was not unhandsome.

"A penny for your thoughts, Mike," said Nancy after a while, imitating the woman's magazine she read.

"I was thinking what a grand opportunity we've got at last to show these people how a school should be run."

Ndume School was backward in every sense of the word. Mr. Obi put his whole life into the work, and his wife hers too. He had two aims. A high standard of teaching was insisted upon, and the school compound was to be turned into a place of beauty. Nancy's dream-gardens came to life with the coming of the rains, and blossomed. Beautiful hibiscus and allamanda hedges in brilliant red and yellow marked out the carefully tended school compound from the rank neighbourhood bushes.

One evening as Obi was admiring his work he was scandalized to see an old woman from the village hobble right across the compound, through a marigold flower-bed and the hedges. On going up there he found faint signs of an almost disused path from the village across the school compound to the bush on the other side.

"It amazes me," said Obi to one of his teachers who had been three years in the school, "that you people allowed the villagers to make use of this footpath. It is simply incredible." He shook his head.

"The path," said the teacher apologetically, "appears to be very important to them. Although it is hardly used, it connects the village shrine with their place of burial."

"And what has that got to do with the school?" asked the headmaster.

"Well, I don't know," replied the other with a shrug of the shoulders. "But I remember there was a big row some time ago when we attempted to close it."

"That was some time ago. But it will not be used now," said Obi as he walked away. "What will the Government Education Officer think of this when he comes to inspect the school next week? The villagers might, for all I know, decide to use the schoolroom for a pagan ritual during the inspection."

Heavy sticks were planted closely across the path at the two places where it entered and left the school premises. These were further strengthened with barbed wire.

Three days later the village priest of *Ani* called on the headmaster. He was an old man and walked with a slight stoop. He carried a stout walking-stick which he usually tapped on the floor, by way of emphasis, each time he made a new point in his argument.

"I have heard," he said after the usual exchange of cordialities, "that our ancestral footpath has recently been closed . . ."

"Yes," replied Mr. Obi. "We cannot allow people to make a highway of our school compound."

"Look here, my son," said the priest bringing down his walking-stick, "this path was here before you were born and before your father was born. The whole life of this village depends on it. Our dead relatives depart by it and our ancestors visit us by it. But most important, it is the path of children coming in to be born . . ."

Mr. Obi listened with a satisfied smile on his face.

"The whole purpose of our school," he said finally, "is to eradicate just such beliefs as that. Dead men do not require footpaths. The whole idea is just fantastic. Our duty is to teach your children to laugh at such ideas."

"What you say may be true," replied the priest, "but we follow the practices of our fathers. If you reopen the path we shall have nothing to quarrel about. What I always say is: let the hawk perch and let the eagle perch." He rose to go.

"I am sorry," said the young headmaster. "But the school compound cannot be a thoroughfare. It is against our regulations. I would suggest your constructing another path, skirting our premises. We can even get our boys to help in building it. I don't suppose the ancestors will find the little detour too burdensome."

"I have no more words to say," said the old priest, already outside.

Two days later a young woman in the village died in childbed. A diviner was immediately consulted and he prescribed heavy sacrifices to propitiate ancestors insulted by the fence.

Obi woke up the next morning among the ruins of his work. The beautiful hedges were torn up not just near the path but right round the school, the flowers trampled to death and one of the school buildings pulled down... That day, the white Supervisor came to inspect the school and wrote a nasty report on the state of the premises but more seriously about the "tribal-war situation developing between the school and the village, arising in part from the misguided zeal of the new headmaster."

CHARTING THE STORY

1 What typical characteristics of indigenous people who have "sold out" to the colonial masters do Michael and Nancy Obi exhibit?

2 The main characters in this story are presented in the first and third parts. What important narrative functions do the minor characters in the second part of the story serve?

3 What destruction is done to the school compound, and how is it made to be a case of the punishment's fitting the crime?

CONSIDERATIONS OF STYLE

1 Compare the descriptions of the school garden "before and after." What are the dominant images in each? Does the story hold any other vivid images for you?

3 What symbolism is implied in the proverb cited by the village priest, "Let the hawk perch and let the eagle perch"? What other symbols do you find in the story?

4 How do the village priest and Michael Obi, as well as the white supervisor and Michael Obi, "speak past each other"? Considering their manners of speech, would it have been possible for any mutually satisfactory understandings to arise?

AFTERTHOUGHTS

1 After all the negative aspects of colonialism are considered, what are some positive things that could be said about a colonial legacy? Cite examples. If you do not consider that anything positive has come out of colonialism, explain your belief.

2 What is Michael Obi's level of education, and how is it appraised by the school authorities? What level of education would you have expected the authorities to have

attained? What does this suggest about the balance of power in the colonial Nigerian educational system?

THE WRITER'S CRAFT

1 In a 1990 interview, Achebe said: "It is inevitable, I believe, to see the emergence of modern African literature as a return of celebration." Discuss how this notion is shown in "Dead Men's Path" and in at least two other stories or poems by Achebe or other black African writers in this anthology.

2 After World War II, Winston Churchill wrote a monumental, three-volume study, *A History of the English-Speaking Peoples,* at a time when those peoples were overwhelmingly white. How would a similar study written today differ from Churchill's?

3 From the point of view of the village priest, write of your encounter with Michael Obi.

ALEX LA GUMA

ALEX LA GUMA *was born in Cape Town in 1925. After completing his formal education at Cape Technical College, he worked as a clerk, factory hand, book-keeper, and journalist. From an early age, he involved himself in South African politics, and was arrested for treason—with 155 others—in 1956. He was acquitted in 1960. He was later detained for five months after the Sharpeville massacre. In 1966, La Guma left South Africa with his family to live in exile in London. He died in 1986.*

His published works include And a Threefold Cord *(1964) and* In the Fog of the Season's End *(1972).*

This story, first published in 1967, is included in the collection A Walk in the Night and Other Stories, *published the following year. Like the other stories in the collection, "The Lemon Orchard"—the jacket notes— "shows, in the starkest terms, the plight of the non-white in South Africa [of the time]."*

PERSPECTIVES

1 The institutionalized system of racial separation in South Africa, called apartheid, ended officially in 1990, when President F W De Klerk unbanned the African National Congress and the Communist Party, desegregated beaches, and ordered the release from prison of black leader Nelson Mandela, who, in 1994, was elected the first native black president of South Africa. What knowledge of this system do you bring to your reading of the South African texts—by Nadine Gordimer, Bessie Head, and Alex La Guma—in this book?

2 Discuss the phenomenon of lynching in the American South, and discuss its relationship to the concept of apartheid.

The Lemon Orchard

The men came down between two long, regular rows of trees. The winter had not passed completely and there was a chill in the air; and the moon was hidden behind long, high parallels of cloud which hung like suspended streamers of dirty cotton-wool in the sky. All of the men but one wore thick clothes against the coolness of the night. The night and earth was cold and damp, and the shoes of the men sank into the soil and left exact, ridged foot prints, but they could not be seen in the dark.

One of the men walked ahead holding a small cycle lantern that worked from a battery, leading the way down the avenue of trees while the others came behind in the dark. The night close around was quiet now that the crickets had stopped their small noises, but far out others that did not feel the presence of the men continued the monotonous creek-creek-creek. Somewhere, even further, a dog started barking in short high yaps, and then stopped abruptly. The men were walking through an orchard of lemons and the sharp, bitter-sweet citrus smell hung gently on the night air.

"Do not go so fast," the man who brought up the rear of the party called to the man with the lantern. "It's as dark as a kaffir's soul here at the back."

He called softly, as if the darkness demanded silence. He was a big man and wore khaki trousers and laced-up riding boots, and an old shooting jacket with leather patches on the right breast and the elbows.

The shotgun was loaded. In the dark this man's face was invisible except for a blur of shadowed hollows and lighter crags. Although he walked in the rear he was the leader of the party. The latern-bearer slowed down for the rest to catch up with him.

"It's cold, too, Oom," another man said.

"Cold?" the man with the shotgun asked, speaking with sarcasm. "Are you colder than this verdomte hotnot, here?" And he gestured in the dark with the muzzle of the gun at the man who stumbled along in their midst and who was the only one not warmly dressed.

This man wore trousers and a raincoat which they had allowed him to pull on over his pyjamas when they had taken him from his lodgings, and he shivered now with chill, clenching his teeth to prevent them from chattering. He had not been given time to tie his shoes and the metal-covered ends of the laces clicked as he moved.

"Are you cold, hotnot?" the man with the light jeered.

The colored man did not reply. He was afraid, but his fear was mixed with a stubbornness which forbade him to answer them.

"He is not cold," the fifth man in the party said. "He is shivering with fear. Is it not so, hotnot?"

The colored man said nothing, but stared ahead of himself into the half-light made by the small lantern. He could see the silhouette of the man who carried the light, but he did not want to look at the two who flanked him, the one who had complained of the cold, and the one who had spoken of his fear. They each carried a sjambok and every now and then one of them slapped a corduroyed leg with his.

"He is dumb, also," the one who had spoken last chuckled.

"No, Andries. Wait a minute," the leader who carried the shotgun said, and they all stopped between the row of trees. The man with the lantern turned and put the light on the rest of the party.

"What is it?" he asked.

"Wag'n oomblikkie. Wait a moment," the leader said, speaking with forced casualness. "He is not dumb. He is a slim hotnot; one of those educated bushmen. Listen, hotnot," he addressed the colored man, speaking angrily now. "When a baas speaks to you, you answer him. Do you hear?" The colored man's wrists were tied behind him with a riem and the leader brought the muzzle of the shotgun down, pressing it hard into the small of the man's back above where the wrists met. "Do you hear, hotnot? Answer me or I will shoot a hole through your spine."

The bound man felt the hard round metal of the gun muzzle through the loose raincoat and clenched his teeth. He was cold and tried to prevent himself from shivering in case it should be mistaken for cowardice. He heard the small metallic noise as the man with the gun thumbed back the hammer of the shotgun. In spite of the cold little drops of sweat began to form on his upper lip under the overnight stubble.

"For God's sake, don't shoot him," the man with the light said, laughing a little nervously. "We don't want to be involved in any murder."

"What are you saying, man?" the leader asked. Now with the beam of the battery-lamp on his face the shadows in it were washed away to reveal the mass of tiny wrinkled and deep creases which covered the red-clay complexion of his face like the myriad lines which indicate rivers, streams, roads and railways on a map. They wound around the ridges of his chin and climbed the sharp range of his nose and the peaks of his chin and cheekbones, and his eyes were hard and blue like two frozen lakes.

"This is mos a slim hotnot," he said again. "A teacher in a school for which we pay. He lives off our sweat, and he had the audacity to be cheeky and uncivilized towards a minister of our church and no hotnot will be cheeky to a white man while I live."

"Ja, man," the lantern-bearer agreed. "But we are going to deal with him. There is no necessity to shoot him. We don't want that kind of trouble."

"I will shoot whatever hotnot or kaffir I desire, and see me get into trouble over it. I demand respect from these donders. Let them answer when they're spoken to."

He jabbed the muzzle suddenly into the colored man's back so that he stumbled struggling to keep his balance. "Do you hear, jong? Did I not speak to you?" The man who had jeered about the prisoner's fear stepped up then, and hit him in the face, striking him on a cheekbone with the clenched fist which still held the sjambok. He was angry over the delay and wanted the man to submit so that they could proceed. "Listen you hotnot bastard," he said loudly. "Why don't you answer?"

The man stumbled, caught himself and stood in the rambling shadow of one of the lemon trees. The lantern-light swung on him and he looked away from the center of the beam. He was afraid the leader would shoot him in anger and he had no wish to die. He straightened up and looked away from them.

"Well?" demanded the man who had struck him.

"Yes, baas," the bound man said, speaking with a mixture of dignity and contempt which was missed by those who surrounded him.

"Yes there," the man with the light said. "You could save yourself trouble. Next time you will remember. Now let us get on." The lantern swung forward again and he walked ahead. The leader shoved their prisoner on with the muzzle of the shotgun, and he stumbled after the bobbing lantern with the other men on each side of him.

"The amazing thing about it is that this bliksem should have taken the principal, and the meester of the church before the magistrate and demand payment for the hiding they gave him for being cheeky to them," the leader said to all in general. "This verdomte hotnot. I have never heard of such a thing in all my born days."

"Well, we will give him a better hiding," the man Andries said. "This time we will teach him a lesson, Oom. He won't demand damages from anybody when we're done with him."

"And afterwards he won't be seen around here again. He will pack his things and go and live in the city where they're not so particular abut the dignity of the volk. Do you hear, hotnot?" This time they were not concerned about receiving a reply but the leader went on, saying, "We don't want any educated hottentots in our town."

"Neither black Englishmen," added one of the others.

The dog started barking again at the farm house which was invisible on the dark hillside at the other end of the little valley. "It's that Jagter," the man with the lantern said. "I wonder what bothers him. He is a good watchdog. I offered Meneer Marais five pounds for that dog, but he won't sell. I would like to have a dog like that. I would take great care of such a dog."

The blackness of the night crouched over the orchard and the leaves rustled with a harsh whispering that was inconsistent with the pleasant scent of the lemons. The chill in the air had increased, and far-off the creek-creek-creek of the crickets blended into solid strips of high-pitched sound. Then the moon came from behind the banks of cloud and its white light touched the leaves with wet silver, and the perfume of lemons seemed to grow stronger, as if the juice was being crushed from them.

They walked a little way further into the moonlight and the man with the lantern said, "This is as good a place as any, Oom."

They had come into a wide gap in the orchard, a small amphitheater surrounded by fragrant growth, and they all stopped within it. The moonlight clung for a while to the leaves and the angled branches, so that along their tips and edges the moisture gleamed with the quivering shine of scattered quicksilver.

CHARTING THE STORY

1 This story contains a number of words or expressions in Afrikaans—the vernacular derived from the Dutch that emerged as a distinct language in the mid-eighteenth

century. Examples include: *verdomte hotnot, sjambok, Waag'n oomblikkie, most a slim hotnot,* and several others. Try to determine the meanings of these terms based on sound, on context, or by other means. Why do you supposed these terms are not italicized in the text? How do these South African words add to the mood of the story, and what do many of them have in common?

2 What seems to have been the captive's specific "crime" that, in the eyes of his captors, merited punishment? What "crime" in a larger sense impelled them to take the law into their own hands and "give him a better hiding" than did the principal and the minister before them?

3 What earlier clues—or, foreshadowing—suggest what the white men may have done with their captive at the end of the story?

CONSIDERATIONS OF STYLE

1 A dog is mentioned at the beginning of the story and near the end. What purposes does the dog serve in the narrative?

2 How do the first two and the last three paragraphs of the story come together as a connected image to create an ambiance for this story?

3 How do the descriptions of the whites' faces in Paragraphs 5 and 19 bespeak their moral depravity?

AFTERTHOUGHTS

1 A web page, *African Writers: Voices of Change,* notes that throughout his fictional writings, "[t]he moral development of [La Guma's] characters is closely tied [to] their potential to improve their country's future." According to this notion, where do the characters in this story fit in?

2 Does this story remind you of other stories, legends, or myths where an innocent man is captured in the middle of the night and set upon by a group intent on violence? If so, what parallels can you draw between this text and the other(s)? What disjunctures?

THE WRITER'S CRAFT

1 What could possibly happen within the next five minutes after the written story ends? Discuss possible scenarios in a small group; then individually or collaboratively elaborate a scenario.

2 Compose a letter to Alex La Guma, who died in 1986, updating him on the social progress that has been made in South Africa since his death. In particular, relate to him how collective action has been instrumental in creating a new, more democratic South Africa.

NGUGI WA THIONG'O

NGUGI WA THIONG'O *was born in Kenya in 1938, christened James Thiong'oNgugi, a name which he later would change in renunciation of Christianity, which he associated with British colonialism. In 1963, he completed the Honors English program he associated at Makerere College in Kampala, Uganda. He was a professor at Nairobi University until 1977, when he was arrested for antigovernment political ideas in the popular play* I Will Marry When I Want, *which he co-authored with Ngugi wa Mirii. In the same year, he decided to write novels in his native Gikuyu rather than in English, and, in 1980, published the first modern novel written in Gikuyu,* Caitaani Muthara-Ini (Devil on the Cross). *He left his native country in 1982 to live in self-imposed exile in London.*

Ngugi wa Thiong'o is a prolific writer—of novels, plays, short stories, political essays, and children's books.

The story "The Return" tells of a political prisoner of the colonial regime who returns to his village, where he finds life—and his own life—inalterably changed. The story originally appeared in his collection Secret Lives and Other Stories *(1974) and is anthologized in Nadezhda Obradovic's anthology of contemporary African short stories,* Looking for a Rain God *(1990).*

PERSPECTIVES

1 Research the Mau Mau Uprising in Kenya in the 1950s. Who were the players in that bitter drama? What events led up to it, and what was its outcome? Its aftermath to this day?

2 In your experience, *can* one ever "go home again"? What seems to underlie many people's desires to be able to return "home" and find everything and everyone the same?

The Return

The road was long. Whenever he took a step forward, little clouds of dust rose, whirled angrily behind him, and then slowly settled again. But a thin train of dust was left in the air, moving like smoke. He walked on, however, unmindful of the dust and ground under his feet. Yet with every step he seemed more and more conscious of the hardness and apparent animosity of the road. Not that he looked down; on the contrary, he looked straight ahead as if he would, any time now, see a familiar object that would hail him as a friend and tell him that he was near home. But the road stretched on.

He made quick, springing steps, his left hand dangling freely by the side of his once white coat, now torn and worn out. His right hand, bent at the elbow, held onto a string tied to a small bundle on his slightly drooping back. The bundle, well wrapped with a cotton cloth that had once been printed with red flowers now faded out, swing from side to side in harmony with the rhythm of his steps. The bundle held the bitterness and hardships of the years spent in detention camps. Now and then he looked at the sun on its homeward journey. Sometimes he darted quick side-glances at the small hedged strips of land which, with their sickly-looking crops, maize, beans, and peas, appeared much as everything else did—unfriendly. The whole country was dull and seemed weary. To Kamau, this was nothing new. He remembered that, even before the Mau Mau emergency, the overtilled Gikuyu holdings wore haggard looks in contrast to the sprawling green fields in the settled area.

A path branched to the left. He hesitated for a moment and then made up his mind. For the first time, his eyes brightened a little as he went along the path that would take him down the valley and then to the village. At last home was near and, with that realization, the faraway look of a weary traveler seemed to desert him for a while. The valley and the vegetation along it were in deep contrast to the surrounding country. For here green bush and trees thrived. This could only mean one thing: Honia River still flowed. He quickened his steps as if he could scarcely believe this to be true till he had actually set his eyes on the river. It was there; it still flowed. Honia, where so often he had taken a bath, plunging stark naked into its cool living water, warmed his heart as he watched its serpentine movement around the rocks and heard its slight murmurs. A painful exhilaration passed all over him, and for a moment he longed for those days. He sighed. Perhaps the river would not recognize in his hardened features that same boy to whom the riverside world had meant everything. Yet as he approached Honia, he felt more akin to it than he had felt to anything else since his release.

A group of women were drawing water. He was excited, for he could recognize one or two from his ridge. There was the middle-aged Wanjiku, whose deaf son had been killed by the Security Forces just before he himself was arrested. She had always been a darling of the village, having a smile for everyone and food for all. Would they receive him? Would they give him a "hero's welcome?" He thought so. Had he not always been a favorite all along the ridge? And had he not fought for the land? He wanted to run and shout: "Here I am. I have come back to you." But he desisted. He was a man.

"Is it well with you?" A few voices responded. The other women, with 5
tired and worn features, looked at him mutely as if his greeting was of no con-

sequence. Why! Had he been so long in the camp? His spirits were damped as he feebly asked: "Do you not remember me?" Again they looked at him. They stared at him with cold, hard looks; like everything else, they seemed to be deliberately refusing to know or own him. It was Wanjiku who at last recognized him. But there was neither warmth nor enthusiasm in her voice as she said, "Oh, is it you, Kamau? We thought you—" She did not continue. Only now he noticed something else—surprise? fear? He could not tell. He saw their quick glances dart at him and he knew for certain that a secret from which he was excluded bound them together.

"Perhaps I am no longer one of them!" he bitterly reflected. But they told him of the new village. The old village of scattered huts spread thinly over the ridge was no more.

He left them, feeling embittered and cheated. The old village had not even waited for him. And suddenly he felt a strong nostalgia for his old home, friends and surroundings. He thought of his father, mother, and—and—he dared not think about her. But for all that, Muthoni, just as she had been in the old days, came back to his mind. His heart beat faster. He felt desire and a warmth thrilled through him. He quickened his step. He forgot the village women as he remembered his wife. He had stayed with her for a mere two weeks; then he had been swept away by the colonial forces. Like many others, he had been hurriedly screened and then taken to detention without trial. And all that time, he had thought of nothing but the village and his beautiful woman.

The others had been like him. They had talked of nothing but their homes. One day he was working next to another detainee from Muranga. Suddenly the detainee, Njoroge, stopped breaking stones. He sighed heavily. His worn-out eyes had a faraway look.

"What's wrong, man? What's the matter with you?" Kamau asked.

"It is my wife. I left her expecting a baby. I have no idea what has happened to her."

Another detainee put in: "For me, I left my woman with a baby. She had just been delivered. We were all happy. But on the same day, I was arrested..."

And so they went on. All of them longed for one day—the day of their return home. Then life would begin anew.

Kamau himself had left his wife without a child. He had not even finished paying the bride price. But now he would go, seek work in Nairobi, and pay off the remainder to Muthoni's parents. Life would indeed begin anew. They would have a son and bring him up in their own home. With these prospects before his eyes, he quickened his steps. He wanted to run—no, fly to hasten his return. He was now nearing the top of the hill. He wished he could suddenly meet his brothers and sisters. Would they ask him questions? He would, at any rate, not tell them all: the beating, the screening and the work on roads and in quarries with an askari always nearby ready to kick him if he relaxed. Yes. He had suffered many humiliations, and he had not resisted. Was there any need? But his soul and all the vigor of his manhood had rebelled and bled with rage and bitterness.

One day these wazungu would go!

One day his people would be free! Then, then—he did not know what he would do. However, he bitterly assured himself no one would ever flout his manhood again.

He mounted the hill and then stopped. The whole plain lay below. The new village was before him—rows and rows of compact mud huts, crouching on the plain under the fast-vanishing sun. Dark blue smoke curled upward from various huts, to form a dark mist that hovered over the village. Beyond, the deep, blood-red sinking sun sent out fingerlike streaks of light that thinned outward and mingled with the gray mist shrouding the distant hills.

In the village, he moved from street to street, meeting new faces. He inquired. He found his home. He stopped at the entrance to the yard and breathed hard and full. This was the moment of his return home. His father sat huddled up on a three-legged stool. He was now very aged and Kamau pitied the old man. But he had been spared—yes, spared to see his son's return—

"Father!"

The old man did not answer. He just looked at Kamau with strange vacant eyes. Kamau was impatient. He felt annoyed and irritated. Did he not see him? Would he behave like the women Kamau had met by the river?

In the street, naked and half-naked children were playing, throwing dust at one another. The sun had already set and it looked as if there would be moonlight.

"Father, don't you remember me?" Hope was sinking in him. He felt tired. Then he saw his father suddenly start and tremble like a leaf. He saw him stare with unbelieving eyes. Fear was discernible in those eyes. His mother came, and his brothers too. They crowded around him. His aged mother clung to him and sobbed hard.

"I knew my son would come. I knew he was not dead."

"Why, who told you I was dead?"

"That Karanja, son of Njogu."

And then Kamau understood. He understood his trembling father. He understood the women at the river. But one thing puzzled him: he had never been in the same detention camp with Karanja. Anyway he had come back. He wanted now to see Muthoni. Why had she not come out? He wanted to shout, "I have come, Muthoni; I am here." He looked around. His mother understood him. She quickly darted a glance at her man and then simply said:

"Muthoni went away."

Kamau felt something cold settle in his stomach. He looked at the village huts and the dullness of the land. He wanted to ask many questions but he dared not. He could not yet believe that Muthoni had gone. But he knew by the look of the women at the river, by the look of his parents, that she was gone.

"She was a good daughter to us," his mother was explaining. "She waited for you and patiently bore all the ills of the land. Then Karanja came and said that you were dead. Your father believed him. She believed him too and keened for a month. Karanja constantly paid us visits. He was of your Rika, you know. Then she got a child. We could have kept her. But where is the land?

Where is the food? Ever since land consolidation, our last security was taken away. We let Karanja go with her. Other women have done worse—gone to town. Only the infirm and the old have been left here."

He was not listening; the coldness in his stomach slowly changed to bitterness. He felt bitter against all, all the people including his father and mother. They had betrayed him. They had leagued against him, and Karanja had always been his rival. Five years was admittedly not a short time. But why did she go? Why did they allow her to go? He wanted to speak. Yes, speak and denounce everything—the women by the river, the village and the people who dwelled there. But he could not. This bitter thing was choking him.

"You—you gave my own away?" he whispered. 30

"Listen, child, child..."

The big yellow moon dominated the horizon. He hurried away bitter and blind, and only stopped when he came to the Honia River.

And standing at the bank, he saw not the river, but his hopes dashed on the ground instead. The river moved swiftly, making ceaseless monotonous murmurs. In the forest the crickets and other insects kept up an incessant buzz. And above, the moon shone bright. He tried to remove his coat, and the small bundle he had held on to so firmly fell. It rolled down the bank and before Kamau knew what was happening, it was floating swiftly down the river. For a time he was shocked and wanted to retrieve it. What would he show his—Oh, had he forgotten so soon? His wife had gone. And the little things that had so strangely reminded him of her and that he had guarded all those years, had gone! He did not know why, but somehow he felt relieved. Thoughts of drowning himself dispersed. He began to put on his coat, murmuring to himself, "Why should she have waited for me? Why should all the changes have waited for my return?"

CHARTING THE STORY

1 What changes have taken place in Kamau's village during his five-year absence? What caused the changes?

2 Why might Kamau wish to withhold from his brothers and sisters the story of his detention, when he was subjected to the abuses of his captors? What do you infer to be the meanings of *askari* and *wazungu* in Paragraphs 13 and 14, respectively? Why do you suppose these Gikuyu words are not italicized in the English text?

3 How does Kamau himself change from the beginning to the end of the story?

CONSIDERATIONS OF STYLE

1 Ngugi is a master of microdescription, a skill immediately evident as the story opens. Analyze the first paragraph, noting how words convey sensory images, which in turn convey the controlling mood.

2 What narrative and symbolic roles does the River Honia play in the story?

AFTERTHOUGHTS

1 What similarities and differences do we find among the struggles of the main characters in Alex La Guma's "The Lemon Orchard" and Ken Saro-Wiwa's "Africa Kills Her Sun" and in this story?

2 In the second paragraph, and at the end of the narrative, Kamau's bundle, which "held the bitterness and hardships of the years spent in detention camps," is featured. In the story, the reader never gets to look inside it, but it is apparently important enough for Kamau to carry and significant enough for its loss to pain Kamau. What might the faded cotton cloth have contained?

THE WRITER'S CRAFT

1 Continue the telling of Kamau's story—as his life enters a new phase, eventually a postcolonial one.

2 Write about a landmark—natural or manmade—of your childhood, such as the Honia was for Kamau. How do you relate to that landmark now that you have moved on, and changed, while it remains the same?

3 Had Muthoni or Kamau's parents been able to write to the authorities, would the outcome of the story have changed? If so, how? Does it appear that they *could* have written? Write a short essay discussing the relevance of literacy to Kamau's situation.

BEN OKRI

BEN OKRI *was born in Nigeria. He is the author of two novels and two collections of stories. He was poetry editor of the magazine* West Africa, *and has worked as a broadcaster with the BBC. In 1987 he received the Commonwealth Writers' Prize for Africa and* The Paris Review *Aga Khan Prize for Fiction. He lives in London. The story takes place in rural Nigeria, in a climate of civil war between the central government in Lagos and the breakaway province of Biafra. The central character is a child, Omovo, who witnesses the violence of war despite adults' attempts to shield him from it.*

"In the Shadow of War" appeared in Stars of the New Curfew, *Okri's first book published in America, in 1988.*

PERSPECTIVES

1. How does war affect adults and children, respectively? Present evidence from conflicts raging in the world today.
2. What do you take to mean the word "civil" in the phrase "civil war"? On the surface at least, isn't the latter term an oxymoron?
3. What would a person's life be like, growing up literally "in the shadow of war," where war is a daily aspect of her or his life? If one has had such experience, is it possible to share it with others in a way they can understand?

In the Shadow of War

That afternoon three soldiers came to the village. They scattered the goats and chickens. They went to the palm-frond bar and ordered a calabash of palm-wine. They drank amidst the flies.

Omovo watched them from the window as he waited for his father to go out. They both listened to the radio. His father had bought the old Grundig cheaply from a family that had to escape the city when the war broke out. He had covered the radio with a white cloth and made it look like a household fetish. They listened to the news of bombings and air raids in the interior of the country. His father combed his hair, parted it carefully, and slapped some after-shave on his unshaven face. Then he struggled into the shabby coat that he had long outgrown.

Omovo stared out of the window, irritated with his father. At that hour, for the past seven days, a strange woman with a black veil over her head had been going past the house. She went up the village paths, crossed the Express road, and disappeared into the forest. Omovo waited for her to appear.

The main news was over. The radio announcer said an eclipse of the moon was expected that night. Omovo's father wiped the sweat off his face with his palm and said, with some bitterness:

'As if an eclipse will stop this war.'

'What is an eclipse?' Omovo asked.

'That's when the world goes dark and strange things happen.'

'Like what?'

His father lit a cigarette.

'The dead start to walk about and sing. So don't stay out late, eh.'

Omovo nodded.

'Heclipses hate children. They eat them.'

Omovo didn't believe him. His father smiled, gave Omovo his ten kobo allowance, and said:

'Turn off the radio. It's bad for a child to listen to news of war.'

Omovo turned it off. His father poured a libation at the doorway and then prayed to his ancestors. When he had finished he picked up his briefcase and strutted out briskly. Omovo watched him as he threaded his way up the path to the bus-stop at the main road. When a danfo bus came, and his father went with it, Omovo turned the radio back on. He sat on the window-sill and waited for the woman. The last time he saw her she had glided past with agitated flutters of her yellow smock. The children stopped what they were doing and stared at her. They had said that she had no shadow. They had said that her feet never touched the ground. As she went past, the children began to throw things at her. She didn't flinch, didn't quicken her pace, and didn't look back.

The heat was stupefying. Noises dimmed and lost their edges. The villagers stumbled, about their various tasks as if they were sleep-walking. The three soldiers drank palm-wine and played draughts beneath the sun's oppressive glare. Omovo noticed that whenever children went past the bar the soldiers called them, talked to them, and gave them some money. Omovo ran down the stairs and slowly walked past the bar. The soldiers stared at him. On his way back one of them called him. 'What's your name' he asked.

Omovo hesitated, smiled mischievously, and said: 'Heclipse'?

The soldier laughed, spraying Omovo's face with spit. He had a face crowded with veins. His companions seemed uninterested. They swiped flies and concentrated on their game. Their guns were on the table. Omovo noticed that they had numbers on them. The man said:

'Did your father give you that name because you have big lips?'

His companions looked at Omovo and laughed. Omovo nodded.

'You are a good boy,' the man said. He paused. Then he asked, in a different voice:

'Have you seen that woman who covers her face with a black cloth?'

'No.'

The man gave Omovo ten kobo and said 'She is a spy. She helps our enemies. If you see her come and tell us at once, You hear?'

Omovo refused the money and went back upstairs. He re-positioned 25
himself on the window-sill. The soldiers occasionally looked at him. The heat got to him and soon he fell asleep in a sitting position. The cocks, crowing dispiritedly, woke him up. He could feel the afternoon softening into evening. The soldiers dozed in the bar. The hourly news came on. Omovo listened without comprehension to the day's casualties. The announcer succumbed to the stupor, yawned, apologized, and gave further details of the fighting.

Omovo looked up and saw that the woman had already gone past. The men had left the bar. He saw them weaving between the eaves of the thatch houses, stumbling through the heat-mists. The woman was further up the path. Omovo ran downstairs and followed the men. One of them had taken off his uniform top. The soldier behind had buttocks so big they had begun to split his pants. Omovo followed them across the Express road. When they got into the forest the men stopped following the woman, and took a different route. They seemed to know what they were doing. Omovo hurried to keep the woman in view.

He followed her through the dense vegetation. She wore faded wrappers and a grey shawl, with the black veil covering her face. She had a red basket on her head. He completely forgot to determine if she had a shadow, or whether her feet touched the ground.

He passed unfinished estates, with their flaking ostentatious signboards and their collapsing fences. He passed an empty cement factory: blocks lay crumbled in heaps and the workers' sheds were deserted. He passed a baobab tree, under which was the intact skeleton of a large animal. A snake dropped from a branch and slithered through the undergrowth. In the distance, over the cliff edge, he heard loud music and people singing war slogans above the noise.

He followed the woman till they came to a rough camp on the plain below. Shadowy figures moved about in the half-light of the cave. The woman went to them. The figures surrounded her and touched her and led her into the cave. He heard their weary voices thanking her. When the woman reappeared she was without the basket. Children with kwashiorkor stomachs and women wearing rags led her half-way up the hill. Then, reluctantly, touching her as if they might not see her again, they went back.

He followed her till they came to a muddied river. She moved as if an 30
invisible force were trying to blow her away. Omovo saw capsized canoes

and trailing waterlogged clothes on the dark water. He saw floating items of sacrifice: loaves of bread in polythene wrappings, gourds of food, Coca-Cola cans. When he looked at the canoes again they had changed into the shapes of swollen dead animals. He saw outdated currencies on the riverbank. He noticed the terrible smell in the air. Then he heard the sound of heavy breathing from behind him, then someone coughing and spitting. He recognized the voice of one of the soldiers urging the others to move faster. Omovo crouched in the shadow of a tree. The soldiers strode past. Not long afterwards he heard a scream. The men had caught up with the woman. They crowded round her.

'Where are the others?' shouted one of them. The woman was silent.

'You dis witch! You want to die, eh? Where are they?'

She stayed silent. Her head was bowed. One of the soldiers coughed and spat towards the river. 'Talk! Talk!' he said, slapping her.

The fat soldier tore off her veil and threw it to the ground. She bent down to pick it up and stopped in the attitude of kneeling, her head still bowed. Her head was bald, and disfigured with a deep corrugation. There was a livid gash along the side of her face. The bare-chested soldier pushed her. She fell on her face and lay still. The lights changed over the forest and for the first time Omovo saw that the dead animals on the river were in fact the corpses of grown men. Their bodies were tangled with river-weed and their eyes were bloated. Before he could react, he heard another scream. The woman was getting up, with the veil in her hand. She turned to the fat soldier, drew herself up to her fullest height, and spat in his face. Waving the veil in the air, she began to howl dementedly. The two other soldiers backed away. The fat soldier wiped his face and lifted the gun to the level of her stomach. A moment before Omovo heard the shot a violent beating of wings just above him scared him from his hiding place. He ran through the forest screaming. The soldiers tramped after him. He ran through a mist which seemed to have risen from the rocks. As he ran he saw an owl staring at him from a canopy of leaves. He tripped over the roots of a tree and blacked out when his head hit the ground.

When he woke up it was very dark. He waved his fingers in front of his face and saw nothing. Mistaking the darkness for blindness he screamed, thrashed around, and ran into a door. When he recovered from his shock he heard voices outside and the radio crackling on about the war. He found his way to the balcony, full of wonder that his sight had returned. But when he got there he was surprised to find his father sitting on the sunken cane chair, drinking palm-wine with the three soldiers. Omovo rushed to his father and pointed frantically at the three men.

'You must thank them,' his father said. 'They brought you back from the forest.'

Omovo, overcome with delirium, began to tell his father what he had seen. But his father, smiling apologetically at the soldiers, picked up his son and carried him off to bed.

CHARTING THE STORY

1 How does the lunar eclipse inform this story?
2 What type of war appears to be going on, and how can one tell?
3 What is the effect of Okri's depicting the soldiers' humane characteristics as well as their darker side? In the end, are they less blemished human beings?
4 How do you suppose the myth about the strange woman—that she had no shadow and that her feet never touched the ground—came to be?

CONSIDERATIONS OF STYLE

1 Find at least three vivid descriptions of ambulatory motion in this story.
2 Where in the story is the image of the bloated corpses floating in the river foreshadowed? What is the significance of the "items of sacrifice" (Paragraph 32) floating alongside? Of Omovo's first impression that the floaters were capsized canoes, then swollen dead animals?
3 Images of light and shadow move through the text. What do light and darkness reveal and conceal?

AFTERTHOUGHTS

1 As an epigraph to the collection that contains "In the Shadow of War," Okri cites an observation by Nigerian poet Christopher Okigbo: *We carry in our worlds that flourish our worlds that have failed.* To which characters in this story do you think the observation most applies?
2 Does the father appear to be aligned with the "side" of the soldiers, in some secret resistance, or neutral? What in the text (or implied therefrom) supports your view?

THE WRITER'S CRAFT

1 Write an essay showing how the war alluded to in this story has affected the attitudes of the various characters: children, parents, soldiers, government functionaries, resisters.
2 Rewrite the forest incident from the point of view of one of the soldiers, or of the woman in the veil.

CHRISTINE CRAIG

CHRISTINE CRAIG *was born in Jamaica. She majored in English at the University of the West Indies. She collaborated with her husband, Jamaican artist Karl Craig, on two children's books, which were published by Oxford University Press in 1970 and 1971. Her works include short stories, non-fiction on feminist and health topics, and a collection of poems,* Quadrille *(1984). Craig has been awarded a fellowship to the International Writers Program at Iowa University. She presently lives in Kingston, Jamaica.*

In this story, a woman who has left "the noise and the warring" of the city finds that even in the solitary life in the hills peace can be elusive. "In the Hills" is included in Her True-True Name: An Anthology of Women's Writing from the Caribbean *(1990).*

PERSPECTIVES

1 What differing connotations are conveyed by the words "alone[ness]," "loneliness," and "solitude"? Describe a context in which you have experienced each state.

2 Were a revolution to arise where you live, what would be your relationship to those on both sides of the struggle? What issues would you have to face? What actions would you feel compelled to take?

In the Hills

Up in these hills the mornings bloom so gently moist, everything so wet with dew and wrapped in pale grey that you want desperately to hold your arms out, to pull it all to you and hold it there for an hour, keep it with you for a space of time. But the sun, busy auntie, rushes out and tidies it all away so quickly you can hardly believe your grey moment was ever there. Later, the busy, rushing sun will spread herself out and reign expansively throughout the hills.

Years before, I had left the heat and the noise and the warring of the city to build my small house here on my mother's land. The land had been new and difficult to work, but now it was yielding up its crops regularly and I had become part of the cycle of planting and weeding and watering and reaping. My nearest neighbour was some few chains away down the hill. A silent old man who kept a few cows and walked the two miles to the village to sell his milk. On Saturday he stayed in the village to get his drinking evening in and on very clear Saturday nights I could hear him singing his way home with unctuous, richly turned psalms.

A few miles further up the mountain lay a forest reserve. Land carefully planted out with firs. I became aware, gradually, that something was going on up there. A coming and a going and sudden noises of jeeps rambling up and down the stony road. The first time I saw them they were clearly city youths. Tight trousers and skinny T-shirts, hair luxuriously uncombed and lazy, slouchy hips, and talking, so much talking all the time. A week later I saw them drilling, soft cat manoeuvres, boys' games played with stony eyes.

Twice a week the big shots came to talk, to stir the blood, to lay strong reasons why they should learn the war game and be prepared to play it out down in the dusty city. These leaders walked like men but their repeated jargon sounded like gun fire under the firs and in silence I watched the scene close up like the stilted figures in a No play.

One of the boys came to my house. He wanted vegetables for the group. 5
I let him have them, making myself sound simpler and more crazy than in the days when I was really ill. Soon they became greedy, they wanted the corn and beans before they were even full. I told them there would be more for all of them if they waited but they said their time was now and they could not wait. One Saturday afternoon a boy came on his own. He asked for nothing but stood silently near my front step and looked around. I took no notice of him and busied myself with my tomato plants, pinching out the first buds so the plant would not bear before it was strong enough. The sun was going down and still he stood there, his dark eyes large and quiet in his thin face. I went inside and made a quick supper for us, bread and plaintain and fresh carrot juice to wash it down. We sat on my verandah until eventually I asked him: 'What is it, are you afraid?'

His thin body moved suddenly, jerkily and he looked at me.

'Yes,' he said. 'I can see no way out.'

He spoke for awhile then of his hot, bitter existence in the city. No job, no money for him. When the big ones spoke it had sounded so simple. Stay with me, learn to hate, learn to kill and you will have a job, you will have a house and you will be free. Free from the oppressors.

He sat there, as the evening turned into night, and he said: 'I am afraid to kill another man. It is a sin to kill. And afterwards, what job can I get that will make me forget what I have done. What pride can I take in my house if I have such a sin in my heart?'

I had no answer of course, I could only watch the lines of his thin body 10
aching with pain as he sat there on my small verandah.

'What do the big shots tell you?' I asked. 'How do they make it seem alright to the others?'

He sighed and I saw the shine of tears in his eyes. 'They say,' he whispered, 'that we are all oppressed, that we cannot all be free to enjoy the new society unless all make the sacrifices. They say we will be heroes and our names will be written in the history books.'

I looked out into the starry sky and heard my old neighbour singing his way home up the hill. 'So, that is a good thing,' I said. 'If none of you have anything now you will have to do something together to get what you want.'

The young boy looked at his hands and then folded them round his body, he suddenly seemed very young indeed. He said: 'Perhaps there is another way. This way, they will get what they want. They will always have us then because we shall have to live with what they have made us create.'

I shivered then, on my small verandah and went inside to fetch a shawl. I suggested we make some hot tea and he came inside and helped me light the lamp. The dirty things from supper still lay on the table in the alcove that I call my kitchen. He fetched some water from the big oil drum out back and washed our few things while I waited for the kettle to boil. He was quick and economical with his movements in the small space which only I had moved in for so many years.

We took our tea back out to the verandah and found to our delight that the moon, which had been struggling up over the hill, had made it to the top and lay, flatly gleaming into our verandah. For the first time he smiled and threw back his head to catch the gleam of the light under his half-closed eyelids. But he grew serious again and blew on his tea to cool it.

'You could leave,' I said, testing him. 'Run away.'

'No,' he said firmly. 'I am in the group now and there is no way out. There was no way out when I was in the city and there will never be a way out for me now.'

The warm tea eased its way past the back of my closed throat. I said, 'I used to live in the city. I had access to money, on terms. I too was in a box, a prison. It took me a long time to find my way out, but I did. You will find your way out in your own time.'

He set the cup down and looked carefully at me. 'I used to think that way once,' he said. And then he was walking down the step and out across my garden and off into the hills.

Up in these hills the mornings are so soft and moist that you want, just for one moment, to gather it all to you. To hold, just for that second a soft, new life before that overriding sun burns and dries it flat away.

CHARTING THE STORY

1 How do the narrator's interactions with the "boys" change over the course of the story? What may account for the changes? How do you predict their interactions will go in the future?

2 How might the trainees' marauding of the narrator's garden be construed as an allegory? How does the young boy fit into the allegory?
3 How do you interpret the narrator's comment in Paragraph 19 that in the city she "had access to money, on terms"?

CONSIDERATIONS OF STYLE

1 Read aloud the first and the last paragraphs as performance pieces. What images do you find yourself emphasizing? What gestures seem automatically to accompany your reading?
2 What moods does the author build in the story? With what images does she create them?

AFTERTHOUGHTS

1 A student, Oksana, wrote so memorably in her personal narrative: "Life is as fragile as a piece of glass, and you never know when it may break." How do the narrator and her young friend—as well as her neighbor "some few chains away down the hill"—attempt to keep the fragile glass of their lives intact?
2 Why does the narrator, in the fourth paragraph, characterize the "big shots" as "stilted figures in a No play"? If you are unfamiliar with the Japanese genre of No drama, you might wish to look it up. What does the usage of this metaphor suggest about the narrator?
3 What do you predict will happen in the near future, after the end of the story? What in the text suggests it?

THE WRITER'S CRAFT

1 Rewrite the incident of the evening from the point of view of the young man, or from that of the old man who lives down the hillside.
2 Researching Jamaica's recent history, write an essay discussing the issues which may have prompted the young man to join with others in political struggle.

Politics and Poetry: Three African Voices

FUNSO AYEJINA

FUNSO AYEJINA *was born in 1950 in Nigeria. He attended the University of Ibadan, the University of Acadia in Canada, and the University of the West Indies. He has returned to Nigeria to teach in the Department of Literature at the University of Ife.*

Ayejina has written poetry, short stories, radio plays, and critical essays. His work is informed by his familiarity with West Indian as well as African cultures. "And So It Came to Pass" reflects a theme common in Ayejina's poetry: the failure of many postcolonial African leaders to live up to their promises. It appears in the collection A Letter to Lynda and Other Poems *(1988).*

PERSPECTIVES

1. Which European powers withdrew from Africa in the early 1960s? Approximately how long had they ruled the continent? Why did colonialism vanish so suddenly? What has been its legacy under successive native African administrations, particularly those of Nigeria, Ghana, and Kenya—the sources of these poems?
2. Since the end of World War II, have any new nations made a peaceful transition from colonial rule to independence? What seems to have encouraged a great deal of violence, greed, and self-seeking in some newly independent nations and less of these evils in others?

And So It Came to Pass

And so it came to pass
many seasons after the death of one Saviour
that a new crop of saviours, armed with party programmes
came cascading down our rivers of hope;
poised for the poisoning of our atlantic reservoir
they sought out the foxes in the family

to whom they gave their thirty pieces of silver
in local and foreign exchange
for the secrets of the passage—
way into the castle of our skins . . .

men we had taken for fearless warriors
as protectors of our secret recipes
suddenly turned crabs, carapace and all
shedding shame like water from duck-backs,
seeing sideways beyond the good of all
to the comfort of the selves;
and with their divination bags of tricks
slung over arrogant shoulders
they crawl over our dreams
under the cover of moonless nights
sidestepping traps, destroying hope
they turn our green august of rains,
of showers with which to persuade crops
towards harvest-circles
around whose fire we would have exchanged
happy tales of toil
into an orgy of furious flames . . .

And so it came to pass
that our saviours gave us a gift of tragedy
for which we are too dumb-struck to find a melody.

CHARTING THE POEM

1 What Biblical references inform this poem? What images of native African culture? What is the effect of juxtaposing the two?

2 The "castle of our skins" (Line 10) is a reference to Barbados writer George Lamming's novel of Caribbean identity. How do you interpret the phrase in the context of this poem?

3 What condition of the country is depicted in the second stanza? In the end, what is the people's response to their "tragedy"?

CONSIDERATIONS OF STYLE

1 What sound devices—especially alliteration, assonance, and consonance—roll through this poem?

2 How are the grammatical sentences of the poem signaled? In what respect do they seem to read like charges in a denunciation?

3 How do images of water and fire play against each other in the poem?

YAO EGBLEWOGBE

YAO EGBLEWOGBE *was born in southeast Ghana in 1937. He was educated at the University of Ghana, where he joined the faculty of the Language Centre, after having taught in secondary schools and teacher training colleges.*

"The Coming of Day," set in the later days of the regime of Kwame Nkrumah, appeared originally in The Wizard's Pride and Other Poems *(1974) and has been anthologized in* A Selection of African Poetry, *K E Senanu and T Vincent, eds (1976).*

The Coming of Day

I
They came with gift and promise
That the day had dawned
And darkness fled. Then higher and higher
The royal sun climbed, while lips cracked
Beneath a dying tree,
And men shaded their doubtful eyes
To see fatality in glory;
The grey dog and brown dog and the young dog,
(It had died) had ceased to bark;
Pastures once rich had become barren
Where fleshy cattle grazed.
And here and there the bleached skeleton
Of a goat reflects the luminous power.

Beneath the blessed silence of a glowing city
Children choked and mothers wept.
A woman stood agape behind the city wall;
Her song is long forgotten.
But noon was yet to come.

One tired cat, pursued by hungry mice,
Had seen a flameless hell
Where ghastly figures sat
Dreaming of night.

II
We were shrouded in mists of grief;

Strained hazy eyes to see
What the stranger had brought:

Certain uncertainties of misshaped minds
That sipped their leisure from the cup
Of human tears; pleasure boats
That sailed on the dark fluid
Of aching eyes till night swallowed us all.
We have seen another morrow;
We have seen other heads
Whose dark foreheads ache with thinking clear;
Men of might who wipe all tears
With a handkerchief of determination.
Before tomorrow they will unweave
The tapestry of deceit.
So may this mist recede
For the coming of day.

CHARTING THE POEM

1. The hopeful mood at the beginning of the poem soon turns to despair. How might this reflect the mood of many Africans in the early days of independence? Why?
2. At the end of Part I, a tired cat is pursued by hungry mice, and hell is flameless, its inhabitants dreaming of night and not day. What is the force of these contradictions?
3. Does the speaker lose or regain hope at the end of the poem? What enabling factors are we left to imagine?

CONSIDERATIONS OF STYLE

1. What is the effect of the several animal images in the first three stanzas? In addition there are images of a woman and of children. Where are the men in this scenario?
2. What are the dominant visual images in Part II? Whose vision is being clouded, and why? Who are the clear-thinking "Men of might who wipe tears/With a handkerchief of determination"?

JARED ANGIRA

JARED ANGIRA *was born in Kenya in 1947. He received a degree in commerce at the University of Nairobi, where he edited the creative magazine,* Busara. *He has published the collections of poetry* Juices *(1970)*, Soft Corals *(1974)*, The Years Go By *(1980)*, *and* Tides of Time: Selected Poems *(1996)*.

"No Coffin, No Grave" is a satirical poem about the assassination of a political leader whose plans for a grand funeral have gone awry.

No Coffin, No Grave

He was buried without a coffin
without a grave
the scavengers performed the post-mortem
in the open mortuary
without sterilized knives
in front of the night club

stuttering rifles put up
the gun salute of the day
that was a state burial anyway
the car knelt
the red plate wept, wrapped itself in blood its master's

the diary revealed to the sea
the rain anchored there at last
isn't our flag red, black, and white?
so he wrapped himself well

who could signal yellow
when we had to leave politics to the experts
and brood on books
brood on hunger
and schoolgirls
grumble under the black pot
sleep under torn mosquito net
and let lice lick our intestines

the lord of the bar, money speaks madam
woman magnet, money speaks madam
we only cover the stinking darkness
of the cave of our mouths
and ask our father who is in hell to judge him
the quick and the good.

Well, his diary, submarine of the Third World War
showed he wished
to be buried in a gold-laden coffin
like a VIP
under the jacaranda tree beside his palace
a shelter for his grave
and much beer for the funeral party

anyway one noisy pupil suggested we bring
tractors and plough the land.

CHARTING THE POEM

1 Where has the politician been gunned down? What is ironic about the site?
2 What attributes of a typical swaggering politician does the poem show? Can you provide examples among Western or other non-African politicians?
3 What Third World War might the speaker be referring to in Line 30?

CONSIDERATIONS OF STYLE

1 How does personification—of the scavengers, the rifles, the car, the red plate—figure in the poem's characterization of the dead politician?
2 What is the significance of the color images in Stanzas 3 and 4?
3 Of what significance is the suggestion of the "noisy pupil" that "we bring tractors and plough the land"?

AFTERTHOUGHTS

1 In what respects do you think foreign intervention—in particular, by the United States and other developed nations—has contributed to the corruption of politics in postcolonial Africa? In what respects did the Cold War fuel the fires of corruption?
2 What is the origin of the term "Third World"? Why has the term fallen out of use? Or has its use shifted to different contexts, as in Mutabaruka's poem *dis poem,* which characterizes itself as "revoltin against 1st world 2nd world/3rd world . . ."?

THE WRITER'S CRAFT

1 Write a poem, an essay, or other work about a revolution gone awry. If you are referring to a particular historical instance, document your research sources; if you

are writing of a fictional composite, note which nation's or nations' post-independence malaise has contributed to your writing.

2 In Cuba, local "Committees for the Defense of the Revolution" abound, a sort of political, but also socioeconomic "Neighborhood Watch." If your own nation achieved its independence through revolution (whether violent or nonviolent), upon what issues might such a "Committee" have focused, and why? If your nation achieved independence in a less dramatic manner, what sort of issues might a "committee for the defense of a peaceful independence" have focused upon?

KEN SARO-WIWA

*Kenule Benson Tsaro-Wiwa—*KEN SARO-WIWA*—was born in 1941 in Bori, Nigeria. He studied at Government College Umuahia (also Chinua Achebe's alma mater) and at University College Obadan, where he began his literary career as editor of the English Department's student magazine and president of the dramatic society. He sought an academic career in drama, but his goals were interrupted by the Biafran War of 1968–1973, during which time he worked as a government civil servant.*

Saro-Wiwa was a prominent leader of his ethnic Ogoni people, whose homeland is both a major food-producing area and the source of millions of barrels of crude oil, vital to Nigeria's economy. He took up the cause of the minority Ogoni—whose interests were not protected by the Nigerian constitution—against the Anglo-Dutch transnational Shell Corporation, which he accused of exploiting the Ogoni while propping up the dictator of General Sani Abacha. Under his leadership, the Ogoni resistance movement was essentially peaceful and focused on environmental and human rights issues. Yet, he was arrested, tortured (Amnesty International declared him a prisoner of conscience), and, on 10 November 1995, executed with eight co-trialists, despite international calls for clemency.

Saro-Wiwa's works include: the story "The Transistor Radio," which won fourth place in the Second BBC African Service Competition in 1971; the novels Basi and Company *(1983),* Song in a Time of War, *and* Sozaboy *(both 1985); and the short-story collection* A Forest of Flowers *(1986). "Africa Kills Her Sun" is from the collection* African Rhapsody, *published in 1994.*

PERSPECTIVES

1. What are some criticisms being leveled against transnational companies currently operating in developing countries? What is your response—active or passive—to such criticisms?
2. What is Amnesty International? What role does it play in the international community?
3. "Deathbed confessions," whether spoken or written, have commonly been considered to be credible utterances, because the person who faces death has nothing to lose, and everything to gain, by telling the truth. Do you agree with this notion? Why, or why not? What events from history, from literature, in everyday life, support your view?

Africa Kills Her Sun

Dear Zole,

You'll be surprised, no doubt, to receive this letter. But I couldn't leave your beautiful world without saying good-bye to you who are condemned to live in it. I know that some might consider my gesture somewhat pathetic, as my colleagues, Sazan and Jimba, do, our finest moments having been achieved two or three weeks ago. However, for me, this letter is a celebration, a final act of love, a quality which, in spite of my career, in spite of tomorrow morning, I do possess in abundance, and cherish. For I've always treasured the many moments of pleasure we spent together in our youth when the world was new and fishes flew in golden ponds. In the love we then shared have I found happiness, a true resting place, a shelter from the many storms that have buffeted my brief life. Whenever I've been most alone, whenever I've been torn by conflict and pain, I've turned to that love for the resolution which has sustained and seen me through. This may surprise you, considering that this love was never consummated and that you may possibly have forgotten me, not having seen me these ten years gone. I still remember you, have always remembered you, and it's logical that in the night before tomorrow, I should write you to ask a small favor of you. But more importantly, the knowledge that I have unburdened myself to you will make tomorrow morning's event as pleasant and desirable to me as to the thousands of spectators who will witness it.

I know this will get to you because the prison guard's been heavily bribed to deliver it. He should rightly be with us before the firing squad tomorrow. But he's condemned, like most others, to live, to play out his assigned role in your hell of a world. I see him burning out his dull, uncomprehending life, doing his menial job for a pittance and a bribe for the next so many years. I pity his ignorance and cannot envy his complacency. Tomorrow morning, with this letter and our bribe in his pocket, he'll call us out, Sazan, Jimba and I. As usual, he'll have all our names mixed up: he always calls Sazan "Sajim" and Jimba "Samba." But that won't matter. We'll obey him, and as we walk to our death, we'll laugh at his gaucherie, his plain stupidity. As we laughed at that other thief, the High Court Judge.

You must've seen that in the papers too. We saw it, thanks to our bribe-taking friend, the prison guard, who sent us a copy of the newspaper in which it was reported. Were it not in an unfeeling nation, among a people inured to evil and taking sadistic pleasure in the loss of life, some questions might have been asked. No doubt, many will ask the questions, but they will do it in the safety and comfort of their homes, over the interminable bottles of beer, uncomprehendingly watching their boring, cheap television programs, the rejects of Europe and America, imported to fill their vacuity. They will salve their conscience with more bottles of beer, wash the answers down their gullets and pass question, conscience and answer out as waste into their open sewers choking with concentrated filth and murk. And they will forget.

I bet, though, the High Court Judge himself will never forget. He must remember it the rest of his life. Because I watched him closely that first morning. And I can't describe the shock and disbelief which I saw registered on his face. His spectacles fell to his table and it was with difficulty he regained composure. It must have been the first time in all his experience that he found persons arraigned on a charge for which the punishment upon conviction is death, entering a plea of guilty and demanding that they be sentenced and shot without further delay.

Sazan, Jimba and I had rehearsed it carefully. During the months we'd been remanded in prison custody while the prosecutors prepared their case, we'd agreed we weren't going to allow a long trial, or any possibility that they might impose differing sentences upon us: freeing one, sentencing another to life imprisonment and the third to death by firing squad.

Nor did we want to give the lawyers in their funny, black, funeral robes an opportunity to clown around, making arguments for pleasure, engaging in worthless casuistry. No. We voted for death. After all, we were armed robbers, bandits. We knew it. We didn't want to give the law a chance to prove itself the proverbial ass. We were being honest to ourselves, to our vocation, to our country and to mankind.

"Sentence us to death immediately and send us before the firing squad without further delay," we yelled in unison. The Judge, after he had recovered from his initial shock, asked us to be taken away that day, "for disturbing my court." I suppose he wanted to see if we'd sleep things over and change our plea. We didn't. When they brought us back the next day, we said the same thing in louder voice. We said we had robbed and killed. We were guilty. Cool. The Judge was bound hand and foot and did what he had to. We'd forced him to be honest to his vocation, to the laws of the country and to the course of justice. It was no mean achievement. The court hall was stunned; our guards were utterly amazed as we walked out of court, smiling. "Hardened criminals," "Bandits," I heard them say as we trooped out of the court. One spectator actually spat at us as we walked into the waiting Black Maria!

And now that I've confessed to banditry, you'll ask why I did it? I'll answer that question by retelling the story of the young, beautiful prostitute I met in St. Pauli in Hamburg when our ship berthed there years back. I've told my friends the story several times. I did ask her, after the event, why she was in that place? She replied that some girls chose to be secretaries in offices, others to be nurses. She had chosen prostitution as a career. Cool. I was struck by her candor. And she set me thinking. Was I in the merchant navy by choice or because it was the first job that presented itself to me when I left school? When we returned home, I skipped ship, thanks to the prostitute of St. Pauli, and took a situation as a clerk in the Ministry of Defense.

It was there I came face-to-face with the open looting of the national treasury, the manner of which I cannot describe without arousing in myself the deepest, basest emotions. Everyone was busy at it and there was no one to complain to. Everyone to whom I complained said to me: "If you can't beat them, join them." I was not about to join anyone; I wanted to beat them and took it upon myself to wage a war against them. In no time they had gotten rid of me. Dismissed me. I had no option but to join them then. I had to make a choice. I became an armed robber, a bandit. It was my choice, my answer. And I don't regret it.

Did I know it was dangerous? Some girls are secretaries, others choose to be prostitutes. Some men choose to be soldiers and policemen, others doctors and lawyers; I chose to be a robber. Every occupation has its hazards. A taxi driver may meet his death on the road; a businessman may die in an air crash; a robber dies before a firing squad. It's no big deal. If you ask me, the death I've chosen is possibly more dramatic, more qualitative, more eloquent than dying in bed of a ruptured liver from overindulgence in alcohol. Yes? But robbery is antisocial, you say? A proven determination to break the law. I don't want to provide an alibi. But just you think of the many men and women who are busy breaking or bending the law in all coasts and climes. Look for a copy of *The Guardian* of 19th September. That is the edition in which our plea to the Judge was reported. You'll find there the story of the Government official who stole over seven million naira. Seven million. Cool. He was antisocial, right? How many of his type d'you know? And how many more go undetected? I say, if my avocation was antisocial, I'm in good company. And that company consists of Presidents of countries, transnational organizations, public servants high and low, men and women. The only difference is that while I'm prepared to pay the price for it all, the others are not. See?

I'm not asking for your understanding or sympathy. I need neither, not now nor hereafter. I'm saying it as it is. Right? Cool. I expect you'll say that armed robbery should be the special preserve of the scum of society. That no man of my education has any business being a bandit. To that I'll answer that it's about time well-endowed and well-trained people took to it. They'll bring to the profession a romantic quality, a proficiency which will ultimately conduce to the benefit of society. No, I'm not mad. Truly. Time was when the running and ruining of African nations was in the hands of half-literate politicians. Today, well-endowed and better trained people have taken over the task. And look how well they're doing it. So that even upon that score, my conscience sleeps easy. Understand?

Talking about sleep, you should see Sazan and Jimba on the cold, hard prison floor, snoring away as if life itself depends on a good snore. It's impossible, seeing them this way, to believe that they'll be facing the firing squad tomorrow. They're men of courage. Worthy lieutenants. It's a pity their abilities will be lost to society forever, come tomorrow morning. Sazan would have made a good Army General anyday, possibly a President of our country in the mold of Idi Amin or Bokassa. The Europeans and Americans would have found in him a useful ally in the progressive degradation of Africa. Jimba'd have made an excellent Inspector-General of Police, so versed is he in the ways of the Police! You know, of course, that Sazan is a dismissed Sergeant of our nation's proud army. And Jimba was once a Corporal in the Police Force.

When we met, we had similar reasons for pooling our talents. And a great team we did make. Now here we all are in the death cell of a maximum security prison and they snoring away the last hours of their lives on the cold, smelly floor. It's exhilarating to find them so disdainful of life. Their style is the stuff of which history is made. In another time and in another country, they'd be Sir Francis Drake, Cortes or Sir Walter Raleigh. They'd have made empires and earned national honors. But here, our life is one big disaster, an endless tragedy. Heroism is not in our star. We are millipedes crawling on the floor of a dank, wet forest. So Sazan and Jimba will die unsung. See?

One thing, though. We swore never to kill. And we never did. Indeed, we didn't take part in the particular "operation" for which we were held, Sazan, Jimba and I. That operation would've gone quite well if the Superintendent of Police had fulfilled his part of the bargain. Because he was in it with us. The Police are involved in every single robbery that happens. They know the entire gang, the gangs. We'd not succeed if we didn't collaborate with them. Sazan, Jimba and I were the bosses. We didn't go out on "operations." The boys normally did. And they were out on that occasion. The Superintendent of Police was supposed to keep away the police escorts from the vehicle carrying workers' salaries that day. For some reason, he failed to do so. And the policeman shot at our boys. The boys responded and shot and killed him and the Security Company guards. The boys got the money alright. But the killing was contrary to our agreement with the Police. We had to pay. The Police won't stand any of their men being killed. They took all the money from us and then they went after the boys. We said no. The boys had acted on orders. We volunteered to take their place. The Police took us in and made a lot of public noises about it. The boys, I know, will make their decisions later. I don't know what will happen to the Superintendent of Police. But he'll have to look to himself. So, if that is any comfort to you, you may rest in the knowledge that I spilt no blood. No, I wouldn't. Nor have I kept the loot. Somehow, whatever we took from people—the rich ones—always was shared by the gang who were almost always on the bread line. Sazan, Jimba and I are not wealthy.

Many will therefore accuse us of recklessness, or of being careless with our lives. And well they might. I think I speak for my sleeping comrades when I say we went into our career because we didn't see any basic difference between what we were doing and what most others are doing throughout the land today. In every facet of our lives—in politics, in commerce and in the professions—robbery is the base line. And it's been so from time. In the early days, our forebears sold their kinsmen into slavery for minor items such as beads, mirrors, alcohol and tobacco. These days, the tune is the same, only the articles have changed into cars, transistor radios and bank accounts. Nothing else has changed, and nothing will change in the foreseeable future. But that's the problem of those of you who will live beyond tomorrow, Zole.

The cock crows now and I know dawn is about to break. I'm not speak- 15
ing figuratively. In the cell here, the darkness is still all-pervasive, except for the flickering light of the candle by which I write. Sazan and Jimba remain fast

asleep. So is the prison guard. He sleeps all night and is no trouble to us. We could, if we wanted, escape from here, so lax are the guards. But we consider that unnecessary, as what is going to happen later this morning is welcome relief from burdens too heavy to bear. It's the guard and you the living who are in prison, the ultimate prison from which you cannot escape because you do not know that you are incarcerated. Your happiness is the happiness of ignorance and your ignorance is it that keeps you in the prison, which is your life. As this night dissolves into day, Sazan, Jimba and I shall be free. Sazan and Jimba will have left nothing behind. I shall leave at least this letter, which, please, keep for posterity.

Zole, do I rant? Do I pour myself to you in bitter tones? Do not lay it to the fact that I'm about to be shot by firing squad. On second thoughts, you could, you know. After all, seeing death so clearly before me might possibly have made me more perspicacious? And yet, I've always seen these things clearly in my mind's eye. I never did speak about them, never discussed them. I preferred to let them weigh me down. See?

So, then, in a few hours we shall be called out. We shall clamber with others into the miserable lorry which they still call the Black Maria. Notice how everything miserable is associated with us. Black Sheep. Black Maria. Black Death. Black Leg. The Black Hole of Calcutta. The Black Maria will take us to the Beach or to the Stadium. I bet it will be the Stadium. I'd prefer the Beach. So at least to see the ocean once more. For I've still this fond regard for the sea which dates from my time in the Merchant Navy. I love its wide expanse, its anonymity, its strength, its unfathomable depth. And maybe after shooting us, they might decide to throw our bodies into the ocean. We'd then be eaten up by sharks which would in turn be caught by Japanese and Russian fishermen, be refrigerated, packaged in cartons and sold to Indian merchants and then for a handsome profit to our people. That way, I'd have helped keep people alive a bit longer. But they won't do us that favor. I'm sure they'll take us to the Stadium. To provide a true spectacle for the fun-loving unemployed. To keep them out of trouble. To keep them from thinking. To keep them laughing. And dancing.

We'll be there in the dirty clothes which we now wear. We've not had any of our things washed this past month. They will tie us to the stakes, as though that were necessary. For even if we were minded to escape, where'd we run to? I expect they'll also want to blindfold us. Sazan and Jimba have said they'll not allow themselves to be blindfolded. I agree with them. I should want to see my executors, stare the nozzles of their guns bravely in the face, see the open sky, the sun, daylight. See and hear my countrymen as they cheer us to our death. To liberation and freedom.

The Stadium will fill to capacity. And many will not find a place. They will climb trees and hang about the balconies of surrounding houses to get a clear view of us. To enjoy the free show. Cool.

And then the priest will come to us, either to pray or to ask if we have any 20
last wishes. Sazan says he will ask for a cigarette. I'm sure they'll give it to him. I can see him puffing hard at it before the bullets cut him down. He says he's

going to enjoy that cigarette more than anything he's had in life. Jimba says he'll maintain a sullen silence as a mark of his contempt. I'm going to yell at the priest. I will say, "Go to hell, you hypocrite, fornicator and adulterer." I will yell at the top of my voice in the hope that the spectators will hear me. How I wish there'd be a microphone that will reverberate through the Stadium, nay, through the country as a whole! Then the laugh should be on the priest and those who sent him!

The priest will pray for our souls. But it's not us he should be praying for. He should pray for the living, for those whose lives are a daily torment. Between his prayer and when the shots ring out, there will be dead silence. The silence of the graveyard. The transition between life and death. And it shall be seen that the distinction between them both is narrow, as the neck of a calabash. The divide between us breathing like everyone else in the Stadium and us as meat for worms is, oh, so slim, it makes life a walking death! But I should be glad to be rid of the world, of a meaningless existence that grows more dreary by the day. I should miss Sazan and Jimba, though. It'll be a shame to see these elegant gentlemen cut down and destroyed. And I'll miss you, too, my dear girl. But that will be of no consequence to the spectators.

They will troop out of the Stadium, clamber down the trees and the balconies of the houses, as though they'd just returned from another football match. They will march to their ratholes on empty stomachs, with tales enough to fill a Saturday evening. Miserable wretches!

The men who shall have eased us out of life will then untie our bodies and dump them into a lorry and thence to some open general grave. That must be a most distasteful task. I'd not do it for a million dollars. Yet some miserable fellows will do it for a miserable salary at the end of the month. A salary which will not feed them and their families till the next payday. A salary which they will have to augment with a bribe, if they are to keep body and soul together. I say, I do feel sorry for them. See?

The newspapers will faithfully record the fact of our shooting. If they have space, they'll probably carry a photograph of us to garnish your breakfasts.

25 I remember once long ago reading in a newspaper of a man whose one request to the priest was that he be buried along with his walking stick—his faithful companion over the years. He was pictured slumping in death, devotedly clutching his beloved walking stick. True friendship, that. Well, Zole, if ever you see such a photograph of me, make a cutting. Give it to a sculptor and ask him to make a stone sculpture of me as I appear in the photograph. He must make as faithful a representation of me as possible. I must be hard of feature and relentless in aspect. I have a small sum of money in the bank and have already instructed the bank to pay it to you for the purpose of the sculpture I have spoken about...

Time is running out, Zole. Sazan and Jimba are awake now. And they're surprised I haven't slept all night. Sazan says I ought at least to have done myself the favor of sound sleep on my last night on earth. I ask him if I'm not going to sleep soundly, eternally, in a few hours? This, I argue, should be our most wakeful night. Sazan doesn't appreciate that. Nor does Jimba. They stand up, yawn, stretch and rub their eyes. Then they sit down, crowding round me. They ask me to read out to them what I've written. I can't do that, I tell them. It's a love letter. And they burst out laughing. A love letter! And at the point of death! Sazan says I'm gone crazy. Jimba says he's sure I'm afraid of death and looks hard and long at me to justify his suspicion. I say I'm neither crazy nor afraid of death. I'm just telling my childhood girlfriend how I feel this special night. And sending her on an important errand. Jimba says I never told them I had a girlfriend. I reply that she was not important before this moment.

I haven't even seen her in ten years, I repeat. The really compelling need to write her is that on this very special night, I have felt a need to be close to a living being, someone who can relate to others why we did what we did in and out of court.

Sazan says he agrees completely with me. He says he too would like to write his thoughts down. Do I have some paper to lend him? I say no. Besides, time is up. Day has dawned and I haven't even finished my letter. Do they mind leaving me to myself for a few minutes? I'd very much like to end the letter, envelope it and pass it on to the prison guard before he rouses himself fully from sleep and remembers to assume his official, harsh role.

They're nice chaps, are Jimba and Sazan. Sazan says to tell my girl not to bear any children because it's pointless bringing new life into the harsh life of her world. Jimba says to ask my girl to shed him a tear if she can so honor a complete stranger. They both chuckle and withdraw to a corner of the cell and I'm left alone to end my letter.

Now, I was telling you about my statue. My corpse will not be available to you. You will make a grave for me, nonetheless. And place the statue on the gravestone. And now I come to what I consider the most important part of this letter. My epitaph.

I have thought a lot about it, you know. Really. What d'you say about a robber shot in a stadium before a cheering crowd? That he was a good man who strayed? That he deserved his end? That he was a scallywag? A ragamuffin? A murderer whose punishment was not heavy enough? "Here lies X who was shot in public by firing squad for robbing a van and shooting the guards in broad daylight. He serves as an example to all thieves and would-be thieves!"

Who'd care for such an epitaph? They'd probably think it was a joke. No. That wouldn't carry. I'll settle for something different. Something plain and commonsensical. Or something truly cryptic and worthy of a man shot by choice in public by firing squad.

Not that I care. To die the way I'm going to die in the next hour or two is really nothing to worry about. I'm in excellent company. I should find myself recorded in the annals of our history. A history of violence, of murder, of disregard for life. Pleasure in inflicting pain—sadism. Is that the word for it? It's a world I should be pleased to leave. But not without an epitaph.

I recall, many years ago as a young child, reading in a newspaper of an African leader who stood on the grave of a dead lieutenant and through his tears said: "Africa kills her sons." I don't know what he meant by that, and though I've thought about it long enough, I've not been able to unravel the fully mystery of those words. Now, today, this moment, they come flooding back to me. And I want to borrow from him. I'd like you to put this on my gravestone, as my epitaph: "Africa Kills Her Sun." A good epitaph, eh? Cryptic. Definite. A stroke of genius, I should say. I'm sure you'll agree with me. "Africa Kills Her Sun!" That's why she's been described as the Dark Continent? Yes?

So, now, dear girl, I'm done. My heart is light as the daylight which seeps stealthily into our dark cell. I hear the prison guard jangle his keys, put them into the keyhole. Soon he'll turn it and call us out. Our time is up. My time here expires and I must send you all my love. Good-bye.

Yours for ever,

Bana

CHARTING THE STORY

1 What reasons does Bana, who is writing the letter, give as justification for his actions; and what political ramifications does his narrative carry?

2 In what ways does Bana reshape the events of his imminent death into an art form? In contrast, how do Sazan and Jimba handle their approaching deaths? What motivations seem to drive each of the three men?

3 What associations does the narrator make with the term "Black Maria" for police patrol wagon? What associations do you make with the popular American term "paddy wagon"?

CONSIDERATIONS OF STYLE

1 Bana frequently interjects "Cool," "You see?" and "Understand?" into his narrative. What other usages from "everyday speech" (conversation as opposed to consciously "literary" writing) do you find? How do they affect your view of him as a polemical writer, seeking to educate Zole (and, by extension, you)?

2 Of what use are the characters Sazan and Jimba? How would the narrative be different, were Bana acting alone? What is gained by having two accomplices whose characterization significantly differs from that of the narrator?

AFTERTHOUGHTS

1 Discuss with your classmates your individual interpretations of and reactions to the eponymous epitaph that the narrator wishes to have put on his grave.

2 If the narrator had had some degree of power to effect change in his country's government, as would be the case in a democracy, what solutions might he have proposed to keep his people's life from being a "waking death" (Paragraph 21)?

3 In Paragraph 17, calling out the images of "Black Sheep. Black Maria. Black Death. Black Leg. The Black Hole of Calcutta," Bana asks Zole to "notice how everything miserable is [still] with us." As a black man writing to a black woman, in the context of a nation in which power rests in the hands of black Africans (the fact that he has mentioned Idi Amin and Bokassa denotes that he is writing well after independence), what point is he making?

THE WRITER'S CRAFT

1 From the point of view of Sazan or Jimba, set down your internal monologue from the time you are loaded into the Black Maria until your death (paying particular attention to the characterization in Bana's narrative).

2 In the mid-1990s, a US talk-show host unsuccessfully lobbied to have an execution televised. Ratings aside—admittedly, a very large "aside"—he argued that Americans' witnessing such an event would help them to have a clearer idea of just what is involved in capital punishment. In an analytical essay, discuss the rationales for and against public execution, using (at least in part) Bana's description of how the crowds would react if indeed they were taken to the Stadium.

Part Five
The Immigrant Experience

I remember that first day of school, my mother with the purest intention,
took two sheets of foil hollowed
with a cup of steamed rice
and a helping of last night's
caldereta: *chunks of potatoes, sliced*
red peppers, and a redder sauce with beef;
and I, with hunger, could not
bring myself to eat.

EUGENE GLORIA, *Assimilation*

ROBERT OLEN BUTLER

ROBERT OLEN BUTLER *was born in 1945 in Granite City, Illinois. Growing up, he worked summers in a blast furnace labor gang, drove taxis, and mixed with the working class people of his town. Still, even as a child he dreamed of becoming an actor, like his father, who was head of the theatre department at St. Louis University. But while attending theatre school at Northwestern University, Butler aspired instead to being a writer, initially of plays, later of novels and short stories.*

In 1969 Butler enlisted in the Army, was taught Vietnamese, and sent to Vietnam as a counterintelligence special agent. While he worked days in an office in Saigon's City Hall, at night he would prowl the streets with the Vietnamese—warm and generous-spirited people who would later populate many of his works, including the novels Alleys of Eden *(1981),* On Distant Ground *(1985),* The Deuce *(1989), and the collection of stories that won him the Pulitzer Prize,* A Good Scent from a Strange Mountain *(1992), from which "Crickets" is taken.*

His other works include the novels Sun Dogs *(1982),* Countrymen of Bones *(1983),* Wabash *(1987), and* They Whisper *(1994), and a collection of stories,* Tabloid Dreams *(1997).*

Butler teaches writing at McNeese State University in Louisiana.

PERSPECTIVES

1 What experience do you bring to the reading of this text concerning a cultural gap between parent and child, whether experienced by you or by someone you know?

2 If you were forced to emigrate from your country and found yourself raising a family in another culture, what aspects of your native culture would you attempt to preserve and transmit to your children? How would you go about this?

3 What games amused you most as a child? How do the games you played as a child differ from those enjoyed by children growing up now?

Crickets

They call me Ted where I work and they've called me that for over a decade now and it still bothers me, though I'm not very happy about my real name being the same as the former President of the former Republic of Vietnam.

Thiệu is not an uncommon name in my homeland and my mother had nothing more in mind than a long-dead uncle when she gave it to me. But in Lake Charles, Louisiana, I am Ted. I guess the other Mr. Thiệu has enough of my former country's former gold bullion tucked away so that in London, where he probably wears a bowler and carries a rolled umbrella, nobody's calling him anything but Mr. Thiệu.

I hear myself sometimes and I sound pretty bitter, I guess. But I don't let that out at the refinery, where I'm the best chemical engineer they've got and they even admit it once in a while. They're good-hearted people, really. I've done enough fighting in my life. I was eighteen when Saigon fell and I was only recently mustered into the Army, and when my unit dissolved and everybody ran, I stripped off my uniform and put on my civilian clothes again and I threw rocks at the North's tanks when they rolled through the streets. Very few of my people did likewise. I stayed in the mouths of alleys so I could run and then return and throw more rocks, but because what I did seemed so isolated and so pathetic a gesture, the gunners in the tanks didn't even take notice. But I didn't care about their scorn. At least my right arm had said no to them.

And then there were Thai pirates in the South China Sea and idiots running refugee centers and more idiots running the agencies in the U.S. to find a place for me and my new bride, who braved with me the midnight escape by boat and the terrible sea and all the rest. We ended up here in the flat bayou land of Louisiana, where there are rice paddies and where the water and the land are in the most delicate balance with each other, very much like the Mekong Delta, where I grew up. These people who work around me are good people and maybe they call me Ted because they want to think of me as one of them, though sometimes it bothers me that these men are so much bigger than me. I am the size of a woman in this country and these American men are all massive and they speak so slowly, even to one another, even though English is their native language. I've heard New Yorkers on television and I speak as fast as they do.

My son is beginning to speak like the others here in Louisiana. He is ten, the product of the first night my wife and I spent in Lake Charles, in a cheap motel with the sky outside red from the refineries. He is proud to have been born in America, and when he leaves us in the morning to walk to the Catholic school, he says, "Have a good day, y'all." Sometimes I say good-bye to him in Vietnamese and he wrinkles his nose at me and says, "Aw, Pop," like I'd just cracked a corny joke. He doesn't speak Vietnamese at all and my wife says not to worry about that. He's an American.

But I do worry about that, though I understand why I should be content. 5
I even understood ten years ago, so much so that I agreed with my wife and gave my son an American name. Bill. Bill and his father Ted. But this past summer I found my son hanging around the house bored in the middle of vacation and I was suddenly his father Thiệu with a wonderful idea for him. It

was an idea that had come to me in the first week of every February we'd been in Lake Charles, because that's when the crickets always begin to crow here. This place is rich in crickets, which always makes me think of my own childhood in Vietnam. But I never said anything to my son until last summer.

I came to him after watching him slouch around the yard one Sunday pulling the Spanish moss off the lowest branches of our big oak tree and then throwing rocks against the stop sign on our corner. "Do you want to do something fun?" I said to him.

"Sure, Pop," he said, though there was a certain suspicion in his voice, like he didn't trust me on the subject of fun. He threw all the rocks at once that were left in his hand and the stop sign shivered at their impact.

I said, "If you keep that up, they will arrest me for the destruction of city property and then they will deport us all."

My son laughed at this. I, of ourse, knew that he would know I was bluffing. I didn't want to be too hard on him for the boyish impulses that I myself had found to be so satisfying when I was young, especially since I was about to share something of my own childhood with him.

"So what've you got, Pop?" my son asked me. 10

"Fighting crickets," I said.

"What?"

Now, my son was like any of his fellow ten-year-olds, devoted to superheros and the mighty clash of good and evil in all of its high-tech forms in the Saturday-morning cartoons. Just to make sure he was in the right frame of mind, I explained it to him with one word, "Cricketmen," and I thought this was a pretty good ploy. He cocked his head in interest at this and I took him to the side porch and sat him down and I explained.

I told him how, when I was a boy, my friends and I would prowl the undergrowth and capture crickets and keep them in matchboxes. We would feed them leaves and bits of watermelon and bean sprouts, and we'd train them to fight by keeping them in a constant state of agitation by blowing on them and gently flicking the ends of their antennas with a sliver of wood. So each of us would have a stable of fighting crickets, and there were two kinds.

At this point my son was squirming a little bit and his eyes were shifting 15 away into the yard and I knew that my Cricketman trick had run its course. I fought back the urge to challenge his set of interests. Why should the stiff and foolish fights of his cartoon characters absorb him and the real clash—real life and death—that went on in the natural world bore him? But I realized that I hadn't cut to the chase yet, as they say on TV. "They fight to the death," I said with as much gravity as I could put into my voice, like I was James Earl Jones.

The announcement won me a glance and a brief lift of his eyebrows. This gave me a little scrabble of panic, because I still hadn't told him about the two types of crickets and I suddenly knew that was a real important part for me. I tried not to despair at his understanding and I put my hands on his shoulders and turned him around to face me. "Listen," I said. "You need to understand this if you are to have fighting crickets. There are two types, and all of us had some of each. One type we called the charcoal crickets. These were very large and strong, but they were slow and they could become confused. The other type was small and brown and we called them fire crickets. They weren't as strong, but they were very smart and quick."

"So who would win?" my son said.

"Sometimes one and sometimes the other. The fights were very long and full of hard struggle. We'd have a little tunnel made of paper and we'd slip a sliver of wood under the cowling of our cricket's head to make him mad and we'd twirl him around by his antenna, and then we'd each put our cricket into the tunnel at opposite ends. Inside, they'd approach each other and begin to fight and then we'd lift the paper tunnel and watch."

"Sounds neat," my son said, though his enthusiasm was at best moderate, and I knew I had to act quickly.

So we got a shoe box and we started looking for crickets. It's better at 20
night, but I knew for sure his interest wouldn't last that long. Our house is up on blocks because of the high water table in town and we crawled along the edge, pulling back the bigger tufts of grass and turning over rocks. It was one of the rocks that gave us our first crickets, and my son saw them and cried in my ear, "There, there," but he waited for me to grab them. I cupped first one and then the other and dropped them into the shoe box and I felt a vague disappointment, not so much because it was clear that my boy did not want to touch the insects, but that they were both the big black ones, the charcoal crickets. We crawled on and we found another one in the grass and another sitting in the muddy shadow of the house behind the hose faucet and then we caught two more under an azalea bush.

"Isn't that enough?" my son demanded. "How many do we need?"

I sat with my back against the house and put the shoe box in my lap and my boy sat beside me, his head stretching this way so he could look into the box. There was no more vagueness to my feeling. I was actually weak with disappointment because all six of these were charcoal crickets, big and inert and just looking around like they didn't even know anything was wrong.

"Oh, no," my son said with real force, and for a second I thought he had read my mind and shared my feeling, but I looked at him and he was pointing at the toes of his white sneakers. "My Reeboks are ruined!" he cried, and on the toe of each sneaker was a smudge of grass.

I glanced back into the box and the crickets had not moved and I looked at my son and he was still staring at his sneakers. "Listen," I said, "this was a big mistake. You can go on and do something else."

He jumped up at once. "Do you think Mom can clean these?" he said. 25

"Sure," I said. "Sure."

He was gone at once and the side door slammed and I put the box on the grass. But I didn't go in. I got back on my hands and knees and I circled the entire house and then I turned over every stone in the yard and dug around all the trees. I found probably two dozen more crickets, but they were all the same. In Louisiana there are rice paddies and some of the bayous look like the Delta, but many of the birds are different, and why shouldn't the insects be different, too? This is another country, after all. It was just funny about the fire crickets. All of us kids rooted for them, even if we were fighting with one of our own charcoal crickets. A fire cricket was a very precious and admirable thing.

The next morning my son stood before me as I finished my breakfast and once he had my attention, he looked down at his feet, drawing my eyes down as well. "See?" he said. "Mom got them clean."

Then he was out the door and I called after him, "See you later, Bill."

CHARTING THE STORY

1 The narrator notes in the third paragraph the similarities between the landscape of the Mekong delta where he grew up and that of the flat bayou land of Louisiana, "where there are rice paddies and where the water and the land are in the most delicate balance with each other." How does the geographical analogy extend to other aspects of Ted's life in America?

2 What symbolic role do the "charcoal crickets" and the "fire crickets" play in this story? What irony does the symbolism ultimately engender?

3 What effect does American consumer culture have on the relationship between father and son? How does the father use it to his advantage? How, in the end, nevertheless, does it separate the worlds that each inhabits?

CONSIDERATIONS OF STYLE

1 Like many ten-year-olds, son Bill seems to be a minimalist in conversations with adults—here namely with his father. Find examples in the story of how Butler conveys the boy's responses through nonverbal behavior rather than through dialogue.

AFTERTHOUGHTS

1 Under what circumstances have you ever changed your name or been "called out of" your name? (The latter is an African American expression referring to misnaming as an intentional insult.)

2 Discuss the effect of changing one's name on a person's sense of identity, considering the various populations that either once have, or sometimes do, change their names in the course of a lifetime.

3 While this story focuses on the father-son bonding between Ted and Bill, what passages suggest that the bond may be stronger between Bill and his mother? What effect might this have on the father-son relationship?

THE WRITER'S CRAFT

1 Retell selected scenes in "Crickets" from the point of view of son Bill, or from that of his mother, who is spoken of, but never speaks herself.

2 Write a short essay on the effects of assimilation upon immigrants, as well as the effects that immigrants' assimilation have on the host population—without once using the expressions "melting pot," "salad bowl," "mosaic," or any other cliché you may have heard to describe this phenomenon.

EDWIDGE DANTICAT

EDWIDGE DANTICAT *was born in Haiti in 1969 and moved to New York City when she was twelve. She graduated from Barnard College and received an MFA from Brown University.*

Her published works include the novels, Breath, Eyes, Memory *(1994) and* The Farming of Bones *(1998), and a collection of short stories,* Krik? Krak! *(1995). Her works evoke both joyful and painful images of her native Haiti, and often focus on the strength of her people—particularly Haitian women—in the face of adversity.*

Blurring distinctions between prose poem and story, this text presents vignettes in the portrayal of the narrator's mother—a "day woman" in New York—alternating viewpoints of mother and daughter. "New York Day Women" first appeared in Krik? Krak! *in 1991.*

PERSPECTIVES

1. Recall a time when you observed a person—for a palpable period of time—who was not aware of being watched. How did the experience affect your perception of the person?
2. The expression *Krik? Krak!* is also a traditional closing to other Caribbean stories:

   Krik? Krak! Monkey break 'e back
   On a rotten pommerac.

   Consult some folk-tale or fairy tale anthologies to find traditional story closings in other cultures. What purposes do these closings serve? In their absence, what devices are used to signal that a narrative has ended?

New York Day Women

Today, walking down the street, I see my mother. She is strolling with a happy gait, her body thrust toward the DON'T WALK sign and the yellow taxicabs that make forty-five-degree turns on the corner of Madison and Fifty-seventh Street.

I have never seen her in this kind of neighborhood, peering into Chanel and Tiffany's and gawking at the jewels glowing in the Bulgari windows. My mother never shops outside of Brooklyn. She has never seen the advertising office where I work. She is afraid to take the subway, where you may meet those young black militant street preachers who curse black women for straightening their hair.

Yet, here she is, my mother, who I left at home that morning in her bathrobe, with pieces of newspapers twisted like rollers in her hair. My mother, who accuses me of random offenses as I dash out of the house.

Would you get up and give an old lady like me your subway seat? In this state of mind, I bet you don't even give up your seat to a pregnant lady.

My mother, who is often right about that. Sometimes I get up and give my seat. Other times, I don't. It all depends on how pregnant the woman is and whether or not she is with her boyfriend or husband and whether or not *he* is sitting down.

As my mother stands in front of Carnegie Hall, one taxi driver yells to another, "What do you think this is, a dance floor?"

My mother waits patiently for this dispute to be settled before crossing the street.

In Haiti when you get hit by a car, the owner of the car gets out and kicks you for getting blood on his bumper.

My mother who laughs when she says this and shows a large gap in her mouth where she lost three more molars to the dentist last week. My mother, who at fifty-nine, says dentures are okay.

You can take them out when they bother you. I'll like them. I'll like them fine.
Will it feel empty when Papa kisses you?

Oh no, he doesn't kiss me that way anymore.

My mother, who watches the lottery drawing every night on channel 11 without ever having played the numbers.

A third of that money is all I would need. We would pay the mortgage, and your father could stop driving that taxicab all over Brooklyn.

I follow my mother, mesmerized by the many possibilities of her journey. Even in a flowered dress, she is lost in a sea of pinstripes and gray suits, high heels and elegant short skirts, Reebok sneakers, dashing from building to building.

My mother, who won't go out to dinner with anyone.

If they want to eat with me, let them come to my house, even if I boil water and give it to them.

My mother, who talks to herself when she peels the skin off poultry.

Fat, you know, and cholesterol. Fat and cholesterol killed your aunt Hermine.

My mother, who makes jam with dried grapefruit peel and then puts in cinnamon bark that I always think is cockroaches in the jam. My mother, whom I have always bought household appliances for, on her birthday. A nice rice cooker, a blender.

I trail the red orchids in her dress and the heavy faux leather bag on her shoulders. Realizing the ferocious pace of my pursuit, I stop against a wall to rest. My mother keeps on walking as though she owns the sidewalk under her feet.

As she heads toward the Plaza Hotel, a bicycle messenger swings so close to her that I want to dash forward and rescue her, but she stands dead in her tracks and lets him ride around her and then goes on.

My mother stops at a corner hot-dog stand and asks for something. The vendor hands her a can of soda that she slips into her bag. She stops by another vendor selling sundresses for seven dollars each. I can tell that she is looking at an African print dress, contemplating my size. I think to myself, Please Ma, don't buy it. It would be just another thing that I would bury in the garage or give to Goodwill.

Why should we give to Goodwill when there are so many people back home who need clothes? We save our clothes for the relatives in Haiti.

Twenty years we have been saving all kinds of things for the relatives in Haiti. I need the place in the garage for an exercise bike.

You are pretty enough to be a stewardess. Only dogs like bones.

This mother of mine, she stops at another hot-dog vendor's and buys a frankfurter that she eats on the street. I never knew that she ate frankfurters. With her blood pressure, she shouldn't eat anything with sodium. She has to be careful with her heart, this day woman.

I cannot just swallow salt. Salt is heavier than a hundred bags of shame.

She is slowing her pace, and now I am too close. If she turns around, she might see me. I let her walk into the park before I start to follow again.

My mother walks toward the sandbox in the middle of the park. There a woman is waiting with a child. The woman is wearing a leotard with biker's shorts and has small weights in her hands. The woman kisses the child good-bye and surrenders him to my mother; then she bolts off, running on the cemented stretches in the park.

The child given to my mother has frizzy blond hair. His hand slips into hers easily, like he's known her for a long time. When he raises his face to look at my mother, it is as though he is looking at the sky.

My mother gives this child the soda that she bought from the vendor on the street corner. The child's face lights up as she puts in a straw in the can for him. This seems to be a conspiracy just between the two of them.

My mother and the child sit and watch the other children play in the sandbox. The child pulls out a comic book from a knapsack with Big Bird on the back. My mother peers into his comic book. My mother, who taught herself to read as a little girl in Haiti from the books that her brothers brought home from school.

My mother, who has now lost six of her seven sisters in Ville Rose and has never had the strength to return for their funerals.

Many graves to kiss when I go back. Many graves to kiss. 35

She throws away the empty soda can when the child is done with it. I wait and watch from a corner until the woman in the leotard and biker's shorts returns, sweaty and breathless, an hour later. My mother gives the woman back her child and strolls farther into the park.

I turn around and start to walk out of the park before my mother can see me. My lunch hour is long since gone. I have to hurry back to work. I walk through a cluster of joggers, then race to a *Sweden Tours* bus. I stand behind the bus and take a peek at my mother in the park. She is standing in a circle, chatting with a group of women who are taking other people's children on an afternoon outing. They look like a Third World Parent-Teacher Association meeting.

I quickly jump into a cab heading back to the office. Would Ma have said hello had she been the one to see me first?

As the cab races away from the park, it occurs to me that perhaps one day I would chase an old woman down a street by mistake and the old woman would be somebody else's mother, who I would have mistaken for mine.

Day women come out when nobody expects them. 40

Tonight on the subway, I will get up and give my seat to a pregnant woman or a lady about Ma's age.

My mother, who stuffs thimbles in her mouth and then blows up her cheeks like Dizzy Gillespie while sewing yet another Raggedy Ann doll that she names Suzette after me.

I will have all these little Suzettes in case you never have any babies, which looks more and more like it is going to happen.

My mother who had me when she was thirty-three—*l'âge du Christ*—at the age that Christ died on the cross.

That's a blessing, believe you me, even if American doctors say by that time you can make retarded babies.

My mother, who sews lace collars on my company softball T-shirts when she does my laundry.

Why, you can't you look like a lady playing softball?

My mother, who never went to any of my Parent-Teacher Association meetings when I was in school.

You're so good anyway. What are they going to tell me? I don't want to make you ashamed of this day woman. Shame is heavier than a hundred bags of salt.

CHARTING THE STORY

1 What physical dangers face the mother as she strolls through the streets of Manhattan? How does she seem to react as she faces them?

2 How does the mother's persona at home differ from her persona at large in the outside world? What effects does this have on her daughter, the unseen observer?

3 "Salt is heavier than a hundred bags of shame" and "Shame is heavier than a hundred bags of salt." How do the images of salt, heaviness, and shame work together thematically in the story?

4 As the daughter follows the mother around, she is presented with many unexpected observations, small mysteries of her mother's activities during the day. Why does the daughter not catch her mother's attention and walk with her? Do you think the daughter would ever tell her mother that she had seen her? Why, or why not?

CONSIDERATIONS OF STYLE

1 From whose point of view does the narrative unfold? What does the author accomplish by her choices of point of view? What relationships can be seen between the daughter's and the mother's words?

2 Characterize the differing styles of speaking of the mother and the daughter. What does each contribute to the story?

AFTERTHOUGHTS

1 The mother has never gone back to Haiti—not even to bury her six sisters. What do you think it would take to convince her to return there, either to visit or to live?

Why do you think she lets the clothes and "all kinds of things for the relatives in Haiti" pile up in the family garage?

2 How do you interpret the thought (in Paragraph 39) that the daughter has as she rides away from the park in the cab: "...it occurs to me that perhaps one day I would chase an old woman down a street by mistake and that old woman would be somebody else's mother, who I would have mistaken for mine"?

3 The perspective of the narrator's father is hardly included, although he is clearly present in their lives. How does this affect the story?

THE WRITER'S CRAFT

1 Write a vignette from the story, in the same setting, but reversing the roles—with the mother secretly observing her daughter.

GEORGE LAMMING

GEORGE LAMMING *was born in Barbados in 1927, grew up on the island, moved to Trinidad in 1947, and taught school there until 1950, when he emigrated to England. He worked as a factory hand before becoming a broadcaster for the BBC Colonial Service. Along with other exiles from the Caribbean—V S Naipaul, Wilson Harris, Derek Walcott, Garfield Sobers—he became an active cultural and political writer. He returned to the West Indies in 1967 to be a writer-in-residence and lecturer at the University of the West Indies. He has served as visiting professor at the University of Texas at Austin and the University of Pennsylvania.*

Lamming's great autobiographical novel, In the Castle of My Skin, *was published in 1953. It was followed by another autobiographical novel, about West Indian emigrants living in England,* The Emigrants, *in 1954. Later novels set in the Caribbean include* Of Age and Innocence *(1958),* Season of Adventure *(1960),* Water with Berries *(1972), and* Natives of My Person *(1979). His essays have been collected in* The Pleasures of Exile *(1960),* The Influence of Africa on Antillian Literature *(written in Spanish, 1972), and* Western Education and the Caribbean Intellectual Coming, Coming, Coming Home *(1995).*

Many of his short stories have been anthologized. "A Wedding in Spring" appears in Global Voices: Contemporary Literature from the Non-Western World *(1995).*

PERSPECTIVES

1. What immigrant communities—especially urban ones—are you familiar with? Have you observed these communities as a member of the non-immigrant majority, or internally, as a "minority"? How do such communities hold together?
2. What sorts of tension afflict the members of a bridal party just before a wedding? Why does tension often attend the happy occasion of a wedding and generally not accompany a funeral?

A Wedding in Spring

London was their first lesson in cities. The solitude and hugeness of the place had joined their lives more closely than ever; but it was the force of similar childhoods which now threatened to separate them: three men and a woman, island people from the Caribbean, who waited in separate rooms of the same basement, sharing the nervousness of the night.

The wedding was only a day away.

Snooker thought he could hear the sweat spilling out of his pores. Talking to himself, old-woman-like in trouble, he started: "Is downright, absolute stupid to make me harness myself in dis mornin' costume.... I ain't no Prince Phillip or ever want to be...."

A pause drew his attention to the morning suit he had rented. The top hat sat on its crown, almost imitating itself. It provoked Snooker. He watched it, swore at it, then stooped as though he was going to sit on it.

"Now what you think you doin'?"

Snooker was alerted. He heard the closing creak of the door and the blurred chuckle of Knickerbocker's voice redeeming the status of the top hat.

Snooker was silent. He watched Knickerbocker hold the top hat out like some extraordinary fruit in his hand.

"Is what Beresford think it is at all?" he said, turning his back on the suit to face Knickerbocker. "My body, not to mention my face, ain't shape for dis kind o' get-up."

"Even de beggar can be king," said Knickerbocker, "an' dis is de kind o' headpiece kings does wear." He cuddled the top hat to his chest. "An' tomorrow," he added, lifting his head towards Snooker, "I goin' to play king."

"You goin' to play jackass," Snooker said sharply.

"So what?" Knickerbocker smiled. "Christ did ride on one."

"Is ride these clothes goin' ride you tomorrow," said Snooker, "'cause you ain't got no practice in wearin' them."

"You goin' see who ride what," said Knickerbocker, "I sittin' in de back o' dat limousine jus' so, watch me, Snooker." He was determined to prove his passion for formal dress. He had lowered his body onto the chair, fitting the top hat on his head at precisely the angle his imagination had shaped. He crossed his legs, and plucked at the imaginary seams of his morning trousers. The chair leaned with him while he felt the air for the leather rest which would hold his hand.

Snooker refused to look. But Knickerbocker had already entered the fantasy which the wedding would make real. His head was loud with bells and his eyes turned wild round the crowd, hilarious with praise, as they acknowledged his white gloved welcome. Even the police had removed their helmets in homage to the splendour which he had brought to a drab and enfeebled London. He was teaching the English their own tune. So he didn't hear Snooker's warning until the leather rest refused his hand and the crowd vanished into the shadows which filled the room. The chair had collapsed like a pack of cards under Knickerbocker's body. He looked like a cripple on his back.

Now he was afraid, and he really frightened Snooker too, the way he probed his hands with fearful certainty under and across his thighs. His guess was right. There was a split the size of a sword running down the leg and through the crotch of the only pair of trousers he owned.

"You break up my bes' chair," Snooker said sadly, carrying the top hat like wet crockery across the room. It had fallen into the sink.

The crisis had begun. Knickerbocker crouched on all fours, his buttocks cocked at the mirror, to measure the damage he had done. The basement was still: Knickerbocker considering his black exposure while Snooker collected the wreckage in both hands, wondering how he could fit his chair together again. They didn't speak, but they could hear, behind the door, a quiet tumble of furniture, and after an interval of silence, the sullen ticking of the clock in Flo's room.

She was alone, twisting her hair into knotty plaits that rose like spikes out of her skull. She did not only disapprove of her brother's wedding but she also thought it a conspiracy against all they had learnt. Preoccupied and disdainful, she saw the Vaseline melt and slip like frying lard over her hands. The last plait done, she stuck the comb like a plough into the low shrub of hair at the back of her neck. She scrubbed her ears with her thumb; stretched the under lid of each eye to tell her health; and finally gave her bottom a belligerent slap with both hands. She was in a fighting mood.

"As if he ain't done born poor," she said, caught in that whispering self-talk which filled the basement night. "Borrowin' an' hockin' every piece o' possession to make a fool o' himself, an' worse still dat he should go sell Snooker his bicycle to rent mornin' suit an' limousine. Gran Gran.... Gawd res' her in de grave, would go wild if she know what Beresford doin'...an' for what...for who he bringin' his own downfall."

It was probably too late to make Beresford change his mind: what with all those West Indians he had asked to drop in after the ceremony for a drink: the Jamaican with the macaw face who arrived by chance every Sunday at supper time, and Caruso, the calypsonian, who made his living by turning every rumour into a song that could scandalise your name for life. She was afraid of Caruso, with his malicious tongue, and his sly, secretive, slanderous manner. Moreover, Caruso never travelled without his gang: Slip Disk, Toodles and Square Dick; then there were Lice-Preserver, Gunner, Crim, Clarke Gable Number Two, and the young Sir Winston. They were all from "back home," idle, godless, and greedy. The she reflected that they were not really idle. They worked with Beresford in the same tyre factory.

"But idle or no idle," she frowned, "I ain't want Beresford marry no white woman. If there goin' be any disgrace, let me disgrace him first."

She was plotting against the wedding. She wanted to bribe Snooker and Knickerbocker into a sudden disagreement with her brother. Knickerbocker's disapproval would have been particularly damaging since it was he who had introduced the English girl to Beresford. And there was something else about Knickerbocker that Flo knew.

The door opened on Snooker who was waiting in the passage for Knickerbocker. Flo watched him in the dark and counted three before leaning her hand on his head. Her anger had given way to a superb display of weakness: a woman outraged, defenceless, and innocent of words which could tell her feeling.

"Snooker."

"What happen now?"

"I want all you two speak to Beresford," she said. Her voice was a whimper appropriate with grief.

"Let the man make his own bed," said Snooker, "is he got to lie down in it."

"But is this Englan' turn his head an' make him lose his senses." Flo crouched lower, tightening her hand against Snooker's neck.

"He keep his head all right," said Snooker, "but is the way he harken what his mother say, like he walkin' in infancy all life long."

"Ma wasn't ever goin' encourage him in trouble like this," Flo said.

"Is too late to change anything," said Snooker, "Except these kiss-me-tail mornin' clothes. Is like playin' ju-ju warrior with all that silk cravat an' fish-shape' frock they call a coat. I ain't wearin' it."

"Forget 'bout that," said Flo, "is the whole thing we got to stop complete."

Knickerbocker was slipping through the shadows, silent and massive as a wall which now rose behind Flo. The light made a white mask over his face. Flo seemed to feel her failure, sudden and complete. Knickerbocker had brought a different kind of trouble. He was fingering the safety-pins which closed the gap in his trousers. He trusted Flo's opinion in these details. He stooped forward and turned to let her judge whether he had done a good job.

"Move your tail out of my face," she shouted, "what the hell you take me for."

Knickerbocker looked hurt. He raised his body to full height, bringing his hands shamefully over the safety-pins. He couldn't understand Flo's fury: the angry and unwarranted rebuke, the petulant slam of the door in his face. And Snooker wouldn't talk. They stood in the dark like dogs shut out.

Beresford was waiting in the end room. He looked tipsy and a little vacant under the light; but he had heard Flo's voice echoing down the passage, and he knew the others were near. It was his wish that they should join him for a drink. He watched the bottle making splinters with the light, sugar brown and green, over the three glasses and a cup. The label had lost its lettering; so he turned to the broken envelope on his stomach and went on talking to himself.

All night that voice had made dialogue with itself about his bride. His mood was reflective, nostalgic. He needed comfort, and he turned to read his mother's letter again.

> ...concernin the lady in question you must choose like i would have you in respect to caracter an so forth. i excuse and forgive your long silence since courtship i know takes time. pay my wellmeanin and prayerful respects to the lady in question. give flo my love and my rememberance to snooker and knick....

The light was swimming under his eyes; the words seemed to harden and slip off the page. He thought of Flo and wished she would try to share his mother's approval.

> . . . if the weddin come to pass, see that you dress proper. i mean real proper, like the folks in that land would have you. hope you keepin the bike in good condition. . . .

The page had fallen from his hand in a moment of distraction. He was beginning to regret that he had sold the bike to Snooker. But his mood didn't last. He heard a knock on the door and saw Knickerbocker's head emerge through the light.

"Help yuhself, Knick."

Beresford squeezed the letter into his pocket while he watched Knickerbocker close in on the table.

"I go take one," Knickerbocker said, "just one."

"Get a next glass if the cup don't suit you."

"Any vessel will do," knickerbocker said.

Knickerbocker poured rum like water as though his arm could not understand the size of a drink. They touched cup and glass, making twisted faces when the rum started its course down their thoats,

"Where Snooker?"

"Puttin' up the bike," Knickerbocker said. "But Flo in a rage."

"She'll come round all right," said Beresford. "Is just that she in two minds, one for me an' one 'gainst the wedding."

"You fix up for the limousine?"

"Flo self do it this mornin',"said Beresford, "they comin' for half pas' four."

"Who goin' partner me if Flo don't come to the church?"

"Flo goin' go all right," said Beresford.

"But you never can know with Flo."

Beresford looked doubtful, but he had to postpone his misgivings.

Knickerbocker poured more rum to avoid further talk, and Beresford held out his glass. They understood the pause. Now they were quiet, rehearsing the day that was so near. The room in half light and liquor was preparing them for melancholy: two men of similar tastes temporarily spared the intrusion of female company. They were a club whose rules were part of their instinct.

"Snooker ask me to swap places with him," Knickerbocker said.

"He don't want to be my best man?" Beresford asked.

"He ain't feel friendly with the morning suit," Knickerbocker said.

"But what is proper is proper."

"Is what I say too," Knickerbocker agreed. "If you doin' a thing, you mus' do it as the done thing is doed."

Beresford considered this change. He was open to any suggestion.

"Snooker or you, it ain't make no difference," he said.

"Then I goin' course wid you to de altar," Knickerbocker said.

Was it the rum or the intimacy of their talk which had dulled their senses? They hadn't heard the door open and they couldn't guess how long Flo had been standing there, rigid as wire, with hands akimbo, and her head, bull shaped, feeding on some scheme that would undo their plans.

"Get yuhself a glass, Flo," Beresford offered.

"Not me, Berry, thanks all the same."

"What you put your face in mournin' like that for?" Knickerbocker said. He was trying to relieve the tension with his banter. "Those whom God join together..."

"What you callin' God in this for?" Flo charged. "It ain't God join my brother wid any hawk-nose English woman. Is his stupid excitement."

"There ain't nothin' wrong wid the chick," Knickerbocker parried.

"Chick, my eye!" Flo was advancing towards them. "He let a little piece o' left-over white tail put him in heat."

"Flo!"

Beresford's glass had fallen to the floor. He was standing, erect, wilful, his hands nervous and eager for action. Knickerbocker thought he would hit her.

"Don't you threaten me wid any look you lookin'," Flo challenged him. "Knickerbocker, here, know what I sayin' is true. Look him good in his face an' ask him why he ain't marry her."

"Take it easy, Flo, take it easy," Knickerbocker cautioned. "Beresford marryin' 'cause he don't want to roam wild like a bush beast in this London jungle."

"An' she, you know where she been roamin' all this time?" Flo answered. Knickerbocker fumbled for the cup.

"Is jus' what Seven Foot Walker tell you back in Port-o'-Spain," Beresford threw in.

Whatever the English girl's past, Beresford felt he had to defend his woman's honour. His hands were now steady as stone watching Flo wince as she waited to hear him through.

"That man take you for a long ride, Flo an' then he drop you like a latch key that won't fit no more. You been mournin' ever since that mornin' he turn tail an' lef' you waitin'. An' is why you set yuh scorpion tongue on my English woman."

"Me an' Seven Foot Walker..."

"Yes, you an' Seven Foot Walker!"

"Take it easy," Knickerbocker begged them. "Take it easy..."

"I goin' to tell you, Berry, I goin' to tell you..."

"Take it easy," Knickerbocker pleaded, "take it easy..."

Flo was equipped for this kind of war. Her eyes were points of flame and her tongue was tight and her memory like an ally demanding vengeance was ready with malice. She was going to murder them with her knowledge of what had happened between Knickerbocker and the English girl. Time, place, and circumstance: they were weapons which now loitered in her memory waiting for release. She was bursting with passion and spite. Knickerbocker felt his loyalty waver. He was worried. But Flo's words never came. The door opened and Snooker walked in casual as a bird, making music on his old guitar. He was humming: "Nobody knows the trouble I've seen." And his indifference was like a reprieve.

"The limousine man outside to see you," he said. "Somebody got to make some kind o' down payment."

The crisis had been postponed.

London had never seen anything like it before. The Spring was decisive, a hard, clear sky and the huge sun naked as a skull eating through the shadows of the afternoon. High up on the balcony of a fifth-floor flat an elderly man with a distressful paunch was feeding birdseed to a flock of pigeons. He hated foreigners and noise, but the day had done something to his temper. He was feeling fine. The pigeons soon flew away, cruising in circles above the enormous crowd which kept watch outside the church; then closed their ranks and settled one by one over the familiar steeple.

The weather was right; but the crowd, irreverent and forgetful in their fun, had misjudged the meaning of the day. The legend of English reticence was stone-cold dead. An old-age pensioner with no teeth at all couldn't stop laughing to the chorus, a thousand times chuckled: "Cor bli'me, look at my lads." He would say, "Ere comes a next in 'is tails, smashers the lot o' them," and then: "Cor bli'me, look at my lads." A contingent of Cypriots on their way to the Colonial Office had folded their banners to pause for a moment that turned to hours outside the church. The Irish were irrepressible with welcome. Someone burst a balloon, and two small boys, swift and effortless as a breeze, opened their fists and watched the firecrackers join in the gradual hysteria of the day.

Snooker wished the crowd away; yet he was beyond anger. Sullen and reluctant as he seemed he had remained loyal to Beresford's wishes. His mind alternated between worrying and wondering why the order of events had changed. It was half an hour since he had arrived with the bride. Her parents had refused at the last moment to have anything to do with the wedding, and Snooker accepted to take her father's place. He saw himself transferred from one role to another; but the second seemed more urgent. It was the intimacy of their childhood, his and Beresford's, which had coaxed him into wearing the morning suit. He had to make sure that the bride would keep her promise. But Beresford had not arrived; nor Knickerbocker, nor Flo.

Snooker remembered fragments of the argument in the basement room the night before; and he tried to avoid any thought of Flo. He looked round the church and the boys from "back home" looked at him and he knew they, too, were puzzled. They were all there: Caruso, Slip Disk, Lice-Preserver, and an incredibly fat woman whom they called Tiny. Behind him, two rows away, he could hear Toodles and Square Dick rehearsing in whispers what they had witnessed outside. There had been some altercation at the door when the verger asked Caruso to surrender his guitar. Tiny and Slip Disk had gone ahead, and the verger was about to show his firmness when he noticed Lice-Preserver who was wearing full evening dress and a sword. The verger suddenly changed his mind and indicated a pew, staring in terror at the sword that hung like a frozen tail down Lice-Preserver's side. Snooker closed his eyes and tried to pray.

But trouble was brewing outside. The West Indians had refused to share in this impromptu picnic. They had journeyed from Brixton and Camden Town, the whole borough of Paddington and the Holloway Road, to keep faith with the boys from "back home." One of the Irishmen had a momentary lapse into prejudice and had said something shocking about the missing bridegroom. The West Indians bristled and waited for an argument. But a dog intervened, an energetic, white poodle which kicked its hind legs up and shook its ears in frenzy at them. The poodle frisked and howled as though the air and the organ music had turned its head. Another firecracker went off, and the Irishman tried to sing his way out of a fight. But the West Indians were showing signs of a different agitation. They had become curious, attentive. They narrowed the circle to whisper their secret.

"Ain't it his sister standin' over yonder?"

They were slow to believe their own recognition.

"Is Flo, all right," a voice answered, "but she not dress for the wedding."

"Seems she not goin'," a man said as though he wanted to disbelieve his suspicion.

"An' they wus so close," the other added, "close, close, she an' that brother."

Flo was nervous. She stood away from the crowd, half hearing the rumour of her brother's delay. She tried to avoid the faces she knew, wondering what Beresford had decided to do. Half an hour before she left the house she had cancelled the limousine and hidden his morning suit. Now she regretted her action. She didn't want the wedding to take place, but she couldn't bear the thought of humiliating her brother before this crowd. The spectacle of the crowd was like a rebuke to her own stubbornness.

She was retreating further away. Would Beresford find the morning suit? And the limousine? He had set his heart on arriving with Knickerbocker in the limousine. She knew how fixed he was in his convictions, like his grandfather whose wedding could not proceed; had, indeed, to be postponed because he would not repeat the words: *All my worldly goods I thee endow*. He had sworn never to part with his cow. He had a thing about his cow, like Beresford and the morning suit. Puzzled, indecisive, Flo looked round at the faces, eager as they for some sign of an arrival; but it seemed she had lost her memory of the London streets.

The basement rooms were nearly half a mile from the nearest tube station; and the bus strike was on. Beresford looked defeated. He had found the morning suit, but there was no way of arranging for another limousine. Each second followed like a whole season of waiting. The two men stood in front of the house, hailing cabs, pleading for lifts.

"Is to get there," Beresford said, "is to get there 'fore my girl leave the church."

"I goin' deal wid Flo," Knickerbocker swore. "Tomorrow or a year from tomorrow I goin' deal wid Flo."

"How long you think they will wait?"

Beresford had dashed forward again, hailing an empty cab. The driver saw them, slowed down, and suddenly changed his mind. Knickerbocker swore again. Then: a moment of revelation.

"Tell you what," Knickerbocker said. He looked as though he had surprised himself.

"What, what!" Beresford insisted.

"Wait here," Knickerbocker said, rushing back to the basement room. "I don't give a goddam. We goin' make it."

The crowd waited outside the church, but they looked a little bored. A clock struck the half-hour. The vicar came out to the steps and looked up at the sky. The man in the fifth floor flat was eating pork sausages and drinking tea. The pigeons were dozing. The sun leaned away and the trees sprang shadows through the early evening.

Someone said: "It's getting on."

It seemed that the entire crowd had agreed on an interval of silence. It was then the woman with the frisky white poodle held her breast and gasped. She had seen them: Beresford and Knickerbocker. They were arriving. It was an odd and unpredictable appearance. Head down, his shoulders arched and harnessed in the morning coat, Knickerbocker was frantically pedalling Snooker's bicycle towards the crowd. Beresford sat on the bar, clutching both top hats to his stomach. The silk cravats sailed like flags round their necks. The crowd tried to find their reaction. At first: astonishment. Later: a state of utter incomprehension.

They made a gap through which the bicycle free-wheeled towards the church. And suddenly there was applause, loud and spontaneous as thunder. The Irishman burst into song. The whole rhythm of the day had changed. A firecracker dripped flames over the church steeple and the pigeons dispersed. But crisis was always near. Knickerbocker was trying to dismount when one tail of the coat got stuck between the spokes. The other tail dangled like a bone on a string, and the impatient white poodle charged upon them. She was barking and snapping at Knickerbocker's coat tails. Beresford fell from the bar on to his knees, and the poodle caught the end of his silk cravat. It turned to threads between her teeth.

The crowd could not determine their response. They were hysterical, sympathetic. One tail of Knickerbocker's coat had been taken. He was aiming a kick at the poodle; and immediately the crowd took sides. They didn't want harm to come to the animal. The poodle stiffened her tail and stood still. She was enjoying this exercise until she saw the woman moving in behind her. There was murder in the woman's eyes. The poodle lost heart. But the top hats were her last temptation. Stiff with fright, she leapt to one side seizing them between her teeth like loaves. And she was off. The small boys shouted: "Come back, Satire, come back!" But the poodle hadn't got very far. Her stub of tail had been safely caught between Flo's hand. The poodle was howling for release. Flo lifted the animal by the collar and shook its head like a box of bones.

Knickerbocker was clawing his rump for the missing tail of the morning coat. Beresford hung his head, swinging the silk cravat like a kitchen rag down his side. Neither could move. Flo's rage had paralysed their speech. She had captured the top hats, and it was clear that the wedding had now lost its importance for her. It was a trifle compared with her brother's disgrace.

The vicar had come out to the steps, and all the boys from "back home" stood round him: Toodles, Caruso, and Square Dick, Slip Disk, Clarke Gable Number Two, and the young Sir Winston. Lice-Preserver was carrying the sword in his right hand. But the poodle had disappeared.

Flo stood behind her brother, dripping with tears as she fixed the top hat on his head. Neither spoke. They were too weak to resist her. She was leading them up the steps into the church. The vicar went scarlet.

"Which is the man?" he shouted. But Flo was indifferent to his fury.

"It don't matter," she said. "You ju' go marry my brother."

And she walked between Knickerbocker and her brother with the vicar and the congregation of boys from "back home" following like a funeral procession to the alter.

Outside, the crowd were quiet. In a far corner of sunlight and leaves, the poodle sat under a tree licking her paws, while the fat man from the fifth-floor flat kept repeating like an idiot to himself: "But how, how, how extraordinary!"

CHARTING THE STORY

1 How, and why, does Beresford plan his wedding to include aspects of both a "back-home" and a proper English one? What problems arise in this undertaking?

2 Why do you suppose Flo does not give her blessing to her brother's union—while their mother, in her letter, certainly seems to. What, eventually, causes her to come around, and how do her reasons compare with those of her mother?

3 Why does the wedding turn into a public spectacle? What roles do each of the bystanders, especially those in the street outside of the church, play in the building of this increasingly absurd event?

CONSIDERATIONS OF STYLE

1 Look up the definition and etymology of *farce*. Cite evidence from this story that clearly categorizes it as farcical.

2 The verbal by-play among Knickerbocker, Snooker, Flo, and Beresford contributes a great deal to the comic mood of the story. What roles does each of them play in the resolution of the "conflict" of the problematic marriage? Who seem to be most aware of the improbability of the coming marriage, and who seem least aware? What does each of them say that gives this impression?

AFTERTHOUGHTS

1 In the last scene, as Beresford and Knickerbocker arrive triumphantly at the church by bicycle, the narrator notes: "But crisis was always near." What are some crises typically facing immigrants in a busy urban setting such as London (or New York, or Toronto, or Sydney . . .)? What do immigrants contribute to the life of such great cities? Do you feel that they are usually rewarded commensurately?

THE WRITER'S CRAFT

1 Write up a brief walking tour, for tourists from out of town—perhaps from the undiversified hinterland—of an immigrant neighborhood in your city, or a nearby one. Which aspects of the neighborhood would appeal to outside visitors? Which would not? Would you selectively "finesse" the latter? Why, or why not?

2 We never see the bride, although it is obvious she is inside, waiting at the altar. Why is she "invisible" in the narrative? How is she characterized *in absentia,* and how would you characterize her, based on all you have read?

CHITRA DIVAKARUNI

CHITRA BANERJEE DIVAKARUNI *was born in 1956 in Calcutta, India, and educated at Calcutta University, Wright State University in Dayton, Ohio, and at the University of California at Berkeley, where she received her doctorate in English literature. She currently lives in the San Francisco Bay area and teaches creative writing at Foothill College in Los Altos Hills.*

Divakaruni has written an award-winning collection of short stories, Arranged Marriage *(1995); four books of poetry, including new and selected poems in* Leaving Yuba City *(1997); two novels,* The Mistress of Spices *(1997) and* Sister of My Heart *(1999); and a multicultural pedagogical reader,* Multitude *(1993).*

"Woman with Kite," originally published in Hurricane Alice *in 1992, is from the collection* Leaving Yuba City.

PERSPECTIVES

1 In your experience, or in the experience of others you know, how does a woman's life change after she becomes a mother? What are the expectations laid upon mothers, as opposed to young girls?

2 What demands do children make upon their mothers, without ever reflecting upon what the mother's inclinations may be?

Woman with Kite

Meadow of crabgrass, faded dandelions,
querulous child-voices. She takes
from her son's disgruntled hands the spool
of a kite that will not fly.
Pulls on the heavy string, ground-glass rough
between her thumb and finger. Feels the kite,
translucent purple square, rise in a resistant arc,
flapping against the wind. Kicks off her *chappals,*
tucks up her *kurta* so she can run with it,

light flecking off her hair as when she was
sexless-young. Up, up

past the puff-cheeked clouds, she
follows it, her eyes slit-smiling at the sun.
She has forgotten her tugging children, their
give me, give me wails. She sprints
backwards, sure-footed, she cannot
fall, connected to the air, she
is flying, the wind blows through her, takes
her red *dupatta,* mark of marriage.
And she laughs like a woman should never laugh

so the two widows on the park bench
stare and huddle their white-veiled heads
to gossip-whisper. The children have fallen,
breathless, in the grass behind.
She laughs like wild water, shaking
her braids loose, she laughs
like a fire, the spool a blur
between her hands,
the string unraveling all the way
to release it into space, her life,
into its bright weightless orbit.

CHARTING THE POEM

1. Why does the mother initially take the kite and get it up into the air? How does the kite become a metaphor for her life as a young wife and mother? Why is she loath to let it go? What does she eventually do with it?
2. Why do the two widows "gossip-whisper" about the young woman's behavior? How do her children react to her?
3. In what ways does this poem exalt the rather humble activity of flying a kite?

CONSIDERATIONS OF STYLE

1. What contrasts—of characters, of setting, of pace, and others—work together to evolve this poem?
2. What "families" of images—of air, water, and fire—attend this narrative within a poem? How do they connect thematically to transform the mother into a free spirit?
3. Why is the woman changed, by the act of flying a kite, into a "sexless-young" girl who lets the wind blow off "her red *dupatta,* mark of marriage"? What is implied by this shedding of her marital status and her sexuality?

AFTERTHOUGHTS

1 Having seen her let the string fly away, what do you envision for the woman afterwards?

2 How does this poem reflect the experience of the Indian woman immigrant in particular and immigrant experience in America in general?

THE WRITER'S CRAFT

1 Had you witnessed this event even as a child, how would you have reacted to the grace of your mother's—to use an expression from Czech writer Milan Kundera—"unbearable lightness of being"? Write about how you would have responded to such a moment.

2 In poetry or in prose, write an encapsulated description of a physical activity that lifts you out of the doldrums and, for the moment at least, raises you to new heights.

Three Poems on the Filipino Immigrant Experience

Typically, immigrants must adapt to their new country by learning a new language, adopting new customs, tolerating differing beliefs and values, and getting used to new kinds of food. The last task is often the hardest, especially when coming from a traditional diet to the "streamlined"—often bland—diet of the United States. Each of the three poems presented here focuses on this experience by Filipino immigrants to the United States. They are taken from the anthology of Filipino and Filipino American poets Returning a Borrowed Tongue *(1995), edited by Nick Carbó.*

PERSPECTIVES

1 How has the American cuisine been influenced by native foods? By immigrant traditions? By technology?

2 If you have ever traveled or lived abroad to another region of your country, what new eating experiences—pleasant or unpleasant—have you had?

MARIA LUISA B. AGUILAR-CARIÑO

MARIA LUISA B AGUILAR-CARIÑO *won the Manila Critics' Circle National Book Award in 1993 for her collection of poetry* Cartography and Other Poems on Baguio. *She received her PhD from the University of Illinois at Chicago.*

Dinakdakan

For Mama Tet

This could be
the supermarket of your dreams,
the shelves slick and
showy with fruit, wide-

mouthed mason jars of herring,
rice grains longer
than your fingernail.

Our shopping cart would quickly swell
with breads whose names till now
were fable: rye, stone-ground
wheat, poppyseed buns;
the brie and Camembert
longed for at Christmas time
instead of the yearly *queso*
de bola; the Spam and corned
beef worth a whole week's pay.

And then I think of you
as on a trip to market long ago:
the marvel was not merely
how the wind lifted our hair,
knifed raw the flesh of our mouths,
wrists, cheeks—how our rubber
boots were worthless in steady rain
and slippery mud.

It was you, plunging a bare
arm into a pail of still-breathing milkfish,
certain which had the sweetest belly;
knowing where to find
tamarind pods cracking
out of their rinds for ripeness,
the lemon grass for boiling
with white rice, the river snails
to steep into a heady broth.
(We extricated these with safety
pins, smacking lips, fingers.)

Among the rows of plastic-sealed,
aseptically packaged food,
I stare and stare, imagining flat,
dried, salted fish-shapes pressed
between the cereal boxes,
fresh blood and entrails forming
a dark pool on the white linoleum.

(Above the click and hum
of computerized cash registers

I hear your singing knife
slice pigs' ears paper-thin,
your fork twirl thick
with clouds of boiled brain and minced
shallots for the evening meal.

CHARTING THE POEM

1 The Tagalog title of this poem can be translated variously as "gossip," "nagging," or, simply, "the urge to tell something." Which meaning(s) might fit this poem best? Why?

2 What in the poem suggests irony in the speaker's opening line to her mother: "This could be/the supermarket of your dreams/ . . . ?

3 Why do you suppose the speaker's kinfolk back home would—especially at Christmas time—sacrifice a whole week's pay to buy expensive imported foods like Brie, Camembert, Spam, and [canned] corned beef? By comparison to these foods, what characteristics of the native Filipino foods does the speaker appear to extol?

CONSIDERATIONS OF STYLE

1 What senses are evoked in the exposition of the US supermarket, and what senses come into play in the discussion of the Philippine *mercado*? Regardless of which one's food is more familiar, which market seems to be the more engaging, and why?

2 The speaker in the poem interweaves images of the US supermarket and the traditional Filipino market in a pattern: Stanzas 1 and 2 focus on the supermarket; Stanzas 3 and 4 on the traditional *mercado*. How does the pattern change in the last two stanzas? To what dramatic effect?

EUGENE GLORIA

EUGENE GLORIA *is a Filipino American. After receiving his MFA in Creative Writing from the University of Oregon, he studied in Manila as a Fulbright Exchange Scholar. His poems have appeared in several journals as well as in the anthology* The Open Boat *(Anchor Books, 1993). His poem "Saint Joe" recently won the Eighty-Ninth Annual Poetry Society of America award. "Assimilation," the poem selected for this anthology, explores food imagery to trace the process of the speaker's enculturation.*

Assimilation

On board the Victory Line Bus
boring down Kennon Road
from a weekend in Baguio
is the bus driver's sideline:
a Coleman chest full of cold Cokes and Sprites,
a loaf sack of sandwiches
wrapped in pink napkin and cellophane.
My hunger sated by thin white
bread thick with mayonnaise,
diced pickles and slim slice of ham.
What's mere snack
for my gaunt Filipino seatmate,
was my American lunch, a habit
of eating, shaped by boyhood shame.
You see, there was a time when I believed
that a meal meant at least a plate of rice
with a sauced dish like *kare kare,*
or *pinakbet* pungent with *bagoong.*
But homeboys like us are marked
by experience of not being part of the whole
in a playground full of white kids lined
on red-painted benches in the fall chill of noon,
lunchpails bright with their favorite cartoons,
and a thermos of milk, or brown paper sacks
with Glad bags of chips, peeled Sunkist,
Mom's special sandwich with crisp leaf of lettuce,
and pressed turkey thick in between—
crumbed with the breakfast table bread.
I remember that first day of school, my mother with the purest intention,
took two sheets of foil hollowed
with a cup of steamed rice
and a helping of last night's
caldereta: chunks of potatoes, sliced
red peppers, and a redder sauce with beef;
and I, with hunger, could not
bring myself to eat.
Ashamed to be more different
than what my face had already betrayed,
the rice, I hid from my schoolmates.

Next morning, my mother grasped
the appropriate combination: fruit,
sandwich cut into two triangles,
handful of chips, my best broken English.
And weeks passed while the scattered rice—
beneath the length of the red-painted bench—
blackened with the schoolyard's dirt.

CHARTING THE POEM

1. How does the opening anecdote about the bus returning from Baguio (a popular mountain resort north of Manila) serve the rest of the poem?
2. How do the school lunches of the speaker and his American peers differ—both in content and style? Why does the speaker brand himself a "homeboy"?
3. How does the mother react to her son's shunning of a Filipino-style school lunch? Does the son's refusal to bring a Filipino lunch to school seem entirely willful?

CONSIDERATIONS OF STYLE

1. What is suggested by the fact that the poem's conceptual divisions—five, say—are not presented in five separate stanzas?
2. What does the last image—of the scattered rice beneath the bench blackened with dirt—say about "assimilation"?

VINCE GOTERA

Born and raised in San Francisco, VINCE GOTERA *spent a considerable amount of time in the Philippines as a boy. He received his MFA and PhD from Indiana University. He has published poems in* Kenyon Review *and* Caliban. *His poems appear also in* The Open Boat *(Anchor Books, 1993).*

In 1994, Vince Gotera published two books: Dragonfly *(a poetry collection) published by Pecan Gravel Press and* Radical Visions: Poetry by Vietnam Veterans, *a literary-criticism book published by the University of Georgia Press. Journals such as* Amerasia, Caliban, Kenyon Review, *and* Ploughshares *have published his poetry.*

Presently, Gotera teaches creative writing and poetics at The University of Northern Iowa.

Pacific Crossing

The pier, a great concrete semicircle,
stretched into San Francisco Bay
like a father's arm around a daughter.
On Sundays, we would venture on that pier,

Mama in her broad straw hat, a country
woman in some rice paddy on Luzon.
In his lucky lime-green short-sleeved shirt, checked
by orange pinstripes, Papa would heft the net.

I would lean over the rail, watch the two
steel hoops—the smaller within the larger,
criss-crossed by heavy twine in diamond shapes—
lift out over the dark water and sink

in a green froth. A small wire cage nestled
in the center of the hoops, containing
chunks of raw meat. Papa would say, "Best bait
is porterhouse. Crabs really go for that."

Sometimes he would let me pull the net up.
The rope slimy and tight in my small hands
and then the skitter and scuttle of claws
on the wooden deck of the pier. Later

at home, I would play the radio loud, hide
that same skitter on the sides of the large
enamel-white Dutch oven, concentrate
instead on the sweetness I knew would come.

One of those Sunday evenings, I dropped in
at my friend Peter van Rijn's house. Dinner
had just been served, and the family rule
was: all the neighborhood kids had to leave.

But I didn't. There was Pete's father, like some
patriarch from a Norman Rockwell painting,
poising his carving knife above the shell—
huge and bountiful—of a red King crab.

I said, "Wait." Their heads swiveled toward me
in shock, as if I'd screamed a voodoo curse.
Old Peter, the daughter Wilhemina, his sons—
Paul, Bruno, Guido, my friend Pete—

the Mom whose given name I never knew:
a good immigrant family. The heirs
of European culture, I always
thought, these direct descendants of Rembrandt.

I said, "Wait." And then I shared the secret
passwords to being a Filipino.
Here is where you dig your fingernails in
to pry the top shell off. You suck this green

and orange jelly—the fat of the crab.
This flap on the underside tells if it's
male or female: pointed and skinny or
round like a teardrop. Here's how you twist off

legs, pincers. Crack and suck the littlest ones.
Grip it here and here, then break the body
in half. These gray fingers are gills—chew but
don't swallow. Break the crab into quarters.

Here you find the sweetest, the whitest meat.

CHARTING THE POEM

1 How do the two families in the poem differ?
2 What impelled the speaker to stay at the van Rijns' house after dinner had been served, "when all the neighborhood kids had to leave"?
3 Does it appear that the van Rijn family has ever correctly eaten a king crab before? What is wrong with this "Norman Rockwell" picture?

CONSIDERATIONS OF STYLE

1 What is the significance of the italics in the poem? Of the solitary last line?
2 What significance do you find in the fact that the narrator/speaker in this poem is Asian, and not European?

AFTERTHOUGHTS

1 Bring to class the food section (which usually appears on a particular day) of a local newspaper. How does it speak ethnographically to American culture, or, more specifically, to the culture of a particular region of the country?
2 If you had to emigrate to another country and adapt yourself to its ways—to its food, its manner of dress, its folkways, leaving behind the things to which you are

accustomed—in what new country might you adapt with the greatest ease? With the greatest difficulty? How have the three poems negotiated their "Pacific Crossings"?

THE WRITER'S CRAFT

1 In poetic form, compose a recipe for a favorite dish that could define you ethnically.

2 Especially if you have not done so before, spend some time in an ethnic grocery store, preferably an East Asian one. Take the time to slowly make your way up and down the aisles, regaling all of your senses. Finally, buy at least one unfamiliar food item, bring it home, and eat it. Then write about it, whether poetically or otherwise.

CHITRA DIVAKARUNI

CHITRA BANERJEE DIVAKARUNI was born in 1956 in Calcutta, India, and educated at Calcutta University, Wright State University in Dayton, Ohio and at the University of California at Berkeley, where she received her doctorate in English Literature. She currently lives in the San Francisco Bay Area with her husband and two sons and teaches creative writing at Foothill College.

Divakaruni has written an award-winning collection of short stories, Arranged Marriage *(1995), four collections of poetry, a novel,* The Mistress of Spices *(1997), and a multicultural reader,* Multitude *(1993).*

Like many of Divakaruni's stories, "Mrs Dutta Writes a Letter" is populated by Indian characters living in America, and concerns itself with the complexities experienced by members of different generations as they straddle the two cultures.

Widowed for three years before she joins her only child (her son Sagar) and his family in California, Mrs Dutta attempts to adjust to American culture and in particular to an American family lifestyle, which she finds at times mystifying.

This story appeared in the April 1998 issue of The Atlantic Monthly.

PERSPECTIVES

1 What aspects of American culture would you expect to be most challenging to an immigrant from a tradition-bound, and family-centered culture like India?

2 What images come to your mind when you think of "India"? Think in particular of food, dress, marriage customs, religion, music, symbols.

Mrs Dutta Writes a Letter

When the alarm goes off at 5:00 A.M., buzzing like a trapped wasp, Mrs. Dutta has been lying awake for quite a while. She still has difficulty sleeping on the Perma Rest mattress that Sagar and Shyamoli, her son and daughter-in-law, have bought specially for her, though she has had it now for two months. It is too American-soft, unlike the reassuringly solid copra ticking she used at home. *But this is home now,* she reminds herself. She reaches hurriedly to turn off the alarm, but in the dark her fingers get confused among the knobs, and the electric clock falls with a thud to the floor. Its angry metallic call vibrates through the walls of her room, and she is sure it will wake everyone. She yanks frantically at the wire until she feels it give, and in the abrupt silence that follows she hears herself breathing, a sound harsh and uneven and full of guilt.

Mrs. Dutta knows, of course, that this ruckus is her own fault. She should just not set the alarm. She does not need to get up early here in California, in her son's house. But the habit, taught her by her mother-in-law when she was a bride of seventeen, *A good wife wakes before the rest of the household,* is one she finds impossible to break. How hard it was then to pull her unwilling body away from the sleep-warm clasp of her husband, Sagar's father, whom she had just learned to love: to stumble to the kitchen that smelled of stale garam masala and light the coal stove so that she could make morning tea for them all—her parents-in-law, her husband, his two younger brothers, and the widowed aunt who lived with them.

After dinner, when the family sits in front of the TV, she tries to tell her grandchildren about those days. "I was never good at starting that stove— the smoke stung my eyes, making me cough and cough. Breakfast was never ready on time, and my mother-in-law—oh, how she scolded me, until I was in tears. Every night I'd pray to Goddess Durga, please let me sleep late, just one morning!"

"Mmmm," Pradeep says, bent over a model plane.

"Oooh, how awful," Mrinalini says, wrinkling her nose politely before 5
she turns back to a show filled with jokes that Mrs. Dutta does not understand.

"That's why you should sleep in now, Mother," Shyamoli says, smiling at her from the recliner where she sits looking through *The Wall Street Journal.* With her legs crossed so elegantly under the shimmery blue skirt she has changed into after work, and her unusually fair skin, she could pass for an American, thinks Mrs. Dutta, whose own skin is as brown as roasted cumin. The thought fills her with an uneasy pride.

From the floor where he leans against Shyamoli's knee, Sagar adds, "We want you to be comfortable, Ma. To rest. That's why we brought you to America."

In spite of his thinning hair and the gold-rimmed glasses that he has recently taken to wearing, Sagar's face seems to Mrs. Dutta still that of the boy she used to send off to primary school with his metal tiffin box. She remembers how he crawled into her bed on stormy monsoon nights, how when he was ill, no one else could make him drink his barley water. Her heart lightens in sudden gladness because she is really here, with him and his children in America. "Oh Sagar," she says, smiling, "now you're talking like this! But did you give me a moment's rest while you were growing up?" And she launches into a description of childhood pranks that has him shaking his head indulgently while disembodied TV laughter echoes through the room.

But later he comes into her bedroom and says, a little shamefaced, "Mother, please don't get up so early in the morning. All that noise in the bathroom—it wakes us up, and Molli has such a long day at work..."

And she, turning a little so that he won't see her foolish eyes filling with tears, as though she were a teenage bride again and not a woman well over sixty, nods her head, *yes, yes*. 10

Waiting for the sounds of the stirring household to release her from the embrace of her Perma Rest mattress, Mrs. Dutta repeats the 108 holy names of God. *Om Keshavaya Namah, Om Narayanaya Namah, Om Madhavaya Namah.* But underneath she is thinking of the bleached-blue aerogram from Mrs. Basu that has been waiting unanswered on her bedside table all week, filled with news from home. Someone robbed the Sandhya jewelry store. The bandits had guns, but luckily no one was hurt. Mr. Joshi's daughter, that sweet-faced child, has run away with her singing teacher. Who would've thought it? Mrs. Barucha's daughter-in-law had one more baby girl. Yes, their fourth. You'd think they'd know better than to keep trying for a boy. Last Tuesday was Bangla Bandh, another labor strike, everything closed down, not even the buses running. But you can't really blame them, can you? After all, factory workers have to eat too. Mrs. Basu's tenants, whom she'd been trying to evict forever, finally moved out. Good riddance, but you should see the state of the flat.

At the very bottom Mrs. Basu wrote, *Are you happy in America?*

Mrs. Dutta knows that Mrs. Basu, who has been her closest friend since they both moved to Ghoshpara Lane as young brides, cannot be fobbed off with descriptions of Fisherman's Wharf and the Golden Gate Bridge, or even with anecdotes involving grandchildren. And so she has been putting off her reply, while in her heart family loyalty battles with insidious feelings of—but she turns from them quickly and will not name them even to herself.

Now Sagar is knocking on the children's doors—a curious custom this, children being allowed to close their doors against their parents. With relief Mrs. Dutta gathers up her bathroom things. She has plenty of time. Their mother will have to rap again before Pradeep and Mrinalini open their doors and stumble out. Still, Mrs. Dutta is not one to waste the precious morning. She splashes cold water on her face and neck (she does not believe in pampering herself), scrapes the night's gumminess from her tongue with her metal tongue cleaner, and brushes vigorously, though the minty toothpaste does not leave her mouth feeling as clean as does the bittersweet neem stick she's been using all her life. She combs the knots out of her hair. Even at her age it is thicker and silkier than her daughter-in-law's permed curls. *Such vanity,* she scolds her reflection, *and you a grandmother and a widow besides.* Still, as she deftly fashions her hair into a neat coil, she remembers how her husband would always compare it to monsoon clouds.

She hears a sudden commotion outside. 15

"Pat! Minnie! What d'you mean you still haven't washed up? I'm late to work every morning nowadays because of you kids."

"But, Mom, *she's* in there. She's been in there forever . . ." Mrinalini says.

Pause. Then, "So go to the downstairs bathroom."

"But all our stuff is here," Pradeep says, and Mrinalini adds, "It's not fair. Why can't *she* go downstairs?"

A longer pause. Mrs. Dutta hopes that Shyamoli will not be too harsh with 20
the girl. But a child who refers to elders in that disrespectful way ought to be punished. How many times did she slap Sagar for something far less, though he was her only one, the jewel of her eye, come to her after she had been married for seven years and everyone had given up hope? Whenever she lifted her hand to him, her heart was pierced through and through. Such is a mother's duty.

But Shyamoli only says, in a tired voice, "That's enough! Go put on your clothes, hurry!"

The grumblings recede. Footsteps clatter down the stairs. Inside the bathroom Mrs. Dutta bends over the sink, fists tight in the folds of her sari. Hard with the pounding in her head to think what she feels most—anger at the children for their rudeness, or at Shyamoli for letting them go unrebuked. Or is it shame she feels (but why?), this burning, acid and indigestible, that coats her throat in molten metal?

It is 9:00 A.M., and the house, after the flurry of departures, of frantic "I can't find my socks" and "Mom, he took my lunch money" and "I swear I'll leave you kids behind if you're not in the car in exactly one minute," has settled into its quiet daytime rhythms.

Busy in the kitchen, Mrs. Dutta has recovered her spirits. Holding on to grudges is too exhausting, and besides, the kitchen—sunlight spilling across its countertops while the refrigerator hums reassuringly in the background—is her favorite place.

Mrs. Dutta hums too as she fries potatoes for alu dum. Her voice is rusty 25
and slightly off-key. In India she would never have ventured to sing, but with everyone gone the house is too quiet, all that silence pressing down on her like the heel of a giant hand, and the TV voices, with their strange foreign accents, are no help at all. As the potatoes turn golden-brown, she permits herself a moment of nostalgia for her Calcutta kitchen—the new gas stove she bought with the birthday money Sagar sent, the scoured-shiny brass pots stacked by the meat safe, the window with the lotus-pattern grille through which she could look down on white-uniformed children playing cricket after school. The mouthwatering smell of ginger and chili paste, ground fresh by Reba, the maid, and, in the evening, strong black Assam tea brewing in the kettle when Mrs. Basu came by to visit. In her mind she writes to Mrs. Basu: *Oh, Roma, I miss it all so much. Sometimes I feel that someone has reached in and torn out a handful of my chest.*

But only fools indulge in nostalgia, so Mrs. Dutta shakes her head clear of images and straightens up the kitchen. She pours the half-drunk glasses of milk down the sink, though Shyamoli has told her to save them in the refrigerator. But surely Shyamoli, a girl from a good Hindu family, doesn't expect her to put contaminated *jutha* things with the rest of the food. She washes the breakfast dishes by hand instead of letting them wait inside the dishwasher till night, breeding germs. With practiced fingers she throws an assortment of spices into the blender: coriander, cumin, cloves, black pepper, a few red chilies for vigor. No stale bottled curry powder for her. *At least the family's eating well since I arrived,* she writes in her mind. *Proper Indian food, puffed-up chapatis, fish curry in mustard sauce, and real pulao with raisins and cashews and ghee—the way you taught me, Roma—instead of Rice-a-roni.* She would like to add, *They love it,* but thinking of Shyamoli, she hesitates.

At first Shyamoli was happy enough to have someone take over the cooking. "It's wonderful to come home to a hot dinner," she'd say. Or, "Mother, what crispy papads, and your fish curry is out of this world." But recently she has taken to picking at her food, and once or twice from the kitchen Mrs. Dutta has caught wisps of words, intensely whispered: "cholesterol," "all putting on weight," "she's spoiling you." And though Shyamoli always says no when the children ask if they can have burritos from the freezer instead, Mrs. Dutta suspects that she would really like to say yes.

The children. A heaviness pulls at Mrs. Dutta's entire body when she thinks of them. Like so much in this country, they have turned out to be—yes, she might as well admit it—a disappointment.

For this she blames, in part, the Olan Mills portrait. Perhaps it was foolish of her to set so much store by a photograph, especially one taken years ago. But it was such a charming scene—Mrinalini in a ruffled white dress with her arm around her brother, Pradeep chubby and dimpled in a suit and bow tie, a glorious autumn forest blazing red and yellow behind them. (Later Mrs. Dutta was saddened to learn that the forest was merely a backdrop in a studio in California, where real trees did not turn such colors.)

The picture had arrived, silver-framed and wrapped in a plastic sheet filled with bubbles, with a note from Shyamoli explaining that it was a Mother's Day gift. (A strange concept, a day set aside to honor mothers. Did the sahibs not honor their mothers the rest of the year, then?) For a week Mrs. Dutta could not decide where it should be hung. If she put it in the drawing room, visitors would be able to admire her grandchildren, but if she put it on the bedroom wall, she would be able to see the photo last thing before she fell asleep. She finally opted for the bedroom, and later, when she was too ill with pneumonia to leave her bed for a month, she was glad of it.

Mrs. Dutta was accustomed to living on her own. She had done it for three years after Sagar's father died, politely but stubbornly declining the offers of various relatives, well-meaning and otherwise, to come and stay with her. In this she surprised herself as well as others, who thought of her as a shy, sheltered woman, one who would surely fall apart without her husband to handle things for her. But she managed quite well. She missed Sagar's father, of course, especially in the evenings, when it had been his habit to read to her the more amusing parts of the newspaper while she rolled out chapatis. But once the grief receded, she found she enjoyed being mistress of her own life, as she confided to Mrs. Basu. She liked being able, for the first time ever, to lie in bed all evening and read a new novel of Shankar's straight through if she wanted, or to send out for hot eggplant pakoras on a rainy day without feeling guilty that she wasn't serving up a balanced meal.

When the pneumonia hit, everything changed.

Mrs. Dutta had been ill before, but those illnesses had been different. Even in bed she'd been at the center of the household, with Reba coming to find out what should be cooked, Sagar's father bringing her shirts with missing buttons, her mother-in-law, now old and tamed, complaining that the cook didn't brew her tea strong enough, and Sagar running in crying because he'd had a fight with the neighbor boy. But now she had no one to ask her, querulously, *Just how long do you plan to remain sick?* No one waited in impatient exasperation for her to take on her duties again. No one's life was inconvenienced the least bit by her illness.

Therefore she had no reason to get well.

When this thought occurred to Mrs. Dutta, she was so frightened that her body grew numb. The walls of the room spun into blackness; the bed on which she lay, a vast four-poster she had shared with Sagar's father since their wedding, rocked like a dinghy caught in a storm; and a great hollow roaring reverberated inside her head. For a moment, unable to move or see, she thought, *I'm dead.* Then her vision, desperate and blurry, caught the portrait. *My grandchildren.* With some difficulty she focused on the bright, oblivious sheen of their faces, the eyes so like Sagar's that for a moment heartsickness twisted inside her like a living thing. She drew a shudder of breath into her aching lungs, and the roaring seemed to recede. When the afternoon post brought another letter from Sagar—*Mother, you really should come and live with us. We worry about you all alone in India, especially when you're sick like this*—she wrote back the same day, with fingers that still shook a little, *You're right: my place is with you, with my grandchildren.*

But now that she is here on the other side of the world, she is wrenched by doubt. She knows the grandchildren love her—how can it be otherwise among family? And she loves them, she reminds herself, even though they have put away, somewhere in the back of a closet, the vellum-bound *Ramayana for Young Readers* that she carried all the way from India in her hand luggage. Even though their bodies twitch with impatience when she tries to tell them stories of her girlhood. Even though they offer the most transparent excuses when she asks them to sit with her while she chants the evening prayers. *They're flesh of my flesh, blood of my blood,* she reminds herself. But sometimes when she listens, from the other room, to them speaking on the phone, their American voices rising in excitement as they discuss a glittering, alien world of Power Rangers, Metallica, and Spirit Week at school, she almost cannot believe what she hears.

Stepping into the back yard with a bucket of newly washed clothes, Mrs. Dutta views the sky with some anxiety. The butter-gold sunlight is gone, black-bellied clouds have taken over the horizon, and the air feels still and heavy on her face, as before a Bengal storm. What if her clothes don't dry by the time the others return home?

Washing clothes has been a problem for Mrs. Dutta ever since she arrived in California.

"We can't, Mother," Shyamoli said with a sigh when Mrs. Dutta asked Sagar to put up a clothesline for her in the back yard. (Shyamoli sighed often nowadays. Perhaps it was an American habit? Mrs. Dutta did not remember that the Indian Shyamoli, the docile bride she'd mothered for a month before putting her on a Pan Am flight to join her husband, pursed her lips in quite this way to let out a breath at once patient and exasperated.) "It's just not *done*, not in a nice neighborhood like this one. And being the only Indian family on the street, we have to be extra careful. People here sometimes—" She broke off with a shake of her head. "Why don't you just keep your dirty clothes in the hamper I've put in your room, and I'll wash them on Sunday along with everyone else's."

Afraid of causing another sigh, Mrs. Dutta agreed reluctantly. She knew she should not store unclean clothes in the same room where she kept the pictures of her gods. That would bring bad luck. And the odor. Lying in bed at night she could smell it distinctly, even though Shyamoli claimed that the hamper was airtight. The sour, starchy old-woman smell embarrassed her.

She was more embarrassed when, on Sunday afternoons, Shyamoli brought the laundry into the family room to fold. Mrs. Dutta would bend intently over her knitting, face tingling with shame, as her daughter-in-law nonchalantly shook out the wisps of lace, magenta and sea-green and black, that were her panties, placing them next to a stack of Sagar's briefs. And when, right in front of everyone, Shyamoli pulled out Mrs. Dutta's crumpled, baggy bras from the heap, she wished the ground would open up and swallow her, like the Sita of mythology.

Then one day Shyamoli set the clothes basket down in front of Sagar.

"Can you do them today, Sagar? (Mrs. Dutta, who had never, through the forty-two years of her marriage, addressed Sagar's father by name, tried not to wince.) "I've *got* to get that sales report into the computer by tonight."

Before Sagar could respond, Mrs. Dutta was out her her chair, knitting needles dropping to the floor.

"No, no, no, clothes and all is no work for the man of the house. I'll do it." The thought of her son's hands searching through the basket and lifting up his wife's—and her own—underclothes filled her with horror.

"Mother!" Shyamoli said. "This is why Indian men are so useless around the house. Here in America we don't believe in men's work and women's work. Don't I work outside all day, just like Sagar? How'll I manage if he doesn't help me at home?"

"I'll help you instead," Mrs. Dutta ventured.

"You don't understand, do you, Mother?" Shyamoli said with a shaky smile. Then she went into the study.

Mrs. Dutta sat down in her chair and tried to understand. But after a while she gave up and whispered to Sagar that she wanted him to teach her how to run the washer and dryer.

"Why, Mother? Molli's quite happy to . . ."

"I've got to learn it . . ." Her voice was low and desperate as she rummaged through the tangled heap for her clothes.

Her son began to object and then shrugged. "Oh, very well. If it makes you happy."

But later, when she faced the machines alone, their cryptic symbols and rows of gleaming knobs terrified her. What if she pressed the wrong button and flooded the entire floor with soapsuds? What if she couldn't turn the machines off and they kept going, whirring maniacally, until they exploded? (This happened on a TV show just the other day. Everyone else had laughed at the woman who jumped up and down, screaming hysterically, but Mrs. Dutta sat stiff-spined, gripping the armrests of her chair.) So she has taken to washing her clothes in the bathtub when she is alone. She never did such a chore before, but she remembers how the village washerwomen of her childhood would beat their saris clean against river rocks. And a curious satisfaction fills her as her clothes hit the porcelain with the same solid wet *thunk*.

My small victory, my secret.

This is why everything must be dried and put safely away before Shyamoli returns. Ignorance, as Mrs. Dutta knows well from years of managing a household, is a great promoter of harmony. So she keeps an eye on the menacing advance of the clouds as she hangs up her blouses and underwear, as she drapes her sari along the redwood fence that separates her son's property from the neighbor's, first wiping the fence clean with a dish towel she has secretly taken from the bottom drawer in the kitchen. But she isn't worried. Hasn't she managed every time, even after that freak hailstorm last month, when she had to use the iron from the laundry closet to press everything dry? The memory pleases her. In her mind she writes to Mrs. Basu: *I'm fitting in so well here, you'd never guess I came only two months back. I've found new ways of doing things, of solving problems creatively. You would be most proud if you saw me.*

When Mrs. Dutta decided to give up her home of forty-five years, her relatives showed far less surprise than she had expected. "Oh, we all knew you'd end up in America sooner or later," they said. She had been foolish to stay on alone for so long after Sagar's father, may he find eternal peace, passed away. Good thing that boy of hers had come to his senses and called her to join him. Everyone knows a wife's place is with her husband, and a widow's is with her son.

Mrs. Dutta had nodded in meek agreement, ashamed to let anyone know that the night before she had awakened weeping.

"Well, now that you're going, what'll happen to all your things?" they asked.

Mrs. Dutta, still troubled over those traitorous tears, had offered up her household effects in propitiation. "Here, Didi, you take this cutwork bedspread. Mashima, for a long time I have meant for you to have these Corning Ware dishes; I know how much you admire them. And Boudi, this tape recorder that Sagar sent a year back is for you. Yes, yes, I'm quite sure. I can always tell Sagar to buy me another one when I get there."

Mrs. Basu, coming in just as a cousin made off triumphantly with a bone-china tea set, had protested. "Prameela, have you gone crazy? That tea set used to belong to your mother-in-law."

"But what'll I do with it in America? Shyamoli has her own set—"

A look that Mrs. Dutta couldn't read flitted across Mrs. Basu's face. "But do you want to drink from it for the rest of your life?"

"What do you mean?"

Mrs. Basu hesitated. Then she said, "What if you don't like it there?"

"How can I not like it, Roma?" Mrs. Dutta's voice was strident, even to her own ears. With an effort she controlled it and continued. "I'll miss my friends, I know—and you most of all. And the things we do together—evening tea, our walk around Rabindra Sarobar Lake, Thursday night Bhagavad Gita class. But Sagar—they're my only family. And blood is blood, after all."

"I wonder," Mrs. Basu said drily, and Mrs. Dutta recalled that though both of Mrs. Basu's children lived just a days' journey away, they came to see her only on occasions when common decency dictated their presence. Perhaps they were tightfisted in money matters, too. Perhaps that was why Mrs. Basu had started renting out her downstairs a few years earlier, even though, as anyone in Calcutta knew, tenants were more trouble than they were worth. Such filial neglect must be hard to take, though Mrs. Basu, loyal to her children as indeed a mother should be, never complained. In a way, Mrs. Dutta had been better off, with Sagar too far away for her to put his love to the test.

"At least don't give up the house," Mrs. Basu was saying. "You won't be able to find another place in case . . ."

"In case what?" Mrs. Dutta asked, her words like stone chips. She was surprised to find that she was angrier with Mrs. Basu than she'd ever been. Or was she afraid? *My son isn't like yours,* she'd been on the verge of spitting out. She took a deep breath and made herself smile, made herself remember that she might never see her friend again.

"Ah, Roma," she said, putting her arm around Mrs. Basu. "You think I'm such an old witch that my Sagar and my Shyamoli will be unable to live with me?"

Mrs. Dutta hums a popular Tagore song as she pulls her sari from the fence. It's been a good day, as good as it can be in a country where you might stare out the window for hours and not see one living soul. No vegetable vendors with enormous wicker baskets balanced on their heads, no knife sharpeners with their distinctive call—*scissors-knives-choppers, scissors-knives-choppers*—to bring the children running. No peasant women with colorful tattoos on their arms to sell you cookware in exchange for your old silk saris. Why, even the animals that frequented Ghoshpara Lane had personality—stray dogs that knew to line up outside the kitchen door just when the leftovers were likely to be thrown out; the goat that maneuvered its head through the garden grille hoping to get at her dahlias; cows that planted themselves majestically in the center of the road, ignoring honking drivers. And right across the street was Mrs. Basu's two-story house, which Mrs. Dutta knew as well as her own. How many times had she walked up the stairs to that airy room, painted sea-green and filled with plants, where her friend would be waiting for her?

What took you so long today, Prameela? Your tea is cold already.

Wait till you hear what happened, Roma. Then you won't scold me for being late—

Stop it, you silly woman, Mrs. Dutta tells herself severely. *Every single one of your relatives would give an arm and a leg to be in your place, you know that. After lunch you're going to write a nice letter to Roma telling her exactly how delighted you are to be here.*

From where Mrs. Dutta stands, gathering up petticoats and blouses, she can look into the next yard. Not that there's much to see—just tidy grass and a few pale-blue flowers whose name she doesn't know. Two wooden chairs sit under a tree, but Mrs. Dutta has never seen anyone using them. *What's the point of having such a big yard if you're not even going to sit in it?* she thinks. Calcutta pushes itself into her mind again, with its narrow, blackened flats where families of six and eight and ten squeeze themselves into two tiny rooms, and her heart fills with a sense of loss she knows to be illogical.

When she first arrived in Sagar's home, Mrs. Dutta wanted to go over and meet her next-door neighbors, maybe take them some of her special sweet rasogollahs, as she'd often done with Mrs. Basu. But Shyamoli said she shouldn't. Such things were not the custom in California, she explained earnestly. You didn't just drop in on people without calling ahead. Here everyone was busy; they didn't sit around chatting, drinking endless cups of sugar-tea. Why, they might even say something unpleasant to her.

"For what?" Mrs. Dutta had asked disbelievingly, and Shyamoli had said, "Because Americans don't like neighbors to"—here she used an English phrase—"invade their privacy." Mrs. Dutta, who didn't fully understand the word "privacy," because there was no such term in Bengali, had gazed at her daughter-in-law in some bewilderment. But she understood enough not to ask again. In the following months, though, she often looked over the fence, hoping to make contact. People were people, whether in India or in America, and everyone appreciated a friendly face. When Shyamoli was as old as Mrs. Dutta, she would know that too.

Today, just as she is about to turn away, out of the corner of her eye Mrs. Dutta notices a movement. At one of the windows a woman is standing, her hair a sleek gold like that of the TV heroines whose exploits baffle Mrs. Dutta when she tunes in to an afternoon serial. She is smoking a cigarette, and a curl of gray rises lazily, elegantly, from her fingers. Mrs. Dutta is so happy to see another human being in the middle of her solitary day that she forgets how much she disapproves of smoking, especially in women. She lifts her hand in the gesture she has seen her grandchildren use to wave an eager hello.

The woman stares back at Mrs. Dutta. Her lips are a perfect painted red, and when she raises her cigarette to her mouth, its tip glows like an animal's eye. She does not wave back or smile. Perhaps she is not well? Mrs. Dutta feels sorry for her, alone in her illness in a silent house with only cigarettes for solace, and she wishes the etiquette of America did not prevent her from walking over with a word of cheer and a bowl of her fresh-cooked alu dum.

Mrs. Dutta rarely gets a chance to be alone with her son. In the morning he is in too much of a hurry even to drink a fragrant cardamom tea that she (remembering how as a child he would always beg for a sip from her cup) offers to make him. He doesn't return until dinnertime, and afterward he must help the children with their homework, read the paper, hear the details of Shyamoli's day, watch his favorite TV crime show in order to unwind, and take out the garbage. In between, for he is a solicitous son, he converses with Mrs. Dutta. In response to his questions she assures him that her arthritis is much better now; no, no, she's not growing bored being at home all the time; she has everything she needs—Shyamoli has been so kind. But perhaps he could pick up a few aerograms on his way back tomorrow? She obediently recites for him an edited list of her day's activities, and smiles when he praises her cooking. But when he says, "Oh, well, time to turn in, another working day tomorrow," she feels a vague pain, like hunger, in the region of her heart.

So it is with the delighted air of a child who has been offered an unexpected gift that she leaves her half-written letter to greet Sagar at the door today, a good hour before Shyamoli is due back. The children are busy in the family room doing homework and watching cartoons (mostly the latter, Mrs. Dutta suspects). But for once she doesn't mind, because they race in to give their father hurried hugs and then race back again. And she has him, her son, all to herself in a kitchen filled with the familiar, pungent odors of tamarind sauce and chopped coriander leaves.

"Khoka," she says, calling him by a childhood name she hasn't used in years, "I could fry you two-three hot-hot luchis, if you like." As she waits for his reply, she can feel, in the hollow of her throat, the rapid thud of her heart. And when he says yes, that would be very nice, she shuts her eyes tight and takes a deep breath, and it is as though merciful time has given her back her youth, that sweet, aching urgency of being needed again.

Mrs. Dutta is telling Sagar a story. "When you were a child, how scared you were of injections! One time, when the government doctor came to give us compulsory typhoid shots, you locked yourself in the bathroom and refused to come out. Do you remember what your father finally did? He went into the garden and caught a lizard and threw it in the bathroom window, because you were even more scared of lizards than of shots. And in exactly one second you ran out screaming—right into the waiting doctor's arms."

Sagar laughs so hard that he almost upsets his tea (made with real sugar, because Mrs. Dutta knows it is better for her son than that chemical powder

Shyamoli likes to use). There are tears in his eyes, and Mrs. Dutta, who had not dared to hope that he would find her story so amusing, feels gratified. When he takes off his glasses to wipe them, his face is oddly young, not like a father's at all, or even a husband's, and she has to suppress an impulse to put out her hand and rub away the indentations that the glasses have left on his nose.

"I'd totally forgotten," Sagar says. "How can you keep track of those old, old things?"

Because it is the lot of mothers to remember what no one else cares to, Mrs. 85
Dutta thinks. *To tell those stories over and over, until they are lodged, perforce, in family lore. We are the keepers of the heart's dusty corners.*

But as she starts to say this, the front door creaks open, and she hears the faint click of Shyamoli's high heels. Mrs. Dutta rises, collecting the dirty dishes.

"Call me fifteen minutes before you're ready to eat, so that I can fry fresh luchis for everyone," she tells Sagar.

"You don't have to leave, Mother," he says.

Mrs. Dutta smiles her pleasure but doesn't stop. She knows that Shyamoli like to be alone with her husband at this time, and today, in her happiness, she does not grudge her this.

"You think I've nothing to do, only sit and gossip with you?" she mock- 90
scolds. "I want you to know I have a very important letter to finish."

Somewhere behind her she hears a thud—a briefcase falling over. This surprises her. Shyamoli is always careful with it, because it was a gift from Sagar when she was finally made a manager in her company.

"Hi!" Sagar calls, and when there's no answer, "Hey, Molli, you okay?"

Shyamoli comes into the room slowly, her hair disheveled as though she has been running her fingers through it. Hot color blotches her cheeks.

"What's the matter Molli?" Sagar walks over to give her a kiss. "Bad day at work?" Mrs. Dutta, embarrassed as always by this display of marital affection, turns toward the window, but not before she sees Shyamoli move her face away.

"Leave me alone." Her voice is low, shaking. "Just leave me alone." 95

"But what is it?" Sagar says with concern.

"I don't want to talk about it right now." Shyamoli lowers herself into a kitchen chair and puts her faces in her hands. Sagar stands in the middle of the room looking helpless. He raises his hand and lets it fall, as though he wants to comfort his wife but is afraid of what she might do.

A protective anger for her son surges inside Mrs. Dutta, but she moves away silently. In her mind-letter she writes, *Women need to be strong, not react to every little thing like this. You and I, Roma, we had far worse to cry about, but we shed our tears invisibly. We were good wives and daughters-in-law, good mothers. Dutiful, uncomplaining. Never putting ourselves first.*

A sudden memory comes to her, one she hasn't thought of in years—a day when she scorched a special kheer dessert. Her mother-in-law had shouted at her, "Didn't your mother teach you anything, you useless girl?" As punishment she refused to let Mrs. Dutta go with Mrs. Basu to the cinema, even though *Sahib, Bibi aur Ghulam,* which all Calcutta was crazy about, was playing, and their tickets were bought already. Mrs. Dutta had wept the entire afternoon, but before Sagar's father came home, she washed her face carefully with cold water and applied *kajal* to her eyes so that he wouldn't know.

But everything is getting mixed up, and her own young, trying-not-to- 100
cry face blurs into another—why, it's Shyamoli's—and a thought hits her so sharply in the chest that she has to hold on to her bedroom wall to keep from falling. *And what good did it do? The more we bent, the more people pushed us, until one day we'd forgotten that we could stand up straight. Maybe Shyamoli's the one with the right idea after all...*

Mrs. Dutta lowers herself heavily onto her bed, trying to erase such an insidious idea from her mind. Oh, this new country, where all the rules are upside down, it's confusing her. The space inside her skull feels stirred up, like a pond in which too many water buffaloes have been wading. Maybe things will settle down if she can focus on the letter to Roma.

Then she remembers that she has left the half-written aerogram on the kitchen table. She knows she should wait until after dinner, after her son and his wife have sorted things out. But a restlessness—or is it defiance?—has taken hold of her. She is sorry that Shyamoli is upset, but why should she have to waste her evening because of that? She'll go get her letter—it's no crime, is it? She'll march right in and pick it up, and even if Shyamoli stops in mid-sentence with another one of those sighs, she'll refuse to feel apologetic. Besides, by now they're probably in the family room, watching TV.

Really, Roma, she writes in her head, as she feels her way along the unlighted corridor, *the amount of TV they watch here is quite scandalous. The children, too, sitting for hours in front of that box like they've been turned into painted dolls, and then talking back when I tell them to turn it off.* Of course she will never put such blasphemy into a real letter. Still, it makes her feel better to be able to say it, if only to herself.

In the family room the TV is on, but for once no one is paying it any attention. Shyamoli and Sagar sit on the sofa, conversing. From where she stands in the corridor, Mrs. Dutta cannot see them, but their shadows—enormous against the wall where the table lamp has cast them—seem to flicker and leap at her.

She is about to slip unseen into the kitchen when Shyamoli's rising voice 105
arrests her. In its raw, shaking unhappiness it is so unlike her daughter-in-law's assured tones that Mrs. Dutta is no more able to move away from it than if she had heard the call of *nishi,* the lost souls of the dead, the subject of so many of the tales on which she grew up.

"It's easy for you to say 'Calm down.' I'd like to see how calm *you'd* be if she came up to you and said, 'Kindly tell the old lady not to hang her clothes over the fence into my yard.' She said it twice, like I didn't understand English, like I was a savage. All these years I've been so careful not to give these Americans a chance to say something like this, and now—"

"Shhh, Shyamoli, I *said* I'd talk to Mother about it."

"You always say that, but you never *do* anything. You're too busy being the perfect son, tiptoeing around her feelings. But how about mine? Aren't I a person too?"

"Hush, Molli, the children . . ."

"Let them hear. I don't care anymore. Besides, they're not stupid. They already know what a hard time I've been having with her. You're the only one who refuses to see it."

In the passage Mrs. Dutta shrinks against the wall. She wants to move away, to hear nothing else, but her feet are formed of cement, impossible to lift, and Shyamoli's words pour into her ears like fire.

"I've explained over and over, and she still does what I've asked her not to—throwing away perfectly good food, leaving dishes to drip all over the countertops. Ordering my children to stop doing things I've given them permission to do. She's taken over the entire kitchen, cooking whatever she likes. You come in the door and the smell of grease is everywhere, in all our clothes even. I feel like this isn't my house anymore."

"Be patient, Molli. She's an old woman, after all."

"I know. That's why I tried so hard. I know having her here is important to you. But I can't do it any longer. I just can't. Some days I feel like taking the kids and leaving." Shyamoli's voice disappears into a sob.

A shadow stumbles across the wall to her, and then another. Behind the weatherman's nasal tones, announcing a week of sunny days, Mrs. Dutta can hear a high, frightened weeping. The children, she thinks. This must be the first time they've seen their mother cry.

"Don't talk like that, sweetheart." Sagar leans forward, his voice, too, anguished. All the shadows on the wall shiver and merge into a dark silhouette.

Mrs. Dutta stares at that silhouette, the solidarity of it. Sagar and Shyamoli's murmurs are lost beneath the noise in her head, a dry humming—like thirsty birds, she thinks wonderingly. After a while she discovers that she has reached her room. In darkness she lowers herself onto her bed very gently, as though her body were made of the thinnest glass. Or perhaps ice—she is so cold. She sits for a long time with her eyes closed, while inside her head thoughts whirl faster and faster until they disappear in a gray dust storm.

When Pradeep finally comes to call her for dinner, Mrs. Dutta follows him to the kitchen, where she fries luchis for everyone, the perfect circles of dough puffing up crisp and golden as always. Sagar and Shyamoli have reached a truce of some kind: she gives him a small smile, and he puts out a casual hand to massage the back of her neck. Mrs. Dutta shows no embarrassment at this. She eats her dinner. She answers questions put to her. She laughs when someone makes a joke. If her face is stiff, as though she had been given a shot of Novocain, no one notices. When the table is cleared, she excuses herself, saying she has to finish her letter.

Now Mrs. Dutta sits on her bed, reading over what she wrote in the innocent afternoon.

> Dear Roma, 120
>
> Although I miss you, I know you will be pleased to hear how happy I am in America. There is much here that needs getting used to, but we are no strangers to adjusting, we old women. After all, haven't we been doing it all our lives?
>
> Today I'm cooking one of Sagar's favorite dishes, alu dum. It gives me such pleasure to see my family gathered around the table, eating my food. The children are still a little shy of me, but I am hopeful what we'll soon be friends. And Shyamoli, so confident and successful—you should see her when she's all dressed for work. I can't believe she's the same timid bride I sent off to America just a few years ago. But Sagar, most of all, is the joy of my old age. . . .

With the edge of her sari Mrs. Dutta carefully wipes a tear that has fallen on the aerogram. She blows on the damp spot until it is completely dry, so that the pen will not leave a telltale smudge. Even though Roma would not tell a soul, she cannot risk it. She can already hear them, the avid relatives in India who've been waiting for something just like this to happen. *That Dutta-ginni, so set in her ways, we knew she'd never get along with her daughter-in-law.* Or worse, *Did you hear about poor Prameela? How her family treated her? Yes, even her son, can you imagine?*

This much surely she owes to Sagar.

And what does she owe herself, Mrs. Dutta, falling through black night with all the certainties she trusted in collapsed upon themselves like imploded stars, and only an image inside her eyelids for company? A silhouette—man, wife, children, joined on a wall—showing her how alone she is in this land of young people. And how unnecessary.

She is not sure how long she sits under the glare of the overhead light, how long her hands clench themselves in her lap. When she opens them, nail marks line the soft flesh of her palms, red hieroglyphs—her body's language, telling her what to do.

Dear Roma, Mrs. Dutta writes, 125

> I cannot answer your question about whether I am happy, for I am no longer sure I know what happiness is. All I know is that it isn't what I thought it to be. It isn't about being needed. It isn't about being with family either. It has something to do with love, I still think that, but in a different way than I believed earlier, a way I don't have the words to explain. Perhaps we can figure it out together, two old women drinking cha in your downstairs flat (for I do hope you will rent it to me on my return) while around us gossip falls—but lightly, like summer rain, for that is all we will allow it to be. If I'm lucky—and perhaps, in spite of all that has happened, I am—the happiness will be in the figuring out.

Pausing to read over what she has written, Mrs. Dutta is surprised to discover this: now that she no longer cares whether tears blotch her letter, she feels no need to weep.

CHARTING THE STORY

1 How does Mrs Dutta's life as a young bride contrast with that of her daughter-in-law Shyamoli/Molli? How does such a strong contrast affect the relationship between the two women?
2 What role(s) does Mrs Basu play in Mrs Dutta's life?
3 Mrs Dutta lived happily on her own for three years after her husband's death. What made her decide to join her son in America after all?
4 At the end of the story, Mrs Dutta's writes in her letter to Mrs Basu that "...in spite of all that has happened,...the happiness will be in the figuring out." What do you think she means by this?

CONSIDERATIONS OF STYLE

1 Throughout the story, Mrs Dutta lapses into monologue, signaled by italics. How do these snippets of text contribute to the telling of the story?
2 How does Divakaruni convey Mrs Dutta's sense of place in America?

AFTERTHOUGHTS

1 At the time this story was published, Divakaruni said in a conversation with an *Atlantic Monthly* interviewer:

> Although I think India is unique and distinct in its nature, it is really just like America. One of the things I hope to show in my writing is that although the *ways* of thinking and doing things are different for Indians and Americans, the *reasons* we think and do those things are often the same.

Find evidence from "Mrs Dutta Writes a Letter" which might clarify that statement.

THE WRITER'S CRAFT

1 The story "Mrs Dutta Writes a Letter" is a case study in cross-cultural maladjustment. Write another such case study based on a personal or an observed experience. First summarize the case. Then analyze the causes of maladjustment. Finally, discuss "what might have been" the case, or how maladjustment might have been averted.
2 Compose another letter from Mrs Dutta—from her regained home in Calcutta, to her son and his family in California. Make the letter both newsy and reflective.

Part Six
Alienation

For the merest instant, then, I saw her. I really did see her, for the first and only time in all the years we had both lived in the same town. Her defiant face, momentarily, became unguarded and unmasked, and in her eyes there was a terrifying hope.

MARGARET LAURENCE, *The Loons*

NADINE GORDIMER

NADINE GORDIMER *was born in the Transvaal, South Africa in 1923. Her mother was English and her father an Eastern European immigrant. She attended the University of Witwatersrand, where she wrote her first short story at age fifteen. She is the author of over a dozen novels and ten volumes of short stories. She has been called "probably the most decorated living female writer," having won the Booker Prize in 1974 and the Nobel Prize for Literature in 1991, as well as numerous French, Italian, German, and American literary prizes. "Once Upon a Time," a cautionary tale with a deceptively innocent title, first appeared in* Salmagundi *and later in her collection* Jump and Other Stories *in 1994.*

PERSPECTIVES

1 Most major cities are known for their relatively high crime rates. What factors—social, economic, and other—contribute to this unfortunate state of affairs? What solutions are being taken by local governments to combat crime?

2 A high crime rate has contributed to the development of a "siege mentality" in many cities. Give illustrations of this from your own experience or from your having heard or read about it.

3 Look up or try to determine from context the following words: rime (Paragraph 5); stopes (Paragraph 7); *baas* (Paragraph 13); *tsotsis* (Paragraph 13).

Once Upon a Time

Someone has written to ask me to contribute to an anthology of stories for children. I reply that I don't write children's stories; and he writes back that at a recent congress/book fair/seminar a certain novelist said every writer ought to write at least one story for children. I think of sending a postcard saying I don't accept that I 'ought' to write anything.

And then last night I woke up—or rather was wakened without knowing what had roused me.

A voice in the echo-chamber of the subconscious?

A sound.

A creaking of the kind made by the weight carried by one foot after another along a wooden floor. I listened. I felt the apertures of my ears distend with concentration. Again: the creaking. I was waiting for it; watiting to hear if it indicated that feet were moving from room to room, coming up the passage—to my door. I have no burglar bars, no gun under the pillow, but I have the same fears as people who do take these precautions, and my windowpanes are thin as rime, could shatter like a wineglass. A woman was murdered (how do they put it) in broad daylight in a house two blocks away, last year, and the fierce dogs who guarded an old widower and his collection of antique clocks were strangled before he was knifed by a casual labourer he had dismissed without pay.

I was staring at the door, making it out in my mind rather than seeing it, in the dark. I lay quite still—a victim already—by the arrhythmia of my heart was fleeing, knocking this way and that against its body-cage. How finely tuned the senses are, just out of rest, sleep! I could never listen intently as that in the distractions of the day; I was reading every faintest sound, identifying and classifying its possible threat.

But I learned that I was to be neither threatened nor spared. There was no human weight pressing on the boards, the creaking was a buckling, an epicentre of stress. I was in it. The house that surrounds me while I sleep is built on undermined ground; far beneath my bed, the floor, the house's foundations, the stopes and passages of gold mines have hollowed the rock, and when some face trembles, detaches and falls, three thousand feet below, the whole house shifts slightly, bringing uneasy strain to the balance and counterbalance of brick, cement, wood and glass that hold it as a structure around me. The misbeats of my heart tailed off like the last muffled flourishes on one of the wooden xylophones made by the Chopi and Tsonga migrant miners who might have been down there, under me in the earth at that moment. The stope where the fall was could have been disused, dripping water from its ruptured veins; or men might now be interred there in the most profound of tombs.

I couldn't find a position in which my mind would let go of my body—release me to sleep again. So I began to tell myself a story; a bedtime story.

In a house, in a suburb, in a city, there were a man and his wife who loved each other very much and were living happily ever after. They had a little boy, and they loved him very much. They had a cat and a dog that the little boy loved very much. They had a car and a caravan trailer for holidays, and a swimming-pool which was fenced so that the little boy and his playmates would not fall in and drown. They had a housemaid who was absolutely trustworthy and an itinerant gardener who was highly recommended by the neighbours. For when they began to live happily ever after they were warned, by that wise old witch, the husband's mother, not to take on anyone off the street. They were inscribed in a medical benefit society, their pet dog was licensed, they were insured against fire, flood damage and theft, and subscribed to the local Neighbourhood Watch, which supplied them with a plaque for their gates lettered YOU HAVE BEEN WARNED over the silhouette of a would-be intruder. He was masked; it could not be said if he was black or white, and therefore proved the property owner was no racist.

It was not possible to insure the house, the swimming pool or the car against riot damage. There were riots, but these were outside the city, where people of another colour were quartered. These people were not allowed into the suburb except as reliable housemaids and gardeners, so there was nothing to fear, the husband told the wife. Yet she was afraid that some day such people might come up the street and tear off the plaque YOU HAVE BEEN WARNED and open the gates and stream in... Nonsense, my dear, said the husband, there are police and soldiers and tear-gas and guns to keep them away. But to please her—for he loved her very much and buses were being burned, cars stoned, and schoolchildren shot by the police in those quarters out of sight and hearing of the suburb—he had electronically-controlled gates fitted. Anyone who pulled off the sign YOU HAVE BEEN WARNED and tried to open the gates would have to announce his intentions by pressing a button and speaking into a receiver relayed to the house. The little boy was fascinated by the device and used it as a walkie-talkie in cops and robbers play with his small friends.

The riots were suppressed, but there were many burglaries in the suburb and somebody's trusted housemaid was tied up and shut in a cupboard by thieves while she was in charge of her employers' house. The trusted housemaid of the man and wife and little boy was so upset by this misfortune befalling a friend left, as she herself often was, with responsibility for the possessions of the man and his wife and the little boy that she implored her employers to have burglar bars attached to the doors and windows of the house, and an alarm system installed. The wife said, She is right, let us take heed of her advice. So from every window and door in the house where they were living happily ever after they now saw the trees and sky through bars, and when the little boy's pet cat tried to climb in by the fanlight to keep him company in his little bed at night, as it customarily had done, it set off the alarm keening through the house.

The alarm was often answered—it seemed—by other burglar alarms, in other houses, that had been triggered by pet cats or nibbling mice. The alarms called to one another across the gardens in shrills and bleats and wails that everyone soon became accustomed to, so that the din roused the inhabitants of the suburb no more than the croak of frogs and musical grating of cicadas' legs. Under cover of the electronic harpies' discourse intruders sawed the iron bars and broke into homes, taking away hi-fi equipment, television sets, cassette players, cameras and radios, jewellery and clothing, and sometimes were hungry enough to devour everything in the refrigerator or paused audaciously to drink the whisky in the cabinets or patio bars. Insurance companies paid no compensation for single malt, a loss made keener by the property owner's knowledge that the thieves wouldn't even have been able to appreciate what it was they were drinking.

Then the time came when many of the people who were not trusted housemaids and gardeners hung about the suburb because they were unemployed. Some importuned for a job: weeding or painting a roof; anything, *baas,* madam. But the man and his wife remembered the warning about taking on anyone off the street. Some drank liquor and fouled the street with discarded bottles. Some begged, waiting for the man or his wife to drive the car out of the electronically-operated gates. They sat about with their feet in the gutters, under the jacaranda trees that made a green tunnel of the street—for it was a beautiful suburb, spoilt only by their presence—and sometimes they fell asleep lying right before the gates in the midday sun. The wife could never see anyone go hungry. She sent the trusted housemaid out with bread and tea, but the trusted housemaid said these were loafers and *tsotsis,* who would come and tie her up and shut her in a cupboard. The husband said, She's right. Take heed of her advice. You only encourage them with your bread and tea. They are looking for their chance . . . And he brought the little boy's tricycle from the garden into the house every night, because if the house was surely secure, once locked and with the alarm set, someone might still be able to climb over the wall or the electronically-closed gates into the garden.

You are right, said the wife, then the wall should be higher. And the wise old witch, the husband's mother, paid for the extra bricks as her Christmas present to her son and his wife—the little boy got a Space Man outfit and a book of fairy tales.

But every week there were many more reports of intrusion: in broad day- 15
light and the dead of night, in the early hours of the morning, and even in the lovely summer twilight—a certain family was at dinner while the bedrooms were being ransacked upstairs. The man and his wife, talking of the latest armed robbery in the suburb, were distracted by the sight of the little boy's pet cat effortlessly arriving over the seven-foot wall, descending first with a rapid bracing of extended forepaws down on the sheer vertical surface, and then a graceful launch, landing with swishing tail within the property. The whitewashed wall was marked with the cat's comings and goings; and on the street side of the wall there were larger red-earth smudges that could have been made by the kind of broken running shoes, seen on the feet of unemployed loiterers, that had no innocent destination.

When the man and wife and little boy took the pet dog for its walk round the neighbourhood streets they no longer paused to admire this show of roses or that perfect lawn; these were hidden behind an array of different varieties of security fences, walls and devices. The man, wife, little boy and dog passed a remarkable choice: there was the low-cost option of pieces of broken glass embedded in cement along the top of walls, there were iron grilles ending in lance-points, there were attempts at reconciling the aesthetics of prison architecture with the Spanish Villa style (spikes painted pink) and with the plaster urns of neoclassical façades (twelve-inch pikes finned like zigzags of lightning and painted pure white). Some walls had a small board affixed, giving the name and telephone number of the firm responsible for the installation of the devices. While the little boy and the pet dog raced ahead, the husband and wife found themselves comparing the possible effectiveness of each style against its appearance; and after several weeks when they paused before this barricade or that without needing to speak, both came out with the conclusion that only one was worth considering. It was the ugliest but the most honest in its suggestion of the pure concentration-camp style, no frills, all evident efficacy. Placed the length of walls, it consisted of a continuous coil of stiff and shining metal serrated into jagged blades, so that there would be no way of climbing over it and no way through its tunnel without getting entangled in its fangs. There would be no way out, only a struggle getting bloodier and bloodier, a deeper and sharper hooking and tearing of flesh. The wife shuddered to look at it. You're right, said the husband, anyone would think twice . . . And they took heed of the advice on a small board fixed to the wall: Consult DRAGON'S TEETH The People For Total Security.

Next day a gang of workmen came and stretched the razor-bladed coils all round the walls of the house where the husband and wife and little boy and pet dog and cat were living happily ever after. The sunlight flashed and slashed, off the serrations, the cornice of razor thorns encircled the home, shining. The husband said, Never mind. It will weather. The wife said, You're wrong. They guarantee it's rust-proof. And she waited until the little boy had run off to play before she said, I hope the cat will take heed . . . The husband said, Don't worry, my dear, cats always look before they leap. And it was true that from that day on the cat slept in the little boy's bed and kept to the garden, never risking a try at breaching security.

One evening, the mother read the little boy to sleep with a fairy story from the book the wise old witch had given him at Christmas. Next day he pretended to be the Prince who braves the terrible thicket of thorns to enter the palace and kiss the Sleeping Beauty back to life; he dragged a ladder to the wall, the shining coiled tunnel was just wide enough for his little body to creep in, and with the first fixing of its razor-teeth in his knees and hands and head he screamed and struggled deeper into its tangle. The trusted housemaid and the itinerant gardener, whose 'day' it was, came running, the first to see and to scream with him, and the itinerant gardener tore his hands trying to get at the little boy. Then the man and his wife burst wildly into the garden and for some reason (the cat, probably) the alarm set up wailing against the screams while the bleeding mass of the little boy was hacked out of the security coil with saws, wire-cutters, choppers, and they carried it—the man, the wife, the hysterical trusted housemaid and the weeping gardener—into the house.

CHARTING THE STORY

1. The story is presented in two parts: a prologue in the first section of the story and the story within a story in the second section. What motivated the narrator to tell herself a bedtime story, even though she was able to rationalize the source of the noises that awoke her in the night?
2. Find examples, among the many, of irony in this story. What does the narrator's frequent use of irony suggest about her attitude toward the characters in her "bedtime" story?
3. The story takes place in a wealthy suburb of a South African city, in which the residents turn their homes into virtual fortresses. Why does this still not deter crime in the area?
4. Can the family's "trusted" housemaid really be trusted in her judgment regarding the fortifying of the home? Why? / Why not?

CONSIDERATIONS OF STYLE

1. What devices does Gordimer use in the prologue to create suspense?
2. What narrative aspects of this story associate it with a typical children's story?

AFTERTHOUGHTS

1. Identify references in the story to a migrant or itinerant work force. What social problems does this phenomenon generate? Discuss such problems in your own society.
2. This story was written during the period of apartheid in South Africa, which Gordimer and other intellectuals vigorously opposed. Are Gordimer's references to this policy direct or somewhat subtle? Explain your answer.

THE WRITER'S CRAFT

1. In an editorial essay, discuss a particular social injustice that you have experienced or witnessed recently. Use a well-drawn illustrative example of the injustice and argue how such a scenario might be repeated.
2. Write a children's story in which you subtly direct criticism toward a particular social injustice. Let the story resolve that injustice—or not.

JACK DAVIS

Born in rural Western Australia in 1917, JACK DAVIS *is an Australian Koori poet, dramatist, and critic. He has served as a distinctive voice of his people, "positioned as he is," notes his page on* OzLit, *"at the end of a long line of oral storytellers and at the beginning of a blossoming written tradition. . . ."*

Davis served as editor of the Aboriginal magazine Identity. *His poetry collections include* The First Born and Other Poems *(1970),* Jagardoo: Poems from Aboriginal Australia *(1978),* John Pat and Other Poems *(1988), and* Black Life: Poems *(1992). His two most important plays are* The Dreamers *(1982) and* No Sugar *(1986); he has also edited the collection* Plays from Black Australia *(1989). Other writings include* A Boy's Life *(1991),* In Our Town *(1992), and* Moorli and the Leprechaun *(1994).*

In this story, two groups of outcasts—a family of Koori Aborigines and a group of leather-clad motorcyclists—exult in their common humanity. This story comes from Paperbark: A Collection of Black Australian Writings *(1990).*

PERSPECTIVES

1 Find a general article about the Koori on the Internet or from another reference source. What is their socioeconomic status in Australia?

2 What is your general impression of motorcycle enthusiasts, or "bikies," as they are called in the story?

White Fantasy—Black Fact

The bus driver was tired. He had been awakened several times during last night's hot summer hours, by the crying of the baby. His wife Anne had walked around with the child seemingly for hours. He hoped she had taken the child around to the Clinic today. After all it was the first summer of the child's existence, and it was really hot. Really hot.

The bus churned along the narrow bitumen road. He heard the slap, slap of the overhanging branches of roadside gums on the rooftop of the bus. His gaze flitted automatically to the approaching bus stop. He slowed the bus, but seeing nobody on the seat, he pushed the gear lever in a quick interchange of movement between foot on clutch pedal and hand on gear lever. The bus growled and surged ahead, sweeping back onto the centre of its laneway.

His mind slid back to the baby. They had called it Peggy Sue after Anne's mother. Anne had been so grateful when he had agreed with the name of their first child, Peggy Sue. He wondered what she would be like when she grew up. He knew she would be pretty. Blonde haired, blue eyed, and with a nice figure. Both him and Anne were well-built. He wondered what she would be character-wise. Anne was a calm practical even-tempered person. While he was almost the complete opposite. He hated untidiness, people with loud voices. He disliked violence, cruelty to animals. Both he and his wife sent money to overseas missions. He thought of the starving millions in Asia, and the resultant death and disease. Cholera, hook worm, sleeping sickness. His mind flitted through the explanatory brochures that he recalled to his mind, which were sent to him and his wife by the overseas mission people. He was glad that he lived in a country that was white, where there was plenty for all, where nobody starved, and everyone was equal. He saw the next bus stop ahead of him and he imperceptibly guided the bus of the bitumen. As he drew almost level with the stop he saw the small group of people. There were eight of them.

One man of indeterminate age, but old, was drunk and coughing, softly but violently. The paroxysms of his coughing shook his bony frame. He was accompanied by a man and woman and five children. The man was also affected by liquor. They were all scruffily dressed and untidy, and a faint whiff of body odour wafted into the interior of the empty bus. The bus driver stared blankly as the small group began gathering their belongings. The old man, his coughing subsiding into sporadic bursts, staggered forward and placed one hand on the bus door. The bus driver looked at the gnarled brown dirty broken finger-nailed hand. He had a mad kaleidoscopic vision of unparalleled sickness right there within the bus.

He thought of little Peggy Sue, her fair skin scabrous with sores. 5
He thought of Anne her body broken, lying in the back-yard. He thought this must not happen, this cannot be. The old man began to heave himself onto the bus, the others ready to climb aboard behind him. The bus driver bent forward and spoke hoarsely, "You are not allowed on this bus, let go the door." The old man glowered at him, replying, "Why aren't I?" The woman lifted her head and stared at the bus driver, she spoke loudly, shrilly. "Why ain't we allowed, we're people ain't we?" The other man evidently her husband chipped in, saying: "Driver you can't stop us from gettin' on that bus. We got money don't worry about us," he opened his hand to show a crumpled two dollar note.

The bus driver rose from his seat and pushed the old man's hand quickly, but firmly, from the frame of the door and then grasping the lever he closed the door. He wrenched the gear stick downwards, and the engine snarled as if in protest against the unexpected call for power. The bus lurched back onto the bitumen sending a cloud of dust and leaves over the little Aboriginal group left standing at the side of the road.

Molly looked at the rapidly receding bus, tears of angry frustration in her eyes. She had to get the baby to the children's hospital that afternoon. She glanced at Peter, her husband, and the old man, her grandfather. She harangued them angrily, her voice rising high above their denunciation of the bus driver. "I told you to stop drinking," she said. "Now if the baby misses her appointment you'll be the one to blame, not the bus driver."

She looked at the long stretch of bitumen, it would be hours before another one traversed the road. The baby began to cry. Molly looked at the four other children. Three were her own. The eldest, Katey, a child of eight, was a parentless stray belonging to some distant relation who through circumstances had become part of her and Peter's brood. She had not wanted to bring them on the long journey from Geraldton to Perth. But as she had no one to leave them with she had been forced to bring them. They also had to bring the old man, grandfather Joshua. It had been his pension day when they had left Geraldton, and his money was needed to assist the group on the long journey. The old HR Holden had travelled well. But near Caversham in attempting a short cut to Guildford it had given up the mechanical ghost.

Peter and Joshua had pushed the car on to the side of the road. After gathering their essential belongings (Joshua carefully retrieved his remaining flagon) and locking the rickety doors, the small group had made their way to the Guilford road and the nearest bus stop. Two-years-old Tandy began whimpering for water. Molly surmised there would be water in the small creek some 159 metres down the road. The old man and Peter lay in the shade. She looked at them in disgust, disregarding her husband's half-hearted offer to obtain water. She emptied the collection of half-eaten food from a can and with the baby on her hip, and the children following, she made her way down the road where a small trickle of weed-covered water meandered slowly under a culvert then through the paddock bordering the road.

Molly and the children stood at the edge of the culvert. She looked dubiously down the sloping reed-covered bank. She spoke softly to Katey, "Looks like you'll have to get the water Katey Doll." The eight-year-old stepped forward eager to help. With the can in her hand she slithered agilely down the bank, her mother and the other children calling directions and encouragement. Katey stepped into the mud her feet making delicious squelching sounds as she wriggled her toes in its coolness. She looked up at the small group above her, white teeth flashing, brown eyes full of merriment, enjoying her endeavours. She stepped toward the roof of the culvert where the water underneath was cleaner, deeper. She placed one slim hand on the woodwork to steady herself, and glanced to find a place to grasp the culvert ledge.

Then for one terror filled second her fingers were a fraction of an inch away from the snake. Her reflexes were instant, but even as she snatched her hand away, it struck, and with such blinding speed and force that its fangs became embedded in the back of her tiny hand, and swinging off balance, Katey Doll screamed and flung the snake in an arc, where it landed some two metres away. Then slithering in the water it vanished among the reeds. Molly saw it all as if in slow motion. She tried to call out but her voice choked off. With the baby in her arms she leapt down the bank. She grabbed the trembling Katey who stood frozen clutching her hand to her crotch. Her eyes were enormous, dilated with fear. "Mummy," she cried, "it bit me, it bit me. Will I die? Oh, Mummy will I die?" And realising the horror and the enormity of it all, the woman and child screamed together.

Peter heard the screaming. With one leap he was standing on the road. He saw the way the children were running towards him, something was amiss. "Gawd," he muttered. "What's happened?" he ran. Upon reaching the culvert he sprang down the bank grabbing Katey. He saw the two long tips in the skin of her hand. He did not hesitate. He pulled the now mute child to a sitting position, and knelt beside her and gripping her wrist tightly, he began sucking heard and deep over the ragged perforations.

Joshua stood on the road, looking at them aghast. Molly handed the baby up to him. She struggled up the bank, calling to the old man. "If a car comes flag it down." Even as she spoke they heard the hum of an approaching vehicle. Molly standing on the road stood waving her hands frantically. The car came fast. Behind it another. Molly screamed her plea. "Stop! Please! Help! Help!" Both cars roared past, the drivers looking at them with the curious detached look of the unconcerned.

Molly sank on her knees and cried, "O God, please help us." The children were all crying. Peter began pulling the trembling Katey up the bank, still endeavouring to suck the poison from the small frail body. They all knelt at the side of the road. They heard the purr of an engine. Joshua thrust the baby into Molly's arms. He stood almost in the centre of the road, his arms waving wildly. Molly breathed a gasping sigh of relief as she saw the car slow to a crawl. It came opposite the old man, who stepped forward to speak to the driver. Then with a screech of tortured tyres it leaped forward, and an epithet, mingling with the sound of laughter, sprang at them like barbed wire from the interior of the speeding car. The old man stood crouched at the side of the road crying hoarsely, "Aw, you bastards, you bloody, rotten mongrel bastards!" Tears of anger flowed down his thin cheeks.

It was obvious now that the poison and shock were having an effect on Katey Doll, her eyes were closed, her breathing shallow, and a small trace of vomit lingered at the corner of her mouth. Peter knew he had to keep her awake. He shook the child hard, her head, arms and legs were marionette like, limp and flaccid. The old man crouched on the road verge, his voice keeping low, in the beginning of a death chant. Molly turned to him and said fiercely, "Stop that! Do you hear me? She can hear you and that'll make her worse." Suddenly, the little group became aware of a sound, a strange and almost frightening sound. Now the noise was around them. The motor bikes were black and gleaming and the riders helmeted, goggled and dressed in black leather. The whole thirty of them had the skull and crossbones emblem stenciled on their jackets. The roar of the bikes began to lessen, becoming staccato as if wolf-like they had to snap and snarl at one another. A thin blonde-haired youth was the first to dismount from his machine and he spoke to the frightened Molly. “What’s wrong lady? Are you havin’ trouble?” Pointing to the tableau of Peter and Katey Doll, Molly replied “My, my little girl, snake bite!” The youth swore softly and yelled: “Christ, where’s the Doc? Get him someone, this kid’s been bitten by a bloody snake.”

A towering red-headed, red-bearded giant of two metres or more threaded his way swiftly through the mass of machines, he knelt beside the exhausted Peter sucking the back of the girl’s hand. He clasped one huge paw on Katey Doll’s wrist and spoke softly to Peter, “Come on let’s have a look, mate.” There were calls from the riders watching intently. “How she doin’ Red Doc?” The man called “Red Doc” (two years at medical school had given him that unofficial title) gently picked up the child. He spoke quickly, quietly. “We have to move fast. Go Bo, Slit Eyes, get going to the nearest phone box, and ring for an ambulance. Tell them to bring anti-venom and to meet us on the northern highway to Perth Hospital.”

Three bikes leapt to life and with a full-throated roar, they swept down the road in a blinding acceleration of rising speed. Big Red Doc climbed onto his enormous Harley with Katey Doll cradled in his arms, her hand with a tourniquet applied, suspended by a belt tied around his neck. He looked at Peter and grinned and said, “Right mate, on the back.” Red Doc spoke to the others. “OK you guys, you organise getting a car and get the rest of these people into town, better bring them to the hospital.”

A half dozen of the bikies with Joshua and the children sat in the waiting room. Everybody was tense not knowing how Katey Doll was faring. The doctors had guessed correctly that the snake was a death adder, usually fatal. They saw the doctor with Peter and Molly walking toward them, and they knew suddenly, everything was alright. Peter spoke first, his hand groping for the massive paw of Big Red. “She gonna be OK. Thanks fellas, thanks a million.” Molly began to cry quietly as reaction set in. The doctor smiling, spoke: “She’s going to be alright. She is a lucky little girl, the only reason she is alive is because she had prompt attention.”

Molly looked at the group of leather-jacketed men and smiling, spoke softly. “You know when you all came down the road this afternoon, I thought you were a pack of devils, but instead you were all angels on chariots, surely sent by God.” Old Joshua looked up and cackled, “And it’s the first time I reckon, they rode motor bikes.”

Slit Eye spoke cheerfully, “Now that’s why we got kicked out of Northam. 20
It was all that ‘upstairs guy’s’ fault.” And in the late hour of the evening, the hospital waiting room echoed their laughter.

CHARTING THE STORY

1 What is the bus driver's erroneous perception of "his people," the Australians? Where in the story is it evident that his views may be widespread among whites in general?

2 Why do the distressed family members fear the approaching motorcyclists? What causes them to change their minds?

3 What may be motivating the bikies to remain in the hospital with the family?

4 Why, according to Slit Eyes at the end of the story, did the bikies really get kicked out of Northam?

CONSIDERATIONS OF STYLE

1 What Australianisms—both white and Koori—do you encounter in the story? How do they affect your reading of it?

2 At what points does the story's point of view shift? What effect does this create?

3 Where in the story does Davis use words that personify various types of motor vehicles—the bus, the cars, and the motorcycles? What is the effect of this figurative device?

AFTERTHOUGHTS

1 What is the significance—linguistically and socially—of the bikies' nicknames Red Doc, Go Bo, and Slit Eyes?

2 What do you consider to be the eponymous "white fantasy" and "black fact"?

THE WRITER'S CRAFT

1 Write an essay or a poem about a social group in your culture, like the bikies in this story, that you feel is misunderstood—though not mistreated—by society at large.

2 Look up the parable of the Good Samaritan in Luke 10:30–37. Write an essay about the parallels between this parable and Davis' story.

ESTELA PORTILLO TRAMBLEY

ESTELA PORTILLO TRAMBLEY *was born in 1936 in Texas. A teacher and a radio talk-show host, she published stories and poems in the 1970s in* El Grito *(*The Cry*), which publishes Mexican American authors' works. She received the Quinto Sol Award in 1972 for literature. Her story collection,* Rain of Scorpions and Other Writings *(1976), was the first published by a Mexican American woman. Among other things, she has also written a play,* The Day of the Swallows *(1971) and a novel,* Trini *(1986).*

"Village" was published in 1989 and is included in the collection A Rain of Scorpions *(1993).*

The story is of a Mexican American soldier serving in the Vietnam War, whose take on that war is influenced by his ancient heritage.

PERSPECTIVES

1 Look up or try to determine from context the following words: barrio (Paragraph 2); Viet Cong (Paragraph 6); garotte (Paragraph 9); napalm (Paragraph 11); carbine (Paragraph 27); purple heart (Paragraph 32); loco weed (Paragraph 41); and chinks (Paragraph 43).

2 If you were in combat and were given an order that you could not, in good conscience, obey, what do you think you would do?

Village

Rico stood on top of a bluff overlooking Mai Cao. The whole of the wide horizon was immersed in a rosy haze. His platoon was returning from an all-night patrol. They had scoured the area in a radius of thirty-two miles, following the length of the canal system along the Delta, furtively on the lookout for an enemy attack. On their way back, they had stopped to rest, smoke, drink warm beer after parking the carry-alls along the edge of the climb leading to the top of the bluff. The hill was good cover, seemingly safe.

Harry was behind him on the rocky slope. Then, the sound of thunder overhead. It wasn't thunder, but a squadron of their own helicopters on the usual run. Rico and Harry sat down to watch the planes go by. After that, a stillness, a special kind of silence. Rico knew it well, the same kind of stillness, that was a part of him back home, the kind of stillness that makes a man part of his world—river, clearing, sun, wind. The stillness of a village early in the morning—barrio stillness, the first stirrings of life that come with dawn. Harry was looking down at the village of Mai Cao.

"Makes me homesick..." Harry lighted a cigarette.

Rico was surprised. He thought Harry was a city dude. Chicago, no less. "I don't see no freeway or neon lights."

"I'm just sick of doing nothing in this goddamned war."

No action yet. But who wanted action? Rico had transformed into a soldier, but he knew he was no soldier. He had been trained to kill the enemy in Vietnam. He watched the first curl of smoke coming out of one of the chimneys. They were the enemy down there. Rico didn't believe it. He would never believe it. Perhaps because there had been no confrontation with Viet Cong soldiers or village people. Harry flicked away his cigarette and started down the slope. He turned, waiting for Rico to follow him. "Coming?"

"I'll be down after a while."

"Suit yourself." Harry walked swiftly down the bluff, his feet carrying with them the dirt yieldings in a flurry of small pebbles and loose earth. Rico was relieved. He needed some time by himself, to think things out. But Harry was right. To come across an ocean just to do routine checks, to patrol ground where there was no real danger...it could get pretty shitty. The enemy was hundreds of miles away.

The enemy! He remembered the combat bible—kill or be killed. Down a man—the lethal lick: a garotte strangling is neater and more quiet than the slitting of a throat; grind your heel against a face to mash the brains. Stomp the ribcage to carve the heart with bone splinters. Kill...

Hey, who was kidding who? They almost made him believe it back at boot camp in the States. In fact, only a short while ago, only that morning he had crouched down along the growth following a mangrove swamp, fearing an unseen enemy, ready to kill. Only that morning. But now, looking down at the peaceful village with its small rice field, its scattered huts, something had struck deep, something beyond the logic of war and enemy, something deep in his guts.

He had been cautioned. The rows of thatched huts were not really peoples' homes, but "hootches," makeshift temporary stays built by the makeshift enemy. But then they were real enemies. There were too many dead Americans to prove it. The "hootches" didn't matter. The people didn't matter. These people knew how to pick up their sticks and go. Go where? Then how many of these villages had been bulldozed? Flattened by gunfire? Good pyre for napalm, these Vietnamese villages. A new kind of battleground.

Rico looked down and saw huts that were homes, clustered in an intimacy that he knew well. The village of Mai Cao was no different than Valverde, the barrio where he had grown up. A woman came out of a hut, walking straight and with a certain grace, a child on her shoulder. She was walking toward a stream east of the slope. She stopped along the path and looked up to say something to the child. It struck him again, the feeling—a bond—people all the same everywhere.

The same scent from the earth, the same warmth from the sun, a woman walking with a child—his mother, Trini. His little mother who had left Tarahumara country and crossed the Barranca del Cobre, taking with her seeds from the hills of Batopilas, withstanding suffering, danger—for what? A dream—a piece of ground in the land of plenty, the United States of America. She had waded across the Rio Grande from Juárez, Mexico, to El Paso, Texas, when she felt the birth pangs of his coming. He had been born a citizen because his mother had had a dream. She had made the dream come true—an acre of riverland in Valverde on the edge of the border. His mother, like the earth and sun, mattered. The woman with the child on her shoulder mattered. Every human life in the village mattered. He knew this not only with the mind but with the heart.

Rico remembered a warning from combat training, from the weary, wounded soldiers who had fought and killed and survived, soldiers sent to Saigon, waiting to go home. His company had been flown to Saigon before being sent to the front. And this was the front, villages like Mai Cao. He felt relieved knowing that the fighting was hundreds of miles away from the people in Mai Cao—but the warning was still there:

Watch out for pregnant women with machine guns. Toothless old 15
women are experts with the knife between the shoulders. Begging children with hidden grenades, the unseen VC hiding in the hootches—village people were not people; they were the enemy. The woman who knew the child on her shoulder, who knew the path to her door, who knew the coming of the sun—she was the enemy.

It was a discord not to be believed by instinct or intuition. And Rico was an Indian, the son of a Tarahumara chieftain. Theirs was a world of instinct and intuitive decisions. Suddenly he heard the sounds of motors. He looked to the other side of the slope, down to the road where the carry-alls had started queuing their way back to the post. Rico ran down the hill to join his company.

In his dream, Sergeant Keever was shouting, "Heller, heller..." Rico woke with a start. It wasn't a dream. The men around him were scrambling out of the pup tent. Outside most of the men were lining up in uneven formation. Rico saw a communiqué in the sergeant's hand. Next to Keever was a lieutenant from communications headquarters. Keever was reading the communiqué:

"Special mission 72...for Company C, platoon 2, assigned at 22 hours. Move into the village of Mai Cao, field manual description—hill 72. Destroy the village."

No! It was crazy. Why? Just words on a piece of paper. Keever had to tell him why. There had to be a reason. Had the enemy come this far? It was impossible. Only that morning he had stood on the slope. He caught up with Keever, blurting out, "Why? I mean—why must we destroy it?"

Sergeant Keever stopped in his tracks and turned steel-blue eyes at Rico. "What you say?"

"Why?"

"You just follow orders, savvy?"

"Are the Viet Cong . . ."

"Did you hear me? You want trouble private?"

"There's people . . ."

"I don't believe you, soldier. But OK. Tell you as much as I know. We gotta erase the village in case the Viet Cong come this way. That way they won't use it as a stronghold. Now move your ass . . ."

Keever walked away from him, his lips tight in some kind of disgust. Rico did not follow this time. He went to get his gear and join the men in one of the carry-alls. Three carry-alls for the assault—three carry-alls moving up the same road. Rico felt the weight and hardness of his carbine. Now it had a strange, hideous meaning. The machine guns were some kind of nightmare. The mission was to kill and burn and erase all memories. Rico swallowed a guilt that rose from the marrow—with it, all kinds of fear. He had to do something, something to stop it, but he didn't know what. And with all these feelings, a certain reluctance to do anything but follow orders. In the darkness, his lips formed words from the anthem, "My country, 'tis of thee . . ."

They came to the point where the treelines straggled between two hills that rose darkly against the moon. Rico wondered if all the men were of one mind—one mind to kill . . . Was he a coward? No! It was not killing the enemy that his whole being was rejecting, but firing machine guns into a village of sleeping people . . . people. Rico remembered only the week before, returning from their usual patrol, the men from the company had stopped at the stream, mingling with the children, old men, and women of the village. There had been an innocence about the whole thing. His voice broke the silence in the carry-all, a voice harsh and feverish. "We can get the people out of there. Help them evacuate . . ."

"Shut up." Harry's voice was tight, impatient.

The carry-alls traveled through tall, undulant grass following the dirt road that led to the edge of the bluff. It was not all tall grass. Once in a while trees appeared again, clumped around scrub bushes. Ten miles out the carry-alls stopped. It was still a mile's walk to the bluff in the darkness, but they had to avoid detection. Sergeant Keever was leading the party. Rico, almost at the rear, knew he had to catch up to him. He had to stop him. Harry was ahead of him, a silent black bundle walking stealthily through rutted ground to discharge his duty. For a second, Rico hesitated. That was the easy thing to do—to carry out his duty—to die a hero, to do his duty blindly and survive. Hell, why not? He knew what happened to men who backed down in battle. But he wasn't backing down. Hell, what else was it? How often had he heard it among the gringos in his company.

"You Mexican? Hey, you Mexicans are real fighters. I mean, everybody knows Mexicans have guts..."

A myth perhaps. But no. He thought of the old guys who had fought in World War II. Many of them were on welfare back in the barrio. But, man! did they have metals! He had never seen so many purple hearts. He remembered old Toque, the wino, who had tried to pawn his metals to buy a bottle. No way, man. They weren't worth a nickle.

He quickly edged past Harry, pushing the men ahead of him to reach the sergeant. He was running, tall grass brushing his shoulder, tall grass that had swayed peacefully like wheat. The figure of Sergeant Keever was in front of him now. There was a sudden impulse to reach out and hold him back. But the sergeant had stopped. Rico did not touch him, but whispered hoarsely, desperately in the dark. "Let's get the people out—evacuate..."

"What the hell..." Keever's voice was ice. He recognized Rico, and hissed, "Get back to your position soldier or I'll shoot you myself."

Rico did as he was told, almost unaware of the men around him. But at a distance he heard something splashing in the water of the canal, in his nostrils the smell of sweet burnt wood. He looked toward the clearing and saw the cluster of huts bathed in moonlight. In the same moonlight, he saw Keever giving signals. In the gloom he saw figures of the men carrying machine guns. They looked like dancing grasshoppers as they ran ahead to position themselves on the bluff. He felt like yelling, "For Christ's sake! Where is the enemy?"

The taste of blood in his mouth—he suddenly realized he had bitten his quivering lower lip. As soon as Sergeant Keever gave the signal, all sixteen men would open fire on the huts—machine guns, carbines—everything would be erased. No more Mai Cao—the execution of duty without question, without alternative. They were positioned on the south slope, Sergeant Keever up ahead, squatting on his heels, looking at his watch. He raised himself, after a quick glance at the men. As Sergeant Keever raised his hand to give the signal for attack, Rico felt the cold metallic deadness of his rifle. His hands began to tremble as he released the safety catch. Sergeant Keever was on the rise just above him. Rico stared at the sergeant's arm, raised, ready to fall—the signal to fire. The crossfire was inside Rico, a heavy-dosed tumult—destroy the village, erase all memory. There was ash in his mouth. Once the arm came down, there was no turning back.

In a split second, Rico turned his rifle at a forty-degree angle and fired at the sergeant's arm. Keever half-turned with the impact of the bullet, then fell to his knees. In a whooping whisper the old-time soldier blew out the words, "That fucking bastard—get him." He got up and signaled the platoon back to the carryalls, as two men grabbed Rico, one hitting him on the side of the head with the butt of his rifle. Rico felt the sting of the blow, as they pinned his arm back and forced him to walk the path back to the carry-all. He did not resist. There was a lump in his throat, and he blinked back tears, tears of relief. The memory of the village would not be erased. Someone shouted in the dark, "They're on to us. There's an old man with a lantern and others coming out of the hootches . . ."

"People—just people . . ." Rico whispered, wanting to shout it, wanting to tell them that he had done the right thing. But the heaviness that filled his senses was the weight of the truth. He was a traitor—a maniac. He had shot his superior in a battle crisis. He was being carried almost bodily back to the truck. He glanced at the thick brush along the road, thinking that somewhere beyond it was a rice field, and beyond that a mangrove swamp. There was a madman inside his soul that made him think of rice fields and mangrove swamps instead of what he had done. Not once did he look up. Everyone around him was strangely quiet and remote. Only the sound of trudging feet.

In the carry-all, the faces of the men sitting around Rico were indiscernible in the dark, but he imagined their eyes, wide, confused, peering through the dark at him with a wakefulness that questioned what he had done. Did they know his reason? Did they care? The truck suddenly lurched. Deep in the gut, Rico felt a growing fear. He choked back a hysteria rising from the diaphragm. The incessant bumping of the carry-alls as they moved unevenly on the dirt road accused him too. He looked up into a night sky and watched the moon eerily weave in and out of tree branches. The darkness was like his fear. It had no solutions.

Back on the post, Sergeant Keever and a medic passed by Rico, already handcuffed, without any sign of recognition. Sergeant Keever had already erased him from existence. The wheels of justice would take their course. Rico had been placed under arrest, temporarily shackled to a cot in one of the tents. Three days later he was moved to a makeshift bamboo hut, with a guard in front of the hut at all times. His buddies brought in food like strangers, awkward in their silence, anxious to leave him alone. He felt like some kind of poisonous bug. Only Harry came by to see him after a week.

"You dumb ass, were you on loco weed?" Harry asked in disgust.

"I didn't want people killed, that's all."

"Hell, that's no reason, those chinks aren't even—even . . ."

"Even what?" Rico demanded. He almost screamed it a second time. "Even what?"

"Take it easy, will you? You better go for a Section eight." Harry was putting him aside like every one else. "They're sending you back to the States next week. You'll have to face Keever sometime this afternoon. I thought I'd better let you know."

"Thanks." Rico knew the hopelessness of it all. There was still that nagging question he had to ask. "Listen, nobody tells me anything. Did you all go back to Mai Cao? I mean, is it still there?"

"Still there. Orders from headquarters to forget it. The enemy were spotted taking an opposite direction. But nobody's going to call you a hero, you understand? What you did was crud. You're no soldier. You'll never be a soldier."

Rico said nothing to defend himself. He began to scratch the area around the steel rings on his ankles. Harry was scowling at him. He said it again, almost shouting, "I said, you'll never be a soldier."

"So?" There was soft disdain in Rico's voice.

"You blew it, man. You'll be locked up for a long, long time."

"Maybe . . ." Rico's voice was without concern.

"Don't you care?"

"I'm free inside, Harry," Rico laughed in relief. "Free . . ."

Harry shrugged, peering at Rico unbelievingly, then turned and walked out of the hut.

CHARTING THE STORY

1 What moral dilemmas does Rico face? How does he solve each dilemma? How much is the reader given to know about the steps he takes from problem to solution, and what may account for the differences in his decision-making process in each dilemma?

2 What sort of education (at home, at school, at boot camp, and "in country") has Rico received, and how is this reflected in his characterization?

3 Why does Rico seem to be the only person who feels the way that he does about the order to "erase" the village?

4 From the context, can you determine whether Rico was a volunteer or a draftee; how might this affect the major decision that he makes, as well as its ramifications upon him?

CONSIDERATIONS OF STYLE

1 What moods does the author establish in the story, and with what imagery and plot events does the author create them?

2 How does the author use dialogue to set up oppositions between characters?

3 Rico's name in Spanish signifies "Rich," and the name of his barrio translates to "Green Valley." How do these significations play out in the story?

AFTERTHOUGHTS

1 As a woman, the author would not have had personal experience of Vietnam War combat. Does this affect the authenticity of the story? If so, why; and if not, why not? Is direct personal experience necessary for such authenticity?

2 If you were to extend the story over the next few months, what would you forecast for Rico? What does the author accomplish by leaving the narrative where she leaves it?

3 How could one relate the following quotation to the story? What are some similarities? Some differences?

> On the morning of March 16th, 1968, soldiers from the U.S. Army's Americal Division entered the hamlet of My Lai 4 in South Vietnam. On the orders of Lt. William Calley, they tortured and murdered hundreds of helpless civilians. They raped the women and girls. It was the moral and professional nadir of the post-World War II U.S. Army. To compound the shame, the American top-ranking officers covered up the crimes. Only after a conscientious young soldier named Ron Ridenhour detailed the massacre in a letter to his congressman did the Army investigate, eventually setting loose a torrent of public outrage.
>
> From "The Legend of Colin Powell" by Charles Lane, 17 April 1995. In *The New Republic Guide to the Candidates,* 1996. New York: Basic Books, 1996, p. 202.

THE WRITER'S CRAFT

1 At Rico's court-martial, you are on the side of the prosecution, or of the defense. Choose a side, and write your opening statement to the court, considering that it is an audience of military officers, likely Vietnam veterans, who have the power to decide Rico's fate, and that in courts-martial, one is *not* presumed innocent till proven guilty.

2 Write a story from the point of view of another character in "Village," setting forth the situation from that person's unique point of view, in the style of language that person would use in order to describe the events and to convey that person's thoughts.

DESMOND EGAN

DESMOND EGAN *was born in the central Irish town of Athlone. He was educated at Mullingar and Maynooth [colleges] and received graduate degrees from University College in Dublin. He served as Poet in Residence at University College (1987), Kansai University, Japan (1986), Creighton University, US (1991–1993), and the University of Sassari, Sardinia, Italy (1994).*

Egan has published twelve collections of poetry and one of prose. His poetry has been translated in eight languages and has received numerous awards. He lives with his wife, author Vivienne Abbott and their two daughters in Great Connell, Newbridge, County Kildare.

These three poems of war and peace reflect a recurring theme in Egan's work. Woven into the poem "Peace" is another of his main themes, the landscape of nature. The poems were found on the Official Desmond Egan Page *in March 1999.*

PERSPECTIVES

1. What were the circumstances surrounding the bombing of Hiroshima, Japan in 1945? What were immediate and ultimate effects of this event?
2. What is the Northern Ireland "question"? What attempts have been made to resolve it? Does a solution seem imminent? Which of the world's institutions today offer the greatest promise for world peace?

Hiroshima

Hiroshima your shadow burns
into the granite of history

preserves for us pilgrims
a wide serious space
where one may weep in silence

I carry in my mind
a glass bullet lodged deep

the memory of that epicentre where
one hundred thousand souls
fused at an instant

and the picture of a soldier
tenderly offering a cup of water
to a burnt child who cannot respond

the delicate paper cranes

CHARTING THE POEM

1. This poem presents a series of images "lodged deep" in the memory of the narrator, one of many "pilgrims." To what senses (sight, hearing, touch, smell, taste) do these images appeal, and what might account for this appeal?
2. What "progression," if any, do you see in each image, in terms of theme, in terms of their effect on the narrator, or in other terms that you find meaningful? What does the poet seem to accomplish in setting forth any sort of progression?
3. Where would you situate the "delicate paper cranes" in the scenario of this poem?

CONSIDERATIONS OF STYLE

1. What devices, words, or ideas does Egan employ to mitigate the gruesomeness of the bombing without diminishing its historical significance?
2. What is the effect of personifying Hiroshima in a dialogue with a "pilgrim" visitor?

The Northern Ireland Question

Two *wee* girls
were playing tig near a car . . .

how many counties would you say
are worth their scattered fingers?

CHARTING THE POEM

1. What is the plot in this sparse poem? Who are the players? What is the poem's resolution?

CONSIDERATIONS OF STYLE

1 What Irish associations arise with each of the images in the poem?
2 Had the poem been longer, more elegiac in tone—and conveying less of the almost-haiku mood—what might have been gained or lost in effect?

Peace

just to go for a walk out the road
just that
under the deep trees
which whisper of peace

to break the bread of words
with someone passing
just that
four of us round a pram
and baby fingers asleep

just to join the harmony
the fields the blue everyday hills
the puddles of daylight and

you might hear a pheasant
echo through the woods
or plover may waver by
as the evening poises with a blackbird
on its table of hedge
just that
and here and there a gate
a bunaglow's bright window
the smell of woodsmoke of lives

just that!

but Sweet Christ that
is more than most of mankind can afford
with the globe still plaited in its own
crown of thorns

too many starving eyes
too many ancient children

squatting among flies
too many stockpiles of fear
too many dog jails too many generals
too many under torture by the impotent
screaming into the air we breathe

too many dreams stuck in money jams
too many mountains of butter selfishness
too many poor drowning in the streets
too many shantytowns on the outskirts of life

too many of us not sure what we want
so that we try to feed a habit for everything
until the ego puppets the militaries
mirror our own warring face

too little peace

CHARTING THE POEM

1 In the first three stanzas, which words convey the speaker's mood? What does his/her mood suggest about the prospects of peace in Northern Ireland?

2 What pattern can one see in Stanzas 1–5, 6, and 7–11? Where does the pattern seem to break in the course of the poem?

CONSIDERATIONS OF STYLE

1 The poet relies heavily on repetition. But repetition of what besides words?

2 How does the image of "Sweet Christ" tie in, perhaps ironically, with the desired "peace"?

AFTERTHOUGHTS

1 Thich Nhat Hanh, a Buddhist monk who has worked actively for peace for over thirty years, writes:

> In the peace movement there is a lot of anger, frustration, and misunderstanding. The peace movement can write very good protest letters, but they are not yet able to write a love letter. We need to learn to write a letter to the Congress or to the President of the United States that they will want to read, and not just throw away. The way you speak, the kind of understanding, the kind of language you use would not turn people off. The President is a person like any of us. (*Being Peace*. Full Circle: New Delhi, 1997, p 79)

In what ways does the monk's approach to peace activism differ from that which we experience in Egan's poems?

2 A popular song of the 1960s, "Last Night I Had the Strangest Dream," written by Ed McCurdy and sung by the Weavers, among others, conveyed the images of world leaders signing a peace agreement, and the "people in the streets below... dancing round and round." Yet the story was firmly lodged in a dream. How do Egan's poems compare with such a dream? What possibilities do you see of such dreams becoming reality, and how do the poems indicate these possibilities—or lack thereof?

THE WRITER'S CRAFT

1 Write a two-to-three-page documented essay on the topic of the effects of war on children. Include in your paper at least one reference from each of the poems presented in this lesson.

2 Write a prose or poetic "love letter," in Thich Nhat Hanh's sense, in response to any of the "crisis locations" in the world. In your letter, try to convey what you gather from Egan's peace poems.

ALBERT WENDT

Born in 1939 in Western Samoa, ALBERT WENDT *is of Samoan and German origin. He has taught literature at the University of the South Pacific in Fiji and at the University of Auckland, New Zealand.*

His extensive writings include novels, collections of poetry, and edited works. "Crocodile" is a fictional memoir of a schoolmistress in a girls' boarding school in New Zealand, narrated by a Samoan-minority student. It contains little of the "sugar and spice and everything nice" that the childhood poem attributes to "little girls."

The story was first published in the collection The Birth and Death of the Miracle Man *in 1968.*

PERSPECTIVES

1 Recall some of the nicknames—flattering and otherwise—you and your peers in middle and high school gave to certain teachers. Did mischievous nicknaming cease when you got to college?

Crocodile

Miss Susan Sharon Willersey, known to all her students as Crocodile Willersey, was our House Mistress for the five years I was at boarding school. I recall, from reading a brief history of our school, that she had been born in 1908 in a small Waikato farming town and, at the age of ten, had enrolled at our Preparatory School, had then survived (brilliantly) our high school, had attended university and graduated MA (Honours in Latin), and had returned to our school to teach and be a dormitory mistress, and, a few years later, was put in charge of Beyle House, our House.

So when I started in 1953, Crocodile was in her fit mid-forties, already a school institution more myth than bone, more goddess than human (and she tended to behave that way!).

Certain stories, concerning the derivation of her illustrious nickname, prevailed (and were added to) during my time at school.

One story, in line with the motto of our school (which is: Perseverance is the Way to Knowledge), had it that Miss Willersey's first student called her Crocodile because she was a model of perseverance and fortitude, which they believed were the moral virtues of a crocodile.

Another story claimed that because Miss Willersey was a devout Anglican, possessing spiritual purity beyond blemish (is that correct?), an Anglican missionary, who had visited our school after spending twenty invigorating years in the Dark Continent (his description), had described Miss Willersey in our school assembly as a saint with the courage and purity and powers of the African crocodile (which was sacred to many tribes). Proof of her steadfastness and purity, so this story went, was her kind refusal to marry the widowed missionary because, as she reasoned (and he was extremely understanding), she was already married to her church, to her school and students, and to her profession.

The most unkindly story attributed her nickname to her appearance: Miss Willersey looked and behaved like a crocodile—she was long, long-teethed, long-eared, long-fingered, long-arsed, long-everythinged. Others also argued she had skin like crocodile hide, and that her behaviour was slippery, always spyful, decisively cruel and sadistic and unforgiving, like a crocodile's.

As a new third-former and a naive Samoan who had been reared to obey her elders without question, I refused to believe the unfavourable stories about Miss Willersey's nickname. Miss Willersey was always kind and helpful (though distant, as was her manner with all of us) to me in our House and during her Latin classes. (Because I was in the top third form I *had* to take Latin though I was really struggling with another foreign language, English, and New Zealand English at that!) We felt (and like it) that she was also treating all her "Island girls" (there were six of us) in a specially protective way. "You must always be proud of your race!" she kept reminding us. (She made it a point to slow down her English when speaking to us so we could understand her.)

During her Latin classes, I didn't suffer her verbal and physical (the swift ruler) chastisements, though I was a dumb, bumbling student. Not for ten months anyway.

However, in November, during that magical third-form year, I *had* to accept the negative interpretations of Miss Willersey's nickname.

I can't remember what aspect of Latin we were revising orally in class that summer day. All I remember well were: Croc's mounting anger as student after student (even her brightest) kept making errors; my loudly beating heart as her questioning came closer and closer to me; the stale smell of cardigans and shoes; Croc's long physique stretching longer, more threateningly; and some of my classmates snivelling into their handkerchiefs as Croc lacerated them verbally for errors (sins) committed.

"Life!" she called coldly, gazing at her feet. Silence. I didn't realize she was calling me. (My name is Olamaiileoti Monroe. Everyone at school called me Ola and *translated* it as Life which became my nickname.) "Life!" she repeated, this time her blazing eyes were boring into me. (I was almost wetting my pants, and this was contrary to Miss Willersey's constant exhortation to us: ladies learn early how to control their bladders!)

I wanted desperately to say, "Yes, Miss Willersey?" but I found I couldn't, I was too scared.

"Life?" She was not advancing towards me, filling me with her frightening lengthening. "You *are* called Life, aren't you, Monroe? That *is* your nickname?"

Nodding my head, I muttered, "Yes—yes!" A squeaking. My heart was struggling like a trapped bird in my throat. "Yes, yes, Miss Willersey!"

"And your name is Life, isn't it?"

"Yes!" I was almost in tears. (Leaking everywhere I was!)

"What does Ola mean exactly?"

"Life, Miss Willersey."

"But Ola is not a noun, is it?" she asked.

Utterly confused, leaking every which way, and thoroughly shit-scared, I just shook my head furiously.

"Ola doesn't mean Life, it is a verb, it means "to live", "to grow", doesn't it?" I nodded furiously.

"Don't you know even your own language, young lady?" I bowed my head (in shame); my trembling hands were clutching the desk-top. "Speak up, young lady!"

"No, Miss Willersey!" I swallowed back my tears.

"Now, Miss Life, or, should I say, Miss To-Live, let's see if you know Latin a little better than you know your own language!" Measuredly, she marched back to the front of our class. Shit, shit, shit! I cursed myself (and my fear) silently. Her footsteps stopped. Silence. She was turning to face me. Save me, someone!

"Excuse me, Miss Willersey?" the saving voice intruded.

"Yes, what is it?"

"I think I heard someone knocking on the door, Miss Willersey." It was Gill, the ever-aware, always courageous Gill. The room sighed. Miss Willersey had lost the initiative. "Shall I go and see who it is, Miss Willersey?" Gill asked, standing up and gazing unwaveringly at Miss Willersey. We all focused our eyes on her too. A collective defiance and courage. For a faltering moment I thought she wasn't going to give in.

Then she looked away from Gill and said, "Well, all right and be quick about it!"

"You all right, Miss To-Live?" Gill asked me after class when all my friends crowded round me in the corridor.

"Yes!" I thanked her.

"Croc's a bloody bitch!" someone said.

"Yeah!" the others echoed.

So for the remainder of my third-form year and most of my fourth year I *looked* on Miss Susan Sharon Willersey as the Crocodile to be wary of, to pretend good behaviour with, to watch all the time in case she struck out at me.

Not that she ever again treated me unreasonably in class despite my getting dumber and dumber in Latin (and less and less afraid of her).

In those two years, Gill topped our class in Latin, with little effort and in courageously clever defiance of Crocodile. Gill also helped me to get the magical 50% I needed to pass and stay out of Crocodile's wrath.

Winter was almost over, the days were getting warmer, our swimming pool was 35
filled and the more adventurous (foolhardy?) used it regularly. Gill and I (and the rest of Miss Rashly's cross-country team) began to rise before light and run the four miles through the school farm. Some mornings, on our sweaty way back, we would meet a silent Crocodile in grey woollen skirt and thick sweater and boots, striding briskly through the cold.

"Morning, girls!" she would greet us.

"Morning, Miss Willersey!" we would reply.

"Exercise, regular exercise, that's the way girls!"

In our fourth-form dormitory, my bed was nearest the main door that opened out to the lounge opposite which was the front door to Crocodile's apartment, forbidden domain unless we were summoned to it to be questioned (and punished) for a misdemeanour, or invited to it for hot cocoa and biscuits (prefects were the usual invitees!). Because it *was* forbidden territory we were curious about what went on in there: how Croc lived, and what she looked like without her formidably thick make-up and stern outfits, and so on. As a Samoan I wasn't familiar with how papalagi (and especially Crocodile) lived out their private lives. I tried but I couldn't picture Miss Willersey in her apartment in her bed or in her bath in nothing else (not even her skin) but in her make-up, immaculately coiffured hair and severe suits. (I couldn't even imagine her using the toilet! Pardon the indiscretion which is unbecoming of one of Miss Willersey's girls!)

The self-styled realists and sophisticates among us—and they were mainly 40
seniors who had to pretend to such status—whispered involved and terribly upsetting (exciting) tales about Crocodile's men (and lack of men), who visited (and didn't visit) her in the dead of night. We, the gullible juniors, inexperienced in the ways of men and sex, found these lurid tales erotically exciting (upsetting) but never admitted publicly we *were* excited. We all feigned disgust and disbelief. And quite frankly I couldn't imagine Miss Willersey (in her virgin skin) with a man (in his experienced skin) in her bed in the widely lustful embrace of *knowing each other* (our Methodist Bible-class teachers's description of the art of fucking!). No, I really tried, but couldn't put Crocodile into that forbidden but feverishly exciting position. At the time I *did* believe in Miss Willersey's strict moral standards concerning the relationship between the sexes. (I was a virgin, and that's what Miss Willersey and my other elders wanted me to retain and give to the man I married).

One sophisticate, the precociously pretentious and overweight daughter of a Wellington surgeon and one of Crocodile's pet prefects, suggested that

Croc's nightly visitors *weren't* men. That immediately put more disgustingly exciting possibilities into our wantonly frustrated (and virgin) imaginations.

"Who then?" an innocent junior asked.

"What then?" another junior asked.

"Impossible. Bloody filthy!" the wise Gill countered.

"It happens!" the fat sophisticate argued.

"How do you know?" someone asked.

"I just know, that's all!"

"Because your mother is a lesbian!" Gill, the honest, socked it to her. We had to break up the fight between Gill and the Wellington sophisticate.

"Bugger her!" Gill swore as we led her out of the locker room. "She sucks up to Miss Willersey and then says Croc's a les!"

"What's—what's a les . . . lesbian?" I forced myself to ask Gill at prep that evening. She looked surprised, concluded with a shrug that I didn't really know, printed something on a piece of paper and, after handing it to me, watched me read it.

A FEMALE WHO IS ATTRACTED TO OTHER FEMALES!!!

"What do you mean?" I whispered. (We weren't allowed to talk during prep.)

She wrote on the paper. *"You Islanders are supposed to know a lot more about sex than us poor pakehas. A les is a female who does it with other females. Savvy?"*

"Up you too!" I wrote back. We started giggling.

"Gill, stand up!" the prefect on duty called.

"Oh, shit!" Gill whispered under her breath.

"Were you talking?"

"Life just wanted me to spell a word for her!" Gill replied.

"What word?"

"Les—," Gill started to say. My heart nearly stopped. "Life wanted to know how to spell 'lesson'?" Relief.

"Well, spell it out aloud for all of us!" And Gill did so, crisply, all the time behind her back giving the prefect the up-you sign.

After this incident, I noticed myself observing the Crocodile's domain more closely for unusual sounds, voices, visitors, and, though I refused to think of the possibility of her being a lesbian, I tried to discern a pattern in her female visitors (students included), but no pattern emerged. Also, there were no unusual sounds. (Croc didn't even sing in the bath!)

Some creature, almost human, was trapped in the centre of my head, sobbing pitifully, mourning an enormous loss. It was wrapping its pain around my dreaming and I struggled to break away from its tentacles. I couldn't. I woke to find myself awake (and relieved I wasn't strangling in the weeping) in the dark of our dormitory. Everyone else was fast asleep.

Then I knew it was Miss Willersey. I knew it and tried not to panic, not to give in to the feeling I wasn't going to be able to cope. I wrapped the blankets round my head. It was none of my business! But I couldn't escape.

I found myself standing with my ear to Miss Willersey's door. Shivering. 65
Her light was on, I could tell from the slit of light under the door. The sobbing was more audible but it sounded muffled, as if she was crying into a pillow or cushion. Uncontrolled. Emerging from the depths of a fathomless grief. Drawing me into its depths.

My hand opened the door before I could stop it. Warily I peered into the blinding light. My eyes adjusted quickly to the glare. The neat and orderly arrangement of furniture, wall pictures, ornaments, and bookcases came into focus. Miss Willersey was enthroned in an armchair against the far wall, unaware of my presence, unaware of where she was and who she was, having relinquished in her grief all that was the Crocodile. She was dressed in a shabby dressing-gown, brown slippers, hair in wild disarray, tears melting away her thick make-up in streaks down her face, her long-fingered hands clasped to her mouth trying to block back the sound.

Shutting the door behind me quietly, I edged closer to her, hoping she would see me and order me out of her room and then I wouldn't have to cope with the new, fragile, vulnerable Miss Willersey. I didn't want to.

All around us (and in me) her grief was like the incessant buzzing of a swarm of bees, around and around, spiralling up out of the hollow hive of her being and weaving round and round on my head, driving me towards her and her sorrow which had gone beyond her courage to measure and bear.

And I moved into her measure and, lost for whatever else to do, wrapped my arms around her head, and immediately her arms were around me tightly and my body was the cushion for her grief.

At once she became my comfort, the mother I'd never had but had al- 70
ways yearned for, and I cried silently into her pain. Mother and daughter, daughter and mother. A revelation I hoped would hold true for as long as I was to know her.

Her weeping eased. Her arms relaxed around me. She turned her face away. "Please!" she murmured. I looked away. Got the box of tissues on the table and put it in her shaking hands. I looked away. Tearing out a handful of tissues, she wiped her eyes and face.

I started to leave. "It is Ola, isn't it?" she asked, face still turned away. In her voice was a gentleness I have never heard in it before.

"Yes."

"Thank you. I'm . . . I'm sorry you've had to see me like this." She was ripping out more tissues.

"Is there anything else I can do?" I asked. 75

"No, thank you." She started straightening her dressing-gown and hair. The Crocodile was returning. I walked to the door. "Ola!" she stopped me. I didn't look back at her. "This is our secret. Please don't tell the others?"

"I won't, Miss Willersey. Good-night!"

"Good-night, Ola!"

I shut the door behind me quietly, and on *our* secret.

Next morning there was a short article in the newspaper about her 80
mother's death in Hamilton, in an old people's home. Miss Willersey left on the bus for Hamilton that afternoon.

"The Croc's mother crocked!" some girls joked at our table at dinner that evening.

Yes, Crocodile Willersey remained married to her school and students until she died in 1982. By becoming a school tradition and a mythical being in the memories of all her students (generations of them) she has lived on, and we will bequeath her to our children.

Miss Susan Sharon Willersey, the Crocodile, I will always think of you with genuine alofa. (And forgive me—I've forgotten nearly all the Latin you taught me!) By the way, you were wrong about the meaning of Ola; it can also be a noun, Life.

CHARTING THE STORY

1 What three stories explain the origin of the girls' rather unaffectionate nickname for their Latin teacher Miss Willersey? How might one account for the fact that each origin story seems to escalate its negative image of Miss Willersey?

2 In the end, what happens to the issue of Miss Willersey's sexual orientation?

CONSIDERATIONS OF STYLE

1 Throughout the story, Wendt employs several devices to represent the speech of his young female narrator: parentheses, italics, and, in Paragraph 51, a whole sentence in upper-case letters. What nuances do the various representations convey about the narrator's style of speaking?

2 Explain the arresting analogy of the swarm of bees "incessant[ly] buzzing... spiralling up out of the hollow hive of her being..." in Paragraph 68.

AFTERTHOUGHTS

1 In what respects might this story be considered a "coming-of-age" story for both Ola and Miss Willersey?

THE WRITER'S CRAFT

1 Write a two- to-three-page memoir of a colorful teacher in your elementary, middle school, or high school. How has your perception of that teacher changed over the years?

2 From the point of view of that person, write a memoir of someone who has been ostracized, or "othered."

SUNITI NAMJOSHI

Born in 1941 in India, SUNITI NAMJOSHI *now lives in Canada and since 1972 has taught at the University of Toronto. Her collections of short stories and fables include:* The Blue Donkey Fables/The Mothers of Maya Diip *(1990),* Feminist Fables *(1981),* The Conversation of Cow *(1985), and* Aditi and the One-eyed Monkey *(1986). Collaboratively with Gillian Hanscombe, she has published the poetry collection* Flesh and Paper.

These two fables both focus on society's discomfiture with the Other. They are included in The Blue Donkey Fables/The Mothers of Maya Diip, *in 1990. We treat the fables here as a single, coherent text.*

PERSPECTIVES

1 Look up the term *fable* in a dictionary or literary reference work. What elements are typically ascribed to a fable? What is the significance of the etymology of the term?

2 What fables, or collections thereof, have you read or heard? When did you come into contact with them? Are they a part of your reading life now, to the same extent as other genres of fiction? If so, what creates their appeal? If not, why not?

The Blue Donkey

Marc Chagall, *The Blue Donkey*

Once upon a time a blue donkey lived by a red bridge. 'Inartistic,' said the councillors who governed that town. 'A donkey who lives by our bright red bridge must be of the purest and silkiest white or we must request that the said donkey be required to move on.' The matter soon turned into a political issue. One party said that the donkeys never had been and never would be white and what was asked of the donkey was grossly unfair. If, on the other hand, the donkey were required to be a nondescript grey (instead of a loud and laughable blue), they would be prepared to accept the solutions as a reasonable way out. But the opposing party found a fault in their logic. 'Just because donkeys have never been known to be white,' they pointed out patiently, 'it does not follow that a donkey is incapable of achieving whiteness. Your argument imposes an arbitrary limitation on the creature's potential.' 'Good heavens!' cried the others. 'Are you suggesting that the donkey's blueness may be a matter of culpable wilfulness rather than a mere genetic mischance?' 'Yes,' responded the logicians. 'Let us confront the creature and you can see for yourselves.'

They approached the donkey, who happened to be munching a bright pink carrot which clashed most horribly with the bright red bridge. 'O Donkey,' they said, feeling they had better get it over with at once, 'we'd like you to turn an inoffensive grey or else move on.' 'Can't and won't,' replied the donkey. 'There you see,' cried half the populace. 'Obviously wilful!' 'No, no,' cried the other half. 'Patently flawed!' And they began to dispute among themselves. The donkey was puzzled. 'I'm a perfectly good donkey,' she said at last. 'What exactly is the matter with you?' 'Your blueness troubles us,' wailed the citizens. 'It clashes with our bridge, as does the pinkness of your carrots. Oh what shall we do? We cannot agree among ourselves.' 'Look again,' advised the donkey. And so they did; they looked and argued and squabbled and argued and after a while most of them got used to the blueness of the donkey and didn't notice it anymore. But a few remained who maintained strongly that blueness was inherent, and a few protested that it was essentially intentional. And there were still a few others who managed to see—though only sometimes—that the Blue Donkey was only herself and therefore beautiful. These last occasionally brought her a bunch of blue flowers which she put in a vase.

Apotheosis

It so happened that in her middle years the Blue Donkey acquired a certain fame. The townsfolk grew quite proud of her. She attracted tourists. Blue Donkey bars and bistros sprouted, and there was a brisk trade in trinkets, T-shirts and Blue Donkey toys. She herself was installed in a stable and in order to see her it became necessary to buy tickets.

At first the Blue Donkey enjoyed the attention, then she grew bored, and then she took to questioning the tourists. 'Why?' she would ask them. 'Why do you come from near and far merely to see me?' The tourists were delighted. 'Because,' they told her, gawping happily, 'because, O Blue and Beautiful One, we admire you so. Your fame has travelled on the four winds.' She felt pleased. It was nice to be famous. And when the tourists pleaded for a snippet of her rare fur, she allowed them to snip and chop as they wished. Soon she began to look scruffy. The townsfolk worried. They shut down the stable and begged her to grow her fur quickly. The Blue Donkey obliged, and then they discovered that her fur had turned a beautiful grey. They were horrified. 'Oh what shall we do?' Someone suggested a blue pane of glass, but the donkey brushed such suggestions aside.

'I am retiring,' she told them firmly.

'But what about us? What can we possibly tell the tourists?' wailed the townsfolk.

'Tell them the truth. Tell them that I have become a legend,' she replied grandly.

'But will it work?' They still looked anxious.

'Of course,' she assured them. 'Truth is dazzling.'

CHARTING THE FABLES

1. Why do the town councillors oppose the blueness of the donkey? What do their arguments say about the "nature" vs "nurture" (or, "culpable wilfulness" vs "genetic mischance") controversy, as regards an *appropriate* color for the donkey? What light does the fable "Apotheosis" shed on the controversy?
2. What social issues or other significances arise out of this debate?
3. What is the Blue Donkey implying when she assures the townsfolk in "Apotheosis" that "truth is dazzling"?

CONSIDERATIONS OF STYLE

1. What values are suggested by the various colors—blue, red, white, grey, pink—alluded to in the fables?
2. What stylistic elements set these fables off as "fabulous"? In other words, what in their manner of telling makes them different from most other short stories?
3. How do Suniti Namjoshi's fables seem different from other fables you have read or heard?

AFTERTHOUGHTS

1. The author prefaces "The Blue Donkey" with the notation "Marc Chagall, *The Blue Donkey*." Look for some of Chagall's paintings in an art book (definitely one with color plates). How would you characterize his art? How does it relate—apart from the subject matter of one of his paintings—to Namjoshi's fables?

THE WRITER'S CRAFT

1. Write a fable inspired by a piece of art by Chagall or another artist of your choice. If you are bringing this writing to a collaborative group, be sure to include a copy—preferably a color copy—of the artwork that inspired your writing.

2 How does the following poem by Emily Dickinson enlarge/expand/elaborate the last line in “Apotheosis”: ‘Truth is dazzling’?

Tell all the Truth but tell it slant—
Success in Circuit lies
Too bright for our infirm Delight
The Truth's superb surprise

As Lightening to the Children eased
With explanation kind
The Truth must dazzle gradually
Or every man be blind—

CATHERINE LIM

CATHERINE LIM *grew up in Malaysia and now lives in Singapore, and works at the Regional Language Center (RELC) training teachers in sociolinguistics and the teaching of literature. She also writes English language instructional materials for use in Singapore's primary schools.*

Lim's works include the novels They Do Return *(1982),* The Serpent's Tooth *(1983),* The Bondmaid *(1997), and* The Teardrop Story Woman *(1998); and several collections of short stories, including* Little Ironies: Stories of Singapore *(1978),* The Shadow of a Shadow of a Dream: Love Stories of Singapore *(1987),* Oh Singapore! Stories in Celebration *(1988), and* Or Else, the Lightning God and Other Stories *(1980), from which this story is taken.*

PERSPECTIVES

1 What images of "mother-in-law" come to your mind from literature and from popular culture? You might want to do an Internet search, as well as consult a dictionary to see what word-associations arise. How do you explain any general trends of response to "mothers-in-law"?

Or Else, the Lightning God

Whenever Margaret didn't have the opportunity to talk to Suan Choo in the office about the problems with her mother-in-law, she telephoned her friend in the evening. And she did so now, reclining on the bed, freshly bathed and talcumed. Eng Kiat wasn't home, and the old one was in her room downstairs, so it was all right to speak as freely as she wanted to Suan Choo. Suan Choo had a mother-in-law too, equally troublesome, and so understood her problem perfectly. Margaret knew that the old one, though she spoke no English, understood the meanings of certain words when she heard them; her small eyes would flash, she would look up sharply when she caught words such as "mother-in-law," "money," "servant," "nuisance," convinced that she was being talked about and criticised. So Margaret, in her conversations with Suan Choo had evolved a new set of terms intended to put the old lady off the scent.

"Mother-in-law" became "dowager" or "antique," "servant" was "domestic." Sometimes failure to find appropriate alternatives forced Margaret to spell out the word, but the element of unnaturalness introduced into the conversation in this way made the old lady, who was very sharp indeed, pause to listen suspiciously.

"Suan Choo, guess what I saw when I came back from work today," she said, managing to light a cigarette with one hand while holding the receiver with the other. "Or rather, what I smelt. There was a foul smell coming from the kitchen. I rushed to see and there was an earthenpot of the Dowager's herbal medicine a-brewing as usual. The stuff had boiled over and was trickling down the sides of my poor cooker. Luckily I came back in time. Otherwise, that wretched thing would have ruined my whole kitchen. This is the third time this week, Choo, that the Dowager's left her Chinese medicine brewing while she goes off I don't know where. Later she came back and had the audacity to ask who had turned off the flame when her medicine wasn't yet properly brewed!"

Suan Choo was able to furnish a similar story of outrageous mother-in-law behaviour, and the two laughed loud and long over the phone. Margaret's cheerful mood was due partly to the doctor's assurance, when she paid one of her regular calls that morning, that he thought her chances for the baby were very much improved by the administration of the new drug. "When Doctor Lee told me to relax and have plenty of rest, I nearly said, 'You must be joking, Doctor. How can anyone relax with a mother-in-law like mine about the place?'" said Margaret and she laughed again. Not all complaints ended on such a cheerful note.

"Suan Choo, would you believe it, the Dowager actually invited a medium to my house?" cried Margaret shortly after, clutching her friend's arm. "A temple medium, one of those weird men who go into a trance and froth at the mouth? She actually made arrangements for a séance in my house! It seemed she wanted to communicate with my dead father-in-law. Imagine my fury. To make my house a den for those eerie people with their joss-sticks and prayer paper and I don't know what else! A good thing I came back in time. I nearly threw away those horrible prayer things of theirs."

No less than a full delivery of her tirade could have eased the pressure of 5
mounting anger, and after Margaret had finished giving an account of the offence, she went into more details.

"They were going to use her room for the purpose. I saw a table already laid out with those evil-looking candles and joss-sticks and glasses of water and what have you. My father-in-law's photo was on the wall—you know, the one taken of him a month before he died—that unnatural ghostly look—you remarked once how eerie it looked, and how the old man's eyes seemed to be following you, remember? Well, they had the photo on the wall, and a paper effigy of the old man, I think, on the table, against the wall—and I don't know what other rubbish. Fortunately, I came home in time to prevent it. Imagine, Choo, calling up the dead in my house. It makes my flesh creep all over. That mother-in-law of mine is driving me crazy, and Dr. Lee tells me to relax—relax, my God!"

Suan Choo, more interested this time in exploring the subject of the supernatural than in contributing to tirades against mothers-in-law, said that her aunt once conjured the spirit of her uncle in a seance and spoke to the dead one through the medium for half an hour. The aunt maintained that the medium's features had taken on those of her dead husband; she swore it was her husband sitting in the room talking to her.

"Why can't these old people leave their dead alone?" cried Margaret in exasperation. "Why must they cause trouble to others by delving into these dark, sinister things which are best left alone? Anyway, I think those people my mother-in-law associates with are a bunch of cheats, that's all. They foist upon her all sorts of herbal medicines and charms and other such rubbish, and she pays through her nose for them. And where does her money come from? Eng Kiat and me, of course! Do you know, Choo, we give that old fool two hundred dollars a month for pocket money, and she still complains it's not enough! She lives with us, there's a servant to attend to her needs, even her new clothes and slippers and umbrellas are bought for her, and she dares complain the two hundred dollars isn't enough!"

The subject of money had become a very sore one, and here Suan Choo was able to join in the complaints with equal energy, for her mother-in-law sponged outrageously on her husband, demanding money for this or for that all the time.

Margaret's anger extended to the brothers-in-law who refused to carry out their share of the duty of supporting the old one.

"There's Eng Loong, I've told you of his miserly ways so often. His business is thriving, and his wife, I hear, is making tons of money in the Stock Exchange, but they don't give one cent to the old lady. It's only the occasional *ang pow* for the Chinese New Year or the birthday, and they think they're hell of a filial," cried Margaret angrily. "Then there's that good-for-nothing Eng Chian—always flitting from one job to another. I suspect he's been borrowing money from Kiat again, but of course that husband of mine will never tell me anything. So everyone comes to Kiat stretching out a long arm and here I am slaving like a fool in the office, helping to support a host of parasites!" Margaret lit a cigarette furiously, then stubbed it out.

"I forgot," she told her friend in a softened tone. "The doctor says I'm not to smoke during this period. Hey, Choo," a smile appeared on her face, "I may have good news to tell you soon. I'm keeping my fingers crossed!"

When her husband returned from his business trip abroad, Margaret was indeed able to tell him the good news and husband and wife rejoiced, for at last, after six years of marriage, Margaret was to have a child.

"There's no need to tell the old lady yet," said Margaret. "We'll tell her only when we're perfectly sure."

They told her a month later, and Margaret was rankled by the cold indifference of her mother-in-law's response.

"Well, it is good for you," she said stiffly. "You've waited six years for a child, and now you're going to have one."

Margaret recollected the old lady's solicitous anxiety when Eng Loong's wife was pregnant; she fussed, she recommended this food and that food, she made bird's nest soup with expensive rare herbs, she was so concerned. And Mee Lian never bought her any jewellery or even a new dress. Margaret heaved in anger at the unjust antagonism of the old one.

But, she told Suan Choo and her other friends, she couldn't care a jot. She was not of that old breed who trembled in the presence of a mother-in-law and sought to please all the time.

"Today things are different," cried Margaret with spirited defiance. "It's not like in the old days when women were subject to their mothers-in-law. I remember my mum telling me that her mother-in-law nagged and scolded her everyday, and if my father wanted to take her out to the *wayang*, he had to get permission from the old gorgon. Today, it's no longer like this, ah, no more! Today, we're working wives drawing good salaries, we're independent, we're educated. Today, *they* depend on us, *they* stretch out their hands for their monthly money. So what is there to be afraid of?" Margaret described, with animation, her happy position, free of any ties of obligation to the old.

"Number One, we're financially secure, we made it on our own without any help from my husband's family," she said. "Kiat's parents didn't spend a cent on his higher education, for he got scholarships and bursaries all the way. I wouldn't want to be in Diana Lau's position. She's living with her rich in-laws; you know that famous big house in Marine Vista with the two huge stone lions at the entrance? That's the family home, and I hear Diana is scared as hell of offending her old father-in-law and mother-in-law. You know the old lady whom we met in Tai Sing Goldsmith the other day, the one glittering with diamonds? Well, I'm glad I don't have a rich mother-in-law like that; it makes things more difficult. Like this, I'm independent, I'm free, I'm not afraid of anybody."

Suan Choo had two small children and whenever she had problems with the servant, her mother-in-law came to help.

"She's quite useless with the children," said Suan Choo, "but at least I have someone in the house with the kids while Gerard and I are at work. I don't have to leave the children at a friend's, like Gek Eng does whenever the servant plays her out."

"Number Two, I don't depend on my mother-in-law to help in the house," said Margaret with energetic triumph. "My Ah Chan is most reliable and manages perfectly, and I don't have children as yet. When my baby arrives, I'm going to get Ah Chan to take care of the baby, and another servant to do the housework. My mother-in-law will never have the occasion to say, 'See, these young people depend on us their elders to see to this and that.'"

Margaret's mother, a small-sized, timid-looking woman, who was rather in awe of her strong-willed, efficient daughter, nevertheless took her aside one morning when she came on a visit, and gravely spoke about respect for the old.

"You mustn't quarrel with your mother-in-law, Margaret," she said with grave solicitousness. "Young people must heed the old; they must not raise their voice against the old. It is not good, Margaret."

Margaret said impatiently, "Mother, I agree with you. I agree with you when the old are reasonable and considerate in their behaviour. But when they are unreasonable and hypocritical and spiteful, when they are never satisfied no matter how much you do for them and criticise you behind your back, then they don't deserve the respect of the young!"

"Margaret, it is not good to talk like this, it is not good at all," said the elderly woman, with a melancholy shake of her head. "I respected my mother-in-law because of her grey hairs though she was cruel to me. The young must respect the old, Margaret, or they will be punished." And she spoke of that punishment reserved for those guilty of filial impiety, the ultimate transgression: they would be struck by the Lightning God. The Lightning God in Heaven heeds the cries of the old.

"What nonsense!" cried Margaret, and now she was really angry. She said sharply to her mother, "Mother, this is the new age. This is not the old age, when you were scared of your mother-in-law and allowed her to trample on you. There is no Lightning God today, Mother—no Lightning God or Thunder God or Kitchen God. They all died long ago."

Margaret had never seethed with such indignation before. She went out and decided to take her mind off the problems besetting her by doing some shopping. She needed some cleansing cream, and if she found something she like to put in the baby's room which was almost ready, she would get it, regardless of cost. For, Margaret thought, why should I stinge on myself and the baby, and let all the money go the spongers? I will not be so foolish.

The shopping afforded her much pleasure, and she bought a very large and very expensive panda for the baby. She wished Kiat were home, so she could show him the delightful toy. Kiat was a good, loving husband, only too soft when it came to his family. She rang Suan Choo to tell her about the shopping and uttered a little scream of surprise and delight when Suan Choo confided that she too was going to have a baby; the doctor had just confirmed it.

"I hope it'll be a boy this time, Choo," said Margaret, very glad for her friend.

"I'm thinking of the servant problem," said Suan Choo. "My mother-in-law's in one of her cranky moods again, and the earlier I get a reliable servant, the better."

And Margaret, rejoicing with her best friend, was in a sufficiently good mood to withstand her mother-in-law's latest assault upon her nerves: the old lady was making a patchwork blanket, and strewn all over her nice, clean marble floor downstairs were small pieces of cloth and bits of thread. The servant Ah Chan complained that that was the third time she had to sweep up the stuff that morning, but Margaret said, "Oh, leave her alone, Ah Chan. Otherwise, she will have something more to complain to the neighbours about." The neighbour who irritated Margaret most was the next-door washerwoman who was always talking to her mother-in-law over the fence. The two women's habit of lowering their voices and nudging each other, each time they thought Margaret was approaching, was most annoying. She was positive the old one talked about her to the next-door gossip, and she was furious. She had complained about this to her husband, but in his characteristic casual manner, he had said, "Aw, leave them alone. They're idle gossips, that's all."

Oh, when will I be rid of my burden? thought Margaret. She knew the old one would always be staying with them for Eng Loong's wife would not have her, and Eng Chian was a good-for-nothing who had difficulty supporting himself. Her Eng Kiat, because he had a good-natured disposition, was taken advantage of by all. Margaret had the idea, as yet not carefully defined as a strategy, of getting rid of the troublesome old one once her baby arrived. There must be some excuse which the coming of the baby could furnish for making arrangements for the old one to live elsewhere. It would be some months before the baby arrived; meanwhile, she would have to put up with the old lady whose ways were becoming intolerable.

"One of these days I shall blow up, I don't care what Kiat says," cried poor Margaret. "The old one's Lightning God can strike me dead if he likes!" She took some comfort from the thought that Suan Choo was also having much trouble with her mother-in-law. Suan Choo had confided, the night before, in a voice shrill with exasperation, that her mother-in-law had unreasonably quarreled with her new servant. The servant had been proving to be so reliable and efficient. Now the servant had left, and she had to start looking all over again for another one. And she was feeling so sick these days, with her frequent vomiting.

"Choo, we are in the same boat," said Margaret. "I keep telling everybody, one of these days I'm going to blow up."

She blew up shortly after this. It happened this way. Margaret was having lunch with an office colleague, who knew her next-door neighbours. It seemed that her mother-in-law had complained to the washerwoman of being ill-treated by Margaret. She was left alone in the house most of the time, she said, and she didn't have proper food.

"No proper food!" gasped Margaret and she could hardly believe what she had just heard. Her refrigerator was always full, her groceries store was stocked to the ceiling with tinned food and dried stuff for the old one to help herself to, and she was complaining of not having enough food!

It seemed, continued the colleague, the washerwoman went over one morning to see the old lady who was sitting at the table eating a bowl of rice porridge with nothing in it but soya sauce. The washerwoman was shocked and asked her why she was eating such meagre food, food not fit for a beggar, whereupon the old one started to weep. It was so pitiful that the washerwoman wept with her.

"Oh, I can't stand this, I can't stand it anymore!" cried Margaret, white with anger. "She gives me endless trouble, I load her with gifts and food and money and she goes around telling people I ill-treat her and starve her! How can I stand this? That gossipy washerwoman has no business to interfere in our affairs. I'm not going to let this pass, I promise you!" Margaret was now weeping in vexed distress. Her friend grew alarmed, for Margaret was six months pregnant now, and it was bad for a woman in her condition to be so distressed.

Margaret stormed home and confronted her mother-in-law. It was raining heavily and she got wet running from the taxi into the house, but she did not bother to dry herself; she went straight in search of the old one who was in the kitchen, and confronted her. Her words of accusation came out in angry torrents; she accused her mother-in-law of ingratitude, of deceit, of injustice to her. Her voice quavered in her anger, her knees trembled beneath her and her hands were cold, for such a situation was something new and, in retrospect, frightening to her. But she stood, firm and strong now, shrill with hurt and fury.

The old one looked up from the table where she was drinking a cup of coffee; she stared at her, first with disbelief, then with silent malevolence. Her mouth was gathered in tight lines of cold fury. Then she stood up. She said to Margaret, "So you dare speak this way to your old mother-in-law? You see the grey hairs on my head, and you dare speak to me in this way? You, who are going to be a mother yourself! You take care!" She pointed a finger at Margaret, her small grey eyes flashing with anger, but Margaret was not to be cowed easily.

"I'm not afraid of you!" she cried in a quivering indignation. "I've had enough trouble from you, and so you get out of my house!"

The old one glared at her, the small grey eyes glittering menacingly.

"You wouldn't dare do this to me if my son were here," she said slowly.

"This is MY house, it was bought in MY name, and I tell you to get out," shrieked Margaret, the hot tears rushing to her eyes.

The old one stood up to her full height, and she said, in a clear, shrill voice, "All right. Listen, then, daughter-in-law. In this house you have treated me like dirt, you have made me feel worse than a prisoner. You follow me about with your eyes when I want to speak to my son, and you are not happy when my son is good to me and gives me money. Don't think I'm not aware of all this! So I leave now, but before I go, let me tell you this. Those who are cruel to their elders will never prosper! They are cursed. I curse you now; you are bearing a child, but I curse you!"

The roar of the rain outside almost drowned her words, but Margaret heard, and a thrill of terror ran through her. But she remained in the standing posture of defiance, though her heart was beating violently. The old one went into her room, put some things into a paper bag and left with an umbrella, in the pouring rain.

By herself, Margaret ran up to her room, threw herself upon the bed and wept bitterly. Oh, how hateful everything was! How simply hateful! Why was she so unlucky as to be suffering all this? In her distress, she put a long distance call to her husband to come home.

When he arrived, the next evening, he found her inert on the bed, the tears falling silently down her cheeks. She clung to him, crying dismally. He was alarmed on the baby's account and soothed her as best he could, but inwardly he was irked: "These women—will they never stop their nonsense." Unable to criticise his wife or mother, he lashed out in full fury against the washerwoman, now seen as the cause of all the trouble.

His task, after he had soothed Margaret and made her comfortable, was to look for his mother and make sure she had come to no harm. And he groaned again to himself, and shook his head, "These women—they give endless trouble."

He was relieved to find that the old one had gone to Eng Loong's house and was now under the care of Eng Loong and Mee Lian. He explained as best he could, the two brothers shook their heads, and Mee Lian bustled about to make her old mother-in-law comfortable, for she had caught cold in the rain.

"So it's me, the villainess, sending out an old white-haired woman into the rain and storm," cried Margaret with a sharp laugh, when Eng Kiat returned and told her of what had happened.

She felt unwell and lay in bed for a long time. She fretted and grew irritable, and snapped at her husband and servant. The nights were more distressful for she couldn't sleep—her head swarmed with troubling thoughts and her heart was charged with troubling feelings. Again and again she saw the old one, standing upright, with hand raised and finger pointing upwards, and heard her shrill cry ring out, "I curse you! You are with child, but still I curse you!"

The glint of malevolence in the old eyes Margaret could never forget. She 55
trembled each time she recollected that glare of malice in the old face, the white hair that had loosened from the knot at the back of her head and floated in stiff strands about the face. It was ghastly. It was horrible. Margaret closed her eyes tight to shut off that evil scene, but it would come back, again and again. In her dreams, it took on a vividness and monstrosity that caused her to wake up screaming; in her dreams, the old one's features assumed a demonic leer and her voice a demonic shriek so that the curse rang piercingly in Margaret's ears. She woke up screaming and clung to her husband sobbing.

"She cursed me, your mother cursed me, and I'm already seven months with child," she sobbed in her fear. Eng Kiat, haggard with sleeplessness, tried his best to soothe her. He kept reassuring her that everything would be all right, that old people, especially uneducated ones like his mother, cursed when they were angry, and said all sorts of bizarre things.

"Her curse was terrible, she meant every word of it," said Margaret. "Yesterday and today," she continued with a sob, "the child inside me did not move. Didn't even stir once. I swear to you, Kiat, our baby hasn't moved for two days!"

A tremor of terror ran through the husband, but he only said, with feigned casualness, "Now, now, that's being morbid, darling, and that's not like you at all. You had a bad experience and are now imagining all sorts of things. I'll take you to see Dr. Lee tomorrow morning. You'll see that everything is all right."

Dr. Lee said that there was nothing wrong. Mother and child were doing well, and all Margaret needed was a lot of rest. On reaching home, Margaret told her husband that she noticed that Dr. Lee looked worried; perhaps he had discovered something about her baby but was not willing to tell her? Eng Kiat said impatiently, "What nonsense!" but Margaret insisted that he took longer than usual to examine her and there was a frown on his face.

She had lost her appetite and was feeling utterly wretched. A frightened look had come into her eyes; in one of her dreams, her baby was stillborn, in another it had arms but no legs. Margaret sat up in bed in the darkness, and put her hands to her mouth to stifle the sobs, for she did not want to disturb her husband in his sleep.

Suan Choo rang up. Margaret hadn't spoken to Suan Choo for days and was glad to hear her friend's voice. Suan Choo spoke weakly. She was in hospital, recovering from a miscarriage. When she hung up, Margaret stood still, her eyes dilated in terror, her hands cold. Suan Choo had quarrelled with her mother-in-law, and this was her punishment. The power of the curse of the old! Margaret picked up the phone again, rang frantically for Suan Choo, and told her, in stricken whispers, what she thought.

"But that's impossible. The quarrel was some time ago, and besides, my mother-in-law never cursed me. Anyway, we are okay now, and she's helping out with the kids," said Suan Choo, terrified nevertheless by the possibility.

"No, no, Choo, you don't believe it, but it's true! I tell you it's true, their curse is powerful!" sobbed Margaret.

She grew distracted, not wanting her husband to be out of her sight, and she told Dr. Lee tearfully that she felt the child was dying inside her or would be born to torment her.

"On the day she cursed me, there was thunder and lightning," she said in an awestricken voice.

She was in a dark building, which was a temple, for there were red pillars and niches in the walls in which a number of gods sat brooding. Some of them were hidden in the shadows, but she knew they were just watching her. The smell of smoke from the giant joss-sticks in a large gold urn on the floor stung her eyes and made her cough a little, and when the tears cleared, she saw, curled round the joss-sticks, snakes of a variety of sizes and colours. They were dull-eyed and their bodies moved slowly, lugubriously, on the joss-sticks, as if drowsed by the fumes. A long time ago, when she was a little girl, she had gone with her mother and aunt to a Chinese temple which housed hundreds of snakes that were supposed to be holy, and she had hidden behind her mother and cried when a snake slowly lifted its head and cast a beady eye on her. Now she looked upon the snakes on the joss-sticks unafraid, for she knew the poison had been taken out of them long ago. They continued to move slowly, ponderously, and then they slithered down to the floor towards her and were all over her, so that she gasped and choked and tried to pull them off. She saw her mother-in-law at a distance, holding a bunch of small joss-sticks in her hand

and getting ready to stick them into the ash in an urn on the temple altar. She called to her mother-in-law to help her pull off the snakes; the old one didn't appear to hear her and went on arranging the joss-sticks neatly in the urn, then some oranges on a plate, and some fragrant flowers in a vases, in readiness for an offering to the temple gods. One of the gods in the niches stirred to life; Margaret called to him to help her disengage the snakes which seemed to have increased in number; two were around her neck; a multitude were on her arms, bosoms, and legs.

"Please—," she choked and the god who had awakened stepped out and advanced upon her. She looked pleadingly at him; his visage was now her mother-in-law's with the glinting eyes and stiff white hair streaming in the storm, now her father-in-law's, with the malevolent leer.

"Please—," sobbed Margaret, and she put her arms protectively round her swollen belly, afraid her child would be harmed.

She woke up, panting, her wet hair clinging to her face and neck.

Dr. Lee took Eng Kiat aside to discuss Margaret's illness and to recommend psychiatric treatment.

"She's under some obsession which is driving her to distraction; it will be bad for the baby," said the doctor and for the first time, Eng Kiat, under enormous pressure for weeks, broke down and wept.

Margaret's mother consulted a temple medium. In a trance, he said that the only thing that could save Margaret's sanity and the child's life was to have the mother-in-law write certain words on a prayer paper which should then be burnt and the ashes put in water for Margaret to drink. Only in this way would the curse be lifted and Margaret's peace of mind restored.

When told of the temple medium's advice, Margaret, drawn, haggard and hollow-eyed, asked in a small pleading voice, "Do you think it'll work? Do you think it'll save my baby?"

The mother-in-law, recovering from her illness in Eng Loong's house and attended by Mee Lian, refused to write the words for the prayer paper.

"Don't ask me to do anything for her, and don't mention her name in my hearing again," she snapped, sitting in a chair in a corner of the room from which she seldom stirred. There was a look of hard resolution in her eyes.

Margaret herself came to plead. She had grown very thin, but her belly was huge and heavy. She was wearing a long housecoat, and a faded woollen cardigan. Eng Kiat had his arm protectively round her shoulders. When she was brought in front of the old lady, she immediately went up with a sob, but the old one turned aside sharply, and refused to look at her.

"Mother, please," sobbed Margaret and could not go on. Her mother and Mee Lian wept with her, and the sons pleaded with the old one to grant them the favour.

She sat still unmoved, her lips tightly compressed, her brow dark with displeasure. When they continued pleading, she moved a hand impatiently and cried out, in shrill petulance, "All right! Give me the paper to write and be gone! Leave me in peace!" The brush was put in her hand, the temple medium's words were dictated by Margaret's mother, and in a few seconds she had finished.

"Now go, all of you!" she cried imperiously. And according to the temple medium's instructions, the prayer paper was burnt, the ashes were dropped into a glass of water, and Margaret drank gratefully, reverently, to the last drop.

CHARTING THE STORY

1 Why are Margaret and Eng Kiat entrusted with the housing and care of Eng Kiat's mother? Does the mother seem to appreciate the fragility of that arrangement? Why/why not?

2 What are some of the old traditions that the "thoroughly modern Margaret" wishes to debunk? How does she go about this?

3 What views of marriage and/or partnership does Margaret seem to hold—in particular as manifested in her angry response to her mother-in-law in Paragraph 46?

CONSIDERATIONS OF STYLE

1 In what respects does Margaret's dream towards the end of the story become the vehicle that resolves the story's conflicts? How would leaving it out have changed the story?

2 Is Margaret set up to be a "sympathetic character," one that a reader is led to identify with? How so/how not?

AFTERTHOUGHTS

1 Comparing this story with Chitra Divakaruni's "Mrs Dutta Writes a Letter," how do the principals in the multigenerational household interact in both similar and in different ways?

2 In 1980, when this story was written, the term "women's liberation" might have been used to describe a phenomenon that ten years later would probably be referred to as "the women's movement," of "the feminist movement." What differing significations do the various terms suggest? Which might appeal most to Margaret?

THE WRITER'S CRAFT

1 Write a letter of farewell from the dying grandmother (Eng Kiat's mother) to her toddler grandchild, connecting him/her to the family history and heritage.

2 From the point of view of the washerwoman or of Eng Kiat, write of the events that led up to the mother-in-law's curse.

MARGARET LAURENCE

MARGARET LAURENCE *was born in Neepawa, Manitoba in 1926. Her mother died when she was four, and her father when she was nine, after which she and her baby brother went to live with their maternal grandfather. Undaunted by the sadness of her loss, she later wrote: "I was an extremely fortunate child... always interested in reading and in writing [and] always had someone there who encouraged me." She graduated from United College (now the University of Winnipeg) in 1947, and in the same year married John Fergus Laurence, a civil engineer. The Laurences lived for a year in England, and five years in Africa (British Somaliland and Ghana), before moving back to Vancouver and later again to England.*

During her African stay, Laurence wrote translations of Somali prose and poetry; a travel book, The Prophet's Camel Bell; *her first novel,* This Side Jordan *(1961); a collection of short stories,* The Tomorrow Tamer *(1963); and a study of Nigerian fiction and drama,* Long Drums and Cannons.

In the ten-year period between 1964 and 1974, she published five more novels and a collection of essays, Heart of a Stranger *(1976). Among her many honors, Laurence received honorary degrees from more than a dozen Canadian universities, was made a Companion of the Order of Canada in 1971, and was the subject of a documentary film,* Margaret Laurence—First Lady of Manawaka, *which was produced by the National Film Board of Canada and premiered in 1971. She died in 1987.*

"The Loons" is anthologized in The Last Map Is the Heart: An Anthology of Western Canadian Fiction *(1989).*

PERSPECTIVES

1 How are "half-breeds" (or *Métis)* generally characterized in popular representations in the United States and Canada? Do the characterizations differ in Canadian and US discourse?

2 What romanticized notions about First Nations or Native Americans are held by others in Canada and the United States, and what accounts for these views?

The Loons

Just below Manawaka, where the Wachakwa River ran brown and noisy over the pebbles, the scrub oak and grey-green willow and chokecherry bushes grew in a dense thicket. In a clearing at the centre of the thicket stood the Tonnerre family's shack. The basis of this dwelling was a small square cabin made of poplar poles and chinked with mud, which had been built by Jules Tonnerre some fifty years before, when he came back from Batoche with a bullet in his thigh, the year that Riel was hung and the voices of the Métis entered their long silence. Jules had only intended to stay the winter in the Wachakwa Valley, but the family was still there in the thirties, when I was a child. As the Tonnerres had increased, their settlement had been added to, until the clearing at the foot of the town hill was a chaos of lean-tos, wooden packing cases, warped lumber, discarded car tires, ramshackle chicken coops, tangled strands of barbed wire and rusty tin cans.

The Tonnerres were French half-breeds, and among themselves they spoke a *patois* that was neither Cree nor French. Their English was broken and full of obscenities. They did not belong among the Cree of the Galloping Mountain reservation, further north, and they did not belong among the Scots-Irish and Ukrainians of Manawaka, either. They were, as my Grandmother MacLeod would have put it, neither flesh, fowl, nor good salt herring. When their men were not working at odd jobs or as section hands on the CPR, they lived on relief. In the summers, one of the Tonnerre youngsters, with a face that seemed totally unfamiliar with laughter, would knock at the doors of the town's brick houses and offer for sale a lard-pail of bruised wild strawberries, and if he got as much as a quarter he would grab the coin and run before the customer had time to change her mind. Sometimes old Jules, or his son Lazarus, would get mixed up in a Saturday-night brawl, and would hit out at whoever was nearest, or howl drunkenly among the offended shoppers on Main Street, and then the Mountie would put them for the night in the barred cell underneath the Court House, and the next morning they would be quiet again.

Piquette Tonnerre, the daughter of Lazarus, was in my class at school. She was older than I, but she had failed several grades, perhaps because her attendance had always been sporadic and her interest in school-work negligible. Part of the reason she had missed a lot of school was that she had had tuberculosis of the bone, and had once spent many months in hospital. I knew this because my father was the doctor who had looked after her. Her sickness was the only thing I knew about her, however. Otherwise, she existed for me only as a vaguely embarrassing presence, with her hoarse voice and her clumsy limping walk and her grimy cotton dresses that were always miles too long. I was neither friendly nor unfriendly towards her. She dwelt and moved somewhere within my scope of vision, but I did not actually notice her very much until that peculiar summer when I was eleven.

"I don't know what to do about that kid," my father said at dinner one evening. "Piquette Tonnerre, I mean. That damn bone's flared up again. I've had her in hospital for quite a while now, and it's under control all right, but I hate like the dickens to send her home again."

"Couldn't you explain to her mother that she has to rest a lot?" my mother said.

"The mother's not there," my father replied. "She took off a few years back. Can't say I blame her. Piquette cooks for them, and she says Lazarus would never do anything for himself as long as she's there. Anyway, I don't think she'd take much care of herself, once she got back. She's only thirteen, after all. Beth, I was thinking—what about taking her up to Diamond Lake with us this summer? A couple of months' rest would give that bone a much better chance."

My mother looked stunned.

"But Ewen—what about Roddie and Vanessa?"

"She's not contagious," my father said. "And it would be company for Vanessa."

"Oh dear," my mother said in distress, "I'll bet anything she has nits in her hair."

"For Pete's sake," my father said crossly, "do you think Matron would let her stay in the hospital for all this time like that? Don't be silly, Beth."

Grandmother MacLeod, her delicately featured face as rigid as a cameo, now brought her mauve-veined hands together as though she were about to begin a prayer.

"Ewen, if that half-breed youngster comes along to Diamond Lake, I'm not going," she announced. "I'll go to Morag's for the summer."

I had trouble in stifling my urge to laugh, for my mother brightened visibly and quickly tried to hide it. If it came to a choice between Grandmother MacLeod and Piquette, Piquette would win hands down, nits or not.

"It might be quite nice for you, at that," she mused. "You haven't seen Morag for over a year, and you might enjoy being in the city for a while. Well, Ewen dear, you do what you think best. If you think it would do Piquette some good, then we'll be glad to have her, as long as she behaves herself."

So it happened that several weeks later, when we all piled into my father's old Nash, surrounded by suitcases and boxes of provisions and toys for my ten-month-old brother, Piquette was with us and Grandmother MacLeod, miraculously, was not. My father would only be staying at the cottage for a couple of weeks, for he had to get back to his practice, but the rest of us would stay at Diamond Lake until the end of August.

Our cottage was not named, as many were, "Dew Drop Inn," or "Bide-a-Wee," or "Bonnie Doon." The sign on the roadway bore in austere letters only our name, MacLeod. It was not a large cottage, but it was on the lakefront. You could look out the windows and see, through the filigree of the spruce trees, the water glistening greenly as the sun caught it. All around the cottage were ferns, and sharp-branched raspberry bushes, and moss that had grown over fallen tree trunks. If you looked carefully among the weeds and grass, you could find wild strawberry plants which were in white flower now and in another month would bear fruit, the fragrant globes hanging like miniature scarlet lanterns on the thin hairy stems. The two grey squirrels were still there, gossiping at us from the tall spruce beside the cottage, and by the end of the summer they would again be tame enough to take pieces of crust from my hands. The broad moose antlers that hung above the back door were a little more bleached and fissured after the winter, but otherwise everything was the same. I raced joyfully around my kingdom, greeting all the places I had not seen for a year. My brother, Roderick, who had not been born when we were here last summer, sat on the car rug in the sunshine and examined a brown spruce cone, meticulously turning it round and round in his small and curious hands. My mother and father toted the luggage from car to cottage, exclaiming over how well the place had wintered, no broken windows, thank goodness, no apparent damage from storm-felled branches or snow.

Only after I had finished looking around did I notice Piquette. She was sitting on the swing, her lame leg held stiffly out, and her other foot scuffing the ground as she swung slowly back and forth. Her long hair hung black and straight around her shoulders, and her broad coarse-featured face bore no expression—it was blank, as though she was no longer dwelt within her own skull, as though she had gone elsewhere. I approached her very hesitantly.

"Want to come and play?"

Piquette looked at me with a sudden flash of scorn. 20

"I ain't a kid," she said.

Wounded, I stamped angrily away, swearing I would not speak to her for the rest of the summer. In the days that followed, however, Piquette began to interest me, and I began to want to interest her. My reasons did not appear bizarre to me. Unlikely as it may seem, I had only just realized that the Tonnerre family, whom I had always heard called half-breeds, were actually Indians, or as near as made no difference. My acquaintance with Indians was not extensive. I did not remember ever having seen a real Indian, and my new awareness that Piquette sprang from the people of Big Bear and Poundmaker, of Tecumseh, of the Iroquois who had eaten Father Brébeuf's heart—all this gave her an instant attraction in my eyes. I was a devoted reader of Pauline Johnson at this age, and sometimes would orate aloud and in an exalted voice, *"West Wind, blow from your prairie nest; Blow from the mountains, blow from the west"*—and so on. It seemed to me that Piquette must be in some way a daughter of the forest, a kind of junior prophetess of the wilds, who might impart to me, if I took the right approach, some of the secrets which she undoubtedly knew—where the whippoorwill made her nest, how the coyote reared her young, or whatever it was that it said in *Hiawatha*.

I set about gaining Piquette's trust. She was not allowed to go swimming, with her bad leg, but I managed to lure her down to the beach—or rather, she came because there was nothing else to do. The water was always icy, for the lake was fed by springs, but I swam like a dog, thrashing my arms and legs around at such speed and with such an output of energy that I never grew cold. Finally, when I had had enough, I came out and sat beside Piquette on the sand. When she saw me approaching, her hand squashed flat the sand castle she had been building, and she looked at me sullenly, without speaking.

"Do you like this place?" I asked, after a while, intending to lead on from there into the question of forest lore.

Piquette shrugged. "It's okay. Good as anywhere."

"I love it," I said. "We come here every summer."

"So what?" Her voice was distant, and I glanced at her uncertainly, wondering what I could have said wrong.

"Do you want to come for a walk?" I asked her. "We wouldn't need to go far. If you walk just around the point there, you come to a bay where great big reeds grow in the water, and all kinds of fish hang around there. Want to? Come on."

She shook her head.

"Your dad said I ain't supposed to do no more walking than I got to."

I tried another line.

"I bet you know a lot about the woods and all that, eh?" I began respectfully.

Piquette looked at me from her large, dark, unsmiling eyes.

"I don't know what the hell you're talkin' about," she replied. "You nuts or somethin'? If you mean where my old man, and me, and all them live, you better shut up, by Jesus, you hear?"

I was startled and my feelings were hurt, but I had a kind of dogged perseverance. I ignored her rebuff.

"You know something, Piquette? There's loons here, on this lake. You can see their nests just up the shore there, behind those logs. At night, you can hear them even from the cottage, but it's better to listen from the beach. My dad says we should listen and try to remember how they sound, because in a few years when more cottages are built at Diamond Lake and more people come in, the loons will go away."

Piquette was picking up stones and snail shells and then dropping them again.

"Who gives a goddamn?" she said.

It became increasingly obvious that, as an Indian, Piquette was a dead loss. That evening I went out by myself, scrambling through the bushes that overhung the steep path, my feet slipping on the fallen spruce needles that covered the ground. When I reached the shore, I walked along the firm, damp sand to the small pier that my father had built, and sat down there. I heard someone else crashing through the undergrowth and the bracken, and for a moment I thought Piquette had changed her mind, but it turned out to be my father. He sat beside me on the pier and we waited, without speaking.

At night the lake was like black glass with a stream of amber which was 40
the path of the moon. All around, the spruce trees grew tall and close-set, branches blackly sharp against the sky, which was lightened by a cold flickering of stars. Then the loons began their calling. They rose like phantom birds from the nests on the shore, and flew out onto the dark, still surface of the water.

No one can ever describe that ululating sound, the crying of the loons, and no one who has heard it can ever forget it. Plaintive, and yet with a quality of chilling mockery, those voices belonged to a world separated by aeons from our neat world of summer cottages and the lighted lamps of home.

"They must have sounded just like that," my father remarked, "before any person set foot here."

Then he laughed. "You could say the same, of course, about sparrows, or chipmunks, but somehow it only strikes you that way with the loons."

"I know," I said.

Neither of us suspected that this would be the last time we would ever sit 45
here together on the shore, listening. We stayed for perhaps half an hour, and then we went back to the cottage. My mother was reading beside the fireplace. Piquette was looking at the burning birch log, and not doing anything.

"You should have come along," I said, although in fact I was glad she had not.

"Not me," Piquette said. "You wouldn't catch me walkin' way down there jus' for a bunch of squawkin' birds."

Piquette and I remained ill at ease with one another. I felt I had somehow failed my father, but I did not know what was the matter, nor why she would not or could not respond when I suggested exploring the woods or playing house. I thought it was probably her slow and difficult walking that held her back. She stayed most of the time in the cottage with my mother, helping her with the dishes or with Roddie, but hardly ever talking. Then the Duncans arrived at their cottage, and I spent my days with Mavis, who was my best friend. I could not reach Piquette at all, and I soon lost interest in trying. But all that summer she remained as both a reproach and a mystery to me.

That winter my father died of pneumonia, after less than a week's illness. For some time I saw nothing around me, being completely immersed in my own pain and my mother's. When I looked outward once more, I scarcely noticed that Piquette Tonnerre was no longer at school. I do not remember seeing her at all until four years later, one Saturday night when Mavis and I were having Cokes at the Regal Café. The jukebox was booming like tuneful thunder, and beside it, leaning lightly on its chrome and its rainbow glass, was a girl.

Piquette must have been seventeen then although she looked about 50
twenty. I stared at her, astounded that anyone could have changed so much. Her face, so stolid and expressionless before, was animated now with a gaiety

that was almost violent. She laughed and talked very loudly with the boys around her. Her lipstick was bright carmine, and her hair was cut short and frizzily permed. She had not been pretty as a child, and she was not pretty now, for her features were still heavy and blunt. But her dark and slightly slanted eyes were beautiful, and her skin-tight skirt and orange sweater displayed to enviable advantage a soft and slender body.

She saw me, and walked over. She teetered a little, but it was not due to her once-tubercular leg, for her limp was almost gone.

"Hi, Vanessa." Her voice still had the same hoarseness. "Long time no see, eh?"

"Hi," I said. "Where've you been keeping yourself, Piquette?"

"Oh, I been around," she said. "I been away almost two years now. Been all over the place—Winnipeg, Regina, Saskatoon. Jesus, what I could tell you! I come back this summer, but I ain't stayin'. You kids goin' to the dance?"

"No," I said abruptly, for this was a sore point with me. I was fifteen, and thought I was old enough to go to the Saturday-night dances at the Flamingo. My mother, however, thought otherwise.

"Y'oughta come," Piquette said. "I never miss one. It's just about the on'y thing in this jerkwater town that's any fun. Boy, you couldn' catch me stayin' here. I don't give a shit about this place. It stinks."

She sat down beside me, and I caught the harsh over-sweetness of her perfume.

"Listen, you wanna know something, Vanessa?" she confided, her voice only slightly blurred. "Your dad was the only person in Manawaka that ever done anything good to me."

I nodded speechlessly. I was certain she was speaking the truth. I knew a little more than I had that summer at Diamond Lake, but I could not reach her now any more than I had then. I was ashamed, ashamed of my own timidity, the frightened tendency to look the other way. Yet I felt no real warmth towards her—I only felt that I ought to, because of that distant summer and because my father had hoped she would be company for me, or perhaps that I would be for her, but it had not happened that way. At this moment, meeting her again, I had to admit that she repelled and embarrassed me, and I could not help despising the self-pity in her voice. I wished she would go away. I did not want to see her. I did not know what to say to her. It seemed that we had nothing to say to one another.

"I'll tell you something else," Piquette went on. "All the old bitches an' biddies in this town will sure be surprised. I'm gettin' married this fall—my boyfriend, he's an English fella, works in the stockyards in the city there, a very tall guy, got blond wavy hair. Gee, is he ever handsome. Got this real classy name. Alvin Gerald Cummings—some handle, eh? They call him Al."

For the merest instant, then, I saw her. I really did see her, for the first and only time in all the years we had both lived in the same town. Her defiant face, momentarily, became unguarded and unmasked, and in her eyes there was a terrifying hope.

"Gee, Piquette—" I burst out awkwardly, "that's swell. That's really wonderful. Congratulations—good luck—I hope you'll be happy—"

As I mouthed the conventional phrases, I could only guess how great her need must have been, that she had been forced to seek the very things she so bitterly rejected.

When I was eighteen, I left Manawaka and went away to college. At the end of my first year, I came back home for the summer. I spent the first few days in talking non-stop with my mother, as we exchanged all the news that someone had not found its way into letters—what had happened in my life and what had happened in Manawaka while I was away. My mother searched her memory for events that concerned people I knew.

"Did I ever write you about Piquette Tonnerre, Vanessa?" she asked one morning.

"No, I don't think so," I replied. "Last I heard of her, she was going to marry some guy in the city. Is she still there?"

My mother looked perturbed, and it was a moment before she spoke, as though she did not know how to express what she had to tell and wished she did not need to try.

"She's dead," she said at last. Then, as I stared at her, "Oh, Vanessa, when it happened, I couldn't help thinking of her as she was that summer—so sullen and gauche and badly dressed. I couldn't help wondering if we could have done something more at that time—but what could we do? She used to be around in the cottage there with me all day, and honestly, it was all I could do to get a word out of her. She didn't even talk to your father very much, although I think she liked him, in her way."

"What happened?" I asked.

"Either her husband left her, or she left him," my mother said. "I don't know which. Anyway, she came back here with two youngsters, both only babies—they must have been born very close together. She kept house, I guess, for Lazarus and her brothers, down in the valley there, in the old Tonnerre place. I used to see her on the street sometimes, but she never spoke to me. She'd put on an awful lot of weight, and she looked a mess, to tell you the truth, a real slattern dressed any old how. She was up in court a couple of times—drunk and disorderly, of course. One Saturday night last winter, during the coldest weather, Piquette was alone in the shack with the children. The Tonnerres made home brew all the time, so I've heard, and Lazarus said later she'd been drinking most of the day when he and the boys went out that evening. They had an old woodstove there—you know the kind, with exposed pipes. The shack caught fire. Piquette didn't get out, and neither did the children."

I did not say anything. As so often with Piquette, there did not seem to be anything to say. There was a kind of silence around the image in my mind of the fire and the snow, and I wished I could put from my memory the look that I had seen once in Piquette's eyes.

I went up to Diamond Lake for a few days that summer, with Mavis and her family. The MacLeod cottage had been sold after my father's death, and I did not even go to look at it, not wanting to witness my long-ago kingdom possessed now by strangers. But one evening I went down to the shore by myself.

The small pier which my father had built was gone, and in its place there was a large and solid pier built by the government, for Galloping Mountain was now a national park, and Diamond Lake had been renamed Lake Wapakata, for it was felt that an Indian name would have a greater appeal to tourists. The one store had become several dozen, and the settlement had all the attributes of a flourishing resort—hotels, a dance-hall, cafés with neon signs, the penetrating odours of chips and hot dogs.

I sat on the government pier and looked out across the water. At night the lake at least was the same as it had always been, darkly shining and bearing within its black glass the streak of amber that was the path of the moon. There was no wind that evening, and everything was quiet all around me. It seemed too quiet, and then I realized that the loons were no longer there. I listened for some time, to make sure, but never once did I hear that long-drawn call, half mocking and half plaintive, spearing through the stillness across the lake.

I did not know what had happened to the birds. Perhaps they had gone away to some far place of belonging. Perhaps they had been unable to find such a place, and had simply died out, having ceased to care any longer whether they lived or not.

I remembered how Piquette had scorned to come along, when my father and I sat there and listened to the lake birds. It seemed to me now that in some unconscious and totally unrecognized way, Piquette might have been the only one, after all, who had heard the crying of the loons.

CHARTING THE STORY

1 Why is Piquette invited to come along with the narrator's family to Diamond Lake, and how does each member of the family react to this prospect?

2 What underlies the narrator's desire to "gain Piquette's trust" and otherwise befriend her? How does their relationship change over the summer? How does Piquette herself change over the years after the summer at the lake, and to what do you attribute her transformations?

CONSIDERATIONS OF STYLE

1 How is Piquette's way of speaking different from Vanessa's, and how does this help to characterize her?

3 What metaphoric significance do the loons have in this narrative? Why is their call particularly haunting to those with ears for it? Why do they disappear? And why is Piquette presented, in the last paragraph, as perhaps "the only one, after all, who had heard the crying of the loons"?

AFTERTHOUGHTS

1 How does turning Diamond Lake into Lake Wapakata, and outfitting it with a "government pier" and all the other *acoutrements,* change it? How does the nationalization of this land connect thematically with Piquette Tonnerre?

2 Grandmother MacLeod characterizes the Tonnerres, in Paragraph 2, as "neither flesh, fowl, or good salt herring." Would she have seen them differently if she had learned that they were, as Vanessa discovers them to be, in Paragraph 22, "actually Indians, or as near as made no difference"?

THE WRITER'S CRAFT

1 In character as Vanessa's father, write notes for Piquette's chart detailing what treatment you would consider appropriate for her, especially considering her family life.

2 Write about a situation you experienced where your preconceptions about another person's cultural background, politics, religion, race, gender, or other characteristics (about which you thought you knew quite a bit) actually got in the way of your knowing that person.

HERB WHARTON

HERB WHARTON *was born in Cunnamulla, Queensland. He began his working life as a drover (an occupation similar to that of the American West's cowboy, but herding sheep more often than cattle). His maternal grandmother was of the Kooma people; both grandfathers were Irish-English. His publications include the novel* Unbranded *(1992) and the story collections* Cattle Camp *(1994) and* Where Ya' Been, Mate? *(1996), from which this story is taken. He is presently a full-time writer, lecturing at universities, leading workshops, and occasionally going abroad, as he did in 1995 to Germany as part of the writers' group in the Experience Australia tour.*

We see in this story that for one hardy opal prospector seeking his fortune in the Australian outback, perseverance pays—and so does luck.

PERSPECTIVES

1 What notions of prospectors (whether for gold, gems, other rarities) do you bring to your reading of this text? To what do you attribute these notions?

2 Think of one of your greatest achievements in life thus far. A goal reached. A dream realized. How did the achievement change you? What about you stayed the same?

A New Wardrobe for Rainbow Jack

In the harsh glare of summer sunlight, shimmering heat waves rose from the unpainted corrugated tin roof of the outback pub as a battered old Land Rover pulled up. A red-faced old man alighted, his clothes covered in a layer of fine red dust. His face was almost hidden by a green bandanna and his hat was pulled down over his eyes. He looked like some outlaw from the American Wild West, but he had not come to rob the pub. He wore the bandanna for protection against the hot summer wind that peeled his lips and made his red face even redder.

The pub seemed silent and empty, except for the old kangaroo dog that scratched itself as it lay on the warped floorboards of the pub veranda. The old man, who was known as Diamond Jim, gazed back towards the dust cloud made by another car approaching from the north. There was still no sound from inside the pub. The door stood open, the windows on either side were propped open with short pieces of wood. Diamond Jim looked towards the windmill and watering trough a short distance away and saw some goats camped in the shade of a mulga tree. By now the dog had stopped scratching and lay still. Diamond Jim lowered the bandanna from his face. The only things that stirred were the dust from the approaching car and a big willy-willy. Diamond Jim watched as the willy-willy went dancing and whirling across the hot red landscape stirring up the fine red dust. The top went spiralling in the cloudless hazy sky, pieces of paper, grass stalks and roly-poly plants caught up in it. *Like devils dancing on their way to hell,* thought Diamond Jim.

He was soon brought back to reality as the fast-approaching car came to a halt with a squeal of brakes not half a metre from where he stood. A thick cloud of red dust arose, enveloping Diamond Jim. He coughed, then cursed at the man who emerged from the battered Holden ute. "Ya silly old bugger. Why don't ya act your age?" he asked the dark man known as Rainbow Jack, who was as ancient as himself.

Rainbow Jack, a mischievous gleam in his brown eyes, slapped his battered old Akubra hat against his leg. More dust rose from his tattered trousers. He put his hat back on then pulled it down tight over his greying hair, and hitched up the piece of cord that acted as his belt, ignoring the tirade of abuse that came from Diamond Jim. "Ya found any opal lately, mate?" asked Rainbow Jack.

"Wouldn't tell ya if I did," said Diamond Jim. "You're always trying to find out where I get me opal. Bet ya haven't found any of that rich opal ya always claim ya know about yet."

"I'm not really looking for opal, old mate," Rainbow Jack replied. "As I've told ya before I only come out bush to wear out me old clothes. I just scratch around out here waiting for the old clothes to wear out completely. When they do, I'll return to the city and buy new ones, then live there until *they* start to wear out. And when they do I'll come back out west again. The outback is a real good place to wear out me old clothes."

Diamond Jim lifted his hat and scratched his balding head, watching Rainbow as he walked through the powdery red bulldust to the veranda where he was greeted by the kangaroo dog. Rainbow patted the dog and talked softly to it, and it licked his dust-covered boots and dirty trouser legs. The floorboards creaked as Rainbow continued on to the bar room door. Following close behind came Diamond. As he walked past the old dog, it began to sniff at his boots and trouser legs. In a flash Diamond Jim spun around and kicked the dog in the guts. "Bloody pan-licking bastard!" he shouted as the dog let out a loud yelp.

Rainbow turned in the doorway and a frown seemed to cross his brow. For a moment his eyes lost their mischievous gleam. As he watched the dog, its tail between its legs, disappear around the corner of the pub, he recalled the not so distant past. *Times sure are changing,* he thought; it seemed only yesterday that his own people were treated like that old dog. Working all day for no wages, then fed on the woodheap after a kick in the guts. Rainbow really felt for that old kangaroo dog.

Inside the pub they were greeted by a big old man who talked with a foreign accent. Breasting up to the bar counter, both men ordered rums and began to talk to the publican, who had lived out here for almost forty years. No-one seemed to know just where'd he'd come from, or how to pronounce or spell his name, which was made up of lots of *x's, y's* and *z's,* but whenever the publican had an argument with anyone he got called "Ya bloody wog bastard," so he was referred to simply as "Woggy." Woggy's real name was spelled with about twenty letters. Most people who lived out here could only read ear marks and horse and cattle brands, made up of just three letters, numbers or symbols. So it was much easier to say "Woggy."

Woggy poured rums for Rainbow and Diamond then asked if they had 10
any opal for sale. Besides being the publican he acted as opal buyer and storekeeper for the few travellers who came along, mostly people who had taken the wrong turn way back in the mulga and become lost. Sometimes stockmen from the big stations came here for their drinking sprees, along with men like Rainbow Jack and Diamond Jim, who scratched for a living, digging for opal in the hard red earth.

Woggy took a jug of water from the smoking kerosene fridge and placed it on the bar. Diamond Jim was so-called because of the drop of sweat that always seemed to hang from the tip of his nose. Even now, as Rainbow watched Diamond unroll on the bar counter a piece of cloth containing some opals, that drop of sweat hung from his nose, and as he talked to Woggy and moved his head from side to side in the dim light of the bar room, the dewdrop changed and became a diamond. With one swipe of his shirt sleeve he wiped it from his nose and began to tell Woggy how good his pieces of opal were. They weren't bad stones, Rainbow thought as he looked closer at the gleaming opal pieces. But they didn't sparkle like the dewdrop that always hung from Diamond Jim's nose.

Woggy, studying the opals, said, "A little bit of colour, but not much."

"Bullshit, there's plenty of colour in these," said Diamond Jim. So they argued about the value of the opals for a while. Then Woggy offered a price for them and Diamond Jim exploded.

"Ya robbing wog bastard. They're worth triple that price."

"Not worth anything, not worth anything!" yelled Woggy, waving his arms around above his head. "No market, no market, no market. Can't sell-em opal at all. No market for the opal."

Diamond Jim, still cursing "robbing Wog bastards," finally accepted 15
Woggy's price for the opal and ordered another round of drinks.

While they argued, Woggy's wife walked in. She was short and squat, barely fitting through the narrow doorway. No-one knew Woggy's wife's real name.

She was always referred to as "the Missus." And whenever she and Woggy had a big argument in their own lingo, everyone would mutter: "Bloody wog bastards, can't even talk English." When the Missus was told that Rainbow and Diamond would be staying for lunch, she waddled out of the bar again.

Woggy and the Missus ran goats for meat and some chooks. They grew their own vegetables and were quite self-sufficient. They had existed out here and adapted to the country and its hardships better than most locally born people, yet still, after forty years in the outback, they were called "bloody wog bastards." *So much for the pioneering spirit of the bush,* thought Rainbow Jack.

Now Rainbow Jack produced a battered Log Cabin tobacco tin, its top dented, the edge pitted with the marks of the hundrds of beer bottle tops it had removed—for the old tobacco tin was truly the bushman's bottle opener. Unscrewing the lid, Rainbow showed Woggy some small pieces of opal, and again there was the shout: "Ya bloody robbing wog bastard!" and they argued until Rainbow Jack accepted Woggy's price, knowing he had to buy petrol from the drums lying scattered on the ground outside, as well as food, which was stacked on shelves behind the bar—bottles of sauce, tinned meat, jam, treacle, tea, peanuts, boiled lollies...Some of the labels had begun to peel from the tins and bottles, some tins were badly dented after being dropped, their sides pushed in, tops bulging, others had no labels whatsoever. But Woggy would try to sell them all, and whenever he did so, another argument began. He always claimed he only made one per cent on the goods he sold; if he bought some item for one dollar he sold it for two dollars, still claiming he made only one per cent. The same with a bottle of rum: he bought it for twenty dollars, sold it for forty dollars—"Still only making the bloody one per cent," Woggy would say, waving his hands in the air, whenever anyone accused him of overcharging.

Rainbow and Diamond soon got tired of arguing with Woggy about the price of opal and the one per cent profit he made on each sale. So they settled down to some serious drinking and arguing with each other. Rainbow was so named because he claimed he always knew where opal ever colour of the rainbow was ready to be dug up, and because of his eyes. They always seemed to glitter with a humorous gleam when he told his tales. Then again, others used to say he was forever chasing a rainbow. Like Diamond Jim, Woggy and the Missus, no-one knew his real name.

Today Rainbow Jack was still trying to convince Diamond Jim he only 20
came outback to wear out his old clothes, not seek his fortune digging for opal; he said he could find opal whenever he wished. This brought a snort of disgust from Diamond Jim, who, whenever he had a few drinks, would tell how he had discovered the richest opal mine in the world. It happened a few years ago, out prospecting in the hills. There Diamond Jim had come across another old opal digger named Rabbit, who earned his name because he lived in the bush and was always digging holes.

Rabbit was blind and close to death when he was found by Diamond Jim. Clutched tightly in his fist was an opal, and with his last breath Rabbit related his story. Telling Diamond Jim not to look on the opal in his hand in sunlight, as that had caused his blindness, Rabbit said he had at last struck it rich after years of gouging in the hills. He told how he had dug that one last hole and discovered his dream. Alas, when he took this piece of opal from the mine and examined it in the sunlight, the opal sparkled and glittered with such intensity that he had been blinded by its brilliance. Then, telling Diamond Jim the location of the mine, and warning him once again not to examine the opal in his hand in the sunlight, lest he suffer the same fate, Rabbit gave one last shudder and died.

Diamond Jim then told how he'd thrown a sugar bag over Rabbit's face, covered the opal with his hat, then taken it from Rabbit's lifeless hand, before placing his body in one of the many holes he had dug while searching for his dream. Diamond Jim filled in the hole and scratched the name *RABBIT* on the blade of the shovel. Then he stuck the shovel handle into the grave as a marker.

That night, back at his camp in the mulga, Diamond Jim walked away from the flickering flames of his campfire and dared for the first time to gaze upon the opal that had been the death of Rabbit. By the dim starlight he took a quick peek and was still almost blinded by the colours that flashed from the opal. Fearing he too would be blinded by the brilliance of it, he hastily covered it and buried it at the butt of a big old gydgea tree. Today he was still undecided what to do with his fabulous opal mine.

"Bullshit," said Rainbow Jack when Diamond Jim had finished telling his story for the hundredth time, wiping a glistening dewdrop from his nose. "I suppose ya only waiting for a dark night to dig up your opal, hey? No good a moonlit night. Maybe too bright. Maybe you go blind, hey?" Although these two men argued whenever they met, they could best be described as the friendliest enemies in the world.

Then Diamond Jim, knowing Rainbow still held to some of his Aboriginal beliefs, said to Woggy, "Funny thing I came across a few days ago out in the scrub. Lotta strange tracks like someone lost his boots then made a pair from emu feathers. Might be it was a Kadaicha. You been run away from home—might be he been looking for you, hey, Rainbow?"

"Fill 'em up again," said Rainbow, not answering Diamond Jim. So they passed the time arguing and telling the tales they told whenever they met. By now half-blotto, they were served a meal of goat meat and fresh vegies from the pub garden. It was the first decent meal they had eaten in a month. They thanked the Missus for the meal and told Woggy he was still a robbing wog bastard. Then, leaving the pub, they got into their cars and drove towards the dry creek behind the pub to find a shady tree and rest from the burning midday sun.

Diamond Jim drove around past the old thunder-box, called a toilet, and the goat yard. On the bank of the creek he pulled up. Seeing a shady tree in the creekbed, he took his swag and water-bag and headed for it. Meanwhile, Rainbow Jack drove further downstream to the big old gydgea tree where he always camped. Here he rolled out his swag and lay down, contented after the rum and his first good meal in ages.

When Rainbow Jack awoke, the sun had lost some of its heat. The trees had begun to cast long shadows across the land. He washed in a rusty tin dish, then walked the short distance back to the pub. He noticed that the goats had returned to the yard; sometimes dingoes prowled around the pub in search of prey, so the goats, unherded, always came home to the yard before sundown.

When Rainbow Jack reached the pub, Diamond Jim was already there, arguing with Woggy. "Where ya been?" asked Diamond Jim. "Looks like ya been patching up ya old clothes. Might be ya'll soon have to head for the Gold Coast and buy some new ones." And he pointed to the holes in Rainbow's shirt and the patches on his trousers.

Rainbow hitched up the piece of cord that was his belt so that it sat 30
higher on his bony hips, then ordered a rum, and they continued to argue.

As the sun set, Woggy started the diesel engine and the single bulb in the bar room flickered alight. Another light on the veranda was turned on. With the light came the insects. Now as they drank, both men complained to Woggy about the insects. "Only bloody place in the world where the insects drink more grog than the men," Diamond Jim said as he pulled a moth from his rum.

"And get drunker," Rainbow said, watching another moth floundering on the bar counter, unable to fly away. So they cursed each other, Woggy and the moths. Charged up like Formula One racing cars rarin' to go, they argued over anything till they were finally shunted from the bar by Woggy.

Each carrying a bottle of rum, they headed for Diamond Jim's camp, staggering past the old toilet and goat yard to the creek bank, where they stood for a moment in the pale light of a crescent moon, looking to where Diamond Jim had left his swag and water-bag beneath the tree in the creekbed. Then, still arguing, slipping and sliding, they started down the steep bank. Eventually, slithering on their backsides, they reached the creekbed and Diamond's swag—and most importantly his waterbag.

Soon Diamond Jim was sitting on his swag, while Rainbow Jack sat cross-legged on the ground, with the water bag and an opened bottle of rum between them. They began drinking from a chipped and badly dented enamel mug. The engine stopped over at the pub and for a while the only sound was the slurred voices of the two men in the creekbed telling each other how close they were to a big rich strike. As they paused for breath and another rum, from a tree nearby they heard a call. *Mope-pope, mope-pope, mope-pope.*

"Listen to that bird," said Rainbow. "He's trying to tell ya something, 35
Diamond. Sounds like 'no-hope, no-hope, no-hope.'"

"Must be you he's calling to, Rainbow, because I know where the richest opal mine in the world is located," Diamond Jim replied.

While they argued and the mope-pope called, from the hills beyond the creek came the mournful howl of a dingo. As the howling came closer the goats in the yard on the creek bank grew restless and began to bleat. The men kept drinking the strong black rum. By now both were very drunk. Rainbow, blurry-eyed, stared at the dewdrop that still glistened on the tip of Diamond Jim's nose in the pale light of the moon as his head moved from side-to-side—until, with one last shake of his head, it disappeared and Diamond Jim toppled sideways onto his swag and began to snore. "Can't take ya grog, ya old bastard," mumbled Rainbow Jack. "Ya gone and crashed on me, hey. Might as well go home."

Rainbow staggered and fell a couple of times before he finally stood erect. Looking at the steep creek bank, he decided to walk along the creekbed until he reached a place near his camp where the bank was not so steep. Starting off in his wobbly old boots, he staggered and fell a couple of times; cursing, he rose and carried on; until just around the bend in the creek he stubbed his toe on a rock and stumbled. Pain shot up his leg and he fell head-first for the last time into the stony creekbed. Then, as Diamond Jim would have said, "Rainbow Jack's lights went out."

By nine o'clock next morning the sun was already a furnace in the cloudless blue sky. Rainbow Jack still lay motionless in the creekbed. Then, as the kangaroo dog whined and licked at his face and hands, Rainbow stirred. He opened his eyes but the harsh glare of the sunlight forced him to close them again. Shading his eyes with one hand, he patted the old dog with the other, trying to remember what had happened and how he'd got here. Peering between his fingers, still shielding his eyes, he saw some hawks, their dark shapes stark against the clear blue sky, circling silently above. *Staring down at me,* Rainbow thought. Then came the grating sound of a crow as it cawed from a tree close by. "Bloody black bastard," muttered Rainbow. "I'm not gonna die." But his head ached and his mouth felt as if all the circling hawks had shit in it.

Then he recalled Diamond Jim and the rum they'd drunk the night before. He felt a lump on his head. *Musta bumped it,* he thought. With a great effort he moved his legs to sit up. A sharp pain raced up one leg. Still swearing, Rainbow eventually sat up and looked at his foot. His ankle was swollen and had turned a bluish-purple colour. Painfully he removed his boot, cursing, and sat stroking his foot. Then he reached for his hat and placed it on his head just as the crow began its loud *Caw, caw, caw* again. "Cawing bastard," said Rainbow, and he picked up a rock, intending to throw it at the crow. But when he moved to throw the stone, the pain became so intense that he dropped it.

Cursing silently to himself, Rainbow saw the cause of his misery. Sticking up about fifteen centimetres above the ground was the top of the rock on which he'd stubbed his foot last night. Frustrated, he picked up the stone intended for the cawing crow and hurled it at the offending rock.

Fragments of the rock and stone smashed on impact. The pain in Rainbow's foot was worse than ever. "Silly old me," he said to the dog. "I can't hurt that bloody rock." But it made him feel better, somehow. And at least he had chipped the offending rock.

Suddenly he noticed a glint like sunlight reflecting on a mirror coming from the chipped rock. He sat there staring for a moment, puzzled by the glint. Still sitting on his backside, he sidled up to the rock and passed his rough hands over the chipped rock face. He saw opal colours changing from red to blue and green. With his heart beating faster, Rainbow picked up another stone and chipped away at the rock face. More colours were revealed. He spat on his hand, then wiped it on the rock. He was almost blinded by the brilliant glitter of colours that came from the rock. It seemed to be alive. A throbbing, pulsating mass of colours.

Rainbow Jack, the taste in his mouth now bearable, ignored his swollen, aching foot and slid over the ground on his backside to a dead stick lying in the creekbed. Then, with the old kangaroo dog following, he hobbled off towards his camp, using the stick to help his progress. The crow, cawing louder and louder at being robbed of its meal, flew away to scavenge elsewhere for its dinner.

Rainbow reached his camp. After quenching his thirst, he poured some water into his upturned Akubra and the kangaroo dog drank its fill. Rainbow took a couple of Aspros to relieve the pain in his foot, then packed his gear, and with some difficulty drove back along the creek bank. Stopping his car, he took a long-handled shovel as a walking stick and stood for a moment staring down at the rock sticking up from the bed of the gravelly, stony creek. On his backside he slithered down the steep bank. Then with the aid of the shovel handle he limped to where his newly discovered opal lay.

Glancing back towards the bank, Rainbow saw the kangaroo dog heading for the cool pub veranda. But Rainbow did not feel the heat as the sun blazed down. Reaching the rock he began to dig and soon had more of its showing. Using the shovel as a lever, he prised the rock loose, then rolled it away from the hole. Turning it over, he took a stone and chipped at the bottom of the rock. Again he saw the flashing colours of opal. He chipped both ends of the rock. Still more glittering colours were exposed.

Rainbow, by now almost drunk with excitement and trying to ignore the pain in his foot, thought to himself: *I wish I had a bottle of rum now. I'd soon get rid of this bloody aching foot.* Bushmen often joked that rum was the cure-all for any ailment—broken legs, broken hearts, influenza, anything at all. The secret was to drink all the rum, then rub the empty bottle on the offending spot. It never failed to work. By the time the rum was finished the patient was incapable of any feeling.

Muttering excitedly to himself, Rainbow Jack sat gazing at the opal and gently stroking it. The rock was about twenty-five centimetres high and he could circle it with his arms. It was too heavy to carry, so still sitting down, he rolled it to the creek bank where he rested for a moment. Then slowly he inched the rock ahead of him up the slope to his battered old ute, where he lowered the tailboard. Then with one mighty heave, straining with all his weight on his good leg, he lifted the rock onto his unrolled swag in the back of the ute. Wrapping the rock in his swag, he drove to the pub.

When Rainbow Jack hobbled into the bar room, still using the long shovel handle as a walking stick, Diamond Jim, already well-primed, yelled, "Where ya been, ya old bastard? Can't take ya grog, hey. Did ya get lost going home last night—or maybe the sun got too hot for ya and burnt ya out of ya swag?" Then Diamond Jim noticed that Rainbow's trousers looked more threadbare than ever. When he'd slid along on his backside, wrestling with the big opal rock, the seat had been completely worn out of his trousers.

"Ya really got the arse out of ya trousers now. If ya not careful you'll get fly-blown as well," said Diamond Jim, pointing to Rainbow Jack's backside.

Rainbow reached behind and felt his bare arse. "Well that's it!" he yelled, slapping his battered Akubra on the bar top. "My clothes have finally worn out. Now I'll hafta head back to the Gold Coast to buy new ones."

"Bullshit," said Diamond Jim. "Ya couldn't find ya way to the nearest waterhole, mate. Ya'd get lost on the way to the Coast."

Rainbow Jack shouted another rum, then said in a serious voice to Diamond Jim: "Well, old mate, I gotta be going. I really do need new clothes. But don't worry, I'll be back as soon as me new clothes start to wear out. Ya know, the bush is really a great place to wear out old clothes. But before I go I'll show you blokes something in my car."

So outside they went. As they followed Rainbow Jack to his car, Diamond Jim laughed as he pointed out to Woggy the bare brown arse showing through Rainbow's worn-out trousers.

The three men stopped at the back of the ute and stared for a moment at the battered old tucker-box, dinted petrol cans, blackened billy-cans and camp-ovens, picks and shovels, old sugar and flour bags. "What ya got in here?" asked Diamond Jim. "Looks like ya taking a heap of old bags and a lotta red dust to the Coast, old mate."

Then Rainbow unrolled his swag—and there before them, on a frayed and threadbare blanket, was the biggest and brightest piece of opal they had ever seen. Diamond Jim and Woggy stared in amazement. Then, with gentle caressing touches of their calloused hands, they began stroking the stone in silence. And they both asked as one in loud excited voices: "Where'd ya find this?"

"In the creekbed," Rainbow told them. "Of course I knew it was there all the time. I was just waiting for my old clothes to wear out before I dug it up. Now I'm off to the Coast." He wrapped the opal back in his swag, then hopped around to the door of the ute where he gave the old kangaroo dog a couple of pats. He placed his aching foot on an old pillow on the floor of the car to shield it from the jarring ride over the rough, corrugated road to the nearest town. So he left the outback pub, with Diamond Jim and Woggy staring in disbelief at the thick red plume of bulldust that rose from Rainbow's ute as he headed for the Gold Coast to find a rich opal buyer, then buy new clothes.

Rainbow Jack sold the opal for millions, bought a house with a walk-in wardrobe and filled it with new clothes. He employed a housemaid and a gardener. Rainbow had the lot. The months passed and as he walked along the beach each morning staring at the ocean and the restless waves rolling ashore, he became restless himself for one more look at the outback. So he hired a chauffeur and a limousine with tv, car-phone, drinks fridge, the works, and headed outback for a visit to Woggy's bush pub.

Nothing seemed to have changed as Rainbow Jack approached the pub in the limousine with the chauffeur in his neatly dressed uniform at the wheel. Heat waves still rose from the red dusty ground creating mirages in the sky. The fierce hot winds still blew, stirring up the willy-willys that seemed to blow across the land forever.

The flash car came to a halt in front of the pub. The chauffeur alighted, then walked around and opened the car door for Rainbow Jack, who stood for a moment in the soft red powdery dust, a white panama hat shading his head from the hot sun. In neatly pressed trousers, starched shirt and polished shoes, carrying a gold-tipped cane, he stood brushing away the flies. As he walked towards the veranda, the old kangaroo dog stirred and growled, scratching itself. Then, as Rainbow called to it in a soft voice, it came forward. Soon the old dog was licking Rainbow's shoes, already covered in dust. Rainbow asked the chauffeur to bring a thick slab of steak from the ice-box in the car. He placed it on the warped floorboards of the veranda.

The Missus appeared. She stared from the doorway in disbelief, first at Rainbow, then at the limousine and the chauffeur, finally at the old dog eating rump steak, then back to Rainbow. Convinced at last this was no mirage, she ushered them into the bar room, where they enjoyed cold drinks served by the chauffeur from the car fridge.

They talked for a while of many things, but when Rainbow asked the Missus about Woggy and Diamond Jim, the smile left her face and her voice became bitter. "They're down the creek digging for opal," she said. "Day after day they're down the creekbed, digging up rocks then breaking them open. Now Woggy only comes home to eat and sleep," she said sadly. "I do all the work here. Opal, opal, opal. That's all I hear about now, opal and more opal."

Rainbow left the chauffeur and the Missus, still mumbling about the opal, sitting in the pub. He took off in the limousine along the creek bank to the big shady gydgea tree where he had camped many times before. Pulling up in the shade of the tree, he got out and walked to the edge of the bank, where he stood for a moment staring in amazement and disbelief at the scene below. The dry bed of the creek was like a scene from a lunar landscape, ptited with small craters where Woggy, Diamond Jim and half a dozen other opal gougers toiled in the blazing sun, digging the rock from the holes. Then with their hammers they chipped away at all the rocks in search of the elusive opal. Watching, Rainbow saw the piles of worthless rocks growing bigger as the men slaved away in the searing heat.

He called and waved to Woggy and Diamond Jim. Like the Missus, they took him for a mirage at first. Rainbow soon convinced them he was real. But they were reluctant to leave their claims. Rainbow eventually coaxed them to the car, then drove them back to the pub, where the chauffeur served more ice-cold drinks from the car fridge.

For an hour or so they talked, until Woggy and Diamond Jim grew impatient to be back digging for opal, confident the next rock they dug up would be like the one Rainbow had found. Then they too could retire to the Gold Coast. So at last they said their goodbyes on the creaking warped floorboards of the pub veranda. Rainbow told them he would return again when his new clothes began to wear out.

As the limousine drove away Rainbow Jack looked out the rear window. Already Woggy and Diamond Jim were hurrying back to the creekbed. The Missus was still standing on the pub veranda. The old kangaroo dog, now full and contented, lay at her feet. Then, as Rainbow watched, the Missus turned and kicked the dog in the guts before she headed for the bar room. *I wonder why she did that,* thought Rainbow Jack. The dog had done nothing to deserve the kick. But if Rainbow could have read the thoughts of the Missus, he would have understood.

The Missus, standing on the veranda watching Rainbow drive away and Woggy disappear down the creek bank, was recalling last night. She had been awakened from sleep by the gentle caressing touch of Woggy's rough, calloused hand. She felt a stirring of passion she had not felt for ages. As Woggy continued to caress her and whisper passionate words, she nestled closer and closer in his embrace. But suddenly her emotions froze and her body went limp as she made out those loving words that Woggy uttered. Over and over he kept repeating: "Opal, opal, opal." Now those words still echoed in her mind. And this was the scene Rainbow Jack left behind at the outback pub as he headed for the Gold Coast to wear out his new clothes.

CHARTING THE STORY

1 How remunerative does the opal prospecting appear to be, at the onset of the story, for Diamond Jim and Rainbow Jack? What would indicate their relative wealth or poverty?

2 What explanations are given of the origin of the sobriquets of the characters Diamond Jim, Rainbow Jack, Woggy, the Missus, and Rabbit? Why do you suppose they never divulge their real names?

3 How do the characters manage to overcome boredom in the harsh isolation of the outback?

4 How credible does Diamond Jim's story of Rabbit and the opal appear to be? Where else in the text do you see discourse to be somewhat at variance with the truth?

CONSIDERATIONS OF STYLE

1 Two types of dogs are depicted in the story—the kangaroo dog and the dingo. What does each type seem to signify in the narrative?

2 Define, or explain by context: willy-willy, roly-poly plants (Paragraph 2); ute (Paragraph 3); swag (Paragraph 27); fly-blown (Paragraph 50). You may wish to consult an Australian slang dictionary, many of which are available on the Internet, as well as an unabridged dictionary.

3 What purposes are served by the author's stressing of images of heat and sun? If the story had taken place in the more temperate winter, what might be lost?

AFTERTHOUGHTS

1 What do you suppose motivated Rainbow Jack to return to the pub at the end of the story? How does his visit affect his old cohorts?

2 To what extent does the issue of race enter into this text? How might the story be different if all of the characters had come from the same background?

THE WRITER'S CRAFT

1 Write about a gainful experience in your life in which luck played a far greater role than perseverance. How did the experience affect your attitude toward perseverance and hard work?

2 Retell an episode from the text from the point of view of Woggy, the Missus, the dog, Rabbit, or the later prospectors.

3 According to some persons, opals are "unlucky" stones. Write a short essay or poem discussing some object that has "bad luck" attached to it, or otherwise carries a "curse" of one sort or another.

VIVIENNE PLUMB

VIVIENNE PLUMB *was born in Sydney, Australia. Since she began writing in 1990, she has won several awards for her work.* The Wife Who Spoke Japanese in Her Sleep, *her first book of short stories, was awarded the New Zealand SA Best First Book Award for 1993. In the same year, her play* Love Knots *was awarded the* Sunday Star-Times *Bruce Mason Playwright Award. She has also published a number of poems, has held a Reader's Digest-NZSA-Stout Research Center Writing Fellowship, and was a founding member of The Women's Play Press.*

This story, the title story in a collection, features a woman whose special powers alter her own life and the lives of those around her.

PERSPECTIVES

1. What is a clairvoyant? A savant? A psychic? What are some examples of such persons you have read about or actually known? What theories have been advanced to explain their superhuman powers?
2. In your experience, or in the experience of others, how does your waking life differ from your sleep life or your dream life?
3. When one person in a relationship develops some particular talent or receives some particular gift, how does this tend to affect the relationship? Is change inevitable; if so, can it be managed—or should it be managed?

The Wife Who Spoke Japanese in Her Sleep

In the winter the nights become long and cold. In Honey Tarbox's house all is hushed on a frosty midwinter night.

Then slowly, slowly, Honey rolls over in her bed and starts to wake. She is speaking Japanese.

'Kyoo wa samui desu ne.'

'What . . . ?' she thinks.

'Ohayo gozaimasu,' she says out loud. The words echo around the cold, still bedroom. Her husband groans,

'Huh, wozzat?'

She stops speaking but her mind keeps turning, rolling around. What did I say, she thinks. She doesn't know it was Japanese. She's the wife who spoke Japanese in her sleep.

At first she didn't speak much Japanese.

Her husband, Howard, stayed awake one night and described what he saw happen. He watched her go to bed. Gradually she fell asleep, then after an hour she started speaking in another language. She spoke for a little time.

When she woke in the morning Honey was amazed to hear Howard's description.

She never felt tired. She was always rested, relaxed. But Howard often looked exhausted.

'The talking keeps me awake,' he said.

At first they couldn't understand which language it was. Neither of them had ever spoken any language themselves other than English. Honey had once gone on a holiday to Fiji but Howard had never travelled.

So one night Howard said he would tape Honey talking in her sleep. The next day they took the tape to the School of Languages which was very close by. They asked to see a teacher. While they sat waiting they watched six goldfish swimming in a large tank.

'Mr and Mrs Tarbox?' said the teacher. She wore spectacles and a maroon cardigan. Her hair was pulled back into a bun. To Honey and Howard she looked very educated.

'How can I help? What would you like to learn? Arabic? Spanish? Lithuanian? Mandarin? We offer them all.'

'Please listen to our tape,' said Howard, his face slightly flushed. He switched on his pocket machine.

'Nan desu ka,' said the voice on the tape. It didn't sound like Honey at all.

'What language is that?' asked Howard. The teacher listened.

'Why it's Japanese,' she said. She listened some more, then laughed. 'Good grief,' she said.

'What is it?' asked Honey.

'Well it's rather rude,' said the teacher. 'I don't think I could give you a direct translation. Where did you get this from?' Howard and Honey looked at each other.

'Umm...' they both said. Honey looked at her shoes, and Howard looked at the ceiling.

'Wait a minute,' said the teacher. 'Now what's she saying?' She leaned forward, concentrating on the tape recording.

'Wow, incredible. Who is this woman? I'd love to meet her. What a wonderful woman she is, she seems to know so much.'

'Why, what did she say?' said Howard. He wriggled on his chair. Honey watched the fish flipping around the tank and waited to hear what the teacher would say next.

'Well it's a kind of speech, about mankind,' said the teacher. 'Sort of prophecies . . . it's hard to describe.'

They all stood staring at each other. The voice on the tape had stopped.

'She says things. She's like a kind of . . . oracle,' said the teacher. "I'd really like to meet her. Is she a friend of yours?'

Howard giggled. Honey looked at the fish. One really big goldfish swam right up to the glass, it's mouth opening and shutting at Honey. 'Oh! Oh! Oh!' it looked like it was saying.

'It's me,' said Honey in a flat voice. 'That tape recording is me.'

'You?' said the teacher. She was obviously surprised. She took her spectacles off and polished them and put them back on again.

'I don't understand,' said the teacher. 'If you speak Japanese, why don't you know what you're saying? Also, excuse me if I appear rude, but that voice doesn't sound like you at all. Hajimemashite. Watashi wa Florica desu. Doozo yoroshiku.' She bowed low towards Honey.

'No, no!' whispered Honey. She backed away. 'I don't understand you! . . . Tell her Howard. Tell her what happens.'

Howard moved closer to Miss Florica and lowered his voice.

'When Honey goes to sleep at night, she speaks like that.' He nodded his head towards the tape recorder. Miss Florica gasped.

'She speaks in her sleep?' Howard nodded.

'And in a language she doesn't understand?'

'Yes,' said Howard. 'We don't know what to do.'

'But do you realise what she's saying?' asked Miss Florica.

'This voice on the tape is making prophecies. On the tape she made some predictions about the government of our country.'

'No!' said Howard. Honey looked away. She was feeling so embarrassed. She wished they'd never come.

'You must have a very special power,' said Miss Florica, 'to be able to perceive things that we cannot. A clairvoyant power.' She smiled at Honey.

But Honey said to Howard, 'Howard, let's leave, I just remembered I left the heater on at home.'

Howard came straight away. He'd never encouraged large electricity bills. Was in fact quite a penny pincher when it came down to it.

'Which heater?' he kept asking all the way back. 'The big one or the little?'

"Oh, Howard, shut up,' said Honey. She withdrew to the bathroom where she ran a long hot bath. She didn't come out until she heard Howard leave for his afternoon class at the Community Institute. (He was learning how to make patchwork.) Now he was retired he had nothing else to do with his time. As for herself, the children had all grown up long ago. She had no hobbies, no pastimes, no job, but now she had this.

She looked at herself in the bedroom mirror. She saw a short, stout woman, with blonde hair. A fleshy, plump body. She pinched the flesh on her face. When she pulled her fingers away, a white mark was left on the sagging pink skin.

She thought she knew what a clairvoyant was.

It was a woman, dressed with a scarf on her head, and wearing rings and 50
jewellery. She had a rich plummy voice, and she waved her hands around in an artistic manner. She'd seen them in old Sherlock Holmes movies. The lights would be dimmed and then, the spirits would come. They would fill the room, knocking over lamps and tables in an effort to make their presence known.

Was she a clairvoyant?

She laughed. She shook her head and her blonde hair fluffed around her head like a halo. What a preposterous idea!

Or in the newspaper. Sometimes she'd seen them in the newspaper. A woman would be called in to assist the police in finding a dead body. CLAIRVOYANT HELPS POLICE it would shout across the front page. And there'd be a photo of her, hand outstretched, eyes shut. Could that be Honey?

Or at school, many years ago. She remembered they had learnt about the Oracle at Delphi. A woman had sat on a sacred tripod over a deep fissure in the earth. The mists of the inner earth would rise and send her into a trance. Then she'd speak, tell everyone all manner of things. She might talk for hours, then collapse exhausted. A priest interpreted her messages. People would come from everywhere to ask her questions. And often her answers were correct.

Honey considers herself. Looks at her hands, not artistic, but capable. 55

She glances at her bed, smoothly made, her fuchsia pink nightdress rolled up and slipped under the pillow. And she wonders what the night will bring.

At nine o'clock that night there is a knock at the door. Howard answers it. Miss Florica is standing on the step, her eyes shining.

'Good evening Mr Tarbox,' she says. She has someone else with her, a friend, another woman. She introduces her as Mrs Brunt.

'Mrs Brunt knows a little of these matters,' says Miss Florica. 'She once had a psychic experience herself.'

Mrs Brunt wears short, black rubber boots, and a thick woollen coat. A 60
black beret is balanced on her large square head.

Honey enters the lighted hall. Howard is excited. He is gabbling to the two ladies. It is apparent to Honey that Howard skipped his patchwork class and went instead to ask Miss Florica here tonight. Honey's shadow falls across the rose patterned carpet. All three stop talking and turn quietly towards her. Howard cleared his throat.

'Honey, I know you won't mind if Miss Florica and Mrs Brunt stay to listen to you. It's in the interest of Science, I'm sure you'd agree.'

The two woman smile and nod their heads. Their heads look strangely loose on top of their wooden necks. Honey stays quiet, she doesn't smile back.

Please themselves, she thinks. She feels in control. All her life she's had nothing. But now, she has this. And this is becoming important, making her important.

'Have they brought me anything?' asks Honey. 65

'Brought you anything?' says Howard.

'Yes, a gift, a present. They must have something.'

The hall light hangs behind her, lighting up her body in silhouette, but they cannot see her face.

'I did bring something,' says Mrs Brunt. She pulls a rectangular object out of her crocheted shopping bag.

'A box of chocs.' She beams.

'That's good,' says Honey. 'If any more people come, Howard, you must ask them for their gift.' She turns away. 'I'll go and make a pot of tea.'

Howard is embarrassed.

'Really, she's never acted like this before... Come in. Come in.' He leads the two visitors into the lounge.

The fringed lamp shines a soft glow over the room. The television is on with the sound turned down and Honey's knitting lies on the sofa.

It isn't long before Honey brings the tea.

'I'll get ready while you all have a drink,' she says. She goes into the bedroom and changes into her nightdress. She sits waiting on the edge of the bed. Howard comes in. He says,

'You go to bed Honey. I won't ask anyone in until you're asleep.'

'Howard,' says Honey, 'what do they want?'

'I think they want to ask you some questions,' he says.

Howard, Miss Florica, and Mrs Brunt, stay waiting in the lounge. The clock ticks on. They make small talk. Mrs Brunt examines Honey's knitting.

'She's dropped a stitch ten rows back,' she says.

Suddenly they hear a voice talking in the bedroom. Miss Florica is on her feet straight away.

'That's Japanese!' she says. Howard leads them at a trot down to the back bedroom. He turns on a bedside lamp.

Honey is lying on her back in the bed. Her arms folded across her chest. Her face is smooth, wiped of all expression. She is apparently fast asleep.

'Komban wa,' says Miss Florica. She bows toward the bed.

'Komban wa,' replies Honey. And a torrent of Japanese follows. She still looks like Honey but she doesn't sound like Honey. The voice is higher, more penetrating.

Miss Florica introduces Mrs Brunt. She presents the box of chocolates and says,

'Tsumaranai mono desu ga, doozo.'

Mrs Brunt smiles.

'Now she'll explain my problem,' she whispers to Howard. Howard pulls over another chair and they both sit down. There is a pause, then Honey says,

'Doomo arigatoo gozaimasu. Watashi wa ureshii desu.' Miss Florica smiles. She talks to Honey for about five minutes explaining Mrs Brunt's problem.

Honey replies, she talks on and on, hardly stopping for breath. The Japanese syllables sound strange to Howard. He crosses and recrosses his legs.

Finally Miss Florica turns back to them both.

'It's wonderful,' she says. 'It's all so clear. Her answer is simple.'

'What did you ask?' says Howard. Miss Florica and Mrs Brunt exchange looks.

'I don't mind if you tell,' says Mrs Brunt. 'I think we can trust Mr Tarbox.' Miss Florica explains.

'Mrs Brunt has a lovely miniature poodle, only three years old. His name is Schnookie. Schnookie is suffering terribly from arthritis and he may have to have plastic ligaments inserted in his front legs. Mrs Brunt was worried about the pain this operation may cause Schnookie, but now I have the answer.'

'And what is that?' asks Howard.

'It has been suggested Mrs Brunt finds a hypnotherapist.'

Mrs Brunt grins. 'What a terrific idea!'

'I'm so glad Honey helped you find the answer to your problem,' Howard says. Miss Florica and Mrs Brunt prepare to leave.

'Do you think Honey could help other people this way?' asks Howard. Miss Florica's face shines. She comes forward and places her hand on Howard's arm in a warm, caring way.

'Without doubt,' she says. 'Without doubt, I think I could say that Honey's advice and predictions could be the light at the end of the tunnel for many people. And I would make myself available any night to translate . . . for a small donation. Think about it, Mr Tarbox, and let us keep in touch.' She squeezes his arm. He opens the front door for them and says goodbye.

The sound of their footsteps fades away into the still, deep night.

The stars hang, glittering fiercely in the cold midnight sky. Howard hears a noise and swings around. It's Honey. She's wearing her fluffy lilac dressing gown.

'Did I do it?' she asks.

'Yes,' says Howard. His voice is low. 'They were very pleased. You were very successful. Miss Florica thinks you could help even more people.'

'I see,' says Honey. 'Tell her she can have thirty percent.' She turns and goes back to the bedroom. Howard comes inside. He's surprised. Honey seems so different, so business-minded, it's not like her. He frowns at the lock, pulls the chain across and slips it into it's tiny slot. Tomorrow he'll ring Miss Florica and make her an offer.

During the next few months the Tarbox home becomes famous. Word gets around, and every night many people arrive at Honey's with a little hope in their hearts. Some have simple questions written on a tiny scrap of paper. Others come escorted by note-taking secretaries who read their questions out for them.

They ask so many things. How to become rich, how to look more beautiful, how to become loved, and how to love. How to be good, to be received into heaven, to die happy. Honey answers them all.

Now Honey wears a beautiful peach pink nightie. She has her hair styled during the day so she will look her best every night. Reporters come and go. Honey is a popular personality to interview. They adore her combination of mystery and modesty. They ask her opinion on everything, her favourite colour (peach), and her favourite food (watermelon). She's even been on daytime chat shows, and has been photographed with many of the famous and well known people who now pass through the portals of her house in search of advice and predictions.

Her predictions are often correct. Her advice, politely and kindly offered, is always well accepted.

The Japanese ambassador has visited several times. The last time he came they talked at length about the future of Japan.

'Are wa sakura desu ka,' he'd said, peering out of Honey's window into the dark night.

'Hai,' Honey had answered. 'Haru desu.' 115

Waiting outside the door in the shadows, Howard had thought to himself how much Honey had changed.

To Howard, she now appears controlled, never flustered. She's always well dressed, her make up well applied. She offers opinions even when they've not been asked for. And she expects Howard to keep accounts that add up.

Howard thinks he liked the old Honey better. She pottered around the house in her fluffy dressing gown. She always looked to Howard for advice about the way to dress, besides everything else. She was warm, caring, and she looked after me, thinks Howard. Now he thinks she's a Dragon Woman.

The business of the accounts upsets him the most. Maths was never his forte and he often makes mistakes. Sometimes, when it all gets too much for him, he seeks Miss Florica's help. In her old cardie and smudgy pink lipstick and her dishevelled bun and glasses, she reminds Howard of the old Honey.

She is pleased to help Howard. She pats his hand and sometimes makes 120
him a pot of tea. She calls him Howard now, not Mr Tarbox.

During the day Honey often likes to sit in the garden. Howard used to look after it. He would mow a flat square in the middle and clip back the rest.

But it's all different now. A young Japanese man, Kenta Yamashita, has offered to build a real Japanese garden for Hoeny. Honey's advice to Kenta about his problems with his mother has so touched him that he comes back all the time just to visit. Now he has offered to build the Japanese garden.

He has planted a cherry tree and wants to pull up all the grass and replace it with raked gravel.

He is setting three large stones in their geomantic positions. The large stones are covered with lichen. They are the mountains, says Kenta. The gravel will be the water. All the elements of life. Honey loves watching the transformation of the garden. She sees it somewhat representative of what has happened to herself. She's looking forward to the complete removal of Howard's dusty geraniums and proteas and the installation of the raked sand. Smooth, flowing, meditative.

One Monday morning Honey wakes earlier than usual. She walks up the hall and into the kitchen.

Howard and Miss Florica are pushed against the sink bench grappling with each other's bodies. Howard's hands are up Miss Florica's blouse. Miss Florica's hands are down Howard's trousers. Their mouths are squashed against each other's. It makes Honey remember the goldfish.

She coughs gently and they both spring apart. Miss Florica blushes.

'I don't know what came over me,' she says.

Howard looks smug. He says nothing. Instead, he leans across Miss Florica and takes two pieces of toast out of the toaster. He butters them evenly and eats them straight away. Miss Florica excuses herself and hurries out of the kitchen.

'Would you like some toast?' asks Howard.

'No,' says Honey. She prefers to eat fish for breakfast these days.

'You're so different now,' says Howard. It's the first time he's ever talked to Honey about the changes in their lives.

'You're not the same Honey I married.'

'We all change,' says Honey. 'From decay grows new life. From the old is born the new.'

'How poetic,' says Howard. Honey pauses, she then replies,

'I must now take this opportunity to thank you for starting me on this path.'

'No worries,' mutters Howard.

That night Honey dons a white sateen nightie. She pins her hair up, adding a flower or two to the arrangement. She applies a little lipstick to her mouth and climbs into bed. She lies still, waiting for Miss Florica to arrive. This is the way they always do it. When Miss Florica comes, she sits over near the window and Honey slowly falls asleep.

Tonight Honey is more voluble than ever. She is funny and witty, and very likeable in this mood. Her *joie de vivre* breaks the language barrier. When her visitors leave they are smiling and laughing. Miss Florica is kept busy. Honey talks at such a rate, she can hardly keep up.

Then suddenly, Honey sits up in her sleep. She has never done this before. Everyone stops what they're doing.

'Howardsan wa doko desu ka,' she says.

'Quick! Call Howard!' shouts Miss Florica. 'This is for him!'

'Watashi wa megami desu. Me ga mienai. Kiri ga mieru. Howardsan ga kiete iku!'

'I can't see. I see a mist,' translates Miss Florica quickly. Her face flushes. 'A disappearance!'

Honey falls exhausted onto her pillows and goes into a deep sleep. Howard cannot be found until the next morning. (He was down at the all-night service station talking to his friend.)

The next week Howard disappears.

No one sees him leave, nor can anyone remember for sure what happened. One day he was there, the next day—zilch! No one had ever taken much notice of him anyway (except Miss Florica).

She is allowed to move into his old room. She touches the razor on his dresser and carefully runs her fingers along the blade. The terylene curtains wave in the breeze coming through the open window. Miss Florica opens the drawers and wonders why Howard never took any spare underwear with him when he left.

Kenta Yamashita has finished Honey's Japanese garden. Ten tons of white gravel and sand was delivered and raked into uniform patterns. Only Miss Florica can remember the particular day that the gravel arrived.

Yes, she can remember the day, the month, and the year (in case she's ever asked). It was the day before Howard disappeared.

CHARTING THE STORY

1 How is Honey characterized at the beginning of the story? How does Honey's sudden strange success transform the lives of the three main characters in this story—Howard, Miss Florica, and Honey herself?

2 If you speak Japanese, or if you know someone who does, translate Honey's Japanese utterances, or have them translated. What additional significations arise, especially about the types of utterances Honey makes?

3 What is Honey's reaction to discovering Miss Florica and Howard "grappling with each other's bodies" in the kitchen? How might the "old Honey" have reacted to this, and why does the "wife who speaks Japanese" react in the way that she does?

4 How do you account for the absence of divine—or other otherworldly—intervention to explain the mysteries in this story? To explain Howard's disappearance?

CONSIDERATIONS OF STYLE

1 The narrative is structured as a succession of vignettes, most of them relatively short, only one of them quite extended. Why might Plumb have written it in this way, rather than as a conventional story, complete with transitions?

2 Where in the text does Plumb employ humor to put the bizarre events into perspective? What is the effect of this?

AFTERTHOUGHTS

1 What human frailties have contributed to Honey's success as a seer? Can you find parallels in contemporary life where individuals have become rich and famous by seemingly giving their followers easy answers to some of life's hard questions?

2 Of what significance is the Japanese rock garden, apart from a likely repository for Howard's body? (You may need to research this.)

3 What is suggested by Honey's speaking in Japanese, rather than in a Maori or Fijian language, or even in Bahasa Indonesian, Malay, or Chinese? What cultural capital is made of the use of Japanese?

THE WRITER'S CRAFT

1 Write an essay comparing how success transforms the lives of the central characters in this story and in Herb Wharton's "A New Wardrobe for Rainbow Jack" and Patricia Grace's "It Was Green Once." What do all three stories tell us about human frailty?

2 Research, or write from your own experience, about the phenomenon of *glossolalia* ("speaking in tongues"), and compare this phenomenon to that experienced by Honey. Are they different? If so, in what ways?

3 An old Zen story relates the tale of a monk who fell asleep and dreamed he was a butterfly. When he awoke, he wondered whether he was a man who had dreamt of being a butterfly, or a butterfly who was now dreaming of being a man. If he were having this conversation with Honey, how might it go? Write their dialogue.

FAY WELDON

FAY WELDON—*christened Franklin Birkinshaw—was born in Worcester, England in 1931. After her parents' divorce, when she was five, she moved to New Zealand with her mother, sister, and grandmother—thus, her self-professed belief that "the world was peopled by females." She returned to England with her mother and received her master's degree in economics and psychology from the University of St Andrews in Scotland. She was briefly married to a man more than twenty years her senior, by whom she may have had the son she raised as a single mother. She married Roy Weldon in 1962 and had three more sons.*

Her first novel, The Fat Woman's Joke, *was published in 1967, by which time she had already written some fifty plays for radio, stage, or television—the best known being* Upstairs, Downstairs *and her adaptation of Jane Austen's* Pride and Prejudice.

She has published over twenty novels, collections of short stories, and newspaper and magazine articles.

Weldon's husband Roy died of a stroke the day after their divorce was finalized, in 1994. She later married Nick Fox, a poet fifteen years her junior. They live in Hampstead, London.

"Chew You Up and Spit You Out" is subtitled "A Cautionary Tale" for good reason. The story first appeared in Woman *in 1989 and is anthologized in the collection* Moon Over Minneapolis *(1991).*

PERSPECTIVES

1 Look up the concept Feng Shui. What is the etymology of the term? How is it commonly used in English? Can it be associated with any religion or cult?
2 What is there in the relationship between a house and its inhabitants that "makes a house a home"?

Chew You Up and Spit You Out

'Well, yes,' said the house to the journalist, in the manner of interviewees everywhere, 'it is rather a triumph, after all I've been through!' The journalist, a young woman couldn't quite make out the words for the stirring of the ivy on the chimney and the shirring of doves in the dovecote. She was not the kind to be responsive to the talk of houses—and who would want to be who wished to sleep easy at night?—but she heard enough to feel there was some kind of story here. She'd come with a photographer from *House & Garden:* they were doing a feature on the past retold, on rescued houses, though to tell the truth she thought all such houses were boring as hell. Let the past look after the past was her motto. She was twenty-three and beautiful and lived in a Bauhaus flat with a composer boyfriend who paid the rent and preferred something new to something old any day.

'Let's just get it over with,' she said, 'earn our living and leg it back to town.'

But she stood over the photographer carefully enough, to make sure he didn't miss a mullioned window, thatched outhouse, Jacobean beam or Elizabethan chimney: the things that readers loved to stare at: she was conscientious enough. She meant to get on in the world. She tapped her designer boot on original flagstone and waited while he changed his film, and wondered why she felt uneasy, and what the strange muffled breathing in her ears could mean. That's how houses speak, halfway between a draught and a creak, when they've been brought back to life by the well-intentioned, rescued from decay and demolition. You hear it sometimes when you wake in the middle of the night in an old house, and think the place is haunted. But it's not, it's just the house itself speaking.

The journalist found Harriet Simley making coffee in the kitchen. The original built-in dresser had been stripped and polished, finished to the last detail, though only half the floor was tiled, and where it was not the ground was murky and wet. Harriet's hair fell mousy and flat, around a sweet and earnest face.

'No coffee for me,' said the journalist. 'Caffeine's so bad for one! What a 5
wonderful old oak beam!' The owners of old houses love to hear their beams praised.

'Twenty-three feet long,' said Harriet proudly. 'Probably the backbone of some beached man o' war. Fascinating, the interweaving of military history and our forest story! Of course, these days you can't get a properly seasoned oak beam over twelve feet anywhere in the country. You have to go to Normandy to find them, and it costs you an arm and a leg. And all our capital's gone. Still, it's worth it, isn't it! Bringing old houses back to life!' The girl nodded politely and wrote it all down, though she'd heard it a hundred times before, up and down the country; of cottages, farmhouses, manors, mansions, long houses: 'Costs you an arm and a leg. Still, it's worth it. Bringing old houses back to life!' Spoken by the half-dead, so far as she could see, but then she was of the Bauhaus, by her very nature.

'What's the matter with your hands?' the journalist asked, and wished she hadn't.

'Rheumatoid arthritis, I'm afraid,' Harriet said. She couldn't have been more than forty. 'It was five years before we got the central heating in. Every time we took up a floorboard there'd be some disaster underneath. Well, we got the damp out of the house in the end, but it seems to have got into my hands.' And she laughed as if it were funny, but the journalist knew it was not. She shuddered and looked at her own city-smooth red-tipped fingers. Harriet's knuckles stood out on her hands, as if she made a fist against the world, and a deformed fist at that.

'So dark and gloomy in here,' the journalist thought and made her excuses and went out again into the sun to look up at the house, but it didn't warm her: no, the shudder turned into almost a shiver, she didn't know why. The house spoke to her, but the breeze in the creepers which fronded the upstairs windows distorted the words. Or perhaps the Bauhaus had made her deaf.

'You should have seen me only thirty years ago!' said the house. 'What a ruin. I must have fallen asleep. I woke to find myself a shambles. Chimney through the roof, dry rot in the laundry extension, rabbits living in the walls along with the mice, deathwatch beetle in the minstrel's gallery, the land drains blocked and water pushing up the kitchen tiles, and so overgrown with ivy I couldn't even be seen from the road. What woke me? Why, a young couple pushing open the front door—how it creaked; enough to wake the dead. They looked strong, young and healthy. They had a Volvo. They came from the city: they had dogs, cats and babies. They'll do, I thought; it's better if they come with their smalls: they'll see to the essentials first. My previous dwellers? They'd been old, so old, one family through generations: they left in their coffins: there was no strength in them; mine drained away. That's why I fell asleep, not even bothered to shrug off the ivy. I woke only in the nick of time. Well, I thought, can't let that happen again. So now I put out my charm and lure the young ones in, the new breed from the city, strong and resourceful. They fall in love with me; they give me all their money: but they have no stamina; I kept the first lot twelve years, then they had to go. Pity. But I tripped a small down the back stairs, to punish it for rattling the stained glass in its bedroom door, and it lay still for months, and the parents neglected me and cursed me so I got rid of them. But I found new dwellers soon enough, tougher, stronger, richer, who did for a time. Oh yes, I'm a success story! Now see, even the press takes an interest in my triumph! Journalists, photographers!' And the house preened itself in the late summer sun, in the glowing evening light.

'I say,' said the photographer to Julian Simley, as he wheelbarrowed a load of red roof-tiles from the yard to the cider house, 'you should get the ivy off the chimney; it'll break down the cement.' The photographer knew a thing or two—he'd just put in an offer for a house in the country himself. An old rectory: a lot to do to it, of course, but he was a dab hand at DIY, and with his new girlfriend working he could afford to spend a bit. A snip, a snip—and worth twice as much, three times, when he was through. Even the surveyor said so.

The house read his mind and sang, 'When *we're* through with *you*, when *we're* through with *you:* you can call yourself an owner, who are but a slave, you who come and go within our walls, for all old houses are the same and think alike,' and the photographer smiled admiringly up at the doves in the creeper, as they stirred and whirred, and only the journalist shivered and said, 'There's something wrong with my ears. I hear music in them, a creaky kind of music, I don't like it at all.'

'Wax,' said the photographer absently, 'can sound like that.'

15

Julian Simley said, 'Christ, is that ivy back again? That's the last straw,' which is not what you're supposed to say when you're telling the press a success story of restoration, or renovation, in return for a hundred-pound fee, which you desperately need, for reclaimed old brick and groceries. 'I haven't the head for heights I had.'

'You fool, you fool,' snarled the house, overhearing. 'You pathetic weak-backed mortal. Let the ivy grow, will you? Turn me into weeds and landscape? Leave me a heap of rubble, would you! Wretched, poverty-stricken creature: grubbing around for money! You and your poor crippled wife, who'd rather fit a dresser handle than tile the kitchen floor! I've no more patience with you: I've finished with you!' and as Julain Simley stood on a windowsill to open a mullioned pane so the photgrapher could get the effect of glancing light he wanted, the sill crumbled and Julian fell and his back clicked and there was his disc slipped again, and he lay on the ground, and Harriet rang for the ambulance, and *House & Garden* waited with them. It was the least they could do.

'He should have replaced the sill,' thought the photographer, 'I would have done,' and the house hugged itself to itself in triumph.

'We can't manage any longer,' said Julian to Harriet, as he lay on the ground. 'It's no use, we'll have to sell, even at a loss.'

'It's not the money I mind about,' grieved Harriet. 'It's just I love this house so much.'

'Don't you think I do,' said Julian, and gritted his teeth against the stabs 20
of pain which ran up his legs to his back. He thought this time he'd done some extra-complicating damage. 'But I get the feeling it's unrequited love.' The house sniggered.

'But how will we know the next people will carry on as we have? They'll cover up the kitchen floor and not let it dry out properly, I know they will.' Harriet wept. Julian groaned. The ambulance came. The journalist and the photographer drove off.

'You want to know the secret?' the house shrieked after them. 'The secret of my success? It's chew them up and spit them out! One after the other! And I'll have you next,' it screamed at the photographer, who looked back at the house as they circled the drive, and thought, 'So beautiful! I'll withdraw the offer on the rectory, and make a bid on this one. I reckon I'll get it cheap, in the circumstances. That looked like a broken back, not a slipped disc, to me,' and the house settled back cosily into its excellent, well-drained, sheltered site—the original builders knew what they were doing—and smiled to itself, and whispered to the doves who stirred and whirred their wings in its creepers. 'Flesh and blood, that's all. Flesh and blood withers and dies. But a house like me can go on for ever, if it has its wits about it.'

CHARTING THE STORY

1 What is it about the rescue and/or rescuers of old houses that Weldon seems to be satirizing in this story?
2 What relationship—ectoplasmic or karmic—do the journalist and the photographer, respectively, seem to have with the house? Which seems to be most aware of the "voice" of the house, and for what reasons?
3 How might this story change if any one of the characters were completely aware of what the house was saying?
4 What, in your estimation, does that wicked old house *want* in its life? Where does it suggest as much?

CONSIDERATIONS OF STYLE

1 What is the effect of Weldon's anthropomorphizing the house in this "cautionary tale"? Of her making the house such a villainous character?
2 Where are irony and humor, particularly black humor, poignant in the text?
3 In Paragraph 13, the house exults: " You can call yourself an owner, who are but a slave, you who come and go within our walls, for all old houses are the same and think alike." Does the language of the house seem contemporary, or is it evocative of an earlier period? If so, where would you "place" it, and why?
4 Why does the house refer to children as "smalls"? How does the house's lexicon differ from that of humans?

AFTERTHOUGHTS

1 Find a magazine similar to the *House & Garden* portrayed in the story, and focus on articles describing the restorations of old houses. What types of discourse are used; what styles of writing do you notice? From the article(s), what can you deduce about the readership of the magazine? Does it seem to be the same sort of audience that would watch television productions about "old house" restoration?
2 Look up the concept *Bauhaus.* How does it counterpoint the kind of house that is speaking in the story? Can a *Bauhaus* flat "chew one up and spit one out"? Were a

Bauhaus flat to speak, what might it say? How might the journalist have been made "deaf" to house-speech by such a building?

THE WRITER'S CRAFT

1 Describe a neighborhood in your city or town in which houses have been restored to reflect their original condition and the original character of the neighborhood. What temporal and demographic changes might make such restoration seem a bit artificial?

2 Considering that some of the restored houses in England, site of this story, are *many* centuries old, how might house-speech differ in other locales, such as the US suburbs? Write from the point of view of such a "tract home."

Our Common Humanity

Part Seven
Nature, Faith, Spirit

But we did not ourselves know what the end was.
People like us simply go on.
We have our flaws, perhaps a few private virtues,
But it is by blind chance that we escape tragedy.

DONALD JUSTICE, *Pantoum of the Great Depression*

GEORGE MACKAY BROWN

GEORGE MACKAY BROWN *was born in Stromness, in the Orkney Islands in the far north of Scotland, in 1921. His first book appeared in 1954. Since then he has published novels (*Greenvoe, Vinland*); collections of stories (*Island of the Women and Other Stories, Winter Tales, Sun's Net*); collections of poems (*Following a Lark: Poems *and with his friend, Swedish photographer Gunnie Moberg,* The Wreck of the Archangel, Orkney: Pictures and Poems*); his autobiography,* For the Islands I Sing: An Autobiography, *published posthumously.*

Brown was deeply rooted in his native Orkney, whose people, history, way of life, and landscape figure prominently in his work.

In this poem, a boy observing a snow shower learns a lesson by each snowflake, unto the trillionth, that falls around him.

PERSPECTIVES

1 In Romantic writing of the Western tradition, nature often teaches humans—at least those who are receptive. What lesson, or lessons, have you been taught by a natural event such as a rainstorm or a snow shower?

2 Has there ever been a time for you when the natural world seemed to take on a personality and become Nature? In what context did this occur?

A Boy in a Snow Shower

Said the first snowflake
No, I'm not a shilling,
I go quicker than a white butterfly in summer.

Said the second snowflake
Be patient, boy,
Seize me, I'm a drop of water on the edge of your finger.

The third snowflake said,
A star?

No, I've drifted down out of that big blue-black cloud.

And the fourth snowflake,
Ah good, the road
Is hard as flint, it tolls like iron under your boots.

And the fifth snowflake,
Go inside, boy,
Fetch your scarf, a bonnet, the sledge.

The sixth snowflake sang,
I'm a city of sixes,
Crystal hexagons, a hushed sextet.

And the trillionth snowflake,
All ends with me—
I and my brother Fire, we end all.

CHARTING THE POEM

1. From how many points of view do we experience the snow shower?
2. What is the effect of the gradual ordering of snowflakes from the first to the sixth, and then the great leap from the sixth to the trillionth?
3. Explain the four references to the number *six* in the sixth stanza.

CONSIDERATIONS OF STYLE

1. What pattern does the poem display in the way each stanza presents the snowflake "speaker"? How does the pattern affect the rhythm of the poem?
2. How do the seven distinct images in each of the seven stanzas of the poem contribute to the reader's understanding of snowflakes? Of Nature in general?

AFTERTHOUGHTS

1. Wallace Stevens gives us "Thirteen Ways to Look at a Blackbird" (1917), a group of thirteen small connected poems that Stevens has called "a collection of sensations" (*Letters,* p. 251). What parallels can one draw between "A Boy in a Snow Shower" and the first four stanzas of Stevens's poem:

I

Among twenty snowy mountains,
The only moving thing
Was the eye of the blackbird.

II
I was of three minds,
Like a tree
In which there are three blackbirds.

III
The blackbird whirled in the autumn winds.
It was a small part of the pantomime.

IV
A man and a woman
Are one.
A man and a woman and a blackbird
Are one.

THE WRITER'S CRAFT

1 If the poem were "A Girl in a Snow Shower," how might it be written? Would it change? If yes, why? If no, why not?

2 Write a poem about some other natural force speaking to woman or man, old or young, boy or girl.

GARRISON KEILLOR

Born in Anoka, Minnesota in 1942, GARRISON KEILLOR *has been in radio since 1963, and is most famous for his long-running* Prairie Home Companion *on National Public Radio. He has written nine books, including* Happy to Be Here *(1982),* Lake Wobegon Days *(1985),* The Book of Guys *(1993), and* Wobegon Boy *(1997). His radio life and his writing life are infused with his mythical small town in Minnesota, Lake Wobegon, "where all the women are strong, all the men are good-looking, and all the children are above average."*

"Sweet, Sweet Corn" is a story built around a hymn about the kind of strict Puritanical Christian church the narrator knew as a boy. The pleasure derived from eating sweet corn fresh from the garden contrasts with the repressive ambiance of church.

PERSPECTIVES

1 Have you ever listened to *Prairie Home Companion?* If so, how do you characterize Keillor's "News from Lake Wobegon" stories and other regular features of the program?

2 What food, for you, is the epitome of grace and beauty as well as fine taste?

Sweet, Sweet Corn

My people were Puritans who came to America in the late 17th century. They came to America in the hopes of discovering greater restrictions than were permissible under English law.

And their dream in the New World was to repress. When things got too lax for them out East, why they moved to Minnesota, where the weather sort of does it for you.

But when it got to be July and August, there was a great sensual pleasure—a great sinful, sensual pleasure—that was ours, and that no Puritan could deny. It was right out back of the house. And that's sweet corn.

This is a little hymn to this beautiful vegetable.

When I come to the end of my last, last day
And I wait for the night to fall;
In a cold green room,
With machines humming low,
And voices, strange voices, in the hall;
Take my hand, Precious Lord,
Lead me on through the night
To Your land of the bright shining morn,
Where Your children will sit
In constant delight
And feed on your fresh sweet corn.

Oh, the fresh sweet corn
That the Lord sent down
So we'd know how heaven will be.
There'll be no grief and no tears,
Just bright golden ears,
Plenty for you and for me.
Oh, we praise You, dear Lord,
For the good, good life
And thanks for the day we were born
And the gifts You have given,
Especially this heavenly fresh sweet corn.

I grew up in a big white house that was about thirty long strides away from a 5
sweet corn field. There were six children in our family and my dad was a carpenter and worked for the post office. And that garden, that half-acre garden, fed us—pretty well—for most of the year. We canned quarts by the hundreds and froze even more.

But what I best remember about that garden was Sunday afternoons when I came home from church, having sat under some hard preaching for a couple of hours, feeling all of the guilt and shame that another human being could possibly put on you.

Trembling and pale and sweating, we came home. And when the chicken was done, and when the cauliflower and the potatoes were boiled to the point where they could do no harm to anybody, and when the water was boiling, we went out back and we picked about 67 ears of that sweet corn.

We stripped off the husks as we walked into the house and put it directly into the water. Got out the chicken. The corn was briefly prayed over and buttered and salted and that was our spiritual food.

I think back on that fresh sweet corn as the greatest, sweetest experience in life. I really learned about being a writer from eating those rows of corn prose there on that roller. Learned how to type doing that.

But more than that, I think that fresh sweet corn, just a few minutes from 10
the sunshine, told you more than a sermon ever could how much God loves us. To give such good things to the least of His children. Such a lovely world we live in. Such grace and such love surrounds us every day. And we knew it when we sat and ate fresh sweet corn. Yes, we did.

Oh we thank You dear Lord
For this good, good life,
And thanks for the day we were born,
And the gifts You have given,
Especially this heavenly sweet, sweet corn.

CHARTING THE STORY

1 It's just corn. How can this vegetable be "a great sensual pleasure"? Against what is this sensuality running riot?

2 How do you interpret the narrator's comment that he learned his craft "from eating those rows of corn prose there on that roller"?

CONSIDERATIONS OF STYLE

1 How does Keillor use humor in order to convey his "Puritan" background? If he had written about it "straight," humorlessly, what would have happened to the corn?

2 How does the hymn "Sweet, Sweet Corn" both partake of and parody hymns in general?

AFTERTHOUGHTS

1 Do you think the narrator's religiously strict ancestors also enjoyed the "great sinful, sensual pleasure" of sweet corn in summer, even though "their dream in the New World was to repress [sensuality]"?

2 While the *Prairie Home Companion* show is broadcast (like corn) all over the United States and Canada, its stock in trade is "Minnesota," and many of its typically "boomer" audience either grew up in the American Midwest or have family roots there. What sorts of knowledge—and indeed, what attitudes in general—does Keillor seem to take for granted in the show's audience?

3 Keillor's singing voice is not commercially slick: it's pleasant, low, with just a bit of a tremulous quaver when he sings solo. Were he to sing with a "professional" voice, how would the hymn come across? (For fun, if you have not heard Keillor sing it, set it to music of all varieties—urban, country, Euro, Las Vegas lounge, Broadway showstopper, world beat—and test its effects.)

THE WRITER'S CRAFT

1. Write a *hymn* to something that does not normally enjoy a place in anyone's hymn book.
2. Write a panegyric to a favorite food. You may want to include some historical information about it. As Garrison Keillor has done with corn, put this food in a loftier category than mere nourishment.

N SCOTT MOMADAY

NAVARRE SCOTT MOMADAY *was born in Lawton, Oklahoma in 1934. His father, Alfred Morris, was a painter and art instructor, and his mother, Mayme Natachee Momaday, née Scott, was a teacher and writer. His father was a Kiowa, and his mother descended from white pioneers and Cherokee. He studied at a military academy before attending the University of New Mexico, where he received his AB in English in 1958. From Stanford University he received his MA in 1960 and his PhD in 1963. He has taught at the University of California at Santa Barbara and at Berkeley, and at Stanford University. He is currently Regent's Professor of English at the University of Arizona, Tucson, where he has taught since 1982.*

A prolific novelist, memoirist, poet, and painter, Momaday has received numerous awards for his work, including a Pulitzer Prize for fiction in 1969 (for House Made of Dawn*).*

"One of the Wild Beautiful Creatures" first appeared in the newspaper The Santa Fe New Mexican *in 1973.*

PERSPECTIVES

1. What are your views about hunting—for food, for sport? Have you hunted, or, if not, would you wish to? Why; why not? Do your attitudes on hunting contrast at all with views that you have about slaughtering livestock for food?
2. Have you ever watched a living creature die? How did seeing death close up shape your views on life itself, or life for these particular circumstances?

One of the Wild Beautiful Creatures

That day the sun never did come out. It was a strange, indefinite illumination, almost obscure, set very deep in the sky,—a heavy, humid cold without wind. Flurries of snow moved down from the mountains, one after another, and clouds of swirling mist spilled slowly down the slopes splashing in slow, slow motion on the plain.

For days I had seen migrating birds. They moved down the long corridor of the valley, keeping to the river. The day before I had seen a flock of twenty or thirty geese descend into the willows a mile or more downstream. They were still there, as far as I knew.

I was thirteen or fourteen years old, I suppose. I had a different view of hunting in those days, an exalted view, which was natural enough, given my situation. I had grown up in mountain and desert country, always in touch with the wilderness, and I took it all for granted. The men of my acquaintance were hunters. Indeed they were deeply committed to a hunting tradition. And I admired them in precisely those terms.

We drew near the river and began to creep, the way a cat creeps upon a sparrow. I remember that I placed my feet very carefully, one after the other, in the snow without sound. I felt an excitement welling up within me. Before us was a rise which now we were using as a blind. Beyond and below it was the river, which we could not yet see, except where it reached away at either end of our view, curving away into the pale, winter landscape. We advanced up the shallow slope, crouching, leaned into the snow and raised ourselves up on our toes in order to see. The geese were there, motionless on the water, riding like decoys. But though they were still they were not calm. I could sense their wariness, the tension that was holding them in that stiff, tentative attitude of alert.

And suddenly they exploded from the water. They became a terrible, 5
clamorous swarm, struggling to gain their element. Their great bodies, trailing water, seemed to heave under the wild, beating wings. They disintegrated into a blur of commotion, panic. There was a deafening roar; my heart was beating like the wings of the geese.

And just as suddenly out of this apparent chaos there emerged a perfect fluent symmetry. The geese assembled on the cold air, even as the river was still crumpled with their going, and formed a bright angle on the distance. Nothing could have been more beautiful, more wonderfully realized upon the vision of a single moment. Such beauty is inspirational in itself; for it exists for its own sake.

One of the wild, beautiful creatures remained in the river, mortally wounded, its side perforated with buckshot. I waded out into the hard, icy undercurrent and took it up in my arm. The living weight of it was very great, and with its life's blood it warmed my frozen hands. I carried it for a long time. There was no longer any fear in its eyes, only something like sadness and yearning, until at last the eyes curdled in death. The great shape seemed perceptibly lighter, diminished in my hold, as if the ghost given up had gone at last to take its place in that pale angle in the long distance.

CHARTING THE ESSAY

1 Why was the author's early view of hunting "exalted"? How does this change by the end of the essay? What might the author get out of a hunting trip today?

2 In moving from scene to scene in this essay, where and how does the tension build, and ultimately let go?

3 How can the boy "sense the wariness" of the geese, and how does this tie in with his reactions to their flight?

CONSIDERATIONS OF STYLE

1 How is the death of the goose related? What mood is evoked in the description in the last paragraph?

2 Of what importance to the essay are the wintry images? Assuming that one may hunt for something at any given time in the year, how do cold, snow, diffused light, and icy waters "work" for this essay?

3 On the whole, this essay works in contrasts. Identify five contrasts that refer to any of the various structural features of the text—such as characters, mood, or imagery.

AFTERTHOUGHTS

1 Of what relevance is the boy's age of thirteen or fourteen years? Had he been much younger, or much older, how would the narrative have changed, and how would the mood have altered?

2 If you were a high-school or middle-school teacher gathering essays to present "pro" or "con" on some issue (such as hunting), and this essay came to hand, with what "side" would you present it, and why?

THE WRITER'S CRAFT

1 From the point of view of one of the boy's relatives, a fellow hunter, write your account of this boy's first hunting trip.

2 About the flight of the geese, the author writes, "Such beauty is inspirational in itself; for it exists for its own sake." In the form of poetry, essay, or fiction, evoke another beauty which exists "for its own sake."

VICTOR HERNANDEZ CRUZ

Poet VICTOR HERNANDEZ CRUZ *was born in Puerto Rico and grew up in New York during the 1950s. He is the author of the collections* Red Beans *(noted among* Best Books of 1991 *by* Publishers Weekly*);* Mainland; Tropicalization; By Lingual Wholes; Rhythm, Content and Flavor; *and* Panoramas *(1997). He appeared on Bill Moyers's televised* Language of Life *poetry series and was a recipient of the Guggenheim Award and the New York Poetry Foundation Award. Considered one of the premier Puerto Rican poets of the day, Hernandez Cruz currently teaches at the University of Colorado at Boulder.*

"Atmospheric Phenomenon: The Art of Hurricanes" is from the collection Panoramas.

PERSPECTIVES

1 Recall an encounter of your own with a powerful act of Nature, such as a hurricane, a tornado, a flood, an earthquake, or other. Aside from observing palpable property damage, what inner feelings did you experience?

2 How are hurricanes typically portrayed in the news media? From the naming of a "tropical storm" to the effects of its landfall (or of its avoidance of the land), what sort of images are conveyed?

Atmospheric Phenomenon: The Art of Hurricanes

Out of Africa arises a silence
To dance with the sky—
Spinning it makes its music in the air
Follows the route of the drum,
Comes toward the Atlantic—
To drink rum in the tropic islets
To use the bamboo as flute.

Big horizon of space upset,
Traveling through moisture and heat,

It has been known to throw steps
Of 200 miles per hour—
And yet a man of the mountains
Observed a miniature orchid
Purple and yellow
Hold on with such a pride
That it withstood the hurricane—
To hang with the Christmas flora,
Months later in our hot winter.

Each hurricane has its name
Its own character—
Hugo was strong and clumsy,
His strokes were like Van Gogh—
Bold and thick.
Pellets that were punches against the doors.
He came in vortex spirals.
Painting the sky of "Starry Night"
Above us.
He was poignant like tropical fruit.
Devouring mangos and guavas at will.
Breadfruit which flavors the tongues of Malaysia,
Enriching the waists of the hula dancers
In the South Pacific whose belly buttons
Hear better than ears.

Breadfruit which fries or boils
Was rolling through the streets
Of small towns surrounded by mountains—
As if Hugo did the favor
Of going shopping for us
With free delivery.

The Lesser and Greater Antilles like
Keys on a saxophone
An acoustic shoot
Each playing their note.
Did he blow?
A high sea note
Crescendo-waves
Coastal blues.
An air of leaves,
A percussion of branches
In the melody
The sound of green.

As if an asteroid fell
From the heavens—
Making all the religious
Churchgoers
Hallelujah onto their knees
To pray in total fright
In the face of death,
As if all that church attendance
Was not enough
To give them the blessings
When finally God sent
An ambassador in the form of a cyclone.

Makes one see that
People act contrary
To the laws of science.

Iris was a bitch—
She flirted from 14° north latitude
To 19° north—zigzagging
Lateral west
All that stripteasing
And she didn't come.
She went north,
Beautiful Iris
With her almond eye—
Full of lusty gusts.

Marilyn had curves—
A buttocky volition,
An axial memory that went down
To her tail.
At first she was a mere
Gyrating carousel on
The horizon—
On the satellite picture
She looked like a splattered
Sunny-side-up egg.
Her eye small
Like a black frijol
A beany socket,
Searching for the Virgin Islands.

Maelstrom of the sky—
A piranha of Carib moisture,

Calypso in the middle eye—
A vision which is also breath.

A hurricane is the heartburn of the sky—
A schizoid space,
A rotating mill of nervous air.
What made it so worried?
How did it become so angry?
The atmosphere sneezes.
God bless you.

A necklace of esmeraldas,
The stairway of islands
We are sitting roosters
Waiting to be caressed
Our turquoise gown
Ripples in the wind.

Why was it that that Friday eve
When the hurricane was coming in
The beauty parlors were full?
Get dressed, María
Permanent your hair—
Luscious Caribee—

Extra starch
In case I hang my head out
To the breeze tonight.
Sand, palm, white rum
And perfume. A band
Of clouds for white shoes.

The islands look like spinach
That fell into a blender.
Whirlpool dancer
Licking the rim of the sun
Achieving the enlightenment
That comes through motion and moisture.

After Marilyn Saint Thomas
Was like a Jackson Pollock painting—
Telephone lines like a plate of spaghetti.
A canvas of pickup sticks
Covered with random-chance zinc roofsheets
Automatic rhythm art of happens improve—
A colorful square of inspiration.

Saint Croix as in the joy in Kandinsky's
Brush,
Lateral strokes pushing the sky
To collapse into molasses.

In the howling screech a thought:
Have the stars been blown away?

Caribbean islands
Sprinkled in the form
Of a crescent moon
Falling into Venezuela,
The land of Simón Bolívar,
The Orinoco
Currency of our blood.

A hurricane clears the earth's
Nasal passages
A hurricane would do Los Angeles some good—
The winds of Luis
Could have been packaged
In banana leaves,
Its eyeball of great
Cinematropic suggestion
Placed right outside Beverly Hills,
Driving through the freeways
Breaking the speed limit,
A vacuum of 100-mile radius
Dispelling contamination—
The picture in motion.

Tainos knew that palm Bohíos
Were portable homes—
When the tempest came
To remove them—
In two days they had them
Back up.

As the wind roars
Like a million ghosts—
Hurakán lingua accents each letter.
Going through in total disrespect
Of industry and technology
And conventional itinerary,
Things disappear.

Hurricanes go west
Then north to be cool.

A spirit which knocked
Down Antillean coconuts
Could still be breeze
Cooling tea in Scotland.
My dear Lord—
What passes through
A fruit of passion—
To sniff among the English.

The horizon was a bowl
For Marilyn to make her stew—
Stir in the escabeche
The ocean soup.
Ancient appearance
Would have been
Below in caves.
Subterranean Church
Next to the hidden river
Flowing in peace—
Allowing the passage
Of Hurakán—
Bowing in respect.

CHARTING THE POEM

1 What imagery does Hernandez Cruz employ throughout this poem to portray the hurricane as art, as noted in the title?
2 How does the etymology of the word "hurricane" enhance its significance in this poem—in particular where Hernandez Cruz refers to "Hurakán"?
3 Hurricanes originate in Africa, follow "the route of the drum" (Line 4), make art out of the Caribbean, then (in Lines 173–74) "go west/Then north to be cool." What may the author be suggesting, apart from the typical trajectory of a hurricane? How might a hurricane be a sort of postcolonial phenomenon?

CONSIDERATIONS OF STYLE

1 In what different ways and to what effect does the poem associate food images with hurricanes?
2 How does the poem depict the destruction wreaked by the hurricane? How might the description of the aftermath of a hurricane differ in a newspaper article?
3 What other "families" of images, repeated metaphors, work their way through the poem, and what may the author be implying with them?
4 To a victim of a recent hurricane, how might the style and metaphors of Hernandez Cruz's poem be received? How destructive of human life do hurricanes appear

to be, in comparison with other "natural disasters" such as floods, tornadoes, and extremes of heat and cold?

AFTERTHOUGHTS

1 Both the meteorologist and the poet refer to hurricanes by their given names: Hugo, Iris, Marilyn. . . . What is the scientist's purpose in doing this? How does the poet embellish this anthropomorphism?

2 Locate a web site designed to inform the public of the danger of hurricanes. What rhetorical devices does the web site use? How, in a decidedly different way, does Hernandez Cruz's poem also prepare the reader psychologically for a hurricane?

THE WRITER'S CRAFT

1 Why would a hurricane "do Los Angeles some good"? What other places, to your mind, could benefit from a visitation of Hurakán? Write an editorial on the topic.

2 Write about a hurricane from the point of view of a Taino (indigenous Puerto Rican), or even from the point of view of a hurricane itself. (If you research the path of an actual hurricane, you may be able to generate more specific details.)

DONALD JUSTICE

DONALD JUSTICE *was born in Miami, Florida in 1925. He earned degrees from the universities of Miami, North Carolina, and Iowa, and conducted postdoctoral study at Stanford. He taught at several institutions—including the universities of Florida, Miami, and Iowa and Syracuse University—before retiring in 1992.*

Justice is the author of eight books of poetry, of which the first, The Summer Anniversaries, *was the Lamont Poetry Selection of the Academy of American Poets in 1959, and* Selected Poems *(1979), for which he won the Pulitzer Prize. He has also published* Oblivion: Essays on Poetry *(1998), and a libretto,* The Death of Lincoln *(1988).*

In 1997, Justice was elected to the Academy of American Poets Board of Chancellors.

A pantoum *is a Malay song form that has been used by French and English poets of the nineteenth century. Justice, it should be noted, received an MA in musical composition from the University of North Carolina in 1947. He also grew up in the Great Depression in a Miami markedly different from that city today, so this is a particularly personal poem that depicts not so much victims or heroes, but ordinary people who managed to survive "[without] plot" and "devoid of poetry."*

PERSPECTIVES

1 What impressions do you have of the Great Depression, and what sources have contributed to your understanding of this period? What aspects of the Depression tend to be emphasized, or even emblematic, and what might account for this?

2 Look up in the Internet or in an encyclopedia an article on the Great Depression of 1929–33. How did this crisis affect both the US and the global economies? What social programs were created to relieve economic distress in the United States?

Pantoum of the Great Depression

Our lives avoided tragedy
Simply by going on and on,
Without end and with little apparent meaning.
Oh, there were storms and small catastrophes.

Simply by going on and on
We managed. No need for the heroic.
Oh, there were storms and small catastrophes.
I don't remember all the particulars.

We managed. No need for the heroic.
There were the usual celebrations, the usual sorrows.
I don't remember all the particulars.
Across the fence, the neighbors were our chorus.

There were the usual celebrations, the usual sorrows
Thank god no one said anything in verse.
The neighbors were our only chorus,
And if we suffered we kept quiet about it.

At no time did anyone say anything in verse.
It was the ordinary pities and fears consumed us,
And if we suffered we kept quiet about it.
No audience would ever know our story.

It was the ordinary pities and fears consumed us.
We gathered on porches; the moon rose; we were poor.
What audience would ever know our story?
Beyond our windows shone the actual world.

We gathered on porches; the moon rose; we were poor.
And time went by, drawn by slow horses.
Somewhere beyond our windows shone the world.
The Great Depression has entered our souls like fog.

And time went by, drawn by slow horses.
We did not ourselves know what the end was.
The Great Depression had entered our souls like fog.
We had our flaws, perhaps a few private virtues.

But we did not ourselves know what the end was.
People like us simply go on.
We have our flaws, perhaps a few private virtues,
But it is by blind chance only that we escape tragedy.
And there is no plot in that; it is devoid of poetry.

CHARTING THE POEM

1 How do the people in this poem face their plight in the Great Depression?
2 The narrator repeatedly refers to "[keeping] quiet about it" (Stanza 4) and other self-silencing images. In particular, what is the significance of the absence of

"verse" (Lines 14 and 17) and of "poetry" (in the last line) in the lives of the people in this poem? How does this poem both reveal and conceal by means of such references?

CONSIDERATIONS OF STYLE

1 The form of the pantoum is apparent in this poem: the second and fourth lines of each four-line stanza become the first and third lines of the next stanza. How does the form of the pantoum lend itself—musically and psychologically—to the subject matter of this poem?

2 Aside from the pantoum form, what other stylistic devices, including breaking slightly from the form, does the author use to convey a sense of "soldiering" through the Great Depression?

AFTERTHOUGHTS

1 John Steinbeck's novel *The Grapes of Wrath* depicts the socio-economic impact of the Great Depression upon one family from Oklahoma, the Joads, who were evicted from their farm and forced to travel westward in search of jobs and survival. The film adaptation, a classic epic drama, ends with the lines:

> *Pa Joad:*. . . we sure taken a beatin'.
> *Ma Joad:* I know. That's what makes us tough. Rich fellas come up an' they die an' their kids ain't no good, an' they die out. But we keep a-comin'. We're the people that live. They can't wipe us out. They can't lick us. And we'll go on forever, Pa . . . 'cause . . . we're the people.

What differences in attitude do you find between Ma Joad and the speaker in Justice's poem?

THE WRITER'S CRAFT

1 Interview a person who has lived through the Great Depression. What stories does he or she recall about that era? Use the material from your interview in an essay about the Great Depression from *your* generation's perspective.

2 A student writing of her relatives' experience in the 1947 Partition that separated India and Pakistan (causing approximately a million deaths) makes the point that her grandmother's is a "marked generation." Looking back over the last several decades (from which survivors remain to this day), write—in prose or poetry—about another such "marked generation" in world history.

KEN LIPENGA

KEN LIPENGA *was born in the south of Malawi. He was graduated from the University of Malawi in 1976, and he now teaches language and literature at Chancellor College.*

Lipenga has published short stories, poems, and critical reviews. "Waiting for a Turn" is from a collection by the same name, published in 1981. The story also appears in African Rhapsody: Short Stories of the Contemporary African Experience, *published by Anchor Books in 1994.*

PERSPECTIVES

1 What are some traditional conceptions of a Hereafter in major world religions such as Hinduism, Judaism, Buddhism, Christianity, and Islam?

2 In many African faith traditions, the world of the "living" coexists with the world of the "dead." What perspectives do you bring to the text of these worlds; how separate are they, ultimately, in your view?

Waiting for a Turn

All roads lead to Sapitwa. All traffic moves toward Sapitwa. Rivers crisscross and point in different directions. But all rivers flow into Sapitwa pool. Tears of laughter and tears of sorrow flow into Sapitwa pool. All enemies meet and shake hands at Sapitwa.

I

There was no question that my Mbambande Tailoring Shop was the most successful in town. Everyone, from platformed young men and bewigged girls to respectable big shots, came to my shop for their clothes. Everyone who wanted the very latest fashion came to Mbambande. Wives refused dresses from their husbands unless they carried the "Mbambande" label. Girls ignored a young man unless they were convinced that his suit was from Mbambande. Children refused to go to school until *abada* bought their school uniforms from Mbambande. Anything without the Mbambande label was old-fashioned. Fragile marriages collapsed beneath the weight of the "Mbambande" label. In short no one was anyone unless they were clothed by Mbambande Tailoring Shop. Such was my success.

All this was a pleasant surprise. There were times, I admit, when I felt genuinely alarmed at my success. For I had not expected anything of the sort when, a few months after leaving the university, I resigned from that insurance job. And here I must give you a little more detail.

I had resigned for two reasons. First, I could not understand why after spending years at the university, I found myself living from day to day, without the slightest sign that I would ever become rich. I am the get-rich-quick type and hadn't the patience to wait till I had crept through all the usual acrobatics that one must perform in order to get raises and rises. I also have a flighty temper, a weakness which wouldn't let me stand being bossed around by someone for the rest of my life.

I saved some money and resigned, planning to start a business of my own 5
where I could boss myself and control the pace of my progress to the top. I chose tailoring. I don't quite know why. It may have to do with the fact that I had always been one for fashions in clothing. But at the time of my decision, I scarcely knew how to operate a sewing machine. I had to take a one-month course at one of the city tailoring shops. Thus I was in every way a novice in the business, and the success which soon came my way was a great surprise.

I think the hunchback appeared at about the time when I was approaching the peak of success and I needed more tailors. He came one morning, and before the day was over we all saw that he was exceptional. Exceptional in his skill and hard work. Give him a piece of cloth to be made into trousers and they would be ready within an hour. Get suspicious and look for faults and you would find none. Customers always went away satisfied. Oh, such a clever, fast tailor I had never seen before.

I was, of course, delighted; not only because his example infected the rest of my staff, but also because I felt his presence would make my business boom. I could already see rival firms withering away as I shot to the top.

Then came the shock. After a week Hunchback came to ask if he could live in the shop, as he could find no accommodation elsewhere. He was serious. But how could I allow this? My shop was on the city's main street, and to allow a hunchback, no matter how skilled and hardworking, to live there would be bad for business. Even without this problem the whole idea was unthinkable. So I said "No," as I am sure any other sane man would have done; but I also told him that I would look into the problem. He said nothing in reply.

The next morning Hunchback came in with his two wives and thirteen children. There was no word of explanation but it was clear that he had decided to move into the shop whether I liked it or not. The arrival of that army of children caused chaos; they roamed everywhere, pulling at the clothing, turning everything upside down, and causing panic and confusion among my tailors. Such rascals I have never seen before. But life is an unpleasant business, and I know such trials ought not surprise anyone. I found it all very painful.

I told Hunchback to leave. But he quietly refused to budge, and generally behaved as though he was only exercising a natural right. Well, I have already confessed that I am not a saint when it comes to keeping my temper on a leash. I kicked the hunchback with a heavy right boot, and, well, I swear I had never thought he was so light. My modest kick sent him clear into the street where he landed on his head, more or less.

I now seemed to be possessed by some evil spirit for I followed him and started clobbering him severely in front of all those people on the street. At this point his thirteen children, all of them very small and apparently of the same age, swarmed over me and started tearing at my clothes. And the people who had quickly gathered in a crowd gasped in amazement. They opened their mouths wide and although they did not say anything in particular I understood the message.

Hunchback, my exceptional tailor, disappeared with his two wives and thirteen children. Where he went, I knew not.

But immediately my business began to decline. It seemed that people generally disapproved of my beating up Hunchback. They also seemed to think that it would have done my business no harm at all to allow the hunchback and his family to live in my shop on Main Street.

I see no harm in begging to differ but, oh, why is life so unpleasant? People stopped coming to Mbambande Tailoring Shop and the ugliest things were said about me. People were earnestly warned off for fear of assault. Some ingenious fellow made the sudden discovery that we were not in fact good tailors at all, that my shop had from the start produced the lousiest tailoring in town. The news spread. Husbands pulled the Mbambande label from the clothes in their households for fear of having them burnt by angry wives. Girls scornfully ignored boys wearing Mbambande clothes. All around I saw smaller shops booming and growing. My tailors complained that their wives threatened to leave them unless they stopped working for "the murderer." The tailors proved how they loved their wives by dropping out one by one.

Darkness settled on my shop. The sewing machines began to rust; a ghostly silence crept in; spiders built empires in dark corners; lizards played on the walls; grass grew fast outside: Mbambande Tailoring Shop was no more.

My wife, an imaginative woman, began to wonder why there was no bread no margarine no meat no soap no this no that in the house. She then proceeded to conclude that I was squandering my money on other women, and even claimed that she knew I had been doing this all along.

I kicked my wife with my favorite right boot, and I had not thought she was so light. My modest kick sent her flying through the door; I followed and angrily beat her up. My children pulled at my clothes, and the people from the neighborhood, who had quickly gathered in a crowd, opened their mouths wide and although they said nothing specific I could see they were not on my side.

My imaginative wife disappeared with the children, took them to her people. Ah, life is an unpleasant business.

Well, there was no going back now. I went into the kitchen and smashed the china. I came out and smashed all the furniture in the lounge. It didn't help. I piled up all my clothing and blankets and set them on fire. The smoke filled my eyes with tears. I turned on the radio full blast, went into a corner of the bedroom, and cried like a six-year-old. That didn't help either, so I took the radio outside and set it on fire while the crowd watched. They watched me in silence, their mouths agape, and when they were satisfied that I had destroyed all several rushed off in a hurry. I knew where they were going.

But they couldn't make a fool of me, for I had already sized up the situation and made the inevitable decision. None in the crowd dared come near me.

I set out for the mountain.

II

I lifted my bruised limbs and turned round to look back. It had been a great climb. Looking back at the world was like looking down a deep well; everything seemed so infinite. I tried to recall a picture of life down there, to come to terms with it, and mark its place in time. But time vanished and desolation grew. I abandoned the effort and became myself again.

I turned to face my new landscape. So the rocky massif glimmering in heavenly silver before me was Sapitwa. School geography books had merely said this was the highest peak in the area, without suggesting any spiritual power. How thrilling it was! How elevating! What better site could I have chosen? Here on Sapitwa I was at the apex, here on Sapitwa I was (at least physically!) above mortals, and this thought made my blood surge with joy. I kept reminding myself that no other mortal had ever thought of this idea.

Long ago, when I was very young in the village, I asked my grandmother why she held the mountain in such reverence, indeed at times even worshiping it.

"Because, son," she said, "the spirits of the ancestors dwell there."

"Where exactly?"

She had laughed before she realized that I was serious.

"Near the top," she had answered.

"But why not on the very top itself, grandmother?"

"Because on the very top, son, dwell the Great Spirits themselves, guarding the Great Abyss."

Imagine! I had selected for the site of my deed the dwelling place of the Great Spirits themselves! I had not been thinking of the conversation with my grandmother when I made that inevitable decision. I only remembered it on arrival before the peak. I was thrilled at the idea of being received by sacred entities. It added a divine dimension to my plan. And this was what I had wanted: an original kind of departure, not something ready-made which you only had to put on when the time arrived. No, a ready-made life was to be rewarded with an original death.

From the landscape it was easy to guess where it must be, the East. There was something ominously inviting about the East, some mystical spell about this region which was associated with sunrise and the Magi. And that was only proper, for was not the leap itself a step toward spiritual renewal? Would not that simple act let me live in the world of Great Spirits? I walked on toward the Abyss, oblivious to all but the spiritual ecstasy eating up my inside. Closer and closer to the Abyss I went, and all along I readied myself for the leap.

But from nowhere four hands suddenly grabbed my neck and arms. A dizzy spell pinned my soul to the ground; I felt like a grasshopper under an elephant's foot. I had feared at the start that I was being followed but had never expected anyone to come this far. I sank into delirium.

Hello my exceptional tailor hello my imaginative wife! Glad to see you two again! What can I do for you? I'll do the impossible for you. Just wait here a moment while I fetch the impossible. But why are your friends' mouths gaping? Why doesn't anything come out of those mouths? Why don't they say something?

My captors had given me some time to recover from the shock, for when I came to they were sitting patiently on a rock beside me. I looked at them, two heavy figures in a strange uniform, and my eyes begged for an explanation.

"Sorry, uncle," said one in a voice all its own. "We didn't mean to be rough with you. Only we thought you might need some help."

His voice was a hen's scratch on a healing wound: it provoked a nausea from the distant past which had somehow managed to pocket itself away. I felt insulted, extremely insulted. I mumbled something about privacy; something about rights to my own property; something about Hunchback being a man. But my voice failed, my will vanished when I realized that the two men did not follow what I was saying.

"Sorry, uncle," said the spokesman. "We don't understand what you are saying, but we don't believe we've anything to do with it. We only want to clear up a certain misunderstanding. I . . . er . . . I take it you're on your way to the Abyss?"

I nodded.

"Then please come this way. You must take your place in the queue . . . I take it you're aware of the queue?"

There was something hovering at the doorway of my mind which I struggled to pin down. The man's voice made me feel as if I was cutting a ludicrous figure in a crowd. I felt like a clown. I felt I was being laughed at. Someone had found that I was a clown and spread the news. It seemed that I was about to be the victim of some mysterious force.

"I take it you're aware of the queue?"

All roads lead to Sapitwa. All traffic roars toward Sapitwa. Rivers crisscross and point in different directions. But all rivers flow into the Sapitwa pool.

Tears of laughter and tears of sorrow flow into Sapitwa pool. Blood sweat and tears flow into Sapitwa pool. The wind blows all fires toward Sapitwa. All roads lead to Sapitwa. Deadly enemies seal their mouths with the sap of the *kachere* tree and swear never to talk to each other. But all enemies meet and shake hands at Sapitwa.

In my head, pictures of a clever Hunchback shrouded in smoke.

"I take it you're aware of the queue."

It was a still, multicolored thread which disappeared into the distance on both sides, a silent river made of faces, black faces, brown faces, white faces, yellow faces, young faces, old faces, middle-aged faces, rich and poor faces looking bored, grim faces of businessmen and beggars, faces of red-eyed prostitutes and professors, faces of bus drivers, faces of drunken old women, faces of banana sellers, faces of international politicians, faces of spear-brandishing warriors, faces of mourning mothers side by side with faces of pilots of bomber planes, faces of convicted thieves, tired faces, happy faces, angry faces, frightened faces, faces, faces, faces; faces of all kinds, standing still in that endless line.

"You see," spokesman was saying, "you've to wait for all these people in front of you. They came here before you. You mustn't jump the queue. It isn't proper. Quite against the rules here."

A mystical experience. We walked on.

"These people you see all came here long before you. Er . . . I wouldn't be wrong to assume that you too, uncle, are on the Quest . . . I mean for a . . . er . . . shall we call it a parting of your own?"

The feeling you get is of transparent nakedness, a feeling such as you experience in a dream where, walking around amid a crowd a short distance from your house, you discover that you are going about stark naked.

"In that case, as you can see, you have company. But we believe in being orderly here. Hence the queue. I take it you don't mind?"

Every particle of the experience hovered on the threshold, like a memory struggling to come clear.

"Good. I thought so. You see, uncle, the moment you appeared there, I knew you were one of us. You have company, you have company. I tell you, it used to be all chaos here, before things were organized. People fighting to get a place at the edge to leap to their end. Some even getting killed before they got a chance to die their chosen death. It was survival of the fittest then, crude brute behavior. That's why it was necessary to have a kind of system."

I think we walked for a year or so. I could not measure the time or distance. But in the end my captor said: "Aha, we're here at last, uncle. This is your place in the queue. Stay here, and wait for your turn."

III

I am still waiting. Been waiting all these years. Gray hairs have raided my head. My front teeth have dropped earthward. Sometimes I feel as if spiders had built empires in the dark corners of my head, and from time to time I think I hear lizards playing hide and seek in my inside. Yesterday I was amazed to see folds on my forehead. These days I avoid making journeys, and when I do I have to rely on my companion the stick. I know that soon I shall have to give up journeys altogether, for my eyes are losing faith.

I am still waiting. My turn has not yet come. They say it will, that we must keep waiting and not lose faith. Last year progress was made: I received The Initiation, and now have a new name. I am at last fit for the Great Abyss. The Great Spirits will receive me! Oh, how I long for the day!

There are many of us here on Sapitwa, and we get new arrivals every day, all on the Quest. If you look over the edge of the peak on the far side, so the young men tell me, you see countless humans clambering to reach the top. Most are young and are on the run for one reason or another. Sometimes I feel the brats ought to be sent back. Their reasons lack depth. But there's no choice, for these youngsters are a force on their own. Only a few months ago, they ganged up and threatened to reintroduce chaos at the Abyss.

I am told that the peaks surrounding Sapitwa are also filled with humans clambering on the Quest. So we are not the only ones after all. It's reassuring, though I don't quite know if the story is true. People can take advantage of your weak eyes and tell you all sorts of lies.

With the growing population here on Sapitwa we had to reorganize ourselves into a kind of community, with leaders and representatives of this and that and the other. Last year came a priest who has been active in establishing a church and school too, because of the many children being born here as we wait our turn. A hospital has also been built and is proving very useful.

I don't know when my turn will come, but I'm certain that more years will pass. While I wait I have found something to fill my time. Over the years it has become necessary to have tailors here on Sapitwa, and my skill was naturally called upon. So, well, I'm not ashamed to say that I have opened a tailoring shop. On the door of my tailoring shop a Sapitwa artist has painted in crude letters: "New Mbambande Tailoring Shop." I have a number of tailors working for me, and among them are two or three who worked for me in the old shop. They came here too. Isn't life a mysterious affair? I have, however, been particularly careful to avoid tailors of the hunchback kind. It is a simple business precaution.

CHARTING THE STORY

1. Taken as three parts of an allegory, how are the typographically marked divisions of the story connected both linearly and internally? Note that these structural features of a text are typically referred to as coherence and cohesion.
2. Which of the "seven cardinal sins"—pride, anger, avarice, envy, gluttony, lust, and sloth—do you think the narrator is guilty of? Why?
3. What request does the hunchback make of the narrator, and why does the narrator turn it down? From his own point of view, is the narrator being reasonable? From

the hunchback's point of view, is his a reasonable request? What are the immediate consequences, and the long-range consequences, of the narrator's expulsion of the hunchback?

4 How does the world of Sapitwa parallel that of the world the narrator has left? Why must "order" be maintained?

CONSIDERATIONS OF STYLE

1 When the narrator relates his treatment of his "imaginative wife," his story repeats nearly verbatim that of his kicking the hunchback. How does this affect your estimation of his "reliability" as a narrator? And what stylistic techniques does the author seem to be employing?

2 What does the river of faces described in Paragraph 46 represent to you?

3 How is Sapitwa characterized by the narrator, by his grandmother, and by those around him at Sapitwa? Overall, does it seem to be an improvement, or not much different, from the world before? What in the narrator's manner of description would make it so?

4 How does irony both inform and amuse in this story?

AFTERTHOUGHTS

1 In Paragraph 50, the narrator describes the "feeling . . . of transparent nakedness . . . such as you experience in a dream where, walking around amid a crowd a short distance from your house, you discover that you are going about stark naked." What might be a Freudian interpretation of such a dream?

2 The early part of Lipenga's story, with its tale of the hunchback, is somewhat reminiscent of Herman Melville's "Bartleby the Scrivener" (where a man hired by the narrator refuses to do anything the narrator wishes him to do, and likewise refuses to leave his employment, replying to all requests with, "I would prefer not to."). How is this story different, and what likenesses between them are apparent? (The Melville story is generally rather easy to find.)

THE WRITER'S CRAFT

1 Write an essay describing a nemesis in your life at some point thus far "on the Quest." Describe changes in your relationship with and greater understanding of your erstwhile nemesis as you became distanced from one another in time.

2 From the point of view of another person on Sapitwa, write of your particular reason for going on the Quest.

3 Rolling the story forward to the time when the narrator is free to take his place at the front of the line, what do you predict will happen? Write a Section IV from his point of view, in as much of his style of writing as you can adopt.

RUKHSANA AHMED

RUKHSANA AHMED *is from Pakistan. Among other things, she has edited an anthology of poetry entitled* We Sinful Women *(London: Women's Press, 1991).*

This story comes from So That You Can Know Me: An Anthology of Pakistani Women Writers *(which was originally published in 1994 by the Pakistan Academy of Letters, and which has been republished in 1997 for the world market in an abridged edition). In it, a young woman seeks help from a forbidden source, a practitioner of women's magic, in order to defend herself against her abusive husband.*

PERSPECTIVES

1. Domestic violence—more often than not, wife beating—is a widespread social problem throughout the world. What structures exist, in both developed and developing nations, to protect the victims?
2. Many religions, particularly Islam, Judaism, and Christianity, condemn the practice of sorcery. What reasons underlie such prohibitions? What practices do they tend to advocate, instead of resorting to magic, if one is troubled?

The Spell and the Ever-Changing Moon

Nisa looked around nervously as she walked along the dusty edge of the road on that suffocating July afternoon. She was in a part of Lahore which she did not know very well but all the landmarks her neighbour *Apa* Zarina had described had kept appearing so far. She tugged at the *burqa* round her shoulders as if afraid of being recognized through its thin georgette veil and the black silky folds that enveloped her neat, compact little figure. It belonged to her unmarried friend Seema and had been borrowed specially for the occasion. This was the first time in her whole life that she had embarked on a mission knowing it wasn't "permitted." She was trembling slightly with guilt and fear. Her breathing and heartbeat quickened as she approached the house.

Just as Zarina had said, it stood at the end of the *kutchi abadi.* A small house, one of the few here which were brick-built. Right outside its entrance was the lean-to of the motorbike repair shop which she had been told to look out for. Two men sat there tinkering with motorbikes which looked too rusty and battered to be repaired. They looked up from their sweaty labour each time a woman went in or out of the green door of Talat's house.

Most of the women who came had their faces covered with shawls or *dupattas* and some, like Nisa, wore *burqas*. But occasionally the men succeeded in catching a glimpse of a young, fresh, female face. In any case they weren't discouraged by the veils and cloaks. If the outline or gait indicated a youngish woman they did their best to get attention by shouting an obscenity or by humming a snatch of film song.

The women had been trained for years to sidestep and ignore this kind of behaviour. So they all scurried past, hastening their footsteps just a little. Nisa, who was skilled in the same strategy, quickened her pace to reach the shelter of the house although she had been fearful of the ultimate step she was about to take. It was for her a house of Evil.

5 She stood for a second looking around the bare courtyard. In one corner was the usual outside tap in its sunken cemented square used for washing. All down the courtyard hung the laundry drying at the remarkable speed that only the brilliant afternoon sun made possible. Hesitating for an instant, she walked into the small room beyond.

Her eyes were blinded by the sudden fragrant darkness of the room as she steadied herself against the door jamb as she stumbled over the stock of shoes near the door. Slipping off her own, Nisa sat down just inside the doorway. She gasped as her eyes began to see.

Talat sat on a low stage with two huge black snakes entwined round her body. She was strikingly good-looking and very fashionable. Her large black eyes were highlighted by the blackest of kohl and her small delicate mouth was painted a brilliant red, matching the nail varnish on her carefully manicured hands. A shapely bosom and a slender waist were clearly outlined through her black lawn *kurta*. She was muttering to herself, eyes closed, body swaying rhythmically, whilst the women round her stared in hypnotized fascination.

Nisa's glance surveyed the room quickly. The sunlight had been shut out. In the dim lamplight she could make out crudely painted pictures of holy faces which she had never seen before. She remembered hearing about distant foreign lands where it was customary to paint portraits of saints, a practice she knew was definitely blasphemous, and she hastily touched her ears in a gesture of contrition. "*Tauba, tauba,*" she sought forgiveness. In one corner burned scented candles emitting whitish clouds of smoke with a cloying sweet smell. On the mantelshelf stood a photo of Talat with her *guru* who looked remarkably young and healthy as he smiled down at her with his hand resting on her head in benediction.

The queue was moving slowly. People were leaving one by one as each managed to get a personal audience with Talat. There was the usual assortment of problems—mother-in-law or daughter-in-law ones, there were patients seeking cures for incurable diseases, the destitute looking for a better future. Whatever their problems, Talat gave them that hope they knew they did not have.

No one seemed to have come alone except Nisa. She trembled again. It would be her turn soon to speak to Talat. She wasn't sure even now what she would say or what she would ask for. She clutched her cheap plastic handbag in a fierce grip under her left arm and in her right hand she held a brown paper bag containing the four eggs she had bought on her way up, according to Zarina's instructions. The sweat from her fingers had formed a damp, dark ring round the base of the paper bag. She wondered uncomfortably if it was going to give way.

As the crowd in the room thinned, Nisa found herself slowly moving nearer to the raised dais. Within half an hour she was face to face with Talat. Nisa looked up into the dark, warm, liquid eyes. Disconcerted by Talat's youthful appearance, she felt for an instant she had made a mistake. Talat's eyes smiled as if they'd read her thoughts.

"How can I help you, my daughter?" she asked, as if a little amused by this belated scepticism. Her manner and her address claimed for herself the supremacy and status which age automatically bestows on everyone in that world, a manner which seemed strangely inappropriate in someone who was perhaps only nineteen or twenty.

But Nisa was overwhelmed by the encouraging sympathy and affection in her voice and felt the tears welling up in her throat. She could only say, "It's my husband . . . ," before she broke down into a fit of sobbing, aware that she was being stared at very curiously. This kind of desperation was always useful as it impressed other clients. Talat soothed her gently and tenderly.

"Hush, my daughter, have faith. I can help you." Her voice was reassuring. She eyed the bag in Nisa's hands and asked in a whisper, "Do you want me to do a *chowkie* for you?" Nisa could only nod an affirmative. Talat proceeded quickly to perform that ritual. Relieving Nisa of the eggs she placed them in a neat square on a small wooden stool. Nisa stopped crying as she watched in fascination. Talat's fingers moved dextrously as she placed a bowl beside the stool and then began to unwind the snakes from her body. She pulled both of them up to the eggs and closed her eyes, rocking backwards and forwards as if in a trance.

Nisa's body stiffened with fear as the snakes stood dangerously close to her for a few seconds, sniffing the eggs and then raising their heads in what looked like vicious contempt. There was absolute silence in the room as everyone watched. Talat came out of her trance and her assistant, a very plain woman of around thirty-five or so, helped her to capture the snakes and put them away in two large, colourful, wicker baskets.

The snakes slithered and hissed as if in protest, but were soon put away. While the other woman was covering the baskets with pieces of black cloth, Talat began to break the eggs one by one into the clay bowl. Nisa tried to watch her but felt compelled to watch the snakes.

Suddenly she heard Talat's voice cursing under her breath and looked fearfully down at the bowl. On top of the cracked eggs floated claws, blood and some strange, noxious and ugly greenish matter.

"Ah, my daughter," Talat exclaimed as she folded her hands and closed her eyes as if to seek help from above. Nisa shuddered and covered her face with both hands in shock and horror.

"You are deep in difficulties, I can see." Talat was shaking her head in concern. "You need the Art to help you. You can change the path of your man, you know. There is a way..."

The pitch of her voice had changed. Nisa was shivering visibly now. Talat leaned closer to Nisa. She whispered confidentially in her ears as the other women stared. Nisa had kept the lower half of her veil stretched across her face but the curious audience could see her anxious brown eyes widen with horror as they hung on Talat's face, drinking in her whispered words.

She felt dumbfounded and shaken. With her finger on the clasp of her handbag she looked at Talat's companion and began fumblingly, "What's the... the fee? What shall I..."

The woman glanced at Talat's face and replied gushingly, "Oh, there's no fee really, *Bibi*. But we do have to take some *nazars* for the snakes, you know. It's ten rupees for the *chowkie, Bibi*." And she continued again quickly, "You know, Talat *Bibi* has to perform a *chilla* many times to get her powers. That's very, very hard work, *Bibi*. And you need *nazars* for the snakes, you know, *Bibi*. It's twenty-five rupees in all."

She was observing Nisa closely as she spoke, the changing expression in Nisa's eyes guiding her in her reckoning of the bill. Nisa pushed the greasy notes with clumsy and clammy fingers into the assistant's eager hands and stumbled to her feet hastily.

Outside, she tripped over the burning stones in the paved courtyard and then on the threshold of the green door. The two men looked up and jeered again but Nisa neither saw nor heard them. She was too preoccupied with those strange whispered words. She saw the bus approaching from the right direction and ran towards it, relieved at not having to wait in the blistering heat near that evil place.

In all her twenty-six years she had never been so shocked by what she had heard or seen. Neither the shock, years ago, of seeing some pornographic pictures that a girl at school had found in her father's trunk, nor that other time when she had woken up in the middle of the night as the family slept on the roof-top and suddenly realized that the neighbours were actually "doing it" could compare. She had blushed into the pillow and covered her ears to block out the muffled sounds. The mental picture of *Chachi* Nuggo's massive breasts flashed in her mind and the thought of Chachaji on top of her embarrassed her even as she remembered it now, almost ten years later.

"It's indecent even to think of it," she reprimanded herself. Her mind returned again to the present and tried to grapple with what Talat had just told her.

"Women," she'd said, "are powerful beings. If you want your man to be utterly in your power all you have to do is give him a drop of your own blood to drink." As Nisa stared at Talat, vaguely apprehensive, she elaborated her meaning. "Menstrual blood has great magical powers, you know. A man can never overcome the spell. He will become a slave to your will."

Nisa shuddered again as she remembered the words with horror and revulsion. The very thought seemed to impure to her, so unclean. She felt certain that the knowledge came from the devil. "I couldn't do such an awful thing, even to Hameed," she mused to herself, wondering longingly for a few seconds about how it would feel if Hameed was indeed a slave to her will. She tried determinedly to shake off the idea.

"*Ammah* was right," she thought. "Never to go to these weird places. They are truly evil . . . there can be no doubt about it."

She really regretted having gone to see Talat. If it hadn't been for Zarina 30
she'd never have done it. "No one really believes in such things these days," she thought. "Yet Zarina's mother does look a lot better now." The justification for the trip also rose from within her heart.

The debate continued in her mind all the way back across town on the bus. It was almost time for *Asar* prayers; the shadows had doubled in length, she noticed, as she got off near the Mini Market and walked round the shops to the row of poky little houses behind them. Her footsteps quickened as she thought of the children being looked after by Zarina.

Her neighbour was full of questions but Nisa could not bring herself to repeat what Talat had told her. She just hedged round the questions and rushed off with her brood, saying she still had the dinner to cook.

She fed the older children and sat down to nurse the younger of her two boys, Zafar. Her mind was still occupied by her afternoon's adventure. She now felt curiously subdued and guilty about it. Zarina had meant well. Indeed, Nisa often felt guilty even about the fact that her neighbours knew the problems she was having with her marriage.

Her mother had always stressed the dignity and value of reserve. "A good woman," she used to say, "knows who to keep the family's secrets. What's the use, anyway, of telling people seven doors away that your month's allowance hasn't quite stretched to the last four days this month? If possible, you manage to survive without letting the world know."

Nisa felt that was indeed where she'd failed to act as a really good wife. 35
Her neighbours on all three sides of her knew her dark secret. Her own family did not know. She was proud of that. Every time someone had come to visit her from her home town, Sialkot, she had kept up appearances quite well. But she hadn't been able to hide the truth from her neighbours.

Each night when Hameed got home, looking drunk and forbidding, she strengthened her resolve to keep out of his way and not to cause a row, but five nights out of ten she failed. He seemed to seek her out as if that was what he'd been waiting for all day. She wished sometimes that he could come home earlier so that the noise of his rowing would be less noticeable. At eleven the whole neighbourhood was quiet and each abusive mouthful he hurled at her could be heard at least three doors away. Sometimes there were flying plates and howling children, if they happened to wake up. A couple of times she had lost control of herself and had begun to scream hysterically with fear.

Anyway, she realized that it had got easier for her since the neighbours knew. Sometimes when the row was a really bad one Zarina would call out to ask if she was all right. The shame of that always got through to Hameed, even if he was really drunk, and it made him stop and go to bed grumbling about interfering busybody neighbours.

His anger and abuse were often followed by an overbearingly vicious assertion of his conjugal rights which Nisa never dared to deny him, and she believed she ought not dare to deny him either. She never resisted him but she resented his heavy-handed impatience. She hated the stink of cheap, home-brewed beer on his breath with all the moral weight of her mother's censure of drinking. And she missed the snatches of wooing from the early days of her marriage.

After the day's wearying labour, it was that physical humiliation borne in silence five nights out of ten which was consuming her. She loathed that physical submission to his will. It had to be done like the housework and the caring of the children. It was her part of the deal, her return for the housekeeping allowance. She didn't argue about that but she bitterly resented his drinking. Though she wouldn't dare argue with him, she was unable to conceal her disapproval. And her tight-lipped hostility aggravated his bad temper. He was riled by her strong sense of moral superiority into an even deeper viciousness. Sometimes this worked for her. He would be too angry to want her afterwards. Sometimes he would be too drunk to notice her aloofness or her lofty anger and he just pleased himself.

That evening as she lay on her *charpoy* in the courtyard staring at the clear night sky, a vision of Talat's face kept intruding into her thoughts. It was a picture of Talat which compelled her imagination. She saw her standing waist-deep in the shallower waters of the Ravi, dressed in black, eyes uplifted to the moon, invoking her powers. Power, the very thought of power seemed so seductive to Nisa in her helpless situation. She had been adventurous that morning but she knew she couldn't be as brave as Talat, though she longed to have some control over her circumstances.

She jumped up as she heard Hameed's footsteps at the door. It was nearly eleven, his usual time. She quickly brought the simmering water on the stove to the boil and tipped the rice in. That night as Hameed launched into his usual nagging and complaining between each morsel of curried lentils and rice, Nisa felt her resolve never to think about magic weakening.

She wondered how much pain it took, how much courage, to pollute a man's cup of tea or glass of iced water. She watched Hameed's lips pressed against the glass of water and shivered. Through her mind flashed a memory of her first-born, Karim, newly arrived, lying across her belly, sticky and a little blood-stained. She had touched him unbelievingly . . . the sight of the drops of blood on the cord hadn't really worried her or repulsed her then. That was the clot of blood that had made him possible, given him life.

"What are you staring at?" Hameed snapped peevishly, and Nisa jumped to her feet again to clear up the plates. Somewhere in the recesses of her mind she had caught a glimpse of herself performing a grossly sacrilegious spell and that glimpse had unnerved her for a few seconds.

All her life she had seen the women around her observing the taboos in this area of their lives. Nisa herself had developed a deep sense of shame over the years through the secrecy and the avoidances. Now it was as though Talat had pulled out a vital brick at the base of that belief.

45 If it really had magical powers, why did women abhor it so, she wondered. She knew she was too simple to work out the answers but the question rose insistently within her heart each month when she menstruated. The abhorrence didn't make sense to her now that she thought about it. After all, they all knew enough about the physical aspect of menstruation. Wasn't there some mild relief when girls "started" or worry when they were "late"?

Seven months passed by with the creeping pace of a prison sentence. Each month she wondered if she would dare. Each month when the moon was full she remembered Talat's eyes, her face aglow in the moonlight standing waist-deep in the waters of the Ravi, and each month the spell seemed less shocking. She thought about herself, her life and her body a great deal in those months. Each time she saw the moon she prayed for a better month, but things did not change. Except for her own attitude to her own body. That changed subtly.

Towards the end of the month, when the money began to run out on the twenty-fifth or thereabouts, a deep bitterness filled her heart. She had to turn to him again to ask him for more and have him spit in her face. They'd always been the worst nights of the month, when his anger had a sharper, more righteous edge to it. But now when that happened she resented him as deeply as he resented the increased expenses.

She had grown weary of her life. The skimping and the managing, the hard work and the violence and finally the humiliating abuse of her body. She began to refuse him. That was the way of wayward women, she'd been taught, but she no longer cared.

Hameed was nonplussed by her refusal, too surprised and hurt to argue or insist at first. But then she began to reject him more frequently and he had to react. Surprisingly, he did not take her forcibly, but became more violent in other ways. It was almost as if he was aware of her newly found veneration for her own body, and had to violate her in some other way.

50 For Nisa those refusals became a small triumph each time. The black eyes, the swollen lips or bruised face became more commonplace for her. Zarina's mother would shake her head sadly sometimes and say, "Oh, that man, *Beti.* God will reward you for your patience. What makes him so angry?"

For Nisa the bruises became an option she preferred to humiliating sex. She wasn't sure that she wanted rewards in heaven; she only wished she had to suffer less on earth.

That spring Zarina's mother became ill again. The doctor came but the old lady was not reassured. She kept talking of Talat and how well her remedy had worked the year before. Nisa came back from their house with her head full of memories of the day she had gone to see Talat.

Talat was no longer an evil practitioner of magic for her. She appeared in her memory as someone gentle and loving, a friend and a sympathizer, who cared for the underdog, for her. The knowledge that Talat had imparted to her of the strange, sinful spell had given her a sense of strength. Nisa had changed from being a shivering, huddled creature into a calmer, thinking woman.

That evening was women's night out. Seema was getting married the next day. They were all getting together to assemble her clothes for her trousseau, ready to be shown to the in-laws the following day. Nisa had found the right moment to obtain Hameed's permission to attend. She went round early, dressed in glittering clothes, her best earrings swinging from her ears, Zafar in her arms and the older two trailing by her side.

The girls were in high spirits, the singing was buoyant and loud. Nisa tried hard to blend into the scene but her laughter was laboured. The same old familiar well-loved tunes were jarringly painful today. The lies they told of marital bliss, of loving husbands and contented days irritated her. Nisa looked around at the little house sadly and remembered her mother's house. She was pulled out of her nostalgia by the sound of Seema's aunt lecturing her on how to cope with her new life. Forbearance and forgiveness were the operative words. That too was all too familiar.

Nisa could restrain herself no longer. She suddenly erupted, "And how much exactly is she really supposed to endure, *Chachi*? How many tears does it take to make a home?" She asked quietly, "If Seema was really drowning in her own tears and being choked by her own screams, would you still not want her to look back to this house?"

Looking a little uncomfortable and annoyed, the aunt said, "Heaven forbid, rather an inauspicious question for tonight, isn't it?"

Other women around them showed an interest in the conversation. Most of them knew about Nisa. Suddenly Nisa felt an arm around her shoulders. It was Seema's mother. The pain beneath the question had communicated itself to her. "No mother could shut her doors behind her daughter forever. If Seema needed help, I would gladly let her in, of course."

Nisa smiled with difficulty and returned to the kitchen for another teapot. Zarina was assisting in the kitchen.

"You know what?" she chirped as she saw Nisa coming in. "I went to Talat's house today to get Anunah's medicine and I found to my great surprise that Talat and her family have disappeared."

"What do you mean?"

"Well, packed up and shot off into the night."

"Why?" Nisa's heart was throbbing.

"Well! The motorcycle mechanic said they had to run because too many people kept returning to demand their money back. It seems she was a fraud."

Nisa was quiet as she walked the short distance back home with Zarina. 65
The children were exhausted. She took their shoes off one by one and then went into the kitchen to cook the rice, still wondering about Talat. At times she could have sworn that she actually felt the power of the magic, the spell she carried within her body. Now she felt lost and bereft again. She kept hoping that the spell she knew about was genuine.

Hameed came in later and more drunk than ever. He attacked her more viciously than usual, taunting her about her finery and the earrings. Nisa, overwrought and frightened, got up hurriedly to leave the room but he pulled her by the arm. She lost her balance, stumbled and fell to the floor. Her head hit the corner of the wooden *chowkie* and began to bleed furiously. There was a terrible clang as enamelled mugs, plates and bowls rolled off the kitchen shelf. The noise shook Hameed. He pulled himself up and tried to help Nisa up.

But she was hysterical. "No! No! No!" she was screaming. "Don't touch me! Don't come near me. I'll kill you. I'll stab you. I'll poison you." Words poured out of her as fast as the blood sprang from her wound. She looked strange in her glittering clothes, blood-stained face and dishevelled hair.

Zarina was knocking on the door furiously. Hameed, bemused and shaken, let her in and went out again himself. At once Zarina took charge. She nursed Nisa's injuries, calmed her down and helped her to bed. The children had slept through the commotion.

The next morning when Nisa woke up everything was quite clear in her head. She knew what she had to do. She packed some things for herself and Zafar in a small steel trunk. The older children were at school. They walked there and back with Zarina's children. She stood on a small stool near the wall and called Zarina to tell her.

"I'm going to my mother's house, *Apa*," she said. "I'm taking Zafar with 70
me. I don't think they will turn us away. If nothing else, I can wash dishes and cook. If Hameed cannot keep Safia and Karim let him drop them off in Sialkot as well."

Zarina nodded tearfully and promised to keep an eye on them for her. For once she did not have the courage to persuade Nisa that she must endure and that he would change. She didn't know of a magic which worked. Nisa had seen a vision she could not forget, she'd felt a power she could not deny. As she turned away and walked out of the courtyard, clutching both Zafar and the silver trunk, her stops were laboriously slow but firm and determined.

CHARTING THE STORY

1. What does Talat advise Nisa to do about her problem? What is Nisa's reaction, at that moment and over the next several months, to this suggestion, as well as to Talat in general, and what does this suggest about Nisa?
2. What does Zarina reveal about Talat, and how does this affect Nisa's feelings about her own "magic"? In the account of the *chowkie*, particularly in Paragraphs 16–17, does what Zarina later tells Nisa seem to have merit? Why or why not?

3 Trace Nisa's transformation from being "a shivering, huddled creature into a calmer, thinking woman" (Paragraph 53). Where in the story would you locate the turning point in this process?

CONSIDERATIONS OF STYLE

1 How does the author use the images of "months" and of "impurity" or "transgression" throughout the text, and how do these images work together?
2 How do the symbols of the snakes, the moon, the eggs, and, in particular, of blood, inform this story?
3 Does the narrative seem to be written by a woman for a female audience? Why, or why not?

AFTERTHOUGHTS

1 Some outspoken young Muslim women (former students of the authors of this anthology) have decried the Western stereotype of, as one of them expressed it, "the veiled Muslim woman chained to the stove." Does this story overturn such stereotype, comply with it, or do both, and in what ways?
2 Compare Nisa's plight with that of Dikeledi in Bessie Head's story "The Collector of Treasures" (in this anthology). Had Talat's magic not been available to Nisa, and she had acted as Dikeledi did to solve her problem, might she have met a similar, or worse, fate?

THE WRITER'S CRAFT

1 Research Qur'anic attitudes on women (preferably from the Qur'an itself, but if you are not Muslim, or don't have access to the Qur'an, you may want to consult websites written by Muslim women—or men) and write a short essay, poem, or story thereby, concerning a course of action for Nisa.
2 Alcoholism in developing countries—even in countries in which alcohol consumption is proscribed by religion—is a problem largely affecting men. Write a paper investigating this problem with reference to the husbands Hameed in this story and Tony in "Midnight Soldiers."
3 From the point of view of Zarina, write a letter to Nisa a few days after Nisa's departure.

HAZEL D CAMPBELL

Born in Jamaica in 1940, HAZEL CAMPBELL *studied at the University of the West Indies. She has worked at the Jamaica Information Service, and has published* The Rag Doll and Other Stories *(1979),* Woman's Tongue *(1985), and* Singerman. *"Easter Sunday Morning" has also been published in* The Faber Book of Contemporary Short Stories *(Mervyn Morris, ed, 1990).*

PERSPECTIVES

1 In your view, are there things that are truly holy—that stand out over and against sacrilege and blasphemy? If so, what are they—or, alternatively, how have concepts such as "holiness" and "sacrilege" lost their meaning?

2 What do you assume to be the essential components of a religion? Does *obeah* (Paragraph 32—check your dictionary for definition/s, and note the etymology) qualify as a religion by your terms?

3 When a proselytizing religion (such as Christianity or Islam) contends with local religious beliefs, what sorts of interactions occur, especially among those who have converted to the "new" religion? For the purpose of this story, you may wish to research the effects of Anglicanism (the Church of England) upon people of the formerly British islands of the Caribbean region.

Easter Sunday Morning

It wasn't me playing the organ that day, you know. It was like those mechanical pianos that play by themselves. My fingers were moving I know but I wasn't responsible. The organ play louder and louder and keep on playing even when the hymn suppose to stop. I didn't even know what was happening down there because my head stiff straight ahead. Lord, it was frightening! And when the notes just start crashing together I was so scared. And then immediately after that I found myself playing 'Praise God' and the people start singing it same time as if I had already introduced it.

Not even rector don't talk about it yet. It's like everybody still trying to understand what happen.

Some of us would like to pretend that it didn't happen.

You notice how church full up since then.

Yes. It's like it was a sign or something. Like the church renewed. It's real scary.

I never felt so in touch with God since I going to church as on that morning. It was frightening.

I sensed trouble the moment she walked through the door.

I sense trouble through the whole service. We were sitting behind her and she was restless the whole time.

It's when the folk group start singing the Zion songs that she really started getting excited. The moment the drums started she start to twitch.

I don't know. I still think it not quite right to sing them Poco songs and beat drum in church. I don't know. I just not comfortable with it.

I don't know either. Mark you, I like accompanying them. You know it's different and I enjoy it. But I not so sure you're supposed to enjoy yourself in church like that. All that clapping and swaying about almost dancing in church, and the drums, I don't know.

The scariest part was how Mass Luke find the bunch of burn up bush right in the middle of the aisle.

You think she came back?

No. They say nobody has seen her since that.

It was the very first time that they were discussing the incident together. Three weeks had passed and the church was still trying to understand what had happened that Easter morning. It was the one time that an incident with so many eye witnesses didn't have different accounts of what had taken place. Everybody gave almost the same details. There were minor differences only in the estimate of the length of time the incident had taken and the organist had fixed the time almost to a second. It was the length of time it took to play the hymn, 'Oh God unseen yet ever near', twice.

The universal sentiment was that nobody knew exactly what had happened but that it was very frightening.

The April Easter Sunday morning had dawned fresh and calm as the dew-covered trees and bushes and meadow-grass in the village of Walkup Hill. Rainfall in March after a long drought had brought an outpouring of the signs of spring from a grateful earth. Easter morning praises could be heard and seen everywhere. Birds twittered and chirped and sang whole songs as they darted from tree to tree. Every bush and every weed was painted with vibrant colours testifying to its joy at being alive.

Walkup Hill was peaceful, content and holy as the church bells at St Peter Anglican Church began to peal, summoning the faithful also to praise God.

Easter morning service was always extra special at St Peter. For some reason which nobody could remember, that particular church had combined a kind of mini Harvest Festival with the Easter service so that in addition to the white lilies and other Easter flowers, the church overflowed with the many other gifts of the earth: red otaheite apples, bright yellow oranges and grapefruits; sugar cane, yams and sweet potatoes. Green bananas hugged each other in large bunches, voluptuous ripe plantains tempted the touch. The sights and smells of the Easter celebrations at Walkup Hill Anglican Church injected a special earthy sensuousness into the worship that no other service had.

When the middle-class people who had moved into the area in and 20
around the village had first attended this service, they had thought 'how quaint'. But they had liked it, so that the only change now was that the baskets were prettier and more artistically arranged by the Decoration Committee and everybody was pleased.

It was like this with many things in Walkup Hill these days, a mixture of old customs and new ways. For the village had been changing from backwoods on the outskirts of the city to a middle-class suburb.

It had started with one man, a lawyer, who had his roots in Walkup Hill and who had built his home right beside one of the many streams which tumbled through the village on their way to the thirsty flatland below. His friends had envied him the peaceful nature of his home far from the city crowds and noises, and since it didn't take more than three-quarters of an hour to reach the city, the villagers found themselves being besieged by requests for land. One enterprising developer had even turned what appeared to be a rocky hillside into a very charming housing scheme.

Now, in the mornings, the narrow road winding out of the village was busy with fancy motorcars and villagers with their donkeys often getting in each other's way as old-timers and newcomers learned to tolerate each other's ways. In truth most of the villagers didn't really mind the change. For one thing the newcomers didn't plant food so the tiny market did good business most of the week and some villagers who used to go to the big market in the nearest town at the foot of the hill now found that they could sell their foodstuff right there in Walkup Hill.

Several village daughters found employment in the new homes. The village shop expanded to take care of the increased demand for goods, and with the cash for the land they had sold, old-timers fixed up their houses or bought more animals and tools and Walkup Hill assumed an air of prosperity which other villages further away envied.

The newcomers also took over leadership of community organizations 25
and since they had money to contribute or were good at fund-raising, these also prospered—like the new Community Hall and the improved cricket pitch, the toilets in the market, and most of all the churches.

Walkup Hill had two churches. Three really—the Methodist Church, St Peter (the Anglican Church) and the Church of the Holy Redeemer of the Resurrection. The last named, a revivalist church, usually had the largest weekly attendance although most of the villagers would tell an outsider that they were either Anglican or Methodist meaning that they had been christened in one or the other.

By coincidence it seemed that many of the newcomers were Anglican and they quickly took over St Peter.

Attendance used to be so small, the church had been looked after mainly by a deacon, a parish rector visiting once a month or less to administer communion and oversee church matters. But in no time at all this changed and it was established that the congregation was large enough and contributing enough to have its own parson. A rectory was built, facilities at the church upgraded, a few additions made and St Peter instead of sitting forlornly on the peak of a hill as it had been wont to do, now stood, its old stone walls softly proud of the new attention and a sparkling new cross on its roof testifying that it was taking over the leadership of the spiritual community in Walkup Hill.

Some of the old-timers who had kept things together through the years of its backwater existence were a little put out by the new leadership which tended to ignore them, not out of malice, but simply because they were anxious to get on with their jobs and were impatient with the slower, more cautious manner in which the old-timers lived their lives.

Anyway, St Peter became the pride of Walkup Hill and many villagers who had ceased attending now resumed their membership to the detriment, in particular, of the Church of the Holy Redeemer of the Resurrection.

One such was Mother White. She had come back to St Peter, she told somebody, because it seemed that the church had got new power, power which she coveted.

Mother White was not an ordinary villager. She could see things and do things—so people said. They didn't actually call her an obeah woman, but it was said that she had strange powers to cure people of strange illnesses. Illnesses which ordinary doctors could not even diagnose. She could take off evil spirits, and a bush bath by Mother White could cure the most serious disease.

But strangely she didn't always practise her calling. Very often she was an ordinary citizen like anybody else. But sometimes...

Once there was a girl given up for dead. She came from another village and her people brought her to Mother White as a last resort. Her case was so hard that Mother White had left her lying in the thatch-covered room where she gave baths and had disappeared for a whole half day searching for the bushes which she needed.

She returned almost exhausted with a tale that the spirit riding the girl had followed her and had tried to prevent her getting the right bushes.

As she told it: 'Everytime I put out mi hand fi pull up the right bush, wha you think come up? Stink weed! A looking guinea hen, a find horse whip! A looking rosemary, a find lovebush! This is a hard case.'

She had kept the half-dead girl for two days giving her baths and potions and the whole thing had ended with a drum ceremony to pin the evil spirit so that it wouldn't follow the girl home.

Since the girl lived far away, the villagers never heard if she had recovered but nobody doubted Mother White's powers.

Until her own son began to act funny.

It was said that he had given a girl in a nearby village a baby and had promised to marry her but during the time that she was sexually unavailable he had taken up with another girl. The baby's mother had 'put something on him' in revenge.

The villagers looked on curiously to see how quickly Mother White would cure her son. But nothing happened. Ceremony after ceremony was held, but, if anything, the boy got worse. One day he ran amok with a machete and was taken away to the asylum in the city.

Had Mother White lost her powers?

It was during this time that she returned to St Peter where she had been a confirmed member a long time before.

The first Sunday morning she appeared in church the newcomers, many of whom had never heard of her, were quite startled.

She was dressed in bleached calico with two or three layers of thickly gathered long skirts. Her head was tied with calico under her hat. When she entered the main doorway she did a kind of curtsy then walked up the aisle to the altar where she made the sign of the cross and spun around three times, her many skirts billowing around her. Then she walked down the aisle stopping at the pew which caught her fancy.

This she did every Sunday morning and at communion time she would be among the first at the rail, where after receiving the sacrament, she would walk straight out of the church and go home without talking to anyone.

After many Sundays witnessing this behaviour the church relaxed since it seemed that she was harmless. Some of the younger members even began to giggle at her performance. Some of the old-timers, however, were apprehensive. Later, they would say that they knew something was wrong from the beginning, but since nobody listened to them any longer . . .

It was a child who first awakened the church to the fact that Mother White was up to no good.

One Sunday morning, on their way home after service, the Wynter family passed Mother White walking her stiff, swift walk through the village centre on her way to her home hidden away in the bushes.

One of the Wynter children suddenly asked, 'Why that old lady don't like the communion, Mama?'

'Of course she takes communion, every Sunday,' the mother answered.

'But she don't drink it,' the child insisted.

'What you mean?'

'Last week I was outside—you member I went to the toilet?—and she came out of church and spit out the communion in a bottle that hide in her skirt.'

Wynter mother and father looked at each other puzzled, then the mother said quickly, 'I'm sure it wasn't that. And, by the way, don't I tell you not to linger when you have to go outside?'

In that way she shifted the conversation from the child's interest in the strange woman. But later she discussed the situation with her husband who thought that there had to be a simple explanation for what the child had seen.

'Why would anyone want to spit out the communion?' he asked. It didn't make sense.

His wife however was sufficiently puzzled to mention it to some other church members the following week, and she asked the same question—'Why would anybody want to keep the wine? It has its place only in church!'

Two old-timers were in the group and didn't contribute to the conversation. However, during the week, the church later learned, a group went to the rectory to tell the parson about their suspicion that Mother White was using the church and the communion for evil purposes. That could be the only reason why she was not swallowing the communion wine but saving it.

The parson, brought up in the city, had a modern scientific mind and was inclined to dismiss the story.

'True, the woman is strange, but each of us has our little ways,' he told them. 'It's just that Mother White is a little more eccentric than most.'

Still they insisted that he should at least observe her so that they could be satisfied that everything was all right. Great harm would come to the church, they predicted, if she was really using the communion for devilish purposes.

When the parson asked what she could possibly do with the communion, they told him in some detail what they knew of her history.

The following Sunday he was away, so communion service was not held. But sure enough, the next communion Sunday, Mother White turned up, went through her usual act and those watching saw how, as she stepped outside the church, she stopped, took a bottle from her pocket and spat out what had to be the communion wine into it. She also wrapped what appeared to be the wafer in a piece of paper, put both in her pocket and walked quickly away.

Parson was surprised and a little worried when he heard this report. He had no choice but to put the matter before the church's Advisory Committee. So he called a special meeting and together with the witnesses they discussed the situation. Nobody had ever heard of such a thing before. They were appalled and a little bewildered and afraid, because the old-timers were talking about obeah and devil dealings and they were not quite sure how to handle Mother White.

It was decided that the parson should seek advice from the bishop but meanwhile they would withhold the communion from Mother White.

As the parson summed it up, 'We can't prevent her from coming to church but we can withhold the communion since we have witnesses that she is not receiving it in the holy tradition of the Church.'

'Suppose she makes a fuss?' somebody asked.

'That would only prove that she was up to no good,' another replied.

It happened that the next communion service was held on Easter Sunday morning.

The church was packed, as usual, on Easter Sunday. Many who hardly attended church during the year made a special effort to be there at Easter and at Christmas. Indeed one of the parson's favourite jokes was to wish some of his audience Happy Easter at Christmas and Merry Christmas at Easter.

So St Peter was full. Old-timers and newcomers dressed up, feeling peaceful and content with the world as they walked in quietly and took their seats.

Easter lilies filled the brass urns at the altar. Brightly coloured fruits and other offerings wooed the congregation into a feeling of worship and praise, for the Decoration Committee had spent a busy Saturday and had outdone themselves with the flower and harvest arrangements. They were both celebrating the resurrection of their Lord and reaffirming his goodness in providing mankind with so many gifts from the earth.

The organist entered and began the soft prelude. The congregation sat in expectation of the grand march up the aisle of the altar boy with the cross followed by the rector and choir. This was one of the few occasions when St Peter followed a formal pattern, for their services tended to be more informal than in many other Anglican churches.

Suddenly there was a rustle at the main door and a harsh voice crying 'Holy is God! Holy is the Lord!'

Everybody turned around and there was Mother White at the entrance.

Her calico skirts looked whiter and stiffer than usual. Beneath tie-head and hat her wizened features glistened from the oils with which she had rubbed her face.

In her hands she held a bunch of dried bush which looked as if it had been slightly scorched by fire. She also had a single dried mandora coconut, large, smoothed like a calabash and shining as if it too had been rubbed with oils. She walked slowly up the aisle and those sitting near could smell white rum and strange oils as she passed.

At the altar rail she plunked her bunch of burnt bush into the midst of the beautiful white Easter lilies, rested the coconut on the ground, made the sign of the cross, spun around three times and then returned down the aisle.

At the end of the aisle near the doorway she spun around three times again, then, counting off seven rows from the door, she indicated to those in the crowded pew on the left side that that was where she intended to sit.

Two people got up and gave her the aisle seat while others shifted uncomfortably. Somehow her presence had introduced a new influence into the church. Many could sense it and it made them uneasy. The smell of alcohol and strange oils were an unwelcome addition to the already heady odours in the church.

One woman, outraged at the ugly bush in the midst of the lilies, plucked it out and went to a side door and threw it angrily outside. Somebody else spirited away the coconut.

Somehow, after all that, the holy procession up to the altar seemed something of an anti-climax.

It was to be an unusual service that morning for the Advisory Committee had decided to get a group of folk singers as part of the entertainment during the service. Many of them felt that the church could do with a little modernizing of the pattern of its service. Some churches, they argued, were even including dance as part of the worship. The Freedom Singers were seated in the front pews and the two drummers were already stationed near the organist waiting to offer their praises in the folk tradition.

Things went calmly enough for the first part of the service. They sang the usual Easter songs of praise and joy for the resurrection of Christ, and the choir did a special number. It was when the drummers for the Freedom Singers struck up that the first obvious signs of trouble began.

The Singers started with 'Me alone, me alone ina de wilderness'.

Those near to Mother White reported that she began to twitch and shake as soon as the drumming started. So much so that two more people left the pew. When they started to sing 'Moses struck the rock', she got up and began to wheel and turn in the aisle.

A few visitors thought that this was part of the entertainment and were delighted. But the parson, who was a red man, turned redder, and many in the congregation began to frown. Mother White was going too far.

Still nobody made a move to try to quiet her or lead her outside as had been done on occasion with certain stray persons who had tried to disrupt the service. And after the drumming ceased she returned to her seat where after a few more twitches she kept quiet and the parson with a feeling of great apprehension began his sermon.

Jesus Christ by his resurrection had enabled Christians everywhere to overcome Evil and the Power of Darkness—was the main message.

Much later when they were still trying to analyse it, the congregation would agree that it was from this point that the battle began. Imperceptibly. Nothing spectacular. Just a heightening of tension in the church; a strangely powerful ring in the parson's voice affirming the power of Christ in a way they had never heard him do before; and quite unexpectedly storm clouds shielding the sunlight so that someone got up and turned on all the lights in the church.

Then came the invitation to communion.

'My brothers and sisters in Christ, draw near and receive His Body which He gave for you, and His Blood which He shed for you. Remember that He died for you and feed on Him in your hearts by faith with thanksgiving.'

Mother White was among the first to move out of the pews to go to the rail to receive the communion.

Organist and congregation prepared to sing 'Let us break bread together on our knees' as usual, but the parson surprised them by giving instructions for the hymn,

O God, unseen yet ever near,
Thy Presence may we feel;

And thus inspired by holy fear,
Before thine altar kneel.

He recited the words as the faithful took their place waiting to receive the body and blood of Christ.

Mother White was second at the rail and when he came to her, the words ‘The Body of Christ given for you’ just would not come out, so he shook his head and whispered, ‘Mother White, I cannot in all good conscience offer you this sacrament.’

There was a pause as Mother White looked in her upturned hands where there was no expected wafer. She looked up at the parson puzzled but he was moving on to the person beside her.

The first most of the congregation knew about what was happening was when she sprang up and began to stamp her feet and shout:

‘I want me communion. I come fi mi communion and I must get it. You have fi gi me.’

For a second there was a shocked silence in the church, the singing petered out and the bewildered congregation wondered what was happening.

The parson repeated loudly so that all could hear, ‘Mother White, I cannot in good conscience offer you this sacrament.’

As if on cue, those who had been in the aisle waiting their turn quickly retreated to their seats as if clearing the battleground as Mother White began to shout and stamp in earnest.

As if on cue too, the congregation took up back the hymn and without knowing why, began to sing louder and louder. The louder she screamed and shouted, the louder the organ played and the louder the congregation sang. When they reached the last verse,

Thus may we all thy word obey
For we, O God, are thine;
And go rejoicing on our way
Renewed with strength divine

they sang with a fervour and belief that most of them had never before felt in their faith.

Meanwhile the parson stood motionless at the altar, the Host still in his hands, his head bowed in prayer.

But still Mother White shouted and when the hymn ended the congregation started it all over again without even a pause. The organ pealed out as it had never done before and the congregation sang as they had never sung before. Small children hugged their parents in fright as Mother White began to foam at the mouth. She spun around not three times but seven times one way and seven times the other. She rolled rapidly on the floor down the aisle and returned as rapidly. She stood up and her body, washed with sweat, shook and trembled. At one point it seemed that her head alone was spinning leaving her body motionless.

And still the congregation sang.

Suddenly, when it seemed that they could get no louder, when it seemed that their very souls were being lifted out of their bodies, the organ made a loud crash of discordant notes frightening everybody, and in the silence which ensued Mother White shook herself violently once more and then quite calmly and peacefully took up her hat which had fallen on the floor and walked out of the door.

And without any directive, organ, parson and congregation burst into the hymn

Praise God from whom all blessings flow;
Praise Him all creatures here below;
Praise Him above ye heavenly host;
Praise Father, Son and Holy Ghost.
Amen.

At Amen, without another word, as if still on cue, without waiting for the established dismissal everybody quietly and quickly left the church and went home.

No lingering to greet each other and exchange talk and comments on the service as usual, for the emotional experience they had just undergone was too much for discussion yet.

Even the parson, who usually stayed until all had departed, left St Peter that morning without a word to any of this flock.

And as they hurried away the rain clouds dispersed and the bright April morning Easter sun streamed down on them once more, warming them and lighting up the cross on the roof of the church triumphant.

CHARTING THE STORY

1 What sorts of changes altered Walkup Hill when it changed "from backwoods on the outskirts of the city to a middle-class suburb"? How did the changes affect St Peter's Anglican Church? How are they relevant to the story's climactic encounter?

2 Why do you suppose many villagers who were members of the Church of the Holy Redeemer of the Resurrection would tell outsiders that they were either Anglican or Methodist—"that they had been christened in one or the other"?

3 In some Christian churches, communion is looked upon as a memorial service that celebrates the union of the people in the congregation and their love for Christ. In other Christian churches, the bread and wine of the communion (often called Holy Eucharist) are viewed as the body and blood of Christ himself. What view of communion is implied by the actions of the parson and the reactions of the rest of

the congregation to Mother White's treatment of the bread and wine she has taken? What sort of "Easter triumph, Easter joy" breaks out at the end?

CONSIDERATIONS OF STYLE

1 Who is speaking in the italicized opening paragraphs of the narrative, and to what effect has the author used this device?

2 Hymns and portions of the liturgy are featured in the narrative. What audience would likely be the most receptive, the most "understanding," of the events in this story? If you are approaching the story from a perspective in which these hymns and words are unfamiliar, how would you react to the rising tension and the triumphant resolution? From which perspectives would the end of the story *not* appear to be a triumph, and why?

AFTERTHOUGHTS

1 What, in your view, may have motivated Mother White to carry off the communion wafers and to spit out the wine in a bottle? What is suggested in the text; what do various members of the congregation, and the parson, fear she is "up to"?

2 Why might "nobody [have] seen" Mother White since the incident? How would someone from outside that community explain it?

THE WRITER'S CRAFT

1 Write about an incident where something sacred—not necessarily in a religious sense—was threatened, and what happened in response to that threat.

2 From the point of Mother White, write your perspective of the event, explaining your motivations, responding to what happened to you in church.

3 In Chinua Achebe's story "Dead Men's Path" (in this anthology), the village priest, referring to the need to respect both traditional and modern religious religious/cultural practices, remarks: "let the hawk perch and let the eagle perch." Write an essay showing the desirability—or the impracticability—of applying such a notion in a multicultural community such as Walkup Hill.

R K NARAYAN

R K NARAYAN, *one of India's foremost writers of novels and short stories, retellings of myths and legends, memoirs, travel writing, and essays, was born in 1909 and has been writing in English since the late 1930s. Many of his stories and novels are set in Malgudi, a fictional South Indian town, maps of which appear in the frontispiece of some of his books.*

"Under the Banyan Tree" is set in a village in the Mempi forest, in the hills above Malgudi. Thematically, it partakes of some Indian storytelling traditions, where a dramatic presentation, often from the epic Mahabharata *or the* Ramayana, *will take several evenings to play out, and not being scripted, is never done the same way twice.*

The main character in the story, Nambi, is a storyteller like Narayan, except that Nambi is "illiterate, in the sense that the written word [is] a mystery to him."

But the tale goes on to show that the process by which he makes up stories in his head is also a mystery, and the ways in which he engages his listening audience bespeak his mastery of his craft.

PERSPECTIVES

1 Discuss your notions of the origins of stories. If you write them, explain how they come into being for you. Or, read others' accounts of how they come up with their stories and discuss them as well. Is there any uniformity to the various origins?

2 In both developing and developed countries around the world, people are living longer and more older people are choosing to stay in the work force. What might be some advantages of older employees? Some disadvantages? Is there an optimal time to retire?

3 Have you recently sat for a three-hour lecture, sermon, speech, meeting, or ceremony? What would be your physical and mental reactions if you had?

Under the Banyan Tree

The village Somal, nestling away in the forest tracts of Mempi, had a population of less than three hundred. It was in every way a village to make the heart of a rural reformer sink. Its tank, a small expanse of water, right in the middle of the village, served for drinking, bathing, and washing the cattle, and it bred malaria, typhoid, and heaven knew what else. The cottages sprawled anyhow and the lanes twisted and wriggled up and down and strangled each other. The population used the highway as the refuse ground and in the backyard of every house drain water stagnated in green puddles.

Such was the village. It is likely that the people of the village were insensitive: but it is more than likely that they never noticed their surroundings because they lived in a kind of perpetual enchantment. The enchanter was Nambi the story-teller. He was a man of about sixty or seventy. Or was he eighty or one hundred and eighty? Who could say? In a place so much cut off as Somal (the nearest bus-stop was ten miles away), reckoning could hardly be in the familiar measures of time. If anyone asked Nambi what his age was he referred to an ancient famine or an invasion or the building of a bridge and indicated how high he had stood from the ground at the time.

He was illiterate, in the sense that the written word was a mystery to him; but he could make up a story, in his head, at the rate of one a month; each story took nearly ten days to narrate.

His home was the little temple which was at the very end of the village. No one could say how he had come to regard himself as the owner of the temple. The temple was a very small structure with red-striped walls, with a stone image of the Goddess Shakti in the sanctum. The front portion of the temple was Nambi's home. For aught it mattered any place might be his home; for he was without possessions. All that he possessed was a broom with which he swept the temple; and he had also a couple of dhoties and upper cloth. He spent most of the day in the shade of the banyan which spread out its branches in front of the temple. When he felt hungry he walked into any house that caught his fancy and joined the family at dinner. When he needed new clothes they were brought to him by the villagers. He hardly ever had to go out in search of company; for the banyan shade served as a clubhouse for the village folk. All through the day people came seeking Nambi's company and squatted under the tree. If he was in a mood for it he listened to their talk and entertained them with his own observations and anecdotes. When he was in no mood he looked at the visitors sourly and asked, "What do you think I am? Don't blame me if you get no story at the next moon. Unless I meditate how can the Goddess give me a story? Do you think stories float in the air?" And he moved out to the edge of the forest and squatted there, contemplating the trees.

On Friday evenings the village turned up at the temple for worship, when 5
Nambi lit a score of mud lamps and arranged them around the threshold of the sanctuary. He decorated the image with flowers, which grew wildly in the backyard of the temple. He acted as the priest and offered to the Goddess fruits and flowers brought in by the villagers.

On the nights he had a story to tell he lit a small lamp and placed it in a niche in the trunk of the banyan tree. Villagers as they returned home in the evening saw this, went home, and said to their wives, "Now, now, hurry up with the dinner, the storyteller is calling us." As the moon crept up behind the hillock, men, women, and children gathered under the banyan tree. The storyteller would not appear yet. He would be sitting in the sanctum, before the Goddess, with his eyes shut, in deep meditation. He sat thus as long as he liked and when he came out, with his forehead ablaze with ash and vermilion, he took his seat on a stone platform in front of the temple. He opened the story with a question. Jerking his finger towards a vague, far-away destination, he asked, "A thousand years ago, a stone's throw in that direction, what do you think there was? It was not the weed-covered waste it is now, for donkeys to roll in. It was not the ash-pit it is now. It was the capital of the king. . . ." The king would be Dasaratha, Vikramaditya, Asoka, or anyone that came into the old man's head; the capital was called Kapila, Kridapura, or anything. Opening thus, the old man went on without a pause for three hours. By then brick by brick the palace of the king was raised. The old man described the dazzling durbar hall where sat a hundred vassal kings, ministers, and subjects; in another part of the palace all the musicians in the world assembled and sang; and most of the songs were sung over again by Nambi to his audience; and he described in detail the pictures and trophies that hung on the walls of the palace. . . .

It was story-building on an epic scale. The first day barely conveyed the setting of the tale, and Nambi's audience as yet had no idea who were coming into the story. As the moon slipped behind the trees of Mempi Forest Nambi said, "Now friends, Mother says this will do for the day." He abruptly rose, went in, lay down, and fell asleep long before the babble of the crowd ceased.

The light in the niche would again be seen two or three days later, and again and again throughout the bright half of the month. Kings and heroes, villains and fairy-like women, gods in human form, saints and assassins, jostled each other in that world which was created under the banyan tree. Nambi's voice rose and fell in an exquisite rhythm, and the moonlight and the hour completed the magic. The villagers laughed with Nambi, they wept with him, they adored the heroes, cursed the villains, groaned when the conspirator had his initial success, and they sent up to the gods a heartfelt prayer for a happy ending. . . .

On the day when the story ended, the whole gathering went into the sanctum and prostrated before the Goddess. . . .

By the time the next moon peeped over the hillock Nambi was ready with another story. He never repeated the same kind of story or brought in the same set of persons, and the village folk considered Nambi a sort of miracle, quoted his words of wisdom, and lived on the whole in an exalted plane of their own, though their life in all other respects was hard and drab.

And yet it had gone on for years and years. One moon he lit the lamp in the tree. The audience came. The old man took his seat and began the story. ". . . When King Vikramaditya lived, his minister was . . ." He paused. He could not get beyond it. He made a fresh beginning. "There was the king . . ." he said, repeated it, and then his words trailed off into a vague mumbling. "What has come over me?" he asked pathetically. "Oh, Mother, great Mother, why do I stumble and falter? I know the story. I had the whole of it a moment ago. What was it about? I can't understand what has happened." He faltered and looked so miserable that his audience said, "Take your own time. You are perhaps tired."

"Shut up!" he cried. "Am I tired? Wait a moment; I will tell you the story presently." Following this there was utter silence. Eager faces looked up at him. "Don't look at me!" he flared up. Somebody gave him a tumbler of milk. The audience waited patiently. This was a new experience. Some persons expressed their sympathy aloud. Some persons began to talk among themselves. Those who sat in the outer edge of the crowd silently slipped away. Gradually, as it neared midnight, others followed this example. Nambi sat staring at the ground, his head bowed in thought. For the first time he realized that he was old. He felt he would never more be able to control his thoughts or express them cogently. He looked up. Everyone had gone except his friend Mari the blacksmith. "Mari, why aren't you also gone?"

Mari apologized for the rest: "They didn't want to tire you; so they have gone away."

Nambi got up. "You are right. Tomorrow I will make it up. Age, age. What is my age? It has come on suddenly." He pointed at his head and said, "This says, 'Old fool, don't think I shall be your servant any more. You will be my servant hereafter.' It is disobedient and treacherous."

15 He lit the lamp in the niche next day. The crowd assembled under the banyan faithfully. Nambi had spent the whole day in meditation. He had been fervently praying to the Goddess not to desert him. He began the story. He went on for an hour without a stop. He felt greatly relieved, so much so that he interrupted his narration to remark, "Oh, friends. The Mother is always kind. I was seized with a foolish fear..." and continued the story. In a few minutes he felt dried up. He struggled hard: "And then... and then... what happened?" He stammered. There followed a pause lasting an hour. The audience rose without a word and went home. The old man sat on the stone brooding till the cock crew. "I can't blame them for it," he muttered to himself. "Can they sit down here and mope all night?" Two days later he gave another installment of the story, and that, too, lasted only a few minutes. The gathering dwindled. Fewer persons began to take notice of the lamp in the niche. Even these came only out of a sense of duty. Nambi realized that there was no use in prolonging the struggle. He brought the story to a speedy and premature end.

He knew what was happening. He was harrowed by the thoughts of his failure. I should have been happier if I had dropped dead years ago, he said to himself. Mother, why have you struck me dumb...? He shut himself up in the sanctum, hardly ate any food, and spent the greater part of the day sitting motionless in meditation.

The next moon peeped over the hillock, Nambi lit the lamp in the niche. The villagers as they returned home saw the lamp, but only a handful turned up at night. "Where are the others?" the old man asked. "Let us wait." He waited. The moon came up. His handful of audience waited patiently. And then the old man said, "I won't tell the story today, nor tomorrow unless the whole village comes here. I insist upon it. It is a mighty story. Everyone must hear it." Next day he went up and down the village street shouting, "I have a most wonderful tale to tell tonight. Come one and all; don't miss it. . . ." This personal appeal had a great effect. At night a large crowd gathered under the banyan. They were happy that the story-teller had regained his powers. Nambi came out of the temple when everyone had settled and said: "It is the Mother who gives the gifts; and it is she who takes away the gifts. Nambi is a dotard. He speaks when the Mother has anything to say. He is struck dumb when she has nothing to say. But what is the use of the jasmine when it has lost its scent? What is the lamp for when all the oil is gone? Goddess be thanked. . . . These are my last words on this earth; and this is my greatest story." He rose and went into the sanctum. His audience hardly understood what he meant. They sat there till they became weary. And then some of them got up and stepped into the sanctum. There the story-teller sat with his eyes shut. "Aren't you going to tell us a story?" they asked. He opened his eyes, looked at them, and shook his head. He indicated by gesture that he had spoken his last words.

When he felt hungry he walked into any cottage and silently sat down for food, and walked away the moment he had eaten. Beyond this he had hardly anything to demand of his fellow beings. The rest of his life (he lived for a few more years) was one great consummate silence.

CHARTING THE STORY

1. How does Nambi let others know when he is ready to tell a story? When and why does he change his method?
2. What oratorical devices does Nambi use to engage his audience?
3. Chart the narrative structure of Nambi's own life story: from his exalted status as the village storyteller; to its turning point; to a sudden climax; and, finally, to closure.

CONSIDERATIONS OF STYLE

1. Does the story present itself as comic, tragic, ironic? Where do you find elements of comedy, tragedy, irony, or any other storytelling mode in this text?
2. Of what significance is the description of the village at the beginning of the story?

AFTERTHOUGHTS

1 One of the Buddha's most famous sermons was the "flower sermon," where he held up a flower in silence. Similarly, the composer Jon Cage's arguably most famous musical composition consisted entirely of rests, so that all one would hear (or see) was the turning of pages. What effects do these "silent treatments" produce upon audiences, and what may account for differences in "reception"?

2 In India a few years ago, the *Ramayana* and *Mahabharata*, till then told in a multitude of ways, were filmed with major actors, dubbed in various languages, and shown on national television. Many people expressed misgivings over the project, among which included the idea that henceforth, people would look to the television version as the "real" one, and that the other versions, ephemeral as they were, might die out. Of what value to those people or to yourself are multiple versions of stories?

THE WRITER'S CRAFT

1 Describe a favorite oral storyteller—in childhood, in school, at present. Compare this person's craftsmanship to Nambi's.

2 Retell the story of Nambi's last story from the point of view of someone in the audience—or perhaps of Goddess Shakti herself.

ZEBUN-NISSA HAMIDULLAH

ZEBUN-NISSA HAMIDULLAH *became famous in the 1940s for her writings, which centered upon East Pakistan, now Bangladesh. She wrote fiction, nonfiction, poetry, and newspaper columns in English.*

"No Music Before Mosque" comes from the Pakistani Short Stories *anthology, published in 1992. The story shows how one's unorthodox expression of faith can be viewed as a crisis of faith.*

PERSPECTIVES

1 In your opinion, what constitutes devout or pious religious practice? At a time devoted to a religious service, what actions would you consider irreverent, and why?

2 Have you ever engaged yourself—or can you imagine doing so—in the aesthetic pursuit of music, art, writing or the like, so passionately that it would become a "religious" or quasi-religious experience for you? Do others who might have done this come to mind?

No Music Before Mosque

Although all bowed their head in prayer, there were two in the mosque that evening whose thoughts were not on Almighty Allah. Even as they did *sida*, Ahmed glanced sideways at his father. The expression he saw on the old face was sufficient to tell him that his father had heard and, this time, would not forgive. And so, although he strove to concentrate on the verses of the *Quran* that fell, parrot-like, from his lips, he found it quite impossible to do so. All he could think of was his youngest brother and all he could hear was the shrill and sweet music of the flute.

Prayers concluded, the congregation began to disperse. Usually Vilayet Ali lingered in the courtyard of the mosque conversing with his friends until it was time for dinner. Not so today. Without so much as a look either to the left or right he hurriedly put on his shoes and walked quickly away and on to the uneven pathway that skirted the rice fields, passed the village pond and went up to his house.

Ahmed followed his father and, as soon as they were out of hearing of the others, Vilayet Ali unleashed his anger. "Did you hear?" he hissed. "Did you hear?" he repeated, so vehemently that even his long grey beard shook with his fury: "By Allah," he swore, looking angrily up at the cloudy monsoon sky, "he shall pay for this tonight."

Little Nazo's chubby hands clasped and unclasped the raw mango nervously. She had been sitting under the mango tree waiting for her father and grandfather for the past hour. It had been lonely there as the shadows lengthened and, because she was afraid and because she wanted confidence, she had picked up a raw mango from the ground where it had fallen during the storm earlier in the day, and bit into it with her sharp, white teeth.

Nazo had run here almost immediately after the sound of the flute had 5
reached her ears. Until that time she had been playing with her cousins putting the rag dolls, that their mothers had made for them from old cotton sarees, to bed on little pieces of matting; and when the *azaan* had commenced, she had gone to the window and from it waved to her father and grandfather as they walked towards the village mosque. Then suddenly the sound had come. The sound of the flute, so sweet and so disturbing. Usually, she loved to hear it and would leave whatever she was doing, clamber on to the window sill and sit gazing up at the tall palm trees, listening.

But now her little heart stopped dead for a second, and her rag doll with its two long plaits of jute dyed black, fell listlessly from her hands. "There will be trouble," she thought, her stomach sickening inside her, "much trouble." And the pupils of her big black eyes dilated with dread as the music of the flute mingled with the rich, sonorous, inspiring sound of the call to prayer.

Slipping away from her playmates, she went to the kitchen where the women of the family were preparing the evening meal. Her mother was stirring a saucepan and, with her cheeks flushed with the heat of the fire and her lips red with the *paan* she had just eaten, she made a pretty picture. Nazo squatted down close beside her and watched her grandmother straining away the water from the boiled rice. A sudden gust of breeze blew the kitchen door wide open and the sounds of the evening came in to them: first the sonorous sound of the *azaan* followed by the sweet shrillness of the flute. The old woman's hands became unsteady as she heard it, and much of the rice slipped out with the water. Hastily she put the pot aside and, going out of the kitchen, stood in the narrow courtyard, listening.

Nazo followed her, and the old woman twisted the ends of her saree nervously. "Allah, have mercy on us!" she cried, "Allah, have mercy on us!" as the sounds of the *azaan* and the flute continued. Her two daughters-in-law had also come out of the kitchen and she turned towards them in her agitation.

"What am I to do?" she almost wailed, "what am I to do with him?"

Nazo's mother strove to speak light-heartedly. "Maybe it is not him at 10
all," she said.

"I'm sure it's not him," soothed the second daughter-in-law, "the last train from the city could not have come in yet."

"Yes," said the old woman cheering up, "he can't have returned as yet, must be someone else."

The *azaan* finished and there was a second or two of complete silence. And then suddenly the sound of the flute came once more towards them, now louder and sweeter. And, even as they heard it, their hearts sank, for they knew that only Ali in the whole village could play the flute as it was being played now.

"God have mercy upon us," whispered the old woman once again, her face full of her anxiety, "his father will not forgive him this time."

Little Nazo's heart fluttered within her as she looked at the fearful faces of the women. "I have told him," the old woman was now almost in tears, "I have told him time and again not to fritter away his time with his flute," she wailed. "I have forbidden him playing it at prayer time. And yet... God forgive me," she moaned, "God forgive me for giving birth to a son who acts like an infidel."

"Don't be so harsh on him, mother," broke in Nazo's mother, "Ali is a good lad and a truthful one."

"Yes," chimed in the second daughter-in-law, "he is gentle and kind and pure of heart."

"But then why does he do these things," his mother moaned, "why will he waste his time playing on the flute instead of attending to his studies like other boys? And why does he persist in playing it during the hours of prayer even though his father has thrashed him for it times without number?"

"Because that's the way he prays," little Nazo spoke almost without realising it, and the women turned towards her in astonishment. "He told me that," she continued, her big black eyes strangely solemn in the little face, her childish voice grave. "He told me that," she went on, "he prays to Allah with his flute. That's his way of telling Allah how much he loves Him..."

The women smiled indulgently at the grave little girl. "Run away and play, you old head on young shoulders," said her grandmother, pinching her chubby little cheek.

Nazo obeyed her grandmother and ran away, but she did not run back to her playmates. Instead, she ran out of the house and turned down the little pathway that led to the village mosque. It was deserted at this late hour and, as the shadows lengthened, little Nazo felt afraid. But she ran on and on until she neared the village pond, and then her pace slackened and little shivers of fear ran down her spine, for she remembered the stories she heard about the *jin* who haunted the pond...

A familiar mango tree gave her fresh courage and, although she could not bring herself to go past the pond alone, she sat down on a stone at the side of it and waited. Small though she was, she was quite clear in her mind as to what she intended to do. She wanted to meet her father and grandfather as they returned from their evening prayers. She knew that her grandfather had special fondness for her, that she was his pet, and she wanted to cheer him up and, if possible, drive the anger from his heart before he reached home.

And so she sat, a solitary little figure, under the tall mango tree. Six years old, that's all she was, but the heart that beat within her was the heart of a woman. And with a woman's compassion she wanted to shield her favourite uncle from his father's wrath.

Sitting there, her little knees tucked under her, biting every now and then into the raw mango so as to still her fears, Nazo thought about her uncle, her youngest uncle whom she loved with the passionate affection that young girls of ten give to their eldest brothers. He was so different to the other boys in the village, so gentle and so kind; yet everybody was so harsh to him, especially grandfather—dear old grandfather who had never once uttered an unkind word to her, but had thrashed this gentle son of his, this child of his old age, so often and so mercilessly.

And almost everytime it had been about the flute. This little Nazo could not understand. She loved the music of the flute, loved the way Ali played it, coaxing so much of the beauty out of the reed. And she wondered why no one else could understand what she understood so fully; that Ali prayed to Allah through his flute. "I speak to God," he had said, when she had asked him about it one day. "I thank Him for all that He has given me, the beauty of the rice fields, the loveliness of the moonlight on the pond, the magic of the monsoon skies and for the sweetness of humans such as you." And then suddenly his voice had turned harsh and hard. "I'd rather pray to God this way," he added, "than mumble prayers that I do not understand."

They were coming, it could not be anyone but them, she told herself as she heard the sound of approaching footsteps, and she bit hard into the mango to ease her fears, jumping up in relief as her father and grandfather came in sight. Quietly she waited in the shadows and then, just as they were almost upon her, she jumped in front of them with a loud "Coo-ee-ee." Both Vilayet Ali and Ahmad were taken by surprise and, for a moment, felt alarmed, until gurgling with laughter Nazo pushed her warm, soft hand into her grandfather's large one, giggled up at him and questioned saucily: "Did I frighten you, grandfather?"

Seeing the chubby little figure laughing up at him, all the anger vanished from Vilayet Ali's heart. "You little bundle of mischief," he laughed, tweaking her ear affectionately, "saucy girl, trying to frighten your grandfather." Ahmad too, laughed out loud; not so much at his daughter's childish prank as at the fact that his father's anger had been blown away. Mighty pleased with herself, Nazo slipped her other hand into her father's and pranced home between the two men, chatting merrily all the way.

Even as they reached the courtyard, her grandmother pounced upon her. "Where on earth have you been, you naughty little girl?" she demanded angrily, all her fears and irritations finding an outlet on the laughing little girl.

"We've been looking for you everywhere. Go at once and have your dinner. Crest-fallen, little Nazo untwined her fingers from the hands of the two men slowly, hoping against hope that her grandfather at least would say something in her defence. But Vilayet Ali had already forgotten all about her.

"Has that rascal come home yet?" he asked his wife angrily. "Ali?" she questioned. "Who else?" he stormed. "Who else but that spoiled brat of your old age would dare so to dishonour the fair name of the family? Who else would dare to play music before mosques?" His face was red again with anger and the family exchanged apprehensive glances with each other. And, even as they did so, the ominous rumble of thunder announced the approach of yet another monsoon storm.

"Had it been any other but my own flesh and blood, I would have beaten 30
his brains out long ago," continued the old man, his wrath increasing as he noted the wrath of the heavens, "but because of you," he glared reprovingly upon his aged wife, "because you are always pampering him and always pleading for the boy, I've been lenient in the past. But, by Allah, this time it is too much! I'm going to beat him until he is black and blue and begs for mercy. And mercy he will get only when he swears never, never to play that cursed flute again. Where is he," he asked suddenly suspicious, "are you hiding him? Are you . . ."

"He has not yet returned," said his wife soothingly, "remember? He went to the city to find out his Matriculation results."

"Of course, he is back," stormed her husband, "didn't I hear the rascal throughout my prayers? Didn't I hear him defying God every single moment I was in the mosque?"

"Perhaps, he was playing his flute on the way home from the station and did not know that the hour of prayer had come, for he is not back home yet," she replied even more soothingly.

"Not home yet!" shouted Vilayet Ali, determined not to allow his anger to be assuaged, "I can tell you why. He must have failed in his exam, that's what he must have done, the young nit-wit. Let him come home, let him come home . . ."

Little Nazo went away with a sinking heart. She did not even join her 35
cousins for dinner, but went straight to her room, curled up on the straw *chattai* and tried to sleep and forget that her darling uncle was going to be severely thrashed that night. But although sleep did eventually come, it was disturbed and fitful and full of nightmares in which not only her beloved uncle, but she as well, was thrashed mercilessly by her grandfather who, in her dreams, had turned into a terrible monster.

It must have been almost morning when unusual sounds awoke her, for the cocks had started crowing. It was, however, still dark in the room although outside in the courtyard lights twinkled from nearly a dozen hurricane lanterns. What on earth is going on, Nazo wondered, as she stood in the doorway watching. There was quite a crowd assembled in the courtyard, all talking excitedly and she noticed the alarmed expression on her father's and her grandfather's face.

It had just stopped raining and rain drops still trickled from the edges of the roof and water came gushing down in torrents from the drain pipes. Nazo noticed that none of them seemed to care that their clothes were drenched, and it was obvious that whatever it was that had happened was sufficiently serious to make standing in the rain at this unearthly hour and getting drenched to the skin, a matter of no consequence.

"He's nowhere!" she heard her grandmother cry in a voice so shrill with terror that she scarcely recognised it, "we've looked for him everywhere even on the roof, but he's nowhere."

"It's him, I told you it was him," Nazo heard a voice she recognised as belonging to the village barber.

"Come on!" her father shouted impatiently, "let's waste no more time." Quickly he began walking towards the fields, the other men following him, their feet slipping sometimes in the slush, their hurricane lanterns swinging to and fro casting eerie circles of light amid the surrounding darkness.

Her grandfather, Nazo noticed, walked slower than usual and he seemed to be breathing deeply as if in pain. But it was obvious that he was straining every nerve to keep up with the younger men. Evading the eyes of the women of the family, Nazo slipped silently away and out of the house through the bushes and joined her grandfather as soon as their home was safely behind them.

Although she was a little afraid that her grandfather might scold her and send her back for coming out at this unearthly hour, she slipped her hand gently into his, for she was greatly concerned at the terrible unhappiness she saw on his face. Vilayet Ali brightened visibly as he saw the child and clasped her warm little hand firmly, as if the touch of it brought him much solace.

Frogs croaked and the little creatures of the night gave forth their music as the men walked down the slushy, narrow pathway in a single file. On and on they went, all of them silent, until at last Nazo realized that they were going towards Ali's favourite tree—the one under which he loved to sit and play his flute and where he had taught her to play a simple little tune.

Suddenly the village barber, who was walking a few paces behind her father, rushed forward and caught Ahmed by the arm. "There" he cried, pointing towards a tall tree, "there it is!" and he lifted high his hurricane lantern and pointed upwards. "See, see!" he cried excitedly. One by one the lanterns were raised and by their light Nazo saw a dearly familiar figure dangling grotesquely from one of its branches.

"Look at the face," cried the barber urgently, rushing forward and raising his lantern on a bamboo pole, "didn't I tell you it was Ali? Didn't I . . . That's his . . . That's his . . ."

"Stop it, stop it, you fool!" cried Ahmed seizing him by the shoulders. The barber turned around impatiently, but the words of anger died on his lips for something in Ahmed's haggard face silenced him, and slowly, shamefacedly he lowered the lantern.

But all of them had seen enough to know who it was that hung there. Vilayet Ali pushed little Nazo roughly aside and rushed towards the tree. As he did so, his foot slipped and he fell flat into the slush and when he stood up again his clothes, that were invariably so spotless, were soiled and sodden and his grey beard bespattered with mud. "It's my son," he cried "it's Ali, my son. Take him down, take him down!" And he burst out sobbing like a little child.

The men averted their eyes from him, while some took him by the shoulders and strove to comfort him. The barber had already climbed the tree and now he took out his sharp shaving knife and cut the rope from which the figure of Ali was hanging. As the limp body fell, Ahmed put up his strong arms to receive it, but even so it fell upon the ground and with the jolt the flute that Ali held so firmly in one of his hands, was jerked out of his stiffening fingers and rolled upon the ground.

All hovered anxiously around the village doctor as he examined the body and, as he shook his head sorrowfully, the sobs of Vilayet Ali became louder and more heart-rending, and many of the men began to wipe the tears that had forced themselves from their eyes. Nazo crept forward and, picking up her uncle's flute out of the slush, began to wipe it with the edge of her garment. Her father saw her, but instead of anger there was relief in his eyes. "Go to grandfather," he whispered before turning and issuing instructions to the others. Then he and three other men lifted the lifeless body and, with two going ahead to light the way, the sorrowful procession began its homeward journey.

Two of Vilayet Ali's friends assisted him along, for the old man was now in a pitiable state of sorrow and remorse with his shoulders stooped as though under the weight of some crushing burden. Seeing him thus with the tears trickling down his face and his grey beard all spattered with mud, the pain in Nazo's heart became unbearable. She felt so full of it that she was afraid her heart would break. Yes, break into a dozen pieces right there on that very spot where she stood, even as she had heard about hearts doing in the stories her darling uncle used to tell her. And yet she could not cry, even though she wanted to, she could not cry; and so she slipped her hand, which usually so warm, was now cold as ice, into his and helped her grieving grandfather along. All the while her eyes, big with the horror of it all, were fixed on the limp figure being carried in front of them.

As they walked with their tragic burden, the villagers talked. Softly, for they did not wish Vilayet Ali to hear. But it was loud enough for Nazo's sharp young ears to follow.

"He was a good lad," said one of them.

"The brightest that this village has ever seen," said the Headmaster gravely. "I had hoped for great things from him."

"But he failed, didn't he?" another asked, "isn't that why he took his life?"

Ahmed grimly silent, biting into his lips to stop his tears, drew in his 55
breath bitterly as the Headmaster said angrily:

"Ali fail? didn't I tell you that he was the brightest boy our village has ever had? I went with him to the city this morning to find out the Matriculation results, and do you know," he lifted his lantern to see their faces better, "he topped the list of the successful candidates!"

"But then why did he do it? Why? Why? Why?" they asked in astonishment, looking at each other and stealing side glances at tight-lipped Ahmed and weeping Vilayet Ali. The question seemed to hover in the air and haunt it, so that even the sound of their feet on the slushy ground and the swing of their lanterns seemed to be asking again and yet again:

"Why? Why? Why?"

The news of the tragedy had spread throughout the village and, as the pathetic procession wended its sorrowful way home, more and more joined them from the surrounding areas so that both sides of the pathway were lined with wide-eyed onlookers in spite of the unusual hour.

Dawn had all but broken and in its soft light the grim, tired faces of the 60
men, the still burden they carried covered with the coarse piece of home-spun that the barber had brought along, and Vilayet Ali's tragic tearstained face and bowed shoulders told their own story. As they reached the edge of the village pond, the rich, soul-stirring sound of the *azaan* rose in the morning air. Inspiring and beautiful, the wonderful words echoed and re-echoed in the stillness. Vilayet Ali's tears ceased as he listened and, lifting his sorrow-filled face to the skies, he began to murmur softly, resignedly: "It is from Allah that we come and unto Him that we return." The words were taken up by the others all along the way, as slowly the mournful procession neared Vilayet Ali's house where the weeping women waited.

Little Nazo let go of her grandfather's hand and, turning sped quickly back in the direction from which they had just come. Swiftly and surely she ran and, though her bare feet went deep into the mud at times or into tiny puddles, she did not fall. And even as she ran, the *azaan* continued, ending almost as she reached the tree on which her beloved uncle had hung himself.

Nazo was out of breath when she reached it. And so she sat down and gazed up at the sky, becoming glorious now with the rosy red rays of the rising sun. The pain in her heart was still unbearable, but she knew that since her heart had not broken into pieces a little while ago it never would. Pushing back the damp curls that had fallen on her little forehead, she looked lovingly at Ali's flute, wiping it carefully once again until not a trace of mud remained. And, as she did so, the tears tumbled out at last. Not in torrents, but gently, slowly. And one dropped down right upon the flute. And with the tears came a little easing of her pain.

Carefully Nazo wiped the tear off the slender reed and pressed it gently to her lips. "I will learn to play it as beautifully as you did," she solemnly told her uncle who was dead. "I will pray to Allah with it even as you did." And gently she put the flute to her childish rose-bud of a mouth, looked up at the glorious dawn and, with an expression of great reverence upon her delicate little face, began to play. But softly, very, very softly, so as not to hurt her dear grandfather!

CHARTING THE STORY

1 How successful is Nazo at diverting her grandfather when he returns from the mosque?

2 Apart from Nazo, does the family seem unanimous in their opinions concerning Ali? In what ways do they show consensus or division (or both)?

3 Proverbs 13:24 of the Bible states: "He that spareth his rod hateth his son: but he that loveth him chasteneth him betimes," or, Spare the rod and spoil the child—a belief obviously held by Vilayet Ali. How does this story put this traditional belief into perspective for you?

CONSIDERATIONS OF STYLE

1 In which passages does the story reflect a six-year-old's point of view, and in which does it seem that an adult is narrating? How does each age-perspective contribute to the development of the narrative?

2 Through the use of dialogue, in their manners of speech, how are the personalities of the characters developed?

3 Hamidullah's prose flows as easily as music from a flute, and one of its musical qualities is alliteration, as in: "the pupils of her big black eyes dilated with dread" and "the rosy red rays of the rising sun." Find other such examples and read aloud the passages in which they are contained—to the enjoyment of your listening audience.

AFTERTHOUGHTS

1 What legacy does Ali leave Nazo, and how does this seem particularly meaningful given that Nazo is a girl rather than a boy? How do you envision her future?

2 Throughout literature or throughout historical discourse, does Ali seem to resonate with other characters or persons? Which come to mind, and in what ways are they similar or dissimilar?

THE WRITER'S CRAFT

1 From the points of view of three bystanders at Ali's funeral, write out the thoughts (spoken or unspoken) of each.

2 If Nazo were to write a song for her uncle, or a poem—either at her age or older—how would she memorialize him?

GRACE OGOT

GRACE OGOT *was born in Kenya's Central Nyanza district in 1930. She was trained as a nurse in Uganda and in England, where she worked first as a midwife and later as a journalist and broadcaster with the BBC Overseas Service. She was Kenya's ambassador to the United Nations and UNESCO and a founding member of the Writers' Association of Kenya.*

Her works include the novels The Promised Land *(1966),* The Graduate *(1980) and* The Strange Bride *(written in Dholuo, 1980), and three volumes of short stories. "The Rain Came" appears in the anthologies* Unwinding Threads *(Charlotte Bruner, ed, 1968) and* Looking for a Rain God *(Nadezhda Obradovic, ed, 1990).*

PERSPECTIVES

1 Look up the terms *fairy tale, folk tale, legend,* and *myth,* and note the salient differences among them. What stories are you familiar with that might fall under these categories?

2 What stories (fictional or otherwise) have you read that feature an innocent character who must die so that others may live? How does one react to the situation of these sacrificial victims? In your view, is this practice ever justifiable?

The Rain Came

The chief was still far from the gate when his daughter Oganda saw him. She ran to meet him. Breathlessly she asked her father, "What is the news, great Chief? Everyone in the village is anxiously waiting to hear when it will rain." Labong'o held out his hands for his daughter but he did not say a word. Puzzled by her father's cold attitude Oganda ran back to the village to warn the others that the chief was back.

The atmosphere in the village was tense and confused. Everyone moved aimlessly and fussed in the yard without actually doing any work A young woman whispered to her co-wife, "If they have not solved this rain business today, the chief will crack." They had watched him getting thinner and thinner as the people kept on pestering him. "Our cattle lie dying in the fields," they reported. "Soon it will be our children and then ourselves. Tell us what to do to save our lives, oh great Chief." So the chief had daily prayed with the Almighty through the ancestors to deliver them from their distress.

Instead of calling the family together and giving them the news immediately, Labong'o went to his own hut, a sign that he was not to be disturbed. Having replaced the shutter, he sat in the dimly lit hut to contemplate.

It was no longer a question of being the chief of hunger-stricken people that weighed Labong'o's heart. It was the life of his only daughter that was at stake. At the time when Oganda came to meet him, he saw the glittering chain shining around her waist. The prophecy was complete. "It is Oganda, Oganda, my only daughter, who must die so young." Labong'o burst into tears before finishing the sentence. The chief must not weep. Society had declared him the bravest of men. But Labong'o did not care anymore. He assumed the position of a simple father and wept bitterly. He loved his people, the Luo, but what were the Luo for him without Oganda? Her life had brought a new life in Labong'o's world and he ruled better than he could remember. How would the spirit of the village survive his beautiful daughter? "There are so many homes and so many parents who have daughters. Why choose this one? She is all I have." Labong'o spoke as if the ancestors were there in the hut and he could see them face to face. Perhaps they were there, warning him to remember his promise on the day he was enthroned when he said aloud, before the elders, "I will lay down life, if necessary, and the life of my household, to save this tribe from the hands of the enemy." "Deny! Deny!" he could hear the voice of his forefathers mocking him.

5 When Labong'o was consecrated chief he was only a young man. Unlike his father, he ruled for many years with only one wife. But people rebuked him because his only wife did not bear him a daughter. He married a second, a third, and a fourth wife. But they all gave birth to male children. When Labong'o married a fifth wife she bore him a daughter. They called her Oganda, meaning "beans," because her skin was very fair. Out of Labong'o's twenty children, Oganda was the only girl. Though she was the chief's favorite, her mother's co-wives swallowed their jealous feelings and showered her with love. After all, they said, Oganda was a female child whose days in the royal family were numbered. She would soon marry at a tender age and leave the enviable position to someone else.

Never in his life had he been faced with such an impossible decision. Refusing to yield to the rainmaker's request would mean sacrificing the whole tribe, putting the interests of the individual above those of the society. More than that. It would mean disobeying the ancestors, and most probably wiping the Luo people from the surface of the earth. On the other hand, to let Oganda die as a ransom for the people would permanently cripple Labong'o spiritually. He knew he would never be the same chief again.

The words of Ndithi, the medicine man, still echoed in his ears. "Podho, the ancestor of the Luo, appeared to me in a dream last night, and he asked me to speak to the chief and the people," Ndithi had said to the gathering of tribesmen. "A young woman who has not known a man must die so that the country may have rain. While Podho was still talking to me, I saw a young woman standing at the lakeside, her hands raised, above her head. Her skin was as fair as the skin of young deer in the wilderness. Her tall slender figure stood like a lonely reed at the riverbank. Her sleepy eyes wore a sad look like that of a bereaved mother. She wore a gold ring on her left ear, and a glittering brass chain around her waist. As I still marveled at the beauty of this young woman, Podho told me, "Out of all the women in this land, we have chosen this one. Let her offer herself a sacrifice to the lake monster! And on that day, the rain will come down in torrents. Let everyone stay at home on that day, lest he be carried away by the floods."

Outside there was a strange stillness, except for the thirsty birds that sang lazily on the dying trees. The blinding midday heat had forced the people to retire to their huts. Not far way from the chief's hut, two guards were snoring away quietly. Labong'o removed his crown and the large eagle head that hung loosely on his shoulders. He left the hut, and instead of asking Nyabog'o the messenger to beat the drum, he went straight and beat it himself. In no time the whole household had assembled under the siala tree where he usually addressed them. He told Oganda to wait a while in her grandmother's hut.

When Labong'o stood to address his household, his voice was hoarse and the tears choked him. He started to speak, but words refused to leave his lips. His wive and sons knew there was great danger. Perhaps their enemies had declared war on them. Labong'o's eyes were red, and they could see he had been weeping. At last he told them. "One whom we love and treasure must be taken away from us. Oganda is to die." Labongo's voice was so faint, that he could not hear it himself. But he continued. "The ancestors have chosen her to be offered as a sacrifice to the lake monster in order that we may have rain."

They were completely stunned. As a confused murmur broke out, 10
Oganda's mother fainted and was carried off to her own hut. But the other people rejoiced. They danced around singing and chanting, "Oganda is the lucky one to die for the people. If it is to save the people, let Oganda go."

In her grandmother's hut Oganda wondered what the whole family were discussing about her that she could not hear. Her grandmother's hut was well away from the chief's court and, much as she strained her ears, she could not hear what was said. "It must be marriage," she concluded. It was an accepted custom for the family to discuss their daughter's future marriage behind her back. A faint smile played on Oganda's lips as she thought of the several young men who swallowed saliva at the mere mention of her name.

There was Kech, the son of a neighboring clan elder. Kech was very handsome. He had sweet, meek eyes and a roaring laughter. He would make a wonderful father, Oganda thought. But they would not be a good match. Kech was a bit too short to be her husband. It would humiliate her to have to look down at Kech each time she spoke to him. Then she thought of Dimo, the tall young man who had already distinguished himself as a brave warrior and an outstanding wrestler. Dimo adored Oganda, but Oganda thought he would make a cruel husband, always quarreling and ready to fight. No, she did not like him. Oganda fingered the glittering chain on her waist as she thought of Osinda. A long time ago when she was quite young Osinda had given her that chain, and instead of wearing it around her neck several times, she wore it round her waist where it could stay permanently. She heard her heart pounding so loudly as she thought of him. She whispered, "Let it be you they are discussing, Osinda, the lovely one. Come now and take me away..."

The lean figure in the doorway startled Oganda who was rapt in thought about the man she loved. "You have frightened me, Grandma," said Oganda laughing. "Tell me, is it my marriage you were discussing? You can take it from me that I won't marry any of them." A smile played on her lips again. She was coaxing the old lady to tell her quickly, to tell her they were pleased with Osinda.

In the open space outside the excited relatives were dancing and singing. They were coming to the hut now, each carrying a gift to put at Oganda's feet. As their singing got nearer Oganda was able to hear what they were saying: "If it is to save the people, if it is to give us rain, let Oganda go. Let Oganda die for her people, and for her ancestors." Was she mad to think that they were singing about her? How could she die? She found the lean figure of her grandmother barring the door. She could not get out. The look on her grandmother's face warned her that there was danger around the corner. "Grandma, it is not marriage then?" Oganda asked urgently. She suddenly felt panicky like a mouse cornered by a hungry cat. Forgetting that there was only one door in the hut Oganda fought desperately to find another exit. She must fight for her life. But there was none.

She closed her eyes, leapt like a wild tiger through the door, knocking her 15
grandmother flat to the ground. There outside in mourning garments Labong'o stood motionless, his hands folded at the back. He held his daughter's hand and led her away from the excited crowd to the little red-painted hut where her mother was resting. Here he broke the news officially to his daughter.

For a long time the three souls who loved one another dearly sat in darkness. It was no good speaking. And even if they tried, the words could not have come out. In the past they had been like three cooking stones, sharing their burdens. Taking Oganda away from from would leave two useless stones which would not hold a cooking pot.

News that the beautiful daughter of the chief was to be sacrificed to give the people rain spread across the country like wind. At sunset the chief's village was full of relatives and friends who had come to congratulate Oganda. Many more were on their way coming, carrying their gifts. They would dance till morning to keep her company. And in the morning they would prepare her a big farewell feast. All these relatives thought it a great honor to be selected by the spirits to die, in order that the society may live. "Oganda's name will always remain a living name among us," they boasted.

But was it maternal love that prevented Minya from rejoicing with the other women? Was it the memory of the agony and pain of childbirth that made her feel so sorrowful? Or was it the deep warmth and understanding that passes between a suckling babe and her mother that made Oganda part of her life, her flesh? Of course it was an honor, a great honor, for her daughter to be chosen to die for the country. But what could she gain once her only daughter was blown away by the wind? There were so many other women in the land, why choose her daughter, her only child! Had human life any meaning at all—other women had houses full of children while she, Minya, had to lose her only child!

In the cloudless sky the moon shone brightly, and the numerous stars glittered with a bewitching beauty. The dancers of all age groups assembled to dance before Oganda, who sat close to her mother, sobbing quietly. All these years she had been with her people she thought she understood them. But now she discovered that she was a stranger among them. If they loved her as they had always professed why were they not making any attempt to save her? Did her people really understand what it felt like to die young? Unable to restrain her emotions any longer, she sobbed loudly as her age group got up to dance. They were young and beautiful and very soon they would marry and have their own children. They would have husbands to love and little huts for themselves. They would have reached maturity. Oganda touched the chain around her waist as she thought of Osinda. She wished Osinda was there too, among her friends. "Perhaps he is ill," she thought gravely. The chain comforted Oganda—she would die with it around her waist and wear it in the underground world.

In the morning a big feast was prepared for Oganda. The women pre- 20
pared many different tasty dishes so that she could pick and choose. "People don't eat after death," they said. Delicious though the food looked, Oganda touched none of it. Let the happy people eat. She contented herself with sips of water from a little calabash.

The time for her departure was drawing near, and each minute was precious. It was a day's journey to the lake. She was to walk all night, passing through the great forest. But nothing could touch her, not even the denizens of the forest. She was already anointed with sacred oil. From the time Oganda received the sad news she had expected Osinda to appear any moment. But he was not there. A relative told her that Osinda was away on a private visit. Oganda realized that she would never see her beloved again.

In the late afternoon the whole village stood at the gate to say good-bye and to see her for the last time. Her mother wept on her neck for a long time. The great chief in a mourning skin came to the gate barefooted, and mingled with the people—a simple father in grief. He took off his wrist bracelet and put it on his daughter's wrist saying, "You will always live among us. The spirit of our forefathers is with you."

Tongue-tied and unbelieving Oganda stood there before the people. She had nothing to say. She looked at her home once more. She could hear her heart beating so painfully within her. All her childhood plans were coming to an end. She felt like a flower nipped in the bud never to enjoy the morning dew again. She looked at her weeping mother, and whispered, "Whenever you want to see me, always look at the sunset. I will be there."

Oganda turned southward to start her trek to the lake. Her parents, relatives, friends and admirers stood at the gate and watched her go.

Her beautiful slender figure grew smaller and smaller till she mingled with the thin dry trees in the forest. As Oganda walked the lonely path that wound its way into the wilderness, she sang a song, and her own voice kept her company.

The ancestors have said Oganda must die
The daughter of the chief must be sacrificed,
When the lake monster feeds on my flesh.
The people will have rain.
Yes, the rain will come down in torrents.
And the floods will wash away the sandy beaches
When the daughter of the chief dies in the lake.
My age group has consented
My parents have consented
So have my friends and relatives.
Let Oganda die to give us rain.
My age group are young and ripe,
Ripe for womanhood and motherhood
But Oganda must die young,
Oganda must sleep with the ancestors.
Yes, rain will come down in torrents.

The red rays of the setting sun embraced Oganda, and she looked like a burning candle in the wilderness.

The people who came to hear her sad song were touched by her beauty. But they all said the same thing. "If it is to save the people, if it is to give us rain, then be not afraid. Your name will forever live among us."

At midnight Oganda was tired and weary. She could walk no more. She sat under a big tree, and having sipped water from her calabash, she rested her head on the tree trunk and slept.

When Oganda woke up in the morning the sun was high in the sky. After walking for many hours, she reached the *tong'*, a strip of land that separated the inhabited part of the country from the sacred place (*kar lamo*). No layman could enter this place and come alive—only those who had direct contact with the spirits and the Almighty were allowed to enter this holy of holies. But Oganda had to pass through this sacred land on her way to the lake, which she had to reach at sunset.

A large crowd gathered to see her for the last time. Her voice was now hoarse and painful, but there was no need to worry anymore. Soon she would not have to sing. The crowd looked at Oganda sympathetically, mumbling words she could not hear. But none of them pleaded for life. As Oganda opened the gate, a child, a young child, broke loose from the crowd, and ran toward her. The child took a small earring from her sweaty hands and gave it to Oganda saying, "When you reach the world of the dead, give this earring to my sister. She died last week. She forgot this ring." Oganda, taken aback by the strange request, took the little ring, and handed her precious water and food to the child. She did not need them now. Oganda did not know whether to laugh or cry. She had heard mourners sending their love to their sweethearts, long dead, but this idea of sending gifts was new to her.

Oganda held her breath as she crossed the barrier to enter the sacred land. She looked appealingly at the crowd, but there was no response. Their minds were too preoccupied with their own survival. Rain was the precious medicine they were longing for, and the sooner Oganda could get to her destination the better.

A strange feeling possessed Oganda as she picked her way in the sacred land. There were strange noises that often startled her, and her first reaction was to take to her heels. But she remembered that she had to fulfill the wish of her people. She was exhausted, but the path was still winding. Then suddenly the path ended on sandy land. The water had retreated miles away from the shore leaving a wide stretch of sand. Beyond this was the vast expanse of water.

Oganda felt afraid. She wanted to picture the size and shape of the monster, but fear would not let her. The society did not talk about it, nor did the crying children who were silenced by the mention of its name. The sun was still up, but it was no longer hot. For a long time Oganda walked ankle-deep in the sand. She was exhausted and longed desperately for her calabash of water. As she moved on, she had a strange feeling that something was following her. Was it the monster? Her hair stood erect, and a cold paralyzing feeling ran along her spine. She looked behind, sideways and in front, but there was nothing, except a cloud of dust.

Oganda pulled up and hurried but the feeling did not leave her, and her whole body became saturated with perspiration.

The sun was going down fast and the lake shore seemed to move along with it.

Oganda started to run. She must be at the lake before sunset. As she ran she heard a noise coming from behind. She looked back sharply, and something resembling a moving bush was frantically running after her. It was about to catch up with her.

Oganda ran with all her strength. She was now determined to throw herself into the water even before sunset. She did not look back, but the creature was upon her. She made an effort to cry out, as in a nightmare, but she could not hear her own voice. The creature caught up with Oganda. In the utter confusion, as Oganda came face with the unidentified creature, a strong hand grabbed her. But she fell flat on the sand and fainted.

When the lake breeze brought her back to consciousness, a man was bending over her. ". . . . .!!" Oganda opened her mouth to speak, but she had lost her voice. She swallowed a mouthful of water poured into her mouth by the stranger.

"Osinda, Osinda! Please let me die. Let me run, the sun is going down. Let me die, let them have rain." Osinda fondled the glittering chain around Oganda's waist and wiped the tears from her face.

"We must escape quickly to the unknown land," Osinda said urgently. "We must run away from the wrath of the ancestors and the retaliation of the monster."

"But the curse is upon me, Osinda, I am no good to you anymore. And moreover the eyes of the ancestors will follow us everywhere and bad luck will befall us. Nor can we escape from the monster."

Oganda broke loose, afraid to escape, but Osinda grabbed her hands again.

"Listen to me, Oganda! Listen! Here are two coats!" He then covered the whole of Oganda's body, except her eyes, with a leafy attire made from the twigs of *Bwombwe*. "These will protect us from the eyes of the ancestors and the wrath of the monster. Now let us run out of here." He held Oganda's hand and they ran from the sacred land, avoiding the path that Oganda had followed.

The bush was thick, and the long grass entangled their feet as they ran. Halfway through the sacred land they stopped and looked back. The sun was almost touching the surface of the water. They were frightened. They continued to run, now faster, to avoid the sinking sun.

"Have faith, Oganda—that thing will not reach us."

When they reached the barrier and looked behind them trembling, only a tip of the sun could be seen above the water's surface.

"It is gone! It is gone!" Oganda wept, hiding her face in her hands.

"Weep not, daughter of the chief. Let us run, let us escape."

There was a bright lightning. They looked up, frightened. Above them black furious clouds started to gather. They began to run. Then the thunder roared, and the rain came down in torrents.

CHARTING THE STORY

1 In what ways is conflict foreshadowed in the opening paragraph? How does the conflict build, and how is it ultimately resolved?

2 What gender-designated roles are depicted in the story?

3 In what respects is the heroine Oganda a rather typical young woman of her age group? In what ways is she privileged?

4 How does this story play its human characters against the forces of nature, the inhabitants of the spirit world, and the dictates of culture?

CONSIDERATIONS OF STYLE

1 This story ascribes especial importance to rain, almost making it the major character whose entrance is delayed till the very end. What other natural phenomena are *dramatis personae* in the drama that is the story?

2 How does the "glittering brass chain" that Oganda wears around her waist serve as an amulet?

3 How much of a surprise does the ending offer a reader? Upon subsequent reading, can one find a foreshadowing of the "deliverance"? Or are the clues ambiguous?

4 If a reader is accustomed to "happy endings," how would his or her reading experience of this story proceed? What does the author seem to expect of her audience's experience with happy endings? Where do you see evidence of these expectations?

AFTERTHOUGHTS

1 What elements of a fairy tale, folk tale, legend, and myth does this story have? Does it have "the right stuff" for a Disney-inspired movie?

2 Compare the Biblical story of Jephthah and his daughter (Judges 11: 1–11, 29–40) with that of the Chief and Oganda. What other scriptural narratives—Judaeo-Christian, Islamic, or other—have you read that seem to resonate with "The Rain Came"?

THE WRITER'S CRAFT

1 Compare how a people's reverence for their ancestors shapes their world view in Chinua Achebe's "Dead Men's Path" and in this story.

2 Compose a contemporary tale of deliverance reminiscent of "The Rain Came."

3 What sort of future do you envision for Oganda and Osinda? Reflect this "life after" in the form of their narrative, written many years later.

BA'BILA MUTIA

BA'BILA MUTIA *was born in Limbe, Cameroon. He has taught African and British literature at the Ecole Normale Superieur of the University of Yaounde, has broadcast his work on African culture and literature on the BBC, and has used Cameroonian folk tales in academic courses and community outreach projects on African culture and thought. He currently teaches in the Liberal Studies Department of Western Washington University in Bellingham, Washington.*

The story "The Miracle" might cause one to pause and consider the "miracles" of faith in our own lives. It has been anthologized in The Heinemann Book of Contemporary African Short Stories, *Chinua Achebe and C L Innes, eds (1992).*

PERSPECTIVES

1 What protections has the Americans with Disabilities Act of 1995 provided disabled persons in the United States? What underlying assumptions about disability are inherent in such legislation?

2 What are some inevitable areas of conflict between native African belief systems and Western-based Christianity, imposed on a continent of diverse peoples by the colonial powers of Europe? Despite such conflicts, has the colonial religious legacy remained in Africa? How has it managed to accommodate native traditions? And vice versa?

The Miracle

Ba'mia waited anxiously for Reverend Father Tabi and his mother to come out of the church. Father Tabi had established it as a routine (after the second mass each Sunday) to come out and mix with the congregation. This particular morning Ba'mia was restless. He took hold of the sturdy ironwood stick with his two hands and hobbled to the school yard, away from the church.

As he pushed the stick to the ground, he hopped on his right leg and dragged his withered left leg after him. He had become so used to the movement that it was now a subconscious, almost acrobatic flow of motion which he executed without effort. The extra weight he exerted on his shoulders had left him with a broad chest and slightly exaggerated biceps and forearms. His thin waist, small stomach, and the baggy look of his left trouser leg, where his full left leg would have been, gave him a waspish appearance which was accentuated by his beady eyes and high cheekbones.

He stood behind the school and gazed down at the raffia palm trees and elephant grass. He knew his mother would be looking for him and, in her usual manner, getting anxious about where he was. He sat down on the grass. It was getting hot, but the grass was dry and comfortable. He placed the ironwood stick beside him and adjusted his withered left leg. A hawk was gliding in the air below him, rising and falling with the wind currents. His eyes tried to follow the stream as it meandered its way through the valley. Out here, alone, he felt at peace with himself.

Manyi looked around and wondered where Ba'mia was. A group of children was playing under the concrete water-tank at the corner of the mission maternity. Ba'mia was not with them. She looked further, towards the Reverend Father's residence. She saw Sister Mary-Jane walking to the mission guest house. The guest house was adjacent to the single-block elementary school. The local congregation stood in front of the old stone church in small groups. The men formed their own groups while the women laughed and chatted with each other. The locally dyed blouses the women wore, their wrappers, the men's handwoven shirts, and the children's *danshikis* looked very colourful. They blended with the hibiscus, marigold, and bougainvillaea to give the mission an atmosphere of heavenly beauty.

Father Tabi moved from one group to another. He shook hands, shared in a joke, listened intently to a family matter, as he moved among the faithful. Then he spotted Manyi.

'Ah, Manyi, where have you been? I was looking for you.'

'Good morning, Father,' Manyi said.

Father Tabi looked at her worried face. 'Is anything the matter?' he asked.

'Yes, Ba'mia,' she said. "I can't find him. I saw him leave the church a short while ago. Father,' she added, 'I'm worried about him. Among the three children I have, he is the only one who's so remote and distant.'

'He's still a child,' Father Tabi explained. 'You worry too much about him. He'll grow out of it.'

'I don't know, Father,' Manyi said reflectively. 'He's almost fourteen years old. Everyone in the family loves him, but it's difficult not to sympathise with his condition.'

'Talking about his condition,' Father Tabi said, 'do you still intend to go to Menda? The Holy Father arrives in the country this week.'

'Yes, Father.' Her face lit up with devotional inspiration. 'Yes. We're lucky to have the Pope visit us at Eastertide.'

Father Tabi smiled. 'Indeed, we are. This is the third nation he's visiting on the continent. We expect him to celebrate Easter Sunday mass in Menda stadium.'

'Easter,' Manyi murmured. 'The Lord's resurrection. The time of miracles, Father,' she said, raising her voice, 'do you think Ba'mia could be healed?"

'Healed?'

'Yes. I want to take him to Menda. His leg could be made whole. It pains me to see him hobble around with that leg. I've always wanted to see him normal, like other children.'

Father Tabi remained silent.

'He can be cured, can't he?'

'It's a matter of faith and God's will,' Father Tabi said. 'You are his mother. If you feel strongly about it, then follow your heart's call. Have you discussed this with his father? You know he doesn't come to church—'

Before Manyi could answer, a boy's voice said, 'Good morning, Father.' They turned round. It was Ba'mia. No one had seen him hobble up to the front of the church.

'Ah, good morning, Ba'mia,' Father Tabi responded. He stretched his arm and shook hands with the boy.

'Where have you been?' Manyi asked him. 'I've been looking all over for you.'

'I'd better leave you two alone,' Father Tabi said. 'Ah, there's Sister Beatrice. I'll have a word with her.'

'Thank you so much, Father,' Manyi smiled.

'God bless you, Manyi.'

'Say goodbye to Father,' Manyi said to the boy.

'Goodbye, Father.' There was a trace of irritation in his voice.

'Goodbye, Ba'mia. Don't forget your catechism classes.'

After Father Tabi walked away, the boy turned to his mother. 'I'm hungry, Mother. Let's go home.'

She wanted to talk to other women and their families, but she changed her mind. She did not want to make the boy feel unwanted. His disability always softened her heart towards him. She waved at some of her friends as she began walking home with Ba'mia.

Gwan-Fumbat was waiting for Manyi when she came back from mass. His house was the only one built with cement blocks and roofed with aluminum sheets. The rest of the homesteads that made up the large Fumbat compound were a scattered cluster of mud-plastered houses roofed with long, dry, savannah grass.

Manyi, his third wife, the mother of his twins, was his favourite. He hoped she would be his last wife. He had married her because he wanted a male child, one who would inherit his name and sustain the unbroken line of the Fumbat lineage.

He had married the second wife because the first had given birth to three girls in succession. She too had three more girls. On his father's insistence, he married Manyi. Her maiden name was Kogah, until she bore the female twins,

Nahgwa and Nahjela. Thereafter, she became Manyi, mother of twins and he Tanyi, father of twins. Twins were a sign of fertility in a woman. Perhaps the seeds of the male heir he was desperately searching for lay in Manyi's womb.

Gwan-Fumbat's father died at eighty-six, two years after the twins were 35
born. Six months after he died, Manyi became pregnant. When she gave birth nine months later, Gwan-Fumbat knew his sacrifices on the family shrine and his repeated appeals for ancestral intervention had not been in vain. It was a baby boy. The long-awaited male heir to the Fumbat lineage had arrived.

But something was wrong. The baby's left leg appeared frail and unusually thin. Gwan-Fumbat's late father had a withered left leg when he was born. But he handled the disability with humour until a logging accident crushed the leg when he was still a young man. Not many people knew the truth about his one leg.

And now, Manyi's baby's left leg too appeared frail and lifeless. There was no trace of recognition on Gwan-Fumbat's face when he came to the Catholic mission maternity to see the baby. Despite the overwhelming evidence, he told himself that the baby's left leg was a temporary condition that would get better with time. He decided to defy tradition and wait for three months—instead of the traditional three weeks—before he would name the child.

Three months later, the visiting medical doctor from the city confirmed what Gwan-Fumbat already knew. The baby's leg hd no circulation, no feeling. It was just a tiny bone and dead tissue. It was a dead leg. The condition was irreversible.

Only then did Gwan-Fumbat order the naming ceremony to be initiated. He paid the late-naming-ceremony penalty of two goats and a drum of palm-oil. He knew it was his father who had returned. So he named the child Ba'mia, father has come back.

It was these thoughts that ran through his mind as the voices of the 40
women and children coming back from mass reached him. He sent one of his older girls to call Manyi.

A few minutes later, Manyi entered his house. She bowed slightly and clapped her hands three times.

'Tanyi,' she said, 'greetings. I hear you want to see me. I just came back from church. I haven't started cooking.'

He acknowledged her greeting and motioned her to sit down on one of the several carved stools around the fireplace. He threw some splinters of wood in the glowing embers of the fire and fanned them with a piece of cardboard. A few flames caught the splinters and crackled into a bright fire. He added bigger pieces of wood and the big yellow flames lit the semi-dark room. He wore brown khaki shorts and a faded jumper. The light from the fire illuminated the face of a man in his late fifties. He had a broad forehead and bushy eyebrows that hung over deep-set eyes. The hair on his head was all grey, and the hands that threw the firewood in the fire were large and thick.

'I didn't call you here because I'm hungry,' he said. He poked the fire with a long piece of wood and stared meditatively at the flying sparks. Then he lifted his head from the flames. He looked at her intently. She was in her mid-forties, but her face did not betray her age. Her angular features, prominent cheekbones and firm breasts only added to her beauty.

He was not used to formalities, so he went straight to the point. 'Where's Ba'mia?' he demanded.

'Somewhere in the compound,' she said. 'Is anything wrong?'

He poked the fire again. The agitated flames lit his face. After a short silence, he raised up his head. 'What's this I hear about you taking Ba'mia to Menda?'

'What is it you want to know?' she retorted.

Her aggressiveness caught him off-guard. Then he laughed. It was a short, sarcastic bark. 'So you're now throwing my questions back at me?' he asked.

'Your question sounds like a riddle. Let me know what's in your mind, and I'll answer you accordingly.'

He laughed again. The laughter faded to a frown and a firm tightening of his lips. He began grinding his teeth. The diminishing flames produced dark shadows on his face.

'Ba'mia belongs to this compound,' he said emphatically, folding his fist into a tight knot. 'His place is here, with the ancestral shrine.'

A gust of wind came through the open door and stirred the fire. There were patches of light and shadows on Manyi's face. She stared defiantly at her husband.

'God has a purpose for him. He belongs to the church. The Holy Father arrives from Rome this week. He's celebrating Easter mass in Menda. This is a chance for Ba'mia to receive a cure—'

'He doesn't need a cure,' he cut in. 'He's not suffering from a disease. He was born that way.'

'He deserves to be normal, like other children.'

'If there's anything he deserves, it's our responsibility to help him accept his condition. It's his right to grow up into a man. Your motherly sympathy will not help him much.'

'You don't understand God's ways—'

'And let me tell you something else. Ba'mia's condition is his personal load he carries from the world of our ancestors.'

'What do you mean?'

'He's a reincarnation of his grandfather.' He ignored the mocking gentleness of her laughter. 'My father too had the same disability,' he carried on.

'But I thought he lost his leg in an accident.'

'He was born with a dead left leg. When Ba'mia was born, I knew my father had chosen to return to the family. His fate was decided before he was born. We can only help him accept it.'

'You have a right to your beliefs,' she said. 'He may be your father, but he's also my son. I feel what he suffers when he hops around on that leg. That's why I'm taking him to Menda.'

There was a tone of finality in her voice. The firewood in the fireplace had been totally consumed by the fire. Gwan-Fumbat poked the fireplace and looked at the hot coals that were left in the ashes. He looked around and saw some firewood. He thought of putting more wood on the dying coals to rekindle the flames, but he changed his mind. He looked up at Manyi.

'There's not much I can do to persuade you,' he said, 'but the truth is never hidden. When it's nightfall, when the day comes to an end, the fowls come home to roost. When Ba'mia grows up, he will know where he belongs.'

It was almost noon. Long rays of sunshine came in through cracks on the wall. They had replaced the light from the dead fire.

'It's almost midday,' Gwan-Fumbat told Manyi, 'and I'm getting hungry.'

Manyi stood up. She felt vindicated. As far as Ba'mia was concerned, she would always have her way. The boy could be Tanyi's reincarnated father; he could be the heir to the Fumbat lineage, but he was still her son.

'I know,' she said. 'I was about to cook some corn *fufu* when you called me.' She was almost at the door now. 'I'll send Nahjela to give you the food as soon as it's ready,' she said, as she stepped out of the door.

When she got to her house, Ba'mia was waiting for her. There was a defiant look on his face.

'What's the matter?' his mother asked him.

'You've been arguing with Father again, haven't you? About me as usual, I'm sure.'

'Everything I do or say is for your interest,' Manyi said.

'You've never given me a choice,' the boy protested. 'Don't I have a chance to talk for myself? Has Father or you ever thought I've got a mind of my own, that I know what's good for me, who I am?'

Manyi kept quiet for a moment. After a while she said, 'I'm sorry, Ba'mia, I never wanted to—'

'I don't want anyone to feel sorry for me,' he blurted. 'I can always take care of myself.' He turned round suddenly, gripped his stick, and hobbled out of the house.

The following Sunday Manyi and Ba'mia got up after the third cockcrow. She wore one of her colourful three-piece wrappers. Her son wore a golden embroided *danshiki* over navy blue trousers. He also had his walking stick with him.

The first bus had already left before they reached the park. The second bus was full even before they got to the park. The third bus took a long while to be filled up. They did not leave the park till seven thirty.

By the time they arrived in Menda at eight o'clock, the streets were jammed with people. The most prominent sight was the variety of school uniforms worn by children all over the city. There were school bands everywhere.

The police mounted roadblocks at every crossroad. They were checking people's identification papers. Ba'mia had been to Menda only four or five times, and he never ceased to be amazed at the novelty of things.

Both sides of the road from the stadium to the Catholic mission premises on the hilltop were already crammed with people. Some had been there as early as three in the morning to have a vantage place at the edge of the road.

Ba'mia and his mother were not so fortunate. They walked as far down towards the stadium as they could. The crowd was so thick that they could not go very far. They finally settled at the outskirts of the crowd, away from the main road itself where the Pope's motorcade would pass.

It was now past nine o'clock. The mass in the stadium had just started. They could hear the choirs from the big loudspeakers that were mounted in the stadium. They found a place and sat down to wait.

The open-air mass was over at eleven thirty. Ba'mia heard the shouts and yells of excitement from the thousands of people who were jammed in the small municipal stadium. He stood up and turned round to his mother. She was dozing.

'Nah Manyi,' he said, shaking her shoulder, 'the service in the stadium 85
seems to be over.'

She stood up, craned her neck, and looked down the road. Small crowds were already trickling out of the stadium. Because of the big population most people had been unable to gain entrance into the stadium. But the throngs of believers lining the road seemed larger than the huge crowd in the stadium. They all waited patiently.

Ba'mia and his mother were pushed back ten or fifteen yards by the ever-increasing crowd. A policeman with a whistle on his lips lashed with a cowhide whip at the feet of the fortunate ones along the road. The crowd pretended to retreat, and the sea of heaving bodies undulated in human waves whose ripples reached Ba'mia and his mother at the back.

Without any warning, the stadium gates were flung open as the flamboyant motorcycle escorts emerged from the stadium. The escort riders were immaculately attired in white. They wore white uniforms, white boots, white goggles, white helmets and white gloves. They had not yet switched on their sirens, but their red lights were flashing. The Pope's walkabout in the stadium had not lasted as long as Ba'mia thought it would. Someone beside him had said they might have to wait for more than three hours under the hot sun.

Ba'mia used the support of his stick to elevate his head another inch or two. When he saw the black Mercedes emerge behind the escort riders, his heart fell. He turned to his mother.

'Father Tabi said the Pope usually walked around and shook hands with 90
the Christians.' There was a note of disappointment in his voice.

'Have faith, my son,' his mother said. 'We didn't come here for nothing. God is on our side. I believe in miracles—'

The boy did not hear her last words. Even as she spoke, the black Mercedes suddenly came to a halt half-way down the road from the stadium. The

Pope came down from the car and was quickly surrounded by aides and government security men. A bishop in a white robe also came out of the car. A slight gust of wind momentarily caught the Pope's white vestment. Instinctively, he reached for his head to keep the white skullcap from being blown away.

'Mother! Mother! Look! He has come out of the car. He's shaking hands with the crowd. Mother—'

'A miracle, my son. Faith. I told you. We must have faith.'

The Pope was just about fifty yards away. Ba'mia tried to think. The crowd in front of him was too thick. If he did not act fast, he would miss the chance of his lifetime. When his mother turned her head towards where he stood, the boy had vanished. Initially she panicked. Then she saw him about five yards away. It was his colourful *danshiki* that caught her eye.

'Ba'mia,' she shouted. 'Ba'mia. This way, not that way. The crowd is too thick over there.' The boy did not hear her. Her small voice was swallowed by the noisy cheers of the crowd.

Ba'mia began heaving and twisting his way through the dense jungle of human bodies. Where the crowd was too thick, he crept in between the legs of the adults. When he stood up again, the edge of the road was about three yards away. He raised himself on the toes of his good foot and managed to support his weight on the stick. He looked up, towards the stadium. The Pope was still walking down the road, stopping here and there, touching the foreheads and hands of the faithful, administering a silent blessing to those who reached out but could not touch him. He was now about thirty yards away.

Ba'mia made up his mind very quickly. He lowered his body and went down on all fours. There were only eight yards of legs and dust between him and the edge of the crowd. He gripped his stick tightly and began creeping forward. The smell of dirty shoes and feet, and the foul taste of raw dust in his throat and nostrils was becoming unbearable. It was suffocating. He thought he would faint. He could not go any further. He crept through the last pair of legs and, without warning, found himself at the edge of the road. He was standing in front of a short fat man who was focusing his camera on the approaching entourage.

'You dirty dusty cripple,' the man swore. 'Get out of my way before I kick you. Don't you see I want to take a picture?'

The boy apologised. It only infuriated the man. 'Get out of my way before I kick you back to the dust.'

Ba'mia moved out of the man's way and took two tentative steps towards the direction of the approaching entourage. He pushed his wooden stick firmly to the ground and raised his neck. Unconsciously he wrapped his paralysed left leg around the stick. He managed to maintain a precarious balance with his healthy right leg.

The Pope was now about twenty yards up the road. The crowd surged forward, yearning to touch his hand. He touched one hand after another, as many as he could. An old haggard woman struggled to catch his attention. Just when she was giving up, the Pope stretched out his right hand and touched her head. Her face broke into a smile and her mouth hung open revealing two rows of black toothless gums.

Some distance away, the motorcade was creeping down the road, keeping an anticipated distance behind the pontiff. He lifted a small baby girl from the arms of her mother and kissed her on the forehead. The child's face wrinkled into a frown and she began crying. He handed the baby back to her mother.

Ba'mia waited apprehensively. He felt his heart throbbing violently against his chest. The Pope was now only a few yards away. The boy held his breath and adjusted the stick to maintain his balance.

Then he jerked his body and darted forward. The police guards and plainclothes security men were completely taken by surprise. They tried to push the boy away. He ducked twice, feinted a fall, and slipped between their legs. He looked up, saw the Pope's flowing white vestment and grabbed it with his left hand. His right hand still clung to his stick. He could not afford to lose it. Two security officers fell on him and tried to pull him away. But he clung to the vestment with all his might.

The Pope raised his hand in a gesture of restraint. The guards and security men hesitated. They stood by in pensive anticipation, waiting for the slightest excuse to pounce on the boy. For a moment, everyone held his breath.

Ba'mia planted his stick firmly on the ground and raised himself upward. He was barely four and a half feet tall. He shifted his body weight to his right foot and, in a quick, sweeping and dramatic motion, took hold of the withered left leg and lifted it effortlessly with his left hand. A murmur of sympathy came from the onlookers.

The Pope laid his right hand on the boy's head and smiled. 'What's your name?' he asked in a thick heavy accent.

'Ba'mia,' the boy barely whispered. He was trying to stop his body from the sudden chills of trembling that had seized him. He coughed and cleared his throat. 'I want you to make me walk upright,' he demanded. His black eyes looked up at the broad face of the Pope.

'I will pray for you...' the Pope began to say.

'But... but,' the boy stammered, in a faltering voice. 'My mother said you are here for God. You speak with him. She said you will make me walk erect.'

There were visible signs of impatience on the faces in the crowd. The motorcade had now caught up with the entourage. The aides glanced at their watches anxiously. The escort riders were revving their engines.

'I speak for God,' the Pope said. 'I am only his voice, his messenger.'

Someone discreetly tapped the Holy Father on his right shoulder. He turned round and an aide whispered into his ear. He barely nodded. He turned round again and looked at the boy's dusty countenance.

There were tears in Ba'mia's eyes. 'I want to walk like other children. Tell God to make me walk properly. Help me with a miracle,' he said.

The black Mercedes pulled up a few feet away from the entourage.

'You are God's miracle,' the Pope responded, 'a miracle of His love and creation. You have to pray to Him.' In a wide, rehearsed gesture he made the sign of the cross over the boy's head. On a second thought, he reached into the pocket of his vestment and brought out a rosary. He handed it to the boy. 'Use this to pray to Holy Mary, mother of God. God will answer your prayers.' Ba'mia took the rosary and slipped it into his *danshiki* pocket.

Another aide came forward and whispered into the Pope's ear again. He moved forward and shook a few hands. When he turned round, television camera crews and a horde of newsmen closed in around him.

A uniformed attendant opened the rear door of the waiting Mercedes. The Pope looked at the waving crowd. He raised his hand in one final benediction.

'What shall I tell my mother?' Ba'mia heard himself shout above the din of the cheering crowd. His voice was swallowed up by the hum of the crowd and threatening throttle of the BMW motorcycles.

The Pontiff's face expanded to one last, memorable smile. Then he stepped into the waiting upholstery of the Mercedes' interior. The uniformed man closed the door mechanically. The motorcade began crawling past the main market, on its way to the Bishop's Residence in the Menda Catholic mission. The escort riders turned on their sirens and flashing lights.

The crowd had already begun breaking up. Ba'mia found himself swallowed up again in a whirlwind of legs, bodies and dust. He did not know when he lost his stick. He crept around in utter desperation and confusion, looking for it. When he located his mother, he was out of breath and exhausted. His face, arms and legs were covered with dust. He began to cough.

'What happened?' his mother asked him.

There were tears in his eyes. She lent him a hand and he stood up erect. His lips trembled. The dust in his lungs made him cough again.

'What happened?' Manyi asked again.

'Nothing,' he said between sobs, 'nothing.'

'Nothing?'

'Nothing happened. I lost my stick.'

'Did you . . . did you see him? Did he touch you?'

'The motorcade is gone,' the boy said, wiping away his tears. 'I'm tired. I want to go home.'

They began walking towards the old road that led to the motor vehicle park. She half-held, half-supported him. They walked in silence. A sudden impenetrable silence has descended on her and the boy. His face had a blank expression. It was as if he was no longer conscious of her presence beside him. He had retreated into an unfathomable world. She did not want to intrude in his private world, so she too kept quiet.

Finally, they reached the park. The minibus that plied the rough, dusty route between Menda and their village was almost full. The passengers paid their fare. The driver started the engine and the bus left the park.

Everyone in the bus was quiet. The monotonous drone of the bus engine was occasionally interrupted by the regular change of gears. Manyi could no longer bear the silence. She glanced at Ba'mia.

'What shall we tell Father Tabi?' she asked, in an effort to break the curtain of silence between her and her son.

'I don't know,' he said. 'And what about my father? What will you tell him?' His voice was flat, without feeling or emotion.

Manyi kept quiet. After a while she said, 'What are you thinking about?' There was a slight trace of desperation in her voice.

'My stick,' he said. 'I will need a new one.' After a while, he reached into his *danshiki* pocket and brought out the rosary. 'Here,' he said, handing it to her. 'You may keep it. The Pope gave it to me.'

'Why?' she asked. 'It's yours.'

He still held the rosary out to her. There was no expression on his face. Manyi took it reluctantly. The bus now began ascending the first of three steep hills before it arrived at the village.

'Tanyi will have to get me a new stick,' he reflected, after a few moments of silence.

'He's your father,' Manyi rebuked him sharply. 'You don't call him Tanyi. It's only the elders who call him Tanyi.'

'I am Ba'mia,' he said softly.

'What do you mean?' she asked.

'Tanyi's father,' he replied. 'I came back to be reborn in the family, to inherit what is rightfully mine—'

'Ba'mia! Don't say such things!' She recoiled back in shock and astonishment. She suddenly went pale. A kind of glow came over the boy's face. His thoughtful, reflective gaze had disappeared. It was replaced by a knowing one. He was radiating a strange aura that stunned his mother.

'I know who I am,' he continued. 'My place is with the ancestors. Tanyi will initiate me in the family shrine to commune with them. But first, he must carve me a new stick.'

Ba'mia did not hear his mother's reply. The driver changed gears and the bus jerked violently. Behind them a thick cloud of dust rose and died down as quickly as the bus's tyres churned it up. Ba'mia closed his eyes and lapsed again into another long silence, listening to the strained drone of the engine.

CHARTING THE STORY

1 How did Manyi come to be Gwan-Fumbat's third wife?

2 How do the differing belief systems of Manyi and Gwan-Fumbat/Tanyi cause them to view Ba'mia's handicap differently? Which of his parents has more strongly influenced Ba'mia's own view of his condition?

3 How does Ba'mia's crisis of faith, in the end, become a "miraculous" gift of faith?

CONSIDERATIONS OF STYLE

1 Which characters in the story does Mutia describe physically in greatest detail? Which psychologically? Citing evidence from the text, how might you account for the difference?
2 What does Mutia achieve by shifting the focus from Ba'mia to each of his parents and to the Pope? Had the story been related from the point of view of any one of them, how would it have changed *vis-à-vis* each character's point of view?
3 How is the Pope characterized? What sort of miracle, if any, could one expect?

AFTERTHOUGHTS

1 Look up the etymology of *miracle*. How does the word's Latin origin shed light on the notion of supernatural intervention in a popular understanding of the term?
2 What significance arises from Ba'mia's losing his stick? In narratives concerning faith-healings, what does one normally hear concerning crutches and other walking aids? How does this story play upon these expectations?

THE WRITER'S CRAFT

1 Having been whisked away to the bishop's residence, the Pope is now writing his account of the day. Staying in character, write your reflections, as Pope, about the day's events.
2 Write an essay on the conflicts between tradition and modernity in postcolonial Africa as depicted in Chinua Achebe's story "Dead Men's Path" and "The Miracle."
3 Compare the notions of ancestral and spiritual connectedness in interpreting and acting upon the reality of the here-and-now in "The Miracle" and in Estela Portillo Trambley's story "Village."

BESSIE HEAD

BESSIE HEAD *was born in South Africa in 1937 to a Scottish mother and a black South African father. She never knew her parents and was raised in a foster home. She attended missionary schools and became a teacher. She also worked as a journalist, eventually falling into the disfavor of the South African government. She went into exile in Botswana in 1964, where she lived haunted by the prospect of being deported back to South Africa.*

Though she attempted to settle into a quiet life of writing and farming, Head's stay in Botswana was often stressful and unsettled, including her being admitted to a psychiatric institution on two occasions. The tensions in her life inform much of her writing, though in the end, her sense of hope and optimism come through. She died in Botswana in 1986 at the age of forty-nine.

Her novels include When the Rain Clouds Gather, Maru, *and* A Question of Power.

The title story in her 1977 collection, "The Collector of Treasures" sheds light on the place of the strong traditional woman in a precolonial, postcolonial, and independent African nation-state.

PERSPECTIVES

1. What images of a precolonial African society come to mind? How might you expect the society to have changed under European—in particular, British—colonialism? What further social changes might you expect to have occurred when a number of new African nation-states were created in the 1960s?
2. Is the killing of another human being ever, in your opinion, justified? If not, why not; and if so, under what circumstances? Upon what do you base your opinion?
3. What attributes about imprisonment and prison life do you bring to this reading? To what sources do you attribute these attitudes?

The Collector of Treasures

The long-term central state prison in the south was a whole day's journey away from the villages of the northern part of the country. They had left the village of Puleng at about nine that morning and all day long the police truck droned as it sped southwards on the wide, dusty cross-country track-road. The everyday world of ploughed fields, grazing cattle, and vast expanses of bush and forest seemed indifferent to the hungry eyes of the prisoner who gazed out at them through the wire mesh grating at the back of the police truck. At some point during the journey, the prisoner seemed to strike at some ultimate source of pain and loneliness within her being and, overcome by it, she slowly crumpled forward in a wasted heap, oblivious to everything but her pain. Sunset swept by, then dusk, then dark and still the truck droned on, impersonally, uncaring.

At first, faintly on the horizon, the orange glow of the city lights of the new independence town of Gaborone, appeared like an astonishing phantom in the overwhelming darkness of the bush, until the truck struck tarred roads, neon lights, shops and cinemas, and made the bush a phantom amidst a blaze of light. All this passed untimed, unwatched by the crumpled prisoner; she did not stir as the truck finally droned to a halt outside the prison gates. The torchlight struck the side of her face like an agonising blow. Thinking she was asleep, the policeman called out briskly:

'You must awaken now. We have arrived.'

He struggled with the lock in the dark and pulled open the grating. She crawled painfully forward, in silence.

Together, they walked up a short flight of stairs and waited awhile as the 5
man tapped lightly, several times, on the heavy iron prison door. The night-duty attendant opened the door a crack, peered out and then opened the door a little wider for them to enter. He quietly and casually led the way to a small office, looked at his colleague and asked: 'What do we have here?'

'It's the husband murder case from Puleng village,' the other replied, handing over a file.

The attendant took the file and sat down at a table on which lay open a large record book. In a big, bold scrawl he recorded the details: Dikeledi Mokopi. Charge: Man-slaughter. Sentence: Life. A night-duty wardress appeared and led the prisoner away to a side cubicle, where she was asked to undress.

'Have you any money on you?' the wardress queried, handing her a plain, green cotton dress which was the prison uniform. The prisoner silently shook her head.

'So, you have killed your husband, have you?' the wardress remarked, with a flicker of humour. 'You'll be in good company. We have four other women here for the same crime. It's becoming the fashion these days. Come with me,' and she led the way along a corridor, turned left and stopped at an iron gate which she opened with a key, waited for the prisoner to walk in ahead of her and then locked it with the key again. They entered a small, immensely high-walled courtyard. On one side were toilets, showers, and a cupboard. On the other, an empty concrete quadrangle. The wardress walked to the cupboard, unlocked it and took out a thick roll of clean-smelling blankets which she handed to the prisoner. At the lower end of the walled courtyard was a heavy iron door which led to the cell. The wardress walked up to this door, banged on it loudly and called out: 'I say, will you women in there light your candle?'

A voice within called out: 'All right,' and they could hear the scratch-scratch of a match. The wardress again inserted a key, opened the door and watched for a while as the prisoner spread out her blankets on the floor. The four women prisoners already confined in the cell sat up briefly, and stared silently at their new companion. As the door was locked, they all greeted her quietly and one of the women asked: 'Where do you come from?'

'Puleng,' the newcomer replied, and seemingly satisfied with that, the light was blown out and the women lay down to continue their interrupted sleep. And as though she had reached the end of her destination, the new prisoner too fell into a deep sleep as soon as she had pulled her blankets about her.

The breakfast gong sounded at six the next morning. The women stirred themselves for their daily routine. They stood up, shook out their blankets and rolled them up into neat bundles. The day-duty wardress rattled the key in the lock and let them out into the small concrete courtyard so that they could perform their morning toilet. Then, with a loud clatter of pails and plates, two male prisoners appeared at the gate with breakfast. The men handed each woman a plate of porridge and a mug of black tea and they settled themselves on the concrete floor to eat. They turned and looked at their new companion and one of the women, a spokesman for the group, said kindly:

'You should take care. The tea has no sugar in it. What we usually do is scoop the sugar off the porridge and put it into the tea.'

The woman, Dikeledi, looked up and smiled. She had experienced such terror during the awaiting-trial period that she looked more like a skeleton than a human being. The skin creaked tautly over her cheeks. The other woman smiled, but after her own fashion. Her face permanently wore a look of cynical, whimsical humour. She had a full, plump figure. She introduced herself and her companions: 'My name is Kebonye. Then that's Otsetswe, Galeboe, and Monwana. What may your name be?'

'Dikeledi Mokopi.'

'How is it that you have such a tragic name,' Kebonye observed. 'Why did your parents have to name you *tears*?'

'My father passed away at that time and it is my mother's tears that I am named after,' Dikeledi said, then added: 'She herself passed away six years later and I was brought up by my uncle.'

Kebonye shook her head sympathetically, slowly raising a spoonful of porridge to her mouth. That swallowed, she asked next:

'And what may your crime be?'

'I have killed my husband.'

'We are all here for the same crime,' Kebonye said, then with her cynical smile asked: 'Do you feel any sorrow about the crime?'

'Not really,' the other woman replied.

'How did you kill him?'

'I cut off his special parts with a knife,' Dikeledi said.

'I did it with a razor,' Kebonye said. She sighed and added: 'I have had a troubled life.'

A little silence followed while they all busied themselves with their food, then Kebonye continued musingly:

'Our men do not think that we need tenderness and care. You know, my husband used to kick me between the legs when he wanted that. I once aborted with a child, due to this treatment. I could see that there was no way to appeal to him if I felt ill, so I once said to him that if he liked he could keep some other woman as well because I couldn't manage to satisfy all his needs. Well, he was an education-officer and each year he used to suspend about seventeen male teachers for making school girls pregnant, but he used to do the same. The last time it happened the parents of the girl were very angry and came to report the matter to me. I told them: "You leave it to me. I have seen enough." And so I killed him.'

They sat in silence and completed their meal, then they took their plates and cups to rinse them in the wash-room. The wardress produced some pails and a broom. Their sleeping quarters had to be flushed out with water; there was not a speck of dirt anywhere, but that was prison routine. All that was left was an inspection by the director of the prison. Here again Kebonye turned to the newcomer and warned:

'You must be careful when the chief comes to inspect. He is mad about one thing—attention! Stand up straight! Hands at your sides! If this is not done you should see how he stands here and curses. He does not mind anything but that. He is mad about that.'

Inspection over, the women were taken through a number of gates to an open, sunny yard, fenced in by high, barbed-wire where they did their daily work. The prison was a rehabilitation centre where the prisoners produced goods which were sold in the prison store; the women produced garments of cloth and wool; the men did carpentry, shoe-making, brick-making, and vegetable production.

Dikeledi had a number of skills—she could knit, sew, and weave baskets. All the women at present were busy knitting woollen garments; some were learners and did their work slowly and painstakingly. They looked at Dikeledi with interest as she took a ball of wool and a pair of knitting needles and rapidly cast on stitches. She had soft, caressing, almost boneless hands of strange power—work of a beautiful design grew from those hands. By mid-morning she had completed the front part of a jersey and they all stopped to admire the pattern she had invented in her own head.

'You are a gifted person,' Kebonye remarked, admiringly.

'All my friends say so,' Dikeledi replied smiling. 'You know, I am the woman whose thatch does not leak. Whenever my friends wanted to thatch their huts, I was there. They would never do it without me. I was always busy and employed because it was with these hands that I fed and reared my children. My husband left me after four years of marriage but I managed well enough to feed those mouths. If people did not pay me in money for my work, they paid me with gifts of food.'

'It's not so bad here,' Kebonye said. 'We get a little money saved for us out of the sale of our work, and if you work like that you can still produce money for your children. How many children do you have?'

'I have three sons.'

'Are they in good care?'

'Yes.'

'I like lunch,' Kebonye said, oddly turning the conversation. 'It is the best meal of the day. We get samp and meat and vegetables.'

So the day passed pleasantly enough with chatter and work and at sunset the women were once more taken back to the cell for lock-up time. They unrolled their blankets and prepared their beds, and with the candle lit continued to talk a while longer. Just as they were about to retire for the night, Dikeledi nodded to her new-found friend, Kebonye:

'Thank you for all your kindess to me,' she said, softly.

We must help each other,' Kebonye replied, with her amused, cynical smile. 'This is a terrible world. There is only misery here.'

And so the woman Dikeledi began phase three of a life that had been ashen in its loneliness and unhappiness. And yet she had always found gold amidst the ash, deep loves that had joined her heart to the hearts of others. She smiled tenderly at Kebonye because she knew already that she had found another such love. She was the collector of such treasures.

There were really only two kinds of men in the society. The one kind created such misery and chaos that he could be broadly damned as evil. If one watched the village dogs chasing a bitch on heat, they usually moved around in packs of four or five. As the mating progressed one dog would attempt to gain dominance over the festivities and oust all the others from the bitch's vulva. The rest of the hapless dogs would stand around yapping and snapping in its face while the top dog indulged in a continuous spurt of orgasms, day and night until he was exhausted. No doubt, during that Herculean feat, the dog imagined he was the only penis in the world and that there had to be a scramble for it. That kind of man lived near the animal level and behaved just the same. Like the dogs and bulls and donkeys, he also accepted no responsibility for the young he procreated and like the dogs and bulls and donkeys, he also made females abort. Since that kind of man was in the majority in the society, he needed a little analysing as he was responsible for the complete breakdown of family life. He could be analysed over three timespans. In the old days, before the colonial invasion of Africa, he was a man who lived by the traditions and taboos outlined for all the people by the forefathers of the tribe. He had little individual freedom to assess whether these traditions were compassionate or not—they demanded that he comply and obey the rules, without thought. But when the laws of the ancestors are examined, they appear on the whole to have been vast, external disciplines for the good of the society as a whole, with little attention given to individual preferences and needs. The ancestors made so many errors and one of the most bitter-making things was that they relegated to men a superior position in the tribe, while women were regarded, in a congenital sense, as being an inferior form of human life. To this day, women still suffered from all the calamities that befall an inferior form of human life. The colonial era and the period of migratory mining labour to South Africa was a further affliction visited on this man. It broke the hold of the ancestors. It broke the old, traditional form of family life and for long periods a man was separated from his wife and children while he worked for a pittance in another land in order to raise the money to pay his British Colonial poll-tax. British Colonialism scarcely enriched his life. He then became 'the boy' of the white man and a machine-tool of the South African mines. African independence seemed merely one more affliction on top of the afflictions that had visited this man's life. Independence suddenly and dramatically changed the pattern of colonial subservience. More jobs became available under the new government's localization programme and salaries sky-rocketed at the same time. It provided the first occasion for family life of a new order, above the childlike discipline of custom, the degradation of colonialism. Men and women, in order to survive, had to turn inwards to their own resources. It was the man who arrived at this turning point, a broken wreck with no inner resources at all. It was as though he was hideous to himself and in an effort to flee his own inner emptiness, he spun away from himself in a dizzy kind of death dance of wild destruction and dissipation.

One such man was Garesego Mokopi, the husband of Dikeledi. For four years prior to independence, he had worked as a clerk in the district admnistration service, at a steady salary of R50.00 a month. Soon after independence his salary shot up to R200.00 per month. Even during his lean days he had had a taste for womanising and drink; now he had the resources for a real spree. He was not seen at home again and lived and slept around the village, from woman to woman. He left his wife and three sons—Banabothe, the eldest, aged four; Inalame, aged three; and the youngest, Motsomi, aged one—to their own resources. Perhaps he did so because she was the boring, semi-literate traditional sort, and there were a lot of exciting new women around. Independence produced marvels indeed.

There was another kind of man in the society with the power to create himself anew. He turned all his resources, both emotional and material, towards his family life and he went on and on with his own quiet rhythm, like a river. He was a poem of tenderness.

One such man was Paul Thebolo and he and his wife, Kenalepe, and their three children, came to live in the village of Puleng in 1966, the year of independence. Paul Thebolo had been offered the principalship of a primary school in the village. They were allocated an empty field beside the yard of Dikeledi Mokopi, for their new home.

Neighbours are the centre of the universe to each other. They help each other at all times and mutually loan each other's goods. Dikeledi Mokopi kept an interested eye on the yard of her new neighbours. At first, only the man appeared with some workmen to erect the fence, which was set up with incredible speed and efficiency. The man impressed her immediately when she went around to introduce herself and find out a little about the newcomers. He was tall, large-boned, slow-moving. He was so peaceful as a person that the sunlight and shadow played all kinds of tricks with his eyes, making it difficult to determine their exact colour. When he stood still and looked reflective, the sunlight liked to creep into his eyes and nestle there; so sometimes his eyes were the colour of shade, and sometimes light brown.

He turned and smiled at her in a friendly way when she introduced herself and explained that he and his wife were on transfer from the village of Bobonong. His wife and children were living with relatives in the village until the yard was prepared. He was in a hurry to settle down as the school term would start in a month's time. They were, he said, going to erect two mud huts first and later he intended setting up a small house of bricks. His wife would be coming around in a few days with some women to erect the mud walls of the huts.

'I would like to offer my help too,' Dikeledi said. 'If work always starts early in the morning and there are about six of us, we can get both walls erected in a week. If you want one of the huts done in woman's thatch, all my friends know that I am the woman whose thatch does not leak.'

The man smilingly replied that he would impart all this information to his wife, then he added charmingly that he thought she would like his wife when they met. His wife was a very friendly person; everyone liked her.

Dikeledi walked back to her own yard with a high heart. She had few callers. None of her relatives called for fear that since her husband had left her she would become dependent on them for many things. The people who called did business with her; they wanted her to make dresses for their children or knit jerseys for the winter time and at times when she had no orders at all, she made baskets which she sold. In these ways she supported herself and the three children but she was lonely for true friends.

All turned out as the husband had said—he had a lovely wife. She was fairly tall and thin with a bright, vivacious manner. She made no effort to conceal that normally, and every day, she was a very happy person. And all turned out as Dikeledi had said. The work-party of six women erected the mud walls of the huts in one week; two weeks later, the thatch was complete. The Thebolo family moved into their new abode and Dikeledi Mokopi moved into one of the most prosperous and happy periods of her life. Her life took a big, wide upward curve. Her relationship with the Thebolo family was more than the usual friendly exchange of neighbours. It was rich and creative.

It was not long before the two women had going one of those deep, affectionate, sharing-everything kind of friendships that only women know how to have. It seemed that Kenalepe wanted endless amounts of dresses made for herself and her three little girls. Since Dikeledi would not accept cash for these services—she protested about the many benefits she received from her good neighbours—Paul Thebolo arranged that she be paid in household goods for these services so that for some years Dikeledi was always assured of her basic household needs—the full bag of corn, sugar, tea, powdered milk, and cooking oil. Kenalepe was also the kind of woman who made the whole world spin around her; her attractive personality attracted a whole range of women to her yard and also a whole range of customers for her dressmaking friend, Dikeledi. Eventually, Dikeledi became swamped with work, was forced to buy a second sewing-machine and employ a helper. The two women did everything together—they were forever together at weddings, funerals, and parties in the village. In their leisure hours they freely discussed all their intimate affairs with each other, so that each knew thoroughly the details of the other's life.

'You are a lucky someone,' Dikeledi remarked one day, wistfully. 'Not everyone has the gift of a husband like Paul.'

'Oh yes,' Kenalepe said happily. 'He is an honest somebody.' She knew a little of Dikeledi's list of woes and queried: 'But why did you marry a man like Garesego? I looked carefully at him when you pointed him out to me near the shops the other day and I could see at one glance that he is a butterfly.'

'I think I mostly wanted to get out of my uncle's yard,' Dikeledi replied. 'I never liked my uncle. Rich as he was, he was a hard man and very selfish. I was only a servant there and pushed about. I went there when I was six years old when my mother died, and it was not a happy life. All his children despised me because I was their servant. Uncle paid for my education for six years, then he said I must leave school. I longed for more because as you know, education opens up the world for one. Garesego was a friend of my uncle and he was the only man who proposed for me. They discussed it between themselves and then my uncle said: "You'd better marry Garesego because you're just hanging around here like a chain on my neck." I agreed, just to get away from that terrible man. Garesego said at that time that he'd rather be married to my sort than the educated kind because those women were stubborn and wanted to lay down the rules for men. Really, I did not ever protest when he started running about. You know what the other women do. They chase after the man from one hut to another and beat up the girlfriends. The man just runs into another hut, that's all. So you don't really win. I wasn't going to do anything like that. I am satisfied I have children. They are a blessing to me.'

'Oh, it isn't enough,' her friend said, shaking her head in deep sympathy. 'I am amazed at how life imparts its gifts. Some people get too much. Others get nothing at all. I have always been lucky in life. One day my parents will visit—they live in the south—and you'll see the fuss they make over me. Paul is just the same. He takes care of everything so that I never have a day of worry . . .'

The man Paul, attracted as wide a range of male friends as his wife. They had guests every evening; illiterate men who wanted him to fill tax forms or write letters for them, or his own colleagues who wanted to debate the political issues of the day—there was always something new happening every day now that the country had independence. The two women sat on the edge of these debates and listened with fascinated ears, but they never participated. The following day they would chew over the debates with wise, earnest expressions.

'Men's minds travel widely and boldly,' Kenalepe would comment. 'It makes me shiver the way they freely criticise our new government. Did you hear what Petros said last night? He said he knew all those bastards and they were just a lot of crooks who would pull a lot of dirty tricks. Oh dear! I shivered so much when he said that. The way they talk about the government makes you feel in your bones that this is not a safe world to be in, not like the old days when we didn't have governments. And Lentswe said that ten per cent of the population in England really control all the wealth of the country, while the rest live at starvation level. And he said communism would sort all this out. I gathered from the way they discussed this matter that our government is not in favour of communism. I trembled so much when this became clear to me…' She paused and laughed proudly. 'I've heard Paul say this several times: "The British only ruled us for eighty years." I wonder why Paul is so fond of saying that?'

And so a completely new world opened up for Dikeledi. It was so impossibly rich and happy that, as the days went by, she immersed herself more deeply in it and quite overlooked the barrenness of her own life. But it hung there like a nagging ache in the mind of her friend, Kenalepe.

'You ought to find another man,' she urged one day, when they had one of their personal discussions. 'It's not good for a woman to live alone.'

'And who would that be?' Dikeledi asked, disillusioned. 'I'd only be bringing trouble into my life whereas now it is all in order. I have my eldest son at school and I can manage to pay the school fees. That's all I really care about.'

'I mean,' said Kenalepe, 'we are also here to make love and enjoy it.'

'Oh, I never really cared for it,' the other replied. 'When you experience the worst of it, it just puts you off altogether.'

'What do you mean by that?' Kenalepe asked, wide-eyed.

'I mean it was just jump on and jump off and I used to wonder what it was all about. I developed a dislike for it.'

'You mean Garesego was like that!' Kenalepe said, flabbergasted. 'Why, that's just like a cock hopping from hen to hen. I wonder what he is doing with all those women. I'm sure they are just after his money and so they flatter him…' She paused and then added earnestly: 'That's really all the more reason you should find another man. Oh, if you knew what it was really like, you would long for it, I can tell you! I sometimes think I enjoy that side of life far too much. Paul knows a lot about all that. And he always has some new trick with which to surprise me. He has a certain way of smiling when he has thought up something new and I shiver a little and say to myself: "Ha, what is Paul going to do tonight!"'

Kenalepe paused and smiled at her friend, slyly.

'I can loan Paul to you if you like,' she said, then raised one hand to block the protest on her friend's face. 'I would do it because I have never had a friend like you in my life before whom I trust so much. Paul had other girls you know, before he married me, so it's not such an uncommon thing to him. Besides, we used to make love long before we got married and I never got pregnant. He takes care of that side too. I wouldn't mind loaning him because I am expecting another child and I don't feel so well these days…'

Dikeledi stared at the ground for a long moment, then she looked up at her friend with tears in her eyes.

'I cannot accept such a gift from you,' she said, deeply moved. 'But if you are ill I will wash for you and cook for you.'

Not put off by her friend's refusal of her generous offer, Kenalepe mentioned the discussion to her husband that very night. He was so taken off-guard by the unexpectedness of the subject that at first he looked slightly astonished, and burst out into loud laughter and for such a lengthy time that he seemed unable to stop.

'Why are you laughing like that?' Kenalepe asked, surprised.

He laughed a bit more, then suddenly turned very serious and thoughtful and was lost in his own thoughts for some time. When she asked him what he was thinking he merely replied: 'I don't want to tell you everything. I want to keep some of my secrets to myself.'

The next day Kenalepe reported this to her friend.

'Now whatever does he mean by that? I want to keep some of my secrets to myself?'

'I think,' Dikeledi said smiling, 'I think he has a conceit about being a good man. Also, when someone loves someone too much, it hurts them to say so. They'd rather keep silent.'

Shortly after this Kenalepe had a miscarriage and had to be admitted to hospital for a minor operation. Dikeledi kept her promise 'to wash and cook' for her friend. She ran both their homes, fed the children and kept everything in order. Also, people complained about the poorness of the hospital diet and each day she scoured the village for eggs and chicken, cooked them, and took them to Kenalepe every day at the lunch-hour.

One evening Dikeledi ran into a snag with her routine. She had just dished up supper for the Thebolo children when a customer came around with an urgent request for an alteration on a wedding dress. The wedding was to take place the next day. She left the children seated around the fire eating and returned to her own home. An hour later, her own children asleep and settled, she thought she would check the Thebolo yard to see if all was well there. She entered the children's hut and noted that they had put themselves to bed and were fast asleep. Their supper plates lay scattered and unwashed around the fire. The hut which Paul and Kenalepe shared was in darkness. It meant that Paul had not yet returned from his usual evening visit to his wife. Dikeledi collected the plates and washed them, then poured the dirty dishwater on the still-glowing embers of the outdoor fire. She piled the plates one on top of the other and carried them to the third additional hut which was used as a kitchen. Just then Paul Thebolo entered the yard, noted the lamp and movement in the kitchen hut and walked over to it. He paused at the open door.

'What are you doing now, Mma-Banabothe?' he asked, addressing her affectionately in the customary way by the name of her eldest son, Banabothe.

'I know quite well what I am doing,' Dikeledi replied happily. She turned around to say that it was not a good thing to leave dirty dishes standing overnight but her mouth flew open with surprise. Two soft pools of cool liquid light were in his eyes and something infinitely sweet passed between them; it was too beautiful to be love.

'You are a very good woman, Mma-Banabothe,' he said softly.

It was the truth and the gift was offered like a nugget of gold. Only men like Paul Thebolo could offer such gifts. She took it and stored another treasure in her heart. She bowed her knee in the traditional curtsey and walked quietly away to her own home.

Eight years passed for Dikeledi in a quiet rhythm of work and friendship with the Thebolo's. The crisis came with the eldest son, Banabothe. He had to take his primary school leaving examination at the end of the year. This serious event sobered him up considerably as like all boys he was very fond of playtime. He brought his books home and told his mother that he would like to study in the evenings. He would like to pass with a 'Grade A' to please her. With a flushed and proud face Dikeledi mentioned this to her friend, Kenalepe.

'Banabothe is studying every night now,' she said. 'He never really cared for studies. I am so pleased about this that I bought him a spare lamp and removed him from the children's hut to my own hut where things will be peaceful for him. We both sit up late at night now. I sew on buttons and fix hems and he does his studies . . .'

She also opened a savings account at the post office in order to have some standby money to pay the fees for his secondary education. They were rather high—R85.00. But in spite of all her hoarding of odd cents, towards the end of the year, she was short on R20.00 to cover the fees. Midway during the Christmas school holidays the results were announced. Banabothe passed with a 'Grade A.' His mother was almost hysterical in her joy at his achievement. But what to do? The two youngest sons had already started primary school and she would never manage to cover all their fees from her resources. She decided to remind Garesego Mokopi that he was the father of the children. She had not seen him in eight years except as a passer-by in the village. Sometimes he waved but he had never talked to her or enquired about her life or that of the children. It did not matter. She was a lower form of human life. Then this unpleasant something turned up at his office one day, just as he was about to leave for lunch. She had heard from village gossip, that he had eventually settled down with a married woman who had a brood of children of her own. He had ousted her husband, in a typical village sensation of brawls, curses, and abuse. Most probably the husband did not care because there were always arms outstretched towards a man, as long as he looked like a man. The attraction of this particular woman for Garesego Mokopi, so her former lovers said with a snicker, was that she went in for heady forms of love-making like biting and scratching.

Garesego Mokopi walked out of his office and looked irritably at the ghost from his past, his wife. She obviously wanted to talk to him and he walked towards her, looking at his watch all the while. Like all the new 'success men,' he had developed a paunch, his eyes were blood-shot, his face was bloated, and the odour of the beer and sex from the previous night clung faintly around him. He indicated with his eyes that they should move around to the back of the office block where they could talk in privacy.

'You must hurry with whatever you want to say,' he said impatiently. 'The lunch-hour is very short and I have to be back at the office by two.'

Not to him could she talk of the pride she felt in Banabothe's achievement, so she said simply and quietly: 'Garesego, I beg you to help me pay Banabothe's fees for secondary school. He has passed with a "Grade A" and as you know, the school fees must be produced on the first day of school or else he will be turned away. I have struggled to save money the whole year but I am short by R20.00.'

She handed him her post office savings book, which he took, glanced at 90
and handed back to her. Then he smiled, a smirky know-all smile, and thought he was delivering her a blow in the face.

'Why don't you ask Paul Thebolo for the money?' he said. 'Everyone knows he's keeping two homes and that you are his spare. Everyone knows about that full bag of corn he delivers to your home every six months so why can't he pay the school fees as well?'

She neither denied this, nor confirmed it. The blow glanced off her face which she raised slightly, in pride. Then she walked away.

As was their habit, the two women got together that afternoon and Dikeledi reported this conversation with her husband to Kenalepe who tossed back her head in anger and said fiercely: 'The filthy pig himself! He thinks every man is like him, does he? I shall report this matter to Paul, then he'll see something.'

And indeed Garesego did see something but it was just up his alley. He was a female prostitute in his innermost being and like all professional prostitutes, he enjoyed publicity and sensation—it promoted his cause. He smiled genially and expansively when a madly angry Paul Thebolo came up to the door of his house where he lived with *his* concubine. Garesego had been through a lot of these dramas over those eight years and he almost knew by rote the dialogue that would follow.

'You bastard!' Paul Thebolo spat out. 'Your wife isn't my concubine, do 95
you hear?'

'Then why are you keeping her in food?' Garesego drawled. 'Men only do that for women they fuck! They never do it for nothing.'

Paul Thebolo rested one hand against the wall, half dizzy with anger, and he said tensely: 'You defile life, Garesego Mokopi. There's nothing else in your world but defilement. Mma-Banabothe makes clothes for my wife and children and she will never accept money from me so how else must I pay her?'

'It only proves the story both ways,' the other replied, vilely. 'Women do that for men who fuck them.'

Paul Thebolo shot out the other hand, punched him soundly in one grinning eye and walked away. Who could hide a livid, swollen eye? To every surprised enquiry, he replied with an injured air:

'It was done by my wife's lover, Paul Thebolo.'

It certainly brought the attention of the whole village upon him, which was 100
all he really wanted. Those kinds of men were the bottom rung of government.

They secretly hungered to be the President with all eyes on them. He worked up the sensation a little further. He announced that he would pay the school fees of the child of his concubine, who was also to enter secondary school, but not the school fees of his own child, Banabothe. People half liked the smear on Paul Thebolo; he was too good to be true. They delighted in making him a part of the general dirt of the village, so they turned on Garesego and scolded: 'Your wife might be getting things from Paul Thebolo but it's beyond the purse of any man to pay the school fees of his own children as well as the school fees of another man's children. Banabothe wouldn't be there had you not procreated him, Garesego, so it is your duty to care for him. Besides, it's your fault if your wife takes another man. You left her alone all these years.'

So that story was lived with for two weeks, mostly because people wanted to say that Paul Thebolo was a part of life too and as uncertain of his morals as they were. But the story took such a dramatic turn that it made all the men shudder with horror. It was some weeks before they could find the courage to go to bed with women; they preferred to do something else.

Garesego's obscene thought processes were his own undoing. He really believed that another man had a stake in his hen-pen and like any cock, his hair was up about it. He thought he'd walk in and re-establish his own claim to it and so, after two weeks, once the swelling in his eye had died down, he espied Banabothe in the village and asked him to take a note to his mother. He said the child should bring a reply. The note read: 'Dear Mother, I am coming home again so that we may settle our differences. Will you prepare a meal for me and some hot water that I might take a bath. Gare.'

Dikeledi took the note, read it and shook with rage. All its overtones were clear to her. He was coming home for some sex. They had had no differences. They had not even talked to each other.

'Banabothe,' she said 'Will you play nearby? I want to think a bit then I will send you to your father with the reply.'

Her thought processes were not very clear to her. There was something she could not immediately touch upon. Her life had become holy to her during all those years she had struggled to maintain herself and the children. She had filled her life with treasures of kindness and love she had gathered from others and it was all this that she wanted to protect from defilement by an evil man. Her first panic-stricken thought was to gather up the children and flee the village. But where to go? Garesego did not want a divorce, she had left him to approach her about the matter, she had desisted from taking any other man. She turned her thoughts this way and that and could find no way out except to face him. If she wrote back, don't you dare put foot in the yard I don't want to see you, he would ignore it. Black women didn't have that kind of power. A thoughtful, brooding look came over her face. At last, at peace with herself, she went into her hut and wrote a reply: 'Sir, I shall prepare everything as you have said. Dikeledi.'

It was about midday when Banabothe sped back with the reply to his father. All afternoon Dikeledi busied herself making preparations for the appearance of her husband at sunset. At one point Kenalepe approached the yard and looked around in amazement at the massive preparations, the large iron pot full of water with a fire burning under it, the extra cooking pots on the fire. Only later Kenalepe brought the knife into focus. But it was only a vague blur, a large kitchen knife used to cut meat and Dikeledi knelt at a grinding-stone and sharpened it slowly and methodically. What was in focus then was the final and tragic expression on the upturned face of her friend. It threw her into confusion and blocked their usual free and easy feminine chatter. When Dikeledi said: 'I am making some preparations for Garesego. He is coming home tonight,' Kenalepe beat a hasty retreat to her own home terrified. They knew they were involved because when she mentioned this to Paul he was distracted and uneasy for the rest of the day. He kept on doing upside-down sorts of things, not replying to questions, absent-mindedly leaving a cup of tea until it got quite cold, and every now and again he stood up and paced about, lost in his own thoughts. So deep was their sense of disturbance that towards evening they no longer made a pretence of talking. They just sat in silence in their hut. Then, at about nine o'clock, they heard those wild and agonized bellows. They both rushed out together to the yard of Dikeledi Mokopi.

He came home at sunset and found everything ready for him as he had requested, and he settled himself down to enjoy a man's life. He had brought a pack of beer along and sat outdoors slowly savouring it while every now and then his eye swept over the Thebolo yard. Only the woman and children moved about the yard. The man was out of sight. Garesego smiled to himself, pleased that he could crow as loud as he liked with no answering challenge.

A basin of warm water was placed before him to wash his hands and then Dikeledi served him his meal. At a separate distance she also served the children and then instructed them to wash and prepare for bed. She noted that Garesego displayed no interest in the children whatsoever. He was entirely wrapped up in himself and thought only of himself and his own comfort. Any tenderness he offered the children might have broken her and swerved her mind away from the deed she had carefully planned all that afternoon. She was beneath his regard and notice too for when she eventually brought her own plate of food and sat near him, he never once glanced at her face. He drank his beer and cast his glance every now and again at the Thebolo yard. Not once did the man of the yard appear until it became too dark to distinguish anything any more. He was completely satisfied with that. He could repeat the performance every day until he broke the mettle of the other cock again and forced him into angry abuse. He liked that sort of thing.

'Garesego, do you think you could help me with Banabothe's school fees?' Dikeledi asked at one point.

'Oh, I'll think about it,' he replied casually.

She stood up and carried buckets of water into the hut, which she poured into a large tin bath that he might bathe himself, then while he took his bath she busied herself tidying up and completing the last of the household chores.

Those done, she entered the children's hut. They played hard during the day and they had already fallen asleep with exhaustion. She knelt down near their sleeping mats and stared at them for a long while, with an extremely tender expression. Then she blew out their lamp and walked to her own hut. Garesego lay sprawled across the bed in such a manner that indicated he only thought of himself and did not intend sharing the bed with anyone else. Satiated with food and drink, he had fallen into a deep, heavy sleep the moment his head touched the pillow. His concubine had no doubt taught him that the correct way for a man to go to bed, was naked. So he lay, unguarded and defenceless, sprawled across the bed on his back.

The bath made a loud clatter as Dikeledi removed it from the room, but still he slept on, lost to the world. She re-entered the hut and closed the door. Then she bent down and reached for the knife under the bed which she had merely concealed with a cloth. With the precision and skill of her hard-working hands, she grasped hold of his genitals and cut them off with one stroke. In doing so, she slit the main artery which ran on the inside of the groin. A massive spurt of blood arched its way across the bed. And Garesego bellowed. He bellowed his anguish. Then all was silent. She stood and watched his death anguish with an intent and brooding look, missing not one detail of it. A knock on the door stirred her out of her reverie. It was the boy, Banabothe. She opened the door and stared at him, speechless. He was trembling violently.

'Mother,' he said, in a terrified whisper. 'Didn't I hear father cry?'

'I have killed him,' she said, waving her hand in the air with a gesture that said—well, that's that. Then she added sharply: 'Banabothe, go and call the police.'

He turned and fled into the night. A second pair of footsteps followed hard on his heels. It was Kenalepe running back to her own yard, half out of her mind with fear. Out of the dark Paul Thebolo stepped towards the hut and entered it. He took in every detail and then he turned and looked at Dikeledi with such a tortured expression that for a time words failed him. At last he said: 'You don't have to worry about the children, Mma-Banabothe. I'll take them as my own and give them all a secondary school education.'

CHARTING THE STORY

1. Specifically, what charges were brought against Dikeledi in court, and what might account for the relative severity (or leniency) of the sentence?
2. What characteristics do you observe among the members of the "sisterhood" in the prison to which Dikeledi has been assigned?
3. The story chronicles an eight-year friendship between Dikleledi and her neighbors the Thebolos. What factors caused this friendship to solidify and to bless the lives of the two families?

CONSIDERATIONS OF STYLE

1. What is the translation of Dikeledi's given name? Why was she so named? How does the name acquire symbolic value in the story?
2. The story begins with Dikeledi's admission into prison and then flashes back to her married life, and to the subsequent development of her relationship with the Thebolos. How would the story change if it had been told in strictly chronological order? Why does Bessie Head begin *in medias res*?
3. How does the manner in which Dikeledi murders her husband inform the story symbolically?
4. How are men and women characterized in the story; and why does the author discuss the precolonial, colonial, and postcolonial eras in connection with gender relations?

AFTERTHOUGHTS

1. In a major way, "The Collector of Treasures" is a treatise on the African man. Do you consider it entirely/essentially fair? Justify your response. Do you think the story could have been narrated just as effectively by a man?
2. Dikeledi is characterized as a "collector of treasures." Discuss this characterization and how it affects the mood of the story. In what other texts have you found characters taking what would commonly be considered an adverse situation and turning it into a field of grace?
3. Contrast this text with any other text that involves prison life (you might consider Aleksandr Solzhenitsyn's novel *One Day in the Life of Ivan Denisovich,* the films *Dead Man Walking, The Birdman of Alcatraz,* the end of George Orwell's *1984,* or some other text). How does this text differ, and why?

THE WRITER'S CRAFT

1. Write an essay comparing men's expectations of women and, conversely, women's expectations of men in intimate relationships.
2. Write a short critical paper on the social, cultural, and psychological dimensions of marital infidelity in "The Collector of Treasures."
3. If Dikeledi were to dictate or write a letter to the Thebolos, what would she write? If she were to make them a present, what would she make (please illustrate it, and write a few paragraphs explaining your choice of item, design, and other artistic details).
4. Defend or question the concept of "justifiable homicide" in a short essay, using this text (and/or others) to augment your argument.

VISHWAPRIYA IYENGAR

Born in 1958, Indian author VISHWAPRIYA IYENGAR *has written extensively as a journalist and as a drama critic as well as in fiction, poetry, plays, and children's literature. She has published frequently in most national daily newspapers in India, and in many journals and magazines, writing of issues of social and political concern, such as that of child labor.*

"Midnight Soldiers" was first published in Truth Tales: Contemporary Stories by Women Writers of India *in 1990. Of a piece with her journalistic work, it addresses the life of a fisherwoman who must, against impossible odds, strive to hold her crumbling family together.*

PERSPECTIVES

1 Western families, particularly in the United States, have addressed today's phenomenon, in industrialized countries, of the "second shift," where wives put in what amounts to an additional "work day" at home in housework after they return from their jobs. In a subsistence economy, where the husband is often unable to find work at all (and generally, like many of his affluent Western brothers, will not do household chores), what would the life of such a man's wife be like?

2 In most families, who tends to get the best of everything, especially in a condition of scarcity? For what reasons?

Midnight Soldiers

I had an ocean. What made of? Good lord—just an ocean! I had a son. I had a giant…

—Frederico Garcia Lorca

Seagulls flew in straight lines. The sky was a hot pale silver light. Blue-green waves smashed against the deserted shore lining the sand with fine slivers of broken shells. In the distance black blobs were curving boat-like on the waves.

The thatched walls of her hut were slipping away at an angle as though they no longer remembered why they had been there. Tony slept sunk in warm noon sands. Matilda watched the sleeping man from the corner of her eye as she unlocked a small black tin box. She opened a cloth pouch and counted some notes.

Tony's mouth was open, drooling, and a little vomit had dried on his chin. Even now, vapors of arrack hung thickly in the air. Matilda slid a tiny key behind the oblong picture of the Ailing Madonna. Angels in lacy white gowns swirled around her. They were telling Mary, Matilda thought, about the grand home in heaven.

Only a scrap of lungi covered his body. In one hand he clutched a crochet tack and his head had rolled over a bundled net. Yesterday, five hundred net-eyes had torn. He had to mend the net before the evening boats went out to sea. Yetta, their baby daughter, slept in the crook of her father's arm. Tony grunted and shifted. The baby, too, moved.

Matilda ran through the burning sands, her outstretched toes, her cal- 5
loused heels stamping flight. The boats were looking bigger moving towards the shore. Matilda watched, her eyes cutting the mist of distance, her palms already weighing the silver bellies of firm fish. Listening to the wind, she reined in her impatience and stood waiting, letting frothy waves wash her feet.

Sweat slipped down from her black-brown waist and clamped the red-black checks to her taut thighs. She dug her feet into the soggy earth and moved shells around with her toes. Salim, the auctioneer, was already at the shore. He folded up his lungi and lit a bidi. A mangy village dog flapped around him, licking his ankles, and more women clustered around. Bleached baskets yawned empty, and in the waiting eyes the homing boats sailed nearer. Salim threw fish bones like arrows. The drowsy dog ran and collapsed on every bone, then turned around and bared his teeth at Salim, wagging a matted tail. He was hoping that Salim would throw him some little fishes when the boats came.

The boats came in, each within a short time of the other. Matilda wandered, peering, waiting for her voice to scream numbers. To wrest in the giddy spiral of the noonday bidding. Salim stared at her with red dead-fish eyes and repeated the last bid, his smile a splinter taunting her reckless spirit. She turned away. More boats would come and then she would get fish cheap. Today she had only thirty rupees. For six months she had tried with an iron will not to borrow money from Salim. But Tony had already sunk them. Last year one whole log had to be replaced for the catamaran. It must have cost seven hundred rupees.

Tony could never repay his debts; in the end it always fell on Matilda. He did not even give her money for rice. He told her he was returning the money his father had borrowed from another moneylender, not Salim. The year of her marriage, his net had been destroyed by a trawler at sea and she had given him her gold bangle to buy another. Now they no longer spoke about their debts. His drunken brawls with moneylenders had become a daily storm that she had learned to live with.

Other fish vendors were walking, running away with baskets full of fish. With fish on their heads they forgot everything. They ran for miles, ten miles, sometimes more, to the market. Only these days fish was expensive, like everything else. It was with great restraint that she was able to put away money for the auction. Paul's medicines and magic brews for Yetta left her with very little money to invest in fish. Staring at the empty sea Matilda prayed fervently for a wonderful catch, for then the fish would be very cheap.

Sniveling and wheezing, Paul came toward her. He wrapped his long thin arms around her slender waist. Babbling warm words on her perspiring skin, he lisped that he was hungry and hesitantly asked for fifty paise. Matilda turned away from the vacant gray-green sea and tripped on her empty basket. A dark anger gripped her thoughts whenever she saw her elder son. His arms and legs were thin. His face and body swollen and bruised. The child kissed his mother's waist and left faint squiggles of green mucus, he pouted his lips and his round eyes shone in anticipation. Matilda slapped the water-bloated cheek. From the back row of huts women walked shorewards. Crows flew low and swift, heralding more boats. Salim turned to her with his red dead-fish eyes. She screamed, guttural and hysterical: "He is lying. He never buys food with the money I give him. He only buys sweets which flies eat. My son is not a fly." Salim was smoothening out the creases from the crumpled notes, the dog was licking the salt from his slippered feet and he kicked it aside, absently. She realized he had not been looking at her, nobody had; Paul was playing a game with tamarind seeds.

Paul was five years old. He had been sick a long time. Only two months ago the Sisters had told her that he had asthma and a disease in his kidneys which could not be cured. She had to wait for his death. The doctors in the big hospital in Trivandrum told her the same. Someone had said that big money, the kind that Matilda would never see in her life, might cure him. Money to buy organs from dying people. "Forget it," they said. "Try and understand, everybody has to die. Some young and some old. Heaven is, after all, a grand place with good food." Stubbornly, she refused to give in. The saints had to save her. Perhaps Tony would catch sharks—many, many sharks which would fetch a lot of money. Money to save Paul. Money to buy many, many kidneys. Carrying the grown child in her arms, she had walked for days to the other end of the coast to visit a famous shrine of the Madonna of Good Health. She prayed for three days, without stopping to eat or sleep. She would never give up hope. Only his wheezing, watery greed made her blind with anguish.

A catamaran was tossing over the banks. The tide was high and the men were pulling the boat with difficulty. They handed the basket over to Salim and Matilda ran towards him. Salim carried the basket, his eyes reflecting the diamond-grill scales of a blue-gray fish. Pulling on his bidi, a twig of ash fell on the midnight scales. Every fish was as large as a grown man's arm. Salim pressed a long fingernail into its flesh. Blood gushed out in red-hot squirts—it was very fresh. He dipped it in sea water and smeared it with sand. Matilda picked up another, she stroked the long fat creature with the palm of her hand, she moved her fingers along the stiff feathery fins. Its mouth was open and the cavity ribbed in circles of orange and red and the tough veins of old blood—black. Sometimes, on each of these big fish, she could make a profit of ten rupees, but today she could not even open the bidding.

Fathima was peering into the basket and her hands clasped a fish tightly. Matilda caught her throat and hissed: "You whore woman, leave my fish alone." Fathima slapped Matilda hard on her face, caught her hair and dragged her down. Matilda twisted Fathima's arm and the older woman shrieked in pain. Salim threw them apart. Panting, a countdown of hurried breathing, and the bidding began. She should not have said that. Salim provoked Fathima to begin the bidding at eighty. Ridiculous. She felt her throat dry and she was shouting numbers that were meaningless. "Ninety, 100, 130." Fathima stared at her, bitterness hammering the black point of her eyes into Matilda's guilt. Salim looked at her with his red dead-fish eyes. Matilda undid the damp knot and counted thirty old notes into his outstretched hand and told him she would give him the hundred tomorrow. The weight of the fish basket on her head was her equilibrium. She felt secure and real. Women with fish were not allowed to ride in buses, so she had to walk fifteen miles to the market.

The other vendors had already reached the ferry, she must hurry. Matilda walked quickly. As she passed the sweet shop she saw Paul, his eyes fixed like a spider on the glass jar, the pink and yellow egg-sweets ballooning into a frightening fantasy. She pressed a coin into his wafer-thin palm. His smile faded into the dusty horizon of his mother's preoccupation.

From the vacant paths that narrowly slit rows of thatched huts, she could 15
see the late noon boats breaking through the high tide and moving into the deep sea for the night fishing. Tony. Tony drunk. Tony sick and vituperative. Tony corroded with seawater. Tony with five hundred torn net-eyes. She turned back home.

The thatched walls were slipping on the sands; each time she had to bend lower to enter. The fumes of arrack were as thick as a whole distillery smashed to smithereens on one man's soul.

She held his smooth mahogany arms and shook him. Flies scattered from his sleeping face and studded the torn coconut matting like nails. His hands were thrown apart like Jesus's. She crossed her heart . . . asking forgiveness. God was no drunkard. She slapped him hard. Startled, his eyes opened like a child's into a nightmare. His lips and teeth meshed in a cobweb of stale saliva. "When will you mend your net? When will you go to sea? After all the fish have been taken by other men? After your children and woman have starved to death?"

Rubbing the stupor from his eyes, his lips warped a smile. She stared at him, enraged and humiliated. She watched him fumble, groan, twisting his perfect body into a thousand trivial distortions. When at last he was able to stand up they stared at each other with the sharp white electric flare of ritualized hatred.

The voices awoke the baby and she began to whimper. Tears moved in soft rivulets over tiny granules of gold sand that were embedded in her cheeks. She turned over on her belly and wriggled a pair of oval bottoms. She discharged a gray gruel clotted with dark blood. Matilda snatched the child away in distress and impatience wishing that there was some way of staying home, away from the market route.

Yetta had had loose motions for days. The mantravadi said a lizard was eating her stomach. She was too small for exorcism and so he had prescribed an herbal brew, but she had not grown any better. She had not taken Yetta to the doctor because she did not believe that those who had given up on Paul could save other human beings. She was also afraid of their predictions. They had told her to care more for Yetta because she would live. But she could not cut love like a fish and divide it between life and death. Matilda threw sand over the excreta and threw the congealed mass outside. She dropped the galvanized iron bucket into the cement well and yanked out the rope in rough jerky movements. Sharp metal rims scraped the mossy walls and she washed the baby in green water. Her basket of fish lay waiting on a stump. She was late for the market. Tony stood watching her and Paul sucked noisily. The egg-sweet made a lump in his bloated cheek and pink saliva dribbled from his mouth.

Covering the basket with bark, she saw that the blood had hardened where Salim had cut the fish with his nail. She began to run, wide, the tendons of her thighs stretching like blades. It was fortunate that she had not invested in sardine or mackerel of which there were quite a lot these days. There would still be a market for her big fish. She walked fast, faster. Matilda felt that dull glow of delight in an unexpected speculation. These days her spirit did not gamble. The fight with Fathima had sent the blood coursing to her brain. She had desperately wanted to sell the basket of big fish today. She was glad that Fathima had started the fight. She did not think Fathima was a whore or even that it was such a bad thing to be a whore. Fathima had helped so much at Paul's first communion. But she did not want her to take the fish today. She was glad that Fathima had helped to start the fight. Salim was a dog. A poisonous dog. She had felt violated when he had intervened. If she were not a Christian she would curse him, she still could, sometime . . . when God wasn't looking. If she had a good sale, she would buy a banana for Fathima's youngest daughter.

Tony dragged his net under the fan shadow of the solitary coconut palm and bent down to work. Between tacks he slurped arrack, throwing back his head to savor the rush of alcohol. A shield of sunlight metalled the child's bloated chest and he sucked, wheezed, sucked and wheezed. "*Aya* Paul, come here and sit next to me. You don't respect me because I drink, huh? You know why I drink, huh? I drink because there is no fish in the sea. See those trawler boats? They take away all the fish and kill the eggs. Because there is no fish for the fishermen those fellows are making arrack instead of fishing. Because they are making arrack instead of fishing, I am drinking instead of fishing. Ha, reason is smart, no?" He slapped the boy's back. "Tell your mother. She will slice your tongue into ribbons." Paul smiles. "You know why we paint our chickens pink? So that vultures don't recognize them. Poor little Paul, you are stupid. Your poor mother, she wanted you to go to school and study to become a bus driver, not some stupid fisherman. I don't care. Kaddallamma is our mother, for her any son of mine is good enough. Go to sea. The sea always has a place for us and our children."

Matilda rubbed the aching tissues of her insteps on the chips of granite that floored the black tar road. She loved to hear the big rumble that buses made and even the delicate squeal of the occasional car. They made the roads a little dirty, splashing water and dust around. Still, they were nice. Nobody moved when those came, they always stood in corners, leaning against walls, watching the huge round wheels turning. A blue bus went past and Matilda watched with a flickering pause of pleasure. Some seven months ago, when Yetta was only two months old, a social worker had come visiting the village. She was fair and pretty. She had worn a white starched sari with a thread border of mango leaves in black. She had worn black and white bangles. Tony had gone fishing when the lady visited her. Matilda was glad that Tony was away. The lady might have got upset if Tony was drunk. Yes, she was glad he was not at home. The lady spoke very softly and clearly and told her intelligent things. She told Matilda that they were all human beings who must live well and be healthy, earn cleverly, spend reasonably and save carefully. Husband and wife should not fight, they should love each other, and Matilda had agreed heartily. The lady had told her that they should have few children, two children, so that they could spend time and attention on making them as wonderful as human beings should be. The lady showed her photographs of families with only two children. They had chairs made of velvet altar cloth and big pictures of crystal bowls filled with grapes, bananas and pineapples. The girl child's long black hair was caught in blue satin ribbons and she was leaning out of a sunny window looking out at a flower and a bird. The boy's small head was heaped with thick black curls and he was wearing a watch on his smooth broad wrist. He was spinning a top. The photograph had caught the spin in a blur. The mother and father were sitting together on the beautiful chairs drinking tea together, in cups and saucers. "They don't fight," the lady told her. "They love each other." The lady's pictures aroused something reverential in Matilda's thin lactating breasts. She went to the big hospital in Trivandrum to have the operation. It wasn't an operation, it was a prayer, a dream of satin ribbons, and of drinking tea together.

She told Tony about it only after she returned from Trivandrum. His eyes contorted with pain, he spluttered for words—spraying her face with angry spittle—a mouth deformed in trying to scream wordless thoughts—about dying wombs and the barren sea mother, Kaddallamma. She could not fathom his fury. Was it rage at some unknown hands turning the secrets of his woman's womb? she asked. He stumbled upon her like a wild animal and beat her with wide palms, a possessed man keeping up the rhythm of his demon. When Matilda had been reduced to the fluid emanations of her anguish he embraced her tightly and fell asleep crying and blabbering, the heavy bones of his chin axing into her chest. The nightmare was never spoken of again.

Lush ferns unfurled in thickets along the river. Matilda stood, cooling her feet, waiting for the ferry. The hot sun draped the lean planes of her shoulder. The slap of water on spade-spooned oars grew louder and she leapt onto the boat. Matilda embraced the big curving basket and hummed a church song.

She paid the boatman and ran, counting the fish in her basket, her excited brain cutting the fish into sharp fractions. She calculated the many permutations and combinations which would determine the price of the day's fish. She prayed that the tiny trawler boat fish from Quilon or the junk fish from purse seiners in Cochin would not flood the markets today. Last Monday she had to bring back a whole basket of unsold mackerel. The baby fish from trawlers were going so cheap that she had been unable to sell her fresh, fully grown fish. The iced fish strangled her prices. Until now she had been able to keep Salim at a distance. Salim had a gang of boys who collected debts at any cost. If she was not able to return that hundred tomorrow. . . . Her stomach contracted.

When Matilda reached the market, it was already in full swing—anticipation of Easter made transactions brisk. Playful, loud sounds curled the air. Matilda saw her treasured customer walk away in the soft pluth-pluth of rubber slippers. Today she wore a voile sari and fresh flowers. She had purchased pomfret, but had Matilda been there she would certainly have bought some big fish. Her crate stall was at its usual place—flung sideways on the garbage heap. Inside was a litter of light white kittens. Matilda lifted them out and placed them gently in a broken pitcher that lay atop the heap. She upturned her crate and placed it in the semicircle of the fish market. The women from her village had already sold three-fourths of their fish. She cursed Tony and Yetta. Two other women were selling the big fish but they only had a few pieces left. She smiled as she washed her crate. The absence of the little pools of melting ice pleased her immensely. With a long iron scythe she slashed the fish into chunks and measured them in her palm. The ache in her shoulder blades eased, the ligaments of her thigh slowly throbbed still. She joined the fray, throwing her voice in a few stray notes, and her eyes watched the slow walk of hesitant customers. She jumped onto the unaware customer with the agility of a leopard. She smiled, flashing perfect orange stained teeth, and pressed her fish upwards to sweet smelling palms. The knot of crisp rupees and new coins grew bigger. She began shouting and selling like a gypsy begins to dance.

The hunchbacked beggar came shuffling and Matilda threw a meaty piece affixed to the still glistening eye into the rattling tin. Night spread around the market square and the vendors walked away slowly. Matilda stretched her arms and arched her spine backwards. She yawned. Scarlet stains patterned her crate and one big fish lay waiting for the nocturnal customer. She peeled tapioca roots and sliced white rims into her basket. Street lights paled against the smoky darkness. Further away, in the main streets, windows lit up sibilant cloaks of intimacy. It was the hour of her loneliness. Wearily clutching the edge of her crate, Matilda lifted herself up and tossed the last fish into the basket. She smoothened the ripples of her lungi and rubbed her sweat with the frayed fabric. Her hands moved massagingly over tired thighs and she pressed the tense roundness of her hips. These days, she looked at her face in the broken jagged bit of mirror and saw age, ghost-like, beginning to weave its thumbprint in fungus silk on her skin. She placed her crate on top of the garbage heap. She gazed at the sealed velvet eyes. One pale gray kitten hung its head out of the broken crack of the earthen pitcher. Gently, Matilda lifted its infant head back into the snug circle of sleeping kittens and sighed.

She walked away from the deserted market square that was marked only by broken crates and rotting vegetables. By dawn, the lepers would have cleared even that. She walked riverwards down a long road to the ferry. Starlight splashed on the coconut palms. The lower branches of yellowed leaves crackled in the breeze and shone more silvery. If she could only cut it now it would be enough to thatch her home. The palms moved their long leaves tantalizingly in the black water. She must thatch her house soon, before the monsoons set in. She would have to pay for the leaves, pay the boy for climbing and pay for the matting. It would cost her five hundred rupees at least. Salim? No. She must not ever borrow. By the time Paul grew up, the tree in her yard would have grown tall. He would climb the tree, cut the leaves and weave thatch mats. She would teach him. Church bells echoed a dull bronze clang over the water. Paul would light the evening lamp. He would kneel before Christ and make the sign of the cross. He would say, "Our Father in Heaven . . ." He would pray for his father at sea and his mother in the market. She stepped out of the ferry thinking, believing, that God delighted in the prayers of children.

She walked slowly, almost at a leisurely pace. There was rice and perhaps she would take a small cut from the big fish and make a curry. She would dry the rest to sell another day. It had been years since the family had tasted the big fish. The sea sounded very rough, there was a strong gusty breeze and Matilda walked with the breeze bouncing her petticoat. The long road was like a tree trunk which branched into lanes that held many homes like fruit. In the darkness the most pleasing sight was the lamplight glowing through them. She turned into a side lane, walking faster, her strides growing longer, heart beating louder. . . . A withering pain wrung the empty space of her heart as her hut stood dark and silent. Church bells clanged in her skull and her mouth tasted tarnished metal. She hurled herself into the hut . . . a cry of dull remorse uncoiling from her belly. "Paul, you Satan's child, where are you? A thousand curses on your demented brain. What do you want? That your father should drown at sea and I writhe under Salim's knife and you die, eh? Do you care, child? Do you care? Then why have you left your home blind at the hour when God looks at us?" The hut was dense with the child's wheezing and he hid along the scalloped shadows. Her fingers shook as she lit the small kerosene lamp. The long paw of waxy light spread slow and quivering over a sleeping baby. Brown, pale and delicate, the child slept very peacefully in a cradle of sand, in the center of the hut. The flame flickered and climbed a wooden cross. Bloodless ivory feet crossed, a black nail running through.

Poor little Yetta, how tired she must have been to sleep such sleep. In her small hands she clutched a yellow egg-sweet. Matilda smiled at her elder son whose face was fraught with anxiety. Taking the small key from behind the picture of the Ailing Madonna she unlocked the black tin box and put the money in. His wheezing disturbed the flame. They had told her he would die soon. They had told her to care more for Yetta because she would live. She could not. She could not believe in the certitude of doctors. The saints were older than the doctors. She stroked the smooth brow of the sleeping child. It was cool, cold, the fever had left her at last.

Matilda picked up the big fish and went outside to cut a slice. She placed it on the flat granite stone and picked up her knife. Even now it etched shadowly silver squares. She pressed the knife a line away from the eye, a cool breeze wafted through the doorway . . . cold, and she crept stealthily back into the hut, sweating with ominous fear. Paul sucked and wheezed. She placed her hands over the boy's mouth and nose and bent her ears over the sleeping girl child. She listened long and hard for a sound that did not escape the stillness. She picked up the child and pressed it deep into her breast. Tiny thin arms fell softly out of the mother's embrace.

Her scream cut the silence like a sword. Women came running out of a hundred lamplit huts. They rushed towards Matilda, despair touching despair. Fathima held her.

They caught the fading embers of her cry and blew into it—a hundred pain-wrought screams. Without pattern or design they filed into rows of two in a line that grew longer as more women came rushing out of the night's immense branches. Matilda stood at the head. In one gnarled hand she held a fish, in the other, a dead child.

The women wept. The sea smashed against the shore in turgid waves. Somewhere in the depth of the ocean Kaddallamma thrashed around her rocky bed emitting a hollow roar that resounded in the women's cries. Paul wheezed, coughed, wheezed again. The sounds mixed.

The long line of midnight soldiers stood transfixed. Where would they burn this fire that always burnt them?

CHARTING THE STORY

1 Following the course of "Midnight Soldiers," what is the process by which a fish goes from the sea to market? Who is involved at each step of the way, and who has the power in each exchange?

2 Why does Matilda ignore the warnings of the Sisters and the doctors that Paul would not live long, as well as the advice of the doctors to "care more for Yetta because she would live"?
3 What is the relevance of the epigraphic quotation by Garcia Lorca to the story?

CONSIDERATIONS OF STYLE

1 What is suggested by the personifications of the walls of Matilda's hut "slipping away at an angle as though they no longer remembered" (Paragraph 2) and the "[b]leached baskets [that] yawned empty" (Paragraph 6)?
2 How is Tony characterized? With whom is he most strongly connected by similarities of image (appearance, actions, etc.)?
3 How does the eponymous metaphor "midnight soldiers" fit the women who fill the story's dramatic last scene?

AFTERTHOUGHTS

1 What is the role of the auctioneer Salim in the economic system which prevails in the story? Why does the repeated description of his "red dead-fish eyes" seem to fit him?
2 How effective are Matilda's prayers and supplications made to be, and how do they relate to the advice that the nuns give her? To which holy figures does she go for help, and what does this suggest about her?

THE WRITER'S CRAFT

1 Write an essay comparing the strategies of family planning in developed and developing countries. For the latter, use evidence from this story.
2 From the point of view of the social worker, write up your own evaluation of Matilda's coping strategies (you may, or may not, decide to characterize the social worker with the ability to see beyond appearances).

ANITA DESAI

The daughter of a Bengali father and a German mother, ANITA DESAI *was born in 1937 in India, grew up in Delhi and went to school there. Growing up, Desai was at home in three languages: German, from her mother; Hindi, the language in Delhi; and English, her language of instruction at the British mission school she attended. By that accident of her education, English became her literary language, the one in which she learned English literature and other literatures in translation, and that in which she wrote.*

Desai has written many short stories and novels, many of which feature at least initially tranquil-seeming domestic venues, behind which swirl powerful, often conflagratory emotions. She has taught at Columbia University, Mount Holyoke and Smith colleges; she currently teaches writing at MIT.

"The Farewell Party," wherein a going-away party for a reclusive couple inspires guests and hosts to most uncharacteristically open up to each other, was originally published in Desai's short story collection Games at Twilight *(1978).*

PERSPECTIVES

1 In your experience, what types of relationships or other connections does the transitory nature of life in a "temporary" venue (such as in a dorm, on a military base, or in a company that frequently transfers its employees) tend to foster?

2 What do you consider to be the ideal ingredients for a successful cocktail party? On the other hand, what factors can turn a party into a disaster?

The Farewell Party

Before the party she had made a list, faintheartedly, and marked off the items as they were dealt with, inexorably—cigarettes, soft drinks, ice, *kebabs* and so on. But she had forgotten to provide lights. The party was to be held on the lawn: on these dry summer nights one could plan a lawn party weeks in advance and be certain of fine weather, and she had thought happily of how the roses would be in bloom and of the stars and perhaps even fireflies, so decorative and discreet, all gracefully underlining her unsuspected talent as a hostess. But she had not realized that there would be no moon and therefore it would be very dark on the lawn. All the lights on the veranda, in the portico and indoors were on, like so many lanterns, richly copper and glowing, with extraordinary beauty as though aware that the house would soon be empty and these were the last few days of illumination and family life, but they did very little to light the lawn which was vast, a still lake of inky grass.

Wandering about with a glass in one hand and a plate of cheese biscuits in another, she gave a start now and then to see an acquaintance emerge from the darkness which had the gloss, the sheen, the coolness but not the weight of water, and present her with a face, vague and without outlines but eventually recognizable. 'Oh,' she cried several times that evening, 'I didn't know you had arrived. I've been looking for you,' she would add with unaccustomed intimacy (was it because of the gin and lime, her second, or because such warmth could safely be held to lead to nothing now that they were leaving town?). The guest, also having had several drinks between beds of flowering balsam and torenias before launching out onto the lawn, responded with an equal vivacity. Sometimes she had her arm squeezed or a hand slid down the bareness of her back—which was athletic: she had once played tennis, rather well—and once someone said, 'I've been hiding in this corner, watching you,' while another went so far as to say, 'Is it true you are leaving us, Bina? How can you be so cruel?' And if it were a woman guest, the words were that much more effusive. It was all heady, astonishing.

It was astonishing because Bina was a frigid and friendless woman. She was thirty-five. For fifteen years she had been bringing up her children and, in particular, nursing the eldest who was severely spastic. This had involved her deeply in the workings of the local hospital and with its many departments and doctors, but her care for this child was so intense and so desperate that her relationship with them was purely professional. Outside this circle of family and hospital—ringed, as it were, with barbed wire and lit with one single floodlight—Bina had no life. The town had scarcely come to know her for its life turned in the more jovial circles of mah-jong, bridge, coffee parties, club evenings and, occasionally, a charity show in aid of the Red Cross. For these Bina had a kind of sad contempt and certainly no time. A tall, pale woman, heavy-boned and sallow, she had a certain presence, a certain dignity, and people, having heard of the spastic child, liked and admired her, but she had not thought she had friends. Yet tonight they were coming forth from the darkness in waves that quite overwhelmed.

Now here was Mrs Ray, the Commissioner's wife, chirping inside a nest of rustling embroidered organza. 'Why are you leaving us so soon, Mrs Raman? You've only been here—two years, is it?'

'Five,' exclaimed Bina, widening her eyes, herself surprised at such a 5
length of time. Although time dragged heavily in their household, agonizingly slow, and the five years had been so hard that sometimes, at night, she did not know how she had crawled through the day and if she would crawl through an-

other, her back almost literally broken by the weight of the totally dependent child and of the three smaller ones who seemed perpetually to clamour for their share of attention, which they felt they never got. Yet now these five years had telescoped. They were over. The Raman family was moving and their time here was spent. There had been the hospital, the girls' school, the boys' school, picnics, monsoons, birthday parties and measles. Crushed together into a handful. She gazed down at her hands, tightened around glass and plate. 'Time has flown,' she murmured incredulously.

'Oh, I wish you were staying, Mrs Raman,' cried the Commissioner's wife and, as she squeezed Bina's arm, her fragrant talcum powder seemed to lift off her chalky shoulders and some of it settled on Bina who sneezed. 'It's been so nice to have a family like yours here. It's a small town, so little to do, at least one must have good friends . . .'

Bina blinked at such words of affection from a woman she had met twice, perhaps thrice before. Bina and her husband did not go in for society. The shock of their first child's birth had made them both fanatic parents. But she knew that not everyone considered this vital factor in their lives, and spoke of 'social duties' in a somehow reproving tone. The Commissioner's wife had been annoyed, she always felt, by her refusal to help out at the Red Cross fair. The hurt silence with which her refusal had been accepted had implied the importance of these 'social duties' of which Bina remained so stubbornly unaware.

However, this one evening, this last party, was certainly given over to their recognition and celebration. 'Oh, everyone, everyone is here,' rejoiced the Commissioner's wife, her eyes snapping from face to face in that crowded aquarium, and, at a higher pitch, cried 'Renu, why weren't you at the mah-jong party this morning?' and moved off into another powdery organza embrace that rose to meet her from the night like a moth and then was submerged again in the shadows of the lawn. Bina gave one of those smiles that easily frightened people found mocking, a shade too superior, somewhat scornful. Looking down into her glass of gin and lime, she moved on and in a minute found herself brought up short against the quite regal although overweight figure, in raw silk and homespun and the somewhat saturnine air of underpaid culture, of Bose, an employee of the local museum whom she had met once or twice at the art competitions and exhibitions to which she was fond of hauling her children, whether reluctant or enthusiastic, because 'it made a change,' she said.

'Mrs Raman,' he said in the fruity tones of the culture-bent Bengali, 'how we'll miss you at the next children's art competitions. You used to be my chief inspiration—'

'Inspiration?' she laughed, incredulously, spilling some of her drink and 10
proffering the plate of cheese biscuits from which he helped himself, half-
bowing as though it were gold she offered, gems.

'Yes, yes, inspiration,' he went on, even more fruitily now that his mouth was full. 'Think of me—alone, the hapless organizer—surrounded by mammas, by primary school teachers, by three, four, five hundred children. And the judges—they are always the most trouble, those judges. And then I look at you—so cool, controlling your children, handling them so wonderfully and with such superb results—my inspiration!'

She was flustered by this unaccustomed vision of herself and half-turned her face away from Bose the better to contemplate it, but could find no reflection of it in the ghostly white bush of the Queen of the Night, and listened to him murmur on about her unkindness in deserting him in this cultural backwater to that darkest of dooms—guardian of a provincial museum—where he saw no one but school teachers herding children through his halls or, worse, Government officials who periodically and inexplicably stirred to create trouble for him and made their official presences felt amongst the copies of the Ajanta frescoes (in which even the mouldy and peeled-off portions were carefully reproduced) and the cupboards of Indus Valley seals. Murmuring commiseration, she left him to a gloomy young professor of history who was languishing at another of the institutions of provincial backwaters that they so deplored and whose wife was always having a baby, and slipped away, still feeling an unease at Bose's unexpected vision of her which did not tally with the cruder reality, into the less equivocal company provided by a ring of twittering 'company wives.'

These women she had always encountered in just such a ring as they formed now, the kind that garden babblers form under a hedge where they sit gabbling and whirring with social bitchiness, and she had always stood outside it, smiling stiffly, not wanting to join and refusing their effusively nodded invitation. They were the wives of men who represented various mercantile companies in the town—Imperial Tobacco, Brooke Bond, Esso and so on—and although they might seem exactly alike to one who did not belong to this circle, inside it were subtle gradations of importance according to the particular company for which each one's husband worked and of these only they themselves were initiates. Bina was, however unwillingly, an initiate. Her husband worked for one of these companies but she had always stiffly refused to recognize these gradations, or consider them. They noted the rather set sulkiness of her silence when amongst them and privately labelled her queer, proud, boring and difficult. Also, they felt she belonged to their circle whether she liked it or not.

Now she entered this circle with diffidence, wishing she had stayed with the more congenial Bose (why hadn't she? What was it in her that made her retreat from anything like a friendly approach?) and was taken aback to find their circle parting to admit her and hear their cries of welcome and affection that did not, however, lose the stridency and harshness of garden babblers' voices.

'Bina, how do you like the idea of going back to Bombay?'

'Have you started packing, Bina? Poor you. Oh, are you having packers over from Delhi? Oh well then it's not so bad.'

Never had they been so vociferous in her company, so easy, so warm. They were women to whom the most awful thing that had ever happened was the screw of a golden ear ring disappearing down the bathroom sink or a mother-in-law's visit or an ayah deserting just before the arrival of guests: what could they know of Bina's life, Bina's ordeal? She cast her glance at the drinks they held—but they were mostly of orange squash. Only the Esso wife, who participated in amateur dramatics and ran a boutique and was rather taller and bolder than the rest, held a whisky and soda. So much affection generated by just orange squash? Impossible. Rather tentatively, she offered them the remains of the cheese biscuits, found herself chirping replies, deploring the nuisance of having packing crates all over the house, talking of the flat they would move into in Bombay, and then, sweating unobtrusively with the strain, saw another recognizable fish swim towards her from the edge of the liquescent lawn, and swung away in relief, saying, 'Mrs D'Souza! How late you are, but I'm so glad—' for she really was.

Mrs D'Souza was her daughter's teacher at the convent school and had clearly never been to a cocktail party before so that all Bina's compassion was aroused by those school-scuffed shoes and her tea-party best—quite apart from the simple truth that she found in her an honest individuality that all those beautifully dressed and poised babblers lacked, being stamped all over by the plain rubber stamps of their husbands' companies—she hurried off to find Mrs D'Souza something suitable to drink. 'Sherry? Why, yes, I think I'll be able to find you some,' she said, a bit flabbergasted as such an unexpected fancy of the pepper-haired schoolteacher, 'and I'll see if Tara's around—she'll want to see you,' she added, vaguely and fraudulently, wondering why she had asked Mrs D'Souza to a cocktail party, only to see, as she skirted the rose bed, the admirable Bose appear at her side and envelop her in this strange intimacy that marked the whole evening, and went off, light-hearted, towards the table where her husband was trying, with the help of some hired waiters in soggy white uniforms with the name of the restaurant from which they were hired embroidered in red across their pockets, to cope with the flood of drinks this party atmosphere had called for and released.

Harassed, perspiring, his feet burning, Raman was nevertheless pleased to be so obviously employed and be saved the strain of having to converse with his motley assembly of guests: he had no more gift for society than his wife had. Ice cubes were melting on the tablecloth in sopping puddles and he had trouble in keeping track of his bottles: they were, besides the newly bought dozens of beer bottles and Black Knight whisky, the remains of their five years in this town that he now wished to bring to their end—bottles brought by friends from trips abroad, bottles bought cheap through 'contacts' in the army or air force, some gems, extravaganzas bought for anniversaries such as a nearly full bottle of Vat 69, a bottle with a bit of *crême de menthe* growing sticky at the bottom, some brown sherry with a great deal of rusty sediment, a red Golconda wine from Hyderabad, and a bottle of Remy Martin that he was keeping guiltily to himself, pouring small quantities into a whisky glass at his elbow and gulping it down in between mixing some very weird cocktails for his guests.

There was no one at the party he liked well enough to share it with. Oh, one of the doctors perhaps, but where were they? Submerged in grass, in dark, in night and chatter, clatter of ice in glass, teeth on biscuit, teeth on teeth. Enamel and gold. Crumbs and dregs. All awash, all soaked in night. Watery sound of speech, liquid sound of drink. Water and ice and night. It occurred to him that everyone had forgotten him, the host, that it was a mistake to have stationed himself amongst the waiters, that he ought to move out, mingle with the guests. But he felt himself drowned, helplessly and quiet delightfully, in Remy Martin, in grass, in a border of purple torenias.

Then he was discovered by his son who galloped through the ranks of guests and waiters to fling himself at his father and ask if he could play the new Beatles record, his friends had asked to hear it.

Raman considered, taking the opportunity to pour out and gulp down some more of the precious Remy Martin. 'All right,' he said, after a judicious minute or two, 'but keep it low, everyone won't want to hear it,' not adding that he himself didn't, for his taste in music ran to slow and melancholy, folk at its most frivolous. Still he glanced into the lighted room where his children and the children of neighbours and guests had collected, making themselves tipsy on Fanta and Coca-Cola, the girls giggling in a multicoloured huddle and the boys swaggering around the record-player with a kind of lounging strut, holding bottles in their hands with a sophisticated ease, exactly like experienced cocktail party guests, so that he smiled and wished he had a ticket, a passport that would make it possible to break into that party within a party. It was chillingly obvious to him that he hadn't one. He also saw that a good deal of their riotousness was due to the fact that they were raiding the snack trays that the waiters carried through the room to the lawn, and that they were seeing to it that the trays emerged half-empty. He knew he ought to go in and see about it but he hadn't the heart, or the nerve. He couldn't join that party but he wouldn't wreck it either so he only caught hold of one of the waiters and suggested that the snack trays be carried out from the kitchen straight onto the lawn, not by way of the drawing-room, and led him towards a group that seemed to be without snacks and saw too late that it was a group of the company executives that he loathed most. He half-groaned, then hiccuped at his mistake, but it was too late to alter course now. He told himself that he ought to see to it that the snacks were offered around without snag or error.

Poor Raman was placed in one of the lower ranks of the companies' hierarchy. That is, he did not belong to a British concern, or even to an American-collaboration one, but merely to an Indian one. Oh, a long-established, prosperous and solid one but, still, only Indian. Those cigarettes that he passed around were made by his own company. Somehow it struck a note of bad taste amongst these fastidious men who played golf, danced at the club on Independence Eve and New Year's Eve, invited at least one foreign couple to every party and called their decorative wives 'darling' when in public. Poor Raman never had belonged. It was so obvious to everyone, even to himself, as he passed around those awful cigarettes that sold so well in the market. It had been obvious since their first disastrous dinner party for this very ring of jocular gentlemen, five years ago. Nono had cried right through the party, Bina had spent the evening racing upstairs to see to the babies' baths and bed-time and then crawling reluctantly down, the hired cook had got drunk and stolen two of the chickens so that there was not enough on the table, no one had relaxed for a minute or enjoyed a second—it had been too sad and harrowing even to make a good story or a funny anecdote. They had all let it sink by mutual consent and the invitations to play a round of golf on Saturday afternoon or a rubber of bridge on Sunday morning had been issued and refused with conspiratorial smoothness. Then there was that distressing hobby of Raman's: his impossibly long walks on which he picked up bits of wood and took them home to sandpaper and chisel and then call wood sculpture. What could one do with a chap who did that? He himself wasn't sure if he pursued such odd tastes because he was a social pariah or if he was one on account of this oddity. Not so speak of the spastic child. Now that didn't even bear thinking of, and so it was no wonder that Raman swayed towards them so hesitantly, as though he were wading through water instead of over clipped grass, and handed his cigarettes around with such an apologetic air.

But, after all, hesitation and apology proved unnecessary. One of them—was he Polson's Coffee or Brooke Bond Tea?—clasped Raman about the shoulders as proper men do on meeting, and hearty voices rose together, congratulating him on his promotion (it wasn't one, merely a transfer, and they knew it), envying him his move to the metropolis. They talked as if they had known each other for years, shared all kinds of public schoolboy fun. One—was he Voltas or Ciba?—talked of golf matches at the Willingdon as though he had often played there with Raman, another spoke of *kebabs* eaten on the roadside after a party as though Raman had been one of the gang. Amazed and grateful as a schoolboy admitted to a closed society, Raman nodded and put in a few cautious words, put away his cigarettes, called a waiter to refill their glasses and broke away before the clock struck twelve and the golden carriage turned into a pumpkin, he himself into a mouse. He hated mice.

Walking backwards, he walked straight into the soft barrier of Miss Dutta's ample back wrapped and bound in rich Madras silk.

'Sorry, sorry, Miss Dutta, I'm clumsy as a bear,' he apologized, but here, too, there was no call for apology for Miss Dutta was obviously delighted at having been bumped into.

'My dear Mr Raman, what can you expect if you invite the whole town to your party?' she asked in that piercing voice that invariably made her companions drop theirs self-consciously. 'You and Bina have been so popular—what are we going to do without you?'

He stood pressing his glass with white-tipped fingers and tried to think what he or Bina had provided her with that she could possibly miss. In any case, Miss Dutta could always manage, and did manage, everything single-handedly.

She was the town busy-body, secretary and chairman of more committees than he could count: they ranged from the Film Society to the Blood Bank, from the Red Cross to the Friends of the Museum, for Miss Dutta was nothing if not versatile. 'We hardly ever saw you at our film shows of course,' her voice rang out, making him glance furtively over his shoulder to see if anyone were listening, 'but it was so nice *knowing* you were in town and that I could count on you. So few people here *care*, you know,' she went on, and affectionately bumped her comfortable middle-aged body into his as someone squeezed by, making him remember that he had once heard her called a man-eater, and wonder which man she had eaten and even consider, for a moment, if there were not, after all, some charm in those powdered creases of her creamy arms, equalling if not surpassing that of his worn and harassed wife's bony angles. Why did suffering make for angularity? he even asked himself with uncharacteristic kindness. But when Miss Dutta laid an arm on top of his glass-holding one and raised herself on her toes to bray something into his ear, he loyally decided that he was too accustomed to sharp angles to change them for such unashamed luxuriance, and, contriving to remove her arm by grasping her elbow—how one's fingers sank into the stuff!—he steered her towards his wife who was standing at the table and inefficiently pouring herself another gin and lime.

'This is my third,' she confessed hurriedly, 'and I can't tell you how gay it makes me feel. I giggle at everything everyone says.'

'Good,' he pronounced, feeling inside a warm expansion of relief at seeing her lose, for the moment, her tension and anxiety. 'Let's hear you giggle,' he said, sloshing some more gin into her glass.

'Look at those children,' she exclaimed, and they stood in a bed of balsam, irredeemably crushed, and looked into the lighted drawing room where their daughter was at the moment the cynosure of all juvenile eyes, having thrown herself with abandon into a dance of monkey-like movements. 'What is it, Miss Dutta?' the awed mother enquired. 'You're more up in the latest fashions than I am—is it the twist, the rock or the jungle?' and all three watched, enthralled, till Tara began to totter and, losing her simian grace, collapsed against some wildly shrieking girl friends.

A bit embarrassed by their daughter's reckless abandon, the parents discussed with Miss Dutta whose finger by her own admission, was placed squarely on the pulse of youth, the latest trends in juvenile culture on which Miss Dutta gave a neat sociological discourse (all the neater for having been given earlier that day at the convocation of the Home Science College) and Raman wondered uneasily at this opening of flood gates in his own family—his wife grown giggly with gin, his daughter performing wildly to a Chubby Checkers record—how had it all come about? Was it the darkness all about them, dense as the heavy curtains about a stage, that made them act, for an hour or so, on the tiny lighted stage of brief intimacy with such a lack of inhibition? Was it the drink, so freely sloshing from end to end of the house and lawn on account of his determination to clear out his 'cellar' (actually one-half of the sideboard and the top shelf of the wardrobe in his dressing-room) and his muddling and mixing them, making up untried and experimental cocktails and lavishly pouring out the whisky without a measure? But these were solid and everyday explanations and there was about this party something out of the ordinary and everyday—at least to the Ramans, normally so austere and unpopular. He knew the real reason too—it was all because the party had been labelled a 'farewell party', everyone knew it was the last one, that the Ramans were leaving and they would not meet up again. There was about it exactly that kind of sentimental euphoria that is generated at a ship-board party, the one given on the last night before the end of the voyage. Everyone draws together with an intimacy, a lack of inhibition not displayed or guessed at before, knowing this is the last time, tomorrow they will be dispersed, it will be over. They will not meet, be reminded of it or be required to repeat it.

As if to underline this new and Cinderella's ball-like atmosphere of friendliness and gaiety, three pairs of neighbours now swept in (and three kochias lay down and died under their feet, to the gardener's rage and sorrow): the couple who lived to the Ramans' left, the couple who lived to their right, and the couple from across the road, all crying, 'So sorry to be late, but you know what a long way we had to come,' making everyone laugh identically at the identical joke. Despite the disparity in their looks and ages—one couple was very young, another middle-aged, the third grandparents—they were, in a sense, as alike as the company executives and their wives, for they too bore a label if a less alarming one: Neighbours, it said. Because they were neighbours, and although they had never been more than nodded to over the hedge, waved to in passing cars or spoken to about anything other than their children, dogs, flowers and gardens, their talk had a vivid immediacy that went straight to the heart.

'Diamond's going to miss you so—he'll be heartbroken,' moaned the grandparents who lived alone in their spotless house with a black labrador who had made a habit of visiting the Ramans whenever he wanted young company, a romp on the lawn or an illicit biscuit.

'I don't know what my son will do without Diamond,' reciprocated Bina with her new and sympathetic warmth. 'He'll force me to get a dog of his own, I know, and how will I ever keep one in a flat in Bombay?'

'When are you going to throw out those rascals?' demanded a father of Raman, pointing at the juvenile revellers indoors. 'My son has an exam tomorrow, you know, but he said he couldn't be bothered about it—he had to go to the Ramans' farewell party.'

One mother confided in Bina, winning her heart forever, 'Now that you are leaving, I can talk to you about it at last: did you know my Vinod is sweet on your Tara? Last night when I was putting him to bed, he said "Mama, when I grow up I will marry Tara. I will sit on a white horse and wear a turban and carry a sword in my belt and I will go and marry Tara." What shall we do about that, eh? Only a ten year difference in age, isn't there—or twelve?' and both women rocked with laughter.

The party had reached its crest, like a festive ship, loud and illuminated for that last party before the journey's end, perched on the dizzy top of the dark wave. It could do nothing now but descend and dissolve. As if by simultaneous and unanimous consent, the guests began to leave (in the wake of the Commissioner and his wife who left first, like royalty) streaming towards the drive where cars stood bumper to bumper—more than had visited the Ramans' house in the previous five years put together. The light in the portico fell on Bina's pride and joy, a Chinese orange tree, lighting its miniature globes of fruit like golden lanterns. There was a babble, an uproar of leavetaking (the smaller children, already in pyjamas, watched open-mouthed from a dark window upstairs). Esso and Caltex left together, arms about each other and smoking cigars, like figures in a comic act. Miss Dutta held firmly to Bose's arm as they dipped, bowed, swayed and tripped on their way out. Bina was clasped, kissed—ear rings grazed her cheek, talcum powder tickled her nose. Raman had his back slapped till he thrummed and vibrated like a beaten gong.

It seemed as if Bina and Raman were to be left alone at last, left to pack up and leave—now the good-byes had been said, there was nothing else they could possibly do—but no, out popped the good doctors from the hospital who had held themselves back in the darkest corners and made themselves inconspicuous throughout the party, and now, in the manner in which they clasped the host by the shoulders and the hostess by the hands, and said 'Ah *now* we have a chance to be with you at last, now we can begin *our* party,' revealed that although this was the first time they had come to the Ramans' house on any but professional visits, they were not merely friends—they were almost a part of that self-defensive family, the closest to them in sympathy. Raman and Bina both felt a warm, moist expansion of tenderness inside themselves, the tenderness they had till today restricted to the limits of their family, no farther, as though they feared it had not an unlimited capacity. Now its close horizons stepped backwards, with some surprise.

And it was as the doctors said—the party now truly began. Cane chairs were dragged out of the veranda onto the lawn, placed in a ring next to the flowering Queen of the Night which shook out flounces and frills of white scent with every rustle of night breeze. Bina could give in now to her two most urgent needs and dash indoors to smear her mosquito-bitten arms and feet with Citronella and fetch Nono to sit on her lap, to let Nono have a share, too, in the party. The good doctors and their wives leant forward and gave Nono the attention that made the parents' throats tighten with gratitude. Raman insisted on their each having a glass of Remy Martin—they must finish it tonight, he said, and would not let the waiter clear away the ice or glasses yet. So they sat on the veranda steps, smoking and yawning.

Now it turned out that Dr Bannerji's wife, the lady in the Dacca sari and the steel-rimmed spectacles, had studied in Shantiniketan, and she sang, at her husband's and his colleagues' urging, Tagore's sweetest, saddest songs. When she sang, in heartbroken tones that seemed to come from some distance away, from the damp corners of the darkness where the fireflies flitted,

Father, the boat is carrying me away,
Father, it is carrying me away from home,

the eyes of her listeners, sitting tensely in that grassy, inky dark, glazed with tears that were compounded equally of drink, relief and regret.

CHARTING THE STORY

1 Why does the farewell party take place in near-darkness? What effects do the darkness and the scattered lights have on the gathering?

2 How do Bina and Raman fit into their local social circle? Had the circumstances of their life been slightly different, do you think they would have related to the others differently? In what way, or why not?

3 Compare the *three* parties that took place on the night of the eponymous farewell party.

CONSIDERATIONS OF STYLE

1 To what sort of audience do you consider this story to be directed? What things does the author seem to expect a reader to have experienced already, to be able to identify with?

2 To what senses does Desai appeal in her unfolding of the farewell party? Classify the images as visual, auditory, olfactory, tactile, and gustatory, and discuss which ones seem to be the most dramatic to you. (This exercise works well if done individually, then collaboratively.)

3 This story contains a number of water analogies: "that crowded aquarium" (Paragraph 8); "another recognisable fish swim[ming] towards her from the edge of the liquescent lawn" (Paragraph 17); "All awash, all soaked in night" (Paragraph 19); and others. Scan the story for more such analogies and discuss how they contribute to its mood, pace, and ambience.

AFTERTHOUGHTS

1 Desai is often noted for her way of presenting her characters, particularly the women, as complex and multilayered. How would you describe Bina, in terms of the way she appears to others, and of her "past" and "present" personae?

2 The song by Rabindranath Tagore that begins

Father, the boat is carrying me away,
Father, it is carrying me away from home

goes back to the days in Bengal (where rivers are often thoroughfares) when a bride would leave her parental home to live with her husband's family, rarely or never to be seen again by her own mother and father. Apart from the fact that Tagore's songs were, and are, tremendously popular in India, why would Dr Banerji's wife sing this one to this small gathering of people?

THE WRITER'S CRAFT

1 Describe a memorable vignette from one of the most memorable parties of your life.

2 Write a letter from Bina to one of the guests at the party, from their Bombay flat at their new posting. After you have written the letter, consider whether Bina would post it.

3 Write of a moment you have experienced where "relief and regret" blended into one.

JOHN HAINES

JOHN HAINES *was born in Norfolk, Virginia in 1924 and studied at the National Art School, the Hans Hoffmann School of Fine Arts, and the American University. He spent more than twenty years homesteading in Alaska, an experience that profoundly shaped his sense of the relation between art and nature. He has taught at Ohio University, The George Washington University, and the University of Cincinnati.*

Haines has published numerous volumes of poetry, the most recent being At the End of this Summer: Poems 1948–54 *(1997). His many prose works include his memoir,* The Stars, the Snow, the Fire *(1989).*

Haines has been honored with the Alaska Governor's Award for Excellence in the Arts, two Guggenheim fellowships, a National Endowment for the Arts Fellowship, and a Lifetime Achievement Award from the Library of Congress. He lives in Helena, Montana.

"Poem for the End of the Century" appeared in the August 1999 issue of The Atlantic Monthly.

PERSPECTIVES

1 What do you infer from the fact that the title of this poem refers to "the end of the century" rather than "the beginning of the new millennium"?

2 What memories and other thoughts do you have concerning New Year's Eve? What images and moods do these associations evoke?

Poem for the End of the Century

I am the dreamer who remains
when all the dreams are gone,
scattered by the millennial winds
and sacked by the roadside.

The solar clock hand stopped:
confusion and fury on the street

—so much idle paper
shredded and tossed aside.

The small, dim shops of the tourist
trade are shuttered and locked . . .
Nightfall, and the buyer turns away.

One more stolen fortune spent:
another century gone
with its fits and desolations—
I leave my house to the creditor wind.

Tell me if you know my name,
whose face I wear, whose stored-up
anger fades to a tentative smile.

I am the one who touches fire,
who rakes the leaves to watch them burn,
and who says once more to himself
on this calm evening of earth:

Awake! The stars are out,
mist is on the water,
and tomorrow the sun will return.

CHARTING THE POEM

1 Would you characterize the speaker as a somewhat otherworldly being, or, rather, very much of the here and now? What images lead to this characterization?

2 Why do you suppose the speaker has chosen to focus on mundane entities—shredded paper, tourist shops shuttered and locked, a pile of burning raked leaves—rather than on the grand-scale achievements, and attendant destruction, of the millennium past?

CONSIDERATIONS OF STYLE

1 Where does the poem take license with conventional "grammaticality" and punctuation? To what effect is this done?

2 Several of the images seem to coalesce about a larger theme of fiscal confusion and disaster. What sort of vision of "millennial winds" has the speaker evoked? Are there any images which do not seem to fit in with the rest? If so, how might the author justify their inclusion?

AFTERTHOUGHTS

1 How did you and your friends and family experience the turning of the millennium? Compare this to "doomsday" accounts of the arrival of the year 1000 (espe-

cially in Europe) and to the more sanguine accounts of the dawning of the year 1900.

2 In the twentieth century, people would sometimes dismiss old-fashioned concepts as being "so nineteenth-century." What do you predict may be dismissed as "so twentieth-century"? When do you think people will start to make these dismissals?

THE WRITER'S CRAFT

1 You have read this poem after the fateful Y2K moment has come and gone. How might your response to it have differed if you had read this poem *before* the turn of the millenium? Write a brief essay comparing expectation and realization before and after the arrival of the new century/millennium.

2 Consider some historical figure who has lived through a turn of the century or a turn of the millennium. From the point of view of that person, write about his or her "turn."

DEREK WALCOTT

DEREK WALCOTT *was born in 1930 in Castries, St Lucia, in the eastern Caribbean. He was raised a Methodist in a largely Roman Catholic society. His father was a painter and his mother a schoolteacher. From his parents he inherited a love of both painting and literature; from his mixed heritage and his British education, he evolved a sense of cultural duality that frequently manifests itself in the themes of his writing. He received a BA from the University of the West Indies in Jamaica in 1953, after which time he devoted his entire adult life to writing. Walcott's prolific literary work includes largely poetry—which he began publishing at fourteen—and drama, as well as critical and cultural essays. He collaborated with songwriter Paul Simon to write the musical* Capeman *in 1998. He won the Nobel Prize for literature in 1992.*

"The Season of Phantasmal Peace" originally appeared in The New Yorker *and is included in the poetry collection* The Fortunate Traveller, *published in 1981.*

PERSPECTIVES

1. If you had to characterize life on earth, particularly as humans have made it, and make it, how would you evaluate our "contribution" to the ecosystem, in a biologic sense, and in a spiritual sense?
2. Of what symbolic significance are birds, in most cultures—the bird kingdom as a whole, not specific birds? How have most humans regarded these creatures?
3. What is implied in saying that peace is "phantasmal"? That it will have a "season"?

The Season of Phantasmal Peace

Then all the nations of birds lifted together
the huge net of the shadows of this earth
in multitudinous dialects, twittering tongues,
stitching and crossing it. They lifted up
the shadows of long pines down trackless slopes,

the shadows of glass-faced towers down evening streets,
the shadow of a frail plant on a city sill—
the net rising soundless as night, the birds' cries soundless, until
there was no longer dusk, or season, decline, or weather,
only this passage of phantasmal light
that not the narrowest shadow dared to sever.

And men could not see, looking up, what the wild geese drew,
what the ospreys trailed behind them in silvery ropes
that flashed in the icy sunlight; they could not hear
battalions of starlings waging peaceful cries,
bearing the net higher, covering this world
like the vines of an orchard, or a mother drawing
the trembling gauze over the trembling eyes
of a child fluttering to sleep;
it was the light
that you will see at evening on the side of a hill
in yellow October, and no one hearing knew
what change had brought into the raven's cawing,
the killdeer's screech, the ember-circling chough
such an immense, soundless, and high concern
for the fields and cities where the birds belong,
except it was their seasonal passing, Love,
made seasonless, or, from the high privilege of their birth,
something brighter than pity for the wingless ones
below them who shared dark holes in windows and in houses,
and higher they lifted the net with soundless voices
above all change, betrayals of falling suns,
and this season lasted one moment, like the pause
between dusk and darkness, between fury and peace,
but, for such as our earth is now, it lasted long.

CHARTING THE POEM

1 Walcott begins the poem with "Then . . ." What is suggested by such an opening? What do you envision that the state of the world may have been before this narration?

2 Why might "all the nations of birds" be selected to lift the earth out of its shadows? In Stanza 1, what different meanings do the various collocations of "shadow/s" suggest?

3 What, exactly, transpires in the course of the narrative? What does the narrator suggest could possibly have motivated the birds to do as they did?

CONSIDERATIONS OF STYLE

1 How do contrasts of imagery work in this poem? In the same vein, where does Walcott use oxymorons such as "icy sunlight" in Line 14 to reinforce a sense of contrast, even contradiction?

2 What emotional responses do the images of sound and light—which predominate in this poem—produce?

3 What is suggested by the fact that the speaker addresses the reader only once as "you"?

4 What images of nationhood, of separate peoples, does the narrator evoke, and to what purposes?

AFTERTHOUGHTS

1 How does this poem's vision of "the end of the world as we know it" differ from that in sacred scripture—Jewish, Christian, Muslim, Hindu—or in ancestral/spiritual oral traditions?

2 A common fable tells the tale of a flock of birds caught in a hunter's net who foil his plans by rising all at once and flying away, net and all. How might this poem partake of the fable? Where does it leave fable behind and become something of its own?

THE WRITER'S CRAFT

1 Write about a moment that shimmers beyond anyone's ability to capture in words. Even half-caught, what might such an instance be?

2 What relevance does this poem have to postcolonial studies? Based upon what you know of Walcott and of postcoloniana in general, what are the birds about?

Credits

p. 3 “It Was a Long Time Before” by Leslie Marmon Silko. Copyright © 1981 by Leslie Marmon Silko. Reprinted from *Storyteller* by Leslie Marmon Silko, published by Seaver Books, New York, New York.

p. 6 Poem titled “Ah Mah” by Shirley Geok-Lin Lim. Copyright © by Shirley Geok Lim. From *What the Fortune Teller Didn’t Say,* West End Press, 1998.

p. 9 “Grandfather at Noon. Lahore, 1957” by Julian Samuel. From PASSAGE TO LAHORE by Julian Samuel. The Mercury Press: Toronto, copyright 1995. Reprinted by permission.

p. 19 “Grandma’s Tales” by Andrew Lam. Reprinted by permission from the author.

p. 25 “Why a Robin?” by Shashi Deshpande. From *The Intrusion and Other Stories.* Copyright © 1993 by Penguin India. Reprinted by permission from Penguin India.

p. 32 “Friend of My Youth” by Alice Munro. From FRIEND OF MY YOUTH by Alice Munro. Copyright © 1990 by Alice Munro. Reprinted by permission of Alfred A. Knopf, a Division of Random House, Inc and McClelland & Stewart, Inc. The Canadian Publishers.

p. 50 “A Rose in the Heart of New York” by Edna O’Brien. From A FANATIC HEART by Edna O’Brien. Copyright © 1984 by Edna O’Brien. Reprinted by permission of Farrar, Straus and Giroux, LLC and David Godwin Associates.

p. 73 “My Mother” from AT THE BOTTOM OF THE RIVER by Jamaica Kincaid. Copyright © 1983 by Jamaica Kincaid. Reprinted by permission of Farrar, Straus and Giroux, LLC.

p. 79 “Anoma” by Punyakanta Wijenaike. Reprinted by permission from Punyakanta Wijenaike.

p. 83 “The Gift,” copyright © 1986 by Li-Young Lee. Reprinted from ROSE: Poems by Li-Young Lee, with the permission of BOA Editions, Ltd.

p. 86 “Goalie” by Rudy Thauberger, from *Our Game* (Polestar Press). © 1988 by Rudy Thauberger and reprinted by permission of the author.

p. 92 “Digging” from SELECTED POEMS 1966–1987 by Seamus Heaney. Copyright © 1990 by Seamus Heaney. Reprinted by permission of Farrar, Straus and Giroux, LLC and Faber and Faber Limited.

p. 95 “The Next Life” from EQUAL LOVE: STORIES BY PETER HO DAVIES. Copyright © 2000 by Peter Ho Davies. Previously published in *Harper’s* Magazine. Reprinted by permission of Houghton Mifflin Co. All rights reserved.

p. 105 “A Family Supper” by Kazuo Ishiguro. Copyright © 1982 Kazuo Ishiguro. Reproduced by permission of the author c/o Rogers, Coleridge & White Ltd., 20 Powis Mews, London W11 1JN.

p. 114 “It Used to Be Green Once” by Patricia Grace. From *Patricia Grace: Selected Stories.* Reprinted by permission from Penguin Books New Zealand Limited.

p. 120 “Jewish Christmas” by Faye Moskowitz. From *And The Bridge Is Love* by Faye Moskowitz. Copyright © 1991 by Faye Moskowitz. Reprinted by permission of Beacon Press, Boston.

p. 125 “The Holiday Season” by Jane Shore. Copyright © 1996 by Jane Shore. From MUSIC MINUS ONE by Jane Shore. Reprinted by permission of St. Martin’s Press, LLC.

p. 133 “For My People” by Margaret Walker. From *This is My Century: New and Collected Poems* by Margaret Walker. Copyright © 1989 by The University of Georgia Press. Reprinted with permission.

p. 137 "El Grupo McDonald's" by Nick Carbó. From *El Grupo McDonald's,* by Nick Carbó. Copyright © 1995 by Tia Chucha Press. Reprinted by permission from Nick Carbó.

p. 140 "Kicking the Habit" by Lawson Fusao Inada. From *Drawing the Line.* Copyright © 1997 by Coffee House Press. Reprinted by permission.

p. 145 "The Day They Burned the Books" by Jean Rhys. From *Tales of the Wide Carribean,* edited by Kenneth Ramchard. Copyright © 1985 by Heinemann Educational Publishers, a division of Reed Educational & Professional Publishing Ltd.

p. 152 "Thread" by Stuart Dybek. Reprinted by permission of International Creative Management, Inc. Copyright © 1998 by Stuart Dybek.

p. 158 "Good Girls are Bad News" by Subhadra Sen Gupta. Extracted from GOOD GIRLS ARE BAD NEWS © 1982 by Rupa. Reprinted by permission.

p. 164 "The Creation" from RATTLEBONE by Maxine Clair. Copyright © 1994 by Maxine Clair. Reprinted by permission from Farrar, Straus & Giroux, LLC.

p. 182 "Death by Music" by Rukun Advani. From *Beethoven Among the Cows.* Copyright © 1994 by Ravi Dayal Publishers, India, distributed by South Asia Books.

p. 195 "Mother Dressmaking" by Craig Raine. Reprinted by permission from the author.

p. 197 "Flying to Belfast" by Craig Raine. Reprinted by permission from the author.

p. 199 "A Martian Sends a Postcard Home" by Craig Raine. Reprinted by permission from the author.

p. 201 "Of Rabbi Yose" by Dannie Abse. From *One-Legged on Ice* by Dannie Abse. Copyright © 1983 by The University of Georgia Press. Reprinted by permission.

p. 203 "Winter Visit" by Dannie Abse. From *One-Legged on Ice* by Dannie Abse. Copyright © 1983 by The University of Georgia Press. Reprinted by permission.

p. 205 "Of Itzig and His Dog" by Dannie Abse. From *One-Legged on Ice* by Dannie Abse. Copyright © 1983 by The University of Georgia Press. Reprinted by permission.

p. 209 "Wonderful People" by Richard Hagopian. From *The Dove Brings Peace.* Copyright © 1944 by Farrar & Rinehart, Inc.

p. 212 "The Tenant" by Bharati Mukherjee. From THE MIDDLEMAN AND OTHER STORIES by Bharati Mukherjee. Copyright © 1988 by Bharati Mukherjee. Used by permission of Grove/Atlantic, Inc. and Penguin Books Canada Limited.

p. 225 "Epithalamium" by Andrew Motion. Reprinted by permission of the Peters Fraser & Dunlop Group Ltd.

p. 226 Sáenz, Benjamin Alire, "The Wedding Feast at Cana" from *Dark and Perfect Angels,* Cinco Puntos Press. Copyright © 1995 by Benjamin Alire Sáenz. Used by permission of the author and Cinco Puntos Press (800-566-9072, www.cincopuntos.com).

p. 230 "The Bridegroom" by Ha Jin. Copyright © 1999 by *Harper's* Magazine. All rights reserved. Reproduced from the July issue by special permission.

p. 247 "Licks of Love in the Heart of the Cold War" by John Updike. From *The Atlantic Monthly,* May 1998 issue. Reprinted by permission from John Updike.

p. 260 "Yellow Woman" by Leslie Marmon Silko. Copyright © 1996 by Leslie Marmon Silko, reprinted with permission of The Wylie Agency, Inc.

p. 270 "Postcard" from SELECTED POEMS II: POEMS SELECTED AND NEW 1976–1986 by Margaret Atwood. Copyright © 1987 by Margaret Atwood. Reprinted by permission of Houghton Mifflin Co. All rights reserved. Also appeared in *Selected Poems 1966–1984* by Margaret Atwood. Copyright © Margaret Atwood 1990. Reprinted by permission of Oxford University Press Canada.

p. 273 "Incompatibilities" by Ted Hughes. From *The Hawk in the Rain* by Ted Hughes. Copyright © 1957. Reprinted by permission from Faber and Faber Limited.

p. 276 "Shanti" by Vikram Chandra. From LOVE AND LONGING IN BOMBAY by Vikram Chandra. Copyright © 1997 by Vikram Chandra. By permission of Little, Brown and Company, Inc.

p. 270 "'Commonwealth Literature' Does Not Exist" by Salman Rushdie. "Commonwealth Literature" (pp. 61–70), copyright © 1991 by Salman Rushdie, from IMAGINARY HOMELANDS by Salman Rushdie. Used by permision of Viking Penguin, a division of Penguin Putnam, Inc., and The Wylie Agency.

p. 315 "The Song of Ourselves" by Chinua Achebe. Reprinted by permission of Harold Ober Associates Incorporated. Copyright © 1990 by Statesman and Nation Pub. Co., Ltd.

p. 322 "Dis Poem" by Mutabaruka. Originally appeared in *The Jamaican Journal,* 24, 2 (March 1992), p. 52, Kingston, Jamaica.

p. 326 "Dead Men's Path," from GIRLS AT WAR AND OTHER STORIES by Chinua Achebe. Copyright © 1972, 1973 by Chinua Achebe. Used by permission of Doubleday, a division of Random House, Inc. and by Harold Ober Associates Incorporated.

p. 331 "The Lemon Orchard" by Alex La Guma. From *A Walk in the Night and Other Stories.* Copyright © 1967 by Northwestern University Press. Reprinted by permission from Northwestern University Press and Reed Educational & Professional Publishing Ltd.

p. 336 "The Return" by Ngugi wa Thiong'o. Reprinted by permission of Ngugi wa Thiong'o: *Secret Lives and Other Stories* (Heinemann, A division of Reed Elsevier Inc., Portsmouth, NH, 1975).

p. 342 "In the Shadow of War" from STARS OF THE NEW CURFEW by Ben Okri, copyright © 1988 by Ben Okri. Used by permission of Viking Penguin, a division of Penguin Putnam, Inc.

p. 347 "In the Hills" by Christine Craig. From *Her True-True Name: Anthology of Women's Writing from the Carribean,* edited by Pamela Mordecai and Betty Wilson. Copyright © 1989 by Heinemann Educational Publishers, a division of Reed Educational & Professional Publishing Ltd.

p. 351 "And So It Came to Pass" by Funso Aiyejina. Reprinted by permission from the author.

p. 353 "The Coming of Day" by Yao Egblewogbe.

p. 354 "No Coffin, No Grave" by Jared Angira.

p. 358 "Africa Kills Her Sun" by Ken Saro-Wiwa. Copyright © 1980 by Ken Saro-Wiwa.

p. 371 "Crickets" by Robert Olen Butler. From *A Good Scent from a Strange Mountain* by Robert Olen Butler, © 1992 by Robert Olen Butler. Reprinted by permission of Henry Holt and Company, LLC.

p. 377 "New York Day Women" by Edwidge Danticat. From *Krik? Krack!* by Edwidge Danticat. Reprinted by permission of Soho Press, New York.

p. 383 "A Wedding in Spring" by George Lamming.

p. 394 "Woman with Kite" by Chitra Divakaruni. From LEAVING YUBA CITY by Chitra Banerjee Divakaruni, copyright © 1997 by Chitra Banerjee Divakaruni. Used by permission of Doubleday, a division of Random House, Inc.

p. 397 "Kinakdakan" by Maria Luisa B. Aguilar-Cariño originally appeared in *Pacific-American Journal,* Spring/Summer 1994 issue. Also appeared in *Returning a Borrowed Tongue: An Anthology of Filipino and Filipino American Poetry,* edited by Nick Carbó. Copyright © 1995 by Coffee House Press. Reprinted by permission from the author and Nick Carbó.

p. 399 "Assimilation" by Eugene Gloria appeared in *Returning a Borrowed Tongue: An Anthology of Filipino and Filipino American Poetry,* edited by Nick Carbó. Copyright © 1995 by Coffee House Press. Reprinted by permission from the author and Nick Carbó.

p. 401 "Pacific Crossing" originally appeared in *Liwanag, Vol. II.* San Francisco: 1995. Also appeared *Returning a Borrowed Tongue: An Anthology of Filipino and Filipino American Poetry,* edited by Nick Carbó. Copyright © 1995 by Coffee House Press. Reprinted by permission from the author and Nick Carbó.

p. 405 "Mrs. Dutta Writes a Letter" by Chitra Divakaruni. Copyright © 1998 by Chitra Divakaruni. From *The Atlantic Monthly,* April 1998. Reprinted by permission from the author.

p. 423 "Once Upon a Time" from JUMP AND OTHER STORIES by Nadine Gordimer. Copyright © 1991 by Feliz Licensing, B.V. Reprinted by permission of Farrar, Straus and Giroux, LLC and Penguin Books Canada Limited.

p. 429 "White Fantasy—Black Fact" by Jack Davis. Appeared in *Paperbark: A Collection of Black Australian Writing* by Jack Davis. Copyright © 1990 by University of Queensland Press.

p. 435 "Village" by Estela Portillo Trambley. From *A Rain of Scorpions* by Estela Portillo Trambley. Copyright © 1993 by Bilingual Press/Editorial Bilingüe, Arizona State University, Tempe, AZ. Reprinted by permission.

p. 443 "Hiroshima" by Desmond Egan. Copyright by Desmond Egan. From ELEGIES, The Goldsmith Press. Reprinted by permission from the author.

p. 444 "The Northern Ireland Question" by Desmond Egan. Copyright by Desmond Egan. From ELEGIES, The Goldsmith Press. Reprinted by permission from the author.

p. 445 "Peace" by Desmond Egan. Copyright by Desmond Egan. From ELEGIES, The Goldsmith Press. Reprinted by permission from the author.

p. 448 "Crocodile" by Albert Wendt. Permission granted by the copyright owner, c/o Curtis Brown (Aust) Pty Ltd., Sydney, Australia.

p. 455 "The Blue Donkey" by Suniti Namjoshi. From *The Blue Donkey Fables/Mothers of Maya Diip* by Suniti Namjoshi. Copyright © 1990 by Penguin India. Reprinted by permission.

p. 456 "Apotheosis" by Suniti Namjoshi. From *The Blue Donkey Fables/Mothers of Maya Diip* by Suniti Namjoshi. Copyright © 1990 by Penguin India. Reprinted by permission.

p. 458 6–10 poem (#1129) by Emily Dickinson. Reprinted by permission of the publishers and the Trustees of Amherst College from THE POEMS OF EMILY DICKINSON, Ralph W. Franklin, ed., Cambridge, Mass.: The Belknap Press of Harvard University Press. Copyright © 1998 by the President and Fellows of Harvard College. Copyright © 1951, 1955, 1979 by the President and Fellows of Harvard College.

p. 459 "Or Else, the Lightning God" by Catherine Lim. From *Or Else, the Lighning God and Other Stories* by Catherine Lim. Copyright © 1980 by Octopus Publishing Group Ltd., Singapore.

p. 470 "The Loons" by Margaret Laurence from A BIRD IN THE HOUSE, copyright 1963 by New End Inc. Published in Canada by McClelland & Stewart. Reprinted by permission of the author's estate.

p. 480 "A New Wardrobe for Rainbow Jack" by Herbert Wharton, from *Where Ya' Been, Mate?*, University of Queensland Press, St. Lucia, 1996. Reprinted with permission.

p. 492 "The Wife Who Spoke Japanese in Her Sleep" by Vivienne Plumb. Reprinted by permission from Vivienne Plumb.

p. 502 "Chew You Up and Spit You Out," from MOON OVER MINNEAPOLIS AND OTHER STORIES by Fay Weldon, copyright © 1991 by Fay Weldon. Used by permission of Viking Penguin, a division of Penguin Putnam Inc.

p. 511 "A Boy in a Snow Shower" by James MacKay Brown. From *Following a Lark*. Copyright © 1995 by John Murray Ltd. Reprinted by permission.

p. 514 "Sweet, Sweet Corn" by Garrison Keillor. From SWEET, SWEET CORN by Garrison Keillor. Copyright © 1992 Athens Music. All rights administered by Sony/ATV Music Publishing, 8 Music Square West, Nashville, TN 37203. All rights reserved. Used by permission.

p. 518 "One of the Wild Beautiful Creatures" by N. Scott Momaday. Copyright © by N. Scott Momaday. Reprinted with permission.

p. 521 "Atmospheric Phenomenon: The Art of Hurricanes" by Victor Hernandez Cruz. From *Panoramas.* Coypright © 1997 by Coffee House Press. Reprinted by permission.

p. 529 "Pantoum of the Great Depression" by Donald Justice. From NEW AND SELECTED POEMS by Donald Justice. Copyright © 1995 by Donald Justice. Reprinted by permission of Alfred A. Knopf, a division of Random House, Inc.

p. 531 "Waiting for a Turn" by Ken Lipenga. From *Waiting for a Turn*. Copyright © 1981 by Popular Publications.

p. 539 "The Spell and the Ever-Changing Moon" by Rukhsana Ahmed. From *So That You Can Know Me: An Anthology of Pakistani Women Writers,* edited by Yasmin Hameed and Asif Aslam Farrukhi. Copyright © 1994 by Garnet Publishing. Reprinted by permission.

p. 549 "Easter Sunday Morning" by Hazel D. Campbell. Published by Savacou Publications, Jamaica.

p. 560 "Under the Banyan Tree," pp. 187–192, copyright © 1969 by R.K. Narayan, from UNDER THE BANYAN TREE by R.K. Narayan. Used by permission of Viking Penguin, a division of Penguin Putnam, Inc.

p. 566 "No Music Before Mosque" by Zebun-Nissa Hamidulla. From *Pakistani Short Stories,* edited by Waqas Ahman Khwaja. Copyright © 1992 by UBS Publishers Distributors Ltd., 5 Ansari Road, New Delhi - 110002, India. Reprinted with permission.

p. 575 "The Rain Came" by Grace Ogot.

p. 584 "The Miracle" by Ba'bila Mutia. From *Heinemann Book of Contemporary African Short Stories,* edited by Chinua Achebe and C.L. Innes. Copyright © 1992 by Heinemann Educational Publishers, a division of Reed Educational & Professional Publishing Ltd. Reprinted with permission.

p. 596 "The Collector of Treasures" by Bessie Head. From THE COLLECTOR OF TREASURES published by Heinemann. Copyright © The Estate of Bessie Head, 1977.

p. 612 Vishwapriya Iyengar, "Midnight Soldiers," in *Truth Tales: Contemporary Stories by Women Writers of India,* edited by Meena Alexander. Kali for Women, New Delhi, 1990 (New York: The Feminist Press at The City University of New York, 1990). The story was first published in *Imprint* (March 1986). Reprinted here by permission of The Feminist Press at The City University of New York and Kali for Women.

p. 622 "The Farewell Party" from GAMES AT TWILIGHT AND OTHER STORIES by ANITA DESAI. Copyright © 1978 by Anita Desai. Reprinted by permission of the author c/o Rogers, Coleridge & White Ltd., 20 Powis Mews, London W11 1JN and HarperCollins Publishers, Inc.

p. 634 "Poem for the End of the Century" by John Haines. Appeared in the *Atlantic Monthly,* August 1999 issue. Reprinted by permission from John Haines.

p. 637 "The Season of Phantasmal Peace" by Derek Walcott. "The Season of Phantasmal Peace" from THE FORTUNATE TRAVELLER by Derek Walcott. Copyright © 1982 by Derek Walcott. Reprinted by permission of Farrar, Straus and Giroux, LLC.

Index of Authors and Titles